rs

I̶'̶l̶l̶ ̶b̶e̶ ̶t̶h̶

✓ Reachout - D²

Shake - B °

✗ Don't Bring Me Do⁻⁰ᵂⁿ

✓ MY GENERATION - D³

✓ HEART ANYMORE ⁻ᴰ

46 Whatever ²

2 Hey Joe - D³

Hungry - B²

30 - Little Girl ³

-D ✓ Good loviu ³
F.

S - Catch the Wind ³

S - There's no Other ³

²-Summertime ²

More praise for
Unrequited Infatuations

"What a wonderful, witty, incisive, moving, authentic, and beautifully written memoir. Stevie Van Zandt's *Unrequited Infatuations* is a heartfelt and soulful tour though Rock 'n' Roll history, politics, and pop culture from the vantage point of a rare talent and singular American life. I loved every page."

—HARLAN COBEN, bestselling author of *Win, The Boy from the Woods, Run Away,* and the Myron Bolitar series

"A glorious trip into the mind of a true Rock 'n' Roll Renaissance man. Stevie's autobiography digs beneath the surface of his music, evolving into something extraordinarily rich and complex. It's part Rock 'n' Roll history lesson, part political thriller, part revelatory dive into the brotherhood of a band. And so much more. What's most impressive is Stevie's self-deprecating honesty. He has the courage to write about his failures, alongside tales of his enormous success. The stories are also wildly entertaining, hilarious, and emotionally devastating. One of the best Rock 'n' Roll books ever written. It belongs on a shelf between Bob Dylan's *Chronicles* and Gerri Hershey's *Nowhere To Run.* A masterpiece."

—CHRIS COLUMBUS, director, producer, and screenwriter

"Steven and I grew up in the same town, two miles apart—unless you count the fact that creatively he was on another planet. Beneath the bandana is the beautiful mind of a polymath: singer, songwriter, actor, activist, arranger, thinker and creator. There is sex, there are drugs, and—thank the Lord—there is rock and roll. Names are named. Mistakes are made. Fights are (mostly) forgiven. And lightning strikes more than once. This is the beautifully told story of a great American life, and I dreaded the arrival of the final page."

—BRIAN WILLIAMS, journalist

"I was expecting a great music book with a bit more depth than most. What I got was the *Tao Te Ching* of Rock biographies! Only it's Lao Tzu with a fabulous sense of humor! This adventure is metaphysically amazing."

—MICHAEL DES BARRES, actor / writer / musician / DJ

"Steven Van Zandt is the ultimate Rock 'n' Roll soldier, an eyewitness to history who has made plenty of his own in the trenches and the studio. His stories of struggle and awakening, the mysteries of creation, and the ties that bind in every great band come at you like a blaze of killer 45s in a true voice of America: part Vegas, part Alan Freed, all New Jersey."

—DAVID FRICKE, journalist, SiriusXM, *Mojo*, *Rolling Stone*

"*Unrequited Infatuations* is as musical, soulful, funny, adventurous, inspiring, and real as the man who wrote it, the one and only Stevie Van Zandt."

—JON LANDAU, journalist, music producer, and manager

"A pleasure for music fans and one of the best entertainment memoirs in recent years.

—*Kirkus Reviews* (starred review)

Unrequited Infatuations

Unrequited Infatuations

Odyssey of a
Rock and Roll Consigliere
(A Cautionary Tale)

Stevie Van Zandt

Edited by Ben Greenman

hachette
BOOKS   NEW YORK

Hachette Books
Hachette Book Group
1290 Avenue of the Americas
New York, NY 10104
HachetteBooks.com
Twitter.com/HachetteBooks
Instagram.com/HachetteBooks

First Edition: September 2021

Published by Hachette Books, an imprint of Perseus Books, LLC, a subsidiary of Hachette Book Group, Inc. The Hachette Books name and logo is a trademark of the Hachette Book Group.

The Hachette Speakers Bureau provides a wide range of authors for speaking events. To find out more, go to www.hachettespeakersbureau.com or call (866) 376-6591.

The publisher is not responsible for websites (or their content) that are not owned by the publisher.

Print book interior design by Jeff Williams

Library of Congress Control Number: 2021940666

ISBNs: 978-0-306-92542-9 (hardcover); 978-0-306-92541-2 (ebook)

Printed in the United States of America

LSC-C

Printing 1, 2021

To Maureen,
my one requited infatuation

Contents

Contents

Overture

The distant music speeds up and slows down like vinyl on a warped turntable, holding, then yielding to the wind's caress, as the soft tinkle of breaking glass and tired car horns recede into the mysterious absence of light that becomes the exotic toxic wasteland beyond the city line, and the echoes of drunken revelry pass through their nightly metamorphosis, transformed on our soundtrack into the leaves softly rustling on the terrace, where on this particularly chilly December night in Greenwich Village our hero contemplates his fate.

It's a vagrant winter and you can't sell consciousness.

Nobody's buying it.

Hell, you can't even give it away!

Is what I'm hearing the icy wind blowing through the dead grey streets? Or are those echoes the sound of ridicule?

Once upon a time, consciousness was hard to come by, and nobody was buying it then either.

Information was rationed out by the clergy, witch doctors, power-drunk elders. People we foolishly trusted to do the understanding and interpret life for us.

Every hundred years or so, somebody would have a revelation and try to share it. They would usually be excommunicated, confined to asylums, or burned at the stake by our grateful society.

Who dug the Buddha when he was around? A bunch of poor homeless acolytes who hoped to someday actually understand what the hell the pleasantly plump man was talking about?

Who'd Jesus have? A dozen guys and an ex-hooker or two?

Socrates and Robert Johnson both got the same reward for their insights. A final toast from the Loving Cup.

No, my friend, you better come with something better to sell than truth.

Something we can use.

Like war, taxes, government, long tiring meaningless work, the phony scorecard of Wall Street, sexual frustration, suffering, false hope, disease, guns, drugs, gasoline, agribusiness, fear, booze, poison, hatred. Give us someone to blame. Fill the vacuum of our spiritual bankruptcy with religion.

We'll buy any and all of that. Speak to us condescendingly as children so we understand. There's a pandemic of stupidity, so no one will notice.

We will follow you anywhere.

Parents, teachers, priests, doctors, politicians, philosophers, poets, artists, gods, Lord Almighty, Holy Spirit, are your obligations so diminished?

Your offspring need suckling and you are busy doing what?

December's Children are orphans.

It's a vagrant winter and you can't sell consciousness.

Prologue

Silence.

He was under a blanket in the back of the car on the floor in the crazy spooky silence.

Nobody spoke. No radio. Just the lazy hum of the motor, and him alone with his thoughts. And ooh daddio, that was not his favorite thing.

His two coconspirators were sneaking him past the military blockade into the black township of Soweto. The "native unrest," as the government liked to call it, erupted every few years, but lately it had become more frequent, and now, constant.

Not coincidentally, the police had become less dependable. They had mixed feelings about beating their own family members and neighbors at demonstrations or turning their backs as people they knew ended up tortured and occasionally murdered in prison.

The government, no longer able to trust the police, had in an unprecedented move brought in the military. They were stationed at every checkpoint in and out of the massive ghetto. Not to protect the inhabitants, but to keep them contained for more convenient slaughter once constructive engagement gave way and the bloodshed levee broke. Tension was at an all-time high. It was no time to be the wrong color in the wrong place. Hence the under-the-blanket thing.

The seemingly endless township had no electricity, so a thick fog of fuel oil and coal smoke hung four feet off the ground, making the mystery and sense of imminent danger even more pronounced. It felt like a *Twilight Zone* ride at a Dostoevsky Disneyland. Or a *Star Trek* landing

3

party where he was the expendable crew guy in the wrong uniform. In this case the wrong uniform was his white skin, dig?

Every country smelled different. In South Africa, the sweet scent of the jacaranda, cane, and banana trees was cut by an occasional breeze that carried traces of an acrid stench, a mix of burning rubber and human flesh that came from tires filled with gasoline, forced on perceived traitors, and lit as a means of execution.

They called it necklacing.

There was also, in the combination of the intoxicating beauty and smoldering hatred, the distinctive scent of revolution. And he loved every scary crazy exhilarating minute of it, baby.

A final showdown was coming and he had a ringside seat.

He was on his way to a very secret and very illegal meeting with the most violent sect of the South African Revolution, the Azanian People's Organization (AZAPO). The plan was to learn how they thought and hopefully gain their endorsement for the strategy he'd come up with to aid their liberation.

In 1984 South Africa, it was illegal for three black men to congregate in the same place at the same time. Illegal for anyone to suggest support for the cultural boycott, especially Blacks (as they were legally designated). And a capital crime to have a gun or to consort with anyone who did.

He was about to violate all of the above.

AZAPO were frontline soldiers, heroes to the struggling masses, terrorists in the eyes of the government.

What he hadn't planned on was that in one hour's time he'd not only be criticizing their strategy for revolution, but making the case for why they should let him live.

How the fuck did a half-a-hippie guitar player get here?

For seven glorious years, Bruce Springsteen and the E Street Band were Rock and Roll's Rat Pack, and he happily and naturally played the Dean Martin role.

If you were even thinking of throwing a party, you called him. That was the extent of his politics. He was the fun guy. The court jester. Always good for a laugh. Sex, booze, drugs, Rock and Roll, and . . . more sex. Yo bartender, another round for the house!

A whole lot had to go sideways to find him under that blanket.

And yet it was all perfectly logical that a Rock and Roller from New Jersey would be risking imprisonment and death. Logical to his new mind. New mind because he had become a different guy.

He'd worked night and day with the E Street Band, proudly contributing to making them the biggest and best in the world. Then, in a moment of clarity (or insanity, take your pick), he had left the band to discover who he was and how the world worked. It was now or never, he knew. Once you take that road to being rich, there ain't no going back. The rich had too much to lose. He chose to take the adventure instead of the money.

What a putz.

Early on in his crazy new journey, he'd made a surprising discovery. He'd found that with proper research he could analyze and find a solution to virtually any political problem, no matter how complicated. Of course, implementing the solution was another matter entirely, but all he was trying to do was collect research to write some songs. At least at first.

He had always known that he had the talent of improving things when it came to art. A song, an arrangement, a lyric, a production. You name it. For years, for others, he had made bad into good, good into great, and great into greater.

It wasn't all roses, by any means.

Even in art, this ability to fix and improve things was both a gift and a curse.

The gift part was obvious.

The curse was twofold. For starters, most people didn't want advice, no matter what they said. They wanted to think they could figure things out themselves. Sometimes they pretended to listen and then ignored the advice. It was also a tough way to make a living, in that it depended on others driving the wagon while he kept the wheels greased, occasionally leaping off to make repairs.

And then there was the biggest drag, which was that he had never been able to apply this beautiful logic to his own life. The frustrations of business constantly drew him away from the pleasures of Art. No matter how he fought it, the delusional devil down inside him was still waiting for that magical, mystical patron who should have shown up by now if they were coming at all.

When he found out that his ability extended beyond art, that it carried into the real world, it came as quite a shock. He considered himself half a moron who had barely managed to finish high school. Not to mention his mind's normal state, which, when not actively doing something, was a chaotic combination of frustration, impatience, self-hatred, or preoccupation with artistic and philosophical puzzles.

That's why artists became artists, wasn't it? To make order out of the chaos? To impose a rationale on the irrational? To answer the unanswerable questions? To create a structure that provided shelter from the contradictory tornados that constantly ravage the mind? Or was it all revenge? Best not go there, he thought. It risked emotional indulgence.

But this new insight, this awareness that he could focus his talent on the larger problems of the world, taught him that his destiny, at least for the foreseeable future, was to be a political Rock Artist.

And not in the way Jackson Browne, Bonnie Raitt, Graham Nash, and John Hall were political. They were heroes. On the front lines. His interest, at least at first, was journalism. Combining his art and journalism. The way Bob Dylan did as a Folk artist. He would be the first to make art about political problems all the time, with every individual song relating to a bigger theme on every album. Nobody had done that, not on a regular basis.

Why not?

Well, first of all, everybody else was too intelligent. It was a career-ending move, and they knew it. He didn't care. In the heat of self-discovery, a career was the last thing on his mind. This blind naivete would turn out to be a self-fulfilling prophecy.

He was interested only in the adventure of learning. His life had started over again, and he had become a seeker. He was in search of truth to absorb, of lies to expose. He was making up for everything he hadn't learned in school and maybe, just maybe, justifying his existence in the process.

When he had embarked on his solo career, he had outlined five albums that handled five different kinds of political problems.

But things had gotten more complicated when his creative passion and his practical research were combined and he was drawn into the real-world issues he was writing about.

South Africa was the best example.

The challenge of the remainder of his life was crystallizing on that back-seat floor.

The car slowed down for a moment, then sped back up. Had they been waved through the checkpoint? It was his second trip to South Africa trying to complete the research for his third solo album.

He should have felt fear under that blanket. But he didn't. All fear had left his being.

He realized it on the long flight from New York. He'd never liked flying. Always a bit squeamish about the turbulence. Suddenly it hit him. He was over it.

He was over it because he'd blown it. He'd worked his whole life to achieve the impossible dream of being a Rock and Roll star. And just as he'd finally, miraculously made it, he had walked away.

From the moment on the plane when he let go of his fear, suicide would be his constant companion and temptation. No longer fearing death, it turned out, was an asset. It let him go places and observe them without giving a fuck about his own safety.

He'd lost his band, his best friend, his career, his way of making a living. Everything. Why? Just to pursue some abstract idea of justifying his existence?

He still wasn't even sure about being a front man. He happened to be quite natural at it, but he just didn't need it. All great front men needed the spotlight. The adoration. The endorsement. The reassurance. The completion of something missing in their souls.

He needed some of those things, but not as much, and not in the traditional way. When he was a kid and fantasized about being in his favorite bands, he was never the front man. He was George in the Beatles, Keith in the Stones, Dave in the Kinks, Jeff in the Yardbirds, and Pete in the Who.

He liked to watch people, to sit at a sidewalk café and just be. All of that vanished when you were in front. You were crowded all the time. You couldn't observe if you were constantly being observed. It brought out his claustrophobia.

And yet here he was, in front, but also under a blanket in back. It was a strange state he'd gotten to. And yet surprisingly liberating. He had an unusual clarity. He felt like he'd finally discovered what he was born to do.

And so, like every mythological Greek hero in denial of the inevitable tragic results, he had set off on his quest. His odyssey. Relentlessly, calmly, and, yes, fearlessly, irrationally determined to fulfill it.

The car stopped.

They were . . . where? All the houses looked the same. Eight members of the executive council of AZAPO, machetes in their waistbands, waited inside to put him on trial.

He looked up from the mist, impenetrable, township shrouded in doom, into the crystal clear African sky. Is this where life began? Or was this where it all ended?

The eternal spirit of the world's original motherland was whispering in his ear.

Destiny awaits!

He smiled to his companions to calm their nerves. Shrugged with acceptance.

And walked in . . .

one

Epiphany

(1950s–1960s)

If you're gonna do something, do it right.

—WILLIAM VAN ZANDT SR., GIVING ADVICE TO HIS LAZY
OLDEST SON (THE UNWRITTEN BOOK)

My first epiphany came at the age of ten, in 1961, in my room at 263 Wilson Avenue, New Monmouth, Middletown, New Jersey, during my fifty-fifth consecutive time listening to "Pretty Little Angel Eyes" by Curtis Lee.

That's what we did in those days.

A song on the radio would stop your life and start it up again. Talk about the perfect relationship completing you? When you were a kid in the '60s, the right song completed you. It made your day.

Owning a great record wasn't optional. You had to have it. That meant convincing your mom to drive you into town and then, with great anticipation and reverence, entering the teenage church / temple / synagogue / sweat lodge known as the record store.

Mine was Jack's Record Shoppe in Red Bank, which had a Music Shoppe on the other side of the street. Getting in early with the British Invasion with that spelling.

It's where I'd buy my first guitar a few years later. Still there, incredibly.

The store was a beautifully constructed place of worship, as ornate and glorious as any European cathedral. I'd go through dozens of bins to find the record I'd heard on the radio, take it to the counter, and give the guy my hard-earned seventy-nine cents. Then, back at home, I'd listen to it over and over again until it became a physical part of me.

We were the second generation of Rock and Roll kids, which meant that we were only the second generation able to play records in the privacy of our own rooms. The 45 rpm single was invented by RCA in 1949 in retaliation for Columbia inventing the 33⅓ rpm LP the year before. Individual portable record players soon followed. Up until then, the record player was in the living room, in the same piece of furniture that held the TV and radio.

If it wasn't for that portable machine, Rock and Roll might never have happened.

A record player in the living room meant kids needed their parents' permission, or at least tolerance, to listen to what they wanted. Without the portable player, the first generation of Rock kids would have never gotten Little Richard, Bo Diddley, and Jerry Lee Lewis past their parents.

The older generation viewed those 1950s pioneers as an odd combination of novelty and threat. Humorous because of their onstage antics, flamboyant looks, and complete lack of talent (as parents defined it), but scary because there was an uncomfortable element of black culture connecting it all. What effect would that have on kids who already had too much time on their hands for their own good?

Rock could have been snuffed out right there!

But it went up to the kids' bedrooms. It isn't my imagination when I say that back in the '60s you didn't just hear records, you felt them. Sound waves entered your body. The needle, dragging through analog impulses miraculously etched into a piece of plastic, somehow had a deeper, more physical level of communication than modern digital music.

I happened to be in London for the twentieth anniversary of *Sgt. Pepper*, and EMI, my label at the time, invited a bunch of us to hear the original four-track analog tapes at Abbey Road. I have never heard anything quite like it before or since. I swear to you, I felt stoned for two days afterward. Drug-free.

There had been great strides breaking through to autistic children with music. They ended when the world went digital.

I remember reading that it took two hundred plays to wear a record out. The high frequencies would finally give up. Technology was no match for teenage passion and perseverance.

I passed that limit often. "Twist and Shout" by the Isley Brothers, "Sherry" by the Four Seasons, "Duke of Earl" by Gene Chandler. Had to buy them again.

So there I was, just getting started on "Pretty Little Angel Eyes," and even though I can't remember what I had for breakfast today, I vividly remember looking out my window, seeing a neighbor, Louie Baron, and experiencing a rush of exultation. The music had released my endorphins in a new and unexpected way.

I wanted to run down the stairs and embrace Louie and tell him he was my friend. And that friendship was everything. And that love and music would save the world. I could see a beautiful future clearly. It was there for all of humankind.

My first epiphany.

I didn't do it, of course. My bliss didn't make me completely stupid. Men didn't embrace other men in those days.

I was always a little slower than most kids, so my ecstasy didn't immediately trigger what should have been obvious curiosity. Who was making the music? How was it made? Could I make it myself? These thoughts wouldn't come for another couple of years. But music would soon replace my religious fervor.

Did I mention I was a very religious kid? I regularly went to Sunday School, accepted Jesus as my personal savior, got baptized at nine or ten. That's how Protestants did it, as opposed to Catholics, who baptize at birth. They don't take any chances.

I was extremely devout there for a couple of years.

Easter Sunrise Service was the test. You had to get up at 4 a.m. to make it to some mountaintop in Highlands by six. I don't remember my parents going to this, only the church elders and a few super extremist types. I liked the respect I got. I could see it in people's eyes. I went two years running, maybe three.

I've always wanted to be the guy who knows. The guy with the inside dope. I was willing to put the work in, to spend the time to find out. At the age of ten, I figured religion was where the answers were hidden.

In addition to that, I obviously had some genetic penchant for metaphysical zealotry. A need to be part of something larger. A sense of wanting to belong is built into human nature; the zealotry part is what separates the holy rollers, and holy rock and rollers, from regular, far more sane civilians.

Looking back, I also could have been trying to impress my new father. I was brought up kind of Catholic, and my mother changed teams when she remarried. Or at least she pretended to. She secretly kept eating fish on Fridays and prayed to Saint Anthony when something got lost.

When I was eight, the only father I would ever know, William Van Zandt, moved us from Boston, where I was born, to New Jersey so I could get on with fulfilling my destiny.

He was a funny kind of guy. Short, tough, quiet, stoic to the max. Ex-Marine, Goldwater Republican. He had a flattened, broken nose from boxing, either on the Marines team or maybe Golden Gloves. He had played trumpet as a kid, but I don't remember him ever playing it. Ironically, or whatever the right word is, trumpet should have been my instrument. But I never had the lungs for it. It's the most evocative instrument to me, especially for film scores. What's better than the opening of *The Godfather*? Or the Miles Davis score of *Elevator to the Gallows (Ascenseur pour l'échafaud)*?

The only records I remember my father listening to on the big living room phonograph were by Arthur Prysock. When he was in a particularly good mood, he would occasionally sing along. He had a good voice.

He spent every Tuesday night with the Society for the Preservation and Encouragement of Barber Shop Quartet Singing in America (SPEBSQSA), now wisely reduced to the Barbershop Harmony Society, or BHS. Thinking back now, I see how his singing with a Barbershop quartet, the Bayshore Four, could have stimulated my lifelong love of Doo-Wop and harmony in general. The Mills Brothers, sons of a member of a Barbershop quartet, and the Ink Spots are considered direct links to the roots of Doo-Wop.

I am deeply embarrassed to admit it, but I don't remember ever having one single conversation with him about his life. What he did as a kid. Who he liked. What his dreams were.

My mother never talked about my blood father. It must have been a bad situation, because people didn't get divorced much in those days. Especially Catholics. And double especially Catholics with kids. I never pictured my mother as particularly rebellious, but that was an extraordinarily rebellious act in those days. He died young is all I know. I should have asked her for more details, but I always felt it would have been disrespectful to my father.

She was a classic '30s/'40s woman. With the big exception of uncharacteristically leaving her husband, she accepted life as it was. No ambition. No opinions. No drama. Followed the rules. Great cook. Easy smile. Always in a good mood when I was young. Society didn't expect much and didn't allow much. Lived for her kids. And at that point, that meant me.

We moved in with her parents, Adelaide and Sam Lento, so I had two uncles and two aunts around to help bring me up. It takes a village . . . of goombahs!

When we split to Jersey, the family followed. Nana Lento said it was because of me, her first grandchild, which was a big deal in Italian families. Since four of her five children ended up living in Jersey, we gathered at her house every Sunday, a short walk from our church, for the classic Italian supper, a mix of lunch and dinner that ran from early afternoon until evening. Wives, husbands, kids—had to be fifteen, sometimes twenty of us.

My father's father was long gone, and all I know is he had turned down a job pitching for the New York Giants before they moved to San Francisco, because it didn't pay enough, and had come in second to Bobby Jones in a golf tournament in South Carolina.

We would visit Nana Van Zandt in Hackensack every month or so, and she was quite a character. She was from one of the Carolinas and looked exactly like Granny from *The Beverly Hillbillies*. So I grew up with grits. Real grits. Just butter, salt, and pepper, thank you, none of that horrible cheese people like to add.

One day I found a warped old acoustic guitar in her attic that my father said had belonged to his father.

My mother's father, Grampa Sam Lento, also played guitar, and he started teaching me the folk song of his village in Calabria in southern Italy.

Not songs. Song. Just one short repeating melody. Maybe he thought that was all I could handle.

Sam was an archetypal traditional Italian shoemaker, and I'd work summers in his shop in Keansburg. He'd have one of our two identical Pop stations, WABC or WMCA, playing loud in the shop. I can still smell the shoe polish and hear the hum of the machines accompanying "Baby, baby, where did our love go?"

Nobody wanted to talk about Sam's origins. All we knew was that he had left Calabria suddenly and ended up with a successful shoe business in the Italian section of Boston before moving down to Jersey.

I'd like to think he got out of the country with some stolen money from the 'Ndrangheta. It would have been totally out of character, but it's a nice fantasy.

Nana Lento, always the life of the party, was Napolitano. Picture Marty Scorsese's mother Catherine in *Goodfellas*. She was always good for a laugh, usually unintentional. Like the time my sister Kathi brought home a Jewish boyfriend for Thanksgiving and Nana sincerely asked if his people also celebrated the holiday. If there's any genetic showbiz in me it comes from her. She was always in a good mood with the rest of us, me especially, but she harassed my grandfather mercilessly. Maybe he'd disappointed her by not ending up successful and rich, the fate of most marriages. Or maybe it was what Nana mentioned to me fairly often, revenge for Sam's mother constantly mocking her accent. Whatever it was, she took it out on him. For forty years.

He just took it quietly. He was another stoic, Italian-style. More *omertà* than stoic, I guess. Old-school. He always had a smile behind his eyes that suggested he knew things he was never gonna talk about. Once again, I wish I'd had more conversations with him.

My blood keeps life interesting.

The Calabrése part is rock-solid. Simple. Not intelligent enough to do what's best for money or career or social standing if it means compromising ideals. No ambition whatsoever. He is satisfied with his position as the laborer. The loyal soldier. Work and family are everything. Just don't fuck with him. He never forgets an insult. It takes a lot to make him mad. But if you do, he will never stop until vengeance is his, no matter what it costs.

On the other side, the Napolitano exists for action. He thrives on wheeling and dealing, fixing and changing things. He has ambition but no patience. Learns on the job. Makes lots of friends. Achieves a foothold, then parlays. He's not as sneaky and conniving as the Sicilians can be, but he's a good actor when necessary.

It is a constant challenge to call on the appropriate balance of blood in the appropriate circumstance.

I had a lucky childhood. Played sports in the park three blocks from my house. I was too small but made up for it by being faster and more fearless than most.

All I really remember is that I couldn't wait to grow up. I hated being a kid. Nothing too traumatic, just hated it in general. Not enough control, I guess.

I wanted to be who I was gonna be and get on with it. I wanted to know what was going on and felt the world was full of secrets kept from us kids.

I did well enough in school. Life was simple and good. The country was as rich as it would ever be. The conversation at the dinner table was about when, not if, the country would go to a four-day workweek. And that was with mostly only one parent working in the middle-class suburbs.

I was completely oblivious to the nation's problems in the '50s and would continue to be when politics exploded in the '60s. The main contractor for our suburban development, who was black, had a son about my age. He became my first best friend. I didn't know black and white weren't supposed to mix, and my mother didn't say anything.

Our idea of fun in those days was riding our bikes behind the mosquito man's truck, its thick chemical toxic fog pouring out the back. I have no idea why I'm still alive. Maybe it was some kind of adolescent vaccine. Maybe the poison made my immune system bulletproof.

Most of the middle-class families had either a pool in the yard or a membership at the beach clubs, or they sent their kids to summer camp. I went to summer camp. It wasn't a sleepover camp. I am a relatively rabid environmentalist, but I was never that comfortable with nature.

A bus picked me up from home at six in the morning and returned me at six in the evening. It's where I learned to swim and learned practical crafts like weaving Indian bracelets and shooting a bow and arrow. My main memory is a jukebox in the outside eating area. I can still hear "Yakety Yak" by the Coasters echoing throughout the entire camp, probably the first Rock song I ever heard.

My only other memory is one of the other kids telling me that he lived behind a drive-in theater so he could watch movies from his room and would see naked women sometimes. I remember being quite impressed and envious at his remarkable good fortune.

I got so tan at camp that a local real estate agent asked my mother to keep me inside because she had lost several sales from people thinking I was black.

My mother told her to get lost. I overheard, so she had to try and explain it to me. "Some people don't like black people," she said.

"Why?" I said.

She didn't know.

I didn't get it then. And I don't get it now.

A few years later, must have been '63 or '64, my neighborhood friends Tom Boesch, Louie Baron, I think Louie's brother Robert, and Ernie Heath, from the only black family in the whole area, went with me to the Keansburg public pool one summer day. We had just gotten there and suddenly Tom says, "Come on, we're leaving." I was like, What happened? He said they wouldn't let Ernie in the pool. That freaked me out completely.

I do remember my father, who was a construction engineer inspector, coming home angry one day. There was the new thing called affirmative action that meant he had to fire a few white guys and hire some black guys at the construction firm. He was as pissed as I'd ever seen him.

Goldwater Republicans were different. They were more like today's Libertarians. The term "Conservative" in those days meant *Mind your own business.* There was no interest in what happened in the privacy of adults' bedrooms, for instance.

That would all change with Ronald Reagan, who was the first to invite religious extremists into the Republican Party and into the political process, technically a violation of the separation of Church and State.

Religious extremism is the reason half of America doesn't believe in equality for women or LGBTQ.

Real Conservatives would have legalized drugs, abortion, you name it, but they didn't believe in federally mandated civil rights. Or federally mandated anything. They believed in states' rights. That's about the only thing that remains in common between the new so-called Conservative Republicans and the true Conservative Republicans of my father's day. If states' rights could override federal laws, we'd still have slavery. So it was a mixed bag.

My father was a hunter, though he didn't go very often.

I went once but I couldn't do it. I don't understand killing defenseless animals and calling it sport. I even think fishing is sickening. Putting a hook in a creature's mouth and pulling it as it struggles to escape? Why is that OK? I am a natural-born vegan, but I hypocritically go off and on it.

Can you imagine me and my father in the same house? We were the Generation Gap.

My political ignorance extended all the way to President Kennedy's assassination, which happened on my thirteenth birthday. All it meant to me was wondering if my party would be canceled.

There was one more defining moment I'll mention before we leave the subject of my father. He was a tough, no-nonsense type of guy, and one day I made a wisecrack to my mother and out of instinct he smacked me hard right across the face.

We were all shocked there for a minute, each for our own reasons.

We were never quite the same after that.

My favorite TV show was *Zorro*. Did that influence my look with the bandana? Probably. I was drawn to heroes, not just Zorro but Tarzan, Conan, John Carter of Mars, Errol Flynn as Robin Hood and Captain Blood, James Cagney as Rocky Sullivan and Eddie Bartlett (heroes!), Paul Newman as Rocky Graziano and Billy the Kid, Marlon Brando as Johnny Strabler in *The Wild One* (my Uncle Sal got me a motorcycle jacket like Johnny's), and James Bond (the only time my father and I ever went to the drive-in together was to see *Dr. No*).

And then there were my more educational mentors: Moe, Larry, and Curly. Abbott and Costello. Maynard G. Krebs. The Bowery Boys. Kookie, Toody, and Muldoon. Soupy Sales. Sgt. Bilko. Sid Caesar. The Marx Brothers. Professor Kelp and Buddy Love. It's a wonder any of us survived.

When *West Side Story* came out in 1961, I went to see it in Red Bank at the Carlton Theater (now the Count Basie Theatre), five or six blocks from Jack's Record Shoppe.

The movie had a profound impact on me in two ways.

First there was the gang thing. It was so cool to us suburban fifth graders that we formed our own gangs and attacked each other with pens during recess. Whoever got written on the most lost.

For me, gangs weren't about conflict or competition. They spoke to my natural impulse to belong to something. I remember getting busted as the ringleader for that one.

It was also the first time I really absorbed Latino music.

I had had a taste of it from the *Zorro* score, Connie Francis's "Malagueña," Ritchie Valens's "La Bamba," Ray Barretto's "El Watusi," and the Champs' "Tequila," but the score of *West Side Story* is my favorite music of all time.

I loved the Sharks. There should be a football team called the Sharks. The New Jersey Sharks. Then we could have the Jets versus the Sharks!

I wanted to be Bernardo with his purple shirt. Pepe. Indio. I wanted to fuck Anita! The dance at the gym and the rooftop "America" scene blow my mind to this day.

Other movie music had a big impact on me too. I'm well aware of the influence of Ennio Morricone's work from the Sergio Leone Westerns ("Standing in the Line of Fire" on *Soulfire*), but every once in a while I'll write a riff and realize it comes from Miklós Rózsa's score for *Ben-Hur* or *King of Kings* or Jerry Goldsmith's score for *The Wind and the Lion*.

I wonder if Jimmy Page knows he got the riff for "Immigrant Song" from Richard Rodgers's "Bali Ha'i" in *South Pacific*?

Or here's a good one. Did you ever wonder where Morricone got the idea for that crazy opening riff in *The Good, the Bad, and the Ugly*? Check out the old Johnny Weissmuller Tarzan movies. But let's keep that to ourselves. What's the statute of limitations for Austro-Hungarian ape-to-ape jungle communication?

Johnny's estate might get ideas . . .

Contrary to popular scientific rumor, the Big Bang that gave birth to the universe did not happen ten million years ago. It happened on February 9, 1964.

To say that Ed Sullivan was an unlikely TV host would be an insult to the word "understatement." Picture Quasimodo attempting to be cute. But stoned. On mushrooms.

He had a Sunday-night variety show that the entire family watched. Same room, same time, on the home's only TV, black-and-white. I remember eventually getting a second TV for our rec room downstairs and the neighbors being awestruck by our wealth and decadence.

Ed made history on a regular basis, drawing something like sixty million viewers weekly. Every show that tried to compete with him failed, partly because other producers didn't realize that people were not only tuning in for the entertainment; they were tuning in to hear Ed mispronounce really famous people's names.

Still, he had a well-booked show, with acts for every age group and taste. The adults got Russian jugglers, Italian opera, Catskills comedians, and Broadway stars. Kids got puppets like Topo Gigio (an act Sullivan took part in), and Ed included something for the teenagers, usually the popular music of the day.

Much to his credit, he had welcomed black acts in the racist '50s, when it wasn't a regular thing.

Bo Diddley made an infamous appearance in 1955.

He had rehearsed "Sixteen Tons," a middle-of-the-road pop cover at soundcheck, but when the show went live he launched into his first single, "Bo Diddley." He got himself a hit single, a career, and a lifetime ban from the show.

A year later, Elvis Presley's first *Sullivan* appearance rocketed him and the new genre of Rock and Roll to the top of the charts. There would be no looking back.

Some would argue Elvis's appearance on *The Ed Sullivan Show* was really the Big Bang of Rock and Roll. But it wasn't mine.

As thrilling as Bo and Elvis might have been, America was not the least bit ready for that February night in 1964 when the act Ed had in mind for the teenagers turned out to be the Beatles.

It was my second epiphany.

The Beatles on *Ed Sullivan* had the cultural impact of a spaceship landing in Central Park. Except that we'd seen spaceships land before in movies like *The Day the Earth Stood Still.* There was no warning or precedent for the Beatles.

They were as alien as anything on that spaceship, completely unique, and in a way that could never happen again. You can only be *that* different once. Everything about them was special. Their hair, clothes, sound, attitude, intelligence, wit, and especially their accent.

But they were mostly different for one very big reason. There were four of them. They were a band.

This was new. Until then, the music business had been made up of individual pioneers like Little Richard, Chuck Berry, and Elvis Presley; Doo-Wop singing groups like the Cadillacs, the Dubs, the Channels, and the Jive Five; Soul groups like the Temptations, the Contours, and the Miracles; and instrumental combos like the Ventures, the Surfaris, and the Tornados. The Four Seasons and the Beach Boys were bands to some degree, playing live and recording with session guys, but they felt anchored to the past, the Beach Boys with their silly high school sweaters and the Four Seasons looking like your Italian uncles.

For me, the first true rock star was Ricky Nelson on *The Adventures of Ozzie and Harriet* when I was eight or nine. I'd look forward to him performing at the end of the episode and be disappointed when he didn't.

Before the Beatles, there had been only one true Rock and Roll band, the Crickets, who had inspired the Beatles to pick a bug for their name. The group released some records as the Crickets and some as Buddy Holly to get twice the radio airplay. And even though it was the same band all along, because of his shocking early death, it was Buddy who would be remembered. I was proud that in 2012 we finally got the Crickets and a bunch of other deserving sidemen into the Rock and Roll Hall of Fame.

The Beatles changed the world literally overnight. There were no bands in America on February 8, 1964. There was one in every garage on February 10.

What was the attraction of bands?

A band communicated something different from what an individual communicated. An individual was all about me, me, me. One personality. One spotlight. You fall in love with that guy or you don't.

Bands communicated Friendship. Family. The Gang. The Posse. The Team. The Squad. And ultimately, the Community. Each kid now had four or five choices about who to relate to. It was like the Three Musketeers (more heroes of mine), but better. All for one, and one for all!

My brother, Billy, was born seven years after me, four years before my sister. The gap was too large to let us share many experiences, and I regret I didn't find a way to spend more time with them.

The main thing I remember is arguing with my brother about which show to watch during dinner. He wanted *I Love Lucy* and I wanted *Star Trek*. Kind of ironic that his first movie when he went to Hollywood was playing an alien on the bridge of the *Enterprise* in *Star Trek: The Motion Picture,* and I ended up loving Latino music probably first introduced to me by Ricky Ricardo!

But my brother and I had one amazing moment. We slept in the same room. At night I snuck my transistor radio under the sheets. One night, on came "I Want to Hold Your Hand," the Beatles' first hit single in the United States. The American record company had turned down their first four singles, all of which were hits in England. Finally, the English parent company, EMI, urged on by Manager Brian Epstein and Producer George Martin, demanded Capitol Records release "I Want to Hold Your Hand."

I was listening. Billy was in the next bed listening also. When the chorus came, and the band hit those incredible high notes on the word "hand," we both burst into laughter. The Beatles communicated the one thing America needed after the assassination of JFK, the one thing that transcended the seven-year difference between me and my brother—unbridled joy. So among other things, I thank them for that moment.

For me, bands weren't just the week's teenage fashion trend or a new type of music or even some way to rebel against the paradise our parents had given us.

This was the beginning of life for me.

Suddenly everything started to make sense. Thank you, I thought. *This* is my species. *This* is my race. My ethnic group. My religion. My language. My creed. My purpose. *This* is *me.*

There was only one slight problem.

The Beatles were a little too good. A little too sophisticated. Yes, they were exciting, and just *liking* them felt like membership in a new tribe. But no matter how good my imagination was, I couldn't really imagine doing what they did.

They were perfect. Their hair was perfect. Their suits were perfect. Perfect harmony. They all sang lead!

This problem would be solved four months later, on June 3, 1964, when I had my third epiphany.

Dean Martin was guest-hosting *The Hollywood Palace,* a *Sullivan*-like variety show with rotating hosts on ABC, the night the Rolling Stones made their American television debut.

I witnessed my past meet my future.

In addition to being Italian American and a fan of Dino, both with Jerry Lewis and in his solo career, I would use his relationship with Frank Sinatra as my future role model in the E Street Band.

That night, Dino made fun of the Stones. Relentlessly. Callously. Obnoxiously as possible. He did it when he was introducing them and after they played a raw cover of Muddy Waters's "I Just Want to Make Love to You."

"They're going to leave right after the show for London," he said. "They're challenging the Beatles to a hair-pulling contest."

This pissed everybody off except me. Bring it up to Keith Richards to this day at your own peril!

Of course Dino made fun of them! He was supposed to! They were new! Young! Loud! Spitting in the face of tradition! Everything his generation despised.

Mick Jagger was a different kind of front man.

There was something about his casual attitude that contrasted with the Beatles' formality. And he didn't play an instrument.

Most white bands just stood there and played. Their guitars functioned as a wall between performer and audience. A front man with no guitar who moved and danced was a black thing. Jagger and Eddie Brigati from the Rascals were big exceptions to the white-guy rule.

Fronting liberated the performer to be the receiver of the energy as well as the transmitter. The Preacher, the Medicine Man, the Mambo, the Houngan, the Mystic, the One Possessed by the Spirit. More intimate. More sexual.

What changed me forever was probably the one thing that galled Dino the most.

Mick Jagger didn't smile.

How dare he display that ungrateful attitude as the Keepers of Traditional Showbiz generously granted him a national audience?

I suddenly understood. I didn't have to be perfect. Or even happy! Just look at them. It wasn't that they were ugly, but they were decidedly . . . simian. You couldn't have called the Beatles "traditional." They changed the world too much for that. But they were conventionally attractive. The Stones were more primitive. Even their clothes seem to be an afterthought. They were the first punk band.

The Beatles showed us a new world; the Rolling Stones invited us in.

It was the spark that would ignite a new way of thinking for me. A world without rules. Without limitations.

Where work isn't alienated from one's identity but *is* one's identity.

The concept of a job as unpleasant labor was instantly transformed. It was a "job" that could be satisfying, rewarding, and fun. Something that you would do for free. And you could get rich doing it? And get laid?

I was so in.

Goodbye school, grades, any thoughts of college, straight jobs, family unity, and American monoculture in general.

The Beatles/Stones exacta would change everything.

My religion had gone from Catholic to Baptist to Rock and Roll Pagan.

Society has never recovered.

And neither have I.

two

The Source

(1965–1967)

You're only as cool as who you steal from.
—THE UNWRITTEN BOOK

Here they come! Run for your lives!

It had started in the '50s, with Americans as economically super-secure Kings of the World. The horny wartime generation filled fresh suburbs with a new subspecies whose evolution stopped somewhere between adolescence and adulthood. They couldn't crank them out fast enough. It didn't take long for this phenomenon to be given a name. It was, as a Roger Corman poster might have read, *The Attack of the Teenagers!*

Represented by the shocking and revelatory ingratitude of Marlon Brando's *Wild One*, the disaffection of James Dean's *Rebel Without a Cause*, the cynical wisdom of the Beat Poets, and the unprecedented integration of the races in Elvis Presley's Rock and Roll, the teenager came fully formed for maximum adult aggravation.

Free, fresh, fearless, and too arrogant (or naive) to know (or care) that there were rules that had governed the previous thousand generations of young people, out they came. Not only with unprecedented discretionary money, but with unprecedented discretionary time to spend it.

The marketplace had to sprint to keep up.

Rock and Roll Records! Transistor Radios! Compact Mobile Phonographs! Cars! Clothes! Guitars! Bikinis! Hula-Hoops! Princess Phones! Pantyhose! Yo-Yos! Birth Control! Drive-In Movies! Malt Shops! Comic Books! Roller Skates!

The bounty was infinite.

But the freedom of the teen life was not. Those pioneering Rock and Roll fans made an impact, don't get me wrong. They set the cars-girls-beach-booze template. But they made a big mistake.

They grew up.

A few would keep their Doo-Wop 45s as a memory of their short but sweet liberation, but most became the society they were rebelling against.

We wouldn't be so easy.

By the time our generation came along, Rock and Roll wasn't a temporary social phenomenon anymore. It wasn't rebellion anymore, or even showbiz. It was a lifestyle.

Something new. And very troubling to the status quo. And guess what. We weren't going to grow up.

Ever.

My first band was the Mates.

Just in case the world didn't realize how influenced we were by the British Invasion.

It was me on vocals, along with Tom Boesch, my best friend growing up, who would turn me on to Bob Dylan, and two richer kids from the other side of the tracks, John Miller and Kerry Hauptli. Tom's father's job was silk-screening, so he created our Beatles-like bass drumhead, complete with a logo, which immediately elevated us above the other local bands.

It was the beginning of the methodology I would adopt for the rest of my life: dive in and learn on the job.

We did a residency at what would become the locally infamous Clearwater pool in Highlands and then faded away for reasons not remembered by me.

The first song I ever sang in public was Dylan's "Like a Rolling Stone." Here is a typical setlist in my handwriting that John kept:

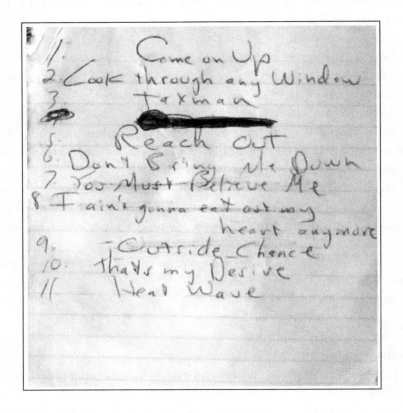

The next thing I remember is joining Buddy Norris's group the Shadows. Cool name. I didn't know it was stolen from England. I wonder if he did.

Around here it gets kind of hazy, but either Buddy invited me to the band rehearsal or John Miller, our former Mates bass player, did.

I met Buddy because he lived at the top of the biggest hill in Middletown, a few blocks from my house. My Aunt Angie, who spoiled her children and occasionally me, had bought me a brand-new thing called a skateboard. It was invented so that landlocked teenagers could enjoy the surf craze the Beach Boys had started. There was even a hit theme song, "Sidewalk Surfin'," by Jan and Dean. Jan Berry, after trying and failing to write a skateboarding anthem, had asked Brian Wilson and

Roger Christian to rewrite the Beach Boys' "Catch a Wave" with different lyrics, which they did.

In addition to lead guitarist Buddy, who greatly resembled Ricky Nelson, and John Miller on bass, the other guys were neighborhood kids, too: Bobby McEvily on drums and Chris Plunkett on rhythm guitar. I brought in Bruce Gumbert who, like every other accordion player—and there were many—had traded it in for a Farfisa or Continental compact organ after the Dave Clark Five did *The Ed Sullivan Show*.

For a couple of years there, Rock TV was spectacular. It started in the '50s when Soupy Sales had the first TV Rock show in Cincinnati. Then Alan Freed had a national show, *The Big Beat*, until Frankie Lymon jumped off the stage and danced with a white girl.

Rock shows exploded for our generation. There must have been ten of them on TV every week in 1965. We had *American Bandstand, Hullabaloo, Upbeat, Shivaree, Where the Action Is*, and *Hollywood a Go Go*, plus the shows hosted by DJs like Murray the K, Clay Cole, Jerry Blavat. Not to mention the variety shows with Pop segments: *Ed Sullivan, The Hollywood Palace, The Red Skelton Show, The Smothers Brothers Comedy Hour, The Dick Cavett Show*, Mike Douglas in the afternoon, Merv Griffin at night.

Impressive, no?

The Shadows made our TV debut, and finale, on *Disc-O-Teen* on Newark's Channel 47. Every local station had their own *American Bandstand* (band lip-synching, kids dancing), and ours was hosted by John Zacherle, a horror-movie host / Rock enthusiast nicknamed "The Cool Ghoul" by his friend Dick Clark. My future wife, Maureen Santoro, a Newark native, danced on the show all the time, so it's possible we overlapped.

We got on *Disc-O-Teen* because we won a local contest. It felt like a taste of the big time.

Rock was not only on radio and TV, but everywhere else. Our generation had more places for teenage Rock bands to play than ever before or since. We had beach clubs, high school dances, VFW halls, even teenage nightclubs like Le Teendezvous. Hullabaloo clubs, named after the TV show, were franchised around the country. The three in our area created a circuit, Middletown to the north, Freehold to the west, Asbury Park to the south, and the beach clubs to the east completed the square. Or more like a trapezoid, in this case.

As a result, the dozen or so bands in our area that got out of the garage were constantly running into each other. Nightlife in those days consisted of two things: playing with your band or going to see some other band.

What else mattered?

There were great local bands. The three biggest were the Mods, with the Lillie brothers, Phil Watson on guitar, and Ray Belicose on drums; the Clique, with the Talarico brothers and Jimmy Barr on guitar; and the Motifs, with Walter Cichon, who looked like a Native American Eric Burdon and would later die in Vietnam.

I had a friend, Mark Romanski, who was in a band with the unfortunate name of the Chlan. Mark was a motorcycle guy, and a spill we took has kept me off bikes to this day. One day in 1966, Mark said, "Let's go see the Beatles." We took the bus to Shea Stadium in Queens, which might as well have been Belgium.

The screaming must have been less noisy than at the previous year's show, because up in the second balcony we could hear the band fine. The very small speakers must have been pointing right at us. The band sounded just like the records, even without any stage monitors. They really were one of the greatest bands in history in every way. We found out later that the stadium wasn't sold out. The first indication Beatlemania was coming to an end. In three years they'd be gone.

Asbury Park was a stopover between New York and Philadelphia, and the biggest acts played Convention Hall: the Who, the Doors, Jefferson Airplane.

I saw the Stones there, with the Texas Blues guitarist Freddie King opening.

There was only one hotel in town, the Berkeley-Carteret, which could have been the location for *The Shining*. After the show, the other kids wanted to look for the Stones. I was not big on this idea. We wandered the endless hallways until we came to an open door. In the room was Freddie King.

My brave comrades urged me forward. Go, they said, get his autograph. I never got the whole autograph thing, but I figured, Let's get it over with. I knocked on the frame. "Excuse me, sir, but could we get your autograph?" He went over to the bed, picked up the pillow, and showed me a gigantic .45.

Never mind.

Never asked for another autograph, never again wanted to meet anybody I liked, and never played a Freddie King lick since.

It was during this period that I met Bruce Springsteen.

Battles of the Bands were regular events, happening every other month or so, so we may have met at one of those. I say that because we were two of the only bands that had Managers, and our Managers became friendly, so they must have met somewhere. But maybe that was later.

Anyway, I think we met at a Shadows gig at the Middletown Hullabaloo, formerly the Oaks, on the exact site of my old summer camp.

A bunch of scraggly, skinny guys with long hair came in, and I knew it had to be a band.

I went over to them during the break.

It was . . . what's the right word . . . inauspicious? Because there was nothing auspicious about us yet. I was fourteen or fifteen, he a year older.

I was wearing a top hat in those days and a huge tie I felt obligated to wear (our drummer's mother had made it), so he probably commented on my attire. Our band was good, so maybe the combination of sight and sound got his attention. I'm sure he invited me to see his band, the Castiles, wherever they were playing next. He didn't have a phone.

The Castiles were from lower-middle-class Freehold, out west, not a town you'd frequent if you could help it. It was one of the towns where the greasers lived. The real hoods. The soon-to-be-big-time gangsters.

It couldn't have been easy for Bruce and the other Castiles to be among the few long-haired freaks in town. Although they had the Motifs as local heroes.

In those days, if you met another guy who was in a band, you were friends. If you both had long hair, you were friends.

And if you both had long hair *and* were in a band, you were best friends.

That was it.

No thunder. No lightning.

Just two misfit kids who had found a common tribe.

It was the beginning of a lifelong brotherly love affair.

I would stay with the Shadows for only a short time. I had started playing guitar and wanted my own band. The minute I got moderately proficient, that's what I did. Within a few months, we had morphed into the Source. Buddy dropped out and John Miller went to college and was replaced by Joe Hagstrom (real name) on bass.

Before John left and changed his name back to his mother's pre-second-marriage name of Britton, he took me to the Red Bank House of Music, which had just gotten in their first Telecaster and was having trouble selling it. I played it and had to have it. The store gave me a good price, probably somewhere around a hundred bucks. I borrowed it from Nana Lento and became the first local Telecaster guy.

I found I had a talent for pulling songs apart and analyzing the pieces. This is where the craft of Arrangement, forever my favorite craft, begins.

Like the Mates and the Shadows, the Source started off playing songs from the top 40 Pop charts—it was the last time the charts were full of great Rock and Soul, not so strangely resembling a typical set of songs that would play in my Underground Garage radio format thirty-five years later. Paul Revere and the Raiders' "Just Like Me," Sam and Dave's "Hold On, I'm Coming," the Turtles' "She'd Rather Be with Me," the Temptations' "Ain't Too Proud to Beg," the Kinks' "Tired of Waiting."

What was different was that the Source was expanding the setlist to include tracks from the albums I had started buying that were being played on the new FM stations. But I didn't mind the AM hits.

They were the coolest songs anyway. That's why I refer to the '50s and '60s as a Renaissance period. When the greatest Art being made is also the most commercial, you're in a Renaissance.

It continues to be fascinating to me that with all the corruption and payola in those days, the best songs somehow made it through. You can't find half a dozen records that should have been hits but weren't! Amazing, really. Let's face it, just like Vegas—which we'll get to in a minute—the music business worked better when the Mafia ran it!

The Source rehearsed in the McEvilys' living room. Our backyards were diagonally across from each other.

Bands like the Source and the Castiles were different from other local groups because, like I said, we had Managers. Theirs was Tex: tall, gangly, cowboy hat, Colonel Tom Parker type. Ours was Bobby's mother,

Big Mama McEvily. The "Big" didn't refer to her size. It referred to her status as the undisputed boss. Picture Ethel Merman in *Gypsy*, only tougher. I wish I'd kept her.

I started going to Greenwich Village on the weekends. I didn't know the history of the place yet, the Beat Poets and the other famous writers

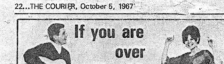

SMASH, SMOKE, TOTAL destruction will be the smash finale as The Source "Freak Out" Friday night at See 'N Surf. Everything will go -- guitars, amplifiers, drums -- promise Sourcers from left Chris Plunkett, Bruce Gumbert, Bob Mc Evily, Steve Van Zandt and Joe Hagstrom.

Article about my band the Source announcing we would blow up our equipment after the show. The ad is about a different gig, a band battle that Bruce's band was also in when we were still the Shadows.

The Courier

Freak out before soul

SEA BRIGHT -- Freak out and soul mixed with some caged go go girls is on the menu at See 'N Surf this weekend.

Leading off Friday night will be The Source in a Freak Out show that goes from 8 p.m. to midnight at which witching hour the popular Middletown group will blow up their equipment with smoke and time bombs. At least that's what they say is going to happen.

Saturday night Go Go girls in cages will add that extra something to the Moment of Truth, featured along with the fabulous Broadways. Soul music is the

sound for Saturday with the Truth group direct from Asbury Park's Hullabaloo and the Broadways who have sung with the Four Tops and appeared several times with the Vick-ters.

The teen beach club snack bar and new Oceanside Surf Shop are open all day Saturday and Sunday and after school hours every weekday. Sundays bands rehearse and surfers surf.

AFS hosting student assembly

MIDDLETOWN -- The American Field Service Club of Mid-

and artists that had frequented those twelve square blocks. All I knew was that Bob Dylan had lived there and written "Positively 4th Street," which was enough for me.

The Cafe Wha? on MacDougal Street (still there) had music around the clock, new bands in the day, more established ones at night. I took the bus in by myself, watched bands, learned what I could, drank alcoholic Brandy Bastards, and made it home for the awkward dinner with the family, as I became more and more of a disappointment.

The bands I saw were a year or two ahead of anything in New Jersey. I was absorbing, and stealing, all I could.

It was a surprise when I started running into Bruce there, the equivalent of running into a Jersey neighbor while on vacation in Sardinia.

"What are you doing here?" I said.

"I come up to check things out."

"Yeah, me too."

Wow, I thought. This guy's as crazy as I am.

We started hanging out and taking the bus into the city together. Before we went, we would go to his room and play records.

It was always a little scary, because we had to pass the kitchen, where his father would often be smoking and staring off into space, occasionally sipping on something. Like my dad, he seemed always on the brink of exploding into violence to vent a lifetime of frustration intensified by having a son who was one of New Jersey's only freaks.

Bruce's father would turn out to be a real sweetheart, just like my own. But those early days were tough going. We were an embarrassment to them. Failures they took personally.

Bruce and I would play each other our favorite records, and he would also play me songs he had written.

I had written only one song. Big Mama had a friend, another Big Mama type, with a terrible Pop song she wanted us to record. If we did, she said, we could record one of our own for the B-side.

Big Mama suggested I write something, so I did. It was called "Traveling," a Rock song with a little Indian flavor, like what George Harrison was bringing to the Beatles. We recorded the terrible Pop song and put "Traveling" on the flip, but it was never released and all the test pressings have disappeared.

No great loss, believe me.

Bruce was taking writing much more seriously. He was already picturing himself as part of the business, even though we were in fucking New Jersey, where our chances of being discovered were only slightly higher than if we were in Tanganyika.

We both had the same crazy dream, but his was advanced dreaming. It was very encouraging.

As I mentioned, I discovered I had a gift for analyzing records and figuring out how they were put together. There turned out to be five crafts of Rock, and they weren't as easy as the Stones made them look.

First Craft: Learn Your Instrument. As a Rock musician, you either get a few lessons in person or you study video of where guys put their hands. Being a front man (singing without playing) is a little more complex. Singing is the easy part. Sing along with your favorite records. But every singer is also an actor. Every lyric is a script, and every song is a movie, performed for the audience. Good singers make it seem like they've experienced what they are singing about, as if it's true, whether it is or not. Some of the greatest singers of all time, like Frank Sinatra, Elvis Presley, Aretha Franklin, and Whitney Houston, never wrote much at all, if anything, but their songs seem autobiographical. While you don't have to take acting or dancing lessons to learn how to inhabit a song, it wouldn't hurt.

Second Craft: Arrangement. Make a list of your favorite songs and then find three or four other guys or girls who share the same vision. That will help you form your band. But now you have to dissect those songs. Your dissection should include an understanding of the lyrics, as Rock is basically a storytelling medium. But arrangement is about asking other questions. What are the chords? What are the instruments being used? What is each one doing, exactly? You will learn which instruments to include and how to configure the song: the verses, the chorus, the bridge, the solo. The rules are there to break. Some songs may start with a chorus, like the Beatles' "Help!" Some songs may not have a bridge, like the Kinks' "All Day and All of the Night." Some songs may not have a bridge or a solo, like the Rolling Stones' "Satisfaction." But understanding how songs are built is central to the craft of arrangement.

Third Craft: Performance. So you're feeling pretty good about your ability with your instrument (though you never stop getting better), your band has learned its favorite fifty songs, and you are ready to get out of the garage. Find a place to play. A venue. If you're over eighteen, it will most likely be a bar. If you're under, you will have to figure it out. Playing live is a whole different animal from rehearsal. It accomplishes three important things. You will learn what effect each song has on the audience, you will learn how to interact with an audience, and you will learn how to interact with your band.

Fourth Craft: Composition. You can now take what you've learned from arrangement and performance and start writing songs. There are really no rules here, but I would make one suggestion. Write with purpose. What do you want the song to do? To be? Do you want it to make people dance? Laugh? Cry? Think? Is your song a question? An answer? A confession? Who are you talking to? Yourself? It helps to have some direction when you're staring at an empty page or screen.

Fifth Craft: Recording. These days most people begin the recording process at home. We did too, usually with a cassette recorder in the middle of the room at rehearsal.

Some people record all on their own. That's both good and bad. There is a chance you'll learn quite a bit and maybe create something fantastic on your own. But most of the time, it takes an army to make a great record. Prince may be the only exception in history to this rule, and even he had help on *Purple Rain.* Everybody else benefits from collaboration. Input from an objective Producer is always helpful. And band members. And Arrangers. I don't care where a good idea comes from—I'll take a suggestion from the studio janitor if it makes the record better. You need help to realize your potential. You can do everything completely by yourself, but most likely you will achieve supreme, profound mediocrity. That's easy. These days everybody is doing that.

But what you want deep down in your soul is to do something great. We may not always achieve greatness, but we should always be reaching for it. Isn't that our best way to show our gratitude for life itself?

Bruce played me his favorite records—Tim Buckley's *Goodbye and Hello,* Van Morrison's *Astral Weeks*—and then an original or two, usually in that same Folk-type genre. Then we'd sneak out to Greenwich Village for more absorbing and more stealing.

My favorite band at the time was called the Source. I liked them so much I stole their name.

They were originally from DC but were living in the Village, where the action was. They would change their name to Kangaroo when they got signed.

John Hall, a future congressman I would help elect forty years later, was their genius bass player, and their guitar player was the amazing Teddy Spelios, the closest thing to Jeff Beck in our world. I still use the two-finger-picks-with-a-flat-pick style Teddy used when he played.

Aside from the mystery of his ridiculous talent, Teddy had the magic tone, a beautiful distorted sound. Bruce was a year or two ahead of me on guitar. I was catching up fast. But neither of us could figure out how Teddy got that tone.

We worked up the courage to ask him one day. He gave us a look to see if we were fucking with him, but he could see we were serious. "Just turn the amp all the way up," he said, predating Spinal Tap by seventeen years. It didn't work for us. Every time we tried it, the pickups would squeal bloody murder.

Then one day Bruce called. "I've got it!" he said. "I've got the tone!" I rushed over. He had found a weird guitar someone had thrown out that fed back the right way, sustaining a note rather than a horrible squeal. It was a major breakthrough.

He was having a tough time finding strings that were long enough because the guitar turned out to be a bass. But he played it for a while.

Bruce's role in the Castiles had grown in the short time I'd known him. A guy named George Theiss had started off as the lead singer, but he had issues occasionally and would refuse to sing, forcing Bruce to step up.

For all our overlap, Bruce and I had our own inclinations, which were reflected in our bands' repertoires. The Source played Rock-Pop like the Who's first album (still my favorite), the Youngbloods, Buffalo Springfield, the Byrds, the Hollies, the Kinks, the Stones, the Beatles.

The Castiles leaned moodier and darker. The Doors, Love, Them, the Yardbirds, the Animals. Between the two of us we had the new revolution covered. And those two complementary sensibilities would show up big-time thirteen years later on an album called *The River*.

Before John Miller, now Britton again, left for college, he came with me and Bruce to the Cafe Wha? one day to see Kangaroo. The guy who opened for them was a black guy doing wild things on his guitar with feedback—in a good way, like the Beatles had started doing and the Who were doing regularly. I didn't pay much attention to his group, Jimmy James and the Blue Flames, which seemed like an out-of-their-environment R&B group that had just dropped acid for the first time. The wild guitar player wouldn't change back to his birth name of Hendrix until he got to England. I was much more interested and anxiously awaiting the new Kangaroo lineup, having heard they had recently added a girl singer.

In between John Miller leaving and Joe Hagstrom coming into the Source, I mentioned to the guys that I would like Bruce to be in the band. He had mentioned having tough times in the Castiles every now and then. But the problem was the way we got to the gigs—our mothers took turns driving us. And since Bruce's mother didn't drive, he couldn't seriously be considered for the band.

There was one brief intrusion of reality into my tunnel vision. Like every other guy my age who didn't go to college, I got drafted.

Everybody had a different idea on how to get out of it. None of them appealed to me. I thought for a minute, Maybe I'll go. But who was I kidding? I couldn't take orders from anybody my whole life. When I got into the draft-board room, I decided to just deal with it.

My anxiety spilled out in a nervous monologue.

I said, "Listen, man. I don't really have the brains to bullshit you, you know? I mean I've heard of people successfully doing that, but I just can't get into it, man, so you've got to, you know, like, help me out here. I'm not that crazy about killing people, I'm being honest with you, as opposed to those guys in the other room, who, you know, can't wait. They are looking forward to killing people, and I've got to believe that's the cats you want. And the room is full of 'em. I, on the other hand, don't have that thing that just wants to kill people. So you're gonna have to explain this to me."

We were the last group and it had been a long day. The guy from the draft board squinted. "Whaddya mean, son?"

"I mean, explain it, sir. What's the story with Vietnam? Start there."

"Well," he says. "It's Communists, boy!"

"OK," I said. "So what's a Communist and why are we killing them? And all the way over there?"

"Well, a Commie is a . . . a . . . a dictator and uh, bad people, son. Bad people. And we're fighting him there so he don't come here."

Really?

"I'm sorry, sir, but I still don't get it. They're coming from Southeast Asia to take over New Jersey? For what? Our tomatoes? I just cannot buy that. They land on Bradley Beach, I'll be the first one there, but I ain't going halfway around the damn world to shoot people just because you say so. All due respect."

He stared at me for a long time. I figured, I'm going to jail. It wouldn't be the first time. The first time was when the local cops planted marijuana on me to try and get the only freak in town off the streets. Luckily, my parents believed me when it was discovered they had loaded the wrong brand of cigarettes. Soon after that I started smoking weed. I figured if I'm already being punished, I might as well do the crime.

Finally . . .

"OK, son."

"Check those boxes in the right-hand column," he said, "and I'd better see you on Bradley Beach when the time comes."

I said, "Yes, sir, you will, sir." And that was that.

Maybe he knew I was trouble. Or maybe I was the small fish that got thrown back into the pond.

I didn't have to hide in a college or run away to Canada. I was free to pursue my impossible dream.

But what were the odds of a kid from New Jersey becoming a Rock star? A million to one?

No. Worse.

three

Upstage

(1968–1970)

> You don't want to piss off anybody from New Jersey. They're
> already pissed off by being from New Jersey.
> —THE UNWRITTEN BOOK

High school was a drag.

Who cared about the Peloponnesian War when John Lennon was inventing feedback for the intro of "I Feel Fine"?

Just ring the damn bell and let me get to band practice.

Contrary to our most delicious fantasies, in New Jersey the girls chasing the Beatles in *A Hard Day's Night* would prefer the sports guys for another five years.

We were at rehearsal one day at Joe Hagstrom's house when he came running in with a music magazine. He opened it, pointed, and declared with shock, "Look! Rod Stewart is white!"

"Get the fuck outta here!"

"It must be the way it's printed."

"The Equals all looked white too."

"I'm telling you," he said. "He's white."

The issue wouldn't be resolved until Stewart came onstage at the Fillmore East.

The Fillmore East was a miraculous Rock oasis that Bill Graham had opened in early 1968 as the East Coast sister to the Fillmore in San Francisco. It was right in the middle of the Lower East Side, Second Avenue and Sixth Street, and the rent must have been right because it was a neighborhood of bikers, dealers, winos, homeless, junkies, and panhandlers.

Graham was a tough, controversial guy, a German Jew whose mother sent him to France to escape the Nazis. He ended up in San Francisco, where he helped invent the new Artform of Rock performance.

He called himself a Producer rather than a Promoter, and rightfully so.

His vision elevated the performance part of our Artform to its highest evolution, a level that, regarding three-act theater bills, has never been equaled.

The shows were a total immersive experience.

You entered a funky but chic chandeliered lobby leading to the main room, which held around twenty-five hundred of the first velvet seats we'd ever seen.

The Fillmore East usually had three acts per show, two shows a night on Fridays and Saturdays. The amazing Joshua Light Show, named for the Engineer and Lighting Designer who created it, Joshua White, was projected on the full-screen back wall. We had never seen anything like it. No one had. Between acts, Graham showed cartoons and newsreels.

The shows were curated by Graham's eclectic but exquisite taste and both reflected and influenced the open-minded hippie era of the late '60s.

Some typical Fillmore East bills:

March 8, 1968 (opening night):

Big Brother and the Holding Company
Tim Buckley
Albert King

April 27, 1968:

Traffic
Blue Cheer
Iron Butterfly

January 9, 1970:

Ike and Tina Turner
Mongo Santamaria
Fats Domino

Unbelievable, right? For five dollars or less!

Anyway, such was the state of Rock journalism circa 1967. We weren't even sure what color our Rock stars were!

At least until May 2, 1969. The Jeff Beck Group, Joe Cocker, and NRBQ. And I feel quite confident positively confirming it now. Rod Stewart is white.

As I entered my senior year of high school, I was blossoming into the full-blown hippie I would be for the next few years, or the rest of my life depending on how you're counting, and my father told me to cut my hair or get out.

So I moved in with my first girlfriend, Susan. Very straight. Very smart. Very cute. The star actress in school. It must have been her theatrical sensibility that attracted her to a freaky nascent underground underdog Rock and Roller. Her mother was a widow and an alcoholic, one of the few adults I could relate to even a little bit. I liked both of them a lot.

Being the school freak meant I was the last guy in high school to have sex. Or at least it felt like that, hanging with guys like Mark Romanski, who knew how to talk to girls, something I never did figure out. I heard he ended up in the CIA. That might be a rumor, but he *was* a clever Robert Culp type. I hope I'm not blowing his cover.

I finally had sex at a party with Susan after close calls with others. It was terrible. Couldn't get the rubber on. Couldn't get it off. Once I moved into her place, we got quite good at it. It was a little kinky because we'd do it in her mother's bed while she was at work.

Then I got kicked out of school because I didn't live at home. Or was I kicked out of the house because I'd gotten kicked out of school? I felt bad for my mother, who was caught in the middle, so I went back home and—forgive me, David Crosby—cut my hair.

Oh, the humanity!

It was traumatic. I even saw sorrow in my mother's eyes. The only good that came out of it was that, since my hair was cut, I figured I might as well join the wrestling team to exact revenge on a kid who had a gang that had been bullying me. The whole thing was over in a day. I joined the team, selected him as an opponent, smashed his face on the floor, broke his nose, and started growing my hair back.

After I reluctantly and meaninglessly graduated from high school (the irony of my giving keynote addresses at education forums these days isn't lost on me), I hooked up with a working band from the Boston area. Gingerbread, I think the name was.

The experience only lasted about three months and was notable for only a few things. I met my second girlfriend, Vivienne, who was French and twenty-five and began my appreciation of older women. Every young boy and girl, of legal age of course, should begin their sex lives with older lovers. It should be treated as an apprenticeship just like anything else. It would be so much more enjoyable. Young kids having their first sex with each other is always pathetic. Mine certainly was. Older cultures used to do that for the boys. But probably not the girls, unfortunately. Society has always been deathly afraid of truly unleashing a woman's sexuality because they know it is infinitely more powerful than a man's.

The diner we ate in had a little jukebox attached to each table, and we played "Ramblin' Gamblin' Man" by the Bob Seger System and Donovan's "Hurdy Gurdy Man" every day.

The only other event of note from that experience was that my Grampa Lento's National acoustic guitar with the resonator was stolen by the other guitar player in the band. I couldn't prove it, but he had been drooling over it, and then one day it was missing.

I was very upset and told Nana Lento. All I had left was a guitar strap, and she asked for it. I'll never know for sure whether she did it or called her sister Zeze in Boston, but an Italian conjurer was approached and issued a *maloik* on whoever took Sam's guitar. (It's like a goombah hoo-doo thing. Every ethnic group has one.)

Cut to forty years later, an E Street Band show in Pittsburgh. On my way to the stage stands Joe Grushecky. "Hey," he said, "I know who has your grandfather's guitar."

"What?!? Don't you fucking leave!" I said as they pulled me onstage.

The story went something like this. Joe was at a funeral, and the widow came up to him and said, "I heard you know Stevie." Yeah, he said. "Well," she said. "I have his grandfather's guitar."

Turns out the *maloik* really worked. The scum that stole it died. Slow, I hope. Then the guy who got it from him died. Then the guy who got it from *him* died. At that point, the widow wisely concluded it was time to return the thing from whence it had come.

My name and address were on a card in the compartment, and the original thief never bothered to take it out. So I got the guitar back.

Gingerbread got boring. The gigs dried up. I moved back with my parents for a minute. And then one night I went to see Bruce play at Le Teendezvous in Shrewsbury, one of those teenage Jersey nightclubs. The Castiles had broken up by then, and he was with one of his new bands, Earth or maybe Child.

At the break, Bruce said, "You heard about this place Upstage?"

I hadn't.

"It's amazing. Down in Asbury. Open 8 p.m. to 5 a.m. All ages. Ask for Margaret."

All I knew about Asbury Park was Convention Hall, where we saw the big bands, and the Battle of the Bands on the roof of the Howard Johnson's where Tim McLoone's is now. We won.

Down I went to check out the Upstage Club.

At the door was Margaret, looking straight out of the '50s, probably in her forties, the owner Tom Potter's wife and the lead singer of Margaret and the Distractions.

"Bruce told me about you," she said. "If you're as good as he says, you'll get upstairs in no time. Now go in, but don't tell Tom I let you in for free."

The beginning of a beautiful friendship.

Upstage was above a Thom McAn shoe store. You climbed a tubular black staircase lit with colorful iridescence to get to the lower floor of the club. That was the café, reserved for auditions and Folk singers.

If you were designated as worthy, you moved up. That meant another long staircase up to the main room, maybe two or three hundred capacity, distinguished by, and locally infamous for, having the amps and PA system built into the black-lit psychedelic walls.

It was the place bands came to jam after the bars closed at 3 a.m., back when jamming was all the rage.

I vaguely remember having to build a band out of whoever was sitting around in the café that day for the audition. One of my first encounters would end up being one of my lifelong closest friends, a soft-spoken, southern-boy bass player named Garry Tallent. I introduced myself and said I was there to audition. He volunteered to play with me.

Big Bad Bobby Williams, the three-hundred-pound biker and drummer with the Distractions, a larger-than-life character in every way, volunteered to play the drums.

We did "Hi-Ho Silver Lining," "Shapes of Things," and maybe a Blues thing like "Rock Me Baby." All Jeff Beck, who was everything to me at the time (and pretty much still is). I'd be forever grateful to Jeff for introducing the world to Rod Stewart, who would be the reason I would become infatuated with Sam Cooke.

I graduated upstairs immediately. As I met more of the Upstage guys, I found out there was a scene in that part of Jersey that I knew nothing about. Bands like the Storytellers (featuring the impish Danny Federici on organ), Sonny and the Starfires (with the lanky and hyperintense Vini Lopez), the Bank Street Blues Band (with the cynical, peripatetic John Lyon), the Blazers, the Moment of Truth (also with Vini, and with Garry Tallent), Norman Seldin's Joyful Noyze, etc.

Sprinkled throughout, sometimes playing with one band, sometimes with another, were hot local guitar players like Billy Ryan, Ricky De-Sarno, Sonny Kenn, Bill Chinook, and Paul Dickler.

In those years, the guitar players ruled because the guitar had become temporarily omnipotent. Hard to imagine now, but for a few years the guitar players were more important than the singers.

Rod Stewart worked for Jeff Beck. Robert Plant worked for Jimmy Page. No shit. Jimi Hendrix's group was called the Jimi Hendrix Experience for a reason, and not because he happened to be the singer. There would be one more example of this ten years later with Van Halen when Eddie gave the guitar its last evolution.

I became one of the kings of the jam, along with Bruce, Ricky, and Billy.

If you jammed all night at Upstage, you made five dollars. The few of us that led the jams got fifteen dollars for four or five hours onstage.

I only worked three nights a week, but I lived off that forty-five dollars a week for quite a while.

When Bruce wasn't commuting back and forth to Freehold, he was sleeping on the beach or in the surfboard shop of his second Manager,

Carl "Tinker" West. I had dropped by once or twice, maybe we rehearsed there with one band or another, but I thought the place was toxic. Literally. The chemicals used to make the boards smelled poisonous. So Bruce and I got an apartment together on Fourth or Fifth Avenue in Asbury Park.

One big loft room. Two mattresses on the floor. Not much else.

We were the original odd couple, as he immortalized in a speech he gave decades later when I was honored by Little Kids Rock.

Of course, when it came to who was Oscar and who was Felix, he lied. When there was no more room in the sink for the pile of dishes, we moved.

Along with Johnny Lyon, Albee Tellone, and Johnny Waasdorp, I got an apartment where Cookman met Kingsley. Johnny Lyon had worked in the post office and played harmonica. Albee was a Singer-Songwriter and guitarist. Waasdorp, who had started the Rogues and then replaced Phil Watson in the Mods, was a brilliant guitar player who switched to piano, gaining the moniker "Hotkeys" in the process. Bruce would stay there sometimes too.

We used the time together to really dig into the roots of Blues. As one of the bedrocks of Rock, Blues music was present in whatever we did. We were introduced to it through the Rolling Stones, but many of the lead guitar developments in Blues Rock came from the trio of guitarists who passed through the Yardbirds.

The first, Eric Clapton, defined modern lead guitar, both in the Yardbirds and in bands like John Mayall's Bluesbreakers and Cream. He influenced everybody who plays a solo to this day. Clapton's successor, Jeff Beck, founded the Jeff Beck Group, which introduced us to both Rod Stewart and Ronnie Wood (on bass at the time, brilliantly) and redefined the guitar player / lead singer relationship. And finally came Jimmy Page, who created the ultimate Hard Rock archetype, Led Zeppelin.

Right in the midst of that, Jimi Hendrix took it all to some new cosmic place. The only other guitar players of similar stature, representing Blues tradition rather than the progressive English style of playing, were Mike Bloomfield with the Paul Butterfield Blues Band and the lesser-known Danny Kalb with the Blues Project.

At Cookman and Kingsley, we traced the genre back from the white cover versions to the black originators.

We listened incessantly to Little Walter, Fred McDowell, Sonny Boy Williamson, Robert Johnson, Howlin' Wolf, Son House, Elmore James, and Muddy Waters. We also started playing cutthroat Risk and Monopoly in our plentiful spare time.

The early signs of a logical part of my brain I wasn't yet conscious of, and which would come in handy later, began to appear. I realized the way to win at Risk was to capture Australia first.

I had also figured out that the key to having a winning pro football team was the offensive line. They were the most important players. Not the quarterback, the running backs, or the wide receivers. Not any of what are still insultingly referred to as the "skill" players. It's the "unskilled" and probably lowest-paid offensive linemen that make the difference.

Our Monopoly obsession would continue onstage when we formed Dr. Zoom and the Sonic Boom a few months later.

One afternoon, a few of us dropped acid and went to see *Yellow Submarine* in New York.

Acid, of course, was lysergic acid diethylamide, or LSD (why not LAD?), and it was still a new thing in East Coast hippie culture. The drug, a strong hallucinogen, had been discovered by Albert Hofmann in 1938 in Switzerland, was used in experiments by the CIA on unsuspecting victims, and found its way to hippie gurus like Timothy Leary, Owsley Stanley, and Aldous Huxley.

I know it's probably hard to believe now, but my generation didn't do drugs to escape from reality. We were seeking enlightenment, the broader understanding of the universe that the Beatles were singing about in songs like "Love You To," "Tomorrow Never Knows," and "The Inner Light." And believe it or not, LSD wasn't illegal nationally until 1968.

Acid affected the mind in ways that gave the user a shortcut to understanding the basics of Eastern philosophy. Think of it as the hippie Google.

I only did three trips, but the second and third were redundant. The first one revealed to me the three truths that would link elementary school science to metaphysics and that remain the basis of my spiritual knowledge to this day:

Everything is alive (preons, the tiniest particles in the universe, are constantly in motion).

Everything is connected (for every action, there is a reaction).

Everything is forever (matter changes form but can never be destroyed).

Yellow Submarine was not only a Beatles cartoon but an incredible work of Art. Returning to childhood was an essential goal in the hippie philosophy as the seeker sought to release the ugliness of the spiritually bankrupt, materialistic adult society. We hippies were trying to get back our sense of wonder and enjoy the beauty of being alive.

As we watched and tripped, all the secrets of the universe were revealed to us. The inherent yin-yang conflict of positive and negative energy talked about by Joseph Campbell, which would be the basis of *Star Wars*, was there. And a lot more.

It took us a while to realize the movie had ended. As we finally got up to leave, we noticed Johnny Waasdorp was still staring at the screen, mouth open. His mind was completely gone.

We got him home, and over the course of the next few days he slowly returned to us, but in the form of a seven-year-old child. He never came back any further than that. We gradually lost touch with him, and some years later heard that he had killed himself. A sad loss of a great friend and enormous talent.

Stick with the Internet.

At a certain point in 1969 or so, Bruce called me and asked if he could switch to the Telecaster.

I know that sounds funny, but growing up when we did, your guitar was your identity. And I was the Telecaster guy. Bruce had his weird converted bass guitar for a while and then a Les Paul, which probably proved to be too damn heavy.

I said OK. I had been trying a Stratocaster out lately and liked it. And anyway, guitar playing was starting to feel kind of over. The Rock world was about to undergo a major transformation.

In 1969 the Beatles had already broken up, but we didn't know it yet. A world without them was going to be psychologically traumatic, and not just for me. They were our generation's leaders, teachers, and inspiration. I don't think the Stones ever quite recovered from having to try a little harder as the number two band in the world.

We were lucky to have had them as long as we did, keeping in mind we met them halfway through their career. They were together for twelve years and put out thirteen glorious albums in seven years of recording. Keeping a great band together that long isn't easy.

Cream did three and a half albums.

The Jeff Beck Group with Rod, Ronnie, Nicky, Mick, and then Tony did two.

Moby Grape did three.

Buffalo Springfield had broken up by the time their third record came out.

The Youngbloods did two, lost Jerry Corbitt, did one more.

The Byrds lost their main songwriter, Gene Clark, by their third album but still managed four more classics.

With a handful of exceptions, the great bands averaged between three and four albums.

Why? Because what made those classic bands classic was the amount of talent. The Temptations had five lead singers! With that much talent, it's hard to keep things together unless you have a Manager who understands that the band matters more than any individual. And that's rare.

Most Managers encourage the lead singer to go solo. More money for them both. And it's easier to control the situation. But the records are never the same. When the harmony voice joining Dave Mason is Stevie Winwood, it's better than when it's not. Traffic is one of the exceptions— they lost Mason after their second album, then did three more great ones.

Only the Rolling Stones, half of the Who, and two-fifths of the Yardbirds remain working from the original bands of the British Invasion. Lead singers abound, which is great, but it's not the same thing.

No matter how you sliced it, as the new decade began, the simultaneous evolution of sociopolitical consciousness and the nascent Artform of Rock was starting to come apart at the seams.

The optimism that began at the Human Be-In and the Monterey Pop Festival in 1967 got damaged at the Chicago riots in 1968, but made a comeback and peaked at Woodstock. It was now unraveling with Altamont, Manson's murders, and the Beatles' breakup.

As the election of Richard Nixon represented society's reluctance to change, and the failure of Rock to change it, the once-bright '60s limped to a politically disappointing dark end, and Rock and politics would go their separate ways for a while.

At the same time, the Renaissance of the '60s would end appropriately with a work of unparalleled genius that would complete the promise of *Sgt. Pepper*, sum up the entire Rock Era of the '50s and '60s, and reveal the pinnacle of the Artform of Rock:

The Who's masterpiece *Tommy*.

So how do we follow that?

four

Southside Johnny and the Kid

In this jungle we're slaves to politics,
And we call ourselves civilized,
If you ain't got the muscle,
Fear gonna run your life.

   —"FEAR," FROM *VOICE OF AMERICA*

Big Danny was having trouble concentrating.

Being a seven-foot-tall, flaming-red-haired, 380-pound real-life leprechaun may have come in handy when negotiating the tense situations encountered in the course of daily existence, but his intimidating girth could not help him now.

He had the option to build more houses on Boardwalk and Park Place, but Obie already had hotels on Marvin Gardens, Albee was building on St. Charles, and Eddie Larachi had swallowed up the railroads and Pennsylvania Avenue.

Big Danny checked again. He was low on funds. It was hard to think with 120 dB of Rock and Roll being blasted into the echoey old barn that was now the Asbury Park Hullabaloo Club. But that was part of the challenge of being a Monopoly Player onstage with Dr. Zoom and the Sonic Boom! This was his job, and he could handle it. He had to. It was the only gig in town.

The fragmentation of Rock wouldn't happen until the early '70s. In the '60s, there were a series of overlapping monocultural trends that happened like clockwork: the British Invasion in '64, Folk Rock in '65, Blues Rock in '66, the Psychedelic Summer of Love in '67, Country Rock in '68, Hard Rock in '69, and (mostly white) Southern-Gospel-Soul-Rock in '70.

Each major city had one main FM station that reinforced the shared artistic sensibility, so the whole country happily, fearlessly, explored the new artistic vistas right along with the Artists as the new Artform created them.

Some Renaissance artists would enter in the year the specific genre fit them—Jimi Hendrix in Psychedelic '67—and some would move from trend to trend, bringing their genius along with them.

Before the Beatles, Artists considered any hit a miracle, and they (and their record company) showed their gratitude by releasing a slightly rewritten version of the same hit as a follow-up single.

The Twist?

Let's Twist Again.

Perfect.

Simple as that.

But the first nine albums by the Beatles were a constantly changing story. They weren't thinking Art. They just did what came naturally. But by doing so they did something they don't get enough credit for—*they invented the concept of musical evolution.*

And in doing so, influenced everyone who followed, artists and audiences alike.

Each new Byrds album branched out into new genres. Every Who and Kinks release broadened the subjects Rock bands could write about. We waited for the next Stones single to vent our teenage frustration and to hear the new guitar tones. Bob Dylan would climb straight up reaching for his artistic persona through *Blonde on Blonde* before abandoning autobiography altogether and settling on his everyman troubadour persona for the rest of his life while continuing to surprise us to this very day.

The Beatles, incredibly, went from "Love Me Do" to "I Am the Walrus" in six short years, and we as an audience went with them, while we as artists/singers/musicians evolved on the backs of their amazing growth and those yearly genre trends, taking a little from this and a little from that as we built our own future identities.

In late 1969, Bruce started Steel Mill, a band that combined Blues Rock, Hard Rock, Southern Gospel Rock, and Roy Orbison's cinematic technique of going new places in a song without repeating where he'd been.

It was Bruce, Vini Lopez on drums, Vinnie Roslin from the Motifs on bass, and Danny Federici on the rare (because it was so gigantic and expensive) Hammond B-3 organ.

The closest thing to compare it to was a combination of early Rascals, Deep Purple, and Rhinoceros, with one voice instead of two.

When Steel Mill started to get popular on the East Coast, Bruce went west to audition for Bill Graham's new Fillmore record label. He didn't get signed, but on his way back he called me. "Vinnie's not working out," he said. "Would you mind switching to bass for awhile until we figure it out?"

My time with Gingerbread had ended and I had nothing better going on. "Sure," I said.

I got the new Dan Armstrong see-through bass and a huge Ampeg amp that I feel like I'm still paying off and jumped in. Our audience kept growing, especially in Jersey and Richmond, Virginia.

I'm not sure where the connection to Richmond came from. Maybe Tinker. But we were big down there. Richmond always felt like spring. Twenty degrees warmer than Jersey. Beautiful buildings and trees. Clean. The girls were lovely, less cynical, and, in those liberated times, very friendly. It was paradise. Bruce and I would drive down there in my '62 ragtop Austin Healey with the bug-eye headlights. No heat. No shocks. Five hours or so, but we didn't care.

Steel Mill was the first time we experienced the thrill of having what I call "live hits."

Bruce's songwriting was improving all the time, and if we got back to a town often enough, certain songs were so immediately accessible that they'd become favorites.

Steel Mill peaked on September 11, 1970, when we returned to the scene of my first experience onstage, the Clearwater Swim Club in Highlands.

There had to have been a thousand people there, maybe more, all having a great, mellow time. For no discernible reason, the Middletown police had bought riot gear, even though there was no crime in Middletown whatsoever, never mind riots.

The pool was set down in a valley, and all I remember was looking up and seeing what I'd seen in a dozen Westerns: we were completely surrounded by Indians up on the surrounding hills!

But these Indians were cops in military riot gear, and I had a Ghost Dance moment as they charged down the hill and brutally attacked the audience. They were beating everyone in sight with clubs and shields for the capital crime of having long hair and *possibly* smoking pot!

In the melee that followed, Danny saw two cops arresting someone and pushed the PA system down on them.

Now Danny was . . . well, picture an older Dennis the Menace, the kind of character who unscrewed the metal plate that held the elevator

Article about the "riot" at Clearwater Swim Club after a Steel Mill concert

The Courier

buttons as we left a hotel because he'd thought of a creative use for it on his B-3.

Anyway, some cops saw him push the PA, and the chase was on. He escaped and had to go on the lam for a while until things cooled off.

For once the neighborhood was on our side, acknowledging the psychotic police chief, Joe McCarthy, had gone too far.

Even though we were getting bigger and bigger, Bruce surprised the hell out of me and decided he didn't want to be the lead singer anymore. He found a guy named Robbin Thompson from a Richmond band called Mercy Flight.

Great guy. But what the fuck?

I guess Bruce was having existential doubts as to which identity would both work commercially and feel comfortable for the rest of his life. I'm still having those moments.

Predictably, that move totally confused Steel Mill's audience and killed whatever momentum we had. Next!

Whoever ran the Asbury Park Hullabaloo Club, also known as the Sunshine Inn (I seem to remember John Scher, who would become the main Jersey Promoter, being involved), got word to us that they could use a house band to open for the big acts coming through town.

We decided to put a band together that included everyone we knew, both guys and girls. Whoever didn't play an instrument could sweep up between songs. Or blow up balloons. Or play Monopoly or Risk onstage. That way, everyone could get some bread. We named the mobile commune Dr. Zoom and the Sonic Boom.

That's when Johnny got his nickname "Southside." He had started dressing like he did on his first album cover, with the hat and shades. Like the Blues Brothers five years later. Bruce started calling him Chicago Johnny. "No," I said, "the action's on the Southside, where the Checkerboard Lounge is, Pepper's, Theresa's, Florence's, the 708, Turner's." And so it was.

I remember opening for Black Sabbath and Humble Pie. I wish now I'd made a point of meeting Steve Marriott, just on the basis of "Itchycoo Park" alone, but I wasn't as big a fan of the Small Faces as I would become. We especially looked forward to the J. Geils Band, because

Geils had slicked-back hair on the band's first album cover, a cool rebellious throwback look. But he disappointed us profoundly by joining the modern world like five minutes before we played with them. Tragic. But Peter Wolf was one of the greatest front men we'd ever seen. Still is. I have a fond memory of opening for Big Brother and the Holding Company and of Bruce running for his life from Janis Joplin, who wanted to fuck him. She scared him to death.

Every month or two, the same group of guys more or less would turn into a different band.

We had the Sundance Blues Band, with Garry Tallent on bass, Big Bobby Williams on drums, Davie Sancious on keys, Bruce on second guitar, and me on lead vocals/guitar.

We had a soul group called Funky Dusty and the Soul Broom, with me leading.

We had a country thing for a minute called the Hired Hands with Albee Tellone up front, which is when I first picked up the mandolin and spent a few months trying to figure out the impossible pedal steel guitar.

We then decided to get into the final '60s genre: southern (mostly white) Soul.

Southern white Soul covered a lot of territory, from the marriage of Blues and Country by the Allman Brothers Band to the Band's creation of what would eventually be called Americana.

But it was Blues combined with Country and Gospel that got our attention: Delaney and Bonnie and Friends, then Taj Mahal (decidedly not white) with Native American Jesse Ed Davis (decidedly not white) on guitar, Ry Cooder, Bonnie Raitt. The ultimate example was Mad Dogs and Englishmen, with Joe Cocker up front and Leon Russell leading the band.

Cocker, the former plumber in the tie-dyed shirt, was a blue-eyed English Soul Man, channeling Ray Charles so intensely that his spastic body appeared to be completing some kind of invisible electric soul circuit.

And the band behind him included horns and chick singers. The Rolling Stones picked up on what was next and included horns and chick singers on their incredible *Exile on Main St.* album and tour.

We found our own chicks and horns. I think Bruce actually went to a local Gospel church to find the girls.

It was around that time that I convinced Bruce to start using his own name.

It was quite recently that he was still debating whether he wanted to be a lead singer at all. This time, I wasn't having it. "Look," I said. "You're gonna be the leader and lead singer and main writer. That ain't gonna change. It'll still be a band, but it's time for you to be recognized." That was me. Always looking out for my own self-interest.

What a putz.

It took a few weeks, but I would not back down. He knew if anybody criticized the idea, I had his back. He finally got over his embarrassment, and we became the Bruce Springsteen Band.

We continued to go down to Richmond regularly, still in my Austin Healey. The take was split nine or ten ways, but I don't remember even thinking about money in those days. Didn't need it. Never spent it. We were as free as we'd ever be in our whole lives. No responsibilities. Typical rent was $150.

Richmond was where the road to stardom would end for the Bruce Springsteen Band. Vini Lopez earned his new moniker, "Mad Dog," by punching our trumpet player in the mouth (where else?). Before the show.

It was the final straw. We'd tried everything. The ship was sailing and we couldn't get a ticket. We were twenty-one, twenty-two, on the verge of too old to be discovered.

Bruce went home to New Jersey to think. I stayed in Richmond, where Southside and I formed a devolutionary Country-Blues Folk duo, Southside Johnny and the Kid. We played Robert Johnson, Son House, Jimmy Reed, Fred McDowell, a cool arrangement of Elmore James's "Look on Yonder Wall." Davie Sancious sat in if there was a piano around, and Garry Tallent occasionally also. We were edging our way back toward being a band, when . . .

Rrrrrrrrrring.

"Stevie, it's Bruce. Come on back. I got signed!"

five

The Business

(1972)

A masterpiece is a thousand good guesses.
— THE UNWRITTEN BOOK

The band era had peaked and fragmented. Nobody was coming to New Jersey to sign us.

So Bruce wises up and gets signed as a Singer-Songwriter, what used to be called a Folk singer, by the legendary John Hammond, no less! The guy who tried to book Robert Johnson at Carnegie Hall for the *From Spirituals to Swing* concerts. He'd been a few weeks too late. Johnson had just been poisoned by a jealous husband or a pissed-off girlfriend. Hammond signed Benny Goodman and Billie Holiday. He integrated Jazz by encouraging Benny Goodman to use Count Basie and Lionel Hampton. He signed Aretha Franklin to Columbia Records for the first phase of her career and then Bob Dylan, known as Hammond's Folly when his first album didn't sell. The label wanted to drop him. "Over my dead body," Hammond said.

The tradition went back to the troubadours of antiquity and coalesced in the Greenwich Village Folk clubs of the '60s where Dave Van Ronk, the Mayor of MacDougal Street, held court at places like the Bitter End, the Gaslight, the Night Owl, Gerde's Folk City, the Purple Onion, the Kettle of Fish, Café Figaro, the Village Gate, and Cafe Wha?

Those folkies followed the path of Woody Guthrie and included Pete Seeger, Fred Neil, Tom Paxton, Phil Ochs, Ramblin' Jack Elliott, Tim Hardin, Tim Rose, Tim Buckley, and Tiny Tim among others.

Then came Dylan, who revitalized and revolutionized Folk music before plugging in and becoming a Rock star. Donovan, Leonard Cohen, and Joni Mitchell had success in his wake, but it was the Beatles signing James Taylor to their new Apple label, which refurbished Folk as the new Singer-Songwriter genre.

Singer-Songwriters seemed to spring up every month in the early '70s: Kris Kristofferson, Jackson Browne, Gordon Lightfoot, Loudon Wainwright III, John Prine. Even Carole King, who had sung on her songwriting demos for more than a decade, was persuaded by Lou Adler to do an album. Which is still selling.

The one big difference between the traditional Folk singers and the new Singer-Songwriters was that the new acts all had hits.

In the '50s, hits were a risk for Folk credibility. The Kingston Trio's "Tom Dooley" was so big it disqualified them as cool. Peter, Paul, and Mary got away with "Puff, the Magic Dragon" because it was rumored to be about drugs and with "Blowin' in the Wind" because it was a protest song and put Dylan on the charts for the first time. That made them cool in perpetuity.

Folk music was never my thing, so I wasn't paying close attention. Bruce was. He figured that he needed a Trojan horse to get into that mysterious fortress called the Business. And so he reawakened his Singer-Songwriter persona.

It was an honest persona. I had witnessed his Folk side in his room in Freehold. It suited his loner aspect, while being in a band forced him to be social, which was healthy.

But at that stage of the game, a Folk singer was not who he needed to be. He had spent too many hours rockin' to stop now. And Pop hits were still a lifetime away. Now that he was signed, he immediately started assembling a band.

From Steel Mill, he took Danny on accordion and organ and Mad Dog, temporarily forgiven, on drums. He decided to use Davie Sancious and mentioned who he was thinking of for bass. "Oh, man," I said. "He ain't right." The best bass player in town was Garry Tallent. He had always been my bass player. I didn't want to lose him. But I also knew that it would be a small miracle if any of us found a way to break out of New Jersey. Bruce was going to have to be the horse we bet on. I suggested Garry.

"You sure?" Bruce said. I could tell that's what he'd wanted to hear all along.

I would also be going up to the session, of course.

Just to see what Fate had in mind.

As we educated ourselves in earnest in that Upstage period, Bruce and I became obsessed with the honking tenor sax solos that provided the break in the middle of virtually every hit record before the Beatles. Where had they all gone?

The unintended consequence of the British Invasion's dominance was that they put all their heroes out of work. The Drifters, Coasters, Doo-Wop, Little Richard—all the Pioneers—and all their sax players, King Curtis, Lee Allen, George Young, Red Prysock, Wild Bill Moore. Working their asses off one day, gone the next.

In our quest for our identity, we felt that if we could find that authentic sound, we could . . . we would . . . well, we didn't know what, but it would somehow be cool by being so uncool, dig? The saxophone would connect us to the already-starting-to-be-forgotten past. Tradition.

We found a wacky white guy, Coz, a '50s Sam Butera swing-type cat who could have come straight out of Louis Prima's band. Fantastic. He had the right sound but looked exactly like William Bendix. And white wasn't right. We kept looking.

Garry said he knew another guy who had played with Little Melvin and the Invaders. We piled into Garry's car. We couldn't all fit in mine, and Bruce didn't even have a license. We drove into the woods—to this day, I have no idea where. A club suddenly appeared. The place was jumping, and we could feel the bass pulsing as we approached the joint. The whole experience already felt surreal, assisted by the ganja that had been passed around in the car.

When we went in, it was like one of those movies where everything stops and everyone stares for a second before the party restarts. We were the only white faces, but I was too intoxicated by the thick, sexy hashish-and-perfume-scented atmosphere to be nervous. Chicks danced on the bar in a haze of smoke. And wait! There it was!

That sound!

Funny how those little mysterious details occupied us. Like the tone of a saxophone. We were seeking energy from wherever we could find it, and pure, cool sound was life-giving energy, whether from our guitars or a sax. The road was strewn with the broken bodies of those who had searched in vain for it. The few who found it were sanctified. With the sudden unprecedented infinite fragmentation, the zeitgeist was losing its equilibrium. We needed something traditional to ground us.

That sound!

Bruce looked at me with the same expression Cristoforo Colombo must have given his first mate when, after thirty-six death-defying days on the ocean, they spotted naked indigenous chicks sunbathing on Grand Bahama beach.

We met the sax player at the break. He was gigantic. He should have been intimidating but he wasn't. High as a kite wouldn't be an accurate description because kites don't fly as high as he was. We told him to drop in at what was to be a short-lived residency at the Student Prince on Kingsley some night, and that was about all the conversation any of us was capable of.

He was even bigger in the light. He even *looked* like King Curtis. He was just so authentic, we couldn't believe our luck. Afterward, I asked Bruce if he'd caught the guy's name.

"Clarence," he said. We laughed about that. I don't know why. Even his name was authentic. "Clarence Clemons," Bruce added.

So Bruce, who'd been signed as a solo guy, immediately pissed off John Hammond, everybody at Columbia, and his new Manager Mike Appel by telling them his thing was having a band! With a sax player! Named Clarence!

By the time I walked into the studio, the powers that be were in no mood for a second guitarist. Who needed the extra expense? And I was nervous enough as it was. I'd practiced a bottleneck part on "For You." I happen to be real good with a bottle—Duane Allman went out of his way to complement me when we played together—but the atmosphere was impossible. They gave me maybe two takes and said forget it.

That was it. I was out.

My best friend was on his way.

But he'd be making the journey without me.

By that point, I had been a bandleader for seven years. So being rejected from Bruce's new band shouldn't have been that big a deal. Even if I didn't want to front, I could just find a singer and start a new band, right?

I didn't.

I was a bit depressed that Bruce hadn't stood up for me. But it was more than that. I liked the idea of being the guy behind the guy. The Underboss. The Consigliere. I wanted to make Bruce the biggest star in the world, and I knew I had certain instincts that complemented the few he lacked.

Plus, it really did feel like the train had left the station. The Renaissance was over. Most of the '60s groups were being replaced by caricatures and hybrids. We were such fanatical purists that we didn't appreciate groups like Aerosmith, who were a combination of the Stones and the Yardbirds. Why take them seriously when we could go see the real Stones and Yardbirds? Who could have imagined that a decade later we'd be desperate for a band to have the good sense to combine those two bands?

There was financial stress as well. I had never paid off the big Sunn amp and the van I bought to carry it around. It was my first rancid taste of the horror of owing money, around $2000, as I recall.

Depression? Debt? Destiny? Whatever the reason, I quit.

My whole family, all my uncles, were in construction. My father called my Uncle Dick and got me a job.

The Calabrése laborer in my blood was ready to jump body and soul into my new life. Maybe I could fit into society after all? My religion of Rock was filled with ungrateful infidels! Who needed it?

I got a cool used Dodge Charger and listened to *Imus in the Morning* every day on my way to work for two years.

I started as a flagman, standing in the middle of the New Jersey Turnpike or Route 287 directing eighty-mile-an-hour morning traffic from four lanes down to two. Then I raked two-hundred-degree blacktop in ninety-degree heat. Carried bricks and bags of mortar. Reinforced bridge abutments. And worked my way up to the jackhammer, which permanently rattled what Rock and Roll had left of my brains.

On weekends I played flag football. One Sunday, reaching for a flag, I dislocated the ring finger on my right hand. Despite on-field surgery (it's still bent), I couldn't work the jackhammer.

So much for the straight life.

Now, let's see, what would be a good way to exercise my finger?

六

Vegas!

(1973)

We need to teach our students how to think, not what to think.
—THE UNWRITTEN BOOK

Shazam!

As if by wizardry!

A cloud of purple smoke and there I was . . .

. . . playing a Wurlitzer electric piano, exercising my inner Banana and my dislocated finger simultaneously.

Youngbloods. Never mind.

The band included some ex-Mods. Not the English kind, but the Rumson kind that was part of the Holy Trinity of Jersey groups, along with the Clique and the Motifs. Both the Mods and the Clique had asked me to join them a year or so before. That respect made me feel like I'd finally made my bones. Locally anyway. I don't know why I didn't join one of them.

As Fate would have it, and she usually does, the drummer in the bar band I joined for physical therapy happened to be the cousin of one of the Dovells. You know, "Bristol Stomp," "You Can't Sit Down," two of the greatest recordings ever made. They needed a backup band for the old-ies circuit, which was touring the country and would play the Flamingo Hotel in Las Vegas.

That's all I had to hear. Vegas, baby! My first Mecca!

Not only was I a Rat Pack fanatic and Mob aficionado, but I was a gambler. I had John Scarne's *Complete Guide to Gambling* near me at all times like a Bible. Scarne was the mathematics genius who figured out the odds of every casino game. He was banned by one casino after another for card counting (which is why blackjack now has a multideck shoe), until he finally wore them out and they hired him.

It was his math that would have encouraged Meyer Lansky to clean up the corruption when Batista made him gambling commissioner in Cuba in the '50s. Lansky realized the house didn't have to cheat to win. They just had to keep gamblers gambling.

So, let's see . . . socks, underwear, Scarne—I was ready. And I went on the road for the second time. Gingerbread. Remember? My grandfather's guitar?

The whole idea of "oldies" was at its peak in 1973. CBS-FM, the first station to create the format, '50s and early '60s music, had started in '72. *American Graffiti* would lead to *Happy Days*. But an ex-DJ, Richard Nader, was probably most responsible for what became the "Rock and Roll revival."

Nader started as a DJ, then worked at the Premier Talent Agency. Instead of embracing the British Invasion, he was pissed off that it was putting his favorite artists out of business. So he quit and started promoting oldies shows. A documentary about them, *Let the Good Times Roll*, came out in '73 and fueled the nostalgia obsession.

It was perfect timing for me.

I couldn't relate to anything going on in contemporary music at that time: Singer-Songwriters, Prog Rock, Heavy Metal, Glam. It was a good time for me to go back to school and complete my education.

I led a four-piece behind the Dovells that also performed as the opening act. Arnie Silver and Jerry Gross were original Dovells. Mark Stevens came soon after as comic relief. Arnie did the bass vocal parts and looked like James Dean. They were like big brothers to me. They old-schooled me in the ways of '60s-style romance. Like putting cologne on one's balls for the blow jobs between sets. It was a different time.

The Dovells wanted to open with a medley. Jerry had sketched it out, and I finished it off. It gave me a chance to actually play those classic records, which taught me more about them than hearing them a million times.

During that year, on the circuit, I met everybody that ever mattered. Little Richard, Bo Diddley, Gary US Bonds, the Shirelles, the Coasters, the Drifters. I was warned to stay away from Chuck Berry, but everyone else was friendly. The Drifters' guitar player, Abdul Samad, showed me some riffs and taught me about Arabic astrology. He did everybody's charts backstage. Lloyd Price, perhaps the most respected artist of them all—Little Richard had replaced *him* when he was drafted—taught me that if you wash the lubricant off the rubber you come slower. You know, life lessons.

I was having a great time, but the artists were all mostly miserable. They hated being called oldies acts. Many of them were in their prime, having regular hits when the Beatles arrived. Bam, over. Just like that. Tragically put out to pasture in their thirties and early forties by the British artists who loved them the most!

The atmosphere was invigorating. The spiritual power of the pioneers, stronger than they knew, scrubbed away any memory of my short construction career and replaced it with the new energy of a musical rebirth.

I figured since I was immersed in my own version of an adult education course, I might as well go all the way and see if I couldn't figure what was wrong with my songwriting.

I'd been writing for years and could never find my way to anything I was happy with. I decided to stop whatever I'd been doing and analyze it.

Where in the Rock world did songwriting begin?

I decided it began with Jerry Leiber and Mike Stoller. They had written countless classics. "Hound Dog" for Big Mama Thornton. "Jailhouse Rock" for Elvis. "Ruby Baby" for the early Drifters and then Dion. "Stand by Me" for Ben E. King. And most of the Coasters' hits.

I decided I would write a Leiber and Stoller song for Ben E. King and the Drifters.

First, I wanted to find a completely original chord change. Nothing crazy, just a new combination. I finally settled on G–D–E minor–C, otherwise known as 1–5–6–4. It must have been used somewhere, but I couldn't find it anywhere.

I wanted a universal theme, so I went with heartbreak. Your girl has walked out. Your once-happy sanctuary has become a cold, lonely place. "I Don't Want to Go Home."

Ben E. King came directly from the Sam Cooke school, so I wrote a Cooke melody, imagining the Drifters doing a call-and-response for the verse. I designed a split structure, verses and bridge like Frank Sinatra talking to the bartender in "One for My Baby," choruses a desperate delusional drunk talking to the girl in his head.

Man, I liked it. I felt like I had unlocked one of the secrets of the universe. I learned that day what I would teach forever in my songwriter master classes: when you get stuck writing for yourself, write a song for somebody else. But I didn't have the courage to give it to Ben E. King. He was friendly, but he was Ben E. Fucking King!

Between out-of-the-way hotels and clubs, we did arenas with the big Nader shows.

It was at a Madison Square Garden soundcheck that I heard Little Richard give what had to be one of the greatest performances of his life. And nobody saw it. It was the peak of his Jive years, when performances consisted of him performing a song or two and then jumping up on the piano, taking his shirt off, and waving it around, doing everything but singing.

For whatever reason, that afternoon, he felt like singing. He did an hour of Gospel, Country, Blues, Rolling Stones ("Jumpin' Jack Flash"!), songs he would never do in a show. He had the greatest voice I've ever heard, almost unrecognizable from his Rock records. It would encourage me to go back and discover his early Gospel records later, but that day it was quite a revelation.

I also caught a miraculous Bo Diddley performance that just for a moment took him back to his prime, although it took a weird-ass time machine to get him there. For most of the year, most shows, he was good but mostly going through the motions. Then, somewhere in the Carolinas, we were both hired for a high-society coming-out party for some rich sixteen-year-old girl. I'd never heard of a coming-out party, unless it was a gay dude celebrating self-liberation. But down south it signified some kind of adulthood. Like a redneck bar mitzvah, I guess.

I don't know if all coming-out parties were at nine o'clock in the morning, but this one was. And at that gig, I saw Bo lose twenty years and suddenly come to life. Surrounded by a hundred sixteen-year-old, very healthy southern girls exploding out of their Alice in Wonderland ball gowns into the hurricane of puberty, Bo gave one of the finest performances of his life. Every move, every lick, every trick made a reappearance, and he invented some new ones. After that, he went back to still great but legendary autopilot and stayed there for the final thirty-five years of his life.

On the road that year, the Dovells turned me on to Bruce Lee. I had never heard of him, but they took me to see *Enter the Dragon* just after he died. Wow. I was hooked. Whenever we were in a city with a Chinatown, I made sure to catch a kung fu movie.

I decided the actor most likely to replace him was a guy named Jackie Chan, who did all his own unbelievable stunts. He didn't make an English-speaking movie for a long time, and when he did he favored comedies, which disguised his true mastery. I had taken some karate but after that year I switched to kung fu, and even learned to fence and box because Bruce Lee recommended it and had included techniques from both in his Jeet Kune Do style. Didn't stick with any of it long enough to get really good, but it was fun.

Out on the circuit, I also got the news that I'd lost my grandfather Sam Lento, the man who taught me how to play guitar. It was my first big personal loss, and it hit me quite hard. I wondered then, and still wonder, why I hadn't asked him more about his life. Two deeply personal memories stand out: going with him to the Italian section of Boston, where the pushcarts still existed in 1955, and going with him to see *The Godfather* when it opened, where he leaned over to translate the Italian-language parts. I felt the pain of the news of his passing in my very soul. I still feel it. I could barely function for days.

Years later I would think back on moments like that and decide the brain must have a built-in limiter. And it works both ways.

I believe your mind cannot remember your most extreme emotions, one way or the other. That's why every time you walk onstage and hear that roar, it's like the first time.

If you truly remembered how bad every tragedy felt, you'd walk around crying all the time. And if you truly remembered how good sex was, you would get absolutely nothing done.

And then, suddenly, there it was . . . the House That Benny Built! (Don't call him Bugsy!)

The Flamingo, baby!

It was thrilling. I had read so much about it that I felt like I'd come home.

The Dovells stayed at the hotel gratis, while we were put up in some cheap motel off the Strip. Even so, I am glad I caught the last year the Mob ran Vegas.

First of all, there were vast tracts of land in between the casinos. Now you can walk the whole Strip rooftop to rooftop. Back then, the town was designed to make money strictly from gambling. Everything else existed to keep you there.

Rooms were around $20. There would be ridiculous all-you-can-eat buffets for like $3.95. With steak and lobster. The lounges and all the entertainment venues were five or six bucks. And Frank Sinatra might walk in spontaneously and entertain you for an hour.

Hookers were technically illegal in Clark County, but that was probably legislated to boost tips to the concierges, bellboys, doormen, parking lot guys, cabdrivers, and probably the janitors, all of whom had a few phone numbers for you.

The drummer bought me my first hooker. Man, was that fun! Why sex isn't legal everywhere I'll never understand. We should learn from the Netherlands and most civilizations through the centuries. Hookers are Angels of Mercy. Sex work is God's work. They are nurses for the socially retarded, therapists for the terminally shy, healers for the physically handicapped. They should be respected and protected from traffickers and pimps.

But Vegas wanted every penny gambled. Everything was a loss leader meant to keep you at that table for just one more hand, one more spin, one more roll of the dice. With no revenue from rooms, food, or entertainment and with the Mob probably skimming 25 percent off the top, everybody *still* got rich!

I couldn't wait to get to the tables to try out the Gambling Craft I had been studying under John Scarne.

I chose blackjack, although craps was the most fun. I played all seven hands. I was wiped out in about thirty minutes. Over two weeks, I continued practicing my gambling trade in all its forms, winning some, losing more. Cured my love of gambling forever.

Onstage, we opened for Frankie Valli one week, Fats Domino the next. I learned Fats was so in debt to the Mob he had to play Vegas every month, and one of the Four Seasons couldn't leave at all.

I was so visibly into the whole atmosphere I must have been glowing. The stage manager took a liking to me and offered a tour behind the scenes.

One afternoon, we went all the way up behind the top balcony. A pinspot picked out a tiny figure onstage, and as the soundcheck began I heard the last kind of music you would ever associate with the Flamingo or Las Vegas. I thought I was hallucinating. You know that weird feeling you get when you hear or see something but it's so out of context you're not sure it is what it is?

It was . . . Robert Johnson?

"You'd better come on, in my kitchen, because it's gonna be raining outdoors."

"Who's that?" I asked the stage manager.

"Dion," he said.

"'Runaround Sue' Dion?" I said.

"Yeah," he said.

I ran down and introduced myself. We hit it off right away. "Man," I said, "you ought to do something with that. First of all, you're great at it. But also, nobody would expect that from you." When I thought about it later, I realized it fit perfectly with what he'd always done. "Ruby Baby," "Drip Drop," "The Wanderer," all Blues.

Unlike some of the other pioneers, Dion refused to be put out to pasture. He never stopped recording, growing, exploring. The difference was he had deep roots he could rely on. That's one of the best things about Art. It speaks to you in a different way every time you visit.

Dion must have been watching the Dovells show from the wings, because afterward he asked if I could play the last couple of shows with him, including Dick Clark's New Year's Show at the Deauville Hotel in

Miami Beach, where the Beatles had played their second *Ed Sullivan Show* and where the Dovells got their name.

The Dovells wanted to manage me. They swore I was destined for greatness. I didn't see it. After a year on the road, the only destiny I was interested in was going home to New Jersey.

But I'd be going back in style!

I absolutely fell in love with Miami and the entire tropical lifestyle. I'll never really understand why I didn't move there permanently at that time.

Since I couldn't live in it, I decided to take it with me. I started wearing Hawaiian shirts and Frank Sinatra / Sam Snead hats and continued to do so when I got back to Jersey in snowy January. Bruce christened me "Miami Steve."

Later, when I became the slightly more serious Little Steven, I would bequeath the entire look to Jimmy Buffett, who I hear has done quite well with it.

seven

Asbury Park—Doubling Down!

I still remember, baby, those wild, desperate times,
Making love in crazy places, while the town around us died,
I played on broken stages, I watched the lonely cry,
You danced in iron cages, for the boys with hungry eyes,
All those wasted lives . . .

    —"I'M COMING BACK," SOULFIRE

A light summer rain fell through the fog that rolled off the ocean. Southside Johnny and the Kid walked down Cookman Avenue, heading east from the neutral zone of Upstage toward the saloon-circuit part of town, where freaks, misfits, and outcasts, and the freedom they represented, had never been welcome.

It wouldn't be quite as dramatic as the walk Bruce and I would take eight years later through Checkpoint Charlie into East Berlin, but it had the similar tingle of trepidation that tickled your balls. You knew you were entering a world where you did not belong.

And trust me, the wall that kept us renegades separated from the bar bands protecting their turf on that saloon circuit was almost as real as the one in Deutschland.

Asbury Park was a crippled ghost town. Its once-proud Boardwalk managed to continue functioning at subsistence level on the weekends. The Ferris wheel, bumper cars, and Madame Marie Castello's Fortune

Telling staggered on. The smell of cotton candy, salt air, and stale pop-corn somehow remained year-round.

Decades of neglect had run the place down, and then things had gotten worse. The town had always had an uncomfortable relationship between the races, black on the west side of the railroad tracks, white closer to the ocean. The riots that followed the assassination of Martin Luther King Jr. had further divided the town and killed it as a resort town forever.

Which added up to cheap rent for us.

I remember being the only guy in the classic gigantic movie theaters watching blaxploitation movies before they tore those beautiful palaces down. I was such a regular I became friends with the projectionist, who showed me how to thread the reels so he could take a break.

When I got home from the oldies circuit, it was January 2, 1974, and I was looking for some steady action. I had some ideas for a new band, but I needed a spark. It would come a few months later, when Bruce, Southside, and I went to see Sam and Dave at the Satellite Lounge.

It was a black club and mostly a black crowd, and Sam and Dave were ridiculously good. Seeing them in that small club, up close, playing "Soul Man," "Hold On, I'm Coming," "I Thank You," and the rest was truly revelatory. We went up afterward and said hello. They were nice, if a little curious about why these white Rock kids were so enthralled.

And that was that. Another epiphany. Johnny and I would become the Rock version of Sam and Dave, with double lead vocals and Rock guitar, integrated with horns. Not Jazz horns or Chicago horns or Blood, Sweat, & Tears horns. Something harder. Stax. Motown. Or what Allen Toussaint was doing in New Orleans. Simple but powerful.

We wanted to be the ultimate bar band. Our version of the Beatles at the Top Ten Club in Hamburg or the Cavern Club in Liverpool. The Stones at the Crawdaddy Club in Richmond. The Animals at the Club a' Gogo in Newcastle-upon-Tyne. The Dave Clark Five at the South Grove Youth Club in Tottenham. The Who at the Goldhawk Social Club in Shepherd's Bush. But with horns.

Even though the Renaissance was over, we thought the old rules still applied. We still thought, naively, that we needed an original identity to justify our existence. Well, now we had one.

Now we had to find a venue.

So Southside and I took that walk.

The Stone Pony, at 913 Ocean Avenue, was as run-down as the rest of town. By late 1974, the roof was half-caved-in from a recent hurricane, and the owners planned to squeeze out whatever they could from the remaining summer season and then shutter the place for good.

It was perfect.

For once the owners weren't in a position of strength. For once they couldn't demand that we wear suits and play what had become mostly mediocre top 40 Pop songs. In that half-caved-in roof I saw an opportunity. "Give us your worst night," I said. "We'll charge you nothing. Niente. Zip. We take the door, you keep the bar. But we play whatever we want." They agreed.

We couldn't have known that one move would alter New Jersey history forever.

Our band played an odd combination of Rock and Soul. A typical set included "Something About You" (by the Four Tops), "Hey Pocky A-Way" (the Meters), "I'm Not Talking" (the Yardbirds), and "Little by Little" (Junior Wells). Plus some Sam and Dave, of course.

We even introduced Reggae to the Jersey shore. *The Harder They Come* had come out. Its soundtrack was like Reggae's greatest hits, and some made it into our set: Jimmy Cliff's "The Harder They Come" and "Struggling Man," Toots and the Maytals' "Pressure Drop," the Slickers' "Johnny Too Bad," a few others.

Each night we played five sets, starting around ten and going until three in the morning. Forty-five on, fifteen off. We would also control the DJ's music before we started and in between sets to keep the vibe consistent.

The only band I knew of that had worked harder than we did before making it was the Beatles.

The first time I interviewed Ringo Starr for my *Underground Garage* show, he told me about his pre-Beatles gig with Rory Storm and the Hurricanes (is that a great name or what!), and how they alternated sets with the Beatles in Hamburg, six sets a night each, twelve hours a night, *seven nights a week—for months at a time!*

That's Fucking Work.

That's how you build stamina. That's how you learn how to perform. That's how you learn each song's effect on an audience. But it's more than that.

Listening to records, no matter how many times, is one thing. Physically playing them over and over is another. The songs get into your bloodstream and muscle memory.

That's one of the reasons the Beatles became such great writers. This was 1960 to 1962, and there just weren't that many songs to choose from. They knew everything that got released. All ninety-nine bands in Liverpool were playing the same songs, which is why they stretched into obscurities like "Devil in Her Heart" and B-sides like "Boys."

It's also why when John Lennon and Paul McCartney started writing, they looked beyond the four or five chords of the pioneers' songbook they had mastered so well. The incredibly inventive B-sections of verses and bridges of their earliest hit records, combined with their seemingly infinite wealth of great melodies, came from the intense repetition of those foundational songs, which transformed their influence from observance to DNA.

Our audience became the most sophisticated bar audience in the country because they got used to responding to songs they'd never heard before. We would always start the first set with a new song, which we would repeat in the final set.

When we threw in an original, we disguised it under a different name. We'd say that "I Don't Want to Go Home" was a B-side of a Drifters' single. Half the crowd had never even heard of the Drifters, so we got away with it.

Plus, the drinking age had recently been lowered to eighteen, so maybe the kids were just happy to be in a bar for the first time!

We made sure the songs were danceable because that was our job. If the audience danced, they drank. They didn't dance, you were out of work.

The job was harder than a decade before. Thanks to Bob Dylan's influence on Rock Artists' intellect and the ever-evolving imaginations of groups like the Beatles, the Byrds, and the Who, Rock audiences had stopped dancing and started listening.

But they still danced in the bars.

The first week we had about fifty people. The second week, a hundred. The third week, two hundred. The fourth, you couldn't get in.

They fixed the roof.

We went to a second night. Then a third. Then they expanded the place by adding an extension to the back wall.

By the end of the summer, we were pulling in a thousand people a night, three nights a week, at three dollars each. Relative to my overhead, I was as rich as I would ever be in my life.

Meanwhile, Bruce's first two albums had come and gone in a flash. He'd moved to Long Branch by then, but no sales meant he couldn't play the showcase venues that recording bands played, so he returned to Asbury to hang around with us.

He fit easily into what we were doing. The songs were mostly familiar to him, and he played along and sang whenever he felt like it.

As it turned out, it was a lot more fun to be out of the music business than in it.

Back on his first album, Bruce had blown everybody's minds by grabbing a postcard off the boardwalk and telling Columbia that that was his cover art. Greetings from Asbury Park? You gotta be kidding, they said. New Jersey was a punchline in an Abbott and Costello routine, not a place you brag about!

I figured if he had the balls to identify with Asbury Park, we should double down. I renamed the band Southside Johnny and the Asbury Jukes. Stolen from the greatest harp player that ever lived, Little Walter and His Jukes.

I didn't want to be the front man all the time, so I split the job with South. He wasn't that crazy about the idea, but he got used to it.

Bruce didn't get it at first. He was used to me fronting my own bands. And South was not an obvious choice. He was a crazy misanthropic manic-depressive who enjoyed being a grumpy, miserable, ne'er-do-well with no responsibilities—more W. C. Fields than W. C. Handy. But he surprised everybody by rising to the occasion.

Soon enough, it was clear that the Jukes had started a scene. The Pony was the hip place to be Tuesday, Thursday, and Sunday nights.

The walls were sweating just like they described in the early British Invasion days. Cocaine hadn't hit the suburbs yet, so it was mostly about booze, with an occasional joint in the parking lot.

I had stopped smoking ganja and hashish by then and had switched to Bacardi 151 rum to feed my Reggae habit. It was also better suited to my main preoccupation offstage, which was sex.

Girls were everywhere. Women's liberation was at its peak. Girls would ask *you* to have sex. I know. Impossible. But it happened. I was there. At one point I had seven regulars in the area and was meeting new ones from North Jersey on the weekends. In between sets. In the office. With the cologne.

My rent was $150 a month, and that was the extent of my expenses. Mattress on the floor. One fork. One plate. One knife, which I got rid of after I rolled over just in time to stop a New Orleans model from plunging it into my chest. Whatever I did, I am quite sure the punishment did not fit the crime.

I'm not sure exactly why, but I suppose I am obligated to explain the origin of my unusual habiliments. On top of the obvious standard hippie/gypsy/troubadour garb, there was an incident that married the bizarre to the bazaar.

One night I was driving a girlfriend home from the Pony, three in the morning, four lanes, when a guy coming the other way crossed over. I switched lanes as quickly as I could, but he drifted right with me. Head-on collision. Not too fast, but I smashed into the windshield, and though I didn't lose consciousness, I needed a few operations. After that, my hair never really grew in properly.

I asked Bruce what he thought. "You've been wearing these bandanas," he said. "Just make it a thing." I did.

We had been slowly working our original songs into the set, creating a unique identity, and felt we had earned the right to make a record. And it was now or never.

I asked Bruce what he thought about Columbia for the Jukes. He said to try Epic Records, which was a subsidiary. He had a guy in mind, Steve "Pops" Popovich, who used to be promotion at Columbia and then became vice president of A&R (that's artists and repertoire, the guys who sign bands) at Epic. Good guy, Bruce said.

Pops not only immediately signed the Jukes but would become one of our most important working partners and one of my best friends for the rest of his life.

He was a legendary character, the last of the Old School promotion guys. His constant companion was a huge cassette blaster, which he used as a lethal weapon. God help the radio program director he caught in a crowded restaurant at lunchtime. The guy would be quietly sipping his piña colada one minute and then bam! Pops would slam the blaster on the table, hit play, and his latest soon-to-be-hit would come roaring out into the cat's face. It was a beautiful thing to behold.

Pops started hanging around with us too. He was making the hour's ride from Freehold and fell in promotion-man love with the whole idea of making riot-ravaged Asbury hip. He even loved the little Italian joint we always ate in, Richie's, and wanted to franchise it.

The scene was picking up steam. Lines around the block every night, fighting to get in, and then seven hundred liberated maniacs dancing their asses off to Rock and Soul and Reggae they had never heard before.

I didn't realize it until years later, but we unwittingly redefined "bar band" forevermore to mean Soul-based Rock, usually with horns. That's not what it meant when we started. It was originally derogatory, an insult for bands that couldn't make it in the music business. It meant, among other things, that their song list was restricted to the top 40.

Rolling Stone used to have a feature where they would review one live show per issue on the back page. In 1976, for the first time, they wrote about an unsigned band, Southside Johnny and the Asbury Jukes at the Stone Pony, Tuesdays, Thursdays, and Sundays!

After that, "bar band" (and its British version, "pub rock") would be used to describe acts like Graham Parker and the Rumour, Elvis Costello and the Attractions, Nick Lowe, Dave Edmunds, Mink DeVille, Huey Lewis and the News. "Bar band" became a compliment for working-class bands who were proud of their traditional roots.

The audience became so used to hearing music they didn't yet know that for years after, national and even international bands with new albums would play the Pony first. They knew they'd have an audience who could react to new music in real time.

It would never be the Kaiserkeller or the Cavern, the Marquee, the Crawdaddy Club, or the Club a' Gogo.

But it was pretty damn cool for Jersey.

eight

The Boss of All Bosses

Greatness isn't born, it's developed. It's a decision
you make every hour or so.
—THE UNWRITTEN BOOK

"We're doing better than your wildest dreams," I said. "Three nights a week, a thousand people a night. We need to make a change."

Stone Pony owners Butch and Jack were scary dudes. The smaller one was six foot five, 280 pounds. They were picking up cases of beer and tossing them to each other for storage like they were cereal boxes.

"What do you got in mind?" asked Jack.

"We want to go to three sets a night from five," I said. "And before you answer, this isn't a negotiation. Agree or we'll go across the street and take the crowds with us. Gabeesh?"

They stopped tossing for a moment and looked at me like I was lunch. Long pause. They started tossing again. Slow smiles. Butch spoke. "OK."

And just like that, we made history a second time. Not only were we the first bar band in New Jersey to play whatever we wanted, but we were the first to break the ironclad five-sets-a-night rule. Our sets became more like what signed bands would do at showcase clubs like the Bottom Line in New York or the Roxy in LA.

I was good at doing business when I had to. The only problem was that I hated it. I wasn't sure what my purpose was on this planet, but it wasn't to become a fucking businessman. I knew I had to find the Jukes a real Manager and Agent.

Good Managers are the hardest to come by, and in my opinion they are the most crucial factor in a band's success. The Mount Rushmore of Artists had a Mount Rushmore of Managers: Colonel Tom Parker, Brian Epstein, Andrew Loog Oldham, and Albert Grossman. Rock would be unthinkable without Elvis Presley, the Beatles, the Stones, and Bob Dylan, and yet everyone in the business laughed at, passed on, or ignored all of them at first. What's the main job of a Manager? Advocacy. If it wasn't for the advocacy, belief, and salesmanship of those four Managers, who knows how history would've been different?

Managers get paid, of course. Management takes 10, 15, even 20 percent of the gross. Agents get 10 percent. The whole concept of gross points is stupid and unfair, but that's the way the business mostly runs, and it's one reason Managers and Agents can do better than their Artists. The difference between Managers and Agents was and is that Managers, the better ones, usually have to invest in their Artists in the beginning, while Agents usually don't.

But without the right Manager, you are inevitably going to have a problem. Most critics would rank the Kinks third or fourth among British Invasion bands, after the Beatles and the Stones. So why were they never as big as the Who? Because their management was busy producing the Troggs when the Kinks toured America. The tour devolved into chaos. The band didn't get paid. They fought with each other onstage. Ray Davies traded punches with a union guy on *The Dick Clark Show,* which led to a ban from the United States for the most important four years of their prime, 1965 to 1969.

That's what happens when you don't have the right management.

As I set out to find the Jukes a real Manager and Agent, I was still acting as de facto Manager. I figured I needed something to make it more fun. An assistant! Just as a joke really. I drafted Obie Dziedzic, our number one fan, to be my first assistant. She turned out to be great, actually, a perfect buffer. She had that Big Mama McEvily quality of taking no shit from anybody. And like Big Mama, she was physically imposing enough to keep anybody in their right mind from fucking with her—and therefore me.

Bruce was recording what could have been his last record for Columbia. He was fighting for his life.

"Come check it out," he said. I made the trek up to 914 Sound Studios in scenic Blauvelt, New York, owned by the legendary Engineer and Producer Brooks Arthur. Not the happiest of memories, since that's where I got kicked out of the band. Bruce was there with Mike Appel, Mike's partner, and a new guy nobody introduced. It turned out to be another visitor, the writer Jon Landau.

They had been working on one song for weeks. Maybe months.

It sounded like it.

The song was like nothing Bruce had ever done before. This thing was *produced*, baby!

They were rightfully quite proud of it. Even Mike Appel was in a good mood.

There's the baritone sax fifths from "Loco-Motion"!

There's the Motown glockenspiel!

There's Phil Spector's doubling of everything!

There's Duane Eddy's baritone guitar riff! (He actually used a six-string bass.)

It was called "Born to Run," and it was a hurricane of sound. More aggressive and more Rock than Spector's wall because of the central guitar riff, which Spector never had.

And quite a complex arrangement, the most ambitious I'd ever heard Bruce do. It brought me back to Steel Mill, where he wrote almost stream-of-consciousness songs that moved unpredictably from part to part.

When we were kids, bands were measured by their ability to imitate hits. Bruce was never great at that. He heard things differently.

As he gained more experience, he came to understand basic theory, the so-called rules that so-called normal Arrangers live by. But it never limited his creativity.

The "Born to Run" bridge sections show how his imagination-gone-wild arranging style, which had been on full display since "Kitty's Back" an album earlier, was now working within basic rules, such as returning to the beginning key. That's what kept the middle section both exciting *and* coherent.

As impressed as I was, I thought the middle section was too complex for Pop. I kept that to myself. He didn't need the Pop charts at that time anyway.

I did comment on one thing, however.

Bruce walked me out of the control room, still glowing with pride. I was thrilled for him. A major breakthrough. And just in time.

"Man," I said. "That is something else!"

"It's been a lot of work, but it's been worth it." He nodded.

"That's such a new chord change for you, that minor chord in the riff. It's so Roy Orbison, which goes well with your new singing style."

He stopped walking. "What minor chord?"

"In the riff. It's great. Like something the Beatles would do."

"You're trippin'!" His smile was starting to slip. "There's no minor in the riff!"

"What do you mean? Of course there is!"

"Here," he said, throwing me a guitar, "play it!"

I played it.

"That's not what I'm doing," he said. He took another guitar and showed me.

"That's cool," I said. "But that ain't what's on the record!"

Without boring you nonmusicians too much, he had been bending the fifth note of the riff, the minor third of the 4 chord, up to the major third of the 4 chord, à la Duane Eddy. But the reverb was obliterating where he was bending the note *to*, so all you heard was where it was coming *from*.

They had been working on it so long that they thought they were hearing what Bruce intended. But it wasn't really there.

"Oh my God," he said, finally understanding. Into the control room he went with the bad news. If they hadn't already thrown me out of the band, they would have thrown me out again.

Either Mike Appel or one of the few believers left at Columbia sent "Born to Run" to Bruce-friendly DJs, including Richard Neer at WNEW in New York, Kid Leo at WMMS in Cleveland, Ed Sciaky at WMMR in Philly, Charles Laquidara at WBCN in Boston. They started playing the hell out of it. Leo ended his shift with it every Friday to send his audience into the weekend inspired. It saved Bruce's career, at least temporarily.

Mike then mortgaged his house to pay for the album. Even given the single's success, Columbia was still considering dropping Bruce. John Hammond had been moved aside, and Clive Davis had gotten bounced after some stupid scandal. The label was sending promotion men into radio stations to take Bruce's records *out* and put in records by their new kid, Billy Joel. No shit.

There were more complications within Bruce's camp. Appel was unsuccessfully pretending to tolerate Landau's presence, which Bruce was suddenly insisting on. And Jon, attempting to assert some control, had moved the sessions to the Record Plant in Manhattan.

One afternoon, Bruce and I were in his apartment in Long Branch. He was always broke, and I usually had a couple bucks in my pocket to give him. I would say loan, but that would falsely imply he paid it back.

"You've got a Manager and a record company now," I said. "That's big-time. Where's the money? What kind of deal do you have?"

He dug out a copy and showed it to me.

"Man," I said, "am I reading this right? It looks like Mike is taking 50 percent."

The only other fifty-fifty deal I had ever heard of was the one Elvis signed with Colonel Tom.

I got the impression that Bruce had never looked at it. I'm not even sure he had a lawyer when he signed it. I started asking more questions. And then he started asking questions.

It wasn't personal. I liked Mike when I first met him and I like him now. I just didn't like him when he was throwing me out of what was going to be the band back in 1972. And even then he was actually doing me a favor. All I missed was traveling around the country in a fucking station wagon.

The real problem with Mike, ultimately, wasn't just the issue of money. Mike came from the tough-guy camp. Lots of management guys in the '50s and '60s were either Mob related or just as tough as the Mob because that's who they were dealing with.

The business was full of them. Peter Grant and his hit man Richard Cole beat up Bill Graham's security guys. Don Arden hung competitors out windows. Mike Jeffery may have had Jimi Hendrix murdered and then got blown up in a plane.

Even Colonel Tom and Albert Grossman were in the tough-guy group. The colonel had possibly killed somebody in his native Netherlands. And who can forget that wonderful image of Grossman and Alan Lomax rolling around in the grass field of the Newport Folk Festival after Lomax declared the Paul Butterfield Blues Band didn't belong there?

But their time had come and gone. The modern Managers are more like David Geffen, Irving Azoff, and Jon Landau. Intellect over muscle. Persuasion over threat.

Plus, Bruce had discovered publishing and found out he didn't control his own songs. A lawsuit ensued, and things were gonna get worse before they got better.

I continued trying to get out of the Jukes business. I met Steve Leber and David Krebs, who managed Aerosmith and KISS and had invented the Rock T-shirt, for promotional purposes only at first, with no thought of selling them. I met Tommy Mottola, who had Hall and Oates and a few others. He had a little bit of that tough-guy thing I liked.

While I was mulling that decision over, I started meeting all the Agents.

Every single one of them started the conversation the same way. "So, you've probably already met with Frank, but here's what we can do . . ."

By the time the fourth guy said it, I was thinking, Whoever the fuck this Frank is, that's the guy I want.

Frank turned out to be Frank Barsalona, the third of the five important guys that would change my life, and another lifelong friend.

After brief semistardom in childhood as an urban yodeler (you heard me right), Frank became a very young Agent at General Artists Corporation (GAC) when Rock was merely a tiny department next to the janitor's closet. The real Agents were dedicated to the "real" showbiz of the time—movies, TV, and singers of Popular standards.

One day, early in 1964, GAC's Rock guy quit, and Frankie made one of the biggest moves of his life. He told the boss he'd like the job. The boss laughed at the kid's chutzpah but cared so little about the teenage market that he tossed him a booking book and said, "Go ahead, kid, knock yourself out."

The conventional wisdom at the time was that Rock and Roll was pretty much over. Elvis had been drafted. Chuck Berry was in jail. Buddy Holly, Ritchie Valens, and the Big Bopper had died. Dion became a junkie. Eddie Cochran was killed and Gene Vincent crippled in the same car accident. Bo Diddley went to Texas to become a US marshal. Little Richard saw Sputnik, considered it a sign from God, and became a preacher, and Jerry Lee Lewis was blackballed because people thought he had married his fifteen-year-old cousin (she was actually thirteen).

One of the first tests they threw at Frank was the difficult, perhaps impossible, job of booking a group from England. One of the agency's big relationships, Sid Bernstein, was all hot about these Brits. If it had been anybody else, they would have ignored him entirely. There had never been a successful *anything* out of England.

The bosses gave it to the kid, so he'd fail and go back to the mail room where he belonged.

Frank talked a Washington, DC, promoter into booking the English group, who happened to be the Beatles, and went down and witnessed the insanity that followed. He decided that not only was teenage Rock not over, it was just getting started.

He quit GAC a month later and started Premier Talent, the first agency dedicated to Rock, and single-handedly changed the world.

I've started to write a book about him a thousand times, and still hope to, but here is how Frank created the infrastructure of the Rock era, which flourished for thirty years:

- He introduced the game-changing concept that the first thing that matters is how good a band is live. Records and radio success will follow. This was a completely original thought.

- He divided the country into regions like Salvatore Maranzano did for the Mob.

- Like Charles Luciano did for the Mob after he whacked Maranzano, Frank stopped using the old Mustache Pete promoters, who hated Rock and were mostly thieves. He put in Young Turks like Don Law in Boston, Larry Magid in Philly, and Ron Delsener in New York, who owed their careers to him.

- He introduced the concept of *longevity* by telling the promoters they would lose money on a new band's first tour, break even or make a little on the second, and make money every tour after that. Sacrifice would be rewarded with loyalty.

The results were amazing. What had once been a novelty was suddenly a legitimate business. Well, maybe not fully legitimate, but a real business. With a future.

I started calling Frank the Godfather. *Capo di Tutti Capi.* Boss of All Bosses.

Frank immediately took on the Jukes. I had an ulterior motive. Bruce was at the William Morris Agency, and from what I could see they were not in Frank's league.

I wanted Bruce with the Godfather, the best with the best, and started making moves to make it happen.

Dion was doing an album with Phil Spector in Los Angeles, and he invited me to a session. Spector sessions were as legendary as the music that came out of them.

I wanted to bring Bruce, but I was a bit trepidatious, as the Cowardly Lion might say.

The press had been making a big deal about the Spector influence in "Born to Run," though in fact it was just one of a number of elements in the production. I wondered how Spector would react. Would he see it as a tribute? A rip-off? He didn't have the most stable reputation even then.

Still, a Phil Spector session at Gold Star with the Wrecking Crew! Engineered by Stan Ross or Larry Levine! Only Jack Nitzsche was missing.

I had to take the chance.

Dion walked us in and put us on the couch facing the studio. The board was behind us, which was a typical studio configuration in those days. That way, guests would be out of the way of the Producers and Engineers.

Spector comes in already talking a hundred miles an hour. He nodded in our direction and began a three-hour Don Rickles–style monologue that would have played well in Vegas.

They'd do a take every half hour or so, and the Engineer made slight adjustments, but the rest of the time Phil went around the room, musician to musician, making musical suggestions in the form of insults or just doing straight-out insults for the fun of it.

He started off with a gallon jug of *paisano* wine, which my grandfather used to drink, and it was gone by the end of the session.

And yes, he was waving his gun around threatening to kill Hal Blaine if he missed the fill going to the third verse again, occasionally screaming, "Don't embarrass me in front of Bruce Springsteen!"

I felt bad for Dion, who was stuck in the vocal booth trying to make a serious record while everybody else was laughing their asses off.

I wonder if anybody ever filmed Phil doing his act. It was shtick, do a take, shtick, do a take, shtick, until it seemed like the song was literally an afterthought. Then, with five minutes left, he'd get a perfect take. The whole thing was a Spector rope-a-dope!

Of course, a picture of us all together would have been nice.

But I never think of these things.

nine

I Don't Want to Go Home

(1975)

Art can provide insight, inspiration, motivation, even
information, but at the very least it communicates you
are not alone.

—THE UNWRITTEN BOOK

The '70s were the worst time in history to record.

Virtually every record sounded great in the '50s and '60s, and they
would sound great again in the '80s and beyond. But in the '70s most
recorded music sounded weird. Artificial. Claustrophobic.

The reason? Engineers had temporarily taken over. There's a reason most Engineers don't become great Producers and most Producers
aren't great Engineers. They require two very different, complementary
sensibilities.

Engineers have relationships with electrons and digits and knobs
and meters, the science of sound, which is one-quarter of the record.

Producers deal with the songs, the arrangements, the performances,
the living, breathing people. They rely on their own taste to shape emotional content. That's the other three-quarters of the record.

For a brief time in the '70s, the Engineers wrested control from the
Producers and the Artists, resulting in total separation of instruments
for the purpose of "complete control."

Lots of padding on the walls! Get those buzzes out of the drums!
More rugs! Separation! Separation! Separation!

Everything that makes Real Music want to throw up.

Then, during the mix, the Engineers would reproduce room sound, resonance, buzzes, and hums to make the records more exciting! Really.

That was the state of the art when I found myself lying on the floor as horns were being overdubbed for Bruce's new song, "Tenth Avenue Freeze-Out."

It was only the fourth time I'd been in a recording studio.

The first time was when my teenage band the Source recorded my first song, "Traveling."

The second time was up at 914 Sound Studios, when I got kicked out of what was going to be the band.

The third time was also at 914, when Bruce played me "Born to Run."

So I was on the floor thinking, This is the big time? This is the music business we've worked our butts off to get in? This boring sound made worse by this terrible horn chart?

I remember Mike Appel looking like he regretted taking out that second mortgage to pay for this catastrophe.

Bruce did the last thing in the world the gang wanted him to do, which was to ask my opinion. "What do you think?"

"Fucking sucks," I said. There was no muffler between my brain and my mouth in those days. All I knew was my friend was trying to make a record and these guys were fucking it up.

Silence. A nervous chuckle or two. But Bruce knew it sucked, or he wouldn't have asked me. "So go fucking fix it then," he said, pretending to be mad so everybody knew who was boss.

So I did, pretending to be the loyal soldier doing his duty to make sure everybody knew he was boss.

This was in the earliest days of the nickname. I myself was a local boss, very respected, and at various points, more popular than he was. When the nickname started, it was just Bruce having fun, imitating Frank Sinatra. Nobody took it seriously until a respected boss like me joined up, which no one could believe, and started referring to him as *my* boss. That's when he became *the Boss*.

By then, I had been arranging the horns for the Jukes for a while. "Tenth Avenue" was a Stax-type song, but they were playing trumpet, tenor sax, and baritone sax, so I separated out the baritone, more of a Motown move (Stax typically didn't use a bari) and gave the trumpet and tenor some simple Memphis Horns–type riffs.

To explain what I wanted, I sang them the parts like I did every day in Jersey. I didn't know the guys were the biggest horn players in New York, the Brecker Brothers and Dave Sanborn. I don't think it would have mattered if I did. I believe they would have taken riff ideas from the maintenance guy just to get the session over with.

According to one of Dave Marsh's books, that was the moment Jon told Bruce that maybe I should join the band. Who knows? We're all making up half of this shit anyway.

On return visits, I managed to catch two of the coolest moments of the entire album. The amazing trumpet and stand-up bass on "Meeting Across the River," with Randy Brecker, again, and Richard Davis, who had played bass on *Astral Weeks*! Whoa. And the full sixteen-piece string section on "Jungleland," of which only about five seconds was used.

The Engineer for those sessions was a skinny, very Sicilian or Napolitano looking, very New York dude named Jimmy Iovine.

Jimmy . . . what can I say? He was a character like most of us, only a little more so. To call his life charmed was . . . well, let's just say that compared to him, Snow White couldn't pick a horse!

Remember *Welcome Back, Kotter*? Picture Arnold Horshack. That was Jimmy. One day, he was an assistant Engineer watching his boss Roy Cicala record John Lennon's *Rock 'n' Roll*, which Phil Spector was producing. Either Lennon or Spector got into an argument with Cicala, who walked. Lennon pointed to Jimmy: "You! Kid! Get in the chair." Jimmy faked his way through it, and suddenly he was the guy that recorded John Lennon. The King of the Parlay had begun his climb.

Jimmy wore Capezio ballet shoes, which no heterosexual from New Jersey had ever seen before, and he became Jimmy Shoes. The shoes were more than a nickname. They symbolized his whole being. He acted like a millionaire when he had absolutely nothing, and it became a self-fulfilling prophecy. He managed to drive a Mercedes and live on Central Park South on an assistant Engineer's income. I shit you not.

No furniture. I remember him, me, and Bruce going shopping for pillows to sit on. We were at the Navarro Hotel right down the block.

And he was sleeping with models, actresses, singers, DJs, while being broke like the rest of us.

I loved this guy. We bonded immediately.

He acquired an additional nickname soon enough, as people began to notice his extraordinary ability to change his personality, chameleon-like, to suit different situations. For a while he became Split-Screen Iovine. But that wasn't used as much as Shoes.

This was also the period where I tried to get Bruce to change the name of the band.

He had started calling it the E Street Band, which I didn't get. Not only did it have no real resonance or meaning, but it was named after the street where Davie Sancious's parents lived—a guy who was no longer in the band!

We had a softball team at the time. No idea how or why. We were pretty good. We'd regularly play and beat other bands like Crosby, Stills, and Nash, who had the disadvantage of not only running around the field but smoking it.

Our team was called the E Street Kings, which combined the name of the band with a line in "Backstreets." I tried to talk Bruce into changing the band name to follow the lyrics.

How much cooler would that have been?

Bruce Springsteen and the Duke Street Kings!

Fuhggedaboudit!

The E Street Band had like seven gigs lined up for when *Born to Run* came out. Bruce had decided to try fronting, singing without playing, so he asked me to play guitar for those shows. It didn't exactly make Southside or Popovich happy, but I told them I needed a break. I wasn't exactly sure what Ms. Destiny had in mind, so I was keeping my options open.

I had mixed feelings about where Bruce was going musically.

My issues started with the piano.

I was never a big keyboard fan, which was why I never got into the entire Progressive Rock genre, except for Procol Harum and the Left Banke, the two that invented it. Piano for me was Nicky Hopkins in the Rock world, Lowell "Banana" Levinger's electric Wurlitzer in the Country/Folk/Rock world of the Youngbloods, or Otis Spann and Lafayette Leake in Blues. A color instrument to complement the guitars. And sometimes not there at all.

Roy Bittan, the E Street pianist, was obviously overqualified for Rock and Roll. And still is! He had that Broadway-meets-popular-standards accompanist style of providing *all* the music, all the time. We had to literally tie one hand behind his back so he would fit into the less grandiose albums that came after *Born to Run*. He was simply too good.

What I didn't realize until later was that Bruce was not intending for us to be a traditional Rock band, making traditional Rock music. He didn't want the instruments playing the traditional roles all the time. He was imagining something else, something bigger. A marriage of Broadway storytelling, Gospel inspiration, and Rock dynamics. So Roy's style was essential.

We all had to adjust. Having both piano and organ indicated a Gospel influence, and like the other two most notable bands that used both piano and organ, the Band and Procol Harum, we were a hybrid from day one.

The church is where theater probably began in the first place. You've got to believe Scorsese's first infatuation with drama had to happen in the Catholic Church. The black Baptist Church is *all* theater.

I'm sure Bruce was absorbing some of the theatricality that had emerged in the Rock world. It had begun with Mick Jagger, who was transformed by his acting role in the film *Performance*, continued with David Bowie, became Glam and Disco, peaked with KISS, Alice Cooper, and George Clinton's Funkadelic, and ended up with Meat Loaf—an actor who modeled his style on a completely fictionalized idea of Bruce, to the point where he used Roy Bittan and Max Weinberg on his breakthrough album.

I didn't get it. Any of it. I was a street kid stuck in tradition, in Rock that was autobiographical and more straightforwardly authentic. It would take me a few years to understand how Art can illuminate life by illusion, abstract expressionism, distortion, surrealism, and exaggeration.

While I had been working a jackhammer on 287, my friend had never stopped searching and would keep reinventing himself until he found the mother lode. It was only an album away.

The *Born to Run* gigs included five days at the Bottom Line, on West Fourth between Mercer and Greene. It's gone now, like so many other of

Rock's sacred sites. It's a damn shame. Rock history should be preserved just like the George Washington Slept Here joints.

That's why I tried to save CBGBs, the historic club where Punk was born, when they came to me at the eleventh hour, even though I knew it was a lost cause. Wouldn't it have been amazing if a hundred years from now some teenage band could play on the stage where the Ramones and Richard Hell invented Punk?

Around that time, I went to the Bottom Line with Bruce to see the Dictators, who had just released their first album, *Go Girl Crazy*. We loved the hilarious brilliance of writer/singer Andy Shernoff (spelled Adny in those days) and the sheer lunacy of the group's MC, Handsome Dick Manitoba, who wore an old wrestling costume and did inexplicable, completely inappropriate intro raps. Humor hadn't existed in Rock since the Mothers' *Freak Out!* ten years earlier. What closed the deal for us was the backing vocalists on their cover of "California Sun."

> *And I'd Mouse,*
> *(And I'd Mouse),*
> *And I'd Robot,*
> *(And I'd Robot),*
> *And I'd Twist,*
> *(And I'd Twist)*
> *And I'd Shistanoobah)*
> *(And I'd . . . what?)*

Bruce had brought back Marlon Brando's leather-jacket look from the *Wild One*, which he'd wear on the cover of *Born to Run* and which the Ramones would soon adopt as a permanent tribute to teenage angst.

As we walked in to the Bottom Line, somebody yelled, "Hey, punk!"

I stopped and turned to Bruce. "I know you're in the business now, so you gotta act civilized, but you want me to go deal with this guy?"

He laughed. "No, it's a new thing. They mean it as a compliment."

He seemed OK with it, so I pretended I understood.

Our Bottom Line gigs were in August 1975, a week of doubleheaders that faced the stiffest of all possible headwinds at that time: the deadly accusation of hype.

Before joining Bruce's camp, Jon Landau had been the king of Rock journalists. After a 1974 show in Boston, he had written in the *Real Paper* that "he had seen rock and roll future and its name was Bruce Springsteen."

The world saw that lavish praise and showed up to put us down. In those days, authenticity still mattered. Hype was the enemy. But in this case, the hype was based on a misunderstanding.

Jon didn't say "rock and roll's future." He said "rock and roll future."

He did not mean that Bruce was, as the Dictators put it, *the next big thing!* He meant that Bruce was evolving Rock by using all the Artforms that came before him. The literature of Dashiell Hammett, Raymond Chandler, and James M. Cain. The films of John Ford, Elia Kazan, and Jacques Tourneur. The poetry of Rimbaud, Whitman, and Ginsberg. The explosive palette of Van Gogh and the formal invention of Picasso. Not to mention the audacity of Little Richard and Elvis Presley, the craft of the Beatles, the sex of the Stones, the social observation of the Kinks, the vision of Pete Townshend and the power of the Who, the blue-collar frustration of the Animals, the confessional lyrical genius of Bob Dylan, the spiritual elevation of Van Morrison, the musical ambition of the Byrds, the dark cinema of the Doors, and the historical breadth of the Band.

That's what Jon Landau meant, if you're asking me.

The pioneers of the '50s invented Rock. The Renaissance acts of the '60s elevated it to an Artform. Bruce was determined to create work that would not only distract, entertain, and transport but also educate, stimulate, and inspire. He wanted to provide irrefutable proof that life had meaning.

If an audience didn't leave a show feeling substantially better than when they arrived, we had failed. The E Street Band was delivering something that hadn't been delivered in its purest form since the Beatles.

Hope. Not hype.

Landau got there in that same article: "On a night when I needed to feel young, he made me feel like I was hearing music for the very first time."

Three hundred people? Four hundred? I don't know how many jammed into the Bottom Line twice a night for five straight days, or how many of them had come to scoff.

But a funny thing happened on the way to the hype. We lived up to it. We blew the audience's mind.

We had a big advantage. We'd been making our bones playing live for ten years by then, and we had done our residency as a dance band at a time when people had mostly stopped dancing. It took extra energy to get the crowd moving, and we carried that energy into the Bottom Line, and every show since.

One other thing happened at the Bottom Line. A big thing.

"Stevie, meet Maureen." It was Twig, aka Mark Greenberg, one of those friends who appeared out of nowhere and seemed like he had always been there. He was on our softball team. And since I don't know where Twig came from or why we even had a softball team, my memory tends to write the whole thing off as a *Twilight Zone* episode or a dream.

Except that I met Maureen.

Wow! Was she fine! Sexy. A New Jersey Brigitte Bardot. Always the prettiest girl in the room. Still is. Smart, too, as it turned out. I always found smart sexy and later found out there's a word for that, "sapio-sexual." And boy, was I a sap for her. All the way.

She had been a ballet dancer and a clothing designer, had gone to an Arts school in Newark and then the High School of Performing Arts in Manhattan. She had an encyclopedic knowledge of '60s music and literature and had studied acting with Herbert Berghof, Stella Adler, and Bill Hickey.

I'd never met anybody quite like her. Before or since.

I started pursuing her immediately. But she managed to fight me off for quite a while. Did I mention she was smart?

After we conquered New York, it looked like Bruce's career wasn't over after all. I figured I might as well stick around to see how the story ended.

The seven gigs I joined for turned into seventeen cities and nineteen shows between New York and October: places like Atlanta, Austin, Chicago, Minneapolis, and Omaha. In Milwaukee, just before we went onstage, the theater had a bomb threat. The place was emptied and every seat checked. It took hours. The rumor was that some white supremacist group thought Bruce was Jewish.

In those early days, the record company threw after-parties in nearly every city. And in Europe, every country. Now if you see the record company once per tour, you're lucky. During the delay, they decided to have the party before the show.

We got plastered. I have never seen Bruce so drunk in public. On our way back to the theater, he decided to climb onto the roof of the car while we were going seventy miles an hour on the highway. I had to use all my strength to hold on to him to stop him.

Onstage, we reverted back to our drunken bar-band days, which were not that far behind us at that point, opening with Chuck Berry's "Little Queenie."

It was one of the best shows ever.

Next stop, Hollywood.

We were ready for our close-up.

ten

LA A-Go-Go

(1975–1976)

True bliss is a perfect drum fill.

—THE UNWRITTEN BOOK

The Roxy was the Bottom Line of LA, the showcase club for serious new contenders.

Rumors had Phil Spector and half of Hollywood in the crowd.

We opened with either "When You Walk in the Room" or "Needles and Pins"?

I know how hard this is to believe, but by 1975 just acknowledging the '60s existed was a revolutionary act. That's how fast music was progressing.

I glanced up midway through the first song and saw Warren Beatty, Jack Nicholson, Jackie DeShannon, David Geffen, and Cher. I didn't look up again.

We were something new for the jaded world of entertainment. We were characters, but the real thing. Journalists were having a hard time believing we weren't some company invention. We had an unusual amount of personality and played real good. A New Jersey bar band. Quite exotic.

Bruce's songs had become even more cinematic with "Born to Run," and the unique combination of elements in his art—a little Dylan, a little Orbison, some James Brown and Van Morrison—kept the cognoscenti off-balance. Onstage, we were a Rock and Roll Rat Pack with me in the Dino role and Clarence a Sammy on steroids.

We had the best light man in the world, Marc Brickman, a street character from Philly. I called him Mookie after we saw *Mean Streets*. Mookie's talent made the songs come alive. He heightened the drama. He made the audience pay attention. And all of it was done with a couple of friggin' Christmas bulbs and a flashlight.

The Roxy had been opened back in 1973 by Elmer Valentine and Lou Adler.

Elmer was a cop in Chicago who "retired" under murky circumstances in the early '60s and took a trip to France, where some friends took him to a new thing, a "discotheque" called Whisky a Go Go. It was a club where a DJ played records and people danced, an adult version of the '50s "record hop," where famous radio DJs appeared in high school gyms.

Elmer liked the idea so much that he came back, moved to LA, and opened his own Whisky a Go Go in the heart of the Sunset Strip. He immediately changed the concept to include live music and installed Johnny Rivers and his group as his house band. Everyone played there: the Byrds, Love, the Doors, Buffalo Springfield.

The Whisky started a nightlife empire. Elmer opened the Trip and, with Lou Adler and Mario Maglieri, the Rainbow Bar and Grill, and the Roxy, which replaced the Whisky as the showcase club for up-and-comers. Including us.

After our Roxy shows, I hung out with Elmer, who took a liking to me. He took me to the exclusive On the Rox club upstairs and threw a Hollywood party at his house in our honor, where he poured me my first hundred-dollar wine.

I didn't know wine could cost that much or taste that good.

He also loaned me one of his beautiful girlfriends for the night. I mean literally. The whole experience was surreal.

It was like walking through a movie. I felt like Peter Fonda in *The Trip*, minus the acid. Or like *Psych-Out* come to life. Jack Nicholson was standing right there!

The LA women were exactly what every Jersey boy dreamed about. Friendly, beautiful, openly sensual, casually sexual, surprisingly intelligent, totally in control of their own destiny, no games, no talking them into anything. They were just there to have a mutually enjoyable experience with you.

They actually made eye contact instead of avoiding it like the East Coast girls, who mostly still treated sexual pleasure as something reluctantly tolerated instead of sought after.

It was a little intimidating at first. You could see why societies down through the millennia had done everything they could to discourage women's true liberation. Unleashed female sexuality is an awesome force of nature. They fully expected to get their orgasms just like you did, so you had to bring it! Fortunately I had developed an early habit of making sure the girls came first, so I left them with nice thoughts about Italian kids from New Jersey. Richie Sambora would thank me later!

LA in the '70s was a rare magical paradise that made this mostly miserable life worth living. Elmer was conscious of that. He knew how to make your day. Loved him a lot.

As close as we were, I didn't find out his single most amazing achievement until I was doing research for my radio show thirty years later.

When he built the Whisky, he had no perfect spot for the DJ booth, so he built a see-through plexiglass cage and suspended it over the dance floor. On opening night, the female DJ didn't show, so Elmer drafted the cigarette girl, Patty Brockhurst, to spin the discs. *Mad Men* didn't make it up.

Patty was West Hollywood uninhibited. The fact that she had a miniskirt on in a glass cage didn't bother her at all. As she played the records, she danced to them, much to the salacious thrill of the boys below. The crowd loved it so much that Elmer built two more cages. One of the girls, Joanna Labean, created the costumes of fringed skirt and white boots. And that's how my lifelong friend Elmer Valentine invented the go-go girl!

Now that's a legacy! Fuck everything else.

My first trip to Cali included a memorable encounter with LA's finest, when I crossed the street and two patrol cars came screeching up. I was ordered against the wall by four cops with guns drawn—for jaywalking!

Playboy wanted to do a profile of me, and I brought Jimmy Iovine with me to the interview. The interviewer asked why Jimmy was there.

"He's one of my guys," I said. Anything went. We were hot. It was fun to be hot. No worries. No rules.

Marty Scorsese invited us to a special screening of *Mean Streets*, partly because of the line in Bruce's "Jungleland," "wounded, not even dead," which was how the movie ended.

He also showed us some dailies of the new film he was starting to work on, *New York, New York*. Jon Landau was friends with Jay Cocks, who would become a lifelong, important friend of mine, and Jay was friends with Marty. It had been Jay and his wife, Verna Bloom, who had introduced Marty to Bobby De Niro.

In those days Bruce always wanted me with him. I was like his little brother, and he knew I was always watching his back. It was always a complementary relationship. He was—he is—a year older, and very much a mentor when it came to the Art and the Business. But there were some things that I did better, like arranging songs, and I always had more street smarts. I was—I am—much more connected to the social world, because I had to work in it, where he was always a bit distant, focusing on creating his own world and living in it.

I drove back from the screening with Marty in his new Lamborghini, and we talked about Marty showing Francis Ford Coppola the Robert De Niro scenes from *Mean Streets*, which convinced Francis that De Niro would be his perfect Young Vito. It was the type of conversation with the type of guy I'd looked forward to my whole life. Things were finally starting to make sense.

One of my big regrets was not staying in touch with Marty. Even though our paths would cross every few years, we never really had a chance to become the close friends we should have been.

We were still in LA when Bruce made the cover of both *Time* and *Newsweek*. In the same week! I couldn't believe it. There was my friend, a local freak, misfit, and outcast like myself, on the covers of two of the country's biggest magazines. That had only happened for a president or two, maybe an astronaut and a few popes!

I remember the *Newsweek* reporter asking the oddest questions, trying to trip us up. She thought we were fabricated, out of central casting. She could not possibly have conceived of the amount of work we had put in, ten years by then, to be secure enough with our craft to appear casual and inevitable.

I bought out both magazines at the newsstand and handed them out to everybody around the Sunset Marquis pool. Bruce was embarrassed to death. He ran and hid in his room and had a nervous breakdown. After all the work he'd put in to make sure he controlled his own destiny, he felt it slipping away. How quickly Fate can deal new cards.

He'd end up climbing up to his billboard on Sunset Boulevard and painting a mustache on himself or something like that.

I loved the covers. While Bruce always had an inner confidence that he'd make it, I didn't. Validation like that was a big relief to me. And to my parents, who could no longer deny that we were onto something.

But then again, that's exactly why I don't like being out front. You gotta deal with shit like that!

Back in New York, Jimmy Iovine told me he had a key to the Record Plant. "We should sneak in after hours and do some demos for the Jukes," he said.

We went in with the band as they were. Kenny "Popeye" Pentifallo, Kevin Kavanaugh, Alan Berger, and Billy Rush. We had horn players coming and going, so I don't remember how or why we ended up getting a horn section from Philly on the actual record.

It was hard to get used to how bad the studio sounded. All I wanted to do was start with how a band sounds when you walk into a room. I thought the outboard equipment (equalizers, compressors) were making things sound phony, so I had Jimmy turn them all off. When I wasn't looking, Jimmy unscrewed all the bulbs and used the equipment anyway. It wasn't the outboard stuff, as it turned out. It was the fucking '70s. Everything sucked.

How different was radio back then? Steve Popovich sent the demos to Kid Leo, the biggest DJ on the biggest station in Cleveland, and the maniac broadcast them and told his audience that Bruce wasn't the only thing happening in Asbury Park. There was a scene.

So since we were already getting airplay, wouldn't it be nice if we actually had an album?

The deal took forever. Luckily, Southside and I were having a good summer at Monmouth Park Racetrack, where his old man (picture

Ernie Kovacs) was teaching us how to read the racing form. So whatever Jimmy couldn't steal, we paid for with our track winnings.

Producing a record is like directing a movie or executive-producing a TV show. You're in charge. And while producing has psychological, creative, and business aspects, there are logistical responsibilities hanging over everything. The physical record is really four parts—composition, arrangement, performance, and sound. You want the first two done before you get to the studio, especially back in those days, when the clock was running to the tune of $150–$200 an hour.

Southside turned out to have a very recordable voice, and Jimmy did a great job. He had a habit of getting up extremely early—that just seemed to be his natural clock—and that led to a habit of dozing off during our sessions, which might start at midnight. I'd wake him up to rewind the tape and then he'd check back out. The hours were no fun for him. I loved him all the more for doing it.

For free of course, by the way. Although I gave Jimmy the first percentage point he ever received. I made it a regular policy to give all my Engineers points after that. And like me, they're all still waiting to collect.

I Don't Want to Go Home took about three weeks mixed.

On that first album, I began my lifelong habit of proudly wearing my influences on my sleeve, bringing in '60s Artists as a way of showing my gratitude and reminding the industry and the audience that they were put out to pasture way too soon. We were hoping to expose them to a whole new generation.

Jimmy and I would go to Umberto in Little Italy after the sessions and strategize taking over the world. This was only a year or two after Joey Gallo got whacked there.

Jimmy says to me, You're a natural at this producing thing. You should do more. Like who? I say. I don't know, he says. Let me think about it.

He set up a meeting with Joey Heatherton. I had lunch with her and she looked unreal. I suggested to her Lorna Bennett's Reggae version of "Breakfast in Bed," originally done by Dusty Springfield. She loved it but it never happened. Very sorry about that.

Then one night Jimmy brought up Ronnie Spector, who was in some kind of early retirement. I suggested we try her on the Jukes album first to see how it worked out.

Then I was talking to Popovich about how much I love New Orleans, and I told him I just wrote a Lee Dorsey / Allen Toussaint song for the Jukes. "Let's get Lee Dorsey," he said. We dragged him out from under the car he was working on in New Orleans (a scene later re-created by Bruce, unknowingly, in one of his videos). On one of our trips, the E Street Band played Lee's Ya-Ya Lounge to help him out. He wouldn't join us onstage until he sold every bottle of beer he had.

Not only did Steve Popovich tolerate us putting our heroes on the records, he encouraged it! I realize now nobody else on earth would have done such a crazy, blatantly uncommercial thing. He did it because it was cool. And he knew what cool was. And didn't give a fuck what the rest of the industry thought. He was a miracle. The perfect guy at the perfect time.

Like most first albums, our material came straight from our Pony sets. We had R&B like Solomon Burke's "Got to Get You off My Mind," Buster Brown's "Fannie Mae" (stolen note for note by the Stones for "The Under Assistant West Coast Promotion Man"), Ray Charles's "I Choose to Sing the Blues," and an album track from Sam and Dave, "Broke Down Piece of Man." We added some comic Doo-Wop for Popeye, I wrote three songs, and Bruce wrote two.

Not a bad first production, considering I jumped in and learned on the job. It even won an award or two. Credit should go to Jimmy, who always knew more than he appeared to know. Like all southern Italians.

Looking back, I have only one thought.

Since we paid for the first Jukes record ourselves, how come we've never seen one dollar in royalties?

Anybody know a good lawyer?

eleven

This Time It's for Real

(1977)

Brewster: You're a very bad man, Walker, a very destructive man!
Why do you run around doing things like this?
—CARROLL O'CONNOR TO LEE MARVIN, *POINT BLANK* (1967)

The crowd had been building for months.

Building toward this night.

New Jersey in general and Asbury Park in particular hadn't had a lot to cheer about lately. A malaise had been suffocating the country since Nixon's reelection in '72. Not quite the Great Depression following the Roaring Twenties, but in some ways worse.

The death of the 1920s was the death of a hedonistic society that could not have gone on forever without violating the philosophy that life is supposed to suck, which I believe was spray-painted on the side of the *Mayflower*.

The death of the '60s was far more profound. It was the death of a dream of a better society, a new way of living and thinking. The hippies were going to finally implement the ideals of the Founding Fathers. We may not have had their intellect, but goddamn it, we had their spirit!

And then that dream disintegrated, with the assassination of one hero after another, the uprising of a frustrated black population (riots, they were called, but they were really a matter of a seventh of our population waiting for the Civil War to end—still are), and the systematic dismantling of activist groups working toward a more equitable society, from the American Indian Movement to the Young Lords to the Black Panthers.

And just for good measure, Nixon took the dollar off the gold standard, which would begin a fifty-years-and-counting decline in the purchasing power of our currency, directly leading to the permanent malaise we all now live with.

Jersey needed some good news.

And it came. A local hero, Bruce Springsteen, was signed. That hadn't happened since the Critters in 1965. Now a second act, Southside Johnny and the Asbury Jukes, had followed. One local celebrity was a surprise. Two were a scene!

Another local boy, a crazy renegade record executive from Freehold named Steve Popovich, who would have everything to do with the success of the Jukes, was going to broadcast the news of this new scene to the entire nation to celebrate the debut album.

A national broadcast out of Asbury Park? Impossible. But there it was.

The first thing the regulars at the front of the long line extending down the boardwalk toward the Empress Hotel noticed was the new faces.

New names too. Not just the Boss, but the King (Jon Landau), the Godfather (Frank Barsalona), the Duke (Dave Marsh), and one obvious gangster, Kid Leo (Kid Leo), who made the Fonz look like Mother Teresa.

Was this a Rock concert or a prizefight?

Ronnie Spector and Lee Dorsey, who were guests on the first Jukes album, were there, and we started the show with a bang.

As the national broadcast approached, Iovine suggested I write a new song for the occasion. It was strange request. Open the show with a song not on the album we're promoting? It didn't make sense, but I liked the idea. It was a good example of his instinctive genius, which would soon make him the big success he became.

What we couldn't have known at the time was that this innocent request would profoundly affect my songwriting for the rest of my life.

Up until "This Time It's for Real," I had been writing typical Soul-based Rock songs. But the unusual circumstance, a national broadcast introducing us to the world, called for a more autobiographical approach. My first.

It was a major turning point in my artistic life, the archetype of the style that would inform all my work in the '80s. I summoned up all my suppressed feelings about our circumstances. The hopelessness of being late for the party, the underdog status of New Jersey, the frustration of nobodies wanting to be contenders. It all came pouring out, a desperate reach for salvation, a last chance at the title.

I will always be grateful to Jimmy for inspiring me. The song was different. It stood out. It wasn't written with another group or artist in mind. It was written for the Jukes.

After the broadcast, the Jukes hit the road for a combination of clubs and festivals. I came and went, sometimes joining them onstage for a few songs. The first festival I ever played was in Cleveland. I was always claustrophobic and never liked crowds. I didn't know the protocols of festivals, where you're supposed to tolerate drunken cowardly pussies throwing shit at the stage. When a drunk threw a bottle at the stage, missing Johnny by an inch, I jumped into the audience and went after him. Lucky for me, security got to him before I did.

The Jukes were building a lifelong audience the old-school way, one gig at a time. We were getting better every day and were anxious to get back into the studio.

And then we were, this time in the hallowed halls of the old CBS studios on Fifty-Second Street, a huge soundstage where many classics had been cut. Dylan's "Like a Rolling Stone," Count Basie, early Sinatra. The room was so big we actually beat the claustrophobic '70s curse.

First albums are always easy. You're recording your live show, probably one you've been doing for years. Add a new song or two, and you've got it. Second albums are made up of new songs that haven't been road tested.

This proved challenging for the journeymen Jukes, whose lack of studio chops started to show.

Remember I said that the process of record production is basically four things: composition, arrangement, performance, and sound.

Drums are the core of the Sound part. They must sound great for everything else to sound great. The drums are also the key to the performance part of the equation. Since overdubbing became the norm in the late '60s, the essential factor in whether a take is a keeper or not is the drums. Everything else can be redone.

When Rock recording started, nobody had the patience or budget to do take after take, waiting for a drummer to play in time or remember the important drum fills. That's why there were so many session drummers, even for acts like the Beach Boys (Hal Blaine), the early Kinks (Bobby Graham), and the Four Seasons (Buddy Saltzman).

One of my trademarks in the early days as a Producer was to make every attempt to record the real band. This one was a challenge.

I had become obsessed with the African music of Babatunde Olatunji, Sonny Okosun, and Fela Kuti, so I took my eye (and ear) off the sacred snare drum sound I had gotten so right on the first album. My bright, crisp, perfect snare became just another African tom-tom.

It worked, though, and was part of the production experience (and experimentation) that would make the first three Jukes albums very different from one another.

If the song "This Time It's for Real" was a mission statement, the rest of the album went back to the mission. Writing Soul-based Rock long after it was fashionable.

The album continued to acknowledge and pay tribute to the Jukes' musical heroes. With Southside equally enthusiastic about the idea, and with the proud, fatherly approval of Steve Popovich and his boss Ron Alexenburg, we reunited the Drifters, the Coasters, and the Five Satins.

Popovich even found Richard Barrett to play on "First Night," my first Doo-Wop composition. Barrett had played piano on the very first Girl Group hit, the Chantels' "Maybe" (and, somehow, bass and drums also—on a two-track recording!). He had worked with Frankie Lymon and Little Anthony and cowritten "Some Other Guy" with Leiber and Stoller, the song the Beatles were playing in the only film clip I've ever seen of them at the Cavern Club.

On the first Jukes album I had written with specific artists and styles in mind, and I continued that idea on the second.

"Some Things Just Don't Change" was in the style of Holland-Dozier-Holland (or Smokey Robinson) writing for the Temptations. "She's Got

Me Where She Wants Me" was straight Curtis Mayfield and the Impressions. "First Night" drew on Doo-Wop in general, though it leaned on Jerry Butler's "For Your Precious Love."

My cowrites with Bruce, including "Love on the Wrong Side of Town" and "Little Girl So Fine," were among my favorites. The huge room gave us a nice fat sound. I found "Without Love" on a recent Aretha Franklin album and did one of my favorite string arrangements, with a sixteen-piece string section, on it. They sounded great.

The room sounded so good I didn't even double the horns.

While Bruce was tangled up in his management lawsuit, we couldn't go into the studio or tour. And Bruce was out of money.

He told us at rehearsal at his house in Holmdel, after which he went to make his usual two-hour phone call with Jon.

There was a general grumbling within the band. We were at subsistence level, getting maybe $150 or $200 bucks a week. Amazing when I think about it now. And some of the guys had been getting outside work, big session respect, and serious offers.

We voted on whether to break up.

When the first three guys voted to leave, I stopped the voting and made a speech. Not exactly Mark Antony, but I needed to buy some time. "Give me a week," I said.

I went to my go-to guys, Popovich and Barsalona.

Pops came back to me twenty-four hours later.

"I got it," he says. "Ronnie Spector and the E Street Band on my new label Cleveland International." I always laughed when he said the label name out loud. You can't be Cleveland *and* International, I'd tell him. "I'll pay double scale for a two-song double session. That'll hold you for a few weeks."

Beautiful.

Popovich even had the song. Billy Joel had written a tribute to Phil Spector and the Ronettes, "Say Goodbye to Hollywood." It hadn't been a huge hit. Billy was still a year or two from having everything he did be a success. But it was perfect for Ronnie.

The day before the session, Billy's wife and Manager stopped me in the CBS hallway. "Who gave you permission to do this? Of course you'll need Billy there. What time are you starting?" I hadn't met Billy yet. He turned out to be a really great guy, but I don't suffer bullies gladly, then or now. And I am big on gender equality.

"Billy won't be needed, thank you," I said and kept walking.

She left in a huff. Maybe a minute and a huff (sorry, Groucho).

An hour later Pops called. "What the fuck did you say?!?" She had called him to curse me out, and not just me but him, Johnny, Bruce, Walter Yetnikoff, Phil Spector, and probably Garibaldi, Fiorello La Guardia, and Pope John II while she was at it.

"Can she stop the record?" I asked.

"No," he said.

"Then fuck her and her uppity fucking spoiled brat Long Island fucking condescending attitude," I suggested.

Truth is, she wasn't wrong. I should have invited Billy to the session, at least to watch. Of course, after our hallway encounter, I couldn't give her the satisfaction. How poor Billy lived with that horror is beyond Buddhism.

And so it transpired that the original Magnificent Seven gathered to make a little history with one of our childhood fantasies and make about a month's salary, which would keep the E Street Band intact until I got to Frank Barsalona.

That was my third string arrangement. I was getting better and better.

Life has its moments.

I wrote the B-side, "Baby Please Don't Go," which Nancy Sinatra would do a great version of a couple decades later.

The session ended the talk of the E Street Band breaking up. I guess that's what was meant by me occasionally being "unintentionally destabilizing."

Right around that time, Ronnie and I had a brief affair. Early on, she wanted to go to Puerto Rico. On the day we arrived, outside by the pool, we ordered our first drinks of the vacation.

I did some research later and found out there are two kinds of alcoholics. The ones that just drink a lot are bad enough. But then there's the kind whose blood has a chemical reaction with just one drink. She was one of those. Terrible. Freaky to witness. Instant change of personality. It's Jekyll-and-Hyde time.

And did I mention we were in Puerto fucking Rico? Which I already despised because the taxi driver tried to hustle me for a couple hundred from the airport, and I'd caught the blackjack dealer dealing seconds and bottoms from a mechanic's grip (remember, I was a gambler), and now I had a girlfriend who couldn't stand up or speak coherently.

Scared the living piss out of me. It remains one of my top ten nightmares of all time.

We made it home, and I got her help and put her on tour with the Jukes. Johnny was on the wagon at the same time.

She ended up OK, and our involvement gave her some much-needed confidence that put her back onstage, where she's enjoyed an entire second career ever since.

To this day, however, whenever she sings "Say Goodbye to Hollywood" live, she introduces it as "the song Bruce Springsteen produced for me."

I'm the invisible man.

What are you gonna do?

twelve

The Punk Meets the Godfather

(1978)

Focus on the Craft, the Art takes care of itself.

—THE UNWRITTEN BOOK

I had been chasing Maureen ever since our Bottom Line gigs in 1975. I finally caught her on New Year's Eve, 1977.

On our first date, I dragged her to the seen-its-best-days Capitol Theatre in Passaic, New Jersey, for a Jukes concert. Every girl's dream of a romantic New Year's! But I felt obligated since it was their first theater gig, a major rite of passage, and I was still their Manager.

After she visited my world, it was time for me to visit hers. What I couldn't have known is that she was about to expand my understanding and perspective of Art from sketch pad to CinemaScope.

Maureen took me to my first ballet at the Metropolitan Opera House.

After playing joints my whole life, I felt like I was walking into the Palace of the Gods. The red plush velvet seats—not ripped and worn and stained like the Fillmore's—the massive velvet curtain, the incredible chandelier that went up as the lights went down. And then . . .

Tchaikovsky!

What a divine discovery. My first real experience with classical music was ballet music at its most exhilarating. Melodic. Dynamic. Enlightening. Supreme. Delicious. A brand-new trip.

The latest epiphany.

The ballet was full-length, my preference ever since. I need a story to be fully immersed and satisfying, no matter how metaphorical or adolescent it might be. *Swan Lake. The Sleeping Beauty. The Nutcracker. Coppélia. La Bayadère.*

I fell in love with Maureen, and with ballet soon after. We caught the end of the last great era, Baryshnikov, Kirkland, and the most extraordinary human being ever to grace a stage, Rudolf Nureyev. I've never felt such charisma from a stage before. He just exuded Greatness.

Maureen's influence wouldn't stop with ballet. She would turn me on to Impressionist Art, too, and we would immediately fuse the two. We began writing "Impressions," set pieces that opened on tableaus of impressionist paintings. The dancers would come to life, perform a short scene, and end up back in the positions of the painting. Like too many of my ideas, I didn't have the machine in place to finance or sell it, which left me with no practical reason to finish it.

What ballet and impressionism shared was that they opened me up to a bigger artistic vista. After experiencing a few amazing ballet performances, being a Rock star could never regain first place in my imaginary goals.

I began to see myself less as a performer and more as a Producer. An Irving Thalberg of Rock, overseeing the big picture as well as the granular details, able to creatively realize something that would thrill, inspire, and enlighten audiences. My comfort zone remained on stages and in studios. It was where I started and where I could do what I knew best. But I was thinking big! Bigger! Biggest!

It would take me thirty-five years to even get close to my new daydreams. But let's not get ahead of ourselves.

Popovich had temporarily saved the E Street Band, but his fix wouldn't last forever. There was only one solution.

I went to the Godfather.

I told Frank that it was time to make the move. I'd seeded the garden, mentioning his name several times to Bruce, telling him Frank stories and about how well we were doing with the Jukes, so it wouldn't be coming out of the blue.

"Talk to Bruce," I told Frank, "or maybe Jon Landau. He's someone Bruce trusts. Or Peter Parcher, his lawyer. Whatever. But we need you right now."

"What can I expect?" Frank asked.

"We need some gigs until this legal problem is settled," I said. "I'm sure Bruce could use some lawyer money; we're broke. We can't record, so the main thing we need is your juice."

"What else?" said Frank, always thorough in those days.

"Well," I said, "I guess if you really want to provide a little extra comfort, you might want to consider grabbing Bruce's new guy at William Morris, Barry Bell. He replaced Sam McKeith, who signed Bruce, and Bruce seems comfortable with him."

Half the band was ready to rebel. The Promoters thought we were damaged goods. The record company was down to a few guys who were keeping the faith. The agency couldn't help. And even the press was moving on to the next potential big thing. We were going no-fucking-where if we stayed where we were.

"We need you to pull the strings of the Promoters until we can get a new record done. Bruce needs your sponsorship, gabeesh? He needs a rabbi. Your endorsement will stop the bleeding. And the entire industry will have to give us a second look, including his own record company."

"OK," Frank said.

I'm not even sure Frank had seen an E Street show. I had taken him to the Stone Pony, where he'd seen Bruce jam, so he'd gotten a glimpse of his charisma. Maybe that was enough. Otherwise he was taking my word, and whoever else's, that we were something special and going somewhere.

I think the amount was a hundred grand. A lot now, a fucking lot then. A lifesaver. And Frank generously brought over Barry Bell, who is still with us.

Next thing you know, we were back on the road. We saw lots of half-empty halls, but we were alive and doing what we did best. And by June '77, we were back in the studio to make the new album, *Darkness on the Edge of Town.*

And a dark experience it was.

There's a documentary, directed by Thom Zimny from Barry Rebo's footage, that more or less covers it, but suffice it to say it wasn't pretty.

The intense life-and-death struggle of *Born to Run,* reaching for greatness, continued unabated.

We all briefly became drug addicts on this one. Except Bruce. He was the only guy I knew who never did drugs. He had his own vice, which was mentally beating the shit out of himself.

I had a drug dealer friend who was making runs to South America. While coke is never completely uncut because of the chemical process of making it, what he brought me was as pure as it could be. At the time, conventional medical wisdom said cocaine wasn't addictive, but I noticed after a while that I couldn't get out of bed without reaching for the vial. I only used for a year before quitting—almost a year to the day, in fact. Still, it helped the band get through the album. Lots of bathroom visits.

As if Jon's new role as Manager wasn't complicated enough, his unique set of skills, knowledge of culture, and experience with psychoanalysis made his other new role equally invaluable as he redefined the role of the Record Producer.

Not that he wasn't musical. He was and is very musical. But the E Street Band largely produced themselves, and I would be taking more responsibility for the music and sound over the next few records.

His far more important role and unique value was in helping Bruce analyze and discover the bigger picture. The themes he would be talking about and his artistic identity.

Bruce even having artistic aspirations was already odd. Very few Rockers were thinking that way. Jackson Browne maybe, and . . . who else?

Even the Beatles didn't think about such things until they were liberated from having to reproduce their songs live, which resulted in *Revolver.* Then their imaginations were free to take them to wonderful new bizarre places as varied as "Eleanor Rigby" and "Tomorrow Never Knows."

In spite of his game-changing accomplishments, Bob Dylan didn't seem to have any artistic pretensions at all.

Was Bruce being influenced by the early writers like Landau and Paul Nelson and Greil Marcus, who were suddenly recognizing and celebrating this new Artform and treating it seriously as such?

Our third generation was the first to inherit Rock as an Artform. The first two generations were working strictly off instinct and traditional definitions of showbiz success. Evolving through some organic inclination.

And because we inherited it, we immediately took it for granted. There were very few thinking of what we do as Art back then, and that's true to this day.

But Bruce was. And Jon. Conversations we thought might've been self-indulgent turned out to be quite fruitful after all.

Jimmy Iovine was still engineering, but from his experience with *Born to Run*, he knew that he'd have tons of downtime during Jon and Bruce's endless conversations. Maybe more than before, since Jon had brought in a wonderful character named Charlie Plotkin to help with the mix. Charlie had some big hits with Orleans (fronted by John Hall) and would do a Dylan album and other things later.

Bruce, Jon, and Charlie had two things in common. They liked to take their time, and they loved to talk. This was a deadly combination for the rest of us. Jimmy, who had attention deficit disorder even worse than me, would have never made it through alive if he hadn't stayed busy. When Bruce, Jon, and Charlie left to talk, Jimmy would tell me to get him when they came back and run down to Studio 2, where he was producing Patti Smith.

I had met Patti once at a party. Jimmy brought her. I was eating an ice-cream cone, and she walked right up to me and knocked it out of my hand. "You shouldn't be eating that shit," she said. It was like talking to Anybodys from *West Side Story*! I would grow to like her by getting friendly with her guitar player Lenny Kaye, who was completely responsible for her being in the Rock world.

The songs on *Darkness* were among Bruce's best so far, and I was proud of my contribution, which was a significant part of the arranging of the songs, but overall the sound of the record was a disappointment to me. I've gotten used to it now, but at the time it sounded stifled, choked to death, and flat, as if it was recorded with close mics in a padded room. Which it was. Nothing close to how the band actually sounded. When the record was reissued in 2010, I begged Bruce to let me remix it. "Are you out of your fucking mind?" he said. "People have been listening to it this way for thirty-five years—we're gonna change it now?!?"

Somewhere during this period, Bruce opened a vein of creativity that had waited years to be spiked. Suddenly, it was as if every song he had heard in his entire life was channeled through him, was rearranged at a molecular level, and came spilling out in song after song. After having only a few outtakes for *Born to Run,* he suddenly was writing forty, fifty, sixty amazing songs per record, and just as quickly rejecting them.

No one had ever done this before.

You're making an album, you write ten good songs and you put it out.

There was no exception to that rule.

I didn't understand it at the time. Now, I realize he was reaching for something new. A theme for the album he couldn't articulate. He was on a roll, and he was going to see where it led.

He was so determined to find a new identity, he began to separate the songs by genre, Art lyrics over here, Pop lyrics over there. No one had ever made that distinction before, and I felt strongly (and wrongly, as it turned out) that it was a mistake.

Songs got discarded, including some of the best ones. There was an entire album of Pop Rock greatness that was shelved for decades, finally emerging on collections of unreleased material and deluxe reissues like *Tracks, The Promise,* and *The Ties That Bind.*

Every outtake a lost argument.

Looking back, it's obvious now that any song resembling a love song or a Pop song wouldn't have made any sense.

With one exception. Early on, we had worked on a song called "Because the Night." It was a different kind of love song, something special, something darker because of its minor key. We spent far more time on it than any other song, and I contributed considerably to the tricky arrangement. I thought it would be our breakthrough.

One day, when Bruce and Jon went to talk, Jimmy motioned to me. "I want you to hear something," he said. I followed him down the hallway and he put me in the Producer's chair. And on came my arrangement of "Because the Night," sung by Patti Smith. That's how I found out it wasn't going on our record. A week's worth of work!

I was happy for Jimmy. The minute I stopped wanting to kill him.

Bruce did what he had to do. And you have to respect the discipline required to throw away songs other artists would build their careers on.

But here's the thing. Bruce didn't just throw away great songs. He changed his entire persona. *Born to Run*, the culmination of his first three albums, not only yielded his signature song but established what should have been his lifetime identity.

The Jersey kid, the ragamuffin rebel underdog, crossing the river and conquering the big city, saving the girl on the back of his motorcycle and riding off to . . .

Well, it was all romantic fiction.

The only remotely autobiographical song, "Tenth Avenue Freeze-Out," immortalized his relationship with Clarence and fantasized conquering the Big City! Which hadn't happened yet.

Bruce had painstakingly constructed an identity over the previous three years . . . and then realized he couldn't live there.

Born to Run had been an album about hope in the midst of despair, about escaping a dead-end life. It was all there in the last line of "Thunder Road": "It's a town full of losers / And I'm pulling out of here to win."

On *Darkness*, Bruce realized that escape was impossible, that he had been running from himself.

He decided to stay and fight.

To confront reality. Yes, the average working life was a struggle, but instead of denying his connection to it, he would stand with the working class. He would speak for them. It might have been a town full of losers, but it wasn't their fault. The game was rigged against them. He was gonna even up the odds.

Darkness was about Bruce accepting that he was his father's son and winning one fight for him. It's a premise I would revisit with the Jukes on "All I Needed Was You," a song I wrote about Johnny and his father based on *Somebody Up There Likes Me*.

The entire setting would flip from *Born to Run* to *Darkness*. From urban / suburban to rural / small town.

Throwing away songs? Try throwing away an entire identity! Try throwing away success! Every entertainer dreams of an audience defining you and liking you. When it happens, you wrap your arms around that miracle, embrace it with all your might, and pray it lasts forever.

It takes some big balls to say, Thank you, folks, I know I asked you to fall in love in with this guy I introduced you to, but I'm still evolving. We're making a U-turn here, and I hope you follow.

I realize now the gestation was so difficult because in many ways, *Darkness on the Edge of Town* was Bruce's first true album.

The first three albums were development in public. Good as they were (and *Born to Run* was magnificent), the identity he found on *Darkness* remained the core of his being from then on.

That's what all those long conversations with Jon Landau were all about, I bet.

But could that same meaningful conversation take place with thousands of strangers? We were about to find out.

Darkness was the beginning of a new template. Say it with the record, sell it with the tour.

From that moment on, we would never again go onstage without the intention of *saying something*. Bruce made sure the shows engaged the entire spectrum of emotions, from confidence to confession, catharsis to comedy, and all of it entertaining. And the soundtrack to that epic movie included a big part of the history of Rock every night.

Those shows required a support system that began with the management of Jon Landau and Barbara Carr and the crew, including exceptional members like Marc Brickman and George Travis.

But the stage was the front line. That was where the battle was waged, where we won or lost, where our job was to inspire and motivate and convince the masses that Rock was more than entertainment.

And we did.

We felt for the first time, after a few false starts, we were in sight of actually becoming Rock stars, which gave the tour a new intensity. After years of being off the road, we were like seven lions released from captivity.

Before that, we were still very much in the bar-band tradition, and graduating to Rock star meant new responsibilities, including finding a signature look, Rock and fashion being married from the beginning.

I had recently seen a triple feature of Sergio Leone's classic spaghetti Westerns and thought, That's it! I had a full-length duster made. No one had ever used that look in a Rock show.

In Saint Paul, the Promoter told me that a young local musician who had just released his debut album was at the show. The name made an impression: Prince. He left before I had a chance to meet him, but you know he was taking notes on my coat!

Every night, Bruce balanced out the darkness of the record with his own exploding exuberance. We transformed "Prove It All Night" into a two-guitar, show-stopping rave-up, among other things. The shows were marathons of ferocity and determination, sometimes stretching past the four-hour mark.

Radio had abandoned us, the industry had forgotten us, and the press had moved on, but we were gonna make sure you remembered that live show for the rest of your life.

Cocaine may have helped keep me going at first, during those months when I had to fly home from the Darkness Tour to record the Jukes' third album, *Hearts of Stone*, but ultimately the drugs started to burn me out.

The third Jukes record continued my evolution of the Rock and Soul hybrid, especially in my writing. I managed seven tracks before I fried, but they were good ones. My influences were beginning to become more integrated, and my songs felt like something new. Even though I was still recording in the '70s and hated the studio I was told had a great room sound but didn't.

I followed the pattern I used on *This Time It's for Real* by opening with an autobiographical song, "Got to Be a Better Way Home." Funny how the story went from "Here we come, breaking all the rules, and we're gonna win anyway" to "Geezus Fuck, the music business really sucks!" over just one year on the road. Musically it was pure Otis Redding.

"I Played the Fool" was all Smokey.

"Take It Inside" borrowed a bit of the Animals but was mostly original, as was "Next to You," which drew on Sam and Dave and the Temptations.

"This Time Baby's Gone for Good" was . . . Gene Pitney meets the Shangri-Las with a variation on a Townshend lyric and a Beatles bridge?

"Trapped Again," a fave I would eventually use myself, was a nod to blaxploitation. Johnny had the title, Bruce picked up a guitar and sang the chorus spontaneously, I did the rest.

Finally, there was "Light Don't Shine."

The other autobiographical number, along with the opener.

That is one fucking depressing song.

My father's barbershop quartet: Joe Dellabadia, Vern James, Jim Black, Dad. *Van Zandt family*

(Facing page):
My mother,
Mary Lento,
in 1945.
Van Zandt family

(Above):
Grandpa Lento and me
in Watertown, 1950.
Van Zandt family

RnR rebel from birth.
Van Zandt family

Sister Kathi, Dad, Ma, Nana Lento, Jake, me, Maureen, brother Billy. *Van Zandt family*

Southside Johnny and legendary R&B singer Lee Dorsey. *Renegade Nation*

Salute! E Street Kings, 1976. *Valerie Penska*

First fan Obie with her two faves. *Billy Smith*

Ronnie Spector with the three Asbury capos. *David Gahr*

E Street Band, New York, 1979. *Joel Bernstein*

The Dimmer Twins. *Renegade Nation*

"The Godfather"
Frank Barsalona.
Renegade Nation

Getting married by Little Richard, New Year's Eve 1982. With best man Bruce and maid of honor Michelle. *Jim Marchese*

Our wedding party. From front: Brother Billy, Jimmy Iovine, Bruce, Harry Sandler, LaBamba, me, Maureen, Sari Becker, Gary US Bonds, Jack Cocks, Michelle Priarone, Obie, Monti Ellison, Maria Santoro, Jean Beauvoir, Max Weinberg, sister-in-law Lynn Angelo, sister Kathi, Ben Newberry, sister-in-law Gail Napolitano, sister-in-law Lori Santoro, Garry Tallent. *Jim Marchese*

(Above): Big Youth, Lou Reed, Reuben Blades, John Oates, Danny Schecter, Jonathan Demme, and Hart Perry. **David Seelig**

(Facing page, top): Honored in Atlanta by Coretta Scott King, Julian Bond, and Vernell Johnson. **African Activist Archives**

(Facing page, bottom): Miles Davis and Arthur Baker. **David Seelig**

(Above): With Bono and Jimmy Cliff.
Reuven Kopitchinski

(Left): At the '86 Grammys.
Ron Galella

(Facing page, top): With Abbie Hoffman and Mark Graham, National Convention of Student Activists, 1988. **Debra Rothenberg**

(Facing page, bottom): T. M. Stevens, '87. **Guido Harari**

With Gary Bonds, '84. *Mark Weiss*

My longtime assistant, Holly Cara Price. *Renegade Nation*

Sopranos premiere, 2000. *Scott Gries*

Nothing but fun working with David Chase on *Not Fade Away*.
Barry Wetcher—Paramount Vantage

Self-pity personified.

I was feeling abandoned by everybody. It could have been the drugs taking their toll, but there was more. Popovich had left to start his own label, Cleveland International Records. Lennie Petze, who had taken over, didn't have the faith. And the big boss, Ron Alexenburg, had his own problems, with his life being threatened by black activists who blamed him for the Jacksons leaving Motown for Epic.

I don't think I realized until that moment how important Steve Popovich had been as a supporter of our whole thing. Who else would have encouraged us to include '60s artists, a completely unfashionable thing to do?

The song reflected my first musical manifestation of unrequited infatuation. After wanting to be in the business my whole life, the business was not returning my love. I needed some commercial success to propel my dreams to the next level. But I kept getting stuck at first base.

Bruce gave me two final songs, "Talk to Me" and "Hearts of Stone," which I made the title track because it summed up the central emotion of the album. (My first thought for the album title was *Broken Hearts of Stone*, but Bruce thought it was too negative, so I left it more vague.)

The Jukes were ready to rerecord Bruce's songs, which we had cut with the E Street Band, but the budget was gone. Amazing how we went through $250,000 per album without a second thought in those days. We make fifty albums for that price at Wicked Cool Records these days. Literally fifty.

So I said fuck it and kept the E Street Band tracks for those two songs. We were one big family anyway, and since the Jukes were between drummers, Max was already playing drums on the album.

Thirty years later we would complete the circle when I gave the tapes to Bruce's Engineer, who took my horns off "Talk to Me" and put them back on his vocal version for *The Promise*.

Hearts of Stone ended up being our most acclaimed album. The Jukes were inches away from breaking through.

But there were obstacles.

The band got very little airplay because Rock radio, having discovered that profit could result from consistency, introduced into Paradise a virus called consultants. The first symptom of this virus was deciding that no bands with horns would be played on FM Rock stations.

Blood, Sweat, & Tears and Chicago didn't have to worry because they made their living in the Pop world, on AM radio. But the Jukes were Rock and Soul, which meant we needed FM radio, which meant we were fucked.

The good news was that even without airplay, we had gotten to the point where we were grossing a million dollars a year on the road. The Godfather was proud of that. I foolishly didn't take any commission as Manager, which I totally deserved, wanting Johnny and the band to make what they could.

But the lack of label support took its toll. After three increasingly acclaimed records, with one of the great live shows in the business, Epic dropped the Jukes to concentrate on Boston, the Jacksons, and "Play That Funky Music, White Boy!"

It was hard to blame them.

But I managed.

Still, *Hearts of Stone* had set the band up nicely for a new record deal, and it seemed like I might get back what I had put in.

At that point, Bruce wanted me with him in a hotel in New York while the *Darkness* drama unfolded, so I had no bills. Everything I made went into the Jukes, and when you added in the management commissions not taken, I was owed a couple hundred grand by then.

Since I hadn't been able to make up my mind on a Manager, I thought the safe thing for the band, and the safest way to get my money back, was to give the band to someone I could really trust, my personal lawyer. That way I could stay involved for management and production advice.

They made a nice new deal and took the money and ran.

I let it go but stayed pissed off for about fifteen years until the Better Days reunion in the '90s.

Which brings up the subject of the great train robberies of Rock. Here are three:

1. It remains one of the great sources of wonderment how Allen Klein ended up owning the first ten Rolling Stones albums. I asked Peter Parcher, who was involved, to explain it to me. He did, in great detail. I still don't get it.

2. The Animals got their first two singles from Bob Dylan's debut album. "Baby Let Me Take You Home" was derived from "Baby, Let Me Follow You Down" (a folk song credited to Eric Von Schmidt but actually written by Reverend Gary Davis, Blind Boy Fuller, or who knows who). And then there was "House of the Rising Sun," which was public domain, which means whoever adapted or arranged it got the publishing royalties. Because there wasn't room for all the band's signatures, only keyboard player Alan Price's name was on the record. When the song became a worldwide hit, Price took the cash and split!

3. Jack Ely, the lead singer of the Kingsmen, sang the classic version of "Louie Louie." Meanwhile, the mother of Lynn Easton, the drummer, registered the band's name. For herself. As the record hit, Easton declared himself the lead singer and Ely and guitar player Mike Mitchell quit. Easton is the only one anyone has ever seen perform it, and he didn't sing it.

Like Nick Tosches said, showbiz—the dirty business of dreams.

We closed out 1978 still on the road with *Darkness*, still fighting for our lives onstage.

We really became a band on that tour. Longevity, if you can survive it, brings unexpected rewards. That's why bands should stay together. It's not just talent, it's loyalty and, over time, history. Four of us originals left.

You can maybe find the talent. You can probably buy the loyalty. But you can't replace the history. And believe me, when it's a bad night—tough conditions, new audience, rainy and cold—or even a particularly good one, you don't want to look to your left and see a gun for hire.

You want to see me.

thirteen

Baptism

(1979–1980)

We essentially do three things. We learn, we teach, we practice
our craft. Any day we do all three of those things is a good day.
—THE UNWRITTEN BOOK

The first time I quit the E Street Band was in 1979, just as *The River*
sessions were beginning.

We were sitting on amplifiers in Studio A at the Power Station, Bruce
and me.

"Listen," I said. "I know your capacity to withstand suffering is
infinite. And the songs keep getting better and better. But I believe
in something called quality of life. For me the journey is as important as the destination. I can't do this thing again. You don't need me
around."

He thought for a minute and said, "Produce it with me."

Just like that. Maybe he had it in mind already.

"For real?" I said.

"For real," he said.

He knew I was a band guy, and it was time to make a band record.
For real. And that's what we did.

The River started the same way as *Darkness*, with the band working out
material at Bruce's house in Holmdel. He would come in every day with

ideas, sometimes just a chorus and a groove, sometimes a verse, rarely more than that.

One of my gifts is the ability to finish songs other people start. Give me thirty seconds and I can hear the whole thing. As satisfying and important as writing can be, my favorite craft is still Arranging.

I won't bore you too much, skip ahead if you want to, but I'll do a quick summary of the four aspects of Arranging.

The configuration of a song. This runs dangerously close to the grey area of composition. Do you repeat a verse? Double the chorus? Add a bridge? A solo? Where do you put them? Do you modulate to add the element of audio surprise?

Choosing which instruments to use. Does a song need an organ? Which kind? B-3? Farfisa? An acoustic guitar? Doubling the electrics? Congas? Tambourine?

What parts do individual rhythm instruments play on the basic track? What's the bass drum beat? The bass line? Should the piano play eighth notes in the chorus? How much distortion should the guitar have?

And the typical horn and string charts.

I loved it all. I sang or played the parts, since like most Rock musicians I don't read or write music.

I took the rough sketches and fed back a bunch of ideas, many of which Bruce used. At worst, my suggestions stimulated another round of ideas. Incredible as it seems, he maintained this pace for months at a time, bringing in three or four new ideas a day.

One day at rehearsal, he played a circular chord pattern in a medium groove. We all fell in. He told Danny to play the Four Seasons riff on the glockenspiel (from "Dawn") and started singing, "Everybody's got a hungry heart."

Then he got his daily Jon call. Everybody was tired, and the call usually meant the day was over. (They're probably still talking right now!) But there was something about the groove. "Let's keep it going," I said.

We got it cooking, and when Bruce came back he was a bit surprised that we were still there and still jamming on what he must have felt was just another chord change.

It was more than that. It was a hook, part of a chorus, and a title. Half the battle, at least. There was something about that phrase, "everybody's got a hungry heart," that felt like the perfect marriage of the personal and the universal. I wasn't going to let it get away. Bruce liked to finish some of the day's songs as homework. "Hey," I said. "Find a few more words for that baby."

As we moved from rehearsal to studio, I stayed fixated on the sound of the record. I had finally figured out why virtually all the drums of the '50s and '60s sounded great and why they all sucked in the '70s.

It began with the way drums were tuned. The older drummers took lessons from jazz drummers, who knew how to tune their drums, but the craft was in the process of being lost.

Then came the way they were struck. Older drummers played with a lighter touch, left wrist up, which allowed the wrist to snap and thereby pop the loosely tuned snares and make them resonate. What most Rock drummers didn't understand was that the harder they hit the snare drum, the smaller it sounds.

Finally, it was the way they were miked. Older drummers were miked with an overhead mic, or one way in front with more distance, which allowed the sound to breathe, capturing the natural sound you hear when you walk into a room and hear a band playing.

John Bonham's drums were the only real exception to the bad-drum sound rule of the '70s because either he or Jimmy Page was smart enough to record his drums in a stairwell with plenty of room sound.

I had my eye on other factors too. The Engineer, for instance. I was looking for an Engineer who could get great sounds and do it quickly. Maureen was familiar with the studio scene from when she was going with Mitch Mitchell, the genius drummer of the Jimi Hendrix Experience, and had traveled from Woodstock to London and back with them. She remembered a guy named Bob Clearmountain, who had impressed her with his speed at a couple of sessions at Media Sound in midtown Manhattan, right across the street from where we lived at the time.

As Fate would have it, Max Weinberg mentioned he was going to the Power Station to do an Ian Hunter album, and the Engineer was going to be Clearmountain. I asked him to pay close attention to two things. Was he using room mics, and how fast did he get a drum sound? The torture of struggling and ultimately failing to get decent drums on *Darkness* was not an experience I intended to repeat.

Max came back with a favorable review, so I suggested to Bruce we use Clearmountain and the Power Station, where the bigger live room would give us a fighting chance to get a sound.

Bruce had switched managers by then. As I previously mentioned, Jon, with his vast knowledge of film, literature, and music, was helping Bruce refine his ideas during the game-changing *Darkness* sessions. They expanded my consciousness just from what I overheard!

Now Bruce had two trusted lieutenants. Jon took care of the record company, career planning, and big-picture conceptualizing, while I was free to focus on the music and the sound. My job, as I saw it, was to make sure every song was a joy to record.

So while they talked, I made the record.

Kidding.

But I had the studio and the Engineer I wanted. I made sure that every instrument sounded right and that everybody was playing the right thing, easy enough with the greatest band in the world. They literally produced themselves.

When the sessions for the new record started, it sounded great right away. This was gonna be fun! Bob was stupid fast, as advertised.

"Roulette" was recorded and mixed on the same day. I regularly got two mixes a day out of Bob when he used the manual, no automation, old analog Neve board. When things got automated later on that damn digital Solid State, everything slowed down. And never sounded as good again! (I'm exaggerating a little. Bob still gets good sounds with the digital crap. And he still does two mixes a day for me!)

The second thing we did was return to "Hungry Heart."

I felt this was our best shot at a hit single since Jimmy Iovine's genius theft of "Because the Night."

But it wasn't that simple. Remember, this was right in the middle of the Rock era, and a hit single had to be organic. If a song was seen as a conscious attempt to get a hit, it could hurt or even kill an artist's credibility. Once a song crossed over to AM, FM stopped playing it. And if you weren't careful, FM would stop playing you, period. Led Zeppelin became FM darlings partly by forbidding Atlantic to release any singles.

The dividing line had been *Sgt. Pepper*. The Beatles, the true kings of Pop/Rock, released no singles from their masterpiece. It made the irrefutable statement: We just single-handedly evolved the Artform we helped invent.

From 1967 through most of the '70s, the new lingua franca of Rock music would be the album. By the '80s, if it felt right, singles returned to the hip column.

"Hungry Heart" felt right. It had a universal sensibility, simplicity with substance. It was also a song that posed its own unique set of challenges.

For starters, it had an unusual structure, in that the verse and chorus were the same, which was very hard to make work if you weren't James Brown. Because of that, I suggested the modulation for the solo. A modulation is simply a key change implemented to surprise the ears. It's part of the fun of Arranging to jump to an odd key and then have to find your way back to where you started. Or not.

The rest of the song came together. For the Beach Boys–style harmonies in the chorus, I suggested we bring in the Turtles, aka Flo and Eddie, aka Mark Volman and Howard Kaylan. I had seen their show at the Bottom Line and loved it. The session made Mark and Howard relevant again. They'd thank me by later overcharging for a Jukes session and reneging on a deal for a benefit, but nobody's perfect.

Then there were the drums. Even tuned, struck, and miked correctly, there was still the challenge of the mix.

The mix is exactly what it sounds like. You take all your tracks of instruments and mix them down to two tracks. You balance the instruments, add equalization (makes the instrument brighter or fatter, etc.), compression, reverb, etc.

I could hear how close we were to the drum sound I wanted. But we weren't quite there. I kept telling Bob to turn up the room mics. He edged them up a millimeter at a time, the way good Engineers were taught. I'm sure he thought I was just the guitar player being a pain in the ass, and that no one had explained to him my new status as co-Producer.

I took Bruce out to the hallway. "Listen, man," I said. "We are close to the promised land, no pun intended. Nirvana is in sight. Bob won't take me seriously until you explain to him I am coproducing this fucking thing, but right now when you go back in push those drum-room mic motherfucking faders all the way up."

He did. And there it was. The sound I'd been looking for my whole recording life. The sound that would influence everybody in the '80s.

Ironically, incredibly, and much to my eternal aggravation, just a few months later some smart-ass invented sampling! After all my painstaking research and experimenting, all they had to do was push a fucking button for an instant magnificent snare. Usually, one of Clearmountain's!

There was one more thing bothering me. Bruce just didn't have a Pop voice.

On *Born to Run* and *Darkness*, he had been writing older than he was, thinking older than he was, and singing older. He made his voice big and dramatic and rough and lived in, which fit the songs perfectly. Remember the singer is always an actor acting out the script that is the song.

But to be a Pop hit, "Hungry Heart" required something else. Never mind that the subject, a guy abandoning his wife and kids, was not exactly ideal for a younger audience. I have always believed lyrics are icing on the cake, mostly ignored by everyone except critics and the most fanatical fans.

For a song to be a hit, it has to *sound* like a hit. Ideally it's a bright, uplifting sound that appeals to a Pop audience that will respond to the ear candy far more readily than the actual substance. So how could we make the record brighter in general?

And then it hit me. Speed the tape up! His big voice would become smaller. Thinner. Younger! Remember the Chipmunks? Same science, taller Artist. I stayed late with Neil Dorfsman, our Engineer.

The song was better faster! I sped it up a little more, and a little more. It took some getting used to, but it felt natural enough. If you'd never heard the original, you'd never notice the difference.

The next day I played it for everybody. They all laughed. When he saw I was serious, Bruce said I might be on to something, but it was too much. They slowed it back down, then sped it up one step at a time until it was a notch slower than my version.

When Charlie Plotkin mastered it months later, he sped it back up that last notch to my original speed and got the credit. It's OK. He's a good guy.

The River had a completely different atmosphere than the previous two albums. Bruce's identity had settled into the rural, stand-and-fight, speaking-from-the-working-class-perspective persona of *Darkness*. Which didn't mean he wasn't still in his write-and-record-a-million-songs-and-find-the-album-in-there-later mode. But at least this batch *sounded* great. So it was a much more pleasant atmosphere for our endless song arguments, which I usually lost. And *The River* was a double album, which meant more room for some fun songs along with the substance.

Bruce kept "Hungry Heart" but threw out classics like "Loose Ends," "Take 'Em as They Come," "Roulette," and "Restless Nights."

Who needs 'em?

I happen to like "Crush on You," but in place of "Where the Bands Are," or "Mary Lou," or "I Wanna Be with You"?

I don't know.

The other subject that was discussed enthusiastically was the treatment of slow songs. Bruce and Jon were together on this, the sparser the better. Bruce was always so concentrated on his writing on the page, with good reason and great results, that I'm not sure he ever fully understood the difference between a song and a record.

My attention deficit disorder couldn't take it. I was constantly trying to add production and arrangement ideas to songs like "Racing in the Streets" and "Wreck on the Highway," and he wanted stark and stoic because that's what the cinematic lyrics suggested.

But a record ain't a movie. It's a fine line how sparse you can make something, without the visual assistance, before you lose an audience. There's no right or wrong here—that's what makes the longest discussions—but according to my ADD, they'd occasionally go too far. Check out the two versions of "Racing in the Street" for a good example. But Bruce preferred erring on the side of desolation. And you have to respect the discipline of sacrificing the musicality of a song to make a point.

Whatever. If he's happy, I'm happy.

I am very proud of *The River*, which remains my favorite "official" album, but too many of the best songs ended up on the second disc of *Tracks*.

We did a couple of benefits in that period.

No Nukes at Madison Square Garden was promoted under the auspices of Musicians United for Safe Energy, or MUSE, which was founded by Jackson Browne, Bonnie Raitt, John Hall, and Graham Nash.

It's where Tom Petty, not known for his wild and crazy sense of humor, delivered his most memorable punch line. The organizers told him that the Garden was Bruce's home turf, so he shouldn't be bothered if he heard the crowd booing. They were just saying "Bruce."

"What the fuck's the difference?" Tom lovingly contributed to infamy.

That benefit was the first political thing I was ever part of. I understand it better now, but back then I didn't get it. What was preaching to the converted supposed to accomplish? How was a concert and audience full of hippies supposed to affect Ronald Reagan's decision-making process?

The best part of the event for me was meeting Jackson Browne, who would become an important major friend and affect my life greatly very soon.

The event would help me when I eventually established my own results-oriented political methodology, which was a better fit for my ADD.

A little later, in Los Angeles, we did a much-needed tribute for Vietnam vets. Bruce had become friendly with Bobby Muller, the president of the Vietnam Veterans of America Foundation, and I was glad he decided to do that one. A friend from my neighborhood, Rod Paladino, had been spit on when he came home from the war, so it was personal to me.

But mainly, we were looking toward to our new record's release. Landau had done his homework, learning the . . . complexities of the Pop world, and that homework ensured my first work as part of the official production team would get its shot.

"Hungry Heart" started up the charts. And as much as the modern Pop world would forever be a foreign planet, having that first hit was quite a thrill. Album sales went from a few hundred thousand to three million. That was around the average ratio of hit singles to the insane album sales at that time. Every hit single meant around three million album sales in the gold rush '80s. Our half-filled theaters turned into sold-out arenas.

When I met Bruce in '65, we were two teenage misfits who shared an impossible fantasy. And now, a decade and a half of hard work later, we'd made it. What a difference the right hit single at the right time made. Of course my gratitude only lasted until our second single bombed. "Fade Away" not being a hit was, as far as I was concerned, a crime against humanity.

We were on top of the world. Audience enthusiasm was unparalleled. And then a traumatic event diluted our bliss. On the first American leg of the tour, on the night we played the Spectrum in Philadelphia, we lost John Lennon.

I remember hearing the news and being surprised by how upset I was. The Beatles had stopped touring in the mid-'60s. They hadn't been a band for a decade. I had never followed their solo work very closely. But it felt like losing a brother or a father.

Brian Jones's death was important to me. Jimi Hendrix's, even more so. But my relationships with those artists had lasted three or four years. The Beatles had been my mentors for fifteen years. Plus, they had been first. They communicated such hope and joy. They saved my life. Lennon's murder hit me so hard that I expected we'd cancel. But Bruce gave me a wonderful speech about how people needed us more than ever in moments like this.

I remember opening with "Born to Run" and crying all the way through it. Once again, we were reminded by History to embrace those rare blissful moments with all your strength when you find them, because who knows what rough beast slouching toward Bethlehem is just around the corner waiting to be born.

fourteen

Checkpoint Charlie

(1980)

Checkpoint Charlie,
Brothers and sisters on the other side,
Livin' in the shadow of a wall so high,
Make me wanna cry, baby.

— "CHECKPOINT CHARLIE," FROM *VOICE OF AMERICA*

Dystopian.

Fifty steps took us from a technicolor *Hogan's Heroes* episode to a black-and-white, postapocalyptic sci-fi flick.

The farmers on the billboards all looked similarly creepy/George Romero, and after a while I started missing the vapid, consciousness-colorizing advertising that I usually despise.

Bruce and I had decided to go through Checkpoint Charlie to East Berlin. While the wall was still up.

I have lots of German friends, some of the sweetest people in the world, but Germans are one of those ethnic groups that can be really scary when they want to be.

And when the nasty fuck at the border takes your passport and says, "OK, you're on your own," it gives you a little shot of anxiety.

We walked in, and within a few blocks we were in the Twilight Zone. Very quiet. We looked at some shops. Not much on the shelves.

We might've gone into a bar and had a drink or something, but I don't remember striking up a conversation with anyone, all of whom reminded me of the Transylvanian townspeople who stop talking when the victims walk into the tavern.

We didn't stay long. The thought of people living in that atmosphere of acute paranoia was quite depressing.

I wrote a song for them.

Sometimes that's all a po' boy can do.

Frank Barsalona had insisted we go to Europe.

We had played just four shows in Europe after *Born to Run*, and none for *Darkness* because of our perilous financial situation. The River Tour went all over Europe—Germany, France, Belgium, England, Scotland, Spain, the Netherlands, Italy, Norway—you name it.

That tour began a love affair with European audiences that continues to this day. But at first, the culture shock was . . . shocking.

It was hard relating to the food, for starters. Not that we cared that much about food in those days, but the only hamburger in Europe was at the newly opened Hard Rock Cafe in London. The *only* burger in ten countries. I shit you not!

And no peanut butter!

And London is all about teatime, right? But ask for iced tea and they looked at you like you're an escaped mental patient and they're considering whether to report you to the authorities or not.

If I had the entrepreneurial gene, there were business opportunities everywhere. Of course, I didn't act on them. But looking back, I always had those kinds of ideas, those entrepreneurial compulsions, flying by in my head.

Thinking about it now, I think there are two reasons to be at least a little bit of a businessman. The first is a totally legit and in fact essential reason, and that is to protect your Art. This is serious. You have to force yourself to understand what the fuck your lawyers and accountants are talking about. If you get lucky, they might be smart and actually care, but you can't depend on that.

The second reason is a little scary.

It is getting into business because you are not confident enough that your own artistic talent will find an audience. I think this is my problem, which by the way has proven to be true.

Without that confidence, deep down you feel what your parents always said, which is that you need the dreaded *something to fall back on.*

I get shivers just writing those words, but it is funny how the older you get, the smarter your parents become.

In Germany, after we left the Twilight Zone and were back on the West Berlin side of the wall, a kid came up to me on the street. "Why are you putting missiles in my country?" he said.

What? Whatever you're smoking, give me some! The kid asked me again.

"Look, friend, come to the show tonight, on me. I'll show you it's a guitar in that case, not a fucking missile."

I walked on and that was that. Except it wasn't. I couldn't get what he said off of my mind. Why was it bugging me so much?

That's the government, not me, I said to myself. I've got nothing whatsoever to do with what my government does. Just because he's a naive foreigner and doesn't know any better, I shouldn't let that get to me. Just because he thinks I live in a democracy . . .

Holy Shit! It hit me.

He thinks I live in a democracy!

And that means—my mind was racing now—that he doesn't know the difference between a congressman and a musician, a Democrat and a Republican. To him, I'm an . . . American.

Whoa. Radical.

I was the least political guy I knew. I couldn't have cared less. I made it through the entire '60s without one single political thought in my head.

But the German kid sent me down a path, and I kept going. If America is putting missiles in Germany, through NATO or whatever, and America is a democracy, then I *am* putting missiles in his country!

A shiver went through my soul.

If I'm putting missiles in Germany, what else am "I" doing? I suddenly had a hunger to do something I had never done through twelve years of schooling. I felt the need to read a book!

When we got home, I went into my local bookstore, Coliseum Books, off Columbus Circle, and bought every book I could find on our foreign policy since World War II. Just my luck, the first one was by Noam Chomsky.

Game over, baby.

The second book was *Bitter Fruit,* by Stephen Schlesinger and Stephen Kinzer, about the CIA's overthrow of Jacobo Arbenz's government in Guatemala in 1954. Now the game was even more over. I felt like a member of the Nazi Party in 1939.

But there it was, America's ongoing nefarious and immoral activity, right in our own hemisphere.

There was a connection between big business, local slave labor, and military dictatorship? Paid for by American tax dollars? We weren't supporting democracy around the world? We were the bad guys?!?

Fuck me, I thought. No way. This is not what the Founders had in mind.

I proceeded to single-handedly keep Coliseum in business for the next ten years or so.

I started feeling the need to do more than just read.

I had to try and expose this hypocrisy. I had to at least let people know that Rock and Roll wasn't in on these decisions!

But how? I wasn't sure.

All I knew was that hearing foreign audiences singing every word of our songs was absolutely thrilling. The power of Rock to communicate was nothing short of revelatory.

Maybe the '60s did leave a legacy we could pick up on after all.

Checkpoint Charlie, the kid with the missiles, the ability of Rock music to carry messages—it was beginning to add up to something.

fifteen

Hemingway Appropriately

(1980–1982)

The way to do is to be.

—LAO TZU

"Come over," Bruce said. "I've been doing some demos for the new album."

Demos? This was new. We had always worked out the songs at rehearsal.

It was him and Mike Batlin, his first guitar roadie, acting as Engineer, with a four-track cassette tape machine!

The whole setup was bizarre.

He then proceeded to play me the wildest bunch of songs I'd ever heard.

They were stark and acoustic and reminded me of the first time I heard Son House or Charley Patton or Robert Johnson or Harry Smith's Folk recordings. I was completely transported to another time, another place.

Thunder Road. Not the song—the movie. I was suddenly with Robert Mitchum, barreling down the backwater dirt mountain roads of Tennessee and West Virginia, avoiding police roadblocks, or in Pretty Boy Floyd's Depression-era Ohio.

It was thrilling. The songs were so authentic that I didn't think about my friend sitting in front of me. But of course he was in them. They were all him, but a new him. Or maybe an old him that was emerging for the first time.

The difference was not just the writing but the acting. Every singer is an actor, whether they know it or not, and suddenly he had become a very good one. He wasn't narrating anymore. He embodied these songs and made them totally believable.

After listening, I was not my usual effusive and opinionated self. I was quiet.

This worried him.

"What?" he said.

I had to choose my words wisely. It felt like an important moment.

"Well, I only know one thing," I said. "And I know it with all my bones. This is an album. And not only that, it's a great album. I've never heard anything quite like it. It sounds like field recordings."

I named names. Harry Smith, Don Law, Alan Lomax.

He laughed. "What do you mean? These are the demos for . . ."

"Yeah, I get it," I said. "You thought these were demos. That's what makes this the most personal, intimate record you or anybody else will ever do. This has got to be released."

He was genuinely surprised. "Well, wow," he finally said. I could tell he knew he was going to have to listen to the songs much more intensely, in an entirely different context. No longer just as an exercise to entertain his friends, but as a potentially finished piece of work.

Everybody else in the band and organization thought I'd lost my mind. Judging from the last two albums, they figured a hundred more songs would follow before a record started to take shape.

We even attempted to cut at least a few of those "demos" with the band.

At the same time, Bruce started bringing in more songs. Or maybe Paul Schrader sent Bruce the script for a potential movie called *Born in the USA*, asking him to write the title song. In using the band to demo it, Bruce realized he had something special.

Those other songs, the ones that weren't the so-called demos, continued on in the spirit of the "live" sound we'd finally achieved on *The River*. It worked so well that we took it to an extreme. We did the album live. If a vocal didn't work, the whole band would play the whole song again. Crazy? Yes. Pointless? Not exactly. The more unrehearsed it was, the more primal it would be.

I worked on fourteen, fifteen, maybe sixteen songs over two weeks. No overdubs. For the mandolin solo on "Glory Days," I picked it up and played it into my vocal mic!

The more the band work came together, the more the so-called demos were taken seriously as a separate album. At least by Bruce— which meant everybody would be on board soon. So we had both the beginnings of our electric follow-up to *The River* and an acoustic album by the Appalachian moonshining Folk singer John Hammond thought he'd signed in the first place.

Hammond had retired from Columbia in 1975, so Bruce and Jon had to break the news to Walter Yetnikoff and Bruce Lundvall, the label heads at the time.

They played it smart. They said, We've got good news and bad news, and they put on a few of the full-band tracks to get them excited, maybe "Born in the USA" and "Glory Days."

I imagine the two executives lit up like Christmas trees, cash registers ringing in their heads.

I can hear Lundvall's mellifluous voice still echoing. "This is wonderful."

"Exactly the right record at the right time. Congratulations!" Yetnikoff (probably) barked.

Jon had to explain that the Rock record was only coming after the label put out this other record.

And then played them *Nebraska*.

I wish I could have seen their faces.

The heads of the biggest record company in the world, jobs always on the line, listening as their most important artist, accompanied by acoustic guitar on a lo-fi cassette recording, convincingly portrayed a serial killer on the frozen tundra of Oklahoma yodeling like a demon drunk on poisoned whiskey!

Ha-ha!

Take that, Beancounters of the Universe!

Anyway, Bruce and Jon pulled it off, and I'm proud that I encouraged the truly solo Folk part of Bruce, which I was probably the first to witness, back in his room in Freehold, to become a semiregular part of his work output—even if it was once again against my self-interest.

It's among the most uncompromising and uncommercial records any major Artist has ever released. It would keep his dignity forever protected and would ensure his credibility would remain forever bulletproof.

I had met Gary US Bonds on the oldies circuit back in '73. Though we never had a real conversation, I liked him a lot. Funny as hell.

Still, when Bruce decided to produce him just after *The River*, I didn't get it. Of all the phenomenal '50s and '60s cats, he had chosen the guy who sounded like he made party records in his garage?

At first, I was just playing as a member of his band. We did "This Little Girl" and "Dedication," and Jon shopped the single around. Everybody passed. That's when Bruce asked me to get involved.

I fixed a few things in the recording, but mostly I brought back Bob Clearmountain to mix it. Bob really got the song popping on that old analog equipment. Every riff from every instrument was perfectly clear. The handclaps were like gunshots, and that was probably ten of us at the most clapping. It would take forty guys with today's digital shit and still not sound as good.

I ended up taking the completed Bonds record to Gary Gersh, who had just joined Jim Mazza at a brand-new company called EMI America. Gary signed Gary and said he wanted more than a single. He wanted a full album. But Bruce was busy doing something, maybe mastering *Nebraska*, which took months. (I'm guessing an hour of work and two months of conversation!) So Bruce gave me the responsibility of doing the album. He'd drop in now and then to see how it was going.

Turns out, Bonds was one of the great Soul singers. There was no way to know it from his party records, but somehow Bruce knew.

Now that we had one of the great singers, I figured, Let's put him together with songs by the greatest songwriters.

There's an art to covering songs. The Beatles and the Stones both did covers through their first *five* albums. That alone should tell young bands how significant that stage of development is.

The Beatles mostly kept the original arrangements but still made the songs their own. How? They were the fucking Beatles, that's how.

The Stones occasionally sped things up, like on their Muddy Waters covers, but otherwise relied on their own strong identity.

The rest of us have to work a little harder. There are five ways an artist can make a cover song their own: change gender, genre, tempo, arrangement, and style.

You don't need all five. You only need one. But let's have a little fun. What are the greatest covers ever?

Joe Cocker's cover of the Beatles' "With a Little Help from My Friends" comes immediately to mind.

Same gender, pretty much same genre, but Joe (or Producer Denny Cordell) slowed it down, changed the arrangement with the organ intro, added Jimmy Page's guitar licks, girl singers, and a couple of classic B. J. Wilson drum fills Ringo would have been proud of. Then Joe sang the shit out of it, sounding like Ray Charles, while Ringo sounded like who we wanted him to sound like . . . Ringo.

Jimi Hendrix's version of Bob Dylan's "All Along the Watchtower" may be the greatest cover of all time. Same gender, different genre. Acoustic Singer-Songwriter Country/Rock changed to powerful electric Rock, slowed slightly, different emphasis on the chords, a few classic guitar solos in the arrangement, and a much more Soul Roots vocal style.

The most dramatic cover of all time would seem to be Trent Reznor's "Hurt," as performed by Johnny Cash. Surprisingly, it's not that different! The original catches Reznor in a rather mellow mood—meaning intensely suicidal, but quieter than usual. Rick Rubin took out the dissonance, changed the instrumentation slightly, lost the noise at the end, and let Cash's immediately identifiable vocal style redefine the context.

So what's the ultimate example of a cover, the one that satisfies all five criteria?

"You Keep Me Hangin' On" by Vanilla Fudge.

It checks *all* the boxes:

☑ Gender: From the Supremes to male Long Island hoods.

☑ Genre: From Soul to Psychedelic Heavy Rock.

☑ Tempo: Slower. A lot slower!

☑ Arrangement: From Funk Brothers precision to B-3 Rock organ, distorted Rock guitar, Rock drums, Rock every-damn-thing!

☑ Style: From foxy-but-tough woman wanting romantic closure to a desperate, tortured man experiencing a Shakespearean tragedy inside a Roger Corman horror movie.

For Gary, I picked songs by Lennon and McCartney ("It's Only Love"), Dylan ("From a Buick 6"), and Jackson Browne ("The Pretender"). I had a Stones song also ("Connection") but ran out of time.

I didn't change the arrangements much, knowing Gary's super soulful voice would turn the songs into his own.

Bruce found "Jole Blon" on a Moon Mullican record, a radical genre shift that Gary pulled off effortlessly, and gave him "Rendezvous," one of our countless outtakes.

He also suggested I contribute a song, and since we didn't have anything particularly personal, I wrote "Daddy's Come Home" for Gary in an attempt to capture the lifelong struggle of the traveling journeyman with a family at home.

Unbelievably, "This Little Girl" went Top Ten. Some things just hit with the public. We followed up immediately with a second record, *On the Line*, bringing in legendary Soul vocalists Ben E. King and Chuck Jackson.

I loved working with the '60s Artists so much that I told Bruce we should start a label and do nothing but that—and buy the Power Station to do it. We could have done it with Sony money, given them distribution. Game over! He was tempted, I could tell. But he couldn't stand the thought of being in a business of any kind. It's a shame. Can you imagine what great records we could have made? Not just with King and Jackson, but with Wilson Pickett, David Ruffin, Little Richard, and who knows who else?

There was no hit on the second album, in spite of containing all new, great Springsteen compositions and being one of my favorite productions.

Nobody heard it.

◆

Ms. Destiny must have been lurking quietly during that first Bonds record, because Gary Gersh approached me to do a solo album.

I had never considered it.

"Let me think about it," I said, and went home to see if I could write some songs that felt like solo material. Nobody needed another sideman singing love songs. I thought about the kid in Germany and all the reading I'd been doing. Would that point me in the right direction?

I've always loved the idea of concept albums. There's something about the whole being greater than the sum of the parts that appeals to me. Bang for the artistic buck. It's part of my love of *big Art*. The bigger it is, the more significant the audience's experience, right? The songs might be great on their own—or the choreography or the lighting or the sets or the costumes—but they're all so much better if they are serving a story or a theme. Give the audience something to think about. Something to take home with them. That's why I was disappointed with *Love*, Cirque du Soleil's Beatles show. Why not make it a story? It's a great one. Begin with the London bombings and post–World War II depression in black-and-white and then blow it away with brilliant colorful fun led by Sgt. Pepper himself! Enhance it, symbolize it, fictionalize it, whatever, but tell an emotionally engaging story, or the show is nothing more than a momentary distraction.

There weren't that many true concept albums.

Frank Sinatra had invented the form with *In the Wee Small Hours*, *Come Fly with Me*, *Only the Lonely*, and others.

But it came to the Rock world with "A Quick One, While He's Away," a nine-minute montage of fragments strung together on the Who's second album at the suggestion of their Producer-Manager Kit Lambert, whose father was a classical composer. It grabbed me right away.

Pete Townshend would take things a step further, loosely connecting the songs with interstitial commercials on *The Who Sell Out* and then go all the way with *Tommy*.

Along the way the Kinks had *Village Green Preservation Society* and then *Arthur*, the Pretty Things had *SF Sorrow*, the Small Faces had *Ogden's Nut Gone Flake*. Some bands did it loosely, like the Stones with *Their Satanic Majesties Request* or Pink Floyd with *The Piper at the Gates of Dawn* (they'd do another loose one, *Dark Side of the Moon*, before tightening things up with *The Wall*).

All were interesting in their own way, but it was the concept that was abandoned after two songs that changed the world forever: *Sgt. Pepper's Lonely Hearts Club Band.*

It didn't matter that the Beatles were beginning to disintegrate or that there were mounting drug problems or that they were working strictly by instinct, by circumstance, or by accident—*Sgt. Pepper's* was the most important concept album of all time. Not the best or fully realized. That honor would forever go to *Tommy.* But the most *important.*

The sounds were fresh and unique, in complete contrast to the lyrics, which were nostalgic and sad, mostly about dysfunctional losers disappointed by life, and printed on the album sleeve for the first time. Why wasn't Columbia doing that on every Bob Dylan album, one has every right to ask?

It felt like the most extraordinary record made by the most extraordinary band, and it was the last time the world of culture was totally united by Popular music.

Don't believe all the revisionist bullshit you read now. Yes, *Revolver* had more innovations and was better song for song, but *Sgt. Pepper* changed the way our entire culture looked at Rock music.

I was there and I can tell you. You could walk down any street in the Western Freakin' World that first week of June 1967, and you would hear it playing.

For me, the walk was from MacDougal to St. Mark's in Greenwich Village, where I heard the record coming out of every head shop, clothing store, restaurant, and car that went by.

It elevated an entire generation's artistic consciousness and changed the world of Popular music from a singles-oriented, Wild West, fly-by-night hustle to a semilegitimate album-dependent business overnight.

We won't see that again anytime soon.

If I was going to have a solo career, I decided all my records would be concept records. I outlined five general themes that would help me investigate the world, put to use some of the books I had been reading, explore the relationships of power and control, and answer some important questions. Who has the power? Why? What does it mean? How much of the government is endorsed by the governed? Is Rousseau's social contract being honored? Who or what controls our destinies?

What is humanity's common ground? How much of a chance do we really have to change things?

The first solo album would look at how the government and various social forces affect the individual in society. It would also allow me to introduce myself as an Artist.

Then the next four albums would investigate how government affects and separates the human Family, how government manipulates various international States, the effect of that on Economy and how it needed to be transformed, and finally the political consequence of spiritual bankruptcy and the role of Religion. That would complete the circle, returning to the individual, but this time from the inside out.

Hopefully, I'd learn something about myself in the process. Who was I? What happened to those of us who grew up in the '60s? Was all that idealism just talk? I would mix in what little I knew about myself, what I believed, my responsibilities as both an American and a global citizen, my loves, my fears, etc.

These were big questions I had never even thought about. By fully embracing the Artist part of my identity, I could start to answer them.

Musically, for my first record, I decided to go back to the sound I had created with the Jukes: '60s R&B-based Rock with a five-piece horn section.

But I didn't continue in a linear fashion, which would have meant starting up where *Hearts of Stone* left off.

Instead I went for something rootsier. I thought the less produced the record was, the more open and honest, and the more direct my route would be to discovering my own identity.

Being a bit of an extremist back then, I recorded the whole album live in one day. I put the band in a semicircle, used the studio monitors hanging from the ceiling instead of headphones, and let it happen. Horns blowing into the drums, monitors blasting the whole mix back into all the microphones—I didn't care.

I used one of the greatest rhythm sections in the world, E Street's Garry Tallent and Max Weinberg. Dino Danelli from the Rascals and Jean Beauvoir from the Plasmatics came in near the end of the recording and became Disciples of Soul on the road. Bruce sang harmonies, though I couldn't credit him because Yetnikoff was on the warpath about something or other.

It worked pretty well, actually, thanks largely to my Engineer Bob Clearmountain, who probably thought I was nuts but was always game. We came back the next day and did the whole album again to see if we could get better takes. We may have used one or two takes from the second day.

I then spent a couple of weeks messing around, mostly to make sure I idiotically spent every penny of the record budget.

I put acoustic guitar on a couple of songs, did my double tribute to Ry Cooder as I added mandolin and slide on "Princess of Little Italy." Added the double guitar solo to "Angel Eyes." Resang the vocals where Bruce sang harmony live with Bruce because I wanted them spontaneous and loose and not Everly Brothers perfect.

If I had it to do over again, I would double some guitars and add some harmonies. Most of the album is one live rhythm guitar! But it holds up as an honest representation of where I was at the time.

There are two kinds of people in the world, my friend. Solo guys and band guys.

I'm a band guy, but in 1982 I was a band guy on the brink of a solo career. It's a paradox I learned to live with but never quite resolved.

The first time your name and picture are about to be put on an album cover, it makes you think. Being a person who'd rather be doing than thinking, I started to wonder what I'd gotten myself into.

It's a big job asking an audience to redefine you. In the world of showbiz you're lucky if an audience even finds you. If and when they do, they define you forever the way they first discovered you. And you're one in a million lucky it happened at all.

E Street fans knew me as Miami Steve, the always-in-a-good-mood party-guy sidekick. If I'd stayed in that role in my solo career, and written music to fit, I probably would have been very successful.

But that was one part of me, and that part had no time for Art. He was too busy fucking and drinking and fucking and drugging and fucking. He had to go.

It was time to introduce a guy the audience hadn't met yet. Well, unless they had been carefully reading the credits on the Jukes records.

This guy wasn't going to be as sure of himself as the other guy.

This guy would be taking a journey into the unknown, alone, to learn about how the world works, and finally learn about himself.

I knew I needed a new identity. But rather than use my own name, I decided to pick another nickname, for several reasons.

First, it suggests that no matter how serious you take the work, you're never going to be too self-righteous about yourself.

Second, it kept me connected to tradition, which I would need as I found my way through this adventure into the mystic.

And third, I believed in the fantasy aspect of show business. I have never related to the regular-guy look that John Fogerty started and Neil Young and Bruce adopted later. I'm not putting it down. It just never worked for me.

Maureen and I went to see the final Cream reunion. Apart from the fact that three-piece bands are by definition fraudulent since they don't record that way, they wore T-shirts and dungarees. For $350 a ticket, maybe you could put a fucking shirt on? If I go see Cream, I want to see the *Disraeli Gears* album cover, goddamn it!

What we do onstage is a complex, complete communication—songs, performance, clothes, lights, production. At its most effective, a great performance can not only transport an audience but transform it, taking them from tearful catharsis to blissful enlightenment. All in the same show. Nothing less. There is an essential element of Fantasy. Of Mystery. Of Masquerade. Theater!

And so I became Little Steven.

Little Anthony was one of my favorite Doo-Wop singers. "Tears on My Pillow" was the first record I ever bought and Little Anthony and the Imperials was the first live Rock show I ever saw. Toms River Roller Rink.

Little Walter was my favorite Blues guy and the greatest harmonica player ever.

And Little Richard was the embodiment and archetype of the philosophy of Rock and Roll freedom. My man. His flamboyant multisexual androgyny said you can be whoever you wanna be. He turned Rock into an Artform that not only tolerated reinvention but demanded it. He opened his mouth, and out came liberation.

As Little Steven, I would become the Political Guy, and release and embody my inner '60s gypsy forevermore.

Would the E Street audience have a problem with my new persona? Yes.

They never would show up.

One of the books I'd been reading was a collection of short fiction by Ernest Hemingway, *Men Without Women.* The stories were about bullfighters and soldiers and boxers and the relationship between identity and profession. I felt that if Ernie had written it in the '60s or '70s, it would have included a chapter about a Rock band, so I used it for the title of my album.

It would be particularly appropriate since Hemingway had committed suicide and I would be committing career suicide with this record. I'm not whining or being morbid, just saying one has to die in order to be reborn.

At the time, MTV had just started. Video budgets were rising every day. I figured that if we were going to spend a quarter of a million each on a few videos, we could make a real movie for the same money, couldn't we? One of my heroes, Roger Corman, did it all the time. Then we could carve the videos out of the film.

I called Jay Cocks and asked him what he thought. "Let's go see a friend," he said. We went to a hotel and took the elevator up, Jay knocked, and there stood John Cassavetes, wearing a tuxedo. Gena Rowlands flashed by in the background.

"I only got a minute," John said. "But the one-minute version of how to protect your work is this: get a script and make sure the Director sticks to it." Highly ironic advice from the king of improvisation! "That's why I direct all my own stuff. It's the easiest way to control it."

What a cool guy.

Why didn't I go back and spend more time with him?

Our script, by John Varnom, was more of a fluid outline describing our actual situation. It was a story about a band that didn't have the money to tour and decided to make a movie instead.

Because EMI didn't want to pay for the whole thing, we shot few scenes for potential investors. Our husband-and-wife Director-Producer team, Derek and Kate Burbidge, did an amazing job with no budget and a tiny guerrilla crew, and actually shot an impressionistic Indie Film, much more than the outline we intended.

We used crew members from E Street, Tony, Bubba G., and Tomasino; an actor friend, Sal Viscuso, who happened to be in town; and Maureen, who played my girlfriend Knuckles.

She was already all over the album—"Forever," "Save Me," "I've Been Waiting," the title track, and "Angel Eyes" with all the ballet imagery:

> *She dances in shadows, she bleeds in tears,*
> *She turns into animals, she disappears,*
> *Surrounded by mirrors while the spirits watch,*
> *They look now, baby, but they can't touch,*
> *The pain is intoxicating if the music is loud enough.*

We took our footage to Cannes, and the Disciples performed there, probably the first band to have done so, but the record company guy who was supposed to organize the investors' meetings didn't. It never got financed and never really got done.

Almost forty years later, when I watched the footage for the first time, I was surprised we'd done as much as we had. The movie feels like a street version of early French New Wave, or like Cassavetes himself. It requires a bit of filling in the blanks, but it kind of makes sense. "A triumph of style and character over exposition!" a fantasy review might've read.

Prince would do it the right way two years later, with *Purple Rain*.

The *Men Without Women* album came out on October 1, 1982.

Nebraska had come out the day before.

Technically, two band guys making solo records, but in very different ways. For me it was just another band with me out front; for him it was a legit solo project.

Anyway, it was a new adventure for both of us.

An exciting moment.

I was not the marrying kind.

How many guys have said that? Possibly all of us.

I loved the single life, answering to no one, no responsibilities, no guilt, no checking in, no schedule, no plans. Also, in the mid-'70s, I'd developed a temporary addiction to *ménages à trois*, which didn't lend itself to marriage except maybe in Persia or somewhere.

But then there was Maureen. I had pursued her since the infamous Bottom Line shows, but once I reached her I really reached her. Three, four, five times a day, for years!

I took her to Venice and proposed under the Bridge of Sighs. If I was going to get married, I might as well do it right. We set a date for December 31, 1982, five years to the day since we had first gone out.

Little Richard had left Rock and Roll to join the ministry, so we talked him into officiating. (Bruce Willis would steal the idea five years later with no credit—you're welcome, pal!)

Percy Sledge sang "When a Man Loves a Woman" as we came down the aisle at an old ballet studio on Manhattan's East Side, Harkness House. Little Milton performed, along with the band from *The God-father* movie. Unfortunately, Little Anthony was working a cruise ship and couldn't get out if it, and Little Walter was long gone; otherwise I would have had all the "Littles."

Bruce was my best man, and the wedding party included (on my side) Jay Cocks, Max Weinberg, Garry Tallent, Jimmy Iovine, Gary Bonds, Jean and Monti from the first version of the Disciples, my brother Billy, my roadie Ben, our tour manager Harry Sandler, and LaBamba from the Jukes. Maureen had her four sisters (Gail, Lori, Maria, and Lynn), her two best friends (Michelle and Sari), my sister Kathi, and my assistant Obie. Jay's wife, Verna, was there, and they brought Marty Scorsese, who kept our ongoing should-have-been-good-friends story line alive. The Chambers Brothers were there too. Maureen knew them from her New York days in the '60s.

I don't remember much else other than that our two hundred guests were augmented by another hundred or so crashing and stealing all the gifts. We had everything taken care of except security.

Fun, though, I'm told.

sixteen

Voice of America

I've been fighting my whole life for the privilege to work.

—"FOREVER," *MEN WITHOUT WOMEN*

Money and me, what can I say? We never got along too good.

The pattern of my life is investing everything I have in what I believe in. Emotionally. All my time. All my talent. All my energy. And, yeah, usually all my money. Because I hate asking other people for money, and, until recently, never had anybody to do the asking for me. And we'll see how long they last.

In 1982, I proceeded to spend what little money I had left after making the movie, taking an eleven-piece band around the world for a year.

Now, the Rock life isn't for everybody. You're basically packing your bags and unpacking them thirty years later. It's a lifestyle that requires dedication, perseverance, patience, ambition, and, most of all, having no desire or ability to do anything else.

People are always saying, Oh, how proud you must be! How righteous to have withstood the slings and arrows of outrageous fortune!

But no. I'm sorry.

I resist all accusations of nobility.

We were bums. Profoundly unsuited for any legitimate type of work. We did have honor for our outlaw profession. And a work ethic. I'll give us that.

So here's a few tips for keeping a band together.

As soon as you can afford it, get separate rooms. This is the one and only rule you cannot follow from the Beatles, who never had their own rooms. Don't ask.

Make sure everybody gets a moment in the spotlight.

Find out what each band member can do and find a way to use it.

If it's a real band with the same members all the time and one or two people are doing most of the writing, and you are successful, share a little bit of the publishing money. It won't kill you.

Try and keep girlfriends and wives—or if you are a Girl Group, boyfriends and husbands—off the road as much as possible. The band needs to bond, especially in the beginning. And the mates should be busy with their own lives anyway.

Keep a diary! How I wish I'd kept a diary. This book is only the 10 percent I still remember!

And I don't mean the fourteen-year-old-girl's Ooh-Joey-looked-at-me-in-math-class-today!-type stuff.

I mean make notes about the towns. Keep track of details about hotels and venues. Restaurants, local promoters, local friends, local journalists.

You'll be coming back to the same towns for the next thirty or forty years, with a little bit of luck. So keep notes, and you will thank me in the morning.

I guess I figured money was something that should be put to use and I could always make more. I don't know where that comes from. We weren't rich growing up. I had a paper route. I caddied, scraped boats in a marina, worked in a box factory, made a few bucks working at my grandfather's shoe repair store.

I didn't waste it either. I got into gambling for a while, but when I realized that in the long run, you couldn't win, I quit. I've always found people who worshipped money utterly repulsive. Still do. Which is why Wall Street doesn't like me very much. And why I can't relate to too many Managers or accountants.

Even before the tour, I had decided our whole Disciples of Soul thing was going to be a concept. I had full-length leather coats made with a variation of the Hells Angels logo on the back. I got permission from the head of the Angels in New York at the time, Chuck Zito, but the coats got us into trouble in Europe, and I had to have a few sit-downs.

I decided that we were going to be the ultimate Rock and Roll rebels—no drugs, no drinking—and that we'd get into amazing shape. To set a good example and prepare for the revolution to come.

This was before hotels had gyms. I had a personal trainer, Phil Dunphy, and we took his equipment out on the road, put it under the bus. When we got to a hotel Phil had the bellmen bring it to a room, which we would convert to a workout room.

Swear to God.

I'm not showing my age too much with all this, am I? I mean now that every Motel 6 has a five-thousand-square-foot gym?

Did I mention milkmen once came to people's houses every morning to personally bring you milk?

Doctors made house calls.

And a truck of the greatest junk food, the Entenmann's of its day—a Dugan's truck just flashed across my mind—would deliver daily ecstasy to your front door in the form of just-made cupcakes, Danishes, doughnuts. I'm not making this up. Let's face it, Americans have never had a chance healthwise.

In that first year, the Disciples did a couple of interesting gigs, like the US Festival, where we went on at 9 a.m.—Bo Diddley time—and the Reading Festival, where they threw bottles at us. We also opened for the Who and U2.

People didn't know what to make of us. Five horns, Rock guitar, a percussionist, multiracial. It was hard to categorize us, so we were better off playing our own gigs rather than trying to open for other bands.

Opening acts work in the Hard Rock world, or any genre where the opener is very similar to the headliner. If you're the least bit unique, you're better off building your own audience from scratch if you can find a way to pay for it. I'm still trying to figure that part out. But I'd rather play to five hundred of my own fans than fifty thousand of somebody else's. You sell more records with your own people, and they stay with you for life.

Plus, all I was interested in was talking about politics, which America didn't get at all and still hasn't. Well, maybe they're starting to get it now. So I started spending more and more time in Europe.

The turning point of my solo career may have come with the very first show.

It was October 16, 1982, on a live TV broadcast called *Rockpalast* in Germany, which went live to something like seventeen countries, was on all night, and was watched by everybody at a time when there were only three channels.

The creator, Peter Rüchel, who would become a lifelong friend, was such a big fan of *Men Without Women* that we headlined the show. Gianna Nannini, described to me as the Italian Patti Smith, opened, then Kid Creole and the Coconuts, then us.

We were a little concerned because we had just found out our record had come out in Germany that day.

We went on and the crowd went crazy. By the end of the show it was bedlam. Our local record company guy, a delightful wild man named Lothar Meinerzhagen (picture Werner Klemperer as Colonel Klink without the uniform), who was one of our true believers, called LA and begged them to support a European tour immediately. He told them the reaction was extraordinary, and the broadcast had gone out to all of Europe.

They turned it down. A life-changing moment. We could have broken all of Europe right then and there. If I'd had a Manager, it would have gotten done.

Kid Creole—who, with all due respect, put the audience to sleep—stayed, toured, broke Europe wide open, and never left.

Meanwhile, I was thinking a lot about that kid in Germany who'd gotten me hooked on politics in the first place. I wanted to find him. And beat the shit out of him.

The tour established the pattern of my entire performance life: having to win people over song by song, since very few songs I've written would ever become even remotely familiar.

The other pattern I would establish was starting to write the next album a few months into the tour. I was so excited about one new song that I took the band into a studio in Belgium on a day off and cut it.

"RocknRoll Rebel," which was going to be the title and lead track of my second album, referred to an incident from earlier that year when my friends and I got kicked out of Disneyland because of how I was dressed. My friends being Maureen, my assistant Obie, and Bruce.

It was my comic version of the Stones' "Street Fighting Man," and the main joke was that my rebellion was about dressing funny and *not* doing drugs. When I sang about being "straight" in the chorus, that's what it was about, not my heterosexuality, which isn't particularly rebellious.

Although, at one point in the early British Rock scene it *would* have been a rebellious act!

I did a radio essay on it, the substance of which was my sincere belief that the day the gay culture abandoned Rock and went to Disco was the day fashion left with them. Glam would be the gay culture's final endorsement of Rock. Before that, the industry was completely dominated by a culture so gay that the Stones' Manager Andrew Oldham told me he had to pretend to be gay just to have a seat at the table!

It began with the London Promoter and Manager Larry Parnes, who discovered talented and attractive young men, changed their names, seduced them (if possible), and tried to make them famous. His stable included Tommy Steele (originally Tommy Hicks), Marty Wilde (Reg Smith), Billy Fury (Ron Wycherley), Vince Eager (Roy Taylor), Dickie Pride (Richard Knellar), Lance Fortune (Chris Morris), Duffy Power, (Ray Howard), Johnny Gentle (John Askew), Terry Dene (Terence Williams), Nelson Keene (Malcolm Holland), and Georgie Fame (Clive Powell), among others.

Then there was the influential Pop and theater songwriter Lionel Bart. Not to mention virtually all of the early Rock Managers, including Brian Epstein (the Beatles), Kit Lambert (the Who), Robert Stigwood (Cream, the BeeGees), Simon Napier-Bell (Yardbirds, Marc Bolan), Billy Gaff (Rod Stewart), Ken Pitt (David Bowie), Barry Krost (Cat Stevens), John Reid (Elton John), among others.

The point being that I believe it was the gay influence that made fashion such an integral part of the Rock music scene, and I miss it.

Am I digressing enough?

After sitting with "RocknRoll Rebel" for a while, I reconsidered making it the title song, or even putting it on my second album. It was going to be the beginning of my completely political phase, and I felt it needed a harder edge musically than my typical Rock or Soul, so I decided to let the horns go. Plus the song had a lot of humor in it, and I felt I also had to let that side of me go for a while. Thirty-six years, to be exact. *RocknRoll Rebel* finally emerged as the title of my box set of early work in 2019.

Part of the rationalization and satisfaction of being a boss working for another boss was the ability to offer suggestions and advice.

I liked being the underboss in the E Street Band. The consigliere. It kept me out of the spotlight but allowed me to make a significant enough contribution to justify my own existence in my own mind. And there was a balance between me, Bruce, and Jon. We had artistic theory and artistic practice covered.

But somewhere in '83, it started to feel like Bruce had stopped listening. He had always been the most single-minded individual, with a natural extreme monogamy of focus in all things—in relationships, in songwriting, in guitar playing, in friends. Was that impulse now going to apply to his advisers?

At the time, I was hurt by the thought that maybe Jon resented my complete direct access to Bruce. I liked Jon a lot and thought he felt the same about me. If anything, I should have been the resentful one, but I wasn't. In the end, I don't think Jon had anything to do with the way things changed. There comes a time when people want to evolve without any baggage. To become something new and different without having to stay connected to the past. This was, I think, one of those moments.

Occasionally you need to be untethered.

Without all this retrospective wisdom, though, Bruce and I had our first fight, one of only three we would have in our lives.

I felt I had been giving him nothing but good advice and had dedicated my whole life and career to him without asking for a thing.

I felt I'd earned an official position in the decision-making process. He disagreed. So I quit.

Fifteen years.

We finally made it.

And I quit.

The night before payday.

It was fucking with Destiny big-time.

Or was it fulfilling it?

Briefly, let's leave emotion out of it and examine the balance sheet of this rather . . . incredible move.

On the positive side, I would write the music that would make up the bulk of my life's work. Had I stayed, in between tours I probably would have produced other Artists. Or continued writing for others. Or both. But I probably would never have written for myself.

I very possibly wouldn't have gotten into politics. Would Mandela have gotten out of jail? Would the South African government have fallen? Probably. But we took years off both of those things.

I got to be in *The Sopranos* and *Lilyhammer*. They probably never would have happened.

I would create two radio formats, a syndicated radio show, two channels of original content for Sirius (which has introduced over a thousand new bands that have nowhere else to go), a record company, and a music history curriculum. Would any of that exist?

It would change Bruce's personal life for the better; that's indisputable.

He would have been on the road for two years. Would he have had the time to hook up with Patti if she hadn't been on the road with him? Would their three wonderful kids exist if I hadn't left?

Patti Scialfa would find the love of her life, a mixed bag for her well-deserved career—a more visible shortcut but forever in his shadow (welcome to the club)—and most importantly, again, would those same three amazing kids exist if she hadn't joined the band to sing my vocal parts?

Nils Lofgren, hired to do my guitar parts, got a very rewarding second career, or third career if you count Crazy Horse, which he well deserved.

So some good things happened.

The negatives?

I lost my juice.

As Chadwick Boseman, playing James Brown, says in the excellent biopic *Get on Up* after he fires his band, "Five minutes ago you were the baddest band in the land; now you're nobody."

Let that be a lesson, kids. And believe me, I am nothing if not *the* cautionary tale.

Never, ever leave your power base.

Not until you have secured a new one.

I not only lost most of my friends and the respect of several different industries, I blew any chance of living a life without ever again having to worry about money.

Who knows what could have been created if I'd had the backing of the masters of the universe, who are nothing but thrilled to invest in the ideas of happy, successful Rock stars?

I might even have been financially secure enough to have kids of my own.

Next life.

Upon leaving the band, I became persona totally non grata. We didn't publicize any bad blood. Not one negative word from either of us. We just said that I had left to pursue my own career, but I was seen as a traitor by virtually everybody. People felt they had to choose sides. Guess whose side they chose?

I didn't think I had much in common with Trotsky, but we were both temporarily written out of history.

seventeen

The Killing Floor

I should have listened,
When my friend said come to Mexico with me,
I should have listened,
When my friend said come to Mexico with me,
I wouldn't be here now children,
Down on the killing floor.

    —HOWLIN' WOLF

Politics in Pop music began with an innocent enough couplet from Bob Dylan.

It was the first two lines of his fifth album, *Bringing It All Back Home*, and it would change the world forever.

The song, "Subterranean Homesick Blues," nodded to Jack Kerouac in its title and made liberal use of the symbolist poetry of Arthur Rimbaud and Allen Ginsberg. It was also the first time Dylan ever recorded with a band that anybody had heard. (He had played with a band a few years before on a B-side.)

He'd been to England and had seen the future of Rock and Roll, and at that stage of the game, its name was the Beatles.

That led him to accept an invitation from Jim Dickson to come see a group he was managing that would soon be called the Byrds. They were already being touted as the American Beatles, and Dylan didn't miss much. He was also aware that the most money he'd ever made was from the publishing royalty from Peter, Paul, and Mary's version of "Blowin' in the Wind."

The Byrds didn't like "Blowin' in the Wind" and didn't want to do it, so Dickson very cleverly invited Dylan to their rehearsal, forcing them to learn it to avoid being embarrassed. They played him their now-classic electric version of his "Mr. Tambourine Man." As the story goes, after Dylan heard the Bach-meets-Beatles version, he said, "Hey, man! You can dance to that!" And history was made.

It would be released five months after his acoustic version and would establish the Byrds as one of the most important bands of the Renaissance, single-handedly create the Folk Rock genre, and put America back on the charts after a year of British Invasion domination.

And by the way, it would be Dylan's only song to reach number one until "Murder Most Foul" fifty-five years later!

"Subterranean Homesick Blues" ushered in Dylan's electric future.

> *Johnny's in the basement mixing up the medicine,*
> *I'm on the pavement thinking about the government . . .*

I consider those the two most important sentences in the history of Rock.

The first line typified Dylan's unique way of having fun with the language, and no one since Allen Ginsberg has loved the English language as much as Bob. It's clever, secretive, metaphorical, streetwise, and hilarious, all at the same time.

What is Johnny doing in the basement?

Is he rolling a joint? Making a batch of grappa? Planning a revolution? Contemplating a paradox? Writing philosophy? Having sex? Denying he's an existentialist?

Bob leaves that up to you.

But the second line changed everything forever:

> *I'm on the pavement thinking*
> *about the government . . .*

What?

Thinking about *what*?

What the fuck does that mean?

All we thought about was sex.

All we knew was love songs.

That's all there was.

That line is the politics-meets-Pop shot heard round the world.

We were kids. We didn't know Folk music, or Country Blues, where ideas like this were commonplace.

Since when were we supposed to be thinking about the government?

Nobody ever thought about the government.

Not in my neighborhood.

Not in my family.

Not in my generation.

Not anybody in my parents' generation either.

So that was it. The Big Bang of political consciousness in Pop.

Bob Dylan had already taken Woody Guthrie's Folkie, Activist agenda to the highest-possible level on his second and third albums with songs like "Masters of War," "A Hard Rain's A-Gonna Fall," and "Only a Pawn in Their Game." But ideas like these were completely alien to Pop music.

So alien, in fact, that Dylan's words would combine with other ingredients—the Beatles' melodies, the Rolling Stones' sexuality, the Byrds' artistic breadth, the Beach Boys' blissful harmony, the Kinks' eccentricities, and the Who's operatic apotheosis—to create the new Artform of Rock beginning that summer of '65.

Over the years, other Rock songs with political consciousness popped up now and then.

Stephen Stills's "For What It's Worth" with Buffalo Springfield, Janis Ian's "Society's Child," Marty Balin and Paul Kantner's "Volunteers" with Jefferson Airplane, John Fogerty's "Fortunate Son" with Creedence Clearwater Revival, and the ultimate example, Neil Young's "Ohio" with Crosby, Stills, Nash, and Young.

In 1971 Marvin Gaye would make history by being the first mainstream major Soul Artist to do not just a song, but an entirely politically themed album, *What's Going On.*

Gil Scott-Heron could get away with it, and the Last Poets, but showbiz conventional wisdom declared politics and religion out of bounds for big stars.

Gaye had to fight Motown's founder and big daddy Berry Gordy all the way to the finish line. In the end, Gordy recognized that Gaye's passion for what his brother was going through in Vietnam and the daily uprisings in every Black neighborhood was not to be denied. Gordy surrendered with a speech that included "One of us will learn something from this." Gordy would be the one learning. The album was a huge hit.

Marvin would contribute to the writing of the record, his gift was his vocal genius. He belonged to that small club of singers that could completely make a song his own whether he wrote it or not. Only a few—Frank Sinatra, Tony Bennett, and Elvis Presley come to mind—share that gift.

His unique combination of Doo-Wop, Blues, Gospel, Soul, and Jazz was on full display in the title track, mostly written by Obie Benson from the Four Tops (they rejected it!) and Motown staff writer Al Cleveland, and continued to be impressive throughout the incredible album.

What would become his signature style of singing background with himself supposedly came from an engineer mistakenly playing back two different takes of a lead vocal at the same time. Marvin loved the accidental interplay and would use it to great effect on what would be his first (brilliant) Production.

In 1971, at the urging of Ravi Shankar, George Harrison organized the Concert for Bangladesh, which combined the consciousness of Dylan with the new political power of the Rock music generation revealed by Woodstock.

But these were one-offs. It wouldn't have made sense at that stage to practice politics full-time. And then came the 1980s.

We had gone from the Nixon era to the Reagan era, with only a brief, failed respite from the neofascism from Jimmy Carter. It seemed like the right time for an entirely political Rock artist.

In the wake of my first album, I put out a single, "Solidarity," to bring attention to the Polish trade union movement of Lech Wałesa, which was struggling to survive at the time. I kept the lyrics universal, referencing the movement only in the title and in a bit of the Polish national anthem I played in the guitar solo.

Horns were gone by then. I had decided to let the subject matter determine the music, which made for a more satisfying artistic marriage—every record would become the soundtrack to a different movie—but was not a good way to build an audience. As if I didn't have enough challenges already with my name change.

But I was possessed. I was on an obsessive unstoppable artistic adventure, no matter how irrational. There was an indescribable rush of adrenaline that came from feeling like I had found a purpose. A justification for my existence.

Surprise juiced the adrenaline considerably. This was not what I'd had in mind for my life. I wanted to be Diaghilev! Irving Thalberg! Orson Welles! Or at least Bob Fosse!

I wanted to Produce Big Things! I was on the path to doing just that. I had produced a massive hit record, and life is all about the parlay. I could have followed that success with producing other major acts or getting any project I could dream up financed for the rest of my life. Now, my significant contribution would be diminished to irrelevancy.

The adrenaline rush of feeling like I was doing the right thing, of having a purpose, fulfilling some sort of unclear but consequential destiny, had a big empty space to fill. And it did. It would get me through the '80s.

Voice of America, the second in my five-album arc, would be about how government affected the family and society in general.

The title track returned to the theme of an earlier song, "Lyin' in a Bed of Fire," but this time I was more aggressively pissed off, demanding action as opposed to merely observing the state of affairs. Talking to myself really, as much as anyone.

"Can you hear me? Wake up! Where's the voice of America?"

Jackson Browne would cover it, much to my elation.

"Justice" expressed my philosophy at the time, which has changed somewhat over the years. I now see a post-terrorism reason to have a worldwide military presence, which I didn't then. What hasn't changed is the need to give priority to the war at home, the lack of justice for our black, Latino, and Native populations.

The centerpiece of the record was "Checkpoint Charlie," about my trip behind the Iron Curtain. There was no better metaphor than the Berlin Wall to describe the way politics fucked with families, literally separating them.

"Solidarity" and "Out of the Darkness" were examples of the we-are-all-connected theme running through all my work, one Reggae, one Rock/Dance/Pop. With "Solidarity," I started embodying different characters' perspectives to make my points more dramatically, taking the every-singer-is-an-actor thing to its next level.

I sent "Solidarity" to Chris Blackwell, hoping he would release it on his Island Records label in Jamaica. Next time I heard from Chris, Black Uhuru had recorded it and had a hit!

"Los Desaparecidos (The Disappeared Ones)" was the story of our government supporting Latin American dictatorships that used their militaries to enforce slave labor for the multinational corporations. The military would "disappear" the troublemakers, meaning anyone trying to unionize or ask for fair wages or better working conditions.

My song was about a mother trying to explain to her young son why his father wouldn't be coming home. That boy would grow up to be the singer of "Bitter Fruit," a song on my next album. In addition to being one of my favorite songs, "Los Desaparecidos" was also one of my favorite records. Clearmountain's mixes were always great. That one was transcendent.

The album also included the most difficult song I've ever written, then or since.

I had a title, "I Am a Patriot," the subject of which was the disgust with political parties that George Washington expressed in his farewell address. I stared at that title for a year, knowing that my work in general would be criticizing our government, quite severely, and that I had to make it clear that it was coming from loyalty to our Founders' ideals and my belief that America was still a work in progress.

It was worth the effort. Jackson Browne, Eddie Vedder, and Kris Kristofferson, three writers I greatly admire, would cover it, much to my honored surprise.

A few months later Bruce called me. "Knowing you, if I didn't call you, we'd probably never speak again," he said. "Let's meet and get past this."

We reconciled.

I played *Voice of America* for him.

He was legitimately impressed.

"You've just been born," he said.

He had new music for me too. In the two years since I was gone, they had recorded a bunch of things and kept three new songs.

He played me one called "Dancing in the Dark" that was going on the record, and then "No Surrender," which he said would be an outtake for a B-side. (He never played me "Bobby Jean.")

"Man," I said. "You got it backwards! Throw that 'Dancing' thing in the trash and not only put 'No Surrender' on the record, but open with it! In fact, make it the damn title! *No Retreat, No Surrender!*"

To me, "Dancing in the Dark" had the potential to destroy his long-fought-for credibility. He had thrown out dozens of classic Rock songs because they very vaguely resembled rapidly-being-forgotten British Invasion songs, and now he was going to release what could easily be interpreted as a *Disco song* to blatantly try and get a hit?

A month or so later we had dinner. "This record is gonna be big," he said. I guess they knew; preorders from retail must have been huge.

"Good," I said. "You deserve it."

But I sensed a little trepidation. Not quite as bad as being on *Time* and *Newsweek* at the same time, but in that same Am I losing control? ballpark.

"I know you felt I'd stopped listening, but I'm listening now," he said. "What do I do with this?"

I thought about it. How could he separate himself from the pack once and for all?

"You have this identity of a working-class hero. With a big record, it's going to be a challenge to maintain that, even though I know that's where your heart is. I'll tell you what." It's funny how when you really need an idea, it comes. "You know how people do big events. Fundraisers. Shit like that? You know, once a year, once a tour?"

"Yeah."

"Well, what if you made every single show in every single city a fundraiser? Donate . . . I don't know . . . some percentage, something. Not once in a while. Every single show."

"Wow," he said. "That's radical. Gotta think about that one."

"Just like you always used to sign every autograph while we waited for hours on the fucking bus, this would connect you intimately to every town."

While he contemplated, I celebrated.

Waiter! More wine! I'm on a roll!

He would do the charity-in-every-city thing, but, luckily, I lost the "Dancing in the Dark" argument.

He not only put it on the album but released it as the first single! And not only released it as the first single, but filmed a stupid video! When I had been in the band, we'd had an understanding that we would *never* do a video. We had a reputation as the best live band around. If you wanted to see us, you'd have to come to the live show to see us!

But just to prove even the world's greatest consigliere can occasionally be wrong, that Rock Disco song and terrible video started the snowball that would roll to twenty million sales and pay my rent for quite a while.

And for the fans, like me, he put "No Surrender" on the record also.

Voice of America, the album of my birth, was suffocated in its crib by the Sony monster as it rolled out the marketing for Bruce's album, now called *Born in the USA,* which was released just four weeks later.

It never occurred to me that that would be his title. Or that the cover and marketing ads would have stars and stripes all over the place, just like my album.

The DJs' attitudes were, Why play an E Streeter when we can play the Boss! No thought at all that both records might have value.

The '80s caught the zenith of what had started as a teenage novelty distraction. We saw Rock record sales no one ever dreamed of and no one would ever see again.

One after the other. Ten, twelve, fifteen million. Michael Jackson, Madonna, Whitney Houston, Tina Turner, Prince, even Phil Collins— each averaging four or five hit singles per album, with each single bringing an additional three million more in album sales.

The era would last until Guns N' Roses's *Appetite for Destruction,* more or less, before slowing down, but it was a wild ride for those fortunate enough to be at the amusement park at the time.

I, once again, was not allowed in. My pirates were not in the Caribbean. They were busy attending the funeral of my very political, very invisible second album.

Still, we hit the road hard. We did *Rockpalast* again, and killed again.

That fall, with the presidential election looming, Ronald Reagan attempted to co-opt "Born in the USA" as a campaign song. Bruce stopped him, but Ronnie was probably responsible for another five, ten million in sales. Misinterpretation can be profitable.

I released another one-off political single with little room for misinterpretation called "Vote! (That Mutha Out)," backed by my only Rap composition so far, "After World War Three." I tried to find Melle Mel to do it, but we wouldn't meet until two years later, so I became Grandmaster Cobra Jones, and rapped it myself.

My research into America's role in the world's problems continued, but I had also started to feel that books weren't enough. I wanted to be there and see things firsthand. Feel them. Taste them. Absorb what was going on down in my bones.

I decided the third album, *Freedom—No Compromise* would use three examples to explore the theme of government's relationships with the people. The three would be Latin America, Native America, and South Africa.

First stop was Nicaragua with Jackson Browne, who had been everywhere years before I was even aware of these issues. Daryl Hannah came with us, and there were some congressmen down there at the same time.

Nicaragua was at a critical point. The Sandinistas, the rebel group that had overthrown the brutal dictator Anastasio Somoza, the US government's good buddy, had been legitimately elected to run the new government. In response, the Reagan administration's security apparatus and "off the book" friends had organized, funded, and trained the biggest group of terrorists ever assembled by a Western power, the Contras. There were about ten thousand of them at their peak. Literally the largest organized terror group until the Islamic State of Iraq and the Levant (ISIL) thirty years later.

The purpose of the Contras was to murder, terrorize, burn villages, and otherwise create as much havoc as possible against the people of Nicaragua.

It's important to keep this history in mind when you hear so many refer back to the universally revered, happy-go-lucky semisenile grandfatherly cowboy, Ronald Reagan.

Nicaragua had been the only country in the area since Cuba to free itself of the outrageous oppression in the region, and now our government was trying to illegally overthrow their internationally monitored elected government.

Regardless of what I thought about the Sandinistas, I decided I had to do everything possible to stop the terrorism against the Nicaraguan people by my government and try to head off the increasingly likely prospect of a military invasion, which would be justified under the pretense of preventing Nicaragua from supplying arms to rebels in El Salvador, who were trying to overthrow their own brutal military dictatorship.

So when Jackson mentioned he was going and invited me, I immediately said yes.

Reagan and his people were also trying to use Costa Rica as a staging area through bribery and threats as a southern front in this illegal war. This in spite of the fact that Costa Rica was the only country in Central or South America that was truly peaceful because they had completely disbanded their military years earlier.

On our trip, we met with various ministers and central committee members who took us around, showing us the improvements they were making and the plans they had.

I pissed off the agriculture minister immediately. He was explaining with great pride that the land was completely liberated, that people and entrepreneurs were free to do anything they wanted with it.

"Anything?" I said. "It is important that we are very clear about what is going on here."

"Yes," he said, "total freedom."

"So I can buy this land right now," I said, "and put a McDonald's up?"

"Well, not exactly, señor." He laughed and tried to change the subject.

I took him aside. "Look," I said. "I'm sure you have a good plan, and it's none of my business, but just be accurate with us. We're going to be reporting back to America, so it's important to be clear. When we say total freedom in America, we mean it literally. You don't. So let's not allow our cultural communication differences to turn us into bullshitters."

Now he was pissed. Discussion over.

Like most governments in the world, about half the Sandinista Directorate were OK and about half were incompetents, ideologues, or idiots. We were told we would meet the president, Daniel Ortega. "Fine," I said, but I really wanted to meet his wife. In politics, as in life, the wife is usually where the real policy action is.

We set up a meeting with Ortega's wife, Rosario Murillo, ostensibly to talk about culture. I asked Jackson if I could meet with her alone because I had an idea that was a little delicate that I wanted to try out. He agreed. I told her Jackson wasn't feeling well, which turned out to be true. Everybody got sick except me. Whenever I took a research trip I would fast to keep my mind clear. If the trip was too long to fast, I would eat as little as possible and never any meat.

I've heard that Rosario Murillo has become controversial in her later years, but back then she was great. Most of the government officials just wanted rubber-stamp approval from whatever mindless liberal happened to come through town, but she gave the impression she really wanted to know what I thought. And I happened to have a few things on my mind.

After a few drinks, I moved off the small talk and suddenly asked her if she loved her husband. She was taken a bit aback but said, Yes, señor, very much. "Well," I said, "you should spend as much time with him as possible, because he's a dead man walking. It's just a matter of time and time is running out."

She knew I wasn't kidding. The idea had probably crossed her mind more than once. She was a very smart woman married to a revolutionary. But she was expecting a pleasant conversation about the Arts, and the reality of what I was saying hit her hard.

She reached across the table, put her hands on mine, looked deeply into my eyes and asked, "What can we do?"

I suggested three things.

"The first thing may sound silly," I said, "but I sincerely believe there is only one way to save him, and to avoid an invasion by my country where a lot of innocent people will be killed. You have to get him out of those Castro fatigues and into a three-piece suit."

Her eyes widened.

" . . . and for him to make a speech at the UN where everyone will see how wonderfully normal and presidential he looks. Television is everything, and image counts more than you can possibly imagine. This is critical. The other two things are not as important, so if you only remember one thing, remember that."

She nodded. I had her full attention.

"OK," I said. "Here's something else." I had read an early draft of the new Nicaraguan constitution and noticed a big problem. There was something in it about the Sandinista Party being the official party of the country and their flag being the official flag. "The rest of the document looks great," I said, "but unless you separate party affiliation from national governance, you're doomed." Multiparty democracy, I explained, meant playing no favorites, regardless of how many war heroes or liberators a specific party had.

"There have been many discussions about this," she replied. I was guessing they hadn't gone well.

Finally, I asked her if she considered herself a Communist. If she had said yes, it wouldn't have thrown me. I'd studied the subject enough to know that there were many strains of communism, some malevolent (China), some benevolent (Italy), some a combination of malice, corruption, and stupidity (Russia).

"No," she said.

"Do any government officials?" She mentioned a few and explained that Fidel Castro was a big hero to the whole hemisphere because of his success in overthrowing Batista. The Nicaraguan Communists, she thought, would have their own party eventually, and they weren't ideologically extreme enough to be a real factor in her husband's plans.

"OK," I said. "It may be too politically complicated. You probably have to placate your extremists on both sides. But here's the third thing. Get a New York lawyer, and the next time the *New York Times* calls you a Communist country or Communist government, sue them!"

I explained to her that in the United States, the word meant something different than anywhere else in the world. "In our country," I explained, "it is a license to kill. Literally. We will send soldiers down here and they will kill your husband and no one will be accused of a crime. Do you understand?"

She nodded pensively, probably thinking she had no shot with the hard-liners on the second two points.

But the first point? Sure enough, soon after we left, there was Daniel Ortega, on TV, addressing the United Nations, looking like he'd just been to James Bond's tailor on Savile Row! I mean he was superfly, baby!

Did it work? Who knows? All I know is we never invaded. Eventually the arch criminal Ollie North got caught, the Contras were disbanded, and US-sponsored terrorism ended. The Sandinistas would go in and out of power, but I didn't care.

We got lucky. As long as innocent people weren't dying or being terrorized with US involvement, I figured our work was done and moved on.

After Nicaragua, Jackson helped set up trips to the Six Nations, Onondaga Reservation near Syracuse, New York, and the Pine Ridge Reservation in South Dakota, the site of Wounded Knee, where I got a crash course in Indian politics, culture, and religion.

The first thing that hit me was how much was going on, and how little attention it was getting from the general non-Indian public. There were (and still are) hundreds of land disputes, denial of access to sacred sites, the disappearing of native languages, grave robbing by museums, nothing less than a political prisoner named Leonard Peltier who remains in jail as I write this in spite of an outrageously unjust trial, and other issues resulting from the 370 treaties that have been broken by the US government.

Not to mention the efforts to store nuclear waste on Indian land, led by Hazel O'Leary, later picked by President Bill Clinton to be secretary of energy!

Many problems revolved around the Native American religion and its relationship to nature. The essence of Indian religion is that the Earth is sacred and all living and nonliving things are equally sacred, to be respected as separate but equal parts of an integrated universe.

Native Americans are the original environmentalists, and issues like pollution and mining have been major issues since gold was discovered in the Black Hills in 1874.

So first of all, why weren't Native Americans and environmentalists working together?

Those issues were intimately connected to the destruction of Native cultures through the "Americanization" of Indian people. Indian children were dragged to American schools, where their culture was literally beaten out of them. The most successfully Anglicized and co-opted were picked to run the US government-imposed "Indian" governments on the reservations, where these no-longer-Indians-except-in-bloodline would sign agreements allowing corporations to mine Indian land in direct violation of the most fundamental tenets of Indian religion.

Any ethnocide has two essential initial components: take the land and kill the language.

The divide-and-conquer strategy of the US government worked beyond the wars of the nineteenth century. In the late twentieth century, when I came on the scene, there was very little communication between the surviving 350 Indian Nations.

To address these issues, I started the Solidarity Foundation with my Native-blood friend Alex Ewen to serve as an information-gathering and networking service between the Indian Nations themselves, the Indian Nations and the non-Indian public, and the Indian Nations and environmental groups. One of our most important goals was to encourage economic development in harmony with the Earth.

This eventually led to the only disagreement I ever had with the Elder's Circle, the far more spiritual Native American version of the Mafia Commission. The issue of gambling had become a major internal struggle in Indian country. The elders of the National Treaty Council were against it for general reasons of morality, but I thought the potential for new revenue was too good to resist.

Maybe it was my New Jersey / Italian American / Rat Pack upbringing, but legal gambling on Indian land seemed to me the answer to all their problems. I figured it's a nonpolluting, enormous source of revenue, and it sure beat selling beads by the roadside to backpackers looking for a weekend commune with nature.

If it was handled properly, I thought it could turn things around for the whole culture. That meant owning and controlling it, using the money to build and maintain Indian-oriented schools and to cure the rampant poverty, unemployment, increasing drug problems, and devastated infrastructure.

I found myself uncharacteristically disagreeing with the Elders, so out of respect, Solidarity Foundation pretty much stayed away from the subject.

As usual, the Elders' instincts were more right than wrong. They were taken advantage of left and right until a kid from New Jersey named Jimmy Allen was brought in by the Seminole Tribe in Florida to help out a small casino of no great consequence that had recently licensed the Hard Rock name.

But more about that later.

eighteen

The Breathless Projectionist

(1984)

I feel like I'm in the world, but not of it.
—THE UNWRITTEN BOOK

I was in Los Angeles in 1983 and went to an Art theater on Melrose to see Jean-Luc Godard's *Breathless.*

Before the movie started, a song was playing. It was different somehow, oddly evocative. After the movie I knocked on the projectionist's door and asked him what it was. "Peter Gabriel," he said. "Biko." I had never heard of either one of them.

A little research revealed that Peter Gabriel had been in Genesis, a Prog Rock group, a genre I had never found my way into, and was now on his own as a solo artist. And Stephen Biko was a black anti-apartheid activist in South Africa who had been murdered in 1977 in prison.

I had already made a list of America's dubious and mostly hidden foreign entanglements since World War II. I added South Africa to the list.

I had a hard time researching the South African situation. The *New York Times* was saying there was reform going on, but it was unclear how much or what it was leading toward.

The history was easy enough.

The Apartheid Policy—the classification and separation of the races—was officially put in place in South Africa in 1948 when the National (white supremacist) Party took power, although the practice dated back as far as the 1800s. The white invaders—first Dutch (Afrikaners), then British and others—decided they were so outnumbered that they'd better figure out a way of controlling what became, basically, slave labor in the mines.

Their solution? They banned black Africans from "Church and State," meaning they couldn't vote, and made virtually all crossing of racial lines illegal.

This policy didn't sit so well with the rest of the world. Beginning in the late 1960s, the United Nations imposed a boycott to isolate South Africa. The National Party needed to figure out a way around the boycott. So they came up with a solution inspired by our Indian reservations.

They divided the unimportant parts of the country into tribal "home-lands" (Bantustans), forcibly moved the black population into them by their tribal affiliation, and declared those areas independent countries. Never mind that South Africa was the least tribal of all the African countries, with the Zulu Nation the only exception. When the black Africans had been removed to these Bantustans, the Nationalists would declare South Africa a democracy and bring the blacks back in as foreign immigrant labor, with no political rights.

Evil brilliance, right?

They forcibly removed over three million black Africans. Knocked their houses down, put their belongings on trucks, and dropped them off in the wasteland of these Bantustans—many of which, by the way, were shaped like no country had ever been shaped. Fragmented, discontinuous, spatter patterns of land whose only purpose was to further divide and weaken the black population.

Much of the world supported the boycott, with three major exceptions: our president, Ronald Reagan, along with the British prime minister Margaret Thatcher and the German chancellor Helmut Kohl. They opposed any significant economic sanctions and isolation, instead favoring a policy they called "constructive engagement," which was little more than a bullshit way of maintaining the status quo in South Africa and pretending things were getting better.

So that was the central question. Was the boycott the right thing to do or not? In 1984, after Nicaragua, I went to South Africa for two weeks. My motive was nonadversarial, at least at first. I went with an open mind, hoping to find proof of the "reforms" the newspapers were talking about.

It was on that flight that it finally hit me. I had blown my life. All my aspirations big and small were finally coming to fruition with the success of the E Street Band, and I blew it. I never liked flying. Suddenly my fear of flying was gone. Completely. Just like that. In fact, my fear of everything was gone. I would express my feelings about suicide in the song "Guns, Drugs, and Gasoline" a few years later, but for now, I would continue down the road to see where it led and try and accomplish something before I ran into the inevitable unbreachable castle wall my once-upon-a-time career lived behind.

My record company at the time, EMI, was accommodating. They undoubtedly assumed that I was willing to violate the boycott and play there. They hooked me up with two guys, one white, one black, to guide me through the country and connect me with whoever I wanted to meet. Both of them were incredibly courageous and helpful, and they shall remain nameless to protect them from repercussions for the multiple crimes they committed on my behalf. Just by being there I was violating the boycott.

I traveled from Johannesburg to Cape Town and ended up in Pretoria. I met with everyone I could, from the labor unions to religious leaders and everybody in between. I met with Archbishop (then Bishop) Desmond Tutu and Cyril Ramaphosa (then head of the Miner's Union, now president of the country). While I was in Cape Town, my guides tried to arrange a meeting with Nelson Mandela, imprisoned on Robben Island, but the authorities wouldn't let me see him. And I couldn't get to the prime minister either.

We even managed a side trip to one of the so-called homelands, one they were promoting as a separate country called Bophuthatswana, and its main attraction, the gambling resort of Sun City.

My companions explained that Sun City had been built by Nationalist investors, principally a man named Sol Kerzner, in collaboration with the apartheid regime, and was an irresistible temptation to those willing to buy the elaborate con and score either a big payday or some inexpensive sex. There was no gambling in South Africa proper, but Bophuthatswana was an "independent country" with its own rules.

My new friends were surprised when I passed on the gambling and hookers and went up to my hotel room. I was absorbing lots of information, so I had to be constantly evaluating whether I had heard something merely interesting or something important. I had just heard something important.

Over the next days, I spoke to as many people on the street as I could, meaning as many as would talk to me. They were reluctant at first. The problem was that it was illegal to say that you were in favor of the boycott. If you did, you could go to jail, which in those days could be a death sentence.

Luckily, they'd never seen anyone like me. My Rock and Roll appearance helped loosen them up, and many of them ended up telling me that they did in fact support the boycott. I played devil's advocate, explaining that boycotts often hurt the very people they are trying to help. Most South Africans didn't care. They felt they were in prison. How much worse could things get? And most of the political parties were in favor of it. Mandela's African National Congress (ANC), the opposition Pan Africanist Congress (PAC), and even the young, militaristic Azanian People's Organization (AZAPO), which had been founded by Steve Biko.

I also spent a good amount of time with a wonderful righteous cat named Johnny Clegg, a local music star whose group, Juluka, fused Zulu styles like *maskanda* and *mbaqanga* with Western Folk and Rock. His feelings about the boycott were more mixed. He understood certain aspects of it, but he wanted his music to be heard worldwide.

If I wanted simple answers, I was in the wrong place. Views were mixed because the situation was more than complex—human rights, politics, and economics were wound around each other, choking off the air supply.

Just before that first trip ended, an incident provided the clarity I needed.

I was in Pretoria, riding in a taxi at dusk. A black man stepped off the curb and my taxi swerved—not to miss him but to hit him. "Fucking kaffir," the driver said. ("Kaffir" means "nigger" in the Afrikaans dialect.)

I was frozen in shock. "Uh, you can let me out here," I managed to mutter.

I walked and walked around the main part of town, absorbing what I'd just seen and what I had seen before that, trying to make sense of all the opinions I had heard. I ended up in a town square staring up at statues of South African military icons. I decided that this evil system couldn't be reformed. The government and its criminal apartheid policy had to be exterminated.

I looked up at the nearest statue. I'm taking you down, motherfucker!

I didn't know how yet.

But I meant it.

I studied my notes on the long flight home—in those days, it was eighteen hours, with connections in Lagos and Paris.

I was determined to keep my promise to the military icon in that Pretoria square. A picture was forming in my unusually clear head. It was obvious that the South African government should not have lasted as long as it had. And I didn't mean for moral reasons.

I was discovering a part of my brain I didn't know existed. The ability to analyze had shown itself in little ways as a kid. I figured out that the way to win at Risk was to capture Australia first. I figured out that the most important part of a football team isn't the quarterback or running back or wide receiver. It's the offensive line that makes all the difference. (And when are they going to stop being called the unskilled part of the team?) It showed up as I took apart songs to understand them better. But never analysis like this. On a global stage.

In spite of all the false bravado presented to a gullible world, a closer inspection revealed that the stability of the South African government was far more fragile than the world was being led to believe.

They couldn't trust their own cops anymore. They were employing the military to keep the increasing unrest down. Little old Cuba was kicking their asses in Angola. And their economy was hanging by a thread, entirely dependent on the kindness of three white supremacist world leaders.

They were surviving in part because the world was ignorant. Nobody knew the extent of the modern slavery that was going on down there. A little publicity and this whole thing would fold like the house of cards that it was.

I began formulating a plan.

My thought was to hot-wire the existing boycott structure. The United Nations had established the basic boycott, but it was moving along at a low hum, largely because the United States, the UK, and Germany were practicing constructive engagement.

The boycott was most effective when it was most visible. That had worked in sports. South Africa had been kept out of the Olympics for decades, which pissed them off profoundly. The grand slam, obviously, would be an enforced economic boycott. If banks cut the country off, it would put a knife in the heart of apartheid and maybe get Mandela out of jail.

And while I couldn't affect the banks directly, I was standing on the bridge that led from the sports boycott to the economic boycott: the broader cultural boycott.

The best course, I figured, was to expose the evil brilliance of the Bantustans: the way black South Africans were shipped off to these phony homelands, stripped of their citizenry, and converted into immigrant labor with no political rights. And the perfect symbol of this policy was the Sun City resort.

Because Sun City was a con!

It was one of the great cons of all time.

It wasn't in a different country. It was the clever way South Africa fooled everybody into thinking they were *not* violating the boycott by playing in Sun City. That's why all the entertainers were vastly overpaid to play it.

That would be my target.

We expose the con, we win.

And with respectful apologies to my man Gil Scott-Heron, this revolution *would* be televised.

I was only home for a little while when I decided I didn't feel I'd covered the subject completely enough to write what I needed. I had to go back. This time I wanted to meet the guys nobody wanted me to meet.

I knew I had to pitch my idea to all the opposition parties, Mandela's ANC, the PAC, AZAPO. After being engaged in research and meetings and politics for the previous three years or so, I'd started to get the hang of it. Just because individuals or groups were on the same side didn't necessarily mean they liked one another.

The conventional wisdom of conflict resolution was to get everybody in the same room and work out differences and negotiate. Not only was that method impossible in this case, with half the parties on the lam, but I didn't believe it would work.

I decided the better strategy was to present a plan and have them all endorse it separately. If everybody agreed with me, they'd be agreeing with each other without the ego conflicts and general infighting and drama that go on with virtually all pro-democracy, anti-fascist groups worldwide. That kind of petty backstabbing is why the bad guys usually win. I wanted to avoid that.

I managed to meet the PAC in New York. They endorsed the idea. That was a big one, one of the two main opposition parties. Once I got back to Johannesburg, I immediately flew to Zimbabwe to meet with the other one, Mandela's ANC.

It was a good thing I had lost my fear of flying, because that flight from Joburg to Harare was one I'll never forget. It was a twenty-seat propeller job, bad enough, but we somehow managed to fly inside a storm the entire time, which meant being hit constantly by monstrous African lightning.

I didn't think I was going to die.

I *knew* I was going to die.

When we somehow made it to blessed terra firma, I saw that the plane had black marks all over the fuselage where the lightning had struck. At that moment, I felt that Destiny had something in mind for me. There's no way that little piece-of-shit crop duster should have survived that flight.

In Harare I floated my Sun City idea to the ANC representative. I explained that publicity, not violence, was the only way to win the war. If nothing else, I would be publicizing their cause and supporting the ANC as the official voice of the opposition. Of course I had said the same thing to the PAC!

The ANC representative liked my plan, as had the representative of the PAC. After a few days of consultation, he gave me its blessing.

I now had an official mandate from the leading revolutionary groups in my back pocket. It would come in handy.

I asked both organizations to give me six months and to try and minimize the violence in the meantime. They said they'd see what they could do.

Back in Johannesburg, I told my (now trusted) companions about my meeting with the ANC. They were impressed. Then I made my request. "OK, boys," I said. "I've been trying to keep you away from the heavy stuff, but I need you to set up one more meeting. And you're going to have to break the law to do it."

"Are you kidding?" one said. "Half the meetings we've already arranged have been illegal. We're in all the way."

What I needed from them was a meeting with AZAPO.

AZAPO was among the most violent of the younger revolutionary groups. Meeting with them was risky, at the very least, and might be fatal.

Word went out, and a guy who knew a guy who knew a guy sent word back that a meeting could be arranged in Soweto. But getting into Soweto was easier said than done. Since violence was on the rise, the government had established a military blockade around the massive ghetto.

Clearly defining and separating neighborhoods was a strategy designed to anticipate the revolution and give the greatly outnumbered government an advantage to commit mass eradication once the revolution inevitably started.

We drove out to Soweto. My white companion and I were covered by a blanket on the floor of the back seat as our black conspirator drove through the blockade.

We stopped.

"We're here."

A ghost emerged from fog, dressed all in white. He motioned for us to follow. The machete in his waistband did not bode well.

My companions took a last glance my way. Their look seemed to say, Are you sure?

I took a moment to fully absorb the absurdity of the situation. Just a few minutes ago in my timeless mind I was sixteen, slowing down my record player to learn Eric Clapton's solo on "Steppin' Out." And now here I was . . . steppin' way the fuck out. I had the urge to laugh out loud. I suppressed it.

There are references to a biblical state of grace that suggest protection by some unseen force. I'm not religious, but I had that tingly feeling.

I smiled. I was sure.

We went in.

Inside, seven or eight guys were crowded into a single room. All of them were dressed in white. All were carrying machetes.

They immediately began berating me. What was I doing? I had violated the boycott simply by being there. As they spoke, they glowered and fondled their weapons, occasionally advancing toward me, threatening me, anything to intimidate me.

I wasn't having it. I was ready. I knew the only way out of this was to communicate supreme confidence. It was out-tough-guy them or die.

"Just fucking relax," I said. I explained that I was there to help, but that I had to see with my own eyes what was happening so I could report back to my people.

The spokesperson told me that they didn't need my help.

"Yes you do," I said. "Do you seriously think you're gonna win this war blowing up radio stations, assassinating rats, and necklacing traitors? The government loves it when you pick up a gun or a machete. They know they can win that fight. You want to commit suicide? Go ahead! But don't pretend you're some revolutionary heroes doing it!"

They were not enjoying this conversation.

"I know how to win this war without spilling a drop of blood," I said more confidently than I felt.

That got their attention.

"OK," the spokesperson said. "What?"

"We win this war on TV!"

They looked around at each other. Who had agreed to meet with this crazy fucker in the first place?

I made my case. It wasn't the easiest argument I've ever made, considering I was pitching a TV war to revolutionaries living in a black South Africa that had a rare nodding acquaintance with electricity!

I explained to them how focusing on Sun City would expose the homeland policy and let us use the cultural boycott to jump-start the economic boycott.

They went to the far side of the room. An intense conversation followed.

My compadres looked like they were mentally writing their wills.

My black companion was picking up some words here and there and whispering to me. The general consensus seemed to be they were being too soft on violators of the boycott. Especially white guys.

I interrupted. "What white guys?" I asked.

They were taken aback. How had I overheard, let alone understood?

They shouted at me. "First Paul Simon. Now you!" Paul Simon had been to South Africa just before me, doing research and recording for what would become *Graceland*. "We should be killing you both!"

"You're being ridiculous," I said. "You can't kill Paul Simon! He's too good a songwriter!" I had no idea of the problems Paul would soon cause me, but I'd like to think I still would have tried to talk them out of killing him.

They didn't laugh.

I played my ace.

"By the way," I said, "the ANC and the PAC have agreed to support me and endorsed my idea."

This sent them back into another intense conversation.

Bringing up the ANC and the PAC was a calculated risk. All the groups were opposed to one another in some way. There were competitive agendas to spare. But I also knew Mandela had a special place in their hearts. That was true of everyone, except Mangosuthu Gatsha Buthelezi, the leader of the Zulu, who wanted to *be* Mandela. Probably still does if he's alive. He would be one of the few leaders that would refuse to meet with me.

"OK," they finally said. "We have no fucking idea what you're talking about"—I'm paraphrasing—"but we'll give you a few months to see what you can do."

In other words, they might as well let me go since they'd never heard of me.

I wasn't important enough to kill.

I told them I would do my best. And I added my usual reminder: By the way, if at all convenient, please stop killing people and blowing shit up for a minute. It will help me help you.

They nodded tentatively.

It was one of my better acting jobs.

nineteen

Revolution

(1985)

The faces of the statues are tainted,
With an unclean righteousness,
But inside they're crumbling,
They know they ain't got much time left,
In Pretoria.

—"PRETORIA," FREEDOM—NO COMPROMISE

On the flight home, I began to feel the weight of my own promises.

Africa was a mess. Fifty countries devastated by colonization, ocean-to-ocean corruption, and endless tribal warfare. But because of the outrageous arrogance of apartheid, South Africa would always be the lightning rod for African injustice. Until that was fixed, the rest of Africa's problems would never be properly addressed.

I knew whatever I wrote about Sun City would be too important to just be another song on my next album. It needed more impact.

I had already decided not to include a song called "Hunger" about the Ethiopian government watching its people starve while they threw a multimillion-dollar anniversary party. Bob Geldof had that subject covered, even though he was selling it as a natural disaster. Which was smart. If you're looking for money, you score more with less controversy.

Up to that time, there had been three anti-apartheid anthems: Gil Scott-Heron's "Johannesburg" in 1975, Peter Gabriel's "Biko" in 1980, and the Specials' "Free Nelson Mandela" in 1984.

I would try and write the fourth.

The idea of a group song began to germinate, one that was more political than the other group anthems like "Do They Know It's Christmas," and "We Are the World." I would write more straightforwardly about the problem—I didn't believe in natural disasters—and include one artist from every genre to show unity.

I got home and started spreading the word. I needed help. Lots of it. I'd opened my mouth and now I had to deliver.

Somehow, a guy named Danny Schechter found his way into my life. Danny would make all the difference for this project. He was a TV Producer, newsman, and rabble-rouser of the first magnitude, infamous in Boston as "Danny Schechter the News Dissector." He had been politically active his whole life and involved with the South African issue for decades.

He would not only be the second Musketeer, the advocate and confidence booster I desperately needed, but the main reason we would reach the political intelligentsia and the world of news journalism. I've never been short of ideas, though paying for them can be a challenge. But the all-important marketing is always the most important hurdle, and without a Manager, my work rarely got any.

Danny and I went to a diner, and I laid out my plan to bring down the South African government. It was the first of a thousand conversations in a thousand diners.

He knew a woman named Jennifer Davis at the Africa Fund who was one of the leaders of the divestment movement. She was an extraordinarily intelligent and heroic South African woman who had gone into exile. She not only guided us politically but promised to help disburse whatever money we made, if we made any at all.

From moment one, I had decided to include Rappers in our group of vocalists. Danny enthusiastically agreed. Rappers were not yet in the mainstream—Run-DMC's "Walk This Way" was a year off—but it was already a rich genre of black artists finally telling it like it was. That wasn't easy, never had been. Even Marvin Gaye and Stevie Wonder had to fight for the right to express themselves politically back in the early '70s, and protorappers like Gil Scott-Heron and the Last Poets never broke into the mainstream.

Industry insiders questioned our decision. As with Rock and Roll forty years earlier, they thought this adolescent novelty would disappear as quickly as it had arrived.

I disagreed. By putting them on this record, we would bestow a credibility on them that we felt they deserved. And to accomplish that, we needed . . .

Our third Musketeer, Arthur Baker.

Arthur had produced Afrika Bambaataa's "Planet Rock"; he not only was a visionary combining early street rapping with European Kraftwerk-style Electronica but had also invented a new career creating dance remixes of Pop hits, including songs from *Born in the USA*. When Danny and I told him what we had in mind, Arthur offered us his studio, his Engineers, his musicians, and, most important, his phone book full of Rappers.

Wow. How cool was that!

Now all we needed was . . . oh yeah, the song!

I went to the apartment of my assistant Zoë Yanakis, where my little Akai twelve-track was set up and where I would write and record the Lost Boys album and *Born Again Savage* four years later, and did the demo for "Sun City."

Political music has a different purpose than the typical song. It's a sacrifice of poetry for prose. A sacrifice of Art for information. With a specific protest song like "Sun City," the challenge would be to explain the situation while still connecting with the listener emotionally.

Most message records were solemn and earnest. I wanted a different tone, a motivational call to arms. I'd been writing politically for three years by then, so the energy was right at my fingertips.

I wrote and recorded the demo quickly, in an hour or two. Then I ran down to Arthur's studio so we could build up the music.

Danny and Arthur listened. "These are just reference lyrics," I said.

"You're crazy," they said in unison. "This is the whole story."

I protested. I thought I could improve them a bit, but they were adamant—and right, by the way.

I made one more concession. Danny felt the subject was going to be a hard sell, so we needed controversy to spice things up. He wanted to mention the names of the Artists who had played Sun City as a way of getting attention.

We went as far as one version of the demo mentioning names before I changed my mind. I decided we needed to take the position that
those who had played had been duped, that they had been offered huge
money ($100,000 per week) and told they were playing in a separate
country. We needed to present a united front. Arguments among musicians would only confuse the public.

I met with members of Queen and others and explained the situation. The bands wanted to know how to get off the UN boycott list,
which was being taken very seriously by the European unions and interfering with tours. "Just tell me right now you won't go back, and I'll deal
with that," I said. I got them all off the list including, with some mixed
feelings, Paul Simon.

As we built our wish list of singers for the project, I looked for interesting artists from all genres, Rock and Soul, Punk and Funk, Salsa and
Reggae, along with less-than-obvious international artists. Big stars were
fine, but they weren't the priority.

My top four names were Peter Gabriel (who had alerted me to the
issue), Gil Scott-Heron (who had been the first to bring it up in song),
Melle Mel (my personal favorite of the Rappers), and Miles Davis (in
my mind, I heard his iconic trumpet both at the beginning and in the
middle of the song).

From there, I built out the list: Bonnie Raitt and Jackson Browne,
George Clinton and Darlene Love. I couldn't leave out David Ruffin,
my favorite living singer, and I kept my ear tuned to political engagement, which led me to Rubén Blades (a best-selling Salsa Artist who had
started out as a law student) and Peter Garrett (an Australian activist
who fronted Midnight Oil). I picked out a line for Bruce and saved it
for him.

Danny and Arthur added names, and we started making calls.

One of my first was to an Artist I respected a great deal for his enormous talent, his incredible sense of humor, and his political vision.
Including him, I thought, would illustrate the difference between our
song and more-mainstream projects. As I dialed, I laughed to myself
at the thought of him singing along with the chorus of "We Are the
World."

Frank Zappa answered the phone.

"Hi," I said, introducing myself. "We're making a solidarity statement about what's going on in South Africa and . . ."

That was all I got out.

"Why would I want to participate in your meaningless bullshit record when all that's going to happen is that you are going to steal the publishing money?"

"No, no. It's . . ."

"I don't want to hear it."

"Frank, listen . . ."

"I've heard it all before!"

His arrogance and obnoxiousness were breathtaking.

I was tempted to remind him he was mixing me up with someone in show business who had something to lose, instead of a kid from Jersey who would happily beat the shit out of him if he ever dared to speak that way to my face.

I didn't even get to mention that I had started a separate publishing company and all royalties would go to the cause.

"Sorry for wasting your time," I said, and hung up.

And I had been such a fan.

My next two calls were to people from the Hard Rock world I knew fairly well. They both turned me down.

After that, I delegated the calls to a far more successful schmoozer, Arthur Baker.

Everybody he called agreed to participate.

Even so, we weren't as organized as Band Aid or USA for Africa. We never knew who was coming. Or when. Or what they would do when they got there.

Danny had had the foresight to bring in our fourth Musketeer, Hart Perry. Hart was tasked with filming the whole process, and he made himself available around the clock. If an artist happened to show up at two in the morning, we'd call Hart and he'd be there in ten minutes.

I look back in wonderment that we pulled it off at all. We didn't have the brains to reach out through publicists or Managers, who probably would have declined anyway. This was not a good career move for an artist.

We recorded a log drum as the click track, the basic rhythm, I threw on a quick rhythm guitar, added two keyboard horn riffs on a synthesizer, and we were ready for vocals.

We started with the Rappers.

Run-DMC came in, looking and sounding just like I hoped they would. When they did the opening line, "We're rockers and rappers united and strong . . . ," their Manager Russell Simmons leaned over to me. "You know, we're thinking about changing it."

"Changing what?"

"The term for what we do," he said. "Rapping."

"What?" I said. "Why? It's been an underground cult, but we're about to introduce it to the world!"

"Yeah," he said. "That's cool. But we feel like it's too limiting."

"What are you gonna change it to?"

"Hip-Hop," he said.

"Get the fuck outta here!" I said. "That is the stupidest fucking name I've ever heard! It'll never catch on!"

As the Rappers did their thing—Kurtis Blow, the Fat Boys, Duke Bootee, and Afrika Bambaataa—we realized we had all these great artists there just to say a few lines. It seemed like a waste. After we got what we needed, we told them to feel free to express their feelings about the subject any way they wanted.

Melle Mel went into the next room for fifteen minutes and came back with an incredible rap. We added news footage, Mandela's speeches, and sound effects, and Arthur turned it into a separate anti-apartheid montage. That was the beginning of the "Sun City" single growing into an album.

The whole thing was wild and spontaneous. The first twenty or thirty artists that came in sang the whole song, not just their line. We sorted it out later.

Peter Gabriel did a chant and layered it and layered it until it was a cool abstract expressionist piece. When we came back the next day, one of our Engineers, Tom Lord-Alge, and Arthur's drummer Keith LeBlanc had added drums to Peter's chant. I put on guitar and synth and Peter's electric violinist Shankar played on the track. Boom! Another song.

Gil Scott-Heron was on the lam at the time. I had to call a phone booth in Washington, DC, at 10 p.m. on Thursdays to talk to him. But when the time came, he showed up and did a great job.

I flew to London to record Ringo Starr and his son Zak, and got a guitar part from Pete Townshend.

And then he walked in.

By some miraculous stroke of luck, Miles Davis was using my old sound man, who was brave enough to bring up our project to him. He didn't do these types of things ever, but this was an important issue to him.

It was one of the thrills of my life when he walked in. Nobody intimidates me, but he came close. He sat next to me as I played him the song. About halfway through, he leaned over. "Hey," he said in that classic rasp, "you want me to play or what?"

I laughed. "Not really," I said. "I was hoping you'd take over as Producer so I can get some fucking sleep!"

That got a rare smile and loosened him up.

He played for maybe five minutes with the mute, which I asked for, and another few minutes without it.

I looked at Arthur, who looked at Danny, who looked at Hart, who looked back at me. This shit just got real. I had planned to use Miles for twenty seconds in the intro and fifteen seconds in the middle, but there was no way we were leaving five minutes of Miles Fucking Davis on the cutting room floor.

I called the Jazz Producer Michael Cuscuna and asked if he could get to the guys from Miles's Second Great Quintet—Herbie Hancock, Ron Carter, and Tony Williams. They all responded. Michael had found Stanley Jordan playing guitar in the subway and brought him in too. They improvised to what Miles had played, and it became a modal monochromatic impressionist masterpiece.

Bono was so inspired by the project that he wrote a new song, "Silver and Gold," which we recorded with Keith Richards, Ronnie Wood, and Stevie Jordan.

A few days afterward Bruce came in to do his line, then we went across the river and filmed the video for "Glory Days" at Maxwell's in Hoboken. Man, was he in a bad mood that day. I had to mug as exaggerated as I could just to make him laugh and loosen him up.

Meanwhile, we had gone from the original half-dozen or so artists I'd imagined to fifty, adding Lou Reed, Jimmy Cliff, Peter Wolf, Bobby Womack, Nona Hendryx, Joey Ramone, Pat Benatar, Hall & Oates, Ray Barretto, Big Youth, Kashif, and more. I wished we'd gotten the Last Poets, Taj Mahal, and Jerry Dammers, but if we didn't have their phone number we didn't pursue them.

And we weren't done.

Earlier in the year, I had gotten a call from Debbie Gold. Everyone knew Debbie. She was like everybody's confidante/intermediary, full of positive vibes. "Stevie. Bob Dylan wants you to produce him."

"Really? When?"

"Now. Get down to the Power Station."

Bob was playing with Sly and Robbie, the famous Reggae rhythm section, and Roy Bittan was there on piano. Bob pointed to a guitar and I joined in.

He had just started singing a ballad called "When the Night Comes Falling from the Sky."

We did a take and went into the control room to listen. I wasn't sure if I was producing or not; Bob hadn't said anything, but I lingered behind and made a quick dozen suggestions to the Engineer—add a mic under the snare, add 2 dB at fifteen hundred cycles on the guitar, put a compressor on the bass, shit like that.

After a second take, Bob turned to me. "What do you think?" he asked.

"Bobby," I said, "to tell you the truth I'm hearing this faster."

"Oh, yeah? Like what?" I showed him, and he joined in and sang along a bit. "I like it," he said, "but I like it slow too."

"How about this?" I said. "We can start slow with the first verse, then, after a drum fill, go to a faster tempo for the rest of the song."

That's what we did. He asked me for a solo, and I told him I was hearing more of a violin or horn melody line. We tried it and he liked it. "That gives me an idea for a cello line underneath," he said. He sang it and I added it to the solo.

His vocal performance was spectacular, his greatest at least since "Tangled Up in Blue" and arguably since *Blonde on Blonde*. I didn't get any credit for producing, which was fine with me. I was just honored to be there. But he didn't put this version on the record! Between him and

Bruce, I was starting to wonder . . . Is it me? Years later, it would appear on his first *Bootleg Series* box set.

We kept trying to get Bob for "Sun City." He had been responsible for the birth of consciousness in Popular music in the first place, and a record like this was unthinkable without him. Late in the game, he finally came aboard. Jackson Browne was able to record him on the West Coast. But with all those extra singers, we had run out of lines. Bob did the same line as Jackson, and we put his line in between lines to fit.

It was the mix of the century. Thirteen reels of tape times 24 tracks means 312 tracks, which had to be reduced to two. The single alone took weeks. Every Engineer in town worked on it. They'd pass out at the board, we'd carry them out, and bring in another one.

We used every studio in town at some point. Ten days into the mix at Electric Lady, the studio flooded, like it did every spring and fall. Nobody had mentioned to Jimi Hendrix that he was building the place over an underground stream. We lost the mix and had to start all over again, but somehow it got done.

Four freaks with no juice, no muscle, and no money had relied on street connections and a good idea to cobble together an artistically coherent album with as diverse a group of artists as had ever been assembled for a cause nobody had heard of yet.

And Jean-Luc Godard and a nameless projectionist will never know what they started.

twenty

Ain't Gonna Play Sun City!

(1986)

When will we finally invite our black population to join
the rest of us in America?

— THE UNWRITTEN BOOK

What if you spent a year planning a party and nobody showed?

I never had an attitude of superiority while doing research in South
Africa, fully aware that America's own civil rights legislation had taken
place only twenty years earlier.

And I knew that by pointing out the extreme racism of South Africa
I would also be commenting on our own ongoing discrimination, which
seemed to be going backward.

So irony of ironies—but not entirely surprising—we were deemed
too black for white radio and too white for black radio.

Nobody would play the fucking record!

Not exactly what I had in mind by "Ain't gonna play Sun City!"

Fuck me.

I had gotten friendly with Bruce Lundvall while making E Street
Band records at Columbia. Lundvall had moved to EMI Manhattan,
signed me for my next record, *Freedom—No Compromise,* and was very
enthusiastic about the issue of South Africa. We licensed "Sun City" to
him for distribution at a higher than usual royalty—although, again, we
weren't doing it for the money.

I knew Bob Geldof had gotten *all* the royalties for the Band Aid record, but I didn't have that kind of juice. I was happy *anybody* would distribute such a controversial project. But we made a good deal.

As I hadn't quite had the chance to explain to Frank Zappa, I had created a new publishing company, Amandla Music, for all the music on the album. The creative process was truly a collaboration, and none of us wanted the job of sorting out who had done what. It didn't matter anyway. None of us would have taken any money from this. The entirety of the record sales and publishing would go to Jennifer Davis and her Africa Fund.

We tried everything to get the record played. Calling stations. Calling in favors. Lundvall hired a few independent promotion men—all to no avail.

We even tried to get to Stevie Wonder's radio station. He was into the issue of South Africa and human rights in general. I took the record there personally, but they wouldn't play it.

There was only one shot left.

We needed a killer fucking video.

Hart Perry brought in Jonathan Demme, the perfect guy for the job and a soon-to-be-lifelong friend. He would eventually do a video for the E Street Band and win the Academy Award for *Philadelphia*, which also got Bruce an Oscar for the title track. We had a quick discussion with him and decided we wanted to capture the energy of an awakened anti-apartheid movement and the unrelenting passion of the record.

As for every aspect of the project, we didn't want it to be slick, though we didn't have to worry about that too much since we didn't have any money.

We decided we'd do the video guerrilla-style, like everything else. We'd shoot it right on the street, no permissions of course, and then have the individuals arrive at a location that represented our common cause and the stronger-together-than-apart symbolism that we hoped would spread throughout the country.

Jonathan was shooting *Something Wild* at the time, and we only had him for one day.

He shot the New York scenes while Hart flew to Los Angeles to get footage of Jackson Browne, Bob Dylan, George Clinton, and Bonnie Raitt.

Then we assembled as many singers as we could in Washington Square for the final scene. To edit the project, we somehow got the hottest video makers in the world at that time, Kevin Godley and Lol Creme. Peter Gabriel might have made the connection.

The conversation I had with them was similar to the one I had with Demme and everybody else: I wanted intense, unrelenting energy.

We gave them what Jonathan and Hart had shot, along with additional footage from another protest rally we had attended and some news footage—some of it stolen, but this was war!

Godley and Creme did an amazing job. In the intro, they used footage of police whipping protestors as a kind of visual percussion, synced to our snare accents, and also devised innovative ripped-from-the-headlines effects to transition from scene to scene. The result was fierce and violent and motivating, exactly what you want in a battle video. Like everyone else—all the Engineers, all the musicians, the crew—they worked for free.

At that moment, MTV was having its own war with the black community.

Since its launch in 1981, it had not played many black videos.

At first, it hadn't played any.

It had taken Walter Yetnikoff threatening to pull all Columbia and Epic product if it didn't play videos from Michael Jackson's *Thriller*. That had been in December 1983. Things had improved since then, but only slightly. Artists like David Bowie and Rick James criticized MTV for maintaining a color line, and the network responded by admitting that it was concerned about losing its midwestern audience.

I met with the entire executive team of MTV. "Listen," I said. "I hear you're having a public relations problem. I might have the solution right here in my pocket."

I laid out the situation in South Africa and our strategy. "You guys can not only go a long way in solving your problems with the black community," I said, "but you can be on the front end of a movement that is going to be sweeping the country. For once, instead of observing history, you'd be making it."

Of course, I was pretty much lying my ass off like usual. But it all turned out to be true.

I played them the video, and they loved it.

If you know "Sun City," it's because of MTV. Or BET, which also played the video frequently. But it's not from radio.

After the video started getting us more visibility, we started doing interviews and performances whenever possible to spread the word. We shut down the Sun City resort overnight, which meant that the cultural boycott finally had teeth—virtually no one broke it after our record and video came out. That was icing on the cake. But it wasn't the cake.

The cake, of course, was the economic boycott. Everything we had done from the beginning was to raise consciousness, knowing the day was coming when there would be important economic legislation that Reagan would not like. The clock was ticking on whether we would achieve critical awareness before Reagan vetoed the legislation. The goal was to establish such a powerful distaste for the injustice that even Saint Reagan's veto would be overturned. That showdown was imminent.

Senator Bill Bradley brought me to the Senate to explain the situation. It was my closest-ever encounter with our most revered lawmakers, and I must confess, it was a little frightening.

Very few senators had Bradley's intellect, and it was obvious most were hearing about the subject for the first time. How could I tell? By the way I had to point out where South Africa was on the map! And that's a country with two clues in its name!

While I waited for the world to change, I managed to sneak in a few side projects.

Southside and I did a benefit in New Jersey for fire victims in Passaic.

Gary Bonds wanted to do a third album, but all I had time for was a single, "Standing in the Line of Fire," which I cowrote with him and produced.

I produced two songs for my friend Stiv Bators and his great band, the Lords of the New Church. My pleasant memory of working with them was only slightly tainted by meeting their Manager, Miles Copeland. I've been very lucky in my life. After all these years in and around a showbiz full of creeps, I've only had to deal with a few. As temporarily as possible.

I didn't spend enough time with Miles for him to achieve official Royal Scumbaggery, but from our first meeting he was one of those arrogant, condescending slimeballs who make you want to take a shower after being in the same room with them.

My friend Brian Setzer needed a song, so we cowrote "Maria," a song about Mexican migrant workers in Texas.

We were honored by Mayor Bradley in LA and then by Coretta Scott King, Andrew Young, Julian Bond, and John Lewis in Atlanta.

Arthur Baker, who was working on music for Demme's *Something Wild*, came to me for a few songs, and I wrote "You Don't Have to Cry," about the gasoline riots in Jamaica at the time, for Jimmy Cliff and "Addiction" for David Ruffin and Eddie Kendricks.

When the United Nations decided to give "Sun City" an award, we sent a big delegation. Between the early Hip-Hop styles and the Rocker looks, we were the wildest bunch to ever enter the super-sanctimonious United Nations. I saw the secretary general, Javier Pérez de Cuéllar, walk in, take a look at us, hand the award to his deputy, and split!

Ha-ha. I thanked him in my speech anyway.

Somewhere in there, I made another run to the West Coast for Jimmy Iovine to write three songs for Lone Justice for their second album, *Shelter*, and got coproduction credit on the record.

Sol Kerzner, the main owner of Sun City, made the mistake of challenging me on *The Phil Donahue Show*, spewing the usual bullshit apartheid talking points.

I squashed him like the cockroach he was.

Peter Gabriel's latest obsession was something called the University for Peace in Costa Rica.

It was connected to the United Nations and run by an ex-ambassador of Costa Rica. As it was explained to me, it was a school to study conflict resolution; how to deal with the collateral damage of conflict, like refugees; and other international issues like that.

Costa Rica had been of particular interest to me ever since I discovered it was the only country in Latin America that wasn't constantly in conflict because they had the incredible wisdom and strength to disband their military.

I was a little dubious about the university, but Peter was way into it, and I was more than happy to help in any way I could. We pulled together a benefit for the University for Peace; Nona Hendryx, Lou Reed, Jackson Browne, and others participated. Hart Perry filmed it.

It was called Hurricane Irene and was held in Tokyo.

You'd have every right to ask, Why Tokyo?

Good fucking question.

All I really remember is that Irene was some kind of goddess of peace, hence the title of the show. Tokyo I can't help you with. To this day it's still the only time I've ever been there, so that was cool.

One memory from that show still makes me smile. I spent a good hour explaining the entire project to Lou Reed: the concert, the benefit, the peace goddess. He listened intently the whole time. "OK," he finally said. "I'm in. I just want to know one thing. Where the fuck is Costa Rica?"

At some point, Peter Gabriel and I combined our bands and performed at the United Nations to celebrate the International Day of Peace, September 21, which was connected to the university, and we were honored by the United Nations for the second time.

We did an anti-apartheid concert in Central Park with the usual suspects—Peter, Jackson, Bono—and new recruits like Bob Geldof, Yoko Ono, and Sean Lennon.

Geldof asked me to perform Bob Marley's "Redemption Song" with him at the upcoming Amnesty International Concert in New Jersey, which would be televised internationally.

After the show at Giants Stadium, I was backstage with Maureen when I looked across the room. "Holy shit!" I said. Maureen, used to me not being impressed by anybody, was impressed.

"Who is it?" she whispered.

"Muhammad fucking Ali!" I managed to get out.

"Why don't you go say hello?" she said. "He's probably friendly."

Are you kidding? I was too shy. And anyway I never liked meeting my heroes, in case they were assholes. A little while later, a well-dressed, cultured gentleman tapped me on the shoulder.

"Excuse me, sir," he said. "Mr. Van Zandt? Please pardon the interruption, Mr. Muhammad Ali would love to meet you, but he's too shy to come over!"

Right?

There he was. His handshake was gentle. His eyes twinkled mischievously. He bent down and whispered in my ear, sounding like Don Corleone. "You did good with South Africa," he said.

"You did good with George Foreman," I said.

He smiled.

So that was a good day.

The year ended big.

In Santa Monica, at a reception organized by Tom Hayden, Bishop Desmond Tutu gave us a special recognition for efforts on behalf of the anti-apartheid movement. I don't think he was an archbishop yet.

Hart Perry and I received the International Documentary Association Award for *The Making of Sun City*. A companion book written by Dave Marsh and a teaching guide went along with it.

And finally, Congressman Ron Dellums's Comprehensive Anti-Apartheid Act of 1986 was passed, by larger margins than we'd imagined.

As expected, Ronald Reagan vetoed it. Republican Richard Lugar stood up and declared that South Africa was tyranny and that all true Americans were against tyranny!

What became of that kind of Republican?

The Reagan veto was overturned.

The dominoes started to fall.

Both the UK's and Germany's pro-apartheid positions were now untenable.

The banks would soon cut off South Africa, just like we wrote it up.

In the world of international liberation politics, this was a rare complete victory.

It was time to get back to work.

twenty-one

Freedom—No Compromise

(1987–1989)

The Art is always greater than the Artist.
—THE UNWRITTEN BOOK

Freedom—No Compromise was not only my most ambitious album but also the first produced the way I would produce somebody else. The first produced by me the Producer, as opposed to me the Artist. That's why Artists should never produce themselves. The Artist takes over and you don't realize it until it's too late.

Prince is the only exception I can think of. A true genius. I crossed paths with him often in 1987, as we both spent most of that year touring Europe. "You stole my coat idea back in 1978, didn't you?" I said the first time I ran into him. He confessed with one of his sly smiles.

His album that year was *Sign O' the Times.* I took the fact that the gang in the title track was named the Disciples as a personal tribute. The tour behind that record was the best Rock show I've ever seen. I went three times, and it blew my mind every time.

The production was the highest evolution of the live, physical part of our Artform I have ever seen. It was Prince's vision, but his production designer, LeRoy Bennett, deserves much of the credit for pulling it off. It was Rock, it was Theater, it was Soul, it was Cinema, it was Jazz, it was Broadway. The stage metamorphosed into different scenes and configurations right before your eyes, transforming itself into whatever emotional setting was appropriate for each song.

On top of that, the music never stopped, for three solid hours. Prince wrote various pieces, or covered Jazz, as interstitial transitions for those moments when the stage was shifting or the musicians were changing clothes. At one point, he even had a craps game break out, which made me laugh—it brought me back to Dr. Zoom and the Sonic Boom and our onstage Monopoly games.

They captured it pretty well on film, but it can't compare. When you're watching a movie, your mind is used to scene changes, different sets and lighting. Live, it's something else. That kind of legerdemain before your eyes is mind-boggling.

And the show was only the beginning of the night for him. He would do the show, then play into the early morning at a local club. At one of the after-show gigs in Munich, he called me up onstage to jam. Me and his dad! We did a Blues, "Stormy Monday" or something. All I remember is twiddling knobs and stepping on pedals, trying to find a tone before the song ended!

I begged him to take the show to the States, but he was in his pissed-off-at-the-record-company period and wouldn't do it.

The show brought me back to the ballet and the Met. There is nothing quite as thrilling as a live event, especially one I could imagine writing, directing, and producing. Music, dancing, acting, set design, lighting—I loved it all. It took me all those years to realize I didn't want to be Jeff Beck or Miles Davis or even Nureyev or Nijinsky.

I wanted to be Diaghilev!

Jerome Robbins!

Bob Fosse!

Fokine! Massine! Bakst!

Back on Planet Earth, I was still leading a band of my own, and a great one. My Rock-meets-Soul formula had evolved into Rock-meets-Funk. Pat Thrall, who had come from Hughes/Thrall and Pat Travers, was one of the great guitar players of all time. I had a bass player, T. M. Stevens, who could compete with Bootsy Collins and Larry Graham. Mark Alexander was a powerhouse on keyboards, and drummer

Leslie Ming had both the technique for the Funk and the power for four-on-the-floor straight-ahead Rock.

We also had an occasional appearance on the "Zobo," an oboe fed through a phaser and fuzz tone and played by my most excellent and versatile assistant, Zoë Yanakis. Zoë married Pat Thrall, and manages the recording studio at the Palms in Vegas, while Pat engineers and produces. Only time in my life two of my best friends married each other! Nice.

When I see concert footage from that time, it baffles me that we weren't huge. If I had a time machine . . . well, I'd do a lot of things, but one of them would be to go back to 1987, slow down my hundred-miles-an-hour-to-nowhere pace, and hire the first good Manager who came through the door.

We could feel success coming, especially in Europe, where we had built up lots of momentum since that first *Rockpalast.*

But we were still losing money on the road, so we had to reluctantly come home every now and then. Frank Barsalona had us open for the Who on our first tour, and in late 1987 we joined U2's Joshua Tree Tour on the East Coast of the United States. The normal hazards of being an opening act applied. Opening accomplished very little.

While I was home, I was asked to endorse Jesse Jackson's presidential campaign. An empty endorsement didn't interest me, but I said that if Jesse would meet with me to see how much our platforms had in common, I'd consider it. To my surprise, he said yes. We had a long conversation about our political ideas, which were very similar, and I ended up redoing "Vote! (That Mutha Out)" as "Vote Jesse In!" (It's in the 2019 *RocknRoll Rebel* box set.) I traveled with Jesse, spending time in black churches for the first time in my life, greatly adding to my education and to my understanding of the community. He ran a strong campaign, won eleven states—including Michigan—and was even the front-runner for a while, but he was beaten at the wire by Michael Dukakis.

Peter Gabriel, or maybe Jim Kerr from Simple Minds, called to tell me they were doing a Free Nelson Mandela Concert at Wembley Stadium, disguised as a seventieth birthday tribute to reach the maximum broadcast audience. Wise move, as it ended up being shown in sixty-seven countries to six hundred million people.

I was surprised an American network picked up on it at all. The consensus among the mainstream media was that Mandela was a terrorist and a Communist. And not just among the right wing. Famous liberal Paul Simon once cornered me at a party and asked how I could be supporting this Mandela character when he was obviously a Communist.

"Really, Paulie?" I said. "You sure?"

"Yes," he said. "My friend Henry Kissinger explained it all to me. Just follow the money!"

"Well, Paul, I know you and Henry are students of revolution, but I have news for the both of you. People fighting for freedom outnumbered by a better-supplied enemy don't really care where the money comes from. And by the way, your buddy Kissinger is not only an unindicted war criminal but was with the Dulles brothers in the early fifties overthrowing Mosaddegh in Iran and installing the shah. That's the direct cause of half of the *real* terrorism on the planet to this day. So when you see him, please tell your friend Henry to stick his Nobel Peace Prize up his fuckin' ass."

To be fair, Paul denies the conversation took place. But it did.

Wembley was a blast, except for one unfortunate moment. I happened to be in the office with the promoter, Jim Kerr, and Peter Gabriel when Whitney Houston's Manager came in. "We thought this was about celebrating a birthday, but we're hearing lots of politics from the stage. We don't want any part of it. We want the Free Nelson Mandela posters covered up or Whitney doesn't go on!" He stormed out.

We looked at each other in shock. I spoke first. "Throw that bitch the fuck off this show right now!"

"We can't," the promoter said. "We sold the show to the networks with her on it."

"Let 'em complain!" I said.

Jim, or maybe Peter, spoke up. "She was the only request from Mandela personally. They had a poster of her in prison and all the prisoners . . . fell in love with her."

We let her perform. It makes me nauseous seeing the documentaries since then proclaiming her as a proud activist who fought against apartheid her whole life.

The American network edited out everything I said onstage and trimmed whatever politics they could in general. Fox, of course. But the telecast was enormously successful and helped cement Mandela's status as a world leader and one of the good guys.

I continued to do favors for friends when I could. I wrote "While You Were Looking at Me," my contemporary companion piece to Sonny Bono's "Laugh at Me," and cowrote two other songs for *Not Fakin' It*, the solo debut of Michael Monroe. Michael, the former lead singer of Hanoi Rocks, was a star waiting to happen, but he was finding the solo path hard, especially without a Manager.

I would make my own solo path even harder with *Revolution* in 1989. Bruce Lundvall was leaving EMI to go to Blue Note. I knew his dream gig was to be a Jazz guy, so I was happy for him. One of the last of the great gentlemen of the music business. But, for me, the corporate curtain had started to fall. You can feed people in Africa, but when you start bringing governments down, people get nervous.

Lundvall had taken a lot of shit from EMI corporate for putting out *Sun City*. The powerful South African branch of EMI had tried to stop it, even calling the home office in London. Lundvall, to his credit and my undying gratitude, ignored them. That may have sped his departure from the label. Who knows? It sped up mine.

Luckily for me, one of the EMI Germany executives, Heinz Henn, was a fan. He had taken over BMG and not gotten the memo that I was bad news, so I went there.

At this point I really let my artistic vision dominate my common sense. I decided the deeper I got into international themes, the more universal the music needed to be. And I decided Rock wasn't the international common ground anymore, that the true world music was either Reggae or dance music.

I should have gone for Reggae, where my biggest successes had been. One song, "Leonard Peltier" was Reggae, but mostly I went deeper into the Funk. Double entendre intended.

I had already gone halfway to dance music on *Freedom—No Compromise*, where I used a drum machine for the first time and some bass synthesizers. It was Rock on top, dance on the bottom.

With *Revolution*, I went all the way. My initial concept was a sci-fi dystopia with music that was all samples, the vocals the only human element crying out from a cold robotic world.

The theme was the government's relationship to the economy and humankind's alienation, not just from its own labor, but from the Earth and all natural law itself.

The main subtheme would be the way the media was increasingly controlling and manipulating all of our lives.

Keyboard man Mark Alexander was the only link to the previous tour. I have no idea why I let the other guys go. They were fully capable of handling this new idea. But in came the very funky Warren McRae, who along with Mark helped with the production and played bass. For the tour we added the very cool Vini Miranda on guitar, and the great Perry Wilson on drums.

I had made the partial transformation to front man for the Freedom Tour and was completely there for *Revolution*. I still did a token solo or two but had basically lost all interest in playing guitar onstage.

The problem, of course, was asking the audience to redefine me yet one more time. It was weird enough that there was very little of what one would call pure Rock left in the set.

The accumulated momentum of the first three albums hit a wall. Nobody understood *Revolution*. And while audiences enjoyed the show, for the first time they were smaller than on the tour before. We soldiered around Europe, doing better in some places than others.

The tour ended in my best country at the time, Italy.

BMG had given me a new publicist, the brilliant Arianna D'Aloja, a classic Italian beauty from a bygone era. Her husband, Giovanni Tamberi, was and is the handsomest man on earth, straight out of Fellini's *La Dolce Vita*. They remain good friends of mine and Maureen's to this day.

On tour, I met my doppelgänger, Adriano Celentano, a legendary Italian singer and character who occasionally hosted a TV show when he felt like it. We had a good time together.

The final gig in Italy was a free show, a protest against the Chinese government for their actions in Tiananmen Square.

Claudio Trotta, the Promoter, asked for a favor. He had a cousin in Sardinia with a band. "Could they . . . ?"

"Yeah," I said. "Sure. Who cares? It's the last gig."

That was it, the entire bill. An unknown Sardinian garage band opening, and us.

It was a beautiful June night in Rome. The band, Arianna, Giovanni, and I walked up to the side of the stage and looked out at an ocean of audience.

It was startling.

"Do you believe this?" Arianna asked, stunned.

Nobody had ever seen so many people in one place before in Italy. It was a goombah Woodstock!

Giovanni testified wildly in Italian, enthusiastically seconding his wife's amazement. I somehow comprehended everything without understanding a single word.

Some estimated the crowd at a quarter of a million, but let's not get Trumpian here. It was a lot.

We went on not knowing what to expect. I had a fabulous audience in Italy, but had 90 percent of this crowd ever heard of me?

Everything came together that night. The new songs, the new show—which had been going over well in spite of being surprising—suddenly seemed to have been written for this event. The title track, "Revolution," was preaching to the converted. Songs like "Love and Forgiveness" and "Sexy" had the crowd dancing and chanting along by the time the second choruses hit.

As the show ended, I stood there drained, thinking . . . This is it.

Like the opening song of the album asked, "Where Do We Go from Here?"

I was experiencing an existential crisis in real time.

I knew I'd never be more popular than I was at that moment. But it was somehow not real. I could not generate revenue. Fuck, I couldn't even achieve my lifelong goal of breaking even!

The people in the crowd were having a great time, but they had nothing to do with my real life.

They were never going to buy my records.

They were never going to buy a ticket to a show.

I had become a symbol of political activism. So now what? Run for mayor of Rome? I had no interest in politics as a career whatsoever.

I soaked it in as long and as deeply as I could.

I had one more record to make to explore the final theme I had outlined seven years and so many lifetimes ago. I needed to fulfill my promise to myself.

But it was over.

And I knew it.

twenty-two

The Hero with a Thousand Faces

(1990)

I don't want realism. I want magic! Yes, yes, magic! I try to give
that to people. I misrepresent things to them. I don't tell the
truth, I tell what ought to be the truth. And if that's sinful, then
let me be damned for it!

—MAUREEN VAN ZANDT AS BLANCHE DUBOIS,
IN *A STREETCAR NAMED DESIRE*

Rome finished off seven years of nonstop action, education, and
evolution.

Every important band ends up with one important member missing.
I was that guy. Shouldn't I have crashed in that plane in Zimbabwe?
Wouldn't that have made more Rock and Roll sense?

I found myself at the outer reaches of the galaxy with my dilithium
crystals depleted.

It was time for one of my meditative trips to a metaphorical desert to
contemplate, reassess, reevaluate, and reenergize.

Only this time, the desert wouldn't be metaphorical.

I had arranged to meet in southern Algeria with the Polisario Front,
the political representatives of the people of Western Sahara, the Sahrawi (sometimes Saharawi). They were camped in Tindouf, a semisafe
distance from the war they were fighting against Morocco.

Yet one more war we were on the wrong side of. Namely, the battle for Western Sahara, which Morocco was—and probably still is—trying to steal.

The situation began with the end of the colonial era in the '70s, when Spain and France withdrew from northern Africa, specifically the Sahara Desert region bordering Morocco, Mauritania, and Algeria. Spain made a deal with Morocco and Mauritania regarding Western Sahara, but they forgot to include the people of Western Sahara in the negotiations.

The Sahrawi are a mix of Berber and Arab, and a bit of indigenous African, and had a history in the region. So began the war between Morocco and Polisario, which Mauritania quickly withdrew from. The United States and France—and, interestingly, Saudi Arabia—backed Morocco, which was dropping white phosphorus, similar to napalm, on the refugee camps. They sought to steal the indigenous people's land and keep the Sahrawi Arab Democratic Republic from the autonomy the International Court of Justice declared they were entitled to.

I wanted to bring attention to their situation, apologize for my country's position, and let them know that there were Americans who cared about right and wrong.

As always, there was a research component as well. My next album was partly about religion, and I wanted to get their views on spirituality. I'd heard they were moderate Muslims like my main interest in the Middle East, the Kurds, who have long deserved their own independent Kurdistan.

I flew to Paris, where friends I had made at *Libération*, the newspaper started by Jean-Paul Sartre, had agreed to accompany me and write about the trip.

We hoped to meet with Mohamed Abdelaziz, the secretary general of the Polisario Front and, again like the Kurds, a secular nationalist.

The first flight stopped in Algiers, and man, was it weird. The Muslim extremists were in an on-again, off-again war with the moderate government, and the vibe was tense.

First of all, there were no women in sight. Not even covered up. And not many cars driving around. Just a lot of guys: all in white, all with the same beards, fierce X-ray eyes, and scowling visages, all leaning against buildings, staring at us.

I realized we were the only entertainment they were going to get that day. Giving us dirty looks was their equivalent of going to a movie or having a drink in a bar or listening to a great record. They couldn't do any of those things.

So they just leaned and looked mean.

It was creepy as fuck. I couldn't wait to get out of there.

The next flight landed in Tindouf, and we were driven hours out into the desert by jeep.

The typical desert isn't like the one in *Lawrence of Arabia*. No golden waves of sand. It's hard and rocky. I couldn't discern any roads or signs of any kind. Nothing. Two or three hours later, a camp appeared out of nowhere. No idea how they found it.

They didn't want us going into the refugee camp itself, so we stayed a distance away on our own.

As we were led to our tent, my dedication to my craft was sorely tested. Not only am I as urban as it gets—Stevie don't camp—but the one thing in the desert that nobody warns you about is . . . the flies. I hate all forms of bugs, and desert flies are relentless. Where the fuck do they come from? Thankfully they took a break at night.

Our hosts served dinner. I followed my usual routine of fasting on a research trip. For three days, I only drank their tea, which was some powerful shit. I was simultaneously tripping and extremely focused.

We met with five or six guys every day. They were never quite sure they could trust us, so they never identified themselves. And with the turbans and beards and shades, I couldn't be sure if one of them was Abdelaziz or not.

They spoke English very well and occasionally spoke French to my companions. I was very well-read in those days, and they were impressed by how much I knew about religion, especially the more mystical eso-teric stuff like Sufism, Kabbalah, monasticism, even Wicca and Yoga. That stuff was my specialty.

They agreed that the secular state, rather than an Islamic state, was what they wanted, which was as important to me then as it is now. I believe everyone who wants a country should have one, but my dedica-tion to human rights will never allow me to endorse Sharia law, which is the problem with Hamas running half of Palestine right now. And the Boycott, Divestment, Sanctions (BDS) movement assholes aren't going to fix it. As I write this, there's Hamas on one side and Benjamin Netanyahu on the other, a perfect storm of neither one wanting the obviously correct two-state solution.

I tried to sleep, but my adrenaline was flowing nonstop, and the caffeine and whatever else was in that tea had me hallucinating.

I walked out into the desert night.

I concentrated and really listened.

Nothing.

I had never heard quiet like that. The silence seemed to elevate whatever North African drug was coursing through my veins.

The sky was ridiculous. An infinite array of galaxies on a vast canvas that only seemed real because of the moving meteors and vibrating constellations.

This must be how astronauts feel as they look out from the moon, I thought.

I had never felt so small, and at the same time so much a part of the universe.

I had read Joseph Campbell's work growing up, including *The Hero with a Thousand Faces*, which I'd penciled in as the title to my fifth album. The experience I was having was the bliss he was talking about.

It felt like the power of all those stars had nowhere to go and nothing to connect to—except me.

I walked until I couldn't see the camp anymore and took off my clothes.

I didn't want anything between me and eternity.

If there was any doubt before, there wasn't now. I was definitely tripping!

I lay down and looked up as my entire body experienced an electric tingling.

I felt like a lightning rod experiencing all of time at the same time.

I could feel the rumbling of the Earth's past and the iridescent buzz of the future.

It left me with an odd sensation. Something I wasn't used to feeling. It took me a while to recognize it. The feeling was . . . hope.

I hadn't felt it so clearly since my first epiphany back in Middletown thirty years earlier. Only now the Angels' Eyes were stars.

If the sky had opened up and invited me in, I would have gone. I had to force myself to return to the planet on which I felt I was mistakenly born.

It was what we would have referred to back in the psychedelic days as a good trip.

By the third day the obvious leader, Abdelaziz or not, was warming up a little. I told him I'd contact his rep at the United Nations and speak to a few congressmen about pulling our support and encouraging a cease-fire, at the very least.

I also suggested teaching the kids English in the camps, which would help them interact with the world community and would someday help their cause. I told him I'd arrange for books to be sent. He liked the idea and said he'd discuss it with the others.

By the third night of communing with the universe, I was clear about what I would do next. I knew my adventure was coming to an end, and I wanted closure. I wouldn't tour again. But I would go out big, creating a postapocalyptic, cinematic, down-and-dirty setting for my fifth, final, and most personal album. The political consequence of spiritual bankruptcy. And I'd throw in the connection between sexual bliss and spiritual enlightenment for a little yin and yang.

The best part? For the first time in many years I suddenly felt like playing guitar again.

I haven't begun to understand it all, but even a quick glance at the mystics of all the different religions—the shamans, the yogis, the saints, the sages, the Lotus Sutra Buddhists, the Kabbalists, the Sufis, the Taoist seers—suggests they have all had their own personal vision of the same immutable, eternal Truth.

One Truth, many names.

Early on in the process of learning about others to learn about myself, I found that religion was the key element in getting to the roots of a culture's identity. It helped me reexamine my own ever-evolving thoughts on the subject as well, which is worth doing every now and then.

When it came time for my fifth album, I knew I was in for the challenge of my artistic life. I had dug deeper and deeper, thought and tested myself, and eventually walked out into the desert and let the universe take me where it wanted to go.

My starting point for the album was recognizing that the essence of spirituality is a connection to something bigger than ourselves. It could be each other, society, the Earth, the metaphysical energy somewhere out there (as Captain Kirk likes to put it), or the ocean of all souls deep inside each of us. There resides the foundation of faith, optimism, brotherhood, society, law, ethics, and whatever else you want to add to the list.

For me, that connection was revealed in the 1960s, which marked the birth of consciousness. Our minds expanded on a mass scale like never before.

Civil rights for minorities, women's rights, gay rights; a politically active youth movement; the belief that questioning your government was a patriotic responsibility; environmental awareness; expansion of Eastern thinking; the end of colonialism; psychoactive substances; and of course, the Renaissance in all the Arts.

That consciousness was founded on a few basic spiritual principles.

The first was our fundamental understanding of our relationship to the Earth, and the vast gap between Western and Semitic religious belief, on one side, and American Indian, African, and Asian belief, on the other.

Genesis 1:28 says, "And God blessed them, and God said to them, 'Be fruitful and multiply, and fill the earth and subdue it; and have dominion.'"

What "God" meant by "subdue" and "have dominion" can (and should) be debated, but Western religion took it to suggest man's superiority over the Earth. Man the conqueror.

The other tradition—American Indians, Africans, Asians—did not believe that humans were superior to the Earth; rather, they believed that they were meant to live in harmony with it. This difference affected how we viewed our most essential relationship and contributed to a fundamental sense of alienation. That alienation was the first component of our spiritual bankruptcy. That was the theme explored more deeply on *Revolution*, but it would overlap with this one.

A second principle was our changing relationship to time. It seemed like there just simply wasn't enough of it anymore. This was true in the late '80s, and it's only gotten worse. Technology was supposed to give us more time, not less. But technology is being developed in ways that outpace the human mind. Information is great, but when we feel the need to know everything as quickly as possible, we can't connect with any of it. We scratch the surface, hold nothing, and move on. Which inevitably leads to the key malady of the twenty-first century, time deficit disorder.

Finally, I saw that we had demystified one of our greatest forces, our Art, and specifically our Rock music.

Art, like Religion, needs mystery. That is how we participate in it. But our society demystifying that mystery has the same effect as music Engineers separating the frequencies with pillows and rugs.

The advent of MTV was the beginning of the end of Rock's importance. The accessibility of videos diluted and in many cases eliminated the experience of seeing a live Rock band. It has also allowed Rock bands to exist without the essential prerequisite of being great live performers. The corporatization of Rock radio dealt another severely damaging, if not lethal, blow. As did consultants, whose only job was to homogenize and eliminate interesting, unique personality. As did lazy, ignorant, short-sighted record companies.

The result, of course, was the waning of the Rock era and the rise of a Pop era that was more vapid, meaningless, superficial, emotionless, soulless, unmemorable, and disposable than any previous era in the history of music.

Most importantly, now that Pop was big business, bottom-line corporate control took precedence over the Art.

Granted, I was a bit jaded, having lived through the Renaissance. But most Pop made after the '60s was wallpaper, a short-term distraction for kids. You could make the argument that Pop was always so. You'd be wrong, but you could make that argument. In the past, though, there was a balance between Rock and Pop. When that balance went away, Pop ruled unchallenged, and Rock became an endangered species in a world where music no longer engaged our senses or our intellect and where there were few artists we could invest in emotionally.

We don't have many Artforms. We can't afford to have one stolen from us, let alone one of the most powerful. Our spiritual nourishment depends upon it.

As I headed into the fifth album, that was my thinking.

I came home and went back to the Akai twelve-track in Zoë's apartment. She engineered (being versatile has always been a prerequisite for working for me!) as I wrote and demoed the album, which I called *Born Again Savage*.

My lifelong roadie Ben Newberry had been Zoë's boyfriend before Pat Thrall. We tried to keep it all in the family! He had gotten a '56 Les Paul for fifty dollars at a yard sale in the early '60s, and I used it on the whole album through a mini-Marshall amp. The guitar was probably worth $250,000 by 1989—and if you'd played it, you'd know why.

I decided to do the '60s Hard Rock record I always wanted to do as a kid. A little Who, a touch of Kinks, a dollop of Cream, a hint of Zep, a spritz of Hendrix, and a lot of Jeff Beck.

Not a keyboard in sight.

It took me a few weeks to write and record, to get the all-important nod of approval from Zoë, and then put it on the shelf, closure accomplished.

I was not into finding a way to tour or seeing if a record company was interested, so it would stay on the shelf for years. But the five albums I'd outlined when I started my artistic adventure of educating and discovering myself while figuring out how the world works were done.

Now what?

My career contemplation was interrupted happily by one of the most incredible events of my lifetime—one that, in spite of all my public bravado, I never thought I'd live to see.

Nelson Mandela was released from prison.

I watched awestruck as he walked out of Victor Verster prison, accompanied by his estranged but loyal wife Winnie. Geez, I thought, maybe Martin Luther King was right after all. Maybe with time the universe does bend toward justice.

The Afrikaners who ran South Africa were smart, and lucky, to keep him alive all those years. It wasn't the obvious move, since his existence gave the majority hope for an eventual overthrow of the government. But by keeping him alive, they avoided an inevitable bloodbath.

And now they were promising a real democratic election to follow!

I couldn't help but feel some pride.

We did it.

Fifty artists, dozens of studio Engineers and assistants, dozens of unpaid musicians, seven songs, one album, the European unions, the United Nations, journalists, college-age protestors, the Wembley Stadium show broadcast to millions, every company that divested, and on and on. Forty-five years of struggle had led to that exhilarating moment.

The South African government would have inevitably fallen. But we took years off their existence, saving who knows how many lives. Preventing how many more Sharpeville and Soweto massacres, how many more deaths in prison.

When we played Johannesburg years later, I met with the ANC and they thanked me again, explaining that it had been critically important that we had acted when we did, because as the government began to anticipate the possibility of Mandela's release, it began putting hallucinogens like LSD in his food to fry his brain. The ANC weren't sure how long he could have survived it.

Tears streamed down my face at my first sight of this new, grey-haired, distinguished Mandela. Looking very presidential already.

Good luck, my friend, I thought. You are walking into a fucking hurricane.

So now I had to at least pretend to plan the rest of my life, knowing full well that's not how my life had ever worked. Nobody was going to be interested in me producing the Hall of Fame show, or anything remotely as grandiose as my imagination, so I decided to go back to my smaller, more practical, first teenage dream.

I would be the guitar player in a band.

I'd write or cowrite and sing some backing vocals but mostly just play guitar. Start from scratch all over again.

And I knew how it would happen. I would write my second-ever Rock album, *Nobody Loves and Leaves Alive*, by a fictitious new group I planned to assemble called the Lost Boys. If *Born Again Savage* had been late-'60s Hard Rock, *Nobody Loves and Leaves Alive* was mid-'60s Rock, early Stones, Them, or (English) Birds. Guitar playing was fun again, so I used a whole different style on this one. No pedals, no distortion, very clean, some slide.

It was gonna be Steve Jordan on drums, a friend of mine named Jimmy on bass. I eventually relented and decided to have a keyboard, so I located my favorite Rock piano player, the legendary Nicky Hopkins. He was into it and told me to call back when we were further along. Tragically, he died a short time later.

Now all I needed was a singer!

I personally auditioned or heard the tapes of no less than four hundred singers. No one was quite right. One record company guy played me a song from a new record he wasn't sure was going to get a release. "What about him?"

"That's the right idea, but what about his group?"

"I don't know. There's trouble in the band, and half the company doesn't know what to do with it."

I asked if I could take it with me.

"Sure," he said. "It's in the out pile."

I called him the next day. "Listen to me. This is a good album, and it should come out."

"You don't want the guy?"

"I like him, but I'm not breaking up this band. They're good. I don't take good bands for granted and neither should you. And besides, I like the name—the Black Crowes."

Long story short, I never found a singer, and the Lost Boys went on the shelf next to *Born Again Savage*.

As the year ended, *Rolling Stone* named the Jukes' *Hearts of Stone* one of the best albums of the previous twenty years and *Sun City* one of the best albums of the decade. We were having a good year with the critics. But truthfully, I've always had good luck with the critics.

If only they had bigger families, I would have come closer to breaking even.

Once again, either Peter Gabriel or Jim Kerr called me to perform at Wembley. This time it would be a fundraiser for Mandela's ANC, with the man himself present!

Meeting him was a trip.

He had a vibe unlike anybody I've ever met before or since. He had an inner glow like I imagined the big religious icons had. I'm talking the Moses, Jesus, Buddha, Muhammad vibration.

That's how intense his quiet energy was.

This would be the beginning of a fundraising trip that would eventually take him to the United States. Five American cities had pledged $500,000 each to Mandela's ANC to help them compete in the first democratic election in South Africa's history, as if they needed it.

New York was one of them.

Bill Lynch, New York mayor David Dinkins's deputy mayor, organized a meeting to prepare for Mandela's arrival.

Suddenly every activist who ever lived laid claim to being intimately involved in the thinking, planning, and execution of the fall of apartheid. And suddenly, America's own racial animus reared its ugly head.

The meeting's mission was to organize as many events as necessary to net the $500,000 pledge.

Harry Belafonte, the legitimate godfather of activists, ran the show, and a lot of the other civil rights activists and community leaders assigned various people to various tasks.

Bill Graham, the most famous Promoter in America, offered to put together a major concert for the event. He was asked a bunch of stupid, insulting questions, read the room, and left. They were working hard to ignore the other three white people, Jennifer Davis, Danny Schechter, and me.

We were an embarrassment to them.

In their minds South Africa was a "black issue."

Only it wasn't. In fact, no racial issue is a "black issue." If there's racial conflict, by definition it involves more than one race, no? Which means the solution must as well.

In all fairness, there were a few in the room, like Harry, who had been vocal about South Africa. A few had protested. A few had signed petitions and cornered an occasional congressman. But there was no one in that room except me, Danny, and Jennifer who had actually *done* anything significant about it.

Still, every time we brought something up we were patronized, condescended to, or ignored.

Danny had to restrain me when somebody directed a disparaging remark toward Jennifer. She had been an anti-apartheid activist *in* South Africa until it became untenable and she went into exile in the States. Along with me, she was the only person who had actually been there.

She had more courage than the whole room combined.

So after a few hours of being insulted and watching the usual bullshit that goes down when a bunch of conflicting egos clash, watching defenses going up because they don't know what they're talking about, nobody really in charge, we gave up and left.

It was fine with me. Our job was done. We got the legislation passed and got the man out of jail. Now the South Africans could speak for themselves.

I didn't even go down for Mandela's inauguration. I was invited to travel on Air Force One or Two, whichever one went.

I didn't want any credit. I didn't do what we did because I'm some kind of nice guy. I'm not. I did it because the idea that my government supported apartheid was an embarrassment to me. And to our American ideals. And I figured we were never gonna get around to the vast number of other human rights violations on the African continent until South Africa was dealt with.

The meeting we walked out of was held a few months before Mandela came to New York.

Cut to the week before he arrived.

Rrrrrrrrring.

"Yeah."

"Bill Lynch."

"What can I do for you, Bill?"

As if I didn't know.

"Can I buy you lunch?"

We met at the Empire Diner. This was the early '90s, when it was still good.

Bill spoke first. "Sorry about how the meeting went down," he said. "I had a lot of politics I had to contend with."

"I understand," I lied.

"We've got a problem."

"No shit? With that roomful of geniuses? I'm shocked!"

I liked Bill. I knew I was probably going to help him no matter what the problem was, but I was going to give him as much shit as I could in the meantime.

"So Mandela gets out of jail," Bill said, "and starts his fundraising trips. Some airport, he's going down the greeting line shaking hands, and one of the hands he shakes is Yasser Arafat's. Somebody snaps a picture. Makes the front page of the *Post*. My Jewish money, which we were depending on, vanishes the next day. We are fucked. We're going to be the only city that stiffs Mandela. And us with a black mayor no less!"

Oh, boo-hoo, I thought to myself.

But he was actually close to real tears.

"You got nothing?"

"Dick." I'm translating.

You gotta love the hybrid language we speak in New York. It's a combination of '50s Jazz Hipster, Italian American Mafia, Ebonics, Spanglish, and Yiddish, regardless of one's ethnic background.

"Oy vey!" I replied, Arafat reference intended.

That brought out a reluctant smile.

"Alright, let me think about it," I relented.

Bill was a tough guy. His eyes were pleading. I didn't like seeing him like this. I walked him out, and he delivered his parting shot. "It's next week."

"Oh good. You had me nervous there for a minute."

One way or the other, I connected up with Bobby De Niro, Spike Lee, and Eddie Murphy. Drew Nieporent, De Niro's partner in the Tribeca Grill, was also involved. I explained the situation.

They came in.

We sold dinner with Mandela at $2,500 a head times two hundred to get the $500,000 we needed.

Miraculously, because of those names on the invitation, we sold it out!

Smokin' Joe Frazier came to the dinner. My good friends Jay Cocks and Verna Bloom were there. Marty Scorsese brought Ray Liotta, who was starring in his new film.

Mandela was supposed to be there at 7 p.m.

At 7:15 my phone rang.

Uh-oh, I thought. Here it comes.

It was Mandela's guy. "Hello, my friend," he starts. "I hear it's sold out!"

"Yeah, baby." I'm thinking, *Don't fucking do this to me.* "The whole shebang cost us thirty-five grand. Everybody worked for free, Bobby and Drew took no profit." *Don't even think about it, you cocksucker.* "And I've got $500K in my hand waiting for you." *Go ahead, say it, motherfucker, say it!*

"That sounds great, comrade," he said. "That sounds great."

Enough bullshit small talk. Say it.

"So listen, Madiba has had a long day and he's very tired. So we're going to skip the dinner."

Man, why can't I be wrong every now and then?

"Just curious," I said. "Where are you right now?" As if I didn't know.

"We're at Harry Belafonte's apartment."

What a surprise. I knew somebody had been in Mandela's ear telling him not to worry about those fucking white liberals—you can step all over them.

"OK, baby," I said matter-of-factly. "No problem. I'll just give everybody their money back."

"What did you say?"

He suddenly wasn't so cool, calm, and collected.

"I said I'm giving everybody their money back. I sold this as dinner with Mandela. If he can't come, I understand. But everybody gets their money back."

"You can't do that! That's ANC money!"

I had had enough.

"Just watch me, motherfucker! This is *my* fucking money until Mandela comes down here and spends some time and shows these people some respect."

"Now wait a minute, comrade. Hold the phone."

Murmur murmur murmur.

"Alright. He's coming down. But he can't stay all night."

"He needs to shake some hands—at the very least the hands of my three partners, Bobby De Niro, Spike Lee, and Eddie Murphy, whose sponsorship made this a success. And he needs to make a speech and show some gratitude for this fucking money. And there had better be an attitude adjustment because, correct me if I'm wrong, but I don't remember owing you a fucking thing!"

And come he did.

In the only conversation I would ever have with him, Mandela asked me what he should say. I'd heard he had a good sense of humor, so I thought he was fucking with me. But he wasn't.

I told him to open with a joke.

No, I didn't. I told him we'd been using "Keep the pressure on" as our slogan to strengthen his negotiating position with the government so they'd keep their promise of a fair election. "Yes, that's good," he said. And he gave a nice speech.

And that, my children, is this week's lesson showing that no good deed goes unpunished.

The ANC got their money.

David Dinkins wasn't embarrassed.

New York City wasn't embarrassed.

Bill Lynch owes me a big favor.

Smokin' Joe Frazier made two cameo appearances on *The Simpsons*.

Goodfellas came out and became a big hit.

Mandela went home and was elected president.

All in all, an unusually happy ending.

Just wish I'd gotten a picture.

But guess who did?

The next morning, as Mandela's plane was taking off, I opened the papers to see his arm around a little guy with a big shit-eating grin.

I guess Paul Simon got over that whole scary dangerous Communist thing.

twenty-three

Seven Years in the Desert

(1991–1997)

There's a bad storm coming,
I believe it's coming our way,
The air is thick and cloudy,
The sky gets blacker every day,
The rebel children are waiting,
Their time is coming soon,
They face no future gamely,
They've got nothing left to lose . . .

— "SAINT FRANCIS," FROM *BORN AGAIN SAVAGE*

Only part of me came back from the desert. The rest of me remained there, forever wandering, searching for . . . what?

The '90s were a lost decade.

For the first time in my life, I had no clear mission.

I'd lost my way, and as usual I wouldn't find it; it would find me.

Mostly what I remember is walking my dog for seven years. Staying connected to little Jake was the one thing that kept me sane. Studying him, learning from his natural instinct to live in the moment. Giving him the best life I could while cursing a God I knew didn't exist for giving the greatest creatures on earth such horrifyingly short life spans.

Maureen helped by keeping me fantasizing about ballet and Broadway.

I'd blown my life twice at that point. First by leaving the E Street Band, and then by treating my solo career as a purely artistic endeavor.

It was an exhilarating ride while it lasted. I felt like I was finally doing what I was born to do, or at least was on the right road, embracing the life of an Artist and beginning to fulfill my destiny. But who was paying the bills? It was a bit unsettling at that stage of the game to still be looking for a steady job.

Spoiler Alert. I'm still looking.

◈

The decade was spent walking my dog and doing occasional favors for friends. Cell phones didn't exist yet. Can you imagine such a thing? But I was easy to find.

Steve Weitzman, (in)famous for booking the legendary club Tramps, called and asked me to produce an album for a Nigerian artist named Majek Fashek.

The connection was Jimmy Iovine. I had smart friends. Some of the smartest in the business. Jimmy was one of them.

He had hooked up with Ted Field, who had an independent film company called Interscope and started a record division. No surprise, given his history of success—Patti Smith, Tom Petty, Stevie Nicks, Dire Straits, U2, etc.

He started off doing Rock records. They all bombed.

This told Jimmy one simple thing: if he couldn't break a Rock record, then Rock was over. Even though there would be another minute of commercial success in the form of Grunge, it was on the way out, and Jimmy knew it.

I clock the Rock era from "Like a Rolling Stone" in 1965 to Kurt Cobain's death. Thirty years of universal bliss. Cobain marked the last time an audience would invest in an artist emotionally to that degree. It was just too painful.

Iovine saw some action in the Salsa-meets-Disco world, but it wasn't his thing. It was too late to learn Spanish. He was from Brooklyn. He was still working on English.

He looked around. What was next?

Hip-Hop!

Uh, yeah, the name had caught on.

Jimmy signed Tupac.

Then, in the ballsiest move since Don Corleone's deal with Barzini, he decided to distribute Death Row Records. And somehow lived to tell about it.

There's street smarts, super–street smarts, and then there's Jimmy Iovine.

I had to shake my head in wonderment! This Italian kid from Red Hook, Brooklyn, which half the Mob called home and where a black man would never dare to walk down the block, became the king of Hip-Hop.

The same year he signed Tupac, he signed Majek Fashek. I ended up producing a great album for Fashek, *Spirit of Love*, an example of how deep Reggae had penetrated African consciousness.

Nobody heard it.

Gary Gersh called with another production job. An Austin, Texas, super-type group that included my friend Charlie Sexton. I was good at making individuals into bands, and Gary knew that.

Charlie was and is one of the great guitar players, but everybody kept trying to make him a Pop star, just because he looked like James Dean. And OK, he happened to drive a '49 Merc, but that was beside the point. He had never made the record he deserved, and I knew I could help him do that.

The band, named Arc Angels after their rehearsal space, was Charlie, another Austin guitar player and singer, Doyle Bramhall Jr., backed by Stevie Ray Vaughan's rhythm section, Double Trouble, Chris Layton on drums and Tommy Shannon on bass.

I thought the job would be nothing but fun.

It wasn't.

I get along with everybody. Because my life got off to a late start, I am constantly preoccupied with songs and scripts I haven't written, shows I haven't produced, hotels and clubs I haven't built, not to mention a detailed unrealized political agenda, so I don't have time for petty conflict. I never start fights, and never even engage in arguments if I can help it. I have to be nonconfrontational, because I'm too extreme. My Calabrése blood has infinite patience until it doesn't, and my Napolitano blood is always ready for a fight to the death over the slightest insult. It's all or nothing at all with me, which most of the time means nothing. I'm too busy to look for trouble. It has to find me.

For some bizarre reason, it found me during the Arc Angels in the form of Doyle Bramhall Jr. Every suggestion was an argument. He never liked anything I said. Didn't laugh or smile once.

Maybe he thought I'd favor Charlie. Maybe he wanted somebody else to produce. I don't know. He didn't want to talk about his problems, and frankly neither did I.

The adversarial zenith came midway through recording, when I suggested that a solo needed a more Bluesy, melodic approach rather than the jumble of psychedelic noise he was making. He sneered. "What do you know about the Blues?"

Ooh—once in a while I still see that face in my dreams.

I bit my tongue. Hard. I didn't bother to explain that by the time he was six years old I had learned, absorbed, and used onstage every guitar lick on every album by Muddy Waters, Little Walter, Sonny Boy Williamson II, Howlin' Wolf, Elmore James, Buddy Guy, Junior Wells, B.B. King, Albert King, T-Bone Walker, Jimmy Rogers, Jimmy Reed, Hubert Sumlin, Charley Patton, Robert Johnson, Son House, Fred McDowell, Lightnin' Hopkins, Slim Harpo, Blind Willie Johnson, Blind Lemon Jefferson, Reverend Gary Davis, John Lee Hooker, and Otis Rush—whom I discussed at length with Stevie Ray Vaughan when I picked him to open for me at *Rockpalast.* The only licks I hadn't played were Freddie King's, and that was because he'd pulled a gun on me when I was a kid.

I had to make a decision. I had promised Gary and Charlie a great record, but if I beat the shit out of this obnoxious motherfucker, it was going to significantly decrease the chances of success.

Anyway, I somehow managed to ignore him, pretend I was a peace-loving professional, and make a great album.

The Arc Angels broke up just after the record came out.

Nobody heard it.

A guy named Allen Kovac called to say that he had taken over as Meat Loaf's Manager when Meat had fallen out with Jim Steinman. Would I write and produce a song?

I'd met Meat Loaf when Steve Popovich defied the industry's conventional wisdom and worked relentlessly for a year to break him. He was a sweetheart of a guy. Happy to help.

I can write a song for whoever asks. No problem. It usually comes to me within a few minutes. If it's a script, the song comes as soon as I read it. If it's a film, as soon as I see it.

But a week went by . . . and nothing. I analyzed the problem.

Meat Loaf was very popular.

He was charming and talented.

But there was one thing he wasn't.

Meat Loaf was not an Artist.

So what was he? I asked myself.

An actor! I answered.

Aha, I thought! I'm not going to write him a song; I'll write him a show!

Of course, I didn't intend to make the Meat Loaf project my life's work, so rather than conceive of a show from scratch, I went in search of a classic that could be adapted.

Meat Loaf was big. Freaky. Kind of awkward in his own skin. He must have been made fun of his whole life. His nickname was Meat Loaf, for crissake!

So with whom in classic literature did he have the most in common?

Bada bing!

Quasimodo!

The Hunchback of Notre-Dame!

Freaky fucking book.

I don't know how it was a hit in 1831. Netflix must have had a slow month. But let me tell you, Victor Hugo definitely had issues. Here's the CliffsNotes version:

An evil fifteenth-century priest wants to fuck an innocent peasant girl who tries her best to avoid him. Meanwhile, a soulful hunchback dude falls in love with her, but she becomes infatuated with some shallow soldier type. The priest gets pissed, and ready for this, *he hangs her!* Like, by the neck until dead.

Hitchcock's *Psycho* and then some!

Maybe that's where he got the idea.

And how's this for a happy ending? The hunchback whacks the priest, finds the girl's dead body, lies down next to her, and starves to death so he can spend eternity with her.

Now is that a hit, or is that a hit?

I guess compared to cholera and bubonic plague, it must have qualified as comic relief.

On top of that bizarre plot, the book takes an endless digression, even worse than one of mine, discussing the cathedral in excruciating detail. Very weird, until you remember the book was actually titled *Notre-Dame de Paris 1482*.

The comings and goings of a bunch of fatally flawed humans will always be temporary, but Notre-Dame Cathedral is forever (or at least until some asshole sets it on fire six hundred years later!). Which makes it the first existential novel, doesn't it? Beats Dostoevsky by thirty years at least!

Anyway, I rewrote it with a happier ending—not a high bar—wrote half the songs, and demoed them with Mark Alexander playing everything and a Meat Loaf soundalike singing. I was quite proud of it. A whole new genre for me, and a step in the theatrical direction I wanted to go. I delivered my masterpiece and . . . silence.

After a few days, Allen and I met. "Meat doesn't want it."

"What?"

"He can't sing it."

"What is he talking about? I wrote it specifically for his voice, in his key, with melodies in his range."

"I'll tell you the truth," he said. "I think the demo guy intimidated him."

Intimidated him?

He was *imitating* him for fucks sake!

Allen shook his head.

No-go.

I thought fuck it, another six or seven songs and I've got a Broadway show. Several Producers loved it and were considering it when Disney put out its animated *Hunchback of Notre Dame*. The Producers assumed Broadway was the next stop, since Disney owned part of it, and ran for the hills.

Nobody heard it.

Kovac had another idea, a reunion record with Southside. Sure, baby. I got nothing but time.

I had seen the Jukes recently, and they had played a knockout new song Southside and Bobby Bandiera had written, "All Night Long."

So I knew I had one good song.

I love a challenge. *Hearts of Stone* had grown in popularity quite a bit in the fifteen years since we'd worked together. Could I beat it?

I wrote a comeback song called, imaginatively, "I'm Coming Back," even though Southside hadn't gone anywhere. It was probably more about me than him.

I wrote something that included Southside's father, who I always liked (Ernie Kovacs, I swear), called "All I Needed Was You." It was based on *Somebody Up There Likes Me*, Paul Newman as Rocky Graziano.

I got a nice melancholy song from Bruce, the kind I could never write myself, "All the Way Home," and to complete the Jersey reunion vibe, I even got Johnny Bongiovi involved, doing a duet on "I've Been Working Too Hard." It was his title so I tried to give him credit, but he wouldn't take it. Very honorable guy. Even when he stole my logo in his early success, he freely admitted stealing it from me. See, that's all we need. A little credit.

Finally, since these reunions weren't gonna happen very often, if ever again, I wanted a song that told our story, like John and Michelle Phillips's "Creeque Alley" did for the Mamas and the Papas. I caught a good one with "It's Been a Long Time."

The album turned out good.

We called it *Better Days*, a title Bruce would unconsciously steal for a song title about a year later.

That's OK. Careful as I've been, I must have stolen dozens of riffs, melodies, and ideas from him over the years. Plus, our songs had opposite messages. His was optimistic: "These are better days." Mine? "Better days are on the way / 'Cause you know and I know / it can't get much worse!"

I was wrong, by the way.

Allen Kovac's record label, Impact, went under, I don't know, five or ten minutes after the record was released.

Nobody heard it.

Aside from the work, which really is its own reward, one other good thing came out of the project. I found a new lifelong friend.

Lance Freed, the son of the legendary DJ Alan Freed, had become one of the last of the great music publishers. He ran Rondor for Herb Alpert and Jerry Moss, the *A* and *M* in A&M Records.

He heard the Jukes' album and called me. "Let's talk," he said.

We met at Elio's restaurant on the Upper East Side.

"This is some of the greatest songwriting I've heard in twenty years," he started off.

Oh, I'm gonna like this dinner.

For those of you wondering what the fuck publishing is, let me explain real quick.

Each time a song is sold or reproduced, it's worth nine cents, half of which goes to the writer and half of which goes to the publisher. The publisher also controls the composition, which in the old days meant literally publishing songs as sheet music. It was the publisher's job to get the music into all those player-piano scrolls and to get them to record companies and singers.

Since the '70s, most songwriters have had their own publishing companies and use publishers to administer songs—to find and collect the money worldwide; they keep a piece of whatever they find. They get a bigger piece if they place a song in a movie, TV show, or commercial. But that's rare.

Back to Elio's.

So there I was, walking my dog and doing favors, no real work in sight, and an hour later a complete stranger gives me a $500,000 advance to administer my music and saves my life.

God bless America.

One of the nice things about this world of showbiz is that no matter how low you go, you're always only one hit away. Or in this case, one heavy executive fan away. Your whole life changes just like that. So there's always an element of hope as we punch and punch and punch the wall, trying to make a crack to let the light in, to quote Leonard Cohen.

Or make a hole big enough to escape from. To quote me.

Bruce had decided to let the rest of the E Street Band go in the late '80s, and by 1992 or so he was putting a band together to tour his new records, *Lucky Town* and *Human Touch*. *Human Touch* had a song called "57 Channels (and Nothin' On)" that Bruce asked me to remix. I added some political content, which gave Reverend Al Sharpton a chance to brag that he had worked with both James Brown *and* Bruce Springsteen.

Bruce invited me to a rehearsal at A&M Studios.

This was his first post–E Street tour, and he was a little bit anxious.

The new band sounded good, and I told Bruce so. He had kept Roy Bittan, and I knew a few of the horn players and Shane Fontayne, who had been Lone Justice's guitarist. Seeing Shane there could only mean one thing—Maria McKee had gone solo.

That was a shame.

I knew Iovine was heading that way. Jimmy was just coming out of his affair with Stevie Nicks and saw Maria as a similar solo star. Usually he was way ahead of me, but this time I disagreed.

Nobody should ever take a band for granted. Bands are miracles. They're rarely perfect, but if a band has that magical chemistry, it should not be fucked with. If you need to do a solo record, do it between band records.

Chris Columbus—no, the other one—called and said he needed a song for *Home Alone 2: Lost in New York*. We agreed that it was the perfect opportunity to finally work with Darlene Love.

I had met her back in 1980, when we were in LA for the River Tour. I ran into Lou Adler, the great record and movie Producer who also co-owned the Roxy. "I've got something on tonight I know you'll like," he said.

"What's up?"

"How about the return of Darlene Love?"

Holy Shit! The greatest and most mysterious of all the Girl Group singers! And we happened to be there at this historic moment? Destiny.

Darlene had quite a history. Back in the early '60s, Phil Spector was in New York looking for songs. Jerry Leiber and Mike Stoller ran their labels, Red Bird Records and Spark Records, along with Trio Music publishing, in the Brill Building at 1619 Broadway, where they'd signed Ellie Greenwich and Jeff Barry. Up the street at 1650, an address often mistakenly included as part of the Brill Building, were Al Nevins and Don Kirshner, whose Aldon Music had the writing teams of Carole King and Gerry Goffin and Cynthia Weil and Barry Mann. (There's more detail about this in Al Kooper's great book, *Backstage Passes and Backstabbing Bastards*.)

As the story goes, Spector was in one building or the other going from room to room, looking for songs. At the time, that's what half the industry did. He saw Gene Pitney playing "He's a Rebel" for Vikki Carr, knew a hit when he heard one, got hold of the demo, and raced to get it out first.

Back then, music publishers were sleazy bastards who gave songs to multiple producers, telling each of them they had an exclusive. Carr's version was slated to come out on Liberty Records. Phil rushed to get his out on his own label, Philles Records (named for Phil and Lester Sill, a major mentor to Leiber and Stoller as well as Phil).

The Crystals, the first successful group on Philles ("There's No Other," "Uptown"), happened to be on the road, so he recorded "He's a Rebel" with a group called the Blossoms, featuring a young singer named Darlene Love—but he credited it to the Crystals.

Historic mistake. The only possible justification was that in those days, independent record companies had trouble collecting from distributors, and Phil felt it was risky to use a new artist's name so early in the new company's life.

Whatever the reason, it screwed up Darlene's life pretty good. She sang on a few more hits (with the Crystals, with Bob B. Soxx and the Blue Jeans, and under her own name) and enjoyed a storied backing-vocal career with the Blossoms, but by the '70s she was out of the business, working as a housekeeper. The greatest singer in the world cleaning toilets! (Check out the movie *20 Feet from Stardom* for a full version of her story.)

And then it was 1980, and Lou Adler was talking to me about her Roxy show. I couldn't wait to tell Bruce.

Not only was Darlene spectacular that night, but she sang "Hungry Heart." Ha!

Backstage, I told her that I thought she belonged in New York. LA was too trendy. People, especially women, became invisible after the age of twenty-one.

And damn if she didn't pack up and move to New York just like that!

I immediately got her a few gigs but could not interest a record company in signing her.

She ended up doing pretty well on her own. She got a couple of off-Broadway shows and then a couple *on* Broadway. Plus a steady movie gig playing Danny Glover's wife in the *Lethal Weapon* movie series.

Now, thanks to Chris Columbus, we were finally going to record together.

Only like fifteen years late.

But it was perfect. No worries about a label or radio airplay. All the song had to do was fit in the movie. And all I had to do was write it.

Chris screened the movie for me, and I wrote "All Alone on Christmas." It's one of the songs I'm most proud of.

Writing anything great is a challenge, obviously, but it is easier to write something original than it is to write a song that is genre specific.

I know that sounds backward. But trust me on this. If you write something original, you're mostly competing with yourself. If you write a Christmas song, you're competing with fucking "Jingle Bells"! With frickin' "Deck the Damn Halls." "Joy to the Motherjumpin' World!" Songs that are embedded in the world's consciousness.

Not to mention that Darlene Love was best known for singing what many regarded as the greatest Christmas rock song ever recorded, "Christmas (Baby Please Come Home)," first on Phil Spector's Christmas album in 1963 and then every holiday season on the David Letterman show.

Since the E Street Band was no longer with Bruce, I called whoever was around, figuring they'd not only be great but could use the work.

Chris wanted to direct the video, so I wrote a script. Clarence Clemons was Santa, with Macaulay Culkin on his knee. "What do you want for Christmas, little boy?" Santa would ask, and Macaulay would say, "All I want for Christmas is Darlene Love!"

Unfortunately, Macaulay's father was a nasty dude and nixed it.

But I finally fulfilled part of my promise to Darlene. It would be another twenty years until I delivered the rest.

Debbie Gold called me again, again about Bob Dylan. "He wants you to come to rehearsal and talk about producing his next record," she said.

"Are you sure this time, Debbie?"

"I was sure last time! I don't know why he didn't give you credit!"

I honestly didn't care. I was just bustin' her balls.

The rehearsal was in California, which meant I didn't know the musicians. West Coast guys were a different breed. Bob counted them in, and they started playing what was, to me, a very weird group of songs. "Light My Fire," by the Doors, "Somebody to Love" by Jefferson Airplane, "A Whiter Shade of Pale" by Procol Harum. It was like a bar-band setlist from 1967. Bob had been hanging out with the Grateful Dead, had recorded a live album with them. Maybe their influence had rubbed off.

When they took a break, Bob came over. "What do you think?"

"Let's take a walk," I said. "Bob," I said, "this might be my last conversation with you, but I've got to be honest. You cannot do this. Unless you're planning on playing somebody's bar mitzvah, you cannot do these songs. I know you're always seeking ways to have less celebrity, to be a normal guy. But you can't be this normal. You're too important."

"I'm just not writing right now," he said.

Every once in a while you find yourself in a situation where you have to do two weeks' worth of thinking in two minutes.

"How about this?" I said. "How about you go back to your roots? The Carter Family, the Seegers, Woody Guthrie, Lead Belly, whatever. It'll have real value. It's where you come from, and you'll be keeping that tradition alive."

He didn't react. It was a lot to consider. He moved his head around, maybe shaking it, maybe nodding, and said he'd think about it.

I left and never heard back from him, but Debbie said I must have got him thinking because he released two records of Blues and Folk standards, *Good As I Been to You* and *World Gone Wrong*. I felt good about that. And she got production credit! Ha-ha! I loved that!

Oddly enough, I had a very similar conversation with Bruce at around the same time. He wanted me to hear a new batch of his songs, so I went down to Rumson.

He played me a few things and said, "I'm not sure I have a single yet."

Whoa! That's a strange thing to say, I'm thinking. I've got to deal with this right now.

"Listen, man," I said, "I don't know what bizarre circumstances have led to you being on the hit single train, but you have to get off it as soon as you can."

"What do you mean?"

"You had some Pop hits, and they're nice when they happen, but you ain't no Pop star and you don't want to live in that world. If you don't have an album in mind, I suggest you go back to your solo acoustic *Nebraska* thing. Where you can own it. Instead of trying to compete with the latest fifteen-year-old refugee from the Mickey Mouse Club!"

He wrote *The Ghost of Tom Joad.* I felt good about that too. On the way out the door that day, I said, "You know, it doesn't seem right that we all seemed to disappear around the same time. Us, Bob Seger, Tom Petty, John Mellencamp, Jackson Browne, Dire Straits, all the '70s Classic Rockers. We asked the audience to make us part of their lives. An essential part. We asked them to fall in love with us. They did. And then we all disappeared. The next time you want to make a Rock record, you should put the band back together. There is nothing you can think of that the E Street Band can't do." That suggestion would take a little longer to land.

I had gotten friendly with Bob Guccione Jr., owner and editor of *Spin* magazine, who invited me to a small gathering. Midway through, I turned around and was suddenly face-to-face with Allen Ginsberg. I told him what an honor it was to meet him, and how he had influenced me, not only in my songwriting but also in my turn to Eastern religion.

Ginsberg stared at me for a minute and then said, "You've been to the mountaintop! What was it like?"

Michael Monroe and I finally pulled off an idea we'd been cooking up for years. We missed the classic Punk bands, so we assembled one with Sammy Jaffa from Hanoi Rocks, an amazing twenty-year-old guitarist named Jay Hening, and a really great drummer named Jimmy Clark.

Sammy came up with the name Demolition 23, from a William Burroughs short story, "The Lemon Kid." The album was the easiest one I've ever made. I wrote it all in two weeks—the words poured out of me so fast I had to consciously stop writing so Michael could get some writer credits—and recording and mixing took another two weeks.

Real Ramones / Sex Pistols–type stuff. Nothing but hits!

I took it around and was told Punk was dead. A year or two later Green Day and Offspring broke big, and Punk wasn't so dead.

Nobody heard it.

We did a residency at the Cat Club, hoping to start a scene. We had a different guest every week—Joey Ramone, Ian Hunter, Andy Shernoff, the occasional Monk or Bad Brain. Adam Clayton from U2 came down one night, and in the course of shooting the shit he asked me what I was doing. I told him I had two solo albums, half a Broadway show, and a Punk album on the shelf. "And I ain't writing anything else until some of this shit gets released!"

I described the most important project, *Born Again Savage*.

"I've got some time," he said. "Let's do it!" You don't see that kind of enthusiasm every day.

We had to fill out the band. Since it was a '60s-style Hard Rock album, how about Jason Bonham on drums? He'll get it!

We found him somehow, and he was into it.

The album, written in '89, recorded in '94, and released in '99, would never have seen the light of day if not for Adam Clayton, and I am forever grateful to him. You too, Jason! It's one of my favorites.

At around the same time, Jean Beauvoir, who had been in the Plasmatics and then the first version of the Disciples, put out a solo album. During Jean's time with me, he had filled the role that I had once filled for Bruce, the right-hand man, the consigliere. But he had ambition. What he wanted most was the thing I wanted least, to be a front man and a star. When he left after *Voice of America* in 1984, the fun kind of went out of it for me, and it was never quite the same again.

By the '90s, we'd gotten past it, and with his new solo album coming out, he wanted a favor. Would I ask Johnny Bongiovi if Crown of Thorns, Jean's band, could open for him in Europe? I talked to Johnny and Richie Sambora, who said Jean could have the gig, but only if I came out and did a few songs with them. They were getting worried about me turning into a hermit. It was touching, actually. So I agreed. One of the three songs I played, "Salvation," was from *Born Again Savage*, the album's only public performance until the rebirth of the Disciples in 2016, twenty years later.

While I was out with Bon Jovi, Chris Columbus called. He had a new movie, *Nine Months*, that needed a song.

I don't know what it is about Chris, but he brings the best out in me. As you travel through life, you meet very few people with blind faith in you. It makes you really want to deliver for them.

In that case, what he brought out of me was what might be my most important song. "This Is the Time of Your Life" is a Stonesy ballad about living completely in the moment, which is the core of my life's philosophy. I wrote it in Milan, in my hotel room, staring out the window at the great Duomo.

The song was supposed to play over the end credits. But when I saw the movie, there was a Van Morrison song there instead. Maybe Chris had gone out to multiple artists, and Van had turned in his song at the last minute?

Who knows. It was . . . awkward. I never asked.

Van's played, and *then* mine played.

I probably inspired a lot of cleanup crews.

Needless to say . . .

Nobody heard it.

Let's see . . . the '90s . . . the '90s . . .

We had a big victory with our Solidarity Foundation, unifying the Indians and the unions and pressuring the Quebec government to cancel the Grande-Baleine hydroelectric dam project.

I started a couple of books that I didn't get very far on. I had titles, though.

The American Identity: Who Are We? Who Do We Want to Be?

That one would have come in handy in 2020.

The Top Ten Coolest Events in Rock History.

And . . .

Frank Barsalona: Godfather of Rock and Roll

I videotaped everybody Frank knew and Frank himself. The tapes tragically disappeared, probably stolen by an insider, and I was so pissed off I couldn't continue. That one still needs to be written by somebody.

Bruce and I inducted Gary US Bonds into the Rhythm and Blues Hall of Fame. That was fun.

Did some liner notes for Dion.

And did some liner notes for Dino.

Dion released an amazing album in 2020, at the age of eighty!

And Dino. What can I say? Read Nick Tosches's book about him.

The first bio I ever read was Edmund Morris's first book about Teddy Roosevelt. Loved it. Teddy became a controversial hero. I wonder how that holds up.

Dave Marsh's book about Bruce, *Born to Run*, and his book about the Who were great also. As was Tim White's book on Bob Marley.

Bruce's *Born to Run* is an exception, but biographies are almost always better than autobiographies, aren't they?

So much for the '90s. Almost.

"Stevie," Zoë said to me on my way out of the office. "Somebody named David Chase on the phone."

twenty-four

A Night at the Opera

(1998)

In the world of show business—no news is always bad news.
—THE UNWRITTEN BOOK

The saga of *The Sopranos* began in Frank Barsalona's office one late summer day in 1997.

Frank wanted to discuss the annual meeting of the Rock and Roll Hall of Fame nominating committee. He was an important member and wanted my opinion on who he should be politicking for induction.

"How many years will go by before they put the Rascals in?" I said.

"They should be in," he said. "But so should Connie Francis!" He lit another More Red cigarette. "For fuck's sake, these guys forget how this whole thing started!"

"Frankie!" I said.

"OK, OK," he said. "I'll see what I can do."

A few years later, he put me on the nominating committee, but back then I needed him to argue my case—meaning the Rascals' case.

Do you believe in Destiny? I don't know if I do either, but let's pretend for a minute. Because if what happened isn't Destiny, I swear it's her stunt double.

Let's count the number of weird things that led from that moment in Frank's office to the *Sopranos* gig.

Frank gets the Rascals into the Hall of Fame by arguing their case at the nominating committee meaning. That's number one.

Then he told me that I should do their induction.

"No fucking way! They deserve better than me!"

He kept asking, and I kept turning him down. That's called ignoring Destiny's advances.

As the ceremony approached, Frank made one final appeal. "You have to do it," he said. "There's nobody else left."

"Alright," I said. "But goddamn it, it's a shame you couldn't find a real celebrity." That was number two.

I had been to a few inductions. They could be pretty grim, overly serious and overly long. I decided to do a little comedy to break the monotony. And because that year, for the first time, the ceremony would be televised—that's number three—I settled on a sight gag. I had one of my wardrobe girls make the same Little Lord Fauntleroy knickers and frilly shirt that the Rascals wore, and I hid the outfit under a long black coat like people were used to seeing me in so nobody would suspect anything.

At that point, the Rascals hadn't spoken to each other for twenty-five years or so. The conventional wisdom was that Eddie Brigati, one of the two lead singers, was the bad guy who had broken the group up, leading to a circular firing squad of lawsuits among him, Felix Cavaliere, and the other band members. I would eventually find out the real story, but that was still fifteen years away.

When I got to the hotel, I saw Dino Danelli, the original Rascals drummer and one of the first Disciples. He was packing his bag. "What's going on?" I said.

"I'm leaving," he said. During soundcheck, the band had started squabbling, and Dino had decided he had better things to do. "Listen," I said. "It took a lot to get you in. It's gonna make me and Frank look very bad if you guys don't perform. The show is in a few hours, and then you'll never have to see them again!"

He stayed. I delivered my speech, which was full of silly punch lines like "To sound that black you had to be Italian!"

The wardrobe reveal got a big laugh.

And who do you think was flipping around and caught the whole bit? David Chase, a television writer and Director looking for new faces for what he swore would be his last TV show. That was number four.

Chase told his people to call me. Georgianne Walken, a prominent casting Director (and wife of Christopher) told me later that she did a Hercule Poirot and tracked me down through the corporate papers of my Solidarity Foundation. That was number five.

Someone at Solidarity brought me a message. "They want you for a TV show," I was told, though I wasn't told which show, what exactly was wanted, or who "they" were.

"Tell them to send a script," I said, knowing it would be as terrible as the scripts I got every day.

At the time, a Native American man named Alex Ewen ran Solidarity for me. His main researcher was a Rhodes scholar named Jeff Wallich, who we called Doc, him being a doctor of probably several disciplines. Doc was one of those eccentric intellectuals, a bizarre and not-quite-socialized genius. At that point he had been in my office for five years, and I didn't remember him ever speaking a word. Maybe he had said hello once.

One afternoon I went to see a movie by myself to clear my head. As the lights went down, the phone rang.

"Steven?" It was a voice I didn't recognize.

"Who's this?"

"It's Doc."

Oh my God, I thought. The office must be on fire. I ran out to the lobby.

"What's the matter?"

"Well," he said. It was already our longest conversation. "I read the script" (number six).

"You what the what?"

"The script on your desk," he said.

I racked my brain. What the fuck?

"You know: *The Sopranos.*"

It clicked, vaguely. The new thing that someone had sent over. "Oh . . . OK?"

"It's great. You've got to consider this."

It was one of the strangest phone calls I had ever gotten. The office burning down would have made more sense. The guy had nothing to do with show business. He was an academic. Why he would even pick up the script was beyond me, let alone call me to offer career advice.

Because the call was so bizarre, I read the script. Doc was right. It was good (number seven)!

But I still wasn't sure why they wanted me. I assumed it was music supervision, or maybe writing original music.

That's when the call came from the man himself. David Chase turned out to be a fan, not only of my work with the E Street Band but also of my solo albums. He told me that he liked the fact that the E Street Band were not nameless, faceless sidemen. "You were the Rat Pack of Rock and Roll," he said. We talked a little more, and then he sprung a question. "So, do you want to be in this show?"

"In it?" I wasn't being slow. Everything else moving a little too fast.

"Yeah, in it. Like an actor in it."

Wow.

"Uh . . . wow." I had a pretty good imagination, but I'd never pictured being an actor. "That's really flattering, but no, not really."

"What do you mean no?"

"I mean I'm not an actor." Maybe I had been in a play or two in junior high, and there was the *Men Without Women* movie, but the closest I had come to real acting was reading for Marty Scorsese for his first attempt at *The Last Temptation of Christ.* Guess which part? A disciple.

"You are an actor," he said. "You just don't know it yet."

I had to think. Did I hear Destiny calling?

"Let's have lunch," I said (number eight).

We really hit it off. Chase was a huge music fan, had drummed in a band when he was young. And I knew some of his shows. I had never seen *Northern Exposure,* but I had watched a few episodes of *The Rockford Files* and I really liked *Kolchak: The Night Stalker.*

At lunch, we got around to talking about the script. I said that I liked it, and he said that he wanted me for the lead, Tony Soprano.

Wow. The lead.

I was interested in the whole Mob thing. I had grown up around it, the suburban side of it anyway. Like knowing where Vito Genovese's summer house was in Atlantic Highlands, bodies washing up on Sandy Hook, running into low-level gangsters running clubs on the Jersey Shore. I had seen every movie, read every book, and gotten a glimpse of the real thing in Vegas.

Other than the obvious jail-and-death part, I never really had a problem with Mob stuff. If the Beatles and the Stones hadn't come along when they did (and if it hadn't been for the end of *Angels with Dirty Faces* where Jimmy Cagney pretends he's gone chicken and begs as they put him in the electric chair), it probably would have been a viable career choice.

I always thought Italians who pretended to be insulted by the association were hypocrites. Like the assholes that banned all of us Sopranos from the Columbus Day Parade and the next year made Paul Sorvino the grand marshal!

The truth is that I never saw the downside of people thinking you're in the Mob. You can get palpable respect just from *playing* Mob guys!

Everybody thought Frank Barsalona was Mob. Of course, my referring to him as "the Godfather" helped perpetuate that fantasy. But it never hurt him.

My friend Tommy Mottola was always rumored to be Mob. That hurt his career all the way to him running Sony!

Morris Levy, the famous music publisher and label owner, wasn't Mob per se, but he definitely did business with them, and he did just fine for thirty or so years before he got busted. (Read Tommy James's excellent book *Me, the Mob, and the Music* for more about that subject.)

Chase and I talked like we had been friends for years, shooting the shit about music and the '60s. I didn't know enough about the acting world to be nervous. I felt very easy come, easy go.

"Not for nothin'," I said, somewhere between the first and second bottle of Brunello. "There is one thing in the script struck me as kind of strange. I grew up in an Italian family. I had a lot of Italian friends. But this mother character? I've never seen any kind of Italian mother like this. I mean, I don't think it's believable."

The mother in the script, Livia, was the most evil, passionless, manipulative character I had ever read, up there with the worst Shakespearean villains. It felt over the top.

"That's my mother," he said.

Stunned silence.

"Uh, what do you mean?"

"That's my mother."

"That's your mother??"

He nodded solemnly.

A million thoughts went through my head. First of which being, That's the end of this gig. My second thought was that if this guy hadn't gone into show business, he would've been a serial killer. Which is almost the same thing except there's less blood spilled in serial killing.

Not only did Chase not fire me even before he hired me, but as we were leaving he said he was more convinced than ever I could do it (number nine). Maureen, the real actor in the family, had studied with both Stella Adler and Herbert Berghof and had continued taking classes at HB for years. I read the scene with her, she gave me a few tips, and by the third time through, she thought I could handle it.

My friend Jay Cocks was the film critic at *Time* before he became the Rock critic, and his wife, Verna Bloom, was an acclaimed actress who had worked with Frank Sinatra and Clint Eastwood. I read with Jay and Verna, too, and they also were encouraging.

Frank Barsalona was careful, as always. He didn't trust any Artform he didn't control, and he knew he would not be there to protect me. "Do you think you can do it?"

"I don't know," I answered truthfully. "This first script is good, yeah, but what if the next one blows? What do I do then?"

He thought about that. "You tell them to fuck themselves and you split! What can they do? Make you act?"

Lance Freed was dead set against it. "You can't do this," he said. "You're an important Rock Artist. You are Mr. Credibility. You could throw away everything you've worked for your whole life!"

Peter Wolf tipped the scales. He had been one of my best friends for years. He left J. Geils at around the same time I left the E Street Band, and we both had Frank as a mentor. Plus, he had seen the film and TV business from the inside when he was involved with Faye Dunaway. We went to dinner and he thought about my plight.

"The thing about TV is, nobody remembers anything," he said. We were somewhere between our spaghetti and our second bottle of wine. "If it's a success, great! If not, no one will even know about it! Do you think anybody remembers Steve McQueen's TV show? Clint Eastwood? Jimmy Stewart? Lee Marvin? Warren Beatty was on *Dobie Gillis* for cris-sake! Definitely do it. Don't overthink it. If it bombs, it bombs. Nobody will care."

So now I had to figure out a philosophy of acting, a concept to make up for my lack of experience. I had heard all the accepted theories from Maureen—Stanislavski, Strasberg, Adler, Meisner, Hagen—frankly, they were beyond my intellect. So I had to make up my own.

I thought about it and decided that every human characteristic exists in everybody. From Gandhi to Hitler. From Wavy Gravy to Trump. The craft of acting (for me anyway) would be digging down and finding the appropriate characteristics of the character to be played. I then inhabit that part of me and bring it to life.

For me there would be one more necessity that lifelong actors may not need, and that was the physical transformation. I knew if I could look in the mirror and see the man, I could be the man.

I went to the gym and put on twenty-five pounds, eventually going to fifty. De Niro made the concept famous, but let me tell you, it worked for me. I said goodbye to the skinny Rocker, figuring I'd never need him again. I walked different, talked different. I didn't want anybody watching the show associating me with my previous profession.

I knew some guys who knew some guys, and I found out where John Gotti got his clothes made. He had just gone to jail, so the tailor suddenly had a lot of time on his hands.

The way I saw the character, he was a traditionalist, so I added a hairstyle that reflected his romantic reverence for the past.

I went down and read for Chase. He loved it. The part was mine. Almost. "We have to go to the West Coast and read for HBO," he said. "It's just a formality."

HBO's LA lobby was filled with other actors reading for various *Sopranos* parts. One guy, I recognized. Younger than me, a little heavy-set, balding. I had seen him in a couple of movies. *True Romance, Get Shorty*, not big parts but memorable ones. He stood out.

I quietly pointed him out to the casting girl, Sheila Jaffe, Georgianne Walken's partner at the time.

"Do you know who that is?" I said.

"No."

"Did you see *True Romance?*"

"Nope."

"Man! Nobody saw that movie! It's a supercool classic!"

"I'll rent it." Sheila was half a wiseguy herself.

"That's the guy who should play Tony Soprano."

Soon enough she would learn this journeyman character actor's name: Jimmy Gandolfini. But when I pointed him out she just looked at me like I had three heads.

And I did, in a sense. The acting world was very different than the music world, far more competitive. In Rock you go to a bar and say that you want to play. If they already have a band, you just go to the next bar. In the acting world, there are only so many parts, and way too many people want them. I'm quite sure no casting person had ever heard an actor say someone else should play the role they were reading for!

"Schmuck!" Sheila said. "You've got the friggin' part!"

"OK, OK, just saying . . ."

I read.

It was a mini–Roman Colosseum vibe, fifteen or twenty HBO people looking down from bleachers and me in the pit waiting for the lions to be released. I wasn't nervous going in, but the environment got me there pretty quick. Still, I got through it.

The next day, some of those bleacher people got back to David. "He's good," they said. "He can be in it. But no way are we giving the lead to a guy who's never acted before. This show is our biggest investment ever!"

The pilot had ended up at HBO because network after network had passed for one simple reason. David insisted on shooting in New Jersey rather than LA or New York. This simply was not done.

David called me to meet him somewhere, maybe the Polo Lounge at the Beverly Hills Hotel. "Sorry," he said. "They won't let me give you the lead. But you can have any other part you want."

"That's OK," I said. The whole thing was still completely surreal. I had spent the time since my Roman Colosseum experience running the opportunity by the people I trusted.

"Listen, David," I said. "I appreciate this opportunity, but I've been thinking about this, and I've got to tell you I've got mixed feelings about taking an actor's job. They train their whole lives. They take classes.

They dedicate their lives to this craft. I've seen my wife do it for years. So maybe it's better I say thank you and go back to where I belong."

He was unmoved. "I'm determined to have you in this," he said. "It just feels right to me. Your relationship to New Jersey is unimpeachable, and Jersey is going to play a major role in this thing. You don't want to take anybody's job? OK, I'll write you in a part. What do you want to do?"

Wow. You gotta love this guy, I'm thinking. He's nuts!

"Well . . . ," I said. Over the years, I had entertained fantasies about TV and the movies, though they ran more to writing and maybe directing. "I've got a treatment I had written about a character named Silvio Dante, an independent hit man, now semiretired, who owns a nightclub but still does diplomacy, conflict resolution, and an occasional special hit for the bosses."

My treatment was set in contemporary times, but both the character and his club lived in the past: big bands, Catskills-type Jewish comics, dancing girls, the whole schmear. All the Five Families had tables at Sil's place. The police commissioner and the mayor too. The intrigue began in the club. It was kind of like a Mob version of *Casablanca*.

David took my idea to HBO and then came back to me with good news, bad news. "They think the nightclub idea is too expensive. So we'll make it a strip club. You'll run it for the family, and you guys will use the back room as your social club / office."

Number ten.

And so, Bada Bing! A TV career was born.

The first meeting with the entire cast was at Silvercup Studios in Long Island City. It was a table read, where the cast goes through the entire script the day before shooting begins. It's a nice tradition because it's the only time the whole cast is together before splitting up into separate scenes.

I flashed on the first time I saw my brother Billy act. He was like, I don't know, twelve? A quiet, unassuming kid. You picture kid actors as the loud extroverted obnoxious type. He barely spoke. Out he comes, Alfred P. Doolittle in *My Fair Lady* singing "Get Me to the Church on Time" in a totally believable cockney accent! Completely blew my mind. I'm thinking, Man, I've got to act tomorrow. I hope I'm half as good as he was. So I'm half daydreaming, half following along, making sure I don't miss my lines, and midway through one of the early scenes, I looked up and directly across the table from me was Johnny Fucking Ola!

The guy who brought the orange from Hyman Roth to Michael Corleone as good luck in *The Godfather: Part II.*

Dominic Chianese. Now our Uncle Junior.

An electric current ran through my whole body.

The Godfather and *The Godfather: Part II* have a special, even sacred place for most of my generation. And for Italian Americans it was the *paisano Tao Te Ching.*

I was gonna be in a show with Johnny Ola! Suddenly the entire experience became real.

The strangest thing was that while I knew almost none of the other actors, they all knew me. I thought they might resent me invading their turf, but they were very respectful. Jimmy Gandolfini, who did get the lead role—luckily for all of us—was great with me right away, and everyone took their cues from him.

It took me a while to get used to the way TV worked.

For starters, you have to learn to accept that if the Director is happy, you're happy. And you have to take their word for it. You don't even see what you're doing. It was quite a shock artistically.

In the music business, you go in the studio, sing or play, go into the control room to listen to it, and do it again. You improve upon it or you don't. Each take has to be compared to the take before it, or the one after it, before you know if it's working. But you judge *yourself.*

Not in the acting world. Nobody wants actors looking at dailies. So I wouldn't see what I was doing for six months or so. I had to learn to live with that.

The other thing was that no one said anything to me. I was looking for a pat on the back, at least. I brought it up to Michael Imperioli. "Nobody's saying anything to me. That's bad, right?"

"No. That's good," he said. "That means you're not a problem."

HBO waited until the last possible moment to commit.

Me and Jimmy. Miss him every day. *Kevin Mazur*

(Facing page):
Gabriella and Silvio.
HBO

Top of the world, Ma!
Mad Magazine

Launch of the radio
show, 2002.
Renegade Nation

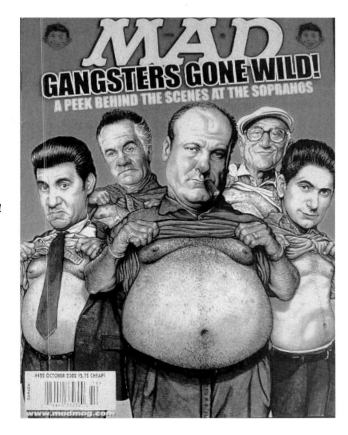

Steve Popovich, last of the great promo men. *Steve Popovich Jr.*

With Scott Greenstein, Keith Richards, Peter Wolf, and Benicio Del Toro, *Sopranos* premiere party, 2001. *Renegade Nation*

Richie Sambora killin' it on the Soulfire Tour. *Wicked Cool Records*

With Dion at the
TeachRock gala,
2019.
Renegade Nation

The Monday Night Football Band I assembled for Hank Williams Jr.:
Clarence Clemons, Bootsy Collins, Rick Nielsen, Charlie Daniels, Joe Perry,
Bernie Worrell, Questlove, Little Richard, Hank, and me. *Renegade Nation*

Jerry Lewis at the Friars Club in 2014. *Renegade Nation*

At the Emmys, 2006. *Steve Granitz*

With Tommy Karlsen Sandum, Ted Sarandos, Trond Fausa, and Fridtjov Saheim, *Lilyhammer* premiere, season two. **Laura Cavanaugh**

Michael Badalucco, Bruce, me, Tony Sirico, and Maureen in the final episode of *Lilyhammer*, my first directing job. **Netflix**

TeachRock seminar between the sound check and the show, Soulfire Teacher Solidarity Tour, Vancouver. *TeachRock*

With Catherine and Marc Brickman and Vinny Pastore at the *Once Upon a Dream* Broadway opening at Richard Rodgers Theater. *Bobby Bank*

Introducing Darlene Love. Renegade Studios, 2015. *Josh Goleman*

(*Above*): Lance Freed and
his sister Sieglinde with
David Porter at the Alan Freed
memorial in Cleveland.
David C. Barnett

(*Right*): With the legendary
Peter Rüchel in 2017.
Renegade Nation

Lowell "Banana" Levinger and Wavy Gravy—three Hippies forever!
Renegade Nation

Disciples of Soul. *Ryan Celli*

The family. *Renegade Nation*

Det. Danny Sprague, my founding partner Det. Kevin Schroeder, Officer Merit Riley, Det. Michael Paladino, Tony Sirico, Det. Brian Hunt, and honoree Jim Allen presenting checks to NYPD With Arms Wide Open and DEA Widows and Children Fund at Little Steven's Policeman's Ball, 2018. *Bobby Bank*

Me (as Wolfie) and Chris Columbus during the filming of *The Christmas Chronicles*. *Netflix*

Dr. Soulfire. *Bob Karp*

As Jerry Vale in *The Irishman*. *Netflix*

What can I say? *Kirsten Donovan*

I had met Robert Wuhl, who had a comedy, called *Arli$$*, on HBO about a sports agent. He invited me to an event for his season premiere the night before HBO's deadline for picking us up.

I'm not much of a socializer, but I thought I would go and talk to the executives, see what I could find out.

The brass were all there: Jeff Bewkes, Chris Albrecht, Richard Plepler. All E Street Band fans. I asked them what was happening with *Sopranos*.

"We've been looking for a partner this entire year," said Jeff. He explained again that the show was a big expense, two or three times what they'd spent on any other show up to that time. "We've had no luck."

"Geez," I said. "We all really love this thing. It's a little eccentric, but it's great."

Eccentric was an understatement. Of course I wouldn't have said it out loud, but I didn't know how commercial it was. A Mob guy sees ducks in his pool, and when they fly away he has a nervous breakdown that lands him in a psychiatrist's office? That's the premise of a hit show?

I went on. "But wouldn't that be good for a network like yours? No offense, give it a little identity?" At the time, HBO had been around forever but remained an unrealized potential. A few original shows, some sports programming, and movies that were mostly R-rated to give people a reason to subscribe. They got no respect whatsoever.

Jeff nodded.

It was hard to read successful executives. That's how they got where they are.

"I'm not saying turn into an Art channel," I said, "but why don't you turn into an Art channel?"

A raised eyebrow.

"You know, Art and porno!"

I got a half grin out of him, and then moved on to Chris Albrecht. Same noncommittal answers. They really hadn't made up their minds.

The next day they pulled the trigger. Pun intended.

We were on HBO!

The network was still fighting David on the title. They thought the audience would assume the show was about the opera. David didn't know what to do, so we strategized in constant multihour conversations, which we've never stopped having.

"That's ridiculous!" I told him. "Tell those fools names become the content. What's the stupidest name of a band you've ever heard? The Beatles! What's the second dumbest? The E Street Band! But nobody thinks they're so dumb anymore now, do they?"

"Yeah, I'll use that," he laughed.

I was still playing golf at the time.

Frank Barsalona had gotten into it and bugged me like crazy to join the torture. My father was a golfer, and one Father's Day I decided to learn so we could spend some quality time together, which we'd never done. We managed to play for a year or two before Alzheimer's got him in 1998. The world's most evil, despicable disease.

I had fifty "The Sopranos Are Coming" shirts printed up, and I gave them out to everybody at a televised MTV charity golf tournament. I was politicking every way and everywhere I could.

HBO wisely gave up and accepted the name.

In some ways, doing a big TV show was the same as doing *Darkness on the Edge of Town*. Lots of downtime. I don't mind working. Waiting, I can't do. Whether I was in the scene or not, I spent my time learning and observing.

Everyone got along OK, but we were a little distant from each other at first. That was the acting world. It wasn't arrogance on anyone's part. There was a tone of humility set from the top down. Jimmy was a character actor, no diva. But I was used to working in a more congenial atmosphere. A cast wasn't a band.

I had written an entire backstory for Silvio, mostly for myself, but I shared it with the writers. Sil was the only character David Chase hadn't created from scratch, and even though I knew he would adjust as we went, I wanted them to have a place to start.

In the fictional bio, I wrote that Sil had grown up with Tony, that they had been best friends since they were kids. In my story, Tony was a year or two older and was always the big-picture guy, big ideas and big ambitions. Sil was a soldier, more street-smart, perfectly happy being underboss as well as consigliere and watching Tony's back. Chase would make Sil older of course, since I was, but keep the consigliere idea intact.

So after seven years in the wilderness, eighteen years after my last semisteady job in the E Street Band, thanks to the caprices of Destiny and only ten twists of Fate, I had finally, miraculously, found a new career. Something I could do for the rest of my life. I was determined to give it my undivided attention and effort.

Rrrrrrrrring.

"Stevie?"

"Yeah."

"Bruce."

"Hey, man."

"It's time to put the band back together."

twenty-five

Cross Road Blues

(1999–2001)

I went to the crossroads, fell down on my knees.
I went to the crossroads, fell down on my knees
Asked the Lord above, "Have mercy now,
*   save Poor Bob if you please."*
—ROBERT JOHNSON, "CROSS ROAD BLUES"

The reasons not to go back to E Street were obvious.

I had a chance at a whole new career as an actor.

That could lead to writing, which I was already doing on the side.

And that could lead to directing, which had always interested me.

And finally, to producing. The big picture. Overseeing all the details of a project. The ultimate goal.

Never mind that in my life plan, I kept getting to first base but couldn't make it to second. And never mind asking an audience to redefine me a third or fourth time. If I wasn't a performer, if what I did was behind the scenes—writing, directing, producing—I would only have to worry about how much an audience liked my work, not how much they liked me.

Another reason not to go back was that the dynamics of the organization had changed.

I'd given up my position as underboss and consigliere when I left. Bruce was now, more than ever, treated by the organization as a solo act. I would have no control or input whatsoever.

How would it feel being a real sideman for the first time? When I left back in the early '80s, Bruce hired Nils Lofgren to play my guitar parts and Patti Scialfa to sing my vocal parts.

So what would my role be in the reformed band, exactly?

The more I thought about it, the more I realized it would be the same as it always was. The role that couldn't be replaced. I would be the lifelong best friend. I was fine with that. In fact, I'd just been cast in the same role in *The Sopranos.*

The bio of Sil I had given the writers had helped them a little bit, but the character was still coming into focus as the show got started. Halfway through the first season, I realized I could use my relationship with Bruce as the emotional basis of Silvio's relationship with Tony, because I knew exactly what the job entailed.

Dreaming together, planning and strategizing, sharing the good times and the bad, suffering the undeserved wrath when bringing bad news that only you could bring because you were the only one who wasn't afraid of the Boss. They were all part of the job. Of both jobs.

Back in the late '80s, years after I had left the band, Bruce had me over to hear his follow-up to *Born in the USA, Tunnel of Love*, at his house in Rumson. I listened. *Tunnel* felt like a solo record, for starters. There were still great songs, but they were smaller in scope, with more personal lyrics. "And what's up with that first song, 'Ain't Got You'?" I asked. "I got this, I got that, and I got Rembrandts on the wall?!?"

"What?" he said. "That's how it is."

"I know you're trying to be funny," I said. "But it's only funny if it's *not* true! If it was a line from a Dave Van Ronk song, we'd all have a good laugh about it, right? Look, I'm sure it's more than a little weird to be rich and famous after almost forty years of being poor and struggling, and I know you're trying to come to grips with how that new reality fits with your working-class persona, but damn!"

"Well," he says, "in a certain way—an exaggerated way—I'm just being honest about my life."

"Honest?" I was getting kind of worked up. "About *your* life? I hate to tell you this, but nobody gives a fuck about *your* life! Your gift, your job, your genius is telling people about *their* lives! Helping them understand *their* mostly fucked-up existence! Letting them know that you under-stand what they're going through and that they are not alone."

"Oh, man," he said. "You're totally nuts! It's just a little humor!"

"People depend on your empathy!" I said. "It's what you do best. They don't want advice from Liberace or empathy from Nelson Fucking Rockefeller! You shouldn't be writing shit like this!"

He said I was crazy, overreacting like I did with everything, that no one else had complained about it. We yelled and screamed for a while and then he threw me out.

It was the second of our three fights.

We got over it.

I was right, of course. Like I always am when it came to giving advice to my friends. Because I care about them. A little too much, to be hon-est. Friendship is a sacred thing to me, and I can't be casual about it. I don't know where that comes from. But I realized early in life that if I'm going to have friends, the friendship has to be defined on their terms. Because nobody is as extreme as me. It's a flaw I can't fix.

So where was I? Oh, yeah. The cons and pros of going back to E Street.

There was the money.

Well, not really, because even though it was more than I made my first year of acting, they would soon even out.

Bruce has always kept us the cheapest concert ticket in the business while doing the most work. It's a Jersey work ethic thing. It was a typ-ically unprecedented moral gesture from Bruce for the benefit of the working class.

But lately it was getting harder and harder to keep the tickets away from the scalpers.

It didn't matter anyway, because my allergy to money would never allow me to make a decision based on it.

No, it was all about the closure.

I shouldn't have left in the first place.

It didn't matter how justified it might have felt at the time, or what I had learned and accomplished since. It felt like I had fucked with Destiny, interrupted what was supposed to be, and abandoned my best friend when he needed me most.

I also felt the band's place in history needed to be secured. We were slowly vanishing from the mass consciousness. When magazines did their annual polls of best bands, or even best American bands, we had always been top five. But recently we had started to slip off the charts.

I wasn't big on competition. But all due respect, shouldn't we be ranked higher than the Spin Doctors?

One day, too, the band should be in the Rock and Roll Hall of Fame, and it would be best to be active if that day was ever to come.

There was a broader principle too. It had occurred to me somewhere along the way that we needed to preserve this endangered species called Rock. And not because it happened to be my main Artform of choice. Because there was something different about the Rock idiom's ability to communicate substance.

Folk music passes along stories and allegories. Blues talks about the conditions of life. Jazz operates through mostly wordless intellect. Soul is all about relationships. Rock has substance and the ability to communicate it worldwide. And that includes its greatest hybrid, Reggae. Bob Marley was the ultimate example. Got to be neck and neck with Muhammad Ali for most well-known human on the planet. Get Tim White's book on Marley. Incredible. I mentioned it once earlier, but I want you to remember it.

It's why I was so interested in Hip-Hop when it started. The early Rappers were carrying on the Rock tradition. Emotional information. Sometimes literal information. Inspiration. Motivation. Education. Melle Mel, Grandmaster Flash, Duke Bootee, Run-DMC, Ice-T, N.W.A., KRS-One, all the way to Public Enemy, Wu-Tang Clan, and Rage Against the Machine.

But Hip-Hop didn't turn out to be as consistent as I hoped it would be. Got a little too comfortable with the hedonism aspect, like Rock before it.

One more reason to go back to E Street?

Bruce.

I liked being with him. Always have. I still got a kick out of him as a performer. He still made me laugh. I still marveled at the fact that my shy best friend had become one of the world's greatest entertainers.

And if we could adapt to being back together, we'd not just get back what we had, but maybe even take it further.

Tony and Sil ride again!

David Chase made my decision a little easier by scheduling my scenes on days off the tour. It was an amazing thing to do and added to the infinite gratitude I already owed him for giving me a new craft.

Of course, my role became smaller if I toured. And I'd never get to write and direct *The Sopranos*.

But for the next seven years I found a way to be in a TV show and a touring Rock and Roll band at the same time.

Flew home and back every day off. Never missed a day on the set, never missed a gig.

Two Bosses, two worlds. One fictional, based on reality, and one real, reinforced by fiction.

A circumstance as improbable as it was unpredictable.

A reconciliation of brothers.

There was work left to do.

twenty-six

Gangster Days / Garage Nights

(2002–2004)

Get really good at one thing, and the whole world
will open up for you.

—THE UNWRITTEN BOOK

Lenny Kaye always had a good imagination.

Which is a big help when one is trying to survive growing up in New Jersey. One of the few subjects I know everything about.

He was in Rock bands like the Vandals by the mid-'60s and simultaneously creating sci-fi fanzines like *Obelisk*.

He was also a successful journalist for *Crawdaddy, Hit Parader,* and *Rolling Stone* while working at Village Oldies on Bleecker Street. That's where he met Patti Smith, which is why you know her name today.

I'm going to briefly digress with a huge mea culpa.

As a member of the nominating committee of the Rock and Roll Hall of Fame I've done OK. But not in 2007.

That was the year I was unable to convince the other committee members that the Patti Smith Group needed to go in, as opposed to Patti Smith solo, because, as history knows full well, there was no such thing as Patti Smith solo.

The reason she made the transition from poet to Rock star was Lenny Kaye, 100 percent.

Ask her!

My comrades remained irrationally unconvinced.

So him not being in the Rock Hall pisses me off every day. There's a growing list of self-disappointments, but it's high on that list.

Before Lenny met Patti, he curated a crazy compilation album for Elektra Records called *Nuggets*. It didn't make any commercial sense, so the label president, Jac Holzman, deserves credit for going along with it.

The album, which originally came out in 1972, was full of '60s artists of no consequence who immediately achieved immortality as ground zero influences on Garage Rock, Pub Rock, and Punk Rock.

Cut to 1998.

Mark "Twig" Greenberg would, from time to time, mention he'd been in a band.

You remember Twig? On our softball team, introduced me to Maureen, became one of my lifelong best friends.

So out came this glorious new Rhino Records edition of *Nuggets*, not just a reissue but a mind-blowing expansion magnificently curated by my friend Gary Stewart that added sixty tracks to Lenny's original double album.

And would you believe it? One of the new tracks was a track from Richard and the Young Lions, which turned out to be Twig's band from the '60s!

Holy Shit.

At the same time, a guy named Jon Weiss, who had been the lead singer of a band called the Vipers in the '80s, had been promoting a series of Garage Rock shows called Cavestomp! that both reassembled classic '60s bands and booked new bands who fit the genre.

He called Twig to reunite the Young Lions, and Twig invited me to the show. I had no idea what to expect. They hadn't played together in like thirty years.

When I got to the Westbeth Theatre on Bank Street, the joint was packed and the crowd was buzzing. Turns out Richard and the Young Lions had attained mythological Garage status, like the Sonics from Tacoma, the Moving Sidewalks from Houston, or Thee Midniters from East LA.

The lights dimmed, the crowd rose up, the walls began to sweat, and on they came, blasting into one of their three singles, "Open Up Your Door!"

Twig was on drums, Louie Vlahakes on guitar, Fred Randall on bass, and Rick Robinson on keyboards. In the center of the stage was a little old man straight out of *Lord of the Rings*, the legendary Richard Tepp, hunched over, mic clutched in his clawlike hands, looking like he was . . . not singing . . . more like summoning demons from hell, resembling not so much Richard the Lionheart as Shakespeare's Richard III. He eloquently croaked out the lyrics, the palpable drama enhanced by the audience's uncertainty of whether or not he would expire before the end of each song.

It was fucking glorious!

I fell in love instantly with the unlikeliest front man in history. He was Johnny Rotten as a three-hundred-year-old sorcerer! Amazing.

Jon Weiss had been struggling with Cavestomp!, so I became his partner to help keep the idea alive. He had been going from one venue to another like a floating craps game staying one step ahead of the cops. We needed a more stable location where our particular audience of freaks, misfits, and outcasts could find us.

I hooked Weiss up with Steve Weitzman, who booked Tramps and had a new venue I thought would be perfect, the Village Underground on Third Street.

Weiss would be at least partly responsible for bringing back the Zombies and the Music Machine, front men like Mark Lindsay from Paul Revere and the Raiders, and many others.

But we never quite jelled. No bad blood, no arguments. It was simply that the longer I knew him, the less I liked him. So after a year or so of monthly shows—and loaning him money he did not pay back—we parted company.

For the first time in a long while I started listening to the radio, and I was underwhelmed by what I heard.

Classic Rock was now a narrow subgenre that consisted of the same five hundred songs. They were great records, but even great records start to lose their luster when repeated that often. And nothing new was allowed into the format to update the repertoire. I mean *nothing*. If the same artist that was played every two hours released a new record, Classic Rock wouldn't play it.

And on top of all that, "oldies" stations were now playing songs from the '70s and '80s!

Uh-oh, I thought. "Oldies" was never meant to be a chronological term. It meant the music of the '50s and early '60s, the original pioneers through their progeny, the Naissance and Renaissance! Worse, sliding the category later and later in time began to erase the '60s themselves, the peak, the pinnacle, the summit of the Artform.

Rock radio disregarding the '50s and '60s because they were too old was the equivalent of a classical music format disregarding Bach, Beethoven, Mozart, and Tchaikovsky because *they* were too old.

The DJs had become as homogenized as the playlists. Their hands were tied. Out of the thousands of DJs playing Rock music in America, I knew of only two, Vin Scelsa in New York and Jim Ladd in LA, who kept playing whatever they wanted. They are both off the air as I write this, though Ladd is forever immortalized by Tom Petty's *The Last DJ.*

Personality vanished too. Most of the educated, experienced, passionate, and interesting voices went to talk and sports radio or were unceremoniously retired. The audience and ratings went with it, but nobody in the boardroom seems to have noted this "coincidence."

Rock radio had shaped my life, saved my life, inspired me, motivated me, given me a reason to live every day when I had nothing to relate to, nothing to do, nothing to hope for. First AM radio, with WABC and WMCA, then FM with WNEW, and oldies with WCBS-FM.

What the fuck happened? For a detailed account, I suggest Richard Neer's book *FM: The Rise and Fall of Rock Radio,* which remains the most accurate explanation of the tragic story.

I don't know why exactly, but I'm attracted to gaps and injustice and have a missionary conversion complex that refuses to tolerate the bland, the banal, and the boring. I have some bizarre flaw that wants the world to be perfect. And colorful. And interesting. And fun.

Suddenly I felt it was time to start a new radio format. Or two.

OK. So if I had the power to create any format I wanted, what would it be?

I knew I had to start with the center of my universe, the British Invasion, which had changed my life and affected virtually everyone else's.

That meant 1964–1967, roughly.

What it also meant was bands.

The British bands were more or less divided between Pop- and Rock-oriented bands, mostly from the north, and the Blues- and Soul-oriented bands, mostly out of London but stretching all the way to Birmingham and Newcastle.

The bands from the north were led by the Beatles and included the Searchers, the Hollies, Herman's Hermits, and Gerry and the Pacemakers from Liverpool and Manchester, along with the Dave Clark Five from Tottenham.

The Blues and R&B groups, mostly from the south, were led by the Rolling Stones and included the Kinks, the Yardbirds, the Animals, the Spencer Davis Group, the Moody Blues, the Who, and Manfred Mann.

I included a few solo artists and duos: Billy Fury, Dusty Springfield, Tom Jones, Petula Clark, Donovan, Billy J. Kramer (the "J." was suggested by John Lennon to toughen him up!), Georgie Fame, Peter and Gordon, and Chad and Jeremy.

And the more obscure but important bands that never invaded: the Pretty Things, the Creation, the Move, the Birds, the Eyes, the Action, and others.

That would be the basis of my format. Along with those core groups, I'd add everybody that influenced the British Invasion, and everybody the British Invasion influenced.

I combined all fifty years of the Rock era (it's now seventy!), and divided my favorite records into categories:

— Blues (Muddy Waters, Howlin' Wolf, Little Walter, etc.)

— Pioneers (Little Richard, Chuck Berry, Jerry Lee Lewis, etc.)

— Doo-Wop (Dubs, Chantels, Little Anthony and the Imperials, etc.)

— R&B (Sam Cooke, Ray Charles, Jackie Wilson, etc.)

— Girl Groups (the Shirelles, the Crystals, the Shangri-Las, etc.)

— Surf and surf instrumentals (Beach Boys, Jan and Dean, the Ventures, etc.)

— Soul (the Miracles, the Impressions, Sam and Dave, etc.)

— British Invasion (those already named, obviously, along with those from the second half of the '60s, including Them, Procol Harum, Traffic, etc.)

— Folk Rock (Bob Dylan, the Byrds, the Lovin' Spoonful, etc.)

— Country Rock (the Youngbloods, Buffalo Springfield, Moby Grape, etc.)

— Psychedelic (the Jimi Hendrix Experience, Jefferson Airplane, the Doors, etc.)

— Blues Rock (Cream, the Jeff Beck Group, Led Zeppelin, etc.)

— Southern Soul (Delaney and Bonnie, the Band, Leon Russell, etc.)

— *Nuggets* (the bands on the original compilation and the reissue, the Blues Magoos, Count Five, the Standells, etc.)

Beyond that, I gave each decade from the '70s its own category and added New Garage.

I then decided how often each category would appear in radio rotation. The Beatles and Stones every hour, Girl Groups every other hour, pioneers every third, and so on.

We might play some of the same bands as Classic Rock radio, but never the same songs. They'd play "Brown Sugar"; we'd play "Confessing the Blues." They'd play "Hey Jude"; we'd play "Doctor Robert." They'd play "Won't Get Fooled Again"; we'd play "The Good's Gone."

Voilà! A new format!

DJ Dan Neer, the brother of DJ Richard, learned how to engineer as I learned how to DJ. We worked hard on the pilot over a couple of months, and sent out 350 copies to every radio station.

It landed on their desks on September 11, 2001.

Yeah—*that* 9/11.

Maureen and I were living on Fifty-Seventh Street at the time. I woke up, put the TV on, and saw a plane sticking out of one of the World Trade Center towers. What the fuck? Had to be a pilot's heart attack, I figured. Or some really drunken asshole . . .

As I was saying to Maureen, "Baby, come here, you gotta see this. Some jerkoff . . ."

Boom! I saw the second plane hit the other.

I was stunned for a minute.

Like the time the white cab driver tried to hit the black guy in Pretoria.

You can't quite put together what your eyes have just told your brain.

Uh-oh. Two ain't no accident.

We were under motherfucking attack!

"Holy shit," Maureen said. "What do we do now? We are in the wrong town for World War III."

My mind was going a hundred miles an hour. No idea what to do. She was so right.

Hearing that a third plane got as far as the Pentagon was not at all encouraging. How many hundreds of billions on defense every year? And some fucking cave dweller drove a plane into the fucking Pentagon?

It understandably took a few weeks before things settled down and radio stations resumed reading their mail.

They all passed.

And I mean all: 350 stations.

I analyzed the situation. I knew I was onto something good musically, but we were obviously going about it all wrong. We were sending the show to the Program Directors, but they didn't run anything anymore. This was America. What's America all about?

Money.

I asked Richie Russo, a radio advertising sales guy and avid record collector (and I mean avid; he has one house for himself and another for his records), "How does this radio racket work?"

He told me they sold advertising by the week and sometimes by the month. I couldn't believe it, but it turned out to be true. Why not by the year?

I started talking to the General Managers. My basic rap was this: If I sell out my weekly two-hour show for a year, would you let your Program Director decide whether he wants it or not?

"Sure," they said.

"OK," I said. "Give me a list of your top ten sponsors." I started calling them, occasionally flying to meet them in person, and got on my first twenty stations, all sold out for a year.

At first, nobody thought that playing that range of music in one place could work, but we proved otherwise. It was just a matter of connecting the dots. And I knew which dots were connected. It's not something an outsider would ever understand, but there was, and still is, a method to the madness.

In the end, the *Underground Garage* show served three main purposes. It made the greatest Rock music in history accessible to future generations. It gave new Rock bands the only airplay they would ever get; we've introduced more than a thousand bands in the last twenty years. And it gave me a chance to say thank you to the greatest generation of Rock Artists. Not only do we play their best music, but if they kept making records (and many of them have—the Rolling Stones, Paul McCartney, Ringo Starr, Dion, the Zombies, the Beach Boys, plus slightly younger artists like Joan Jett and Cheap Trick), there was at least one place that would play it.

We brought in a friend of Dan Neer's, Mark Felsot, to be our in-house syndicator, and off we went.

We peaked at 130 affiliates in the United States alone, and although we're off that peak now, we make up for it by being in a hundred countries on the American Forces Network.

In our second year BBC Two offered me $20,000 per show before I got the chance to say they could have it for free! We shook hands, and I got on a plane. Tragically, by the time I landed, they'd changed their mind. They suddenly didn't want it at any price and never told me why. But we belong there. BBC Two covers the entire UK. We play more great British music than they ever will!

We had amazing ratings those first few years, with no promotion whatsoever.

I was touring with the E Street Band during the first years of the format, so wherever I was, I made a point of visiting my affiliates and going in to record stores and asking if there were any local bands making records. We were checking out everything.

Rock was at an all-time low when we started. We knew every Rock record that was being released worldwide. That's how few there were then.

It became a clear case of "If you build it, they will come." Each band that heard themselves on the radio for the first time was motivated to improve. Every next record was always better.

It had to be the same when Ronan O'Rahilly started Radio Caroline and changed history.

Ronan was born in Dublin in 1940. He was the grandson of Michael O'Rahilly, a leader of the Easter Rising in the fight for Irish independence in 1916—so he had rebel's blood.

He came to London in 1957 to study acting. By 1963, he was running a club called the Scene and managing Georgie Fame and Alexis Korner.

The BBC didn't play much Pop music at the time, so English fans had to try and dial in Radio Luxembourg; that was spotty at best, and the station's broadcast time was legally bought by the major record companies.

Out of frustration, Ronan bought a seven-hundred-ton Danish passenger ferry and anchored it in international waters, and Radio Caroline (named after President Kennedy's daughter) broadcast the British Invasion back to Britain.

England desperately needed it.

In America, we had great AM radio from the mid-'50s until 1967 and great FM radio after that. The British depended on getting records from seagoing servicemen or ordering them through the mail (like the very enterprising, very young Mick Jagger).

The historic significance of what Ronan did cannot be overstated.

His grateful Nation considered him such a threat for having a direct connection to teenagers that—the rumor went—the government seriously considered having him assassinated.

The rumor went on to say that it was his good taste that saved him. Half the Special Air Service listened to his station and refused to whack him!

A similar thing happened to Frank Sinatra: The Mob helped Joe Kennedy get JFK elected and the first thing Bobby Kennedy did was go after organized crime. Sinatra had been the intermediary in the deal, so the Mob debated whether to take him out to teach the Kennedys a lesson. But Sam Giancana and several others supposedly said they liked Sinatra's voice too much, so they let it go.

The bottom line is, Art saves lives!

After word of a possible hit leaked, the wrong kind of hit, Ronan became a paranoid recluse, relocating constantly for the rest of his life. After quite a search, I found him and actually got him out to see an

E Street show in the early 2000s. Only time I met him. Great guy. A hero who deserves a statue in Trafalgar Square. Though he might have been more comfortable in SoHo.

Meanwhile, back on *The Sopranos*, Jimmy Gandolfini wasn't handling being a leading man very well. It just wasn't his natural inclination. He was a character actor, a great one, and that's what he liked doing.

He wasn't used to the long dialogues he had to do regularly with Lorraine Bracco, who played his psychiatrist.

In film, you might do two pages of script a day. In TV, you might do five or six or seven. And half or more of those were Jimmy! One paragraph is a lot to memorize. Try it.

We'd work from six in the morning to nine or ten at night, and then he'd have to go home and learn the next day's work.

Your brain is like a muscle, so it does adapt, but at first the work seemed impossible. So he quit every day. Sometimes disappear for a few days.

We'd take turns going out drinking with him. Sometimes it was me. Sometimes it was Michael Imperioli. Sometimes Stevie Schirripa once he came in, Bobby Funaro, a teamster or two.

Jimmy wanted out.

We'd have the same conversation at least once a month.

"Look," I'd say to him, "how many good movies you see last year?" He'd say, Like ten. "OK," I'd say, "if you're lucky, you're gonna get one of those, right?" Right. "You're not gonna get two, are you?" Probably not. "So you do that movie in between seasons. You don't lose a thing."

"Yeah," he'd say. "I guess." Then skip out for a few days anyway.

But he always came back.

I talked to David about it after the third or fourth time. "David," I said, "you have created like twelve interesting characters, every one of which could have their own spin-off series. Everyone would watch them. Can't you lighten up on Jimmy a little bit?"

Nope. David just fell in love with Jimmy. Could not get enough. And you really couldn't blame him. Jimmy was playing an exaggerated version of David himself, complete with mother issues. *The Sopranos* was the most effective therapy David could get!

During those first seasons, we were also watching Nancy March-and battle the horror of emphysema. The minute a scene ended, they slapped an oxygen mask on her. I'm sure that helped me and Tony Sirico quit smoking. I had smoked from my teens until 1977, and then from 1982 on, to the point where I was up to three packs a day. Quitting was hard. Without smoking, I had no energy. I couldn't concentrate. It used to be that you could give me a pot of coffee and a pack of cigarettes and I could write ten pages in a sitting. Suddenly, nothing. It panicked me for a while because I was writing a twenty-five-page script every week for my radio show. I literally could not write for weeks. Not a word. Slowly, my body worked it out.

But how hip were David Chase and HBO for hiring someone with emphysema? Just hiring someone older was unusual. My brother Billy was in TV the whole first half of his life (he's got a great book about it, *Get in the Car, Jane!*), and he was a big fan of older actors, but the networks always gave him a hard time about hiring them.

And Sil got a new wife. Sort of. During the first season, we only saw his wife a few times. As Sil's character developed, David decided he was not only the consigliere but also a kind of ambassador to the outside world. So as the writers emphasized the "showbiz" connection in the family (after all, he was running a strip club!), they decided I needed more of a trophy-type wife, maybe a former showgirl.

When they decided to recast, either Georgianne or Sheila called Maureen and suggested she audition. Like I said, she's actually the actor in the family. I've seen her do serious drama: Tennessee Williams, Miller, Ibsen. She went down and read with a hundred other girls. That was one of the things about the show. They didn't do any favors. Edie Falco's mother auditioned to play her character Carmela's mother and didn't get the part. I never knew Maureen had auditioned until she got the part.

It was fun for her to revisit the old neighborhood—she grew up in Newark, right near where the show is set. Unfortunately, Maureen and I didn't get to be on-screen together much. There was one arc late in the show when Tony was in the hospital and Silvio was temporary boss, and we had a few nice scenes together. Otherwise, she was with the girls and I was at the Bing.

Over those first seasons, the cast warmed up to each other. We were mostly all from Jersey or New York. I was determined to do whatever I could do to turn the Sopranos into a Rock band.

Speaking of which, I happened to be in an actual Rock band at the time.

When the E Street Band was in Zurich, we spent a night off seeing a Bob Dylan show at the Hallenstadion. About halfway through, a guy came over to me and Nils and said Bob wanted us to play the encore.

I don't usually do it, but sitting in with someone onstage usually includes rehearsing something at soundcheck, but this was parachuting blindly into the chaos.

I walked on and said hi to my friend Charlie Sexton, who was just beginning his run with Bob's band. A roadie was desperately trying to hook up a guitar and amp for me. The audience was on their feet going nuts. Bob came over. "Hey," he said. "I saw you on TV!"

"Yeah, Bob. I'm doing some acting now."

"Oh, man. You were wearing a wig!"

"Yeah, well . . ." My mother had said something similar. She had watched an entire scene with me and rewound the take only because my voice sounded familiar. "You see, the character . . ."

The roadie was trying to adjust the guitar strap. I was half talking to Bob and half adjusting the tone to something in between a clean rhythm and a dirty lead in case he threw me a solo.

"Man, I wasn't sure it was you!"

Bob was so comfortable on the road that he might as well have been in his living room. That's how he arranged his band onstage. Very close to each other, like a club, even though he was playing a ten-thousand-seat arena.

"Well, that's the idea, Bob . . . uh . . ." The crowd was screaming louder. "How about I tell you all about it a little later?"

We played "Not Fade Away" and never did finish the conversation. Always memorable seeing Mr. Dylan.

One day a guy came to me from this new thing called XM Satellite Radio. My radio show had been on for a few years, kicking ass all over the country.

The XM guy said he wanted my show on this new satellite format. He wasn't offering much.

"First of all," I said, "to create my two-hour weekly show, I had to create an entire format. I have a whole channel ready to go."

"Whoa," he said. "Let's not get ahead of ourselves!"

As we talked, I realized that he thought he was in the hardware business—that the ultimate purpose of the company was selling radios!

"You don't understand what you've got here," I said. "You should be *giving* the radios away. The money is gonna be in the monthly content subscriptions. That's the business model of the future. HBO proved it!"

He looked at me like, Why do I even bother talking to these idiotic Artists?, and said he'd get back to me.

I wasn't holding my breath.

Chris Columbus recommended me to Joe Roth for music supervision on a movie called *Christmas with the Kranks*, and Joe became a good friend.

We staged a national *Underground Garage* Battle of the Bands, which aired on MTV.

Joe Strummer died, and Bruce and I played a tribute to him on the Grammy telecast with Dave Grohl and Elvis Costello.

Meanwhile, my friend Scott Greenstein got a gig at the rival satellite radio company, Sirius.

I met Scott sometime in the '90s; I would run into him from time to time at clubs and events. We became friendly. One night at a party, he asked if I could give him a little advice.

At that time, Scott was a lawyer at Viacom, and he wanted to make a move. He asked how he could make a connection to MTV.

"You don't want to be at MTV," I said. "They're on their way out of music. They're doing teenage reality programming, and it's gonna be a whole different scene. What other offers you got?"

He rattled off a bunch of companies.

"Wait," I said. "What was that last one again?"

"Miramax," he said.

"Well," I said. "Let me tell you something. Through learning the hard way, I've come to realize creating content is only half the story. Marketing is the other half. Except it's actually not two different things. It's two halves of the same thing."

I was a little bit of an expert in this area. I had been creating things my whole life that nobody knew about.

"I only know one thing about Miramax. Whenever they have a new movie out, I always know about it. That means whoever is calling the shots has real balls and knows what he's doing."

So Scott took the gig at Miramax with the infamous Weinstein brothers. After a few weeks, he came back for more advice. He had never been in a situation like this; one minute a lawyer was pushing papers around, the next he was in the social center of showbiz, celebrities, Agents, Managers, Publicists, all that. It was disorienting.

"You want to get things done?" I said. "Make contact with the Artists directly. Get close to the people who matter. The actors and Directors. Everybody else, the Managers, Agents, lawyers, accountants—they're all a pain in the ass. It's part of their job. What they do best is say *no. Fershtay?*"

I've given a lot of people a lot of good advice. Sometimes they take it, sometimes they don't. I have never seen a guy learn so fast in my whole freakin' life as Scott.

He went from a quiet shy lawyer nobody had ever heard of to the schmooze king of the world in like two years, and he ended up the number three guy at Miramax.

Let me say right here that neither Scott nor I ever witnessed anything having to do with Harvey Weinstein's horrifying sex life. When the news came out, we could not believe it was the same guy.

But other things began to worry me.

Scott had become close with the actors and Directors, like I suggested, and Harvey began to take advantage of Scott and use him as his hit man. Since Scott was friends with everybody, Harvey let *him* deliver the bad news.

Harvey was very good at knowing what was commercial, but he started to get heavy-handed, pissing off Directors and Producers by editing their pictures without their involvement.

I believe it came down to a Sean Penn project. Harvey was fucking with Sean. Scott had gotten friendly with Sean, as I was (my brother Billy had been in the movie *Taps* with him), and now Scott was caught between Sean and Harvey.

"Scott," I said. "That's it. I suggested you go there, now I'm telling you to get out. You've come a long way in a very short time, but you're gonna blow all your relationships if you stay there one minute longer. Your reputation has to be one where you are always on the side of the Artists and not the company. Get the fuck out."

Once again, Scott wisely listened. He got another gig at USA Films, won an Oscar or two, and eventually ended up as a consultant at Sirius.

XM, the first satellite radio company, was promoting the hell out of itself, something Sirius has never learned to do to this day.

"What can we do?" Scott said to me. "How do we compete?"

I looked at the existing content at both networks. "Everybody's treating this thing like it's regular terrestrial radio in the sky," I said. "It's a new medium. What would be hip is new-style content. Like mine for a start, which is ready to go."

"Obviously," he said. "But what else?"

I gave him a list of ideas, from a poetry channel that would feature the Beats and more (Langston Hughes, Kerouac, Maya Angelou, Ginsberg, Amiri Baraka, Ferlinghetti, the Dark Room Collective, Nikki Giovanni, etc.), to TV channels on the radio like CNN, to music channels devoted to individual artists.

"Why do that?" he said. I told him regular radio wasn't playing the greatest music ever made anymore. And since the Renaissance was over, there were only a finite number of truly great artists. They needed to be accessible at all times for future generations.

"You will be the museum where the Rembrandts, Renoirs, and Dalis hang," I said. "Where on radio can you hear Frank Sinatra? Elvis Presley? Nowhere. The Beatles? The Stones? On a regular basis? Only on my station. The best artists, from the Byrds to Led Zeppelin to Springsteen to U2 to Pearl Jam, should have their own stations."

No matter what was trendy, I said, people still wanted to hear the greatest music ever made.

"And by the way, I have a second format ready to go."

A quick digression (I should call this book *Unrequited Digressions*).

Ten years earlier, Lance Freed, my publisher, had sent me to Nashville to meet a wild dude named David Conrad who was running his Nashville office. I love characters, and he was one.

At the time, a new guy named Billy Ray Cyrus had a monster hit, "Achy Breaky Heart." The single was so big that the wiser executives felt he needed his next record to establish some credibility, or he'd be a flash in the pan. They asked me to write a song for him.

I didn't have the heart to tell them that if you don't start with credibility, it's a long slow climb up that mountain, but what the hell, I went. I had nothing better to do. Plus I was feeling grateful to Lance.

Billy was in the studio working on a new album. He turned out to be a really great guy. Probably as confused about what I was doing there as I was.

After the session, his band was packing up. "What's going on?" I said.

"We've got a gig tonight," he said.

"A gig? In the middle of recording?"

"Yeah. You don't do that in the Rock world?"

Fuck no.

We got to the arena. The crowd was coming in, and his band was setting up their own equipment.

In front of everybody.

I was appalled.

"Billy," I said. "What the fuck? You have a big hit. You're a big star. This is your *band*. They don't have to do that anymore, if they ever did!"

"Well," he said, "we have kind of an old-school Manager and he likes to save money, I guess."

After the show, the artist was obligated to go to a special fan area and sign autographs for an hour or two!

The Country world was sure different.

During that trip, I met Tony Brown, who had been Elvis Presley's piano player and was now a successful Producer running his own company. I was expressing my shock that Johnny Cash was no longer welcome at Country Radio.

"I can't get anything I do on the radio anymore!" he said. "George Jones, the Mavericks, Emmylou Harris."

"How do you establish a new format?" I asked him.

"Damned if I know," Tony laughed, "but if you ever figure it out, let me know. We sure could use it."

While I was there, I wrote Billy Ray a cool song that he didn't use. Somebody somewhere in Nashville has a hit sitting in a desk drawer waiting to happen.

And, by the way, Billy ended up doing just fine, and I'm very happy about his continued success. Nice when the good guys win.

So I started the format Tony was waiting for; I called it "Outlaw Country." It begins with the classics: Johnny Cash, Waylon Jennings, Willie Nelson, Kris Kristofferson, David Allan Coe, at the least. I added all three generations of Hank Williams; Alt-Country like Jason and the Scorchers, Uncle Tupelo, Drive-By Truckers; in-betweeners like Emmylou Harris, Delbert McClinton, Dwight Yoakam; newer Country like Sturgill Simpson, Kacey Musgraves, Jason Isbell, Margo Price, Hellbound Glory; and, finally, the Country side of Rock, the Byrds, Dylan, Buffalo Springfield, the Youngbloods, Moby Grape, the Flying Burrito Brothers, the Band, the Eagles, Jackson Browne, and Bruce.

How could the Band have no format? They had one now. But I didn't know what to do with it until almost a decade later, when I told Scott Greenstein that I had a second format ready to go.

"Don't you think we should get the first one going first?"

"Nope. This is too important to wait another minute."

For both formats, I wanted DJs who were either old-school or could tell stories firsthand.

My first call was to Wild Bill Kelly, whose completely insane format on WFMU was inspirational. He had worked there for like thirty years for free, so I felt good giving him his first paycheck.

I got my old friend Kid Leo out of the record-company business and back where he belonged, on the radio. He also became my Program Director until he moved to the Carolinas and Dennis Mortensen took over.

Andrew Loog Oldham had stolen the Rolling Stones from Giorgio Gomelsky and had publicized and produced their crucial first five years. I offered gigs to both Andrew *and* Giorgio, but only Andrew took it. Giorgio just wanted to talk. Andrew became my morning guy until he wasn't. Michael Des Barres, the Marquis MDB, enjoys that position now.

I tried to talk Jerry Blavat, one of the last of the legendary DJs, into it, telling him he would become a legend to a whole new generation, but he said he really couldn't relate to anything after 1959.

On the Country side, I knew I wouldn't be able to watch the channel as closely. A girl named Gloria who worked for me recommended Jeremy Tepper as Program Director. I got lucky; he got it right away and has done a great job ever since.

Again, I wanted characters, personalities who could deliver stories in first person, and I got them. Cowboy Jack Clement, Elizabeth Cook, Steve Earle, Shooter Jennings—and who the hell else would hire Mojo Nixon?

And so Underground Garage (Channel 21) and Outlaw Country (Channel 60) were born, and Sirius Satellite had its first two original formats.

By 2004, my syndicated *Underground Garage* format had really come together, and it became obvious to us that we should celebrate our uniqueness with an annual festival, broadcast on Sirius.

I entrusted the planning to Alex Ewen, who had started out as Director of my Solidarity Foundation and had pretty much taken over all my businesses.

We had quite an impressive lineup, I must say. A lot of reunions.

Iggy and the Stooges, the New York Dolls, Bo Diddley, the Strokes, Nancy Sinatra, Big Star (band), the Pretty Things, the Creation, the Electric Prunes, the Chocolate Watchband, the Chesterfield Kings, the Pete Best Band, Joan Jett, the Dictators, and twenty-five others.

We were snakebit right from the start.

First of all, we had two deaths before we started. A few months before our festival, the New York Dolls had reunited for a show in London curated by Morrissey. A few weeks after that, the band's bassist, Arthur Kane, came down with a flu and went to a doctor in LA. It wasn't a flu. It was leukemia. Two hours later he was dead.

Richard Tepp, lead singer of Richard and the Young Lions, also succumbed to leukemia, just days after we had finished recording the vocals for the band's first proper album.

But we soldiered on. I had a vision for the festival. There hadn't been a 3-D movie in a long time—and maybe never a concert film shot in 3-D—so I wanted to bring it back. Chris Columbus was going to shoot it, and we had a distribution deal under discussion. The day of the concert,

Chris received word that his young daughter had fallen off an exercise machine and injured herself. He rushed home to Chicago.

Even though Chris had positioned the cameras and designed the entire shoot, because he didn't actually physically shoot it, the deal fell through.

That same morning, Hurricane Danielle changed direction and headed straight toward New York.

Weathermen advised everyone to stay home.

Those brave enough to come to Randall's Island that day saw a miraculous and historic lineup of artists, along with equally historic technical difficulties.

I designed the show to resemble the old Alan Freed / Dick Clark multiact shows. We had a special rotating stage built so that one act could go right into the next. The stage broke after the third band, Davie Allan and the Arrows, so we went crazy with changeovers all day, but we got it in.

Even given the headaches and hurdles, there were so many highlights: Alex Chilton's Big Star, the reunited Creation, the rarely seen Pretty Things, Bo Diddley still rockin' thirty years after we'd done the debutante party, Nancy Sinatra with sixty go-go girls choreographed by Maureen, and Iggy running and leaping onto the huge 3-D camera.

We'll never see it because the amazing footage from the show, 3-D and video, was stolen or lost.

And the next morning, my main man Alex's last act as an employee was to inform me that he'd slightly miscalculated: I'd lost $3 million, and the union guys, who you really don't want to fuck with, were looking for me.

Making history can be an expensive hobby, but what a glorious disaster!

A few days later I went for a drive to clear my head.

I chose the Palisades, the most scenic of New York's outer arteries. After the first few miles I started to relax. The leaves were turning—autumn has always been my favorite season—and the quiet hum of the Cadillac's four hundred horses made for a smooth-as-silk magic carpet ride. It was as close to a perfect afternoon as I was likely to have for the next little while. The pretty girl sitting next to me was just a bonus. The only slight damper on the day was knowing that in just a few more miles I was going to have to kill her.

It was always depressing when a character was eliminated from *The Sopranos* because the cast had grown very close and you knew you would not be seeing that person again very often, if ever.

Drea de Matteo was very popular and her character, Adriana, was one of the show's more sympathetic, so it was a grim event indeed having to be the bastard who took her out. She had cooperated with the Feds and left us no choice.

It was the most difficult thing I've had to do as an actor.

Adriana came across as a tough broad on the screen, but when you put your hands on her in real life she was . . . a woman. Dragging her roughly out of the car made me physically sick. I despise bullies of all stripes. It's just in my DNA. And guys who assault women in any way are among the lowest of the low in my book.

Drea, a pro, told me not to hold back. "If this is gonna be my last scene," she said, "let's make it memorable!"

So I had to really concentrate and become that guy, get in that frame of mind. Completely eliminate my own thoughts and feelings. I just had to keep telling myself that Silvio was a traditionalist. There was no mercy for betrayal. Male or female, didn't matter. I had to rough her up for a couple of hours. Tough, tough day.

After it was done, we let ourselves collapse and lay down in the leaves, both of us mentally and physically exhausted.

"You just won your first Emmy," I said.

She sighed. "I certainly fucking hope so."

twenty-seven

A Wicked Cool Super Bowl

(2005–2009)

The old Kings and the Princes so recently dethroned,
Were prophets once upon a time, their words the law of the land,
They used to look so regal in their psychedelic colors,
There is no place for them now in the land of the bland . . .

—"FACE OF GOD," FROM BORN AGAIN SAVAGE

Scandinavia had become the Rock and Roll capital of the world.

The reason was subtitles. In much of Europe, TV and movies were dubbed. Scandinavian TV and movies were broadcast in their original language and subtitled, which meant Scandinavians grew up hearing and learning English. Since it was the universal language for both airline pilots and Rock and Roll bands, Scandinavians could make records that got played on the only Rock format that existed. Ours.

The Underground Garage channel played about twenty bands from the region, more than from the rest of Europe combined (minus the UK). We played the Cocktail Slippers from Norway, Hawaii Mud Bombers from Sweden, the Breakers from Denmark, and many more.

Scott Greenstein would even be knighted by the Swedish king for supporting Swedish music . . . played on our station.

Those bands and others urged me to start a record company because nobody had American distribution. We didn't foresee that the digital domain was literally around the corner and would make territories irrelevant.

We started Wicked Cool Records and signed a dozen bands just in time to catch the end of the record business and lose a bunch of money. At first, I mostly just picked the acts we signed and worked on the singles, but at some point I realized I had to be hands-on all the way to keep our quality consistent, and I started going through every demo, making suggestions on every song.

Two guys run my world. Dennis Mortensen took over from the legendary Kid Leo as Program Director of the SXM Underground Garage channel and has done an absolutely brilliant job making us better and better every single day. He runs the station with assistance from Olivia, Rebecca, and Casey. He also produces my weekly radio show and runs Wicked Cool Records with Louis Arzonico, who does everything else—websites, graphics, album covers, videos, archives, pictures, bios, speeches, scripts, three publishing companies, and the like. Devanshi does the books and Jeremy does whatever else is needed.

I don't possess the authoritarian gene, so the office staff come and go when they please and take days off when they want. I figure they are all adults and can get the job done without someone watching them.

I only offer one word of advice to them: anticipate. You anticipate, you win.

The one person missing is the one whose job it is to make money. So we don't. The entire operation runs at a deficit.

Wicked Cool follows the same philosophy as the Underground Garage radio format. No absolute rules, but each act, like each record, needs to have a connection to the Renaissance.

The original idea was to cross the generations, link older songwriters and Producers with young Artists. I loved it when Richard Gottehrer, who started out as a Brill Building songwriter and was in the Strangeloves, produced the Raveonettes, and when the Cocktail Slippers covered a Greenwich/Barry song.

We never realized my original vision for the company. Jeff Barry, Russ Titelman, Carole King, Barry Mann, Andrew Oldham, Cynthia Weil—all should have been producing records for us. Shel Talmy. All he did was the Kinks' first four albums and the first album of the Who, still my fave. We never did hook up a production for him. A shame.

But we have always encouraged the generations to work together in the name of connecting the dots. Old Wisdom with Young Energy.

Speaking of wisdom, the wisest friend I had, Frank Barsalona, was showing early signs of the most tragic of all diseases, dementia. He had developed a strange obsession with fishing golf balls out of the water hazards between holes. "Go ahead," he'd say. "I'll catch up." He kept them, too, to the point where he had a garage full.

At first, it was funny. Then he started spending more and more time doing it, and it was less funny. By the time he stopped playing altogether and just fished, we were quite concerned. Justifiably so, unfortunately.

There's nothing worse than watching someone you've known all your life disintegrate before your very eyes. I discussed it with Frank's wife, June, and their daughter, Nicole, my goddaughter and assistant at the time, and decided we needed to move quickly to get Frank into the Rock and Roll Hall of Fame. We spoke to Jann Wenner and Jon Landau, who agreed.

A few years earlier, when Frank had been honored by the TJ Martell Foundation, June and Nicole had asked me to make a speech as Silvio Dante. They wanted a repeat performance of that for the Hall of Fame induction. I brought bodyguards Jimmy Gandolfini and Steve Schrippa to give Frank the royal treatment he deserved.

Frank just barely made it through his acceptance speech. I stood close by, quietly urging him on. It would be his last public appearance.

Once he stopped recognizing people, I stopped going to see him. I felt so bad for June and Nicole, but I loved him too much to watch him fade away. I'd watched it up close with my father and one time was too many.

Everybody in the music business, what's left of it, and everybody who got rich from it when it existed, owes a profound debt of gratitude to Frank Barsalona.

I had tried to extend his legacy. Our company covered a lot of ground: agency, management, record company, radio production, TV production, live events, publishing, publicity, marketing, and more. I hoped that Nicole would eventually run the company. I had trained her as best as I could, though she was pretrained, born with a booking book in her crib. She eventually got tired of the business carnage—everything we tried seemed to come up short of the finish line—and left to try management, which she's doing great at.

Renegade Nation, our parent company, was on a roll for a minute there, though we never solved our basic problem, which was not having someone whose job it was to actually make money.

We had a lot of so-called salesmen come and go, but I always wondered why they insisted on a salary if they were so good at selling. I paid them a 20 percent commission, and not one of them sold dick for what was, at the time, the biggest independent radio show in the world. I finally had to do what I liked least in the world: find us some sponsors to keep the radio show going and pay for the tours we wanted to do.

It's interesting what willpower can do. It's the tiniest part of who we are and the most important. Every once in a while I have to stop and think about how it powers us.

Who exactly are we, after all?

What are we?

We're four things.

We are our genetic makeup, our inclinations, talents, gifts. You can sing in tune or you can't.

We are our environment. You grow up in a loving environment or you don't.

We are our circumstances. You're born rich in Chicago or poverty-stricken in Uganda.

And we are our willpower.

Those first three factors are big, probably between 30 percent and a third each, which leaves us somewhere between 10 and 1 percent for willpower. The part we actually control.

We always think we're making decisions. I do not personally believe that. I think most of who we are is decided very early. Environment and circumstances can change as we grow up and that can affect us. But in the end, it's how we use that little bit of willpower that matters.

In the worst-case scenario, you could have genes, environment, and circumstances stacked against you, 99 to 1. But against all those odds you can still win.

I think about my friend, the late John Lewis, who I met during the Sun City years, when he was a newly elected congressman. John was born one of ten kids of sharecroppers in Nowheresville, Alabama, and ended up as the head of one of the Big Six groups that organized the history-making March on Washington in 1963. He helped pass the Voting Rights Act in 1965 and served in Congress for thirty years.

The voting rights legislation was gutted in 2013 by a Supreme Court that also tolerated gerrymandering and has been slowly losing its way for years. As I write this, a seventh practicing Catholic has been confirmed for the Supreme Court.

Our sacred separation of church and state has been slowly but surely disappearing ever since Reagan. Hopefully by the time you read this, there will be a new stacked court with six new justices who are all atheists or agnostics.

Why six? Because right now the religious extremists on the Court outnumber the others six to three. Assume one of the new justices fools you—there's always one—making it seven to three. We will need the other five to outnumber them eight to seven.

That will give us a shot at equality for women and for the LGBTQ community, not to mention democracy, all of which are rapidly disappearing. And speaking of the last of these, we will also hopefully have a new stronger voting rights act with John Lewis's name on it.

My moments of great willpower don't compare to John's, but I've gotten things done that I shouldn't have been able to. As long as it was for someone else. Or a good cause. And Renegade Nation had one. I took the energy I had previously invested in politics and redirected it toward the support, preservation, and creation of Rock and Soul. It was an endangered species, and something had to be done.

If you've been around long enough, it's easy to be cynical about this world we find ourselves living in. One quick happy story.

As I think I mentioned, as soon as we started Wicked Cool Records the entire record industry as we knew it basically ended. No more record sales. So we're thinking, How are we gonna survive?

We are going to have to survive by licensing our music to commercials and film. No sooner had we said that then one of my guys comes running in in a panic. I just made a deal for a commercial, he says, but the ad agency wants to own the publishing!

Ohhhh! You've got to be fucking kidding me. That's really the end. It's the last income we have left. This will spread like wildfire and kill what's left of the business. Who is the agency? Deutsch, he says. Find out who owns it or who runs it and get them on the phone.

Much to my pleasant surprise on the phone comes Donny Deutsch.

"Donny, I got to talk to you."

"Great," he says, "let me talk to my schedule girl . . ."

"No, Donny, I mean like right now."

"Right now?" he says. "Like now now?"

"Yeah, come on, I'll buy you a cup of coffee. Where are you?"

"I'm over here by the Four Seasons on Fifty-Seventh."

"I'll see you in the bar in ten minutes."

Never met the guy before, never spoke to him. He shows up, I explain the situation, and he fixes it. No argument. No demand for publishing. And life went on, damaged but survivable, thanks to him.

So every once in a while you find a guy like that.

They give you hope.

The Hard Rock Cafe was the first sponsor of the radio show, and, chief willing, still is as you read this.

The Hard Rock is owned by the Seminole Tribe of Florida, the rockingest Indians ever, and managed by one of my closest friends, Jimmy Allen.

The Seminoles had started Indian gambling in 1979 with high-stakes bingo, and within minutes everybody with an Indian great-grandmother opened a casino.

Where there's action, guess who follows? Right. Every Mob guy, wannabe Mob guy, hustler, and con man, many of whom successfully robbed every Native American tribe blind for decades.

Every tribe, that is, except the Seminoles, who had the wisdom to hire Jersey: Jimmy Allen, literally the Last Boy Scout.

At first, the Seminoles' only connection to the Hard Rock organization was that they had licensed the name for their casino in Hollywood, Florida.

Jimmy and I were having dinner one summer night at Morandi in the Village. As part of the license deal, he explained, they had international audit rights, which gave them a look at the books. "So I'm looking," he said, "and I see that our little casino is a big piece of their profits worldwide. I think I'm gonna try and buy the Hard Rock."

I almost choked on my artichoke.

"The whole fucking thing?"

"Yeah, why not?"

He talked to the chief of the Seminoles, who said let's rock! And bada bing, a billion bucks later, give or take, they owned it. Jimmy has probably tripled the value by now.

We held our first Halloween a-Go-Go show at the Hard Rock in Times Square, featuring Rocket from the Crypt, Gluecifer (a Norwegian Hard Rock band, no relation to the Russian hackers . . . I don't think), and Bobby "Boris" Pickett, with Maureen's dancers, the Garage Girls a Go-Go.

Then we got a sponsorship from Rolling Rock for a twenty-city tour. It was a great concept. We picked four Rock bands, one from each decade, fully paid for by sponsors like Rolling Rock and Dunkin' Donuts to keep ticket prices low. And not obscure bands either. We lined up acts like the New York Dolls, the Zombies, the Romantics, the Chesterfield Kings, and more. We boarded all the musicians onto a bus, wrapped it, and barnstormed the country.

We went back to the Hard Rock for New Year's Eve a-Go Go.

New Year's programming back then was totally boring, and I wanted to take over the holiday.

I had lunch with Hugh Hefner at the Playboy Mansion. "Check it out," I said. "New Year's Eve from here. Televised." I explained that our thing was a retro-'60s vibe, which he loved. "We bring in like five bands from different decades and use Playboy Bunnies as go-go girls. What do you think?"

"I'm in!" he said.

Next, I thought, it was on to the easy part, the TV sale. Keep in mind, there was maybe one pretty lame New Year's show at the time. Needless to say, we would have owned New Year's forever.

Nobody wanted it.

Nobody.

Sometimes I think, *I am so on the wrong fucking planet!*

I mean, look around.

Could life be any more fucking boring?

What the fuck happened to evolution?

What happened to fun?

Somebody had a connection at ESPN and heard they were up for something new, since New Year's happened to be a dead time on their station in those days.

I asked Johnny Pasquale, the manager of the Hard Rock Cafe in Times Square, if anybody had ever used the top of the marquee for a show. Nobody had.

The cafe was right under where the ball dropped. Being on that marquee is one of the coolest experiences you'll probably never have.

You are in it, baby. In the heart of the monster that is New Year's Eve, but also securely above it. Big screens in every direction, stages below, confetti raining down. A trip and a half.

So did I secure the marquee for future New Year's gigs forevermore? Of course not. Now Johnny rents it out for hundreds of thousands of dollars, and I can't get back in.

Our 2005 Rockin' *ESPN's New Year's Eve*, the world's best-kept secret due to zero promotion, managed to be third in the ratings that night. I cohosted with Stuart Scott. We just made things up as we went along.

We did a second Halloween show the next year, this time down at the Hard Rock in Hollywood, Florida. We called it Cheap Trick or Treat. Featuring guess who? It was also Roky Erickson's first gig out of Texas after coming back from the horrendous horror of being locked up—for five years for two joints—and after receiving shock treatments as if it was the snake-pit 1950s. He survived somehow and put on a great show.

Back in 2002, Congress, in its infinite wisdom, had passed the No Child Left Behind Act. They did this because American math and science scores had dropped to somewhere between those of farmers in Rwanda and baboons on the Yucatán Peninsula, but our legislators hadn't figured out that in order to prepare for these endless tests, the schools would start canceling all the Arts classes.

If anyone had checked, they would have found out that kids who take music class do better in math and science.

And somebody should also have explained that *testing isn't learning.* But for that to happen, somebody would have had to work for a living and . . . think. A concept rapidly disappearing in our disintegrating society.

The music teachers of America get to me somehow, probably through a lady named Susan McCue, who was working for Senate Majority Leader Harry Reid. Susan was and is my connection to Washington, DC.

The teachers told me that all the music classes were being cut. Could I go check it out and see if anything could be done about it?

Susan hooked me up with Ted Kennedy and Mitch McConnell. Separately, of course. And as I like to say, tragically, Ted Kennedy is no longer with us, and tragically, Mitch McConnell still is.

But both were very nice that day. I was probably the only meeting they had that wasn't about asking for money.

Teddy gave me a long rap about how all the way back to the Greeks, the Arts have always been included in education, and Arts classes being cut was an unintended consequence of improved science testing, but there wasn't a damn thing he could do about it anytime in the near future.

McConnell basically said the same thing, without the Greek rap of course.

I reported the bad news to the teachers. "But listen," I said. "I've got an idea. With our screwed-up priorities, the government is not going to put instruments in kids' hands for a while. We'll have to find another way to do that." We would eventually do that with Little Kids Rock. "How about we do a music history curriculum and sneak it into all the different grade levels? It can be cross-curricular, taught in music class, history class, English class, social studies. The best part is, it will work for all the students, not just musicians, and we can keep the Arts in the DNA of the education system."

They thought about it for a few days and then endorsed the idea.

My first step toward realizing the curriculum was to create another foundation, Rock and Roll Forever.

My second step was to assemble an impressive advisory board before I moved on to the third step, the extremely unpleasant task of raising money. I went to Bruce and Bono and Marty Scorsese, all of whom agreed to be on the board.

I'll always be grateful, because their participation meant that step three was less unpleasant than I feared. In fact, it was one of the two greatest meetings I've ever had. I met one of the loves of my life, Susie Buffett, who, in thirty minutes, on the strength of my idea (and, I'm sure, impressed by the board), gave me $2 million. And the Rock and Roll Forever foundation, whose main initiative would be the TeachRock. org music history curriculum, was born right there.

I quickly outlined two hundred basic lessons to get us started, hired Warren Zanes away from the Rock and Roll Hall of Fame as my first director, and started looking for teachers to write lesson plans. It would take ten years and a few directors to get the curriculum on the right track. It had to be bulletproof, since we'd only get one chance. We eventually got there.

Over that span, we kept promoting Rock any way we could. We made history by having an actual Garage Rock Chart in none other than *Billboard* frickin' magazine! And I wrote a column every week for eighty-three straight weeks before the editors regained their senses.

We did a very freaky residency at a bar called Hawaiian Tropic Zone in Times Square. It was the perfect setting for us. Fake palm trees, waitresses in grass skirts and bikinis, tropical drinks. Kitsch City! We ran horror films on the walls constantly, sometimes right on the bands while they were playing. It was fabulous.

Wackiest, wildest, campiest gig ever.

Only lasted six weeks; the owner got busted for sexually harassing the waitresses.

Bikinis, Garage Rock, and drinks with umbrellas.

A volatile combination.

June 10, 2007, was a day that shall live in infamy: the final broadcast of *The Sopranos*. Episode 86.

The cast had been making appearances at casinos, breaking records everywhere. We had become so big with the right kind of crowd, the whales and the wiseguys, that we were doing boxing numbers, Ali numbers, Tyson numbers, Mayweather numbers.

Jimmy Allen decided to throw a party at the Hard Rock in Florida. He invited five thousand of his closest friends and every international whale to watch the final episode with the entire cast.

It was one awesome event.

Jimmy constructed a tent with a giant screen on the property, about a fifteen-minute walk from the hotel. We assembled with security to walk out together. There had to be like five thousand people there, stacked twelve to fifteen deep on both sides, screaming and shouting and applauding the whole way. I leaned over toward Jimmy and Lorraine. "If you ever wondered what it feels like being a Rock star, this is it."

As I watched, I thought about the coming final scene of the episode, which was also the final scene of the series. Chase hadn't told the cast exactly how the show would end. The script just said that Tony played a song on the jukebox. We were all seeing it for the first time.

More specifically, I was thinking about the two-week wrestling match I'd had with David over what that last song should be.

I had four songs in mind, and made my best pitch for each.

My first suggestion, Bruce's "Loose Ends," might have been a little too on the nose, but it would have been cool. My other three were Procol Harum's "The Devil Came from Kansas" (coolest song ever), the Left Banke's "Pretty Ballerina" (would have worked beautifully as juxtaposition), and the Youngbloods' "Darkness, Darkness," which would have reinforced the ominous vibe.

After ten years and seven seasons of the most amazing music ever used on a TV show, David wanted to use fucking Journey!

Ohhhh! As we used to say.

Nothing wrong with Journey, of course. They made terrific records, had one of the best singers in Rock, and were huge.

But that was the problem. David had turned a lot of people onto much more obscure music through the eighty-six episodes, and the show had the reputation of having the coolest music on TV.

His final argument?

"Look," he said. "Tony is a Classic Rock guy. That's what he would have played."

End of discussion.

The day after the finale aired, I appeared on my Miami radio affiliate's big nationally syndicated morning show, where I heard a straight hour of complaints, consternation, and downright insults about the surprise ending.

People wanted to know what had happened, they'd thought their electricity went out, blah, blah, blah . . .

After an hour, I started fighting back. "OK, smart-asses," I said. "You don't like that ending, let's hear yours!"

Silence.

"Here, let me help you, did you want Tony to die?"

Grumble, grumble, well . . . no . . .

"Did you want Carmela to die?"

Uh . . . no.

"One of the kids maybe?"

No!

So maybe it wasn't such a bad ending after all?

By the time the radio show ended, the whole country had started to come around. David Chase had dodged the final bullet and regained his genius status.

Years later, *Vanity Fair* did a retrospective on the show and talked to actors and writers. Inevitably, the reporter got to the big question: "How did it really end? What happened?"

"OK," I said. "I've been asked this a thousand times, and I'm gonna settle it once and for all right now. You are going to get the scoop! This is the last time I will ever answer this, so sharpen your pencil."

The reporter got visibly excited.

"You wanna know what really happened?"

"Yes," he said.

"Alright. This is it. Are you ready?"

He was.

"The Director yelled cut and the actors went home."

Any excuse to go to Cannes, I'm there.

Nice is nice. Èze. Monte Carlo. Right into Portofino. Over to Barcelona. The entire Mediterranean coastline is one big groovy paradise, and I don't know why I don't live there.

All my life I've wanted to live on the beach. Came close in Miami many times. Lauderdale. But the hurricane thing—man, I don't know.

None of those problems in the Mediterranean.

I just wish I spoke the language. Italian. French. Spanish. Any of them.

I've tried. Maureen and I took Italian lessons for a while. The teacher was a crab. Very formal. Italian is all about informal expressions, and she was more by the book. If we'd actually learned what she taught us, the only people in Italy who would have understood us would have been about a dozen college professors in Milan.

I keep those fantasies alive in my mind, though. Living on the beach, and speaking at least one of those languages. I tell myself I've got to save something for my old age. So I'm saving that.

And the opera.

And breaking even.

And finding out who killed the chauffeur in *The Big Sleep*.

So in 2009, when I was invited to give a keynote address at the Cannes Lions International Festival of Creativity sponsored by the advertising world, I took it.

"The Future of Advertising" was the theme that year. Maybe that's the theme every year. I don't know.

A lot of people invite me to do speeches.

Once.

They rarely invite me back because my tendency is to tell them the truth with the hope of planting a seed or two that might result in a positive change.

In this case, this was the seed I planted. "Listen," I said,

You want to hear about the future of advertising? There is none.

Advertising is nothing but an aggravating pain-in-the-ass interruption that people feel they have to tolerate. The minute they find content without it, they will flock there.

HBO is the business model of the future. That's where it's at. The future is subscription. So you guys should focus on product placement and "Presented by"–type things like on Public Broadcasting channels. Limited-interruption-type programming. Other than that? Your future is sitcoms, reality programming, and Fox News.

They probably weren't thrilled to hear they were passé, but I got a big hand.

Once, like I said.

The E Street Band had been asked to play the Super Bowl for years, but in the old days, the audience was a mile away. Bruce wisely held out until they agreed to allow the audience to be right up against the stage the way we liked it.

That finally happened in Tampa, for Super Bowl XLIII.

I didn't care about the game. All I wanted to see was how the hell they assembled that stage so fast!

It was wild to witness. Like a hundred ants coming out of every possible gate with a piece of staging and zip, zip, zip, there it was.

The performance was timed like the Normandy Invasion, to the second. Thirteen minutes exactly is my recollection.

I wasn't at the meeting with the NFL and the production people, so I was a little surprised when Bruce came back with the setlist: "Tenth Avenue Freeze-Out," "Born to Run," and "Glory Days."

"Uh, not for nothing," I said, "but don't we have a new album coming out the week of the Super Bowl?"

"Yeah," he said.

"Well, call me crazy, but this Super Bowl thing seems like it could be a promotional opportunity!"

"We've got no time. Everybody decided on those three songs."

I thought about it for a minute.

"How about we leave out the second verse of every song? It'll buy us a minute or two, and we can throw in a bit of the title track, 'Working on a Dream.'"

And that's what we did.

We killed.

Bruce ended with a slide, a tribute to Pete Townshend. And if our cameraman hadn't caught him, we'd be looking for a new front man.

On the way out, Bruce looked into the camera and said, "I'm going to Disneyland!"

I thought to myself, Maybe they'll let you in this time.

And you know, to this day, no one has ever come up to me and said anything about those missing verses.

It could make you wonder why we work so hard on those lyrics.

Anyway, not a bad way to end a decade.

The E Street Band was back.

twenty-eight

Lilyhammer

(2010–2013)

> Life requires constant vigilance against love of humanity turning
> into profound frustration, resentment, and disgust. In other words,
> let's face it, most people are assholes.
>
> —GAUTAMA BUDDHA, THE FIFTH NOBLE TRUTH

American Idol was the kind of show the Rock world loved to put down at
every opportunity.

It was accused of being Phony! Fabricated! Superficial! Instant Stardom! A false picture of the realities of the business.

I only caught an episode or two, but Maureen liked it, and I figured
any show that introduced Smokey Robinson to a new generation was
OK by me, since at this point in our history, an era that future generations will look back on with pity, most of our world is phony, fabricated,
superficial, and full of instant stardom.

Jimmy Iovine was serving as head mentor, and he asked me to come
on as an assistant mentor. Not exactly my world, but I figured Maureen
would get a kick out of it, and it ended up being fish-out-of-water fun.
I enjoyed trying to find the common ground between traditional Rock
and the modern Pop world more than I thought I would.

I tried to share my experience as best as I could. Sometimes a brief
comment; when appropriate, a lengthier explanation that I thought
might prove useful if they ended up with a real career.

Mostly I focused on song choice. How to pick material that reflected their vocal style and sensibility. It wasn't easy for the singers, because after getting our advice, they had only twenty minutes or so to learn a song they had probably never heard before in their lives.

Can't remember whether it was me, Nigel Lythgoe, or Maureen who suggested it now, but I remember Joshua Ledet knocking me out with the Bee Gees' "To Love Somebody."

Maureen got friendly with quite a few of the singers on *Idol*, and David Cook surprised her with the gift of a puppy. It was a Cavalier King Charles Spaniel like our first dog Jake, this one named Edie.

I was not thrilled with this because half of me went with Jake when he left us, so I assured Cook that when Edie leaves, he would be leaving with her.

"Why didn't you drop off a couple of kids while you're at it?" I snarled. The first time he came to the E Street dressing room, I said, "Where's my gun?" just to scare the shit out of him.

Of course I love her more than life itself (I added Sedgwick to her name), but I'm not the only one who hopes she lives forever.

I also had a good year at the Hall of Fame.

Selection is a Darwinian process. No, that's not fair to Darwin—it's more ruthless than that. It's always a challenge, as each member of the nominating committee suggests two names, and then tries to talk the other twenty-five or so members into voting for our suggestions rather than their own!

Those first fifty names get winnowed down to fifteen or so, and that list goes out to the hundreds of members of the Hall of Fame plus I'm not sure who else, and they vote it down to five.

In 2011, I brought up the Hollies and, miraculously, got them in. I say "miraculously" because it's hard as hell. And it really pisses me off when honorees don't show up, because show up or not, I guarantee it will be the first sentence of their epitaph.

At the time, I was making a case for writers, based on the simple truth that our entire industry begins with the song. I had brought it up before and gotten nowhere, but this time I had extra passion in my argument, having recently lost my friend Ellie Greenwich. "Are we going to wait for them all to die?" finally got through.

A few writers were already in—Jerry Leiber and Mike Stoller, Carole King and Gerry Goffin, Willie Dixon, and the amazing Motown team of Holland-Dozier-Holland—but that year we managed to induct Jeff Barry and Ellie, Barry Mann and Cynthia Weil, Mort Shuman (his writing partner Doc Pomus was inexplicably in without him), Jesse Stone, and Otis Blackwell.

The committee tragically and arbitrarily cut off my list, leaving out Jerry Ragovoy, Luther Dixon, Dan Penn, Burt Bacharach and Hal David, Neil Sedaka and Howard Greenfield, and Bert Berns. We would get Bert in a year or two later.

I have a great deal of clarity when it comes to who deserves to be in, because, once again, I am quite sure that a Renaissance took place, and it was finite.

Everything important, essential, and truly original came from the '50s and '60s.

That doesn't mean nothing great came after. Lots did, and it should be recognized. But without the Naissance of the '50s and the Renaissance of the '60s, none of the rest would exist.

The further we get from those decades, the harder it is to justify the relevance of the pioneers when programming the Hall's televised induction ceremony. That is the frustration of trying to institutionalize historical significance, which ostensibly is our job, while simultaneously having to make a TV audience happy.

I once again suggested our meetings be broadcast live so the audience can witness the process and stop questioning the legitimacy of the decision-making.

I spend half my life defending the Hall of Fame and Jann Wenner, who everyone likes to blame for everything when he doesn't even attend the meetings!

The system is becoming more challenging, but it's still functioning. When it inevitably breaks down, I hope the executive committee has the wisdom to recognize the dysfunction and replace it with a new system that works as well or better.

It's an institution worth preserving, and I consider it an honor to be a part of it.

But if Junior Walker and the All Stars, Goldie and the Gingerbreads, Procol Harum, Big Mama Thornton, the J. Geils Band, Mamie Smith, Taj Mahal, Joe Cocker, the Runaways, Johnny Burnette and the Rock and Roll Trio, the Shangri-Las, Shel Talmy, and Mickie Most don't get in soon, I'm going to burn the fucking place down.

When Wicked Cool signed the Cocktail Slippers, a five-piece, all-female Rock band from Norway, I decided to produce the record with assistance from Jean Beauvoir, and I wrote two songs for it. We were told of a great mixer in Bergen, Yngve Leidulv Sætre, so we went to the west coast of Norway to mix it at his Duper Studios. Beautiful city, surrounded by mountains, like one of those snow globes.

During the mix, an assistant came in to the studio to tell me that there was a couple with a baby in the lobby wanting to say hello.

I courageously went down to the lobby, hoping it wasn't mine.

Kidding.

The couple was Eilif Skodvin and Anne Bjørnstad, and the baby, theirs, was nursing. Norwegians, conservative in every other way possible, like to do that in public.

They were TV writers, they said, and they had written a show for me.

Hey now! Talk about your pretty special celebrity-type flattery. You don't hear that one every day.

What's the pitch?

Eilif: A New York wiseguy goes into witness protection and chooses Lillehammer, Norway. Crime and comedy ensue.

Oh man!

"I just played a gangster for ten years," I sadly said.

"Well, think about it."

"OK, but I'm almost finished with the mix and will be going back to New York soon."

"We really want you to do this, and to be very involved. You would not only star, you would be one of the Executive Producers and writers."

"And of course do the music if you want to," Anne added.

The baby gurgled encouragement.

"The head of Rubicon, our production company will come to you if you want to continue the discussion."

"OK."

They left. Baby too.

I knew I couldn't do it.

It was partly a matter of taking on a similar role for my second acting job. What serious actor trying to maintain credibility would do that?

But it was mostly about the business.

It felt like my various projects were on a roll that could be close to the breakthrough I had been working toward for years. But they needed me to be there.

We had *Little Steven's Underground Garage* syndicated in over a hundred cities but had never achieved full sponsorship. The two 24/7 channels on Sirius required constant attention. We had the record company, which was trying to adjust to the advent of streaming. We had the management company, three publishing companies, the music history curriculum, live local shows, and national tours.

Plus, I had a really big idea for a website, a combination of a game and an educational tool that would have revolutionized both of those worlds. It was struggling to be born as a result of an ongoing war with the scumbag website creators, who kept robbing me blind.

Whenever I told them, "This is not what I wanted and not what you said you were going to do," they always referred me to some fine print in the contract. Hundreds of thousands of dollars later, I was no closer to my goal than when I started. And it was a billion-dollar idea that could've paid for everything. (Still is, by the way.)

So there was all that to consider. On top of that, everybody I knew tried to talk me out of it. My Agent, my friends, my own office.

"Now let me get this straight," they said in unison. "You're coming out of maybe the most important TV show in history, and you're going to do a local show in a country nobody can find on a map?"

What can I say? Whoever heard of somebody starring in a local TV show in a foreign country? It was going to be difficult to resist the adventure.

Once again, it felt like Destiny at work. And I'd fucked around with that lady enough as it was. I mean, come on! A Norwegian couple show up on the west coast of absolutely nowhere and say they've written a TV show for you? You gonna brush that off as just another day at the office?

The key was when they said I'd be one of the writers and Producers. I felt that that was enough protection to go for it.

Still, when the head of the production company, who shall remain nameless for reasons that will soon be obvious, came to my office in New York, I really did try to say no.

He walked in with a few guys and I thought for a minute a rugby match had broken out. He had a wild, working-class hooligan vibe, and though he turned out to be Swedish, he had mastered what I came to recognize as the Norwegian negotiating style, which involved pretending to be a dumb farmer as a way of concealing strategic thinking and a massive ego. I liked him.

He opened the conversation by pleading poverty, standard practice for all who have ever controlled the purse strings, but just as quickly he told me that it would be one of the most expensive shows in Norwegian history and the featured show on the country's biggest network. He also said I would have complete artistic control. Within reason.

No money, huh? Let me end this right now, I thought.

"OK then," I said. "I want 50 percent of the back end."

I said it as if it was my standard deal. You know—me, Spielberg, Hanks.

He didn't even blink an eye.

"OK."

Alarm bells should have gone off right then and there.

There were three or four of my people in the discussion, and I tried not to look directly in the eyes of any of them.

Uhhh . . . (think, man, think!) "And one more thing." (The kid's got balls, you've got to give him that.)

Blank stares. Scandinavians probably make great poker players.

"I've got all these businesses going on, as you can see."

They had gotten the tour earlier, seen it all, half the office full of employees, the other half taken up by a full-blown recording studio.

"So if I do this, I can only work every other week."

I figured that was that. Nobody's budget could handle that.

They spoke to each other in Norwegian.

"OK," he said.

Well, now I was fucked.

I had just scored the two most incredible deal points in TV negotiation history.

I was doing this show.

Eilif and Anne started coming to New York for brainstorming sessions.

I would find out later that even though Eilif and Anne had sold the show to me as a Norwegian *Sopranos*, Rubicon had sold the show to NRK—Norway's PBS or BBC—as a local family comedy. It would be the artistic challenge of my life to marry those two ideas and satisfy those two audiences.

Right from the start Eilif and Anne had big ambitions. They wanted a big international show, they said, but few in Norway thought the way they did. That's why they had taken the unprecedented step of casting a foreigner as a star. They asked me how could they make it work internationally?

As it happened, I knew exactly how to do that. "My friends," I said, "I watched it happen not once, but twice, in, of all places, New Jersey. Not dissimilar to your own residence. In fact, at one point in history, you could say New Jersey was the Norway of America!"

Without the money. Or the mountains. Or the snow. Or . . .

In any case here's what I knew, and what I told them.

As evidenced by the successful instincts of both Bruce Springsteen and David Chase, the way to be international was to be as local as possible. Counterintuitive, but true. Turns out, people are very curious. They want to know about things that they . . . don't know about.

So I wanted every detail about Norwegian life they could think of. Every eccentricity. Every cultural nuance. Everything they were embarrassed about or proud of. The more granular the local detail, the bigger the show would be.

"We can do that!" they said.

We got down to work.

From the start, there was a question of tone. The two of them were mainly comedy writers, brilliant ones as it turned out, but I didn't want to do that. I could not casually make fun of wiseguys and then make my living portraying them. Not if I wanted to keep living in New York.

It was going to have to be a dramedy, with serious moments in it too, and the humor would have to come from the characters and the circumstances. I didn't want anybody trying to be funny. It would be harder to write, but if we could pull it off it would give the show longevity.

There was also a question of language. How much English should we use? We had to make the Norwegian audience happy, but we also wanted the potential of an international audience.

We decided whoever I was speaking to would speak English in return, and we would see what else felt right as we went. We had to hope the audience would buy the idea that my character understood some Norwegian but didn't speak it. This is actually the case for many foreigners who live there because the language is a difficult one. Surely Gene Roddenberry borrowed Norwegian for the Klingon mother tongue. Take my fricative, please! Plus, Norwegians really do speak perfect English.

My character, who I named Frankie "the Fixer" Tagliano, would look very similar to Silvio Dante, but he needed to have a completely different personality for the show to work.

First of all, he needed to be a real boss. On *The Sopranos*, Silvio was the only character that *didn't* want to be the Boss, and he had to be conservative and careful to balance Tony Soprano's capricious impulsiveness. As a result, he was always on guard, not fully neurotic but always a little nervous.

Frankie was much more outgoing, brazen, and aggressive, with no fear whatsoever. In this way, he was more similar to Tony than Silvio, and his new environment, a practically crime-free Norway, only emboldened him.

There was also the matter of how he had ended up in Norway in the first place. In their version, he had fallen in love with Lillehammer because of the Olympics—beautiful scenery, beautiful girls—and chosen it as his new home. To fill out the backstory and make it feel authentic, I suggested we base the show loosely on the John Gotti scenario, which was still fresh in my mind at the time.

Gotti's *caporegime* (captain, his immediate boss) was Aniello Dellacroce, a street guy everybody respected who was expected to move up to Boss when Carlo Gambino died. Instead, Gambino surprised everybody by selecting a glorified accountant named Paul Castellano, thinking it

would be good for the family business, which was investing in legit en-
terprises along with the usual criminal ones.

Long story short: Dellacroce died, and with no one left to stop him,
Gotti whacked Castellano, got away with it (no one can kill a boss without permission from the Commission), and became the Boss himself.

We flipped that scenario. Frankie was considered such an implicit
threat that the new Boss tried to have him assassinated.

This came as a shock. The whole neighborhood loved Frankie, and
Frankie loved being loved. Whenever someone had a problem, Frankie
would fix it. Need a parking ticket taken care of? Go see Frankie. Base-
ball tickets? Go see Frankie. Landlord raising your rent? Go see Frankie.
In fact, he was so universally beloved that when the new boss tried to kill
him, he ended up testifying against him, something Silvio could never
have done.

And the whole thing freaked him out so much that he made his deal
to go to Lillehammer instead of the usual Arizona or Utah or wherever
Mob guys go where they can never find good Italian food again.

As we started to shoot, I learned that there were some significant cultural
differences.

First of all, the budget was considerably smaller than I expected.
They were do-it-yourself to the max. No sets. Every scene was on location, except the Flamingo Bar, which was the Quality Hotel's existing
bar in Olavsgaard made over for the show. I wrote it into the script my
first day as a way to get bands into the show, and as a defense against the
audience going snow-blind.

The production would borrow people's houses to use as our base
and give us a place to change. We'd be getting dressed, and the kids
would come home from school. "Hi, Mom!" It was . . . different.

I was accustomed to changing in a trailer, which I had on every fifth
location or so. During the brief negotiations with Rubicon, the trailer
kept coming up, over and over again. I couldn't understand why. Turns
out I had ended up with the only trailer in Norwegian TV history. They
just don't go in for that American diva–type stuff.

The trailer ended up being a shit two-banger they had to bring in
from Belgium and couldn't be used in half the locations. The other

actors approached it like the *2001* obelisk. Of course, I told everyone to use it, not realizing it was something unique.

The government in Norway supports the Arts, as does pretty much every country except ours, and the actors were very flexible. They'd do our show during the day, shoot a movie at night, do a commercial on the weekend, and do theater, both Ibsen and children's, between seasons.

And they were all amazing. Great actors would take even the smallest parts, which I knew would give the show depth and longevity.

As brilliant as Eilif and Anne were at casting, they were equally good at knowing exactly how much self-deprecating humor a Norwegian audience could take, and how much cultural comedy international audiences needed.

Nobody knew a thing about Norway, which was perfect. Most Americans think it's a city in Sweden. You can't name one Norwegian product or celebrity to this day, can you? Didn't think so. A-ha doesn't count because they had to move to London to have a hit.

So we could be as surreal as we wanted to be. Ironically, the stuff the international audience thought we made up was actually normal Norwegian behavior. Like a driver's license taking months to get or fathers being forced to leave work and stay at home for a month with new babies.

We filmed about a quarter of the time in Lillehammer, which I fell in love with and whose name Eilif and Anne intentionally misspelled to be more incorrectly American.

It's a tiny town. The first thing that hit you was, How the fuck did they have an Olympics here? Everything important was just a few blocks from my hotel. Walk a block in either direction, and you'd find our two favorite bars: Nikkers, where we'd play table sand hockey and in the spring enjoy the back area that looked down on a pretty stream that leads to the Car Museum; and the Toppen Bar at the top of an old grain silo, which makes the best Stevie colada (piña colada with half a shot of Kahlúa) you'll ever have with snow on the ground.

Equally close was one of the city's half-dozen great restaurants, the Bryggerikjelleren (I told you—Klingon), whose exterior we used as the entrance of the Flamingo.

The Olympic ski jump is the only place that's a fifteen-minute drive away. Everything else is a short walk—even the pedestrian street that we would turn into a reindeer racetrack, complete with Keith Richards soundtrack, in one of my favorite episodes.

Filming in Lillehammer was a fundamental part of the show. It said so right in the title. But the producer, Anders Tangen, kept scheduling Oslo because it was cheaper. He kept running out of money by spending foolishly on the wrong things. He couldn't grasp the concept that fans of the show from all over the world would watch to see our Lillehammer locations.

I made it a point to film in the harshest winter months. Luckily, there were plenty. In an average winter, Lillehammer got between six and ten feet of snow. After a while, they had no place to put it, so they steamrollered it. The road just got imperceptibly higher as the winter went on.

It got so cold that the snow would freeze twice. When the moon was out I looked out my hotel window, the snow on the ground sparkling as far as I could see.

Absolutely magical.

One freezing February night—and I mean five below zero, Fahrenheit—I looked out the trailer window and saw about ten extras dancing around a spontaneously constructed fire.

"Is that some Norwegian actor–type ritual?" I asked the Director.

"Yes," he said. "It's called keeping warm!"

Such eccentricities were cute, but enough was enough. The next night, a tent was erected, with heat and an actual craft-service table with more than a pot of coffee and a bag of apples!

The contrast between our countries' filming process was made all the more dramatic to me when I flew home each week to work on David Chase's movie, where the craft service resembled your average 7-Eleven.

I learned everything I needed to know about Norway's TV culture. Namely, that they didn't have one. It was strictly a film culture transplanted to TV. What's the difference? I'm glad you asked. One big difference: in film, the Director is the boss. On TV, it's the writer.

I was usually the only writer on the set, because Eilif and Anne were off writing the next episode or casting. Too many times, I had to explain to the Director that the script wasn't an outline. If it said the scene ended when Frank sat down, the scene ended when Frank sat down. In the TV world, there's no time for philosophical discussions on the set. I welcomed all input, but not during shooting.

Another difference was that the actors were used to improvising.

I explained that since I came from the David Chase school of writing, every fucking word was sacred! So no improvising. If they had an idea, I wanted to hear it, but I didn't want to be surprised. "And by the way," I said, "if you're improvising in Norwegian, my character might understand you, but I don't!"

But after a while, I ended up enjoying the way their method of continuous creativity carried all the way to "Action!" We learned from each other and found a compromise. And being the only writer-Producer on the set—checking lighting, adjusting wardrobe, rewriting constantly—helped me a lot as an actor. I didn't have time to think. As soon as the camera rolled, I was just there, in the moment, no time for second-guessing.

About six weeks into filming, I started noticing a distinct dearth of grips and gaffers (yes—I am a little slow). And where were the production assistants? Why was the makeup man also the hair guy? And why was he carrying one of the cameras as we went from one location to another?

I called a meeting with everybody, including the elusive head of Rubicon. By the end of the discussion, I had come to the realization that something was rotten in the state of Norway and that we could not afford to shoot the show we had written.

I called my Agent and told him to book meetings with American networks. "I'll be in LA in two weeks," I said.

Why two weeks?

Because somehow, we had to make a trailer out of the first six weeks of shooting that would be impressive enough to get us an American deal. We didn't have one single completed episode.

It took four or five drafts. I knew what we needed to even have a chance: a little violence, a little sex appeal. We had been pretty much filming chronologically, which helped. In the end, Eilif and Anne and their editors did a great job, and off I went to Never-Never Land to try and score an American deal to save the show.

And my ass.

twenty-nine

Once upon a Dream

(2013–2014)

Warriors of the rainbow unite,
From the darkness of the wasteland,
Open up the inner light,
Oh, Great Spirit, your breath gives life,
I hear your voice in the wind,
I come before you as a child,
Seeking strength and wisdom . . .

—"BALANCE," FROM *REVOLUTION*

I called my Agent and told him to book an appointment with Chris Albrecht, who had moved from HBO to Starz.

I had learned a few things since I'd made my genius Spielberg-Hanks, 50-percent-of-the-back-end deal.

The naive Norwegian rugby farmer had hustled me. He was the con in Rubicon.

What he knew, and I didn't, was that the company would have given me 100 percent of the back end because Norway had never sold a show to anybody. Ever. There had never been a back end in Norwegian history.

I also found out that the "biggest budget in Norway" was somewhere around $750,000 per episode, equal to a decent reality show budget in the United States but nowhere close to the $3–4 million spent on the sixty-minute American dramas that were our competition.

I played Chris the trailer we'd cobbled together.

"I love it!" he said.

Wow.

"Chris, that's great. All I need is a million an episode and I can get it done."

"Brother, I'll give you two million an episode, but you have to wait until next year."

Oh man.

"Chris, you don't understand. We started production. I need the money now to finish."

"Fuck, I've got nothing left this year. All I can do is like half a million."

Fuck was right.

"I honestly don't think it can be done for that. I can get big bang for the buck over there, but not that big. Let me get back to you."

Chris had been my best shot. We knew each other. I could trust him. But I couldn't wait. We were already shooting.

And so I went to my second meeting of the day, with some unknown company called Netflix. I had read a single article about them. They were a Blockbuster-type movie-rental company about to start creating content, and they had just made their first deal with Kevin Spacey to star in a remake of a British political show.

There were only two names mentioned in the article: Reed Hastings, the tech genius who had perfected streaming (whatever that was), and the new content guy, Ted Sarandos.

A few weeks before, as Eilif and Anne struggled to finish the trailer, I'd made a phone call.

"Hello? You have reached Netflix."

"Hi. Stevie Van Zandt here. Ted Sarandos, please."

He got right on.

"Hey, man! This is Ted! Really good to talk to you!"

"Hi, Ted. I hear you're looking for stuff?"

"Yes, we're just getting started."

"I've got something."

"Great. Come on in."

That was it. The call that would lead to the greatest business meeting of my life.

My Agent and I walked across the street to Netflix.

The receptionist brought us in to Ted, who greeted me with the same enthusiasm he'd communicated on the phone. I wasn't used to liking

LA executives. They all seemed to be full of shit. Probably because most of them were. They were all smiles and compliments and never said no, but the deal never got done and you never found out why.

Ted was different. There was something unusually normal about him. Real confidence, not the phony LA kind. I liked him right away.

I explained that *Lilyhammer* was unique, to say the least. It was a bit of an experiment. My Agent's eyes were telling me to shut the fuck up, but I wanted Ted to know what he was buying.

I laid it all out. The ultimate fish-out-of-water premise, a gangster sent by witness protection to a country with no crime. The local color, dialogue in Norwegian with subtitles when I wasn't speaking. The unique tone of the show, both familiar and freaky at the same time.

"Sounds good!" Ted said.

Super cool. Nothing but positive vibes.

I showed him the trailer.

"I'm in," he said.

Man, I remember thinking, I'm having a heck of a day. I should leave here and go straight to the track.

I was still trying to talk Ted out of it. "You're starting a whole new company. Are you sure you don't want it dubbed or something?"

He shook his head. Norwegian was perfect, he said. They were planning on being the first truly international content network, and this would be their first international content.

Ted made his offer. "I'll give you a million an episode, and we'll do a two-year deal, eight episodes a year."

Holy Fuck! Maybe there was a God after all.

As far as I knew, this might have been the first two-year deal in TV history. They never did that, even with hits.

On the way out he put his arm around me. "Oh, one more thing. We're gonna be putting all the shows up at once."

That interrupted my groove for a minute.

"What do you mean?"

"You know how HBO has the whole season in the can before the first episode airs? Well, instead of broadcasting one week at a time, we'll put them all up at the same time."

I had to think about that one.

"Geez, Ted, are you sure that's the right move? I mean, you labor and suffer and someone can watch a year's worth of work all in one night? That seems a little weird."

"Oh yeah? You mean like working on a record album for a year and someone listens to it in an hour?"

Son of a bitch! He was right.

"You son of a bitch! You're right!"

And so, for the second time in TV history, I'd find myself at the medium's crossroads.

The Sopranos would change not only HBO but TV in general. For the first time in history, it would replace film as the go-to medium for creators of serious adult content.

And *Lilyhammer* would make Netflix the first truly international distributor and the preferred network for all future international content.

I didn't know that yet. All I knew for sure was that I had met the guy I'd be making TV with for the rest of my life, and I was not about to let him down.

When I returned to Norway to tell the head of Rubicon about Netflix, I was all smiles and expected the same in return. Amazing news, right?

Silence.

Hello? Did you hear what I just said? I saved the show. You know the budget you lied to me about? I just tripled it!

Rugby finally confessed. "There are a few other things you should know," he said.

What could possibly break my groove?

Turns out he was not your run-of-the-mill con man—he was a full-blown Scandinavian Zero Mostel.

Remember my incredible Spielberg-Hanks deal?

The one where I had 50 percent of the back end?

Well, I had 50 percent.

NRK had 50 percent.

The German distributor had 50 percent.

And probably a bunch of horny old ladies had 50 percent each.

How's that for a groove breaker?

Eilif, Anne, and I had lunch with the executives at NRK. Surely they'd see the brilliance of the deal?

Not exactly.

They explained that they rarely broadcast a series for more than one year. And on the rare occasion when they did renew a series, it only aired . . . wait for it . . . every *other* year.

I took my hands off the cutlery at that point. I was rapidly losing confidence in my ability to suppress the urge to slash someone's throat. I just couldn't decide if it would be one of theirs or my own.

We got our second season. Norwegian audiences were too enthusiastic to be denied. But of course, with that whimsical year off in between.

Every once in a while, Lady Destiny takes pity on me.

Ted at Netflix was cool about waiting, figuring that word of mouth would serve us well.

And Bruce decided to tour exactly when I would have been shooting the second season of *Lilyhammer*.

All I missed was a month in Australia. The first Australian trip for the reunited E Street Band had been a rare disaster. The power went out like three times during our opening gig. Not only did that show never get its momentum back, the entire tour never quite got on track.

For that second trip, Bruce took Tom Morello in my place, and that tour the band broke through.

Beautiful.

We lost Clarence Clemons in June 2011. He had been in bad shape for a while, but it was still a shock.

We'd lost Danny Federici in 2008. I still look over every once in a while and see him there. Who ever heard of somebody dying from skin cancer? It's still hard to believe.

Replacing original band members and keeping a band relatively the same is impossible. A band changes when members change. If it changes enough, you may have to even change the name of the band.

With Bruce's name up front we didn't have that problem. For us, continuing in a way that made sense was a profound challenge. Could we keep enough continuity to make a smooth transition and not disrupt the audience's expectations and experience?

In a way, the transition had already been happening. Clarence and I were always part of the show, the shtick, but I had been doing more of it lately because Clarence had to sit down for most of the show. The running-around-the stage vaudeville had shifted toward me and Bruce.

But Clarence's iconic solos were still central to many songs. Would an audience be reluctant to applaud someone new playing them? Would it feel like an insult to Clarence's memory?

The perfect solution dropped in our laps.

Clarence's nephew Jake.

Who, as it happened, could play the saxophone.

There would be no conflict about giving love to a blood relative.

The only problem was that Jake had established the beginnings of a career. He sang, played guitar, and wrote songs. The saxophone wasn't even his first instrument.

Bruce and I talked it over.

"Listen," I said. "We cannot have him stand in Clarence's spot. It's simply going to be too much for the kid. I know he has to play those solos, but let's go out with a horn section to camouflage him a little bit."

"Makes sense," Bruce said.

"And maybe he doesn't play every solo. Eddie Manion can play a few, to ease the pressure. Whoever solos can come out of the horn section and then go right back into it."

Rehearsals went well, but I could tell Bruce wasn't quite settled. After one of the rehearsals, he called me as I drove back to the city. "I don't know."

"What's the matter?" But I already knew.

"Jake."

"Talk to me."

"I think he wants to have his own career. I feel like I'm forcing him to do this. Like he's doing it out of obligation."

"Look, I'm sure he's nervous," I said. "Big shoes to fill. Literally. And he may not know it yet, but he's gonna love this. He's used to playing clubs. Just wait until he looks out at fifty thousand people screaming his name. He'll have an entirely new outlook on life."

Bruce wasn't sold. I could tell.

"Let me just suggest one thing," I said. "Two things."

"Go."

"You're always accusing me of being an extremist, but guess what? *You're* the extremist! OK, maybe we're both right, but we don't have to marry Jake forever. And Jake may not wanna marry us forever."

"I'm listening."

"Let's look at this as a transitional moment. Just this tour and then we see what happens. Maybe later we'll transform ourselves into some other thing, but right now he can keep the heart of the E Street Band intact. We are extremely lucky that he exists. I'm not sure what we would've done without him."

I could hear him thinking in the silence.

I went on. "The audience wants to grieve Clarence. We all do. But at the same time they'll see that his spirit is alive in Jake. That gives everybody something to celebrate instead of every night feeling like a funeral."

Plus, I told him I would talk to Jake and explain that he could pursue a solo career in between E Street tours. "I'm a little bit of an expert in this area. So we'll not only see how good and dedicated he is, but how smart. Because if he's smart, he's gonna embrace this opportunity with both arms."

More silence.

"OK," he finally said. "I hear you. I'll think about it."

He thought about it, and Jake was in. And man, did he rise to the occasion. He got better every single show.

Turned out to be a good kid.

Smart too.

I had another successful year at the Hall of Fame, where a cabal of us talked the rest of the voters into combining the Faces and Small Faces into a single candidate.

The Small Faces were the Faces' incredible predecessor, one of the five important British Invasion bands that never invaded. Combining the two was the only way to get Steve Marriott, the Small Faces' vocalist and one of the greatest white Soul singers ever, into the Hall—he was unlikely to get in with his other band, Humble Pie. I would try the same trick combining Free and Bad Company, who also had two common members, singer extraordinaire Paul Rodgers and the great drummer Simon Kirke, but that hasn't worked yet.

A few years earlier, Maureen had discovered an organization called Little Kids Rock that bought guitars for kids who couldn't afford them. It was started by a San Francisco teacher named Dave Wish. They wanted to honor me, but I'm generally not crazy about that kind of thing, and they honored Clarence instead. Maureen, who went to the ceremony, said it was nice but the organization needed help.

When Clarence left us, Little Kids Rock named their yearly honor after him. The first Clarence Clemons Award went to Lady Gaga, who told Maureen and me that she used to wait on us at Palma on Cornelia Street in the Village.

After Gaga, I told Dave Wish that I would accept the honor but that the show needed to be more elaborately produced. He didn't quite know what I had in mind, but I knew they could do better than the forty grand a year they were raising.

To make the show more interesting, we decided to have a bunch of artists do the honoree's songs. My year, performers included Bruce, Elvis Costello, Darlene Love, Tom Morello, Dion, and Jesse Malin. The next year, Joan Jett was honored by Cheap Trick, Billie Joe Armstrong, Gary Bonds, Kathleen Hanna and Ad-Rock. And Darlene Love's year brought out Elvis Costello, Brian Wilson, and Bill Medley.

We got them up to a million dollars net, and I moved on.

Meanwhile, David Chase, the man most responsible for making TV the go-to medium for the whole world of serious content, leaves TV and decides to make his first feature film. He decided on something small and personal. All due respect to my padrone, it felt like a Stevie move.

As a teenager, David had been a drummer in a band in New Jersey before he split to LA, went to film school, and got into TV. That was right around the time when the Beatles changed everything.

His movie, *Not Fade Away*, was largely autobiographical, exploring the tricky dynamics of being in a teenage band, and it was also about David meeting and falling in love with the girl who became his wife, Denise.

Midway through the writing, the script stalled, and he put it on a shelf. At around that time he asked me what I was working on, and I played him a new song called "The St. Valentine's Day Massacre" and later simplified to "St. Valentine's Day." As much as I love Bob Dylan's work, it was the only overtly Dylanesque song I'd ever written. I intended it for Nancy Sinatra, but for some unknown reason never got it to her and instead we cut it with one of my Wicked Cool bands, the Cocktail Slippers.

"Wait a minute," David said. "Play that again." He was always complimentary, but this was different. Turns out the timeline I'd used for the relationship in the song, Thanksgiving, Christmas, and New Year's, was the same one he had used for his movie. It brought the project back to life for him, and he finished the script.

I tried to talk him out if it.

I tried to reason with him, using the same arguments that people had used to try to talk me out of *Lilyhammer.*

"David, you just did the greatest TV show of all time. You can do anything you want right now. You can make Paulie Walnuts a Marvel Comics superhero and get a $200 million budget. Then you can make your small personal film. You'll have a built-in audience ready to go."

"I don't want to make *Big Pussy Versus the Martians,*" he said. "I want to do what I want to do."

Fuck me.

I figured if I couldn't talk him out of it, I had to help him make it.

My job was to evolve the Twylight Zones, as the band would be called, through their various stages of development, leading to their one moment of glory, my St. Valentine's song.

The first question was, Do we find musicians who could act? Or actors who could sing and play? I leaned toward the former, David toward the latter. He needed great acting more than great musicianship. "Can you turn actors into a band in four months?" he asked.

"Maybe. But I've got to warn you. There is a certain DNA consideration at work here."

"What do you mean?"

"You can sing in tune or you can't. You can keep a beat or you can't. There are some things you cannot learn."

David found two actors, Jack Huston and John Magaro, who *could* sing, and we started giving them lessons right away. Pat DiNizio from the Smithereens came in to teach Jack guitar, and Andy White taught John drums. I needed an older drum teacher because I wanted Magaro to learn the old-school Jazz way of playing with his wrist up.

If Andy's name sounds familiar, it's because he had been hired by George Martin to play on the first Beatles' single "Love Me Do." It was a common practice then, since most band member drummers weren't consistent enough and there was a very limited amount of time to get it right.

Max Weinberg had found Andy working in a North Jersey music store some years earlier. Lord knows how he recognized him, but Max works in mysterious ways. We found and hired Andy.

He was in his early eighties at the time and took the bus in every day from Caldwell, New Jersey. Sweet, sweet guy.

Max, Garry Tallent, Bobby Bandiera, and I recorded the music for the soundtrack, and I sang guide vocals for the actors.

By the time we shot the movie, the Twylight Zones had become a real band. I had fantasies of them playing film festivals after movie screenings.

The festivals that never happened.

Lilyhammer was the most popular show in Norwegian history, drawing one million viewers out of a national population of five million. It was the prime minister's favorite show. He would tweet to be left alone for an hour because "I am watching *Lilyhammer!*"

The tightrope act had worked. We had satisfied the NRK audience that wanted comedy and the Netflix audience that wanted more. We had made Norwegian viewers feel like the show was theirs while drumming up international appetite for Norwegian content for the first time.

In the wake of that success, I had to call Harvey Weinstein.

Miramax had gotten worldwide distribution, outside the United States, for *Not Fade Away*.

I had suggested to David that he release the movie in Europe first. It was more a European art-house film than a blockbuster, more *400 Blows* than *Transformers 5*. Rock and Roll still had some cultural capital in Europe. And though *The Sopranos* was big everywhere, as an auteur

David was more appreciated over there. No Jerry Lewis jokes, please; I agree with the French!

Break *Not Fade Away* in Europe, I figured, and maybe, just maybe, we'd have a shot at home.

So while David was discussing the domestic release with Paramount, I called Harvey. "Listen," I said, "I've got a really big show on in Norway right now. Let's do David's premiere there. Red carpet and the whole schmear! The entire cast of my show will come, we'll fly over a few Sopranos for fun, plus the prime minister is a fan. I know half his cabinet. I bet they'll all come too."

"Yeah, yeah, yeah," Harvey said. "Good idea. Let's make it happen."

It never happened.

The movie went straight to eight-track in the States. Another beautiful piece of work blowing in the wind. This time it wasn't mine, but I felt very bad for David. He and the film deserved better.

Nobody saw it.

The entire three seasons and four years I was in Norway, I loved everything about the country, the people, and the mystery of both. I wanted to leave something meaningful behind. I felt there was enormous untapped potential, and my natural instinct as a Producer was to realize the potential of everyone and everything I saw.

Norway is a very complicated place, and many of the complexities are buried deep.

You could vacation there for the rest of your life and never catch a hint of what is actually going on in the hearts and minds of Norwegians. The longer you are there, the less you know.

The complexity starts with wealth and how it's used.

Norway is one of the richest countries in the world, a well-kept secret. Up until 1972 or so, it was a nation of simple, mostly happy farmers. Well, happy might be a stretch. Content maybe. There's a reason Ibsen's plays aren't a laugh a minute.

Then one day, up from the ground came a-bubblin' crude. Oil, that is. From the sea, actually, but then you can't do the *Beverly Hillbillies* theme sing-along. And if Flatt and Scruggs ain't the ultimate name for a Bluegrass duo, I don't know what is!

So somebody struck oil, and what did they do? They tried to give it to Sweden, of course. Who promptly turned it down. Probably a relative of the schmuck who decided not to quarantine.

So, against their better nature, Norway became crazy rich.

I'm only half kidding about their nature. Norwegians are not all that comfortable being rich. Hard as it may be for Americans to understand, it is simply not a materialist society. No flashy cars, no designer clothes. Even at the homes of the richest Norwegians, no expensive paintings, no Louis XIV chairs, no kooky $50,000 lamps.

As rich as they are—and it's Saudi rich, I shit you not—they don't spend it. On anything. Individually or as a country.

There are potholes in the streets. The trains break down every month or two. Costs are high, taxes are high. With trillions in the bank. Or whatever the next thing after trillions is.

On the other hand, they guarantee free health care and education, from womb to tomb. No homelessness. No poverty. No crime (until Frankie Tagliano showed up!). Really scary socialism!

And don't fall for the we're-just-dumb-farmers routine, like I did. They're in the European Union, but they're not. They use it for trade, but they keep their own currency, which helped them avoid all the recession problems everybody else had a few years back.

Endlessly fascinating place. I miss it. If we could restart *Lilyhammer*, I'd go back in a minute.

One of the secret keys to the deeply mysterious Norwegian sensibility is a philosophy called *Janteloven*.

I won't do a whole big discussion about it—that's why God created Google—but among other things, it suggests that a society is healthiest when everyone is equal.

Radical! I know.

Extremist *Janteloven* acolytes look down on any Norwegians who think or act as if they are superior to anyone else.

Ambition ain't cool.

They make a huge exception, however, for sports stars. As long as they win, they can enjoy as much celebrity as they want.

And foreigners get a pass, luckily. So everybody loved me! And I loved them right back. Not in spite of, but because of all their eccentricities. Many of which we put in the show.

I got friendly with the cultural minister at the time, Trond Giske—and still am—introduced by either Stine Cocktail Slipper or Cecilie Launderette, both members of Wicked Cool bands.

Giske wanted to encourage the Arts and interaction with the rest of the world. I would make speeches occasionally, with his support, trying to explain the difference between equality and equal opportunity, which is one of our proudest American ideals we've never lived up to.

I always spent part of my speeches trying to encourage investment in a new industry—namely, entertainment. The existing industries—fishing, shipping, oil—all centered on the coastline. The interior didn't have a whole lot going on. Wood, maybe. Lots of trees.

When that industry wanes, what can be done? Art can be done. Culture can be done. A town like Notodden in Telemark is a good example. When its industry dried up, it started a Blues festival that has since become legendary in the Blues world.

The same could happen with TV and film. There's room for half a dozen production companies spread out in the countryside.

It only takes one hit show, or one group of talented craftspeople, to make a production company a success.

I had a joke in my speeches: "You'd better hurry and get something going before you run out of oil." Later I changed it to "You'd better start a new industry before oil is banned worldwide, which is in sight. Me and Greta Thunberg hope."

The message wasn't received in a simple way. Norway isn't simple. There were people who thought more or less the way I did and wanted to encourage everybody to realize their potential.

But most Norwegians were just fine being isolated. They had no interest in interacting with the rest of the world. They don't like tourists. They don't need TV. Just give them a cabin in the woods and snow to ski on.

I managed one victory in my battle to promote the film and TV industries.

I became friendly with Jo Nesbo, an amazing author of Norwegian noir / crime fiction. To understand how popular Jo is, you'd have to visit the Oslo Airport, where his books take up the space of an average New Jersey suburban house.

As I was trying, mostly in vain, to bring the TV and film industry to Norway, Jo decided to sell the movie rights to his latest book after years of resisting.

I seized the moment and met with both the prime minister and then cultural minister (by then, the one after Trond). "Jo Nesbo has just agreed to a film deal," I said.

"We heard." They were being polite.

"Every scene of his book takes place in Norway. But if you don't create a film incentive right now, the film will be made in the Czech Republic, or even worse, Iceland!" I continued in my best Cagney. "I sure wouldn't be in your shoes on Election Day if that happens," I said, half joking. Not.

There are complex film incentives having to do with tax breaks, but there's a simple version too. Say a movie company comes to town and spends money. They can rent equipment and production facilities if they're available, but there are expenses even without that: hotels, restaurants, electricians and carpenters, location scouts, extras, etc. The company keeps receipts, and the town gives back part of the expenses, maybe 20 percent, maybe 25. The town cannot lose, because without the movie the money would not have been spent at all.

In this case, Norway was the town. And they did implement the incentive for Nesbo, though I don't know if they kept it. A fleeting triumph.

I started doing master classes for the university in Oslo and the film school in Lillehammer, specializing in subjects that were rapidly becoming irrelevant, crafts like songwriting, arranging, producing. If I do it again, I'll add blacksmithing, Viking navigation, and the care and feeding of dragons.

I tried to organize the first international TV festival, not just a marketplace and showcase but workshops and, overall, a more produced and entertaining convention than what I witnessed at MIPCOM in Cannes, where me and Kiefer Sutherland were the only actors.

But it was hard to get investors interested. I've never been good with them. I explain what I'm doing and answer questions, and then it's up to them. But many investors want to be chased. They want their asses kissed. I guess you're supposed to call back and ask, That discussion we had the other day, any thoughts? Or some schmoozy bullshit like that. I just can't do it.

I also encouraged adding a TV class at the film school in Lillehammer. I explained again that except for a few dozen Oscar contenders and documentaries, the film world would soon be all comic books and video games.

They looked at me like I was nuts.

One of the things I'd been working on during my trips back to New York was reuniting the Rascals in a meaningful way.

Barbara Carr and Dave Marsh held a yearly fundraiser for the Kristen Ann Carr Fund to support sarcoma research. It was named for their daughter, who had died in 1993. The event is a massive meet and greet at the Tribeca Grill, and it usually consisted of just a dinner and a few speeches.

But Kristen Ann had been a real firecracker, full of energy, and the year the fundraiser honored me and Maureen, we thought the night should reflect her energy somehow.

Way back in 1980, Gary Bonds's Manager John Apostol had brought me in to try and get the Rascals back together. It was basically impossible; but I gave it a try every five years or so. The Kristen Ann Carr fundraiser was another try.

"What the hell?" Maureen said. "They won't reunite for their own good; maybe they'll reunite for someone else's good."

And sure enough, that's what happened. That night was the first time they'd done a full set in thirty years, having barely survived the three songs at the Hall of Fame.

For years, every Promoter had told me that the Rascals were the Holy Grail of reunions! Now that I'd done it, no one was interested. It was too late, they all said. The group had been away too long.

There was one place where it wasn't too late. *Jersey Boys* was a big hit on Broadway, and the Four Seasons were a generation *before* the Rascals.

I came up with an idea that I would end up calling *The Rascals: Once upon a Dream.*

I would film the band members telling their stories.

Meanwhile, I would produce the band's live show like no one had ever heard them.

Then they would play in a theater, and between songs the stage would go dark and their interviews would appear on a massive screen behind them. We would film some staged segments as well.

It would be a hybrid, but it could work.

I called Marc Brickman, who had been Bruce's first light man back in the day and had gone on to do lighting for everyone from Pink Floyd to Paul McCartney and even to light the Empire State Building.

Marc had just done the interior light design for the Capitol Theatre in Port Chester, New York. Peter Shapiro, who had refurbished the place after having great success with Brooklyn Bowl, turned out to be one of the world's truly classic characters. Like from another dimension. When we described our project, he took maybe five seconds to think and said, "Debut it here."

With a venue secured, I started writing the show. I needed to sequence the songs to tell a story, to rotate through different perspectives, to build and release tension.

We taped the band for the interview sections, and Marc designed visuals to transport the audience back to the '60s during the songs.

I wanted to start with a film clip of a little girl. I had a helluva time casting her until one day, at the office, I glanced down in the elevator and saw the cutest thing I'd ever seen on her way to ballet class. She turned out to be the daughter of Graydon Carter and Anna Scott, and they graciously allowed her to be cast.

The show would be my masterpiece. It gave the audience a much more satisfying evening than just guys standing there playing their hits. Marc and I started thinking of all the groups we could do next.

The opening night at Peter's theater will always be one of the most thrilling moments of my life.

Because Brickman's technology took up the entire back row, the soundboard was in the middle of the audience.

The lights went down.

I snuck down the aisle and took my place.

I gave the sound man a smile of confidence I didn't feel and tried to remember how to breathe.

There was an intro to my script narrated by Vinny Pastore, then music, then more narration, then Graydon's daughter, and then it happened . . .

The entire audience laughed. At something I wrote!

An electric current shot from my fingertips to my balls to my toes and back.

Marc ran down the aisle in a crouch with an ecstatic look I've never seen on anybody's face before or since.

"This is gonna work!" he whispered loudly.

He was right. The interviews were amazing in large format, more intimate than onstage banter could possibly be. The songs sounded better than ever. I suddenly understood the whole theater thing. The Writer thing. The Producer thing. The Director thing. All at once. It was my Diaghilev moment.

It took me a few songs to stop crying.

This was what I'm on this planet to do.

I'd finally found it.

thirty

The Golden Nymphs

(2014–2015)

Awop bop aloobop awop bam boom!
—LITTLE RICHARD

SC. 1-01 INT. FLAMINGO BAR,
FRANK'S OFFICE—DAY
ON BLACK.

SNOW REMOVAL GUY (O.S.)

I believe in Norway. I've always said it's the best
country in the world ...

(A man in his fifties, THE SNOW REMOVAL GUY, appears. We open
with a close-up of his face, then slowly zoom out.)

SNOW REMOVAL GUY (CONT'D)

... But with all the idiots we let in, I'm not
so sure anymore. Those damn politicians opened a
refugee camp next to my house. That was two months
ago and I haven't slept since.

(We pull back and see that the Snow Removal Guy's wearing
overalls. Next to him sits a German shepherd. The dog has a
funnel on its head. We begin to glimpse the silhouette of
FRANK TAGLIANO.)

SNOW REMOVAL GUY (CONT'D)

The other afternoon, I went to tell them a thing
or two. I brought the dog—I was polite and all,
but they refused to turn down the music. Carita's
sensitive, so she started barking. That's when one
of them smacked her with a belt.

(He fights back his tears.)

SNOW REMOVAL GUY (CONT'D)

Broke her jaw. Carita has always loved bones, but
now she can't eat anything but soup. I told the
police, but they do nothing.

(He starts to cry. From behind we see Frank signal with his
hand for someone to give the man a Kleenex. He blows his nose
and regains control.)

SNOW REMOVAL GUY (CONT'D)

People tell me there is only one person who can
help in situations like these: Johnny Henriksen.

FRANK

Why did you go to the police? Why didn't you come
to me first?

SNOW REMOVAL GUY

I didn't want to get in trouble ...

FRANK

I understand. You grew up in the old Norway.
Paradise. Everybody made a good living. Everybody
was taken care of. Well, that's gone. It's a new
world, my friend.

SNOW REMOVAL GUY

I know, but all this happened before ... before ...

FRANK

Before what?

SNOW REMOVAL GUY

Before I understood what kind of man you are.

SC. 1-02 INT FLAMINGO BAR,
FRANK'S OFFICE—DAY

(Frank smiles with satisfaction and rises. We see the room;
others are present. Arne, Torgeir, and Jan get up as well.
The Snow Removal Guy follows Frank, and Frank lays his arm
over his shoulder.)

FRANK

Good. Someday, and that day may never come, I may
call upon you to shovel some snow. Until that day,
accept this as a gift on the weekend my kids are
baptized. We'll look into your problem.

SNOW REMOVAL GUY

Thank you, thank you.

FRANK

And please: I understand Norwegian.

SNOW REMOVAL GUY

    (in Norwegian)
Of course.
    (to the dog)
Happy now eh, Carita? The man is so nice to us!

FRANK

Now if you don't mind, I'd like to go to my kids' prechristening party.

(The Snow Removal Guy is escorted out by Jan.)

FRANK (CONT'D)

    (straightening his tie in the mirror)
What a putz.

Just before season 2, Eilif and Anne were rattling off ideas they had gathered in the off-season. "Wait, wait," I said. "What was that last one?"

"Torgeir wrecks a gangster's Ferrari?"

"No, before that."

"We replicate the opening of *The Godfather*?"

I could see the whole scene immediately. "Eilif! This is fucking genius! This is not only gonna be great; it's a device we can use all the time!"

In that season 2 opening, Baard Owe played the Snow Removal Guy, the Bonasera the Undertaker role, and did a great job, except he was speaking English with absolutely no accent.

I was already pissed. I had told the Director, the Director of Photography, and the Production Designer to study *The Godfather* because I wanted everything to match exactly. But when I walked in, the lighting was all wrong and the furniture was in the wrong place.

I had to stop production and completely redo it. I got the distinct impression the Norwegians never quite grasped the significance of *The Godfather*'s place in cinema history, let alone in Italian American history.

And then there was the English. I said to the Director, "I need to hear the actor's Norwegian accent."

"He has no accent," the Director proudly told me. "He speaks English perfectly!"

"Yeah, man, I'm grokkin' that, that's really cool." I was starting to lose it. "But check it out. We're in Norway, doing a Norwegian parody of *The Godfather*, so he needs to have a Norwegian accent or it's not funny, dig? If he ain't gonna sound as Norwegian as he, in fact, is, I could have fucking filmed this in fucking Staten Island and slept in my own fucking bed tonight, gabeesh?"

He got it. And I love it.

❖

During the second season of *Lilyhammer*, the completely opposite expectations of the audiences of NRK and Netflix started to take their toll.

Specifically, they started to take their toll on the relationship between me and Eilif and Anne. I was told from the beginning that we would be doing a Norwegian version of *The Sopranos*, more or less. We needed the "cultural differences," but we also needed sex, violence, nudity, and language that would be expected on any subscription network.

I had an enormous obligation to Ted, who was trusting me to deliver a great show for a subscription audience. That meant adult subjects, adult depth, adult characters, and yeah, adult language, sex, and violence.

Eilif and Anne must have been getting pressure from the network because suddenly, everything I wrote was an argument. And even if I understood fighting for every act of violence—Norway was less tolerant of violence than the States—fighting for every sex scene or nude shot started to wear me out.

I had to remind them that Netflix was paying two-thirds of the budget and that the expression "tits and ass" did not refer to women breastfeeding or showing a baby's ass during a diaper change!

It was a crazy combination of contradictory goals and working methods, and sometimes it felt like me against a whole country, but in the end we somehow created a completely original hybrid dramedy and managed to satisfy both Norwegian and American viewers. Plus the international audience, which eventually included 130 countries.

And most important to me, I delivered what I promised to Ted Sarandos, who had staked his company's new content creation on me with blind faith, without notes or second-guessing.

We'd accomplished more in a few years than the entire Norwegian film and TV industry had in the previous fifty in regards to introducing the country's enormously talented artists to the world.

I wasn't exactly expecting dual citizenship or my own cabin in the woods, but not one of the big brass at NRK ever thanked us, visited the set, or seemed to know we existed. We never received one dollar from a very generous government that funded anybody and everybody that even called themselves an Artist.

The creeping tension among the creative team lifted when our second season was nominated by the International TV Awards in Monte Carlo in two Comedy categories, Best Show and Best Leading Man. The competition for the awards, the Golden Nymph Awards, included the whole planet. Just being nominated was amazing.

Would you believe it? Our little local show, underfunded and underpublicized, won both awards? We beat everybody in the world. Shows with three times the budget and big celebrity stars and massive publicity.

The only bummer was that no one was there from Netflix to enjoy it with.

Ted deserved to be there. He had gambled on us and won big. The ballsiest TV executive in history should have taken a bow. I had justified his faith. I wanted to celebrate with him.

In spite of our amazing victory, NRK was not planning on a third season. Remember, they hadn't even wanted the second one.

Luckily for us, NRK got a new boss, Thor Eriksen, who arrived just in time. He was a friend of Trond Giske, the former cultural minister, who set up a dinner the night before Thor was starting his new job. Jo Nesbo joined the three of us. Thor turned out to be a real fan and gave us a very, very rare Norwegian third season.

Ted was into it.

Netflix was going to start expanding worldwide, and I suggested what Ted had undoubtedly already thought of: since they already had a local show in Norway, they should make Norway the first country they expanded to. It was a template they could use everywhere. They literally owned the concept of international cross-fertilization at that point. They'd invented it with *Lilyhammer*, and it was a great strategy.

Start a local show when you start broadcasting in a new country, and then share all your international content. Just make sure you have a worldwide license, which is where HBO and many international franchisers fucked up. They may have had a presence in many countries, but they gave up control to the local territories. Big mistake.

By Netflix's third show, *Orange Is the New Black*, they had surpassed twenty years of HBO's subscribers in three short years.

That third season continued to broaden the show's creative horizons. It opened in Rio, which gave us new sights to see and new music to play.

We were taking our reputation as the first international show seriously. There was simply no country or ethnic group we wouldn't hesitate to corrupt!

While *Lilyhammer* was beating the odds in Norway, my Rascals show was fighting a losing battle back home. The investors never showed up. *Once upon a Dream*, despite being an artistic triumph, had become my usual financial nightmare.

It was the same story as always. I have never been able to raise money for my own projects. I can do it for others, but not myself. I spend every penny I have while I wait for lawyers or investors or sponsors or donors or patrons, because if I don't do that I would never create anything.

And I need to work constantly. I simply cannot function at the normal speed of this planet. The minute I stop moving, I start dying. That's the pattern of my life, and hard as I try, it never changes. I do what I have to do and then try to get it paid for after the fact.

I don't like it. I don't like it one bit. I do not like living this way. I don't have some martyr complex. I come to win.

I always wonder what would have happened to *Once upon a Dream* with a Manager. Maybe they could have gotten me money up front. Then again, I know from experience that nobody has any imagination. No matter how well you describe something, how passionately, how specifically, investors won't be convinced until they have seen it themselves.

Still, as we moved the show to Toronto and then to the rest of the United States, it worked better than we could have dreamed.

The show actually transcended the Rascals themselves. Our real achievement was transporting the audience back to the '60s for two hours.

We spoke to audience members after the show, and they all had the same questions.

What happened?

What happened to joy?

What happened to hope?

Back in the '60s those questions were asked, and answered, every day. In spite of the turmoil of chaos and protest marches and urban unrest and the Vietnam War and assassinations, we felt every tomorrow would be better than yesterday.

Optimism, man. Anybody remember that? The evolution of consciousness, the combination of joy and hope, the thrill of unlimited possibilities. That's what we had experienced in the '60s, and what we brought back with the show.

We had big plans beyond the Rascals. There were so many bands that conveyed the spirit of their time and that had endless stories to tell. Marc and I figured we'd be doing the Eagles next. Then the Who. The Temptations. A Kinks reunion (after the Rascals, nothing would be difficult).

There was no end in sight, and our new template could change the entire future of the Rock and Soul business for the remaining Renaissance Artists.

But then, unbelievably, as Marc took the show on the road, the poisonous relationships in the Rascals, the band dynamics that we had analyzed and filmed and laid out for the world to see, surfaced again.

Three out of four band members started acting like they had just been thawed from four decades of suspended animation, and they resumed being the assholes they always were.

One of the lead singers, Felix Cavaliere, who I'd thought was a friend, had seemingly decided the money he was making—more money than he'd ever made in his life—wasn't enough. He got two of the other guys, Dino Danelli (who had been in the Disciples for two years) and Gene Cornish (whose rent I'd paid for more than a year to keep him from literal homelessness), to go along with him.

The fact that this very costly show was losing money didn't seem to matter to them. The fact that I had written, directed, and produced, at my own expense, a Broadway show that let them showcase their greatness—a greatness that the world had long since forgotten—and restore their place in history also didn't seem to matter to them.

The fact that it was the best they'd ever sounded, even going back to their prime, didn't seem to matter to them.

Apparently what mattered to them was their egomania. I think what was particularly galling to Cavaliere was the fact that each member of the group was getting a separate standing ovation. I don't think he could stand that. To me it seemed like he felt, with absolutely no rational basis, that he'd always been a one-man show.

As it turned out, he was just using the entire two years of the show's run to raise his feeble solo fee. It went $5,000 per gig to $25,000 per gig, and he returned happily to what was, to my mind, a pathetic version of the music he was playing when I'd found him on the oldies' white chitlins circuit three years earlier.

For forty years, the conventional wisdom had been that the breakup had been caused by Eddie Brigati, the second lead singer, and his decision to capriciously quit the band. As it turns out, Brigati was the only one with any sense of honor, and he had originally split to preserve the integrity and dignity of the group, even after his publishing was stolen and his royalties had diminished to nothing.

Not only was the show the best creative work I've ever done, but I felt an additional sense of accomplishment at bringing Eddie Brigati, one of the most beautiful, soulful cats who has ever lived, back from cultural exile. His voice, confidence, and reputation were restored, and his corrected important place in history was secured forevermore.

A few years later, Maureen and I designed a cabaret act for Eddie—I supplied the Rock and Roll songs; she made a list of the best show tunes—and we played that at the Cutting Room in New York. We were proud of that show, and especially proud of Eddie, who really stretched to make that radical transition.

Along with the second death of the Rascals, actual death started to become a regular part of my life.

In the spring of 2012, my mother passed away after suffering horribly for months with complications from diabetes. She hadn't had any quality of life for years. The kindest, simplest woman I knew, she had lived a life of preliberation, old-school obligation. No fun since she was a kid, when, as the oldest of the five children of an Italian family, she became the de facto responsible mother.

I wish that I'd had more conversations with her. My father too. I was just too self-centered. Felt under siege my whole life. Always behind, always running to catch up, never quite getting there. Why couldn't I relax long enough to talk to my own parents?

My mother's passing was bookended by other deaths. We lost Steve Popovich, my early champion, in the summer of 2011, and Frank Barsalona, my mentor and one of my best friends, succumbed to his dementia in November 2012. And then, in June 2013 we lost Jimmy Gandolfini. David Chase called me in Spain with the news.

Jimmy's death was a huge loss to the industry, but I felt it personally. We had been looking to open a restaurant/bar together. We had been talking about the fact that there were no places like the old Columbus, Paulie Herman's joint, where people in the business, actors, musicians, and writers, could hang out together.

I had also talked to him about filming a scene for *Lilyhammer*. It was going to be a dream sequence where Frankie wanders through a blizzard and comes upon a cabin in the middle of nowhere. He knocks. The door opens, and there's Jimmy, Edie Falco, Jamie-Lynn Sigler, and Robert Iler. And Jimmy says, "Sil! You too!"

David Chase had even agreed to direct it.

I began to develop a method to cope with all these deaths.

Denial.

We spend most of our lives breaking down our defenses and trying to confront the truth. When you're young, denial is the enemy of quality of life. But as you get older, it becomes your friend. I have no real sense of time. I go long periods without seeing my friends, and when I do see them, we pick up our conversation where we left off. It's like the five or ten years apart never happened.

So when I lose a friend now, I try to avoid the funeral, unless the family really needs me there. Because in my mind, I keep all my friends alive. I tell myself it's just that our schedules aren't crossing at the moment.

Eventually . . . they will.

One other way to keep people alive is to respect their memory and history or to support institutions that do. The Rock and Roll Hall of Fame, for all its flaws, remained important for that reason.

The Hall mostly gets its mission right. Over the years, I had campaigned for the inclusion of Managers, starting with the Mount Rushmore of Managers: Colonel Tom Parker, Albert Grossman, Brian Epstein, and Andrew Loog Oldham. We got Epstein and Oldham inducted in 2014.

Colonel Tom and Albert Grossman were deemed too controversial. It's a shame. Just as the Art is always better than the Artist, the Manager's historical impact is always more important than the Manager.

There was one ugly moment when the Hall decided it didn't want Alan Freed's ashes anymore, despite the fact that Freed was the reason the Hall was in Cleveland in the first place. Instead of the situation being handled calmly and with dignity, it was dealt with in an unnecessarily disrespectful way.

I didn't learn about the situation until it was too late. Lance Freed was distraught. He is the gentlest, kindest soul I have ever met, completely unaccustomed to adversarial situations.

"Let's turn this into a positive thing," I said. Years earlier, Maureen had read about Rudolf Nureyev's grave. The next time we were in Paris, we went to the Russian Cemetery and found it. It was amazing. A stone mosaic that looks exactly like one of Nureyev's Persian, tapestry-woven kilim rugs. You would swear it was a blanket until you touched it.

I told Lance about it and suggested having the same artist, if we could find him, create a gigantic jukebox as the gravestone for his father.

Lance loved the idea. He started looking for real estate while I looked for the sculptor.

I found out the Nureyev grave had been created by Ezio Frigerio, the former set designer from the Paris Opera. And, incredibly, we found him! He was a hundred years old, but he was into it.

I connected him with Lance, but the cost of commissioning and shipping something that large turned out to be prohibitive, so Lance decided to have somebody in Cleveland do it.

But it turned out great.

That same year, the E Street Band finally made it into the Hall of Fame. We were inducted by Bruce, who had been in as a solo artist since

1999, and in his speech he admitted that I was right when I'd said the band should have gone into the Hall before he went in as a solo artist.

That had been the third of our major fights.

It was a stunning admission. I give him a lot of credit for admitting he was wrong. Especially in such a public fashion.

I had been promising Darlene Love that I would produce an album for her since I met her in Los Angeles in 1980.

Maureen and I would go see her perform at least once a year.

We were sitting in the audience at the old B. B. King Blues Club and Grill on Forty-Second Street in Times Square when Darlene did a Gospel number, "Marvelous" by Walter Hawkins, and as usual, wiped out the entire audience, including me.

This time I just snapped.

"People have got to hear her do this song," I said to Maureen.

"Well, why don't you do something about it?" she said. "You've been waiting for the right time to work with her. But there's never gonna be a right time."

After the show I talked to Darlene backstage. "What are you doing tomorrow?"

"Nothing."

"We're going in the studio."

"What are we doing?"

"We're doing 'Marvelous.' The rest we'll figure out as we go."

The next day I started calling every great songwriter I knew. "I'm doing Darlene Love's debut album. Write her a song!"

Elvis Costello sent me four songs in forty-eight hours, which was very encouraging. The legendary Cynthia Weil and Barry Mann wrote Darlene a great song. Bruce gave me two.

I got a cool song from Joan Jett. One from Michael Des Barres. And Linda Perry wrote a great one.

I had a good opener in mind. A song from my second solo album called "Among the Believers." Never got much attention, but I knew it would resonate with Darlene's faith.

Jimmy Webb sent his song in, and it was great but not quite "Mac-Arthur Park," so I made up an instrumental middle section that made it more epic, which is what we needed.

Darlene had always resented Phil Spector taking "River Deep, Mountain High" away from her and giving it to Tina Turner because they were fighting at the time. She wanted to do it. I was like, uh, Darlene, you know that's known as Spector's greatest record, right?

"I don't care," she said. "We can beat him, Stevie!"

Fuck me.

Now I'm not big on remakes to begin with. As we discussed, a cover has to be either spectacularly different, or simply spectacular, and I wasn't so sure we could be either one.

I solved it with a *West Side Story* intro and by bringing out every riff you remembered and a few more. And then, oh yeah, there was the greatest singer in the world with fifty years of pissed off ready to explode.

As the story goes, Phil quit the business when his greatest record wasn't a hit. Ironically, if he had let Darlene sing it, it would have been. Darlene's Gospel voice can handle the upper registers and smooth those notes out, where Tina's Bluesy R&B voice breaks up in a way that scares little young teenage girls to death. And that was and is the Pop audience.

I later played it for Jeff Barry. He gave me a look I'll never forget.

"I can't believe you had the balls. But goddamn if you didn't pull it off!"

The last thing I did is what I always do when I produce an album. I wait until the end and see what else is needed. This one felt like it could use one more Gospel song. I stayed up late listening to the Soul Stirrers and woke up with "Jesus Is the Rock That Keeps Me Rolling." Dave Clark happened to be in town just after we recorded it and flipped over that one. He said it was the greatest song I had ever written and would be the one that would "ironically live on forever in every church long after your atheist ass is gone!"

I made an amazing deal with Rob Stringer at Sony. I'll forever be thankful that he had so much belief in what he was hearing that he agreed to put out a seventy-three-year-old woman's debut album.

Once we signed with Sony, I figured that was it. The album, *Introducing Darlene Love*, would not only be nominated for Album of the Year but would win going away. I was quite sure no other album could touch it. And since everyone had seen *20 Feet from Stardom*, the Oscar-winning documentary about background singers that featured Darlene, this album would complete the story. A perfect, beautiful, happy ending to an extraordinary career.

We weren't even nominated.

Nobody heard it.

With around three episodes left to shoot in our third season, I got the call from Ted.

The business had gotten too complicated to continue. Was there anything I could do? No, he said, nothing we could do.

Netflix had come a long way since my first promo tour where I promised to bring the stock price back from 47 to 100! I even did CNBC and explained to Maria Bartiromo what Netflix was, because I knew all the stock market freaks watched her. They're creating content, I explained. Why? she asked.

Knowing the show was ending gave me a chance to write in a bit of closure.

In the third-season finale, the show that would be our last, Tony Sirico returned as my older brother Antonio the Priest. Maureen returned as Frank's ex. And Bruce made his acting debut as Frank's middle brother Giuseppe, a mortician and part-time hit man.

For most of the run of the show, Eilif and Anne were only comfortable with me doing first drafts of the last show of each season. They were afraid I was going to hijack things into triple-X pornography. For the third season, not only did I write the first draft, but after seven seasons of *Sopranos* and three seasons of *Lilyhammer*, I finally got to direct.

I had always thought directing TV was the job of a traffic cop. Very limited creativity as opposed to film because the show had to look the same every week. But there was more creativity than I expected, and I enjoyed it more than I thought I would. With the big picture taken care of by the writing, I enjoyed getting into the granular details, the nuances of the actors' performances, timing, expressions, tone, and texture, all the more challenging since they were mostly speaking in Norwegian! And I was able to include more Lillehammer locations, which we should have been doing all along if the producer hadn't been an asshole.

I finally got back to the *Godfather* for inspiration, using Fredo's execution as a model for Fridtjov's. Next time you watch it, note that I did not show Fridtjov actually being shot. You just hear it. Just in case we got another year through some miracle, there was no way I was gonna lose one of our best actors.

As we were packing up in Norway and heading for New York for the final few scenes, which would include Bruce's scenes, the Producer, Anders Tangen, turned to me. "By the way," he said, "we're out of money. If you want to shoot the New York scenes, you're going to have to pay for it."

I had caught Anders overspending on various things over the previous two years, building unnecessarily elaborate temporary sets and overpaying for locations, and ratted him out regularly to the heads of the production company to no avail. This was his revenge, I suppose.

"I hope you are joking."

"No, we're broke."

I called my Agent. He may have been completely incompetent until then, but I was sure he would rise to the occasion and finally use the muscle of his major agency to put Anders in his place!

"What do you want me to do about it?" he said.

Those were his actual words.

As if I could make that up.

"Sorry for bothering you."

I hung up.

He was so fucking fired.

I paid the $180,000 to film the New York scenes, because without them the show would've made no fucking sense. Plus, nobody involved seemed to have the intelligence level to recognize that after years of being pursued by every major Director and Producer, Bruce Springsteen, arguably the biggest star in the world, was giving us his acting debut.

Unfortunately, his appearance would barely be noticed, never mind publicized, because by the time the episode was broadcast, the show had been canceled.

For those New York scenes, I needed someone to play Pasquale, the son of the Mob boss Uncle Sal. Maureen suggested a young actor she'd directed in a play, Nicky Cordero, and I proudly got him his Screen Actors Guild card. Nick would go on to star on Broadway in *Rock of Ages, Waitress, Bullets Over Broadway,* and *A Bronx Tale,* and he would be our most personal loss to the COVID pandemic, murdered by a scumbag ex-president and a political party that doesn't believe in science.

The last piece of the finale was the music. I used a Procol Harum song, not "The Devil Came from Kansas," which I'd suggested for the *Sopranos* finale, but the melancholy "A Salty Dog," which summed up my feelings of leaving both Norway and Netflix, two relationships that would mean so much to my life and that still feel as though they have been only temporarily interrupted.

And I ended the series with another *Sopranos* suggestion, Bruce's "Loose Ends," which also gave the episode its title.

I don't know what lies ahead, but don't forget about me, Norway. We're not done yet.

Ironically and incredibly, that third season of *Lilyhammer* won the Golden Nymph for the second year in a row for both Best Comedy Series and Outstanding Actor in a Comedy Series. That had never happened in the thirty years of the award's existence.

This time, I felt it necessary to apologize to Sir Ian McKellen for beating him. His performance in *Amadeus* remains my most memorable Broadway experience among the rest of his extraordinary life's work.

All the other shows congratulated us. Producers offered me guest spots on everything. But the one group I wanted to see was missing again. Where was Netflix?

Even if they didn't want to continue because of the vast business complications and unscrupulous nature of the partners of the show, I still wish the man who made it all possible would have been there to take a bow.

What balls to gamble on a first show with one American actor and subtitles.

Not only would the meeting with Ted Sarandos forever be my best business meeting of all time (the meeting with Susie Buffett wasn't business), but he was one of the few truly courageous, visionary leaders in a cowardly, myopic business.

He deserves every bit of Netflix's success.

It hurt me to my soul that he wasn't there.

thirty-one

Ambassador to the Court
of Ronald McDonald

(2016–2017)

Write, Act, Paint, Play, Perform, Work, Think, Speak, Live with
Purpose. Or hide under the bed until checkout time.
—THE UNWRITTEN BOOK

Thanksgiving of 2015 Bruce announced there would be no E Street
Band tour in 2016.

We were onstage in January.

As any Tour Manager doing arena tours or bigger knows, that is a
physical, mental, and spiritual impossibility.

For George Travis, our Tour Manager, the impossible took only six
weeks in this case. That's six *fucking* weeks, if you're keeping score.

Find fifty or sixty crew members that aren't booked. Find venues that
aren't already booked. Contact the band and the rest of the touring
party and inform them that whatever they thought they were doing,
they are not doing. Hotels. Planes. Trucks. Buses. Flights. Customs. Staging. Sound. Lights. Screens.

In six weeks. Try it.

George started as a truck driver. Depending on how long the drive
was to the next show, drivers would often work during the show as rig-
gers and spotlight operators.

George was a rigger. They're the crazy mamajamas that climb up high to secure hanging points for lights and sound and screens. Real high. With no net.

He worked his way up, or down in this case, to being the flashlight guy as the band walked on the stage. Might not seem like much, but it put him in contact with humans—well, the band anyway—for the first time, which was a risky move for his immediate superior, in this case Marc Brickman, our light man and production head.

Suppose George said the wrong thing to the wrong guy at the wrong time? Suppose the Boss didn't like his face? Or the shirt he was wearing? A bad flashlight guy could fuck up an entire show! "I like him," I told Marc. "I think he's destined for bigger things."

"Ain't we all," he mumbled with his typical sincere cynicism.

George eventually became Tour Manager, one of the very best.

The River Revisited was my second favorite tour ever, after the original River Tour, because that album has my favorite material. It's also got Bruce's best singing. He is one of the greatest white Soul singers of all time, but since that's not his favorite part of his identity, he only becomes that guy every once in a while. Much to my eternal aggravation, he takes that gift totally for granted.

On this tour he was that guy every night, which was awesome to behold. As a Student Prince advertisement from 1971 said, he was "That Sensational Soul Man."

Featuring the "Hoochi-koochi Guitar Player Steve VanZadt"! And "Pro-Football in Color"!

Bruce managed to ruin my personal fun a little bit by deciding not to do the full *River* album in Europe.

"Why?" I asked, disappointed that some of our greatest audiences wouldn't be seeing one of our greatest shows.

Too many slow songs for stadiums, was the answer.

Now Bruce has to sing the songs, so if he doesn't feel like singing that many slow songs, that's that. But the implication that the audience wouldn't like it was simply incorrect.

I was in in LA having dinner with the very cool *Game of Thrones* guys David Benioff and D. B. Weiss sometime in 2015. They asked if I wanted to go with them to see the Rolling Stones, who happened to be doing the entire *Sticky Fingers* album. "I don't know," I said. "Let me think about it." *As if!* It was phenomenal, and afterward I told Charlie Watts, "This will be the greatest tour you've done since Exile in '72!"

"No it won't," he said in his famous deadpan delivery. "What you just saw was the only time we're doing the whole album. Mick says it's too many slow songs for stadiums. Maybe you can talk to him."

No thanks.

The thing was, I'd spent the entire '80s in Europe, seeing dozens of shows, and half of the biggest Rock acts did nothing *but* slow songs. The Eurovision Song Contest, the single biggest event in Europe, is nothing but slow songs.

Yes, *Sticky Fingers* has a lot of slow songs. But look at what they are! "I Got the Blues," "Sister Morphine," "Moonlight Mile," "You Gotta Move." Not to mention "Wild Horses."

And yes, *The River* has lots of slow songs, but they are "Independence Day," "I Wanna Marry You," "The River," "Point Blank," "Fade Away," "Drive All Night," and . . . well, maybe they had a point.

Anyway, if those two front guys feel the same way about something . . .

I felt really bad the River Revisited Tour had to skip one of my favorite parts of America, North Carolina. For some reason the audiences in the Carolinas are among the most enthusiastic audiences for us in the country. I think they saw our brand of northern bar band as something slightly exotic. It was almost like playing Europe.

But North Carolina had just passed their ridiculous bathroom bill, the first of the Orwellian-titled religious freedom bills. The legislation that had nothing to do with religious freedom and everything to do with imposing extremist religious ideas on a rapidly disappearing Separation of Church and State society.

As soon as they passed the bill, we decided we had to show solidarity with the LGBTQ community and so couldn't play the state. We helped lead a boycott of artists, athletes, and professional organizations to make the point that the North Carolina political leadership was living in the past and needed to be voted out. The boycott worked, to some degree— they adjusted the law without quite fixing it—but within a few months it became impossible to stay away from states that were imposing fanatical anti-LGBTQ legislation. There were just too many.

When the River Tour hit London, Maureen came over. It was her favorite town in her favorite country. She could live there permanently, and I've been promising her at least an apartment there for years, but I keep blowing it. The festival was one apartment. The Rascals show was another. Maybe we'll get there eventually, but between me and you— come here a little closer; I have to whisper—I like visiting and living in hotels better.

We had tea with Bill and Suzanne Wyman, and they invited us to his eightieth birthday party. They are the original odd couple, Bill quietly bemused by much of the modern world and Suzanne as wild and kinetic as can be.

A couple nights later I went to see the soul singer Madeline Bell at Ronnie Scott's Jazz Club with Leo Green, one of our Promoters from Live Nation. "When you coming back to London?" Leo asked.

"We come every year for Maureen's birthday in November and sometimes stay through Christmas, but Bill Wyman just invited us to his birthday party in October."

His eyes lit up. "That's the same week as my Blues Festival. Why don't you throw a band together and headline one of the nights?"

Wow . . . I had to think about that one.

I hadn't fronted a band since the '80s, but doing the Darlene Love album and the *Lilyhammer* score had given me a whole new set of musician friends.

There are two kinds of musicians in the world, band guys and session guys. Band guys are the ones you grow up with and start out playing with, and if you're lucky, you hit on some magical chemical combination.

Session guys are professionals. They play in time, and they play in tune.

The members of the Rolling Stones (and almost every other important band you can name) could not find work as session musicians if their lives depended on it. You're more likely to be overqualified for Rock than underqualified.

What bands have is personality. And chemistry. Alchemy. Every great band is a matter of individual eccentricities blending in different ways with unpredictable, inconsistent, occasionally glorious results.

Session guys generally don't have strong musical personalities. They are trained to take on the personality of the Artist they're working with. That's what makes them valuable. A session guy may be (and often is) the craziest mofo you'd ever want to meet in real life. But at a session he's going to adapt.

In recent years, I had started meeting more of a third type, a hybrid of the first two—session guys that perform live.

There was some precedent. When Rock and Soul began, the revue-type shows used session guys because there were multiple acts, and the band had to read the charts, be great, fast, and consistent. There was no performance requirement per se. They were in the background and just played.

All the big shows had them. The Alan Freed shows, Murray the K shows, Dick Clark shows, the Motown Motortown Revue. Even Soupy Sales emceed a revue show. Those revues needed bands, and they couldn't use the labels' house bands. There were exceptions. Booker T. & the M.G.'s did Stax tours, since they played on most of the records. And that had to be some Funk Brothers on the twelve-year-old Stevie Wonder's live and incredible "Fingertips." But if the house band was on the road, who was left to make the damn records?

Beyond Rock, the Popular standards artists who toured—Frank Sinatra, Tony Bennett, Jerry Vale, or in-betweeners like Tom Jones, Shirley Bassey, and Engelbert Humperdinck—brought along a Music Director, and maybe a drummer, and then hired most of the musicians in each city as they went.

The drummer was often there for shtick as much as for sticks.

It was left to solo artists who lived in the Pop world but had Rock roots or unusual complexity to begin taking true session guys on the road. Artists like Paul Simon, Sting, Linda Ronstadt (half of her band was session guys; the other half turned into the Eagles!). Or even Jeff Beck these days, who requires supreme musical excellence to keep up with him.

I took that path. I had drafted Marc Ribler to be Darlene's Musical Director and brought in higher-level musicians to mix with a few of her old band and excellent singers, Ula Hedwig, Milton Vann, and Baritone Williams. When Leo Green asked me to throw together a band, I decided what the hell. This crazy gig might be fun.

I could do some Paul Butterfield things with the horns, which nobody hears anymore. I could do some of Mike Bloomfield's Electric Flag stuff, which nobody's ever heard live. I could do regular Blues like Little Walter and Howlin' Wolf, and maybe even some blaxploitation for a jazzier change of pace.

Suddenly, I was actually looking forward to this thing!

I called Darlene. "Baby, I've got to borrow Marc back for a minute. I'm actually gonna do a gig!"

"Of course!" She was the coolest.

And it was only one gig. I thought.

Marc put an excellent band together: Richie Mercurio on drums, Jack Daley on bass, and Andy Burton on keys. I added Eddie Manion and Stan Harrison, who went all the way back to the Jukes, on horns.

At rehearsal, along with the Blues and covers, I threw in some of my own songs, which I hadn't sung or even thought about since the '80s.

As I started to sing them, the strangest thing happened. I couldn't make it through a song without beginning to cry. I had to stop for a minute and figure out why. I realized it had been so long since I'd sung them that there was no distance between the emotions that created the songs and the process of performing them. I was literally living the words as I sang them. Feeling the melody and the chord changes with no buffer.

I had heard Maureen talk about the acting theory of "sense memory" from her classes in the old days, but it suddenly occurred to me that that theory may be built on a faulty assumption.

Sense memory theory suggested that when actors needed to cry in a scene, they should think back to an incident in their life that made them cry and use it. But what I found out was if you're really in the moment, you *can't* use it. You can't act. You can't speak. You can't sing. Your throat tightens up. You need a little distance.

When I told Bruce about it, he had a deeper explanation, the result of his forty years of therapy, which was that I was feeling a combination of guilt and despair at having abandoned my children (my songs) for decades.

He probably had a point. He always does.

Either way, it took me a couple of weeks to be able to get through the songs.

I got one of the great phone calls of all time in 2016.

"Stevie?"

"Yeah."

"Chita Rivera."

Wow!

"I'm doing my debut at Carnegie Hall and I want you to perform with me."

"Me?!?"

"Yes, please, darling—you'll make my show so cool!"

Ha-ha! As if her show could be any cooler. Me and Maureen have been catching her show for years and it just gets better and better.

She is the best part of show business personified, and not a bad résumé either—*West Side Story, Bye Bye Birdie, Chicago, Sweet Charity, Pippin, The Rink, Kiss of the Spider Woman,* and more.

We sang a duet on James Taylor's "Secret O' Life." I think that's about as nervous as I've ever been onstage. But it worked out great.

At around the same time, my friend Kenny Schulman, who had been involved with the New York Ronald McDonald House for years, asked for my support.

There are many reasons I'm quite sure there is no such thing as an anthropomorphic white guy with a beard up in the sky looking down personally on all eight billion of us, especially football players that score a touchdown, but the main one is kids with cancer.

"It's God's will," say the religious extremists that make up way too much of our country.

Really?

I feel sick whenever I see them. They wear bandanas when they get chemo, so many years ago I thought it would be nice if wearing the bandana wasn't an embarrassment but a badge of coolness.

So we created very colorful "Little Steven's Magic Bandanas" and told the kids that wearing one made them Rock stars.

I called John Varvatos, who called Tommy Hilfiger, and they also designed bandanas, which was supercool. Every celebrity and clothing designer could and probably would design a bandana if approached. It really makes the kids feel better psychologically.

Kenny loved the idea, and so did the executives at the Ronald McDonald House, and they made me the first Ambassador of Ronald McDonald House in New York to promote the whole thing.

Made it, Ma! Top of the world!

Maybe they'll make it a national campaign eventually.

If it makes these kids feel 1 percent better, it's worth it. All it takes is our will. Not that of God, who is busy making sure Rappers win Grammys.

Leo's Blues Festival gig was at a joint called the Indigo at the O2, part of the O2 Arena complex, which has the coolest configuration of a theater I've ever seen. Nice big stage, big dance floor, but then it has a huge, steeply raked balcony much closer to the stage than any I've ever seen. It made a 2,500-capacity theater feel very intimate.

Our best friends in London, Karl and Anita Sydow, brought Dave Clark, who emceed the evening for us, and the response from the eight hundred or so punters was fabulous.

Doing my own music after all those years was quite emotional for me, and I'll never forget that evening.

Richie Sambora was playing next door at the arena, so I joined him onstage and he joined me. He's one of my best friends, and I don't get a chance to see him often enough.

We went to watch Jeff Beck, who was also playing and was his usual amazing self. It was interesting to see Jimmy Page, not so bad himself, in as much awe as we were.

Backstage, I asked Jeff if he knew how annoying it was that he never missed, no matter how crazy a lick he was going for.

"That's what *you* think," he said. "I've just learned to cover it up well!" He was lying, I'm sure, to keep me from jumping off London Bridge.

As Richie and I were leaving, Leo stopped us. "Come say hi to Van Morrison," he said.

I'd never met him, but I'd heard . . . things. And I never like to take chances meeting my heroes.

"Thanks, Leo," I said, "but no thanks. I've heard he can be a bit . . . well, shy. And so am I."

"You don't understand," Leo said. "He asked for you. He wants to meet you." Richie and I went into his dressing room. Van was in a great mood. A sweetheart really. He talked about getting off the road and going back to his roots. Just grabbing a residency at some local pub and living the rest of his life that way.

After a few minutes our mutual shyness started to take over.

There happened to be a vacuum cleaner sitting there.

"Van," I said, "I don't know any better way to show my gratitude for all the pleasure your music has brought me through the years, so I'm just gonna clean up a bit for you." I started vacuuming his room.

His Tour Manager said it was the most he had seen Van laugh in ten years.

Bill Wyman's eightieth birthday party was filled with Rock celebs: Robert Plant, Bob Geldof, and Mark Knopfler, among others. Mark and I talked about our mutual friend Lance Freed, who had administered Mark's publishing along with mine for years. Lance had left Rondor to venture off on his own.

"Have you heard anything yet?" Mark asked me, as anxious as all of Lance's friends were to be back with him. Quite a compliment, considering that Dire Straits had been among the biggest bands in the history of European Rock. Mark hadn't needed a publisher for forty years. But like the rest of us, he was perfectly willing to give up an administration fee just to hang out with Lance. That's how cool Lance is.

After the party, it was time to get back to E Street, where the River (or at least River-ish) Tour would resume in Australia in January.

But the gig felt so good and the band was so amazing that I couldn't shake the experience. Something significant had taken place. "Hey," I told Marc Ribler, "I've got a month or two off. Why don't we make an album just for the hell of it? No heavy lifting. We can record a bunch of the songs I've written for others through the years." The rehearsal alone had already sounded like an album.

He was down. The band was into it. I talked to Bruce to see what he thought. He said it was a great idea. And that's what we did.

Every album I've ever done has a theme and a concept. In this case, the title said it all: *Soulfire*. A summation of the songs written for others that combined the raw power of Rock with the emotional depth of Soul, in the process creating something uncategorizable and uniquely uncommercial!

I mostly picked songs that still had emotional resonance for me. There were two that Southside had recorded, "I'm Coming Back" from the '90s, which obviously made sense, and "I Don't Want to Go Home," Johnny's signature song, which I rearranged back to the way I'd originally pictured it for Ben E. King and the Drifters. I did an Ennio Morricone arrangement for "Standing in the Line of Fire" from the third Gary US Bonds album, and finally my own version of "St. Valentine's Day" from both the Cocktail Slippers and David Chase's Twylight Zones. I still hope to do it with Nancy Sinatra, who I wrote it for.

I also did some new writing, finally finishing what had been going to be the first song on my first album forty years earlier, "The City Weeps Tonight." My idea back then was to introduce myself as a new artist by going chronologically through the history of Rock and Soul genres, beginning with Doo-Wop. But then I decided to go political.

The other new song on *Soulfire* was "I Saw the Light," a song I'd written for Richie Sambora and his partner at the time, Orianthi. I had talked with Richie casually about producing them. I thought they were a great couple, and I wanted to make them the Delaney and Bonnie of Hard Rock. I could see it, hear it, clear as day.

Richie was in New York with his daughter, who was going to NYU, and he was supposed to come over a dozen times to hear the song and discuss the album. He never made it.

By the time Richie and I reconnected, they were doing an album with Bob Rock and had like thirty songs. I figured they didn't need me or my song, put it on the shelf, and found it again just before I made *Soulfire.*

I always wonder what would have happened if Richie had come over that day and we'd grabbed Orianthi and gone into my studio four blocks away and cut that song.

I'd never recorded a cover on a solo album, but I happened to be listening to an Etta James record and heard "Blues Is My Business," written by Kevin Bowe and Todd Cerney.

" . . . and business is good."

Is that a classic fucking hook or what?

I wanted to fill out the set with something Jazzy so the horn players could blow, and I also wanted to do my favorite blaxploitation song, Bodie Chandler and Barry De Vorzon's "Down and Out in New York City," the *Black Caesar* theme by the Godfather of Soul himself, James Brown. I combined the two ideas by coming up with a cool Jazzy theme we could riff off of that fit right in.

As I contemplated my return to the music business, I promised myself that I was going to do things right. I knew most of the problems of my professional life had come from not having a Manager.

I called Scott Borchetta.

I had met Scott at Jimmy's wedding in 2016. I didn't know much about him other than that he had started the Big Machine label in 2005 and almost immediately hit the lottery with Taylor Swift, but I liked the way he carried himself.

Shortly after we met, Scott asked me to mentor on *Idol* again, where he had taken over from Jimmy. I had gotten away with it once and nobody had gotten hurt. A second time seemed risky. But Maureen made me do it again, and it was fine again. All I remember is La'Porsha Renae turning down my suggestion of Jerry Ragovoy's "Stay with Me," despite my encouragement. She would have won with it!

The experience was uneventful except that Jennifer Lopez, who was one of the judges, didn't have a clue who I was. Totally understandable;

why should she? But Maureen felt she was being disrespectful and went after her on Twitter. That was entertaining for a minute. Luckily J-Lo remained clueless about me all over again when I did a commercial with her for the 2020 Super Bowl, so there was no bad blood. I even changed the script to subtly hype her latest movie.

When I called Scott Borchetta, we reminisced for a minute about *Idol.* Then I got to the point. "Hey, man, I'm kind of coming back into the business. I know you're mostly a record company guy, but if you have a little time, do you want to be my Manager?"

"Wow." Not a call he was expecting. "Yeah! Sure! Let's meet in Nashville."

In NashVegas, Scott brought in a guy named Ken Levitan and another guy. Scott explained he was busy with Big Machine but would get involved with anything important. Levitan, his management partner, would handle the day-to-day.

Ken then introduced me to the other guy, who would actually be handling the day-to-day. Now I was two levels down from what I'd had in mind. But what the hell, everybody seemed enthusiastic.

So they became my first real Managers. Great, I thought. I don't have to say no to the many offers I get, most of which are from acquaintances. I can now send those people to management, who can be the bad guys and turn them down.

I explained it was going to take me a minute to make the enormous adjustment to being a front man, so we needed to take it slow.

Instead, they started saying yes to everything being offered. TV shows. Gigs. Record deals. Everything.

It's a typical management methodology to get some revenue on the books quickly to make everybody feel like the Managers are doing something, but it didn't work for me.

They made a record deal with Bruce Resnikoff at Universal that was the worst deal I've ever seen, but I was determined not to scare them away by interfering.

They assured me it was a good deal for those days. I told them that just a year earlier I had made a fifty-fifty ownership/partnership deal for Darlene Love, a seventy-three-year-old legend releasing her debut album, which was the kind of thing you could do if you had already paid for the record, which I had also done with *Soulfire*. "Well," they said. "This is the best Universal will do."

Long story short, *Soulfire* came out and it was obvious within three months that the management thing just wasn't gonna work, so I let the Managers go.

The first thing I did after they were gone was meet with Bruce Resnikoff. Incredibly, it was the first time anyone had met with Universal to discuss *Soulfire*. Again, this was three months after it came out, as opposed to six months before, when the marketing plan meeting should have happened.

It took me all of sixty seconds to renegotiate the record deal to a fifty-fifty partnership.

Which reminded me why I didn't have a Manager, but it was still depressing. Everybody else had one. I just wanted to be normal.

Bruce would turn out to be a very important and loyal new friend. I had known him casually for years. I almost did the Darlene Love album with him. But what would be the most productive three years of my life were due directly to his faith and belief in my work. And I'll never forget that.

When the E Street Band returned from Australia, Bruce told me he had put together a small one-man biography-type show for the Obamas, which he planned to expand and take to Broadway.

I figured it would be a good time to do a new TV show. I called whichever horse I was riding on the merry-go-round of Agents at the time to make a TV deal for one of my five scripts, and I also met with Chris Columbus and Joe Roth to see if they had anything for me.

While that was going on, Maureen and I were put on the board of the Count Basie Theatre. The Basie had a special place in my heart because when I was a kid it had been my local movie theater, the Carlton (when I wasn't at the drive-in in Holmdel). It was in Red Bank, the place where I bought my records and first guitar at Jack's.

Maureen was busy teaching acting to the dancers at American Ballet Theatre at that time, but she agreed to be on the board because she also had a special place in her heart for the Carlton/Basie from when she'd danced there as a kid with the New Jersey Ballet.

The Basie was fundraising to expand the theater into a block-long Arts center. They had shown me the design, which I didn't like. Why did it have to be so boring? Why not make something iconic like Gaudí's apartment buildings or Saint Basil's Cathedral or even the guitar-shaped hotel Jimmy Allen was building at the Hollywood, Florida, Hard Rock? Who wanted another fucking accountant's office building?

They had promised me a club in the complex, which would be the first Little Steven's Underground Garage.

That appealed to me. I had always wanted to start a really cool franchise where people in the business could hang out no matter what town they were in. Of course, it wasn't just a club I had in mind. More like a club/bar/restaurant/hotel/casino. I can't help it, I just think small.

I have offered to design something like this for my friends at the Hard Rock for the last twenty years or so. No takers yet. People who design hotels should come to people like me, who have spent their whole lives living in them.

As it turned out, the Basie people would end up using my name for fundraising and then not giving me the club after all. But I didn't know that yet when they invited me to an investor lunch.

The investor they were courting had said he would invest if I came to the meeting. So I came, and he did.

We got to talking, and he asked what I was doing. I told him I had just recorded an album for the first time in twenty-five years.

"Hot damn," he said. "You have to take it on the road!"

"Nice thought," I said. "But there's no plan to do that right now. It's a big sound. Five horns, three girl singers. It's too expensive a proposition."

"That's alright," he said. "I've been around long enough to know that greatness usually costs."

Indeed!

Could I have finally stumbled upon the patron of my dreams?

Ms. Destiny was visiting again, and since I wasn't confident about getting a new TV show, I started seriously considering going back on the road.

But could I get my head back into being a real onstage front man after all these years?

Oh man. That was gonna take a minute.

thirty-two

Soulfire

(2017–2018)

I leave you with this. My father was a proud ex-Marine Goldwater
Republican. He wouldn't recognize the party now. I paraphrase
Barry Goldwater as a tribute to my late father. "Extremism in
defense of the environment is no vice, and moderation in pursuit
of stopping pollution is no virtue." Lead us into a green future,
reach for greatness, nothing less, and make sure you have some
fun along the way. Life should never be boring. Congratulations,
go get 'em.

—RUTGERS COMMENCEMENT SPEECH
CLOSING REMARKS, MAY 14, 2017

. . . And with that I became a doctor!

It made my Jewish mother so proud!

Oh wait, I was Catholic turned Baptist turned Rock and Roll Pagan.
But she would've been proud anyway.

No, it ain't that kind. Not a sawbones. Just an Honorary Doctor of
Fine Arts. Still nice. I think it was the mysterious Susan McCue's idea.
She pops up in my life every ten years or so and does a good thing, then
disappears back into the camouflage of behind-the-scene politics in DC.

Meanwhile, the prospect of a Soulfire Tour was looming, but instead
of rising to the occasion, I was having a nervous breakdown. I was in
the worst shape of my life. I had been going steadily downhill since my
friend and trainer Clay Burwell had moved to South Carolina. I went on
YouTube and watched a concert video to remind me of my 1987 self. It

was depressing on two levels. I sure wasn't that guy anymore. And how could that band have not broken through?

There was only one way I was getting on that stage. I had to convince myself I was merely a presenter. An MC. More like the Big Band leaders of the '40s. Over time, I talked myself into it, and out we went for a tour that would take us around the States, to Europe, to Australia.

The shows went well, but I was disappointed with how meaningless I had become in the marketplace. We barely averaged a thousand people a night, if that.

It never ceases to amaze me how my many lives don't cross over. The E Street Band sells out three stadium shows in Dublin, which is 180,000 people. But when my band comes to town, about a thousand people show up. They are great, wildly enthusiastic, but, you know? I fully realize it's a different thing, but wouldn't you think I would get 1 percent of the E Street audience? One fucking percent!

Or take *Lilyhammer*. We drew an audience of one million people a week out of a Norwegian population of five million. I probably could have been elected mayor of Oslo. But when I played there with my band—my very, very, very good band, by the way—I got the same thousand people. Maybe.

That's a tenth of 1 percent.

So I had to adapt to that disappointment very quickly and accept it as just another part of my lifetime of penance, which I attributed to the big mistake of my life, my very public career suicide from which there was no redemption or salvation.

Most fascinating was the realization that we were playing to entire audiences who were there strictly out of curiosity. A few fans came because of my older solo records, E Street, or TV, but most of them didn't recognize one single song.

I had to cling to something, so I proudly held the Frank Barsalona flag high as I became the only artist in modern history with a touring party of thirty-five and absolutely no hits.

Now I can't see your face to see if your expression is one of pity or wonderment, but, believe it or not, there were some advantages.

For starters, I never disappointed anyone in the audience by not playing their favorite song!

(Buying that?)

Not having to do anything was liberating.

(How about that?)

The only trick is that I had to win the audience over every single song, or they would split.

I took pride in the fact that we did just that. No one left a Disciples show early or unsatisfied. And there were bright spots. Our German audiences were as enthusiastic as ever. The only explanation I can come up with is that we were still getting dividends from the *Rockpalast* broadcasts all those years ago, which were created by my lifelong friend Peter Rüchel.

I began a new Disciples tradition by having a band dinner after every show to solidify our esprit de corps. Everybody got along great anyway, so it was a good way to wind down the evening. Andrew, our wardrobe person, doubled as our social organizer, party planner, and minister of fun. He tried to book the restaurant of the hotel we were staying in, so people could just stumble from the table into an elevator.

Tom Petty died just as the tour was starting, which hit me harder than I would have expected. Tom had worked with Jimmy Iovine in the late '70s and early '80s, and Bruce and I had gone to see him perform at the Bottom Line, but I don't think Tom and I had spoken more than three sentences to each other our whole lives. Still, we were the same age and had the same influences, so there was an unspoken connection between us, and we did each other favors whenever possible. He gave me a song for *Lilyhammer*, for instance.

Tom died the day after the Las Vegas massacre, so his passing was barely mentioned in the news. That bothered me so much that I decided to open my show with one of his songs just to keep him alive a few more months.

During the same tour, we did tributes to Greg Allman and Malcolm Young.

These days, every tour seems to have way too many tributes.

Somewhere in that period, the Kennedy Center Spring Gala called for me to participate in a tribute to John Lennon. I wasn't sure what I could contribute, and I was about to turn it down when Maureen suggested I do a Rock arrangement of "Working Class Hero."

As soon as she said it, an idea hit me right away. That's how these things usually work. My brain takes everything it knows on the subject and throws it against the wall that instant. Sometimes I get a Rothko, sometimes a Renoir, and sometimes a kindergarten finger painting.

I got a Pissarro with this one.

When Lennon recorded "Working Class Hero," he was at the peak of escaping from his past, shedding everything he was and did. So out went melody and chord changes and arrangement and production and emotion. He wanted things stark. Primal. A complete focus on the lyrics and no distractions.

I decided to see what would happen when the arrangement and production were added back in, but without changing his melody or emotional intention.

When I got down to DC, the gig immediately became a success when I found that I was sharing a dressing room with Taj Mahal! One of my heroes and favorite artists and somebody I'd always wanted to meet.

We bonded over our always-with-us mutual friend Steve Popovich, who Taj had worked with at Columbia Records. I told him he should do the Notodden Blues Festival in Norway. He was a ball and still texts me now and then.

At the Hall of Fame that year, I finally got to introduce the Rock Hall Jukebox. I had proposed the idea years before as a way of acknowledging important singles, especially if the Artists who'd recorded them were unlikely to make the cut. "Louie Louie" by the Kingsmen, was the ultimate example. Every up-and-coming high school and bar band played it to death (Dave Marsh wrote one of the greatest and most important Rock books with that title), and it reigned as *the* Garage Rock Anthem until it was usurped by Van Morrison's "Gloria," written for his group Them. The Shadows of Knight beat them to the hit in America, but neither group was likely to make it into the Hall.

I thought the jukebox idea had been forgotten, but out of nowhere this year the executive committee finally decided to do it. I inducted the first class of songs in 2018, which included "Louie Louie," of course, along with "Rocket 88," "Rumble," "The Twist," "A Whiter Shade of Pale," and "Born to Be Wild." The next year, they added "Maybe," "Tequila," "Money," "Twist and Shout," "Leader of the Pack," and "Gloria."

Some people wanted to limit the jukebox to artists who would never be inducted, but I had to keep hope alive for Link Wray (who is a lot more than a one-hit wonder), Procol Harum (who along with the J. Geils Band and Johnny Burnette and the Rock and Roll Trio are frankly embarrassing omissions as of this writing), the Shangri-Las, and Them. And of course the Isley Brothers were already in.

And Bruce inducted me into the New Jersey Hall of Fame (didn't know there was one) in a class that included the Four Seasons, Debbie Harry (not Blondie? Does the whole band have to be from Jersey?), Steve Forbes, journalist Anna Quindlen, astronauts Mark and Scott Kelly, and the Cake Boss—Buddy Valastro.

Now there's a dinner party.

Once the miraculous sponsorship money for the Soulfire Tour ran out, I figured that my artistic rebirth was over, and I refocused on my TeachRock.org curriculum.

We had achieved the hundred-lesson goal I had set as a benchmark for announcing the program, but even with Scholastic Magazines, PBS, and HBO as partners, we weren't gaining traction.

I called a foundation meeting. After some not so-great-ideas came and went, our board chairman, David Roth, spoke. He had seen the short sponsored tour. "This show is a living embodiment of the TeachRock curriculum. Why don't we use the tour as a way of publicizing it and registering teachers?"

Good idea.

We put aside five hundred tickets per show to give to teachers for free, ran a workshop between the soundcheck and the show, and registered thirty thousand teachers. The Rock and Roll Forever Foundation sponsored the tour. The extra-nice surprise was how great an audience the teachers were. Totally wild.

Our curriculum must have been getting around, because I was being asked to speak at a lot of education-related events. I gave the keynote address at the New Jersey School Boards Association summit in Atlantic City the day after we played the new Hard Rock Casino.

The casino was Donald Trump's old place, which Jimmy Allen had bought for the Seminole Tribe for practically nothing. It was so shoddily constructed, like everything Trump built, that whoever bought it knew they'd only be able to keep the shell.

Not an easy thing to do by the way, losing money with a casino. That takes a special talent.

And speaking of Indians, Chris Columbus called (too soon?). He was doing a Christmas movie called *The Christmas Chronicles*. Kurt Russell was playing Santa, and even though the original script didn't have a song, Chris wanted to put one in.

Not only that, he wanted the Disciples to be in the movie! In the story, Santa ends up in jail, and in a scene like something in an old Elvis movie, Santa breaks into a song, and the other prisoners, us, become his band.

In fact, it was very much like an old Elvis movie, because Chris decided to use Leiber and Stoller's "Santa Claus Is Back in Town," one of Presley's hits.

Chris asked me if I knew any Elvis impersonators who could sing the song that I would produce.

"Not for nothin'," I said, "but haven't I heard Kurt Russell sing before? Didn't he play Elvis in a movie?"

"Well," Chris said, "I asked him. Kurt says he's not a singer. He doesn't have any confidence in his voice."

"Do me a favor," I suggested. "Have Kurt sing along with the record, just a verse or so. Record it on your phone and send it to me."

He did. It was great. I called back and told him to put Kurt on the line. "Kurt," I said, "I've got good news and bad news. The good news is—you can sing. The bad news is—you can sing. So now you've got to take a trip to NYC!"

I was in the middle of an album, so Kurt and Chris came down. After a long conversation, with Kurt stalling as long as he could, we did it. After the first take, I looked at Chris. Chris looked at me. "Chris," I said. "I'm a picky motherfucker. I was ready to go all night. I have absolutely nothing to say. That was fucking perfect."

"I thought so too," he said. "But I just thought maybe I was willing it into existence!"

We spent the next hour or two adding little moments I knew would make the scene jump, figuring out Kurt's improvs and Santa magic, like commanding instruments to appear and disappear. It was a completely surreal fantasy scene, so we could do anything we thought of. And who on earth is better at magic tricks than Chris Columbus?

The movie was the first Netflix flick not to have a theatrical run. Everyone thought Ted had finally gone too far, until it premiered on Thanksgiving and every family with a kid under fifteen tuned in, giving the movie the equivalent of a $200 million opening day. Kurt was spectacular as the first working-class Santa. And kids started recognizing Maureen on the street just for playing the tambourine in the jail scene.

Within a few months, it was time for the sequel. This time Chris wanted an original song. I held my mind back from jumping into composition mode until I read the script. It was amazing. Man, I thought, if people loved the first one, wait till they get a load of this. I had a song in mind within fifteen minutes.

The song was a duet between Santa and a lady in an airport. "Who do you think we should use for the lady?" Chris asked.

"I'll give you three guesses," I said.

He only needed one. "Darlene was the first name I brought up," he said. "They said I can't use her because she's in some other Christmas movie this year."

"What? Who the fuck would have the balls to question *anything* you say?" I was truly flabbergasted (and I don't use that word every day!). "If you wanted to use Moms Mabley, the only comment should be 'Good thinking, Chris!'"

"I'd love to use Darlene; you know that."

"Look," I said, "I know you're one of the nicest guys in the world, that you respect everybody, but I am not and do not. With your permission, I'm going to use her anyway. Don't tell them who it is. Just tell them if they can find somebody that sounds as good as the mysterious lady I recorded, I'll happily replace her."

Chris went along with it. I had her open up the song with a vocal riff that I knew no one could do except her. Her and Ronnie Isley in 1960, that is—it was a fun little tribute to the "Now wait a minute" Ronnie had improvised in the middle of "Shout!" It had nothing to do with the song, just a way of Darlene's character getting everyone's attention in the scene.

When Kurt came in, he laughed. "Thanks a lot," he said. "You know I don't love my voice to begin with, and now you got me doing a duet with the world's greatest female singer! You're a real pal, Stevie!"

"Don't worry about a thing!" I confidently pretended.

Everything went fine. Darlene and Kurt did their usual fantastic jobs. The studio accepted the song. Then I got a call from Chris, who had just hung up with the film company's lawyers. He didn't get depressed often, but I could tell he was upset. "They flagged the opening riff," he said. "They say we have to change it."

Oh, come on, man! Do the fun police ever fucking sleep?

"You have got to be fucking kidding me."

"Nope."

"Fuck them. We ain't changing shit! Give me a couple of days."

I called Ronnie Isley. He couldn't believe it either, but he didn't want to deal with it, so I strategized with his wife. She was very nice and very understanding, and after a muffled, hand-over-the-receiver conversation, she told me that while they had no problem with it, the publisher was the one who needed to make the call.

Lance Freed helped me find him. "Listen, my friend," I said. "This ain't a negotiation. The 'Shout' riff has absolutely nothing to do with the song I wrote. I can lose it in an instant. It's just a little tribute to the Isleys, who we love, and a reminder of a classic song that might find its way to a new audience. And I cannot believe I have to get permission for a sixty-year-old improvisation in the first place!"

He was cool. He gave us permission, and that was that. There are some good guys out there.

Crisis averted.

But the licensing of songs to TV shows and movies is a larger problem that must be seriously reconsidered.

The acquisition of existing songs to accompany scenes in film and TV falls to the music supervisor. That had been one of my many jobs on *Lilyhammer*. During the three seasons of the show, licenses got more and more expensive.

I knew things had gotten out of control when I asked for one of my favorite Doo-Wop songs, "Don't Ask Me to Be Lonely" by the Dubs, and they came back with a $30,000 price tag! Are you fucking kidding me? Nobody but me and Marty Scorsese even remember this song!

That's the modern reality of publishing. There's no regard for the quality of the project or for whether an association with the TV show or movie will be good for the song.

None of that. Just a twenty-five-year-old kid looking at a list of songs with numbers next to them. Numbers just as likely to have been determined by a computer as by a human being.

Pretty soon, these great songs are all going to be irrelevant. Because when me and Scorsese and Tarantino and David Chase and a few others stop working, nobody's gonna know about the classic songs of the '50s and '60s. They will have priced themselves out of existence.

There was a time when songs in movies and TV shows were considered promotion only. Nobody expected to make money from them. Do you think there would've been all those Rock TV shows if they were being charged for the songs they played?

There's the story of Scorsese putting "Be My Baby" in *Mean Streets*, not even knowing he needed permission. Somebody in Phil Spector's office reported the theft to Phil while he was working on John Lennon's *Rock and Roll.* As the story goes, Lennon told him to leave it in. Scorsese was a cool up-and-coming New York kid that Yoko had turned him onto. So Phil left one of the classic moments in cinema history intact.

I'm proposing this as a place for the discussion to begin.

There should be a set price for song use.

No permission necessary.

A percentage pool like on Broadway. Based on the budget of the project. Maybe it costs a little more if it's used as an opening theme or over the closing credits, although closing credits are annoyingly covered up by advertising or go to the next episode these days.

There should be no negotiation needed.

Let the music of the Renaissance once again fill the air and enrich our lives!

Somebody better start dealing with this soon, or else it's going to be Motown what? And Rolling Stones who? Before you know it.

thirty-three

Summer of Sorcery

(2019–2020)

All my life one of my greatest desires has been to travel—
to see and touch unknown countries, to swim in unknown seas,
to circle the globe, observing new lands, seas, people, and ideas
with insatiable appetite, to see everything for the first time and
for the last time, casting a slow, prolonged glance, then to close
my eyes and feel the riches deposit themselves inside me calmly
or stormily according to their pleasure, until time passes them at
last through its fine sieve, straining the quintessence out of all
the joys and sorrows.

—NIKOS KAZANTZAKIS, *REPORT TO GRECO*

A funny thing happened on the Soulfire Tour.

An album is not the end of the artistic process. It's the script for the live show that follows. Onstage, you can amplify and extend the theme of the record—assuming of course it has one. The raps between and even during songs can amplify and expand the ideas. Bruce began this practice and now I find it an essential part of the process.

Halfway through the tour, as I was reabsorbing my long list of life's work, new ideas started to come to me. After twenty years of being down, the radar went back up.

Damn! Was I going to make a new album?

At first the ideas were bits and pieces. A melody. A chord change. A rhythm. The important part for me was the overall concept, and in this case I knew what I *didn't* want to do before I knew what I did want to do.

I did not want to make another political record, even though that's all I'd ever done. I wrote and sang about politics in the '80s because most of what was going on was hidden. The news didn't dominate our lives like it does now. You could go months without even thinking about the government. Can you imagine such a thing? Meanwhile, Reagan and his henchmen were engaging in criminal activity that needed to be brought into the light of day.

Now, most of the government's extensive criminal activity isn't covered up at all. There's not even an attempt to do so. The government brags openly about kidnapping kids and putting them in cages. The crimes, along with the ongoing murder count from COVID, are on the news every day.

Politics suddenly became redundant.

I also didn't want to make an autobiographical record. Enough about me already. But I needed a concept, some kind of boundaries in order to focus.

How could I be most useful? That's a question every Artist has to ask. I thought I could carry on the theme of the Soulfire Tour. The spiritual common ground of music. The world was becoming desperately in need of common ground. I would try and continue providing some.

It looked like the album would come out in the summer of 2019. That got me thinking about the season. This was to be my artistic rebirth, and spring and summer were the Earth's yearly rebirth. Maybe I could combine the two ideas. We needed something to celebrate.

I also wanted to capture human experience, especially the times when life was most open and exciting. A teenager's first love. The thrill of breaking out of school, going to the beach for the first time after a long winter, watching a new band, seeing a great movie, reading an amazing book—plus the fantasy of lots of incredible sex!

The music was the next question. If I was going to make a new record, what genres, styles, and artists did I want represented?

The Disciples may have started off as a collection of mostly strangers, but it had become a real family. I saw us as a modern version of the ultimate cool group, the first band you'd want at a summer celebration, Sly and the Family Stone. Sly had shown up in my work before, mostly as a vocal influence ("Revolution," "Liberation Theology"). Now it was time to bring his band's influence to a song that celebrated the common ground of diversity ("Communion").

My old hero Sam Cooke always served me well, going back to "I Don't Want to Go Home," and he came through for me again, twice ("Love Again," "Soul Power Twist").

I always dug Tito Puente and the whole Latin Salsa thing. You can hear it in the instrumental break of "Los Desaparecidos" and in its sequel, "Bitter Fruit." We took that groove to the next level ("Party Mambo").

A change of pace with a little Bossa-Nova-meets-Samba for the mellower Latin side, an outtake from the Brazilian sequence in *Lilyhammer* ("Suddenly").

Some James Brown Funk, which I had gone deep into on *Revolution* ("Gravity," "Education").

I loved the whole Girl Group thing, which is where songs like "Love on the Wrong Side of Town," "Among the Believers," and "Love and Forgiveness" had come from ("A World of Our Own").

Some Blues ("I Visit the Blues").

A little funky blaxploitation ("Vortex").

A touch of Little Richard, Chuck Berry, and the Beach Boys ("Superfly Terraplane").

And a taste of new territory in the form of some *Astral Weeks*–era Van Morrison ("Summer of Sorcery").

And voilà!

I worked with my in-house graphics genius Louis to create my favorite album cover ever, by anybody, a tribute to my favorite childhood Artist, Frank Frazetta. Frazetta did the covers of the books I loved as a kid, Conan and Tarzan and John Carter of Mars. They had a common theme of heroes finding their way to triumph through mysterious, dangerous worlds. I wanted to infuse the record with that same sense of adventure. Like my life had.

I credit the loyalty of this band—Marc Ribler, Jack Daley, Richie Mercurio, Andy Burton, Eddie Manion, Stan Harrison, Ron Tooley, Ravi Best, Clark Gayton, Tania Jones, Sara Devine, Jessie Wagner, and Anthony Almonte—with giving me a secure foundation that allowed my creativity to rise again like Lazarus.

This would be the first time I'd ever made two albums in a row with the same band. It was exciting.

I'd always wondered how I would evolve if I had the chance. The first five albums showed growth, but it was horizontal, five different soundtracks in five different genres. This was the first time I got to do what every other band does, which was to grow vertically. The Stones and the Ramones made basically the same album every time, but with different songs. I loved that. I envied that. Get the sound right the first time and stick with it.

What I envied was being satisfied in one creative discipline and sticking to it. Next life.

Summer of Sorcery was released in May 2019, exactly thirty years after my last solo album of original material, *Revolution.*

The Summer of Sorcery Tour turned out to be its own exhilarating energy source. We lit up a darkening world for a few precious months.

The only real disappointment was that it proved that the old road to success had been forever washed away. We were going back to cities where we'd slayed with the Soulfire Tour, and the same number of people showed up. Sometimes even fewer.

This never would've happened in the old days. The entire industry was built on coming to town and knocking them out, knowing that everybody in the audience would bring three friends next time you came back.

The Soulfire band couldn't have been any better or gotten a better response.

The Sorcery Tour was even better.

I had to admit to myself that the fantasy of some triumphant return was simply not in the cards. Much less the comeback of a never-was!

It was too late. Too expensive. I should've made sure I had that one hit when I had the chance. I made sure Bruce had one. And one makes all the difference.

Ladies and Gentlemen, Jimmy Buffett! Casino owner!

Bruce released an album called *Western Stars* in the summer of 2019. It had been finished for a little while, and he referred to it as his Burt Bacharach album because it had a great deal of orchestration.

When first I heard it, about a year before it came out, I told him he needed to stop calling it that. "What it is, really, is your Jimmy Webb album." That was the closest style that came to mind.

Kind of Country. Rural. Cinematic. Small stories in big vistas. Bruce never ceased to impress me when he stretched out artistically.

The Disciples were in Europe when the record came out. I was doing lots of press, and *Western Stars* was coming up quite often—and not in a good way. I was quite surprised. I'd never before heard a negative word about Bruce's work, especially in Europe.

I found myself defending him with the journalists, an odd and unexpected turn of events.

"You a Bruce fan?" I asked.

"Yes of course!" They were effusive.

"Well, this thing called Art is funny." I had their attention. "Sometimes it can be coy. Coquettish. Sometimes it wants to be courted. The good news is, it's forever. No deadlines. No panic. A work of Art may not choose to speak to you now, and then reveal the secrets of the universe to you ten years from now."

Where was this going?

"So as a fan of Bruce, you've enjoyed, what, forty years of good work? And you've probably noticed that he has some insight and knowledge and talent and wisdom that you don't?"

They nodded.

"I'll be back in a year or two and we'll speak again. In the meantime, while I'm gone I want you to consider one simple thing."

They leaned in.

"Maybe there's nothing wrong with this record. Maybe the problem is with you."

While I was on the road for *Summer of Sorcery*, hearing all the negative reaction, I thought the album could use a little bit of what Jimi Hendrix did for Dylan's *John Wesley Harding*. I worked up a version of "Tucson Train" just for fun as a commercial for his upcoming movie, which he didn't need.

It occurred to me that Rock had truly redefined the significance of chronological time. I personally knew seven different artists still working in their eighties. Dion had just made an album, at the age of eighty. The next generation, in their seventies, were still doing great work. Looking at the substance, there's a certain kind of work that can't be done until you're an elder. I did a radio break on it. I called it "Wisdom Art."

Artists of our generation just seem to be defying science and continuing to do work they couldn't have done when they were younger. In music. In film. Suddenly, everybody's Picasso a little bit!

I happened to be in LA for Bruce's seventieth birthday party. We went into a back room away from the crowd, and I played "Tucson Train" for him. Happily, he dug it.

I went back to the party, to a table in the yard. Francis Ford Coppola came in and sat at the table next to mine. I had been trying to reach him for a couple of years. I had a script that I thought would be of particular interest to him. Just as I was working up the courage to say hello, Leo DiCaprio sat down. He and Francis immediately got into an intense discussion, the kind that you could tell would last for two hours.

As I was cursing my fate, Bob Dylan and his girlfriend sat down next to me. As I have mentioned, my encounters with Bob are brief and bizarre but always interesting. I'm never sure if he knows that the musician me and the actor me are the same guy.

I decided to have a little fun. I turned to his girlfriend. "I'm gonna let you in on something I bet nobody's told you about Bob."

He gave me half a nervous glance.

"You've heard about how his songwriting changed the entire Pop music world and helped create a whole new Artform. Fine. But nobody talks about how Bob was one of the great fingerpickers back in the day."

She smiled. "Really?"

Bob looked relieved.

I went on. "Next time you listen to Bob's early records, listen carefully to what's happening with his guitar playing. Keep in mind those records were made live. He didn't play the guitar and then come back and sing later. He's doing that fancy playing and singing all at the same time. It's very difficult to do, and no one has ever given him credit for it. Until this moment."

She was impressed.

Bob then told me a story I hadn't heard before. The first time he went to England, it was to act in a TV play! While he was there, he visited London Folk clubs, where the artists were one degree closer to the source than what we had in America. Those visits, he said, inspired his second album, *The Freewheelin' Bob Dylan*, where he first made his reputation as an unparalleled songwriter.

A few weeks after Bruce's party, Bob called to invite me to his show at the Beacon Theatre. Back in the day, you always knew who was in town. Always. It was a big deal! Now, Artists and bands come and go through town and you never even know it. It was good to see Charlie Sexton, still part of Bob's band after twenty years. And Bob did me the honor of an impressively lengthy shout-out from the stage. Marty Scorsese, too, who I didn't see.

Since I have spent much of this book and this last phase of my career avoiding specific political party issues, I do feel obligated to mention a few of the things that I've been carrying around for forty years while thinking about these issues.

I'll put the full political platform of ideas on some website somewhere, which makes sense since websites get adjusted from time to time. But here are nine quick items that I would implement if I were king of the forest:

1. Design the Future

   - Organize a forum of futurists, visionaries, and social engineers.
   - Design the future, then train people in the right jobs to build it.

2. Poison-Free by 2030

   - Set a ten-year, Kennedy-moon-shot-type goal: poison-free by 2030.
   - Government should partner with fossil-fuel and military industries as they transition to a sustainable green economy.

3. Eradication of "Black Communities"

- The biggest scam ever perpetrated on the black community by the white community was convincing them that black neighborhoods were their idea. It's time to invite black Americans to join the rest of America by eliminating all so-called black communities.

- End poverty, racism, crime, unarmed shooting deaths, black-on-black crime, and overpopulated prisons and recidivism once and for all with one bold move, dismantling "black" neighborhoods.

- Incentivize the immediate neighbors and integrate the poor into middle-class neighborhoods, *not* with low-cost housing but given equal equity.

4. Become a Democracy

- The tragic *Buckley v. Valeo* Supreme Court decision of 1976 declared the spending of money to be protected by freedom of speech in the First Amendment. This officially made us a Corporatocracy and led to the antidemocratic Citizens United legislation and the ridiculous protection of corporations as if they were individual human beings. The issues where money speaks loudest win, while the issues that don't put enough money in politicians' pockets or campaigns die in silence.

- There will never be meaningful gun control, a poison-free environment, justice for the working class, or true democracy in America until *Buckley* is reversed.

5. Women's Rights and Protection

- Pass the long-overdue Equal Rights Amendment.

- End the vast majority of rape and sexual assaults by mandatory martial arts training from kindergarten up for girls only.

- Yes, boys should be taught to respect girls. And yes, there needs to be more female owners and executives. But sexual assault will never stop until women can physically defend themselves.

- Sex should be legal. If our ambition is to become the freest, healthiest country in the world, sex should be legal and available to whoever wants it whenever they want it. Sex Workers of all sexual preferences should be licensed and protected. The inability for most of society to have sex leads to irrational misogyny, inexpressible frustration, and dangerous violence. Sex being illegal is unfair to the disabled, the introverted, and the socially retarded, which turns out to be most of us. It is only our religious extremism by a vocal minority that maintains the hypocritical laws that outlaw sex. No truly healthy society in the history of the world has ever attempted to outlaw such a fundamental function of human nature.

6. Immigration Reform

- Institute a Marshall Plan for Central America.
- The first question that should be asked is, Why are they coming here? Yes, some come for the money, but most come because of conditions in their homeland.
- We need to help clean up government corruption, insist on land reform, invest in businesses, and help get rid of the gangs and crime.
- Believe it or not, most people would prefer to stay in their homelands.
- Most of the eleven million undocumented immigrants who are here have jobs that are a vitally important part of our economy. They should be made citizens.

7. Education Reform

- Integrate the Arts into all disciplines, all grade levels, all schools.
- End all forms of bullying and intimidation.
- Recognize that testing is not learning.

- Means-test college tuition, with college free for all households with incomes below $250,000.
- Discover and encourage inclination.
- Raise teacher standards and compensation.
- Prioritize public education over charter schools.

8. Prison Reform

- End privatization of the prison industry—perhaps the most insane policy ever created by a society. Hey, everybody! Let's make crime profitable!
- Redesign new prisons so prisoners never come in contact with another prisoner.
- Reconfigure prisons to include all-day computerized classrooms with their own separate outside areas. Accomplishment will eventually earn a human teacher.
- Create education incentives for early release. Inmates would begin their education on the Internet and then earn a live teacher, on the other side of the glass, of course.
- Release all drug-related criminals.

9. Paying for This

- If we are the kings of capitalism, why are we the only government that isn't in business? Why is our only revenue taxes? As we transition out of fossil fuels and reduce the military to a smaller but faster and more effective force appropriate for the modern world, the government should partner with both industries, providing tax incentives to transition into a green economy, and keep half the profits.
- Other new revenue would come from a small tax on stock transactions, say, ten dollars per, which would add another $60 billion plus that should go directly toward the debt.

There's a lot more if you're interested.

Social media reform, beginning with forcing people to use their real names.

Gun control, health care, police reform (not defunding), additional justices on the Supreme Court who aren't religious, the creation of transitional homeless villages, etc., etc.

One of the biggest challenges over the next few years will be to recognize that white supremacists, militia members, and QAnon psychotics have infiltrated every level of law enforcement and every branch of our military.

It will be an essential element of the strategy to bring the Civil War, 160 years and counting, finally to a conclusion.

The police must police themselves, something they have never been particularly good at, and purge anti-American, antidemocratic, anti-equality, antiscience individuals from the law enforcement part of our society.

As if that wasn't challenging enough, our country may be facing the biggest decision in our civil rights history.

Unless we find a way to deal with social media's ability to distribute information faster than we can absorb, evaluate, and understand it, a quality-of-life issue that goes back to the advent of television, we may soon have to choose between free speech and democracy.

A manipulated public receiving contradictory "facts" will not be able to find enough common ground for democracy to stand on.

Let's face it, our country was founded as a male-dominant white supremacist Christian nationalist country with an asterisk. The asterisk being—"*not for nothin', but some of the guys feel guilty about it."

We had been way too slowly but sensibly progressing and diversifying ever since the Constitution endorsed slavery and said women are basically men's property, until recently, when the Republicans decided, Screw it, let's forget about progress and the more enlightened ideas of our more enlightened Founders; let's embrace our inner KKK, foment and manipulate a grievance culture, and proudly *become* the White Supremacist Christian Nationalist Party.

When a GOP attorney was asked in early 2021 to justify the voter-suppression laws they were trying to pass all over the country, he actually said out loud that "democracy disadvantaged the Republicans"!

The good guys who thought they won the Civil War never put the final stake in the heart of racism, and the appeasement continues as I write this.

Well, that's enough politics to get a conversation started.

The Summer of Sorcery Tour felt like a personal triumph. If it's my last solo tour, I'm OK with that. It was a gift made possible by the bizarre circumstance of finding a way to register teachers.

The theme of finding a way to love, finding common ground, celebrating diversity, being a patriot and a globalist simultaneously—those were all messages that were the exact opposite of the ones coming out of a malignant, immoral, anti-American, criminal White House. Those messages needed to be articulated, loud and clear. Particularly with the sickening knowledge that hate had a 45 percent approval rating.

What can a poor boy do?

We led by example. The Disciples' love for each other was apparent in every moment of the show. Communicating a philosophy of love as hope and music as spiritual bond in an atmosphere of manipulation; of vicious, violent, sick conspiracy theories; of *fear*; and of the paranoid insanity of white grievance was indeed sorcery.

The same philosophy ran through *Letter to You*, the new E Street Band album we recorded immediately after the Disciples' tour. I interpreted it as Bruce's love letter to both the E Street Band and his first band, the Castiles—he was indeed the last man standing.

It was the first time Bruce knew exactly what the album was about before he wrote it. The importance of being part of a band. Of looking out for each other. Of solidarity. That sped the artistic process up considerably. He wrote it in a couple of weeks, and we recorded it in four days.

Rediscovering Rock's power was step one. But all of us were getting older. We needed to pass it on. Instilling its lessons, its energy, its intelligence and spirit in a new generation was our only hope.

The day before the pandemic shut down New York, I flew out to California with Bill Carbone, current executive director of my foundation; Michael-Ann Haders, our main fundraiser; and Randa Schmalfeld, who, along with Christine Nick, is our Arts Integration Sorceress. We were visiting a partner school, seven hundred kids, in kindergarten through sixth grade, all using our curriculum.

People talk about an out-of-body experience. Well, I definitely had one that day.

After working on this thing for fifteen years, it was amazing to be able to see it come to life, to see how into it those kids were. And the teachers too. Enthusiasm everywhere I looked. It made me feel a little better about the world.

Most of what I have planned has never happened, and most of what I've done pretty much remains invisible, but this curriculum has a shot to go all the way.

The Arts really are our common ground. Worldwide. It's what brings us together.

If we can integrate the Arts into every aspect of every curriculum of every school, our depressed society has a chance of returning to the optimism of the '60s.

We were evolving as a species. You could feel it in the air, hear it in our music, see it in the colors of our clothes and Art, and celebrate it in our sexual liberation. It was the birth of consciousness, a second enlightenment, and it's been stolen from us by immoral economic greed and irrational religious extremism. We've got to win it back.

The curriculum is my way of saying thank you to that period, and to all the people who turned me on to Art and gave me dreams to believe in: the Beatles and Rolling Stones and the other Renaissance bands and Artists, Maureen, Bruce, Steve Popovich, Frank Barsalona, Lance Freed, Chris Columbus, David Chase, Ted Sarandos, and too many friends to name who continue to strengthen and sustain that Spirit of Love.

My initial ambition for education was quite modest. All I wanted was for every kid in kindergarten to be able to name the four Beatles, dance to "Satisfaction," sing along with "Long Tall Sally," and recite every word of "Subterranean Homesick Blues."

The rest will take care of itself.

Epilogue

He squinted, trying to see through the smoke. He flashed back to . . . How many lifetimes did it take to get from Soweto to Spanish Harlem? From revolutionaries brandishing machetes to hundreds of people in '50s fancy dress. Equally surreal. Once again he had to ask, How the fuck did I get here?

He'd read Charles Brandt's *I Heard You Paint Houses* three times.

There wasn't one Mob book he hadn't read.

But Brandt's was one of the best. It felt authentic. The facts would be disputed, but he didn't really care. He appreciated Greatness and this book had it.

And now, he stood on a stage in a smoky ballroom in Spanish Harlem about to satisfy a lifelong ambition. He was about to act in a Martin Scorsese movie. It was based on Brandt's book and renamed *The Irishman.*

With a lot of his favorite actors, no less.

He wouldn't be playing any of the famous gangsters he'd read about—Rothstein, Luciano, Bonanno, Profaci, Lucchese, Gambino, Genovese, Lansky, Siegel, Capone.

He was playing Jerry Vale, one of the greatest of all the Pop standard crooners, and one of Scorsese's favorites. The real Vale had been in both *Goodfellas* and *Casino* and would have been in *The Irishman* if he hadn't passed away.

It would be only a few seconds of screen time, but it was probably his last chance to work with Marty, and it was definitely the last scene in film history that would include De Niro, Pacino, Pesci, and Keitel.

It had been forty-two years since Marty had screened *Mean Streets* for him, thirty-four years since Marty had come to his wedding, thirty-three years since he'd read for the aborted first attempt of *Last Temptation*, and twenty-seven years since Marty had come to his Mandela dinner. He felt Destiny had a checklist, and this was definitely on it.

He finished the scene, and went right to the airport to fly to London, where his European tour was opening the next night.

That's it, he thought during the flight.

He'd never top that.

It took exactly twenty-four hours for it to move to second place on the Peak Moments of His Life chart.

The next day, during soundcheck at the Roundhouse, everything was running late.

His loyal and trustworthy Tour Manager, Gary Trew, was trying every trick in the book to get him offstage so they could let in the biggest audience of the tour. Three-thousand-plus people.

Just then, his driver Ray, back in New York, called him to say that Paul McCartney, who he also drove, had mentioned he was planning on coming into London with his wife Nancy to see the show.

He told Gary to hold everyone off. He needed fifteen more minutes.

It was an extreme long shot, but just in case, he wanted to have something ready.

He had the horns, so he considered "Got to Get You into My Life." Then he remembered Paul was the world's biggest Little Richard fan, that he never would've heard of Little Richard if it hadn't been for Paul and the Beatles, so he worked up a quick Little Richard arrangement for "I Saw Her Standing There."

He ran it once and told his orchestrater, Eddie Manion, to refine the horn charts.

That was that.

Just in case.

The crowd started to file in. He was happy to see the brilliant Ray Davies, who he had interviewed on his radio show; the always-smiling face of Suzanne Wyman (Bill was stuck in his studio); Jeff Jones, who ran the real Apple and his wife, Susan. And then there were Paul and Nancy.

He waited for Paul to say hi to Jeff, and then he took him aside. "Listen, man," he said, "you work constantly and don't get a chance to socialize much. So don't even think about coming onstage or anything like that. Just relax tonight and have a good time."

"Cool, man." Paul seemed to appreciate that.

Paul and Nancy sat with Maureen, who told him later that they were quite animated throughout the whole show.

As he was taking a bow before the encore, his roadie ran up and yelled in his ear, "Paul is coming up."

Holy Fuck.

He flashed back to when they'd first met. It had only been five or six years before. Paul had acknowledged him while he was on his way up to the stage to get inducted into the Rock and Roll Hall of Fame. He gave him one of those famous McCartney winks and a "Good job, brother" as he sped past.

At Hyde Park, Paul had joined the E Street Band just long enough to have the plug pulled when they went five minutes past curfew. Then Paul had invited Bruce and him to come onstage at Madison Square Garden.

But joining him and his band? On his stage? It meant more than the world to him. More than he could ever express.

What an incredible endorsement.

What profound validation.

One of the most thrilling moments of his life.

Paul came up. As he looked across the stage at the older but somehow unchanged face, he thought back to when he was thirteen, listening to the first albums he ever bought, trying to learn the chords to play along with them, trying to unlock the mysteries of the universe.

That kid felt like a freak. That kid knew he was a freak. A freak who didn't fit in and was never gonna fit in. And as that kid, that freak, contemplated the void before him, suddenly there was hope.

The Beatles. A whole new world.

Their communication of unbridled joy would be the foundation of the optimism of the Renaissance.

That thirteen-year-old dove headlong into the warm bath of those vinyl grooves, the spiritual shelter of those sacred three-minute Upanishads. He was seeking enlightenment, a search that never stopped.

It was the template, the philosophy, the mission that would inform his best work.

Freedom—No Compromise.

Once upon a Dream.

Summer of Sorcery.

And that night at the Roundhouse, that kid, older now, saw the reason he was alive standing right beside him.

He felt the adrenaline rush of infinite, eternal gratitude.

His latest and greatest epiphany.

Maybe he'd finally found somewhere he really did belong.

And he'd been there all along.

Acknowledgments / Thank-Yous

This book is dedicated to

MARY, BILL, KATHI, AND BILLY VAN ZANDT,
NANA AND GRAMPA LENTO, NANA VAN ZANDT,
AND MAMA MARIE SANTORO, MATRIARCH OF THE
SANTORO CRIME FAMILY (otherwise known as my in-laws)

FRANK BARSALONA
The Godfather who changed the world

STEVE POPOVICH
Who put me in the Record Business

PETER RÜCHEL
The German genius who broke the Disciples of Soul in Europe

VERNA BLOOM
Always inspiration and encouragement

NICKY CORDERO
So brilliant, gone way too soon

OBIE DZIEDZIC AND HOLLY CARA PRICE
My loyal assistants

Thank-Yous

I want to thank my editor Ben Greenman, who proved to be invaluable and who, like all great editors (I would imagine), doubled as my much-needed psychotherapist during a period of unimaginable daily distractions (and a psycho therapist was what the job required!).

I want to thank my music Agent Steve Martin, who found my Managers David Simone and Winston Simone, who then found both my Agent for everything, Jon Rosen at William Morris Endeavor, as well as my book Agent Marc Gerald, who suggested my editor Ben Greenman and then found my publisher, Ben Schafer.

Thank you, Louis Arzonico, for dealing with the pictures and the art.

I want to thank the Magnificent 7 plus 1 who made all the difference in my life—Bruce Springsteen, Steve Popovich, Frank Barsalona, Lance Freed, David Chase, Ted Sarandos, Susie Buffett, and Bruce Resnikoff.

My overworked but never overpaid attorney, Rob DeBrauwere.

The consigliere's consiglieres—Jimmy Iovine, Jay Cocks, Peter Wolf, Maxie Weinberg, Scott Greenstein, Richie Sambora, Zoë Thrall, Backstretch Billy Rapaport, Nicole Barsalona, June Barsalona, Richie Russo, Dennis Mortensen, and Louis Arzonico.

The E Street Band.

All of the Disciples of Soul musicians and crews through the years.

Thank you all.

I am compelled to thank the Trump Kakistocracy, the most extraordinarily incompetent, malevolent, ignorant, and embarrassing government in history for providing the nine months of quarantine that allowed me to give birth to this unlikely fable.

And most profoundly I thank my wife, Maureen, for sticking with me after the fun-loving Rock and Roller she married turned into a boring workaholic and for tolerating my inability to stay in one place long enough to earn the respectable lifestyle she deserves as I continue my lifelong quest to break even or, at the very least, find a steady job.

And, oh yeah, our dog, Edie, the only life form that truly loved the quarantine and wrote every word with me.

Index

Midnight Hour - 3
Taxman - D 1
Devil w/ Blue - D 2
Come on up 3
Look through my
Heat Wave - 9 2
Nowhere man = D
Mustang Sally 1
Jenny Ride 1
Lonely too long -
I can't Keep from
S - My Girl - D 0 1
Talk Talk - B 2
Give me Love -
Gloria - Unison 3

Ladies and Gents

Ladies and Gents

Public Toilets and Gender

EDITED BY

Olga Gershenson and
Barbara Penner

TEMPLE UNIVERSITY PRESS | PHILADELPHIA

Temple University Press
1601 North Broad Street
Philadelphia PA 19122
www.temple.edu/tempress

Copyright © 2009 Temple University
All rights reserved
Published 2009
Printed in the United States of America

Text design by Kate Nichols

♾ The paper used in this publication meets the requirements of the
American National Standard for Information Sciences—Permanence
of Paper for Printed Library Materials, ANSI Z39.48-1992

Library of Congress Cataloging-in-Publication Data

Ladies and gents : public toilets and gender / edited by
   Olga Gershenson, Barbara Penner.
      p. cm.
   Includes bibliographical references and index.
   ISBN 978-1-59213-939-2 (hardcover : alk. paper) — ISBN 978-1-59213-940-8
   (pbk. : alk. paper)
   1. Public toilets—Social aspects. 2. Sex discrimination. 3. Gender
   identity. I. Gershenson, Olga, 1969– II. Penner, Barbara, 1970–
   GT476.L34 2009
   628.4'508—dc22
                                                                    2008051659

2 4 6 8 9 7 5 3 1

Contents

Foreword

JUDITH PLASKOW

When I was a graduate student at Yale in the late 1960s, my first act as a feminist was to participate in taking over the men's room in the stacks of the Yale Divinity School library. The small restroom—one urinal and one stall—was the only lavatory in the library, and women had to leave the building and walk a considerable distance in order to find a toilet. We staged a day-long sit-in, planted flowers in the urinal, and declared the facility unisex, which it remained until the library was refurbished.

Ten years later I joined the faculty of Manhattan College, just six years after it first admitted women. My female colleagues had many stories to tell about the administration's failure to plan for adequate women's bathroom space as part of the preparation for coeducation. The faculty member who was the most vocal advocate for women's toilets was known as the "toilet lady" and treated as if she were crazy. The first lavatory to be reassigned as a ladies room turned out to have a row of urinals and no stalls! To this day, there is only one single-occupancy women's toilet on the floor with the largest number of women faculty members.

My experiences at Yale and Manhattan set me thinking about the ways in which toilets both reflect and enforce societal assumptions about gender and serve as important sites of struggle for social change. Issues surrounding toilets are located at the intersection of the inescapable materiality of the human body and the ways in which the body's demands are culturally and symbolically elaborated in relation to multiple social hierarchies. On one hand, elimination is a basic physical reality that, in the words of poet Marge Piercy, "only the dead find unnecessary."[1] All human beings need to urinate and defecate, and excretion is potentially a great leveler, linking all persons in our common humanity. As a seventeenth-century English poem to the chamber pot quipped, "To kings and queens we humbly bend the knee, / but queens themselves are forced to stoop to thee." A young black man growing up in the South under segregation expressed himself in similar terms: "All these white folks dressed so fine / Their assholes smell just like mine."[2] On the other hand, despite the fact that excretion is a fundamental biological demand, there is no culture in which it is unmediated by social structures. Like the body's other equally powerful imperatives—its needs for food and sleep, the finality of death—elimination serves as a foundation around which societies elaborate the distinctions and rules that help constitute power relations in a particular time and place. Indeed, precisely because urination and defecation are so necessary, so ordinary, and so daily, the rituals surrounding them serve as extraordinarily effective, generally subliminal mechanisms of socialization. Children coming of age in the segregated South were taught their different places in society not only by the "White" and "Colored" signs on toilet doors but also, for whites, through the very availability of public toilets and, for blacks, through the frequent absence of facilities that forced people who were away from home to urinate in the open. Little girls crossing their legs and waiting with their mothers on endless bathroom lines absorb important lessons about what it means to live in a society in which the built environment consistently fails to reflect women's experiences and needs. In addition, girls are being conditioned to accept their peripheral status quietly and patiently.

Given both the physical importance of toilets to a livable environment and their powerful symbolic and social meanings, it is striking how relatively little academic or public discussion has been devoted to the subject. The topics of gender, sexuality, and the body have been all the academic fashion for four decades, but the issue of toilets seems to be surrounded by the same embarrassment and taboos that generate toilet jokes in the wider culture. Feminist theory and activism are no exceptions to this general rule. Despite the fact that feminists have been centrally concerned with revaluing the body, and especially the female body, since the publication of *Our Bodies Ourselves* in 1971, they have had little to say about elimination as a fundamental aspect of human embodiment. Moreover, the many local actions that have been fought on behalf of toilet equity—my experience at Yale being one of numerous examples—have not been part of any broader, visible feminist campaign for equal toilet provision.

That is why I was so delighted to learn that Olga Gershenson and Barbara Penner were venturing into forbidden territory by editing a volume exploring the issue of public conveniences from multiple gendered perspectives. *Ladies and Gents*, the first full-scale academic exploration of toilets and gender, is at the cutting edge of a new interest in toilets that at last seems to be generating public discussion of the subject. The book offers convincing evidence that toilets provide a vehicle for exploring questions of ideology, power, embodiment, social justice, gender, race, class, sexuality, and physical ability in ways that might actually have an impact on the quality of daily life. In assembling a rich and lively collection of articles on planning, legal campaigns, cross-cultural encounters, linguistic conventions, art, design, and popular culture, the editors convey both the extraordinarily interdisciplinary nature of the subject of toilets and the fruitfulness of exploring it through a wide variety of lenses. Gershenson and Penner clearly demonstrate that, for all that the topic has been trivialized and mocked, it remains a potent window into broader social attitudes and structures.

Each of the essays in *Ladies and Gents* offers a specific example of how the seemingly narrow theme of public conveniences opens up into large and important social questions. Dealing with subjects as varied as the place of toilets in issues of school safety in sub-Saharan Africa; a legal action brought on behalf of women prisoners in Michigan that triggered intense toilet anxieties on the part of the court; and the context, reception, and legacy of Marcel Duchamp's infamous urinal, the contributors manage to shed light on the ways in which spaces designed to serve the real needs of real bodies become sources of intense cultural anxiety and sites for constructing and maintaining gendered power relations.[3] Gershenson and Penner's superb Introduction places the essays in a larger context by providing an overview of the multidisciplinary literature relevant to the study of public toilets. They begin with a series of telling vignettes focused on toilet controversies (including the indignation and abuse that met their own "Call For Papers") that reveal some of the complicated issues and feelings evoked by this highly charged topic. They then survey the growing body of work in different fields whose authors have until now proceeded largely in ignorance of and isolation from each other. Their essay provides a valuable map of the potentially new area of "toilet studies" and demonstrates how much it has to gain from and contribute to multidisciplinary conversation. Indeed, it is difficult to think of another subject that has the potential to bring academics, activists, planners, filmmakers, building-code supervisors, and others together at the same table to discuss an issue in which everyone has a stake. The editors also make clear that, despite the ridicule and resistance they experienced in working on *Ladies and Gents*, the book appears at a historical moment in which there seems to be a new interest in and openness to talking about public conveniences. That openness should help to bring this groundbreaking volume the attention it deserves.

I have many hopes for *Ladies and Gents* and the new appreciation of toilets that it promotes and heralds. I share the expectations of the editors that the book will encourage further research on toilets and enrich conversations in many disciplines. Beyond this, I hope that serious (though not solemn) attention to the multifaceted significance of toilets will foster social action and lead to greater mindfulness of elimination as a dimension of embodied experience. At particular historical moments and in different locations, the absence of toilet facilities has signaled to various subordinate social groups that they are outsiders to the body politic and that there is no room for them in public space. Issues of toilet access thus have the potential to bring together activists in a range of social movements, who, by addressing the ways in which inequalities of power are manifest in this mundane but crucial arena, could do much to make communal spaces more livable and just. Moreover, part of the task of speaking publicly about the need for more toilets involves examining the profound anxieties that surround our basic bodily functions and that lead us (in Freud's words) to withhold from them "the attention and care which [they] might claim as . . . integrating component[s] of [our] essential being."[4] Is it too much to hope that beginning to address toileting in its symbolic, social, and material complexities could even lead to a new acceptance and enjoyment of a basic physiological need?

Notes

1. Marge Piercy, "To the Pay Toilet," *Living in the Open* (New York: Alfred A. Knopf, 1976), 82.

2. The poem is cited in Dan Sabbath and Mandel Hall, *The First Taboo* (New York: Urizen Books, 1977), 219. The second comment, made by a boyhood friend of Richard Wright's, is cited in Leon F. Litwack, *Trouble in Mind: Black Southerners in the Age of Jim Crow* (New York: Alfred A. Knopf, 1998), 414.

3. Claudia Mitchell, "Geographies of Danger," Chapter 3; Jami Anderson, "Bodily Privacy, Toilets, and Sex Discrimination," Chapter 5; Robin Lydenberg, "Marcel Duchamp's Legacy," Chapter 10, herein.

4. Sigmund Freud, "The Excretory Functions in Psychoanalysis and Folklore," *Collected Papers*, vol. 5, ed. James Strachey (London: Hogarth Press, 1950), 88–89. The comment comes from Freud's preface (1913) to the German translation of John Bourke's *Scatologic Rites of All Nations*.

Acknowledgments

This work had a long and occasionally difficult gestation period. We are grateful to the many friends, supporters, and colleagues whose good wishes, indignation, and laughter kept our spirits up and encouraged us to persist, especially Harvey Molotch and Judith Plaskow. Additional thanks must go to Caryn Aviv, Ruth Barcan, Iain Borden, Ben Campkin, Clara Greed, Peter Greenaway, Robyn Longhurst, Steve Pile, Robert A. Rothstein, and Salman Hameed for their helpful advice and to the entire Wobbler group for rooting for the project. We are also indebted to our authors for their patience and good humor. We are particularly grateful to Alex Schweder and the San Francisco Museum of Modern Art for giving us permission to use Alex's fabulous *Bi-Bardon* on our cover; this work was made with the generous support of the John Michael Kohler Arts/Industry Residency program. Thanks also go to Mary K. Lysakowski for administrative support. Finally, our most sincere thanks go to Micah Kleit and the team at Temple University Press, who recognized the viability and value of the project and enthusiastically ushered it out into the world.

Introduction: The Private Life
of Public Conveniences

OLGA GERSHENSON AND
BARBARA PENNER

In 2004, when we decided to edit this essay collection, we began by formulating a short "Call For Papers." It read:

> Public toilets are amenities with a functional, even a civic, purpose.
> Yet they also act as the unconscious of public spaces. They can be a
> haven: a place to regain composure, to "check one's face," or to
> have a private chat. But they are also sexually charged and trans-
> gressive spaces that shelter illicit sexual practices and act as a cul-
> tural repository for taboos and fantasies.

> This collection will work from the premise that public toilets,
> far from being banal or simply functional, are highly charged
> spaces, shaped by notions of propriety, hygiene and the binary
> gender division. Indeed, public toilets are among the very few
> openly segregated spaces in contemporary Western culture, and
> the physical differences between "gentlemen" and "ladies" remains
> central to (and is further naturalized by) their design. As such, they
> provide a fertile ground for critical work interrogating how con-
> ventional assumptions about the body, sexuality, privacy, and
> technology can be formed in public space and inscribed through
> design.

> We welcome papers which explore the cultural meanings, histo-
> ries, and ideologies of the public toilet as a gendered space. Any
> subject is appropriate: toilet design and signage, toilet humour and
> euphemisms, personal narratives and legal cases, as well as art sited
> in public toilets. We also welcome the submissions of design and art
> projects that expose the gendered nature of the "functional" toilet
> spaces and objects.

We circulated the CFP among the usual suspects—a number of academic Listservs and Web bulletin boards. This was a routine academic procedure. However, very soon we discovered that something unusual was happening. We started to find an excessive amount of mail in our in-boxes—and very peculiar mail, not what one expects in response to a CFP. The mail fell in two categories: people either liked our idea (passionately) or disliked it (passionately). Some called our project long overdue and inspiring. Others said that our project was an immoral, even scatological, perversion and a waste of public funds. Our fifteen seconds of fame or, more accurately, notoriety had begun.

Our CFP was featured in the mainstream press and electronic op-ed pages. The *Wall Street Journal* (Taranto 2005) published an opinion column with the amusing if predictable title "How to Earn Your Pee h.D." The *Boston Globe* soon followed up with the more tediously titled "Academia Goes down the Toilet" (Beam 2005). The next day this piece was reprinted by *International Herald Tribune*, and then the real mud slinging began. Many prominent conservative Web sites or blogs weighed in with indignant responses. The commentators included defenders of high culture such as *The New Criterion* (Kimball 2005), defenders of Reaganesque principles and grass-roots conservatism such as *Human Events Online* (Custer 2005) and *Free Republic* (TFFKAMM 2005), and defenders of traditional family roles such as *Independent Women's Forum* (Allen 2005). Among other honors, our project was named the *Young America Foundation's* second-greatest campus outrage of 2004–2005. It even made the satirical *Private Eye's* Pseuds Corner and is now immortalized on the feature's Wikipedia site.

Given that both of us had written about political debates surrounding the provision of public toilets, we would have been naïve to think that this book would be totally uncontroversial. Nonetheless, the sheer number of those who rejected the legitimacy of our inquiry was a surprise. Ninety years after Marcel Duchamp's *Fountain* (1917), we found ourselves in the midst of a toilet controversy of our own. Even stranger than the media commentary on the CFP was the fact that we ourselves became the subject of hundreds of sneering, baffling, and sometimes hilarious attacks on blogs and Web sites such as rantburg.com and barking-moonbat.com. Olga Gershenson received a fax at her department that summed up the tenor of these comments. Calling our CFP "a shocking revelation," our faxer wrote:

> It gives one a startling glimpse at where we stand today in higher education. I'd say your invitation for contribution for the edited collection . . . pretty well encapsulates the ridiculous preoccupation with trivia affecting the elite ivory towers of post-modern academia. I was also taken aback by your obvious fascination with the scatological and its association with sexual practices. . . . Has Aristotelian philosophy now given way to scholarly discourses on toilet

bowls, outhouse designs and architecture? . . . Are these places where you now do your best thinking?

Why did our CFP touch a nerve? People managed to project into our 226-word CFP a vast range of disparate if interconnected problems, ranging from the decline of privacy rights to the promiscuous triumph of gender studies and queer theory, the rhetoric of diversity, and equal rights legislation. Whatever their objection, they tended to come from a very particular, conservative group of people, largely within the United States, who were part of the general post-9/11 swing to the Right. Insofar as anything united them, it was the complaint that our project symbolized the degradation of publicly funded higher education, and, like our faxer, they fondly recalled a prefeminist and pre-postmodern era when idealist academic enquiries prevailed.

It is hard to understand how a discussion of a ubiquitous public space would automatically invalidate an inquiry's scholarly status, unless we see it as an issue of control. The outraged attacks on this project must be seen both as an attempt to police the boundaries of what is acceptable and what is unacceptable within both academia and society at large and as an effort to ensure that certain things remain "in their place"—unspeakable—or spoken about only in a certain fashion. Most of those who objected to our project believe that the mere mention of the toilet, with its invocation of the body, gender, and sexuality, contaminates the purity of academia. This belief infuses the gleefully vitriolic piece by the right-wing Townhall.com columnist and college professor Mike Adams, titled—wait for it—"Piled Higher and Deeper." Adams writes:

> In Gershenson and Penner's call for papers, the phrase "Any subject is appropriate" really sums it up. "Glory holes" used to facilitate anonymous sex in university restrooms and profane poems on the walls of bathrooms are no longer a source of embarrassment for professors and administrators. There is no longer a need to cover them up with putty and spray paint. Now, they are just another form of diversity to be celebrated. Break out the rainbow flags! (2005)

Despite his gleaming "breastplate of righteousness," Adams is remarkably *au courant* with the lingo and practices of what the British call "cottaging" and North Americans call "cruising." Thanks to the obsessive media coverage of Idaho senator Larry Craig's toe-tapping antics, these terms are much more familiar to the world. But Adams's eagerness to tell his readership about "glory holes" (nowhere mentioned in our CFP) is revealing. In its explicit evocations, Adams's piece follows the prurient logic of sensationalistic journalism that cheerfully exposes "secret" practices even as it condemns them or, in Adams's case, preaches concealment. His commentary draws heavily on metaphors of contamination, cleaning, and covering up. Graffiti should be covered up. Gay sex in public toilets should be covered up too, though not with spray paint and putty but with denial. Adams concludes cryptically but apocalyptically: "To tolerate filth is one thing, to celebrate it is another. That is where we stand today in higher education. We are knee deep and getting deeper" (2005). The final statement encapsulates the contradictions at the heart of Adams's piece. It remains unclear why we should not publicly discuss things that, as Adams admits, take place in public places, unless we relate it to the well-worn conservative belief that sex should always be a "private" matter—the "don't ask, don't tell" philosophy. More puzzling still: in what way does Adams actually think he is "tolerating filth"—anonymous gay sex, graffiti, diversity, and, astonishingly, blasphemy, all messily lumped together in this article?

We obviously stand on the opposite side of the fence on these matters. But, partisan politics aside, why should public toilets be a focus of an academic inquiry? Many of the contributors to this volume make forceful cases for the need for clean, safe, accessible, and well-designed public toilets, whatever one's color, sex, age, or status, and reinforce that this should be a priority for governments, school administrators, and design professionals alike. At a time when public provisions are in steep decline in the West and, when provided, often look like defensive fortifications, armored with antisocial deterrents, this message is a crucial one. Yet why is it so difficult to put into practice? Without denying the very real practical concerns surrounding public toilets to do with security, hygiene, and vandalism, we argue that in order to open up discussions in a meaningful way, we must also enter the realm of representation—as many of the contributions to this volume do—and delve into the practical, rhetorical, legal, ideological, and historical reasons why it is uncomfortable for people to talk about toilets. It is only by understanding the private or unconscious life and meanings of the public toilet that we can make sense of why toilets are so consistently controversial; how they are so integrally bound up with other issues, from women's rights to gay sexual identity, that it is often impossible to invoke one without invoking them all; and why they have been the subject of so many passionate debates, controversies, and design and art interventions throughout the modern era.

Public Toilets—Public Controversies: Three Stories

We start our discussion with three stories that, taken together, refract the identity issues that emerge from public toilet debates. The first deals with the introduction of public women's lavatories in Victorian London.[1]

Historically, shared public latrines have been a feature of most communities, and this continues to be true in developing countries such as Ghana, China, and India. Private, sex-segregated lavatories were a modern and Western European invention, bound up with urbanization, the rise of sanitary reform, the privatization of the bodily functions, and the gendered ideology of the separate spheres. As historian Deborah Brunton explains, in the nineteenth century, public conveniences such as paving, lighting, and fire services were taken over by civic authorities as part of their remit to ensure "the free and safe circulation of goods and people" (2005, 188; see also Laporte 1993). From the 1840s, concerns about public health gave the issue of public toilet provision practical and moral urgency, while their successful installation by George Jennings at the Great Exhibition in 1851 gave them the official seal of approval (Wright 1960, 200). However, the vast majority of public facilities were for men only: whereas large cities in Scotland provided male facilities beginning in the 1820s, for instance, female conveniences were not constructed until the 1860s (Brunton 2005, 191). The lack of "resting places" significantly limited women's mobility in the city: in the words of a contemporary, "Either ladies didn't go out or ladies didn't 'go'" (quoted in Rappaport 2000, 82). In response, the Ladies' Sanitary Association and concerned members of the public campaigned for the establishment of women's conveniences at high-traffic spots. One such spot was the junction of Park Street and Camden High Street in the London Vestry of St. Pancras (Penner 2001).

It was at that junction that the local government decided to build a women's lavatory. Residents and omnibus proprietors strenuously objected. They did not limit themselves to words—the wooden model of a lavatory built at the site was vandalized under the pretense that it was "obstructing the traffic." On September 5, 1900, a deputation presented itself to the local government to demand an end to construction. Its members complained that a women's lavatory would lower their property values and challenged the need for such facility, falsely claiming that the majority of women passing through the intersection lived nearby and could relieve themselves at home. Finally, one of the members admitted he simply "didn't want such a place under his own window" (Penner 2001, 41). Another called it an "abomination." As a result, despite the persistence of the lone female member of government and the advocacy of another male member, George Bernard Shaw, the site was abandoned. It was not until December 1905, after five years of stalling, that the decision to build a women's bathroom at Park Street was made.

What drove the strong opposition to the women's lavatory? Architectural historian Barbara Penner explains that "the members of the deputation clearly felt that the proposed convenience's capacity to shock and offend was caused less by its function than by the sex of its future users" (2001, 41). Sanctioning the women's lavatory effectively sanctioned the female presence in the streets, thus violating middle-class decorum and ideals of women as static and domestic. Moreover, "owing to its provocative corporeal associations, a female lavatory evoked the spectre of sexuality which . . . encompassed a nebulous constellation of issues above and beyond sexual conduct itself" (Penner 2001, 45). By making women's bodies and their "private" functions publicly visible, the lavatory threatened to transform its users into "public women." These evocations surfaced in the smirk and ridicule that accompanied the debate in the Vestry, allowing punning slips from lavatory to brothel. Class also played a significant role as fears surfaced that the lavatory might become an arena in which the ladies who shopped promiscuously mixed with factory or flower girls—presuming, of course, that the latter could pay the facility's prohibitive (and also controversial) penny charge (2001, 45).[2]

The second story takes place about half a century later and deals with the racial desegregation of public bathrooms in the United States. It illustrates the importance of toilets for the construction and presentation of social identities. The setting was the Western Electric Company plant in Baltimore, Maryland, during World War II. The trouble started in February 1942, when, following a change in plumbing code, the company adopted a policy against the segregation of public facilities (Ohly 1946). The union, consisting of white members, demanded segregation. When its requirements were not met, the union went on strike. As the Western Electric produced combat communication equipment, the strike had military consequences. Therefore, by order of the president, the secretary of war took possession and operated the plant. Despite the government's intervention, employee attendance and the level of production fell (Ohly 1946). Only after the union leader, who would not budge on the segregation issue, and some administrators were relieved of their duties were the War Department representative and the union able to reach a compromise:

> The company undertook to construct new and enlarged locker room and toilet facilities. A plan was worked out whereby the lockers would be assigned in blocks. Though there was no formal agreement, the intention to assign lockers to white employees which would adjoin each other and to Negro employees which would also adjoin each other was announced. Though there would be no segregation by rule in the use of toilet facilities, it was apparent that each employee would use that nearest his locker, which would result in a sort of voluntary separation. (Ohly 1946, 2)

While not being racist *de jure*, the compromise reinforced segregation *de facto*. The case is instructive in and of itself: the anxieties surrounding bathroom desegregation led to the strike at the nine-thousand-employee plant, a strike that compromised national interests, required presidential seizure, and was stopped only when the key figures were fired. The threat of being mixed with the Other was so great that people were ready to risk their livelihoods. It is telling that the case of Western Electric was not unique, as the war up-ended existing social distinctions and led to racial mixing in intimate spaces. Eileen Boris notes that white fears of catching venereal diseases from blacks in newly integrated facilities underpinned many protests (Boris 1998, 93–95).

During the civil rights movement of the 1950s and 1960s, locker rooms and bathrooms continued to be the main obstacle to desegregation at many workplaces. Many court cases concerning the segregation of public facilities were decided throughout the 1950s and 1960s and as late as the 1970s (for instance, *James v. Stockham*, 1977). Fears over sexual mixing also drove objections to the Equal Rights Amendment to the U.S. Constitution, which was not ratified because, among other reasons, the right wing claimed it would mandate unisex bathrooms (De Hart 1991, 255–56). Observing their role in the ERA's defeat, in fact, Gore Vidal listed ladies' rooms as one of several "tried-and-true hot buttons" in the Right's arsenal—a button that, as our experience has demonstrated, remains hot today (1979/1993, 542).[3]

The third story is contemporary and begins when previously invisible categories of people began successfully to demand public facilities that reflected their needs. First in line were people with disabilities (sometimes with attendants) and parents (with young children of an opposite sex): both groups required access to gender-neutral bathrooms. While single-user unisex bathrooms have always been a feature of airplanes and trains, as a result of the campaigns by disabled persons and parents, at least one such toilet can usually be found in public places such as theaters, gyms, and restaurants today. But when transgender and other gender-variant people joined the queue for toilet provision, anxieties about gender and sexuality immediately surfaced.

College campuses were the stage for these controversies and pitted conservative administrations against more radical student bodies. Campuses are places where many young people are grappling with their identities, sexual and political, and where new social trends emerge and are tested. Practically, too, bathroom provision is more of a concern for students, as they often live on campus and do not have access to other facilities. For some time, transgender students have voiced their reservations about the use of gender-assigned bathrooms, where they risk being insulted, mocked, attacked, and even arrested. However, only a handful of campuses provide unisex bathrooms and gender-blind floors in residence halls, and their introduction is often divisive. One notable dispute started at the University of Massachusetts Amherst (UMass), when a student group called Restroom Revolution suggested establishing several unisex public bathrooms on campus, arguing that transgender or gender-variant students and faculty members should be able to use the facilities in classroom buildings, and especially in the dorms, without fear of verbal or physical harassment.

Restroom Revolution's proposal provoked a poignant debate on campus that lasted over two years. At first, the administration seemed responsive and promised to establish two unisex bathrooms in the residence halls. But no action resulted. Restroom Revolution then renewed their campaign, researching legal issues around the group's cause, organizing publicity on campus and in the media, and networking with other schools dealing with similar issues. They wrote an open letter to put political pressure on the administration. Simultaneously, they flooded the campus bathrooms with posters bearing mottoes such as "Do you know that you are sitting in a seat of privilege?" Hundreds of students signed a petition in support of the group. The group also secured the support of several important student organizations. This debate went public on the pages of the student papers and even in the *Boston Globe*, which featured a largely sympathetic article (Gedan 2002).

The issue was widely debated off campus too. While the conservative Traditional Value Coalition was, unsurprisingly, outraged ("individuals with mental problems should not be allowed to dictate social policies at a university" [Sheldon 2002]), at the opposite end of the political spectrum, the online Independent Gay Forum also voiced reservations about the campaign, noting that transgendered people faced much greater problems (e.g., assault and murder) than toilet access (Miller 2002). However, the main objection to the unisex bathroom, at least in the media, was on the grounds of public morality. According to the UMass conservative student newspaper, Restroom Revolution was using a frivolous issue to promote their morally unacceptable behavior to a naïve public: "Gender-neutral bathrooms are neither an issue of safety nor comfort for transgender students; they are merely a means for homosexual activists to influence campus with their immoral ideals and to break the traditional gender barriers that normal students hold" ("The Politics of Pee" 2002). In short, the objectors feared that unisex bathrooms might undermine traditional gender divisions. The derision and open hostility with which the request for provision and gender variance itself was met revealed deep-seated fears about sexuality as well as gender. The following quote from an online discussion in the progressive campus newspaper was depressingly typical: "If you want to be a woman, have some backbone and go get Mr. Happy chopped off. Until you feel strong enough to change yourself because of your beliefs, then don't you dare expect everyone else to change to cater to your needs" (Pierce 2002). Still, the Restroom Revolution campaign persisted until the summer of 2003, when two single-stall bathrooms (on a campus of thirty thousand people) were designated as unisex.

Despite the contemporary setting and a different agitating body, the story of the Restroom Revolution strongly echoes the other two we have considered: a change to existing toilet arrangements was proposed; a fierce, sometimes violent response occurred; and an uneasy, ambiguous resolution was imposed. In all cases, the debates turned on what the philosopher Louise Antony calls "weird and interesting 'nerve-hitting' issues . . . that people insist are too trivial to warrant discussion even as they make clear that they'd rather die than countenance any alteration" (Antony 1998, 3). Changes to existing toilet arrangements are explosive because they recognize, accommodate, and, hence, legitimate the presence of a social group who customarily "make do" and remain invisible at the level of representation.

As these stories remind us, refusing people toilet access remains a remarkably effective form of social exclusion, and in defiance of basic human rights, toilets have become a potent means of further marginalizing social untouchables. Urban theorist Mike Davis observed that public toilets "have become the real frontline of the city's war on the homeless. Los Angeles, as a matter of deliberate policy, has fewer public lavatories than any other major North American city," thereby preventing the homeless and poor—many of whom are recent immigrants—from having clean water for drinking or washing (1992, 233–34). Toilets have also routinely been deployed to deny status. For instance, the first women's bathroom on the U.S. Senate floor was established only in 1992. Before that, female senators, at the risk of missing a vote, had to run downstairs to share a public restroom with tourists, a degrading reminder that the rightful occupant of the Senate was traditionally male (Quindlen 1992). Even more recently, the lack of women's bathrooms was used as an excuse to ban women's access to military academies (Faludi 1994). The use of a bathroom of the "wrong" sex could get one arrested (Belkin 1990). And, as we have seen, transgender and other gender-variant people still face difficulties in their access to sex-segregated public bathrooms because they do not conform to societal expectations of "male" and "female" (Feinberg 1996; Bornstein 1998; Vade 2001). The bathroom emerges as a space of "discipline" in Foucauldian terms, a space that represents "an unintentional cultural strategy for preserving existing social categories" and maintains our most "cherished classifications" (Cooper and Oldenziel 1999, 8). In the disputes arising over access to public bathrooms, then, we glimpse a social script that is normally implicit. But we also glimpse the possibility—the necessity—of imagining a different kind of script.

Ladies and Gents: Approaches to Public Toilets and Gender

Public toilets are among the last openly sex-segregated spaces that remain in our society and, crucially, among the last spaces that people *expect* to be sex-segregated. Moreover, toilets reflect and shape the binary division between men and women as well as "proper" relations between people of the same sex. As such, public toilets are important and revealing sites for discussions of the construction and maintenance of gender, sexual identity, and power relations in general. Public toilets shape everyday urban experience on both an individual and collective level through their provision, location, and design. For instance, public toilets not only inform a woman's ability to move comfortably through a city but also define what her "needs" are perceived to be by those in power and how she is expected to conduct herself publicly. These built-in assumptions, in turn, can promote a sense of belonging or of alienation: for instance, Muslim men might find the design of Western men's urinals excludes them just as surely as steep sets of stairs exclude people in a wheelchair.[4]

Thus, in this volume we argue that toilets are best seen as spaces of representation. They are places where marginalized social groups strive for visibility and where cities strive for credibility. Thinking of public toilets in this way explains why they feature prominently in so many activist struggles and building campaigns. Campaigns by disabled groups for improved access have been very successful, resulting in the 1990 Americans with Disabilities Act and the U.K. Disability Discrimination Act 1996 (Greed 2003, 162–72; Kitchin and Law 2001, 287–98). The Chinese investment in public toilet provision, especially in advance of the Beijing Olympics, is another well-known example (Geisler 2000; George 2008, 156–58). Indeed, public conveniences remain an important emblem of civility and progress and provide a focus for reformist efforts throughout Asia and India, for instance, through the World Toilet Organization (Greed 2003, 124–29) and the Sulabh Sanitation Movement (George 2008, 100–21). They also remain a rallying point for activist groups in Europe seeking to improve conditions for women. For instance, since 2004 the Belgian initiative "Do Not Silence My Bladder" has effectively protested the lack of female toilet accommodation in Ghent through high-profile poster campaigns, media coverage, publications, petitions, marches, and the installation of a female urinal at the city's annual arts festival (de Vos 2005, 16–17).

Yet public toilets do not always represent "authorized" or regulatory discourses about civility, sanitation, and sexuality. The way they are used, experienced, and imagined can be equally transformative and transgressive: public toilets permit private moments away from public surveillance; they provide a space for communication, solidarity, or resistance, especially among women; and they act as repositories of behaviors and fantasies that can destabilize norms or social categories (Morrison 2008; Gordon 2003). They are also sites regularly associated with sexual expression through practices such as graffiti or cottaging (Houlbrook 2001, 2005; Otta 1993). This oscillation between respectability and its opposite explains why authorities and ordinary citizens frequently regard public toilets with suspicion.

In articulating this point of view, we draw on recent multidisciplinary literature about gender, space, and the body that opens up suggestive new perspectives on public toilets. The vast majority of literature specifically on toilets to date, while informative and amusing, is largely anecdotal, documentary, or technical in nature (Reynolds 1946; Wright 1960; Lambton 1995; Horan 1996; Hart-Davis 1997; Muntadas 2001; Gregory and James 2006; Carter 2007). Most architectural studies of toilets, too, emphasize aesthetic or formal issues over social or environmental ones (Schuster 2005; Wenz-Gahler 2005) However, several pioneering and influential exceptions must be mentioned. The first is Alexander Kira's 1966 *The Bathroom*, one of the few serious twentieth-century studies of the toilet, which attempted completely to rethink bathroom design according to the principles of ergonomics while taking into consideration all aspects of human lavatory requirements, physical and psychological; his revised edition in 1976 includes a substantial section on public toilet design and use that remains pertinent today (Kira 1976, 190–237). Its twenty-first-century equivalent is the planner and campaigner Clara Greed's important *Inclusive Urban Design: Public Toilets* (2003). And journalist Rose George's recent *The Big Necessity* (2008) urgently makes the case that any integrated solution to the global water and sanitation crisis must involve open and frank discussions of toilet use and design, whether flush or biogas.

George is particularly critical of "the absence of academic curiosity" around toilets (2008, 151). In fact, the situation is not as bleak as she believes. Since the 1980s, a critical strand of academic literature has discussed toilets in relation to sex segregation and accessibility and their repercussions for social justice, citizenship, and inclusive urbanism (Banks 1990; Cavanagh and Ware 1990; Greed 1995; Edwards and McKie 1997; Cooper et al. 2000; Daley 2000; Anthony 2001; Case 2001; Cowen, Lehrer, and Winkler 2005; Ings 2007). In the last fifteen years, a small but growing body of work on toilets and sexual identity has also emerged from such disciplines as cultural geography, anthropology, sociology, and queer theory. And toilets have provided a useful focus for the growing body of interdisciplinary work on dirt, filth, and waste (e.g., Cohen 2005; Campkin 2007). Strikingly, however, with the significant exception of Clara Greed and Harvey Molotch, few scholars seem to have a sense of working in a "field" in which others are also active. After our "Call For Papers," for instance, we received countless e-mails that began: "I had no idea anyone else was doing work on this topic."

In order to forge connections between these multidisciplinary discussions, we have provided an overview of key literature that precedes this volume. Our aim is not to build an exhaustive list but rather to give readers the contours of the field as it has emerged and developed, especially in recent years. Not all the literature discussed here specifically raises issues of gender, yet it is relevant in that it opens up a discussion of the construction of social categories and sets the stage for the more historically and culturally specific considerations of gender, space, and identity found in this volume.

Toilets and Equal Rights: From Philosophy to Practical Politics

Since the nineteenth century, feminist campaigners have been well aware of the importance of space to female independence. Questions of spatial organization and access have long been integral to their thinking, as expressed, for instance, by Virginia Woolf's plea for *A Room of One's Own* (1929). In our own time, African American legal scholar Taunya Lovell Banks calls for feminists to recognize access to public toilets as a feminist issue, stating, "We must realize that continuing inequality at the toilet reflects this male-dominated society's hostility to our presence outside of the home" (1990, 267). Banks implicitly invokes the logic of the 1970s feminist slogan "the personal is political," which recognizes how the distribution of everyday duties and spaces institutionalizes sexism, disadvantages women, and reinforces normative notions of femininity. Considering the question of sex-segregated toilets as part of a larger discussion of patriarchy, philosopher Richard Wasserstrom concluded that they were just "one small part of that scheme of sex-role differentiation which uses the mystery of sexual anatomy . . . to maintain the primacy of heterosexual sexual attraction" central to patriarchal power relations (1977, 594). Believing this structural injustice to be incompatible with a good society, he called for the "eradication of all sex-role differences" (1977, 606). Yet as the feminist philosopher Louise Antony astutely observes, most people, feminists included, continue to believe that an "equitable accommodation to gender," rather than its elimination, is all that liberation requires (1998).

Even efforts to provide equitable accommodation prove tricky where toilets are concerned. Viewing the provision of public toilets—or lack thereof—as a form of sex discrimination, sociologist Harvey Molotch pointed out a paradox: due to female toilet needs and uses, distributing space equally between men's and ladies' rooms actually produces "an unequal result." The queues that result from women's longer visits to the toilet (studies show that women take, on average, twice as long as men) place women under "special burdens of physical discomfort, social disadvantage, psychological anxiety" when in public (Molotch 1988, 129). Working from the principles of affirmative action, Molotch argues that unless the cultural demands of society change—something he clearly hopes for—only "an asymmetric distribution of space" will improve the situation and provide "equality of opportunity" among the genders (1988, 130).

Molotch's argument anticipates the rationale behind "potty parity" legislation passed in various U.S. states in the 1980s and 1990s, whose most prominent champion is lawyer John Banzhaf III (1990). In 2002, in the hope of establishing improved female toilet provision as a federal statutory and constitutional right, Banzhaf filed a complaint against the University of Michigan for providing insufficient facilities for women in its planned renovation of Hill Auditorium. Banzhaf argues that the university's failure to provide restrooms that accommodate the "immutable biological differences" between men and women constitutes "illegal sex discrimination and sexual harassment" (2002, n.p.).[5] He also proposes that inadequate provision for women may constitute a violation of the Equal Protection clause of the U.S.

Constitution, which mandates that "state-owned facilities cannot treat members of two different classes differently" unless to do so serves "important governmental objectives" (Banzhaf n.d.). Banzhaf assumes that the "important governmental objective" served by sex-segregated toilets is maintaining the privacy of the two sexes but rejects this as an adequate defense for making women wait longer to perform the same function as men (n.d.).

Although potty parity can represent real gains for women, some elements of Banzhaf's case give one pause. By insisting on "immutable biological differences" between the sexes, such decisions act culturally to reinforce patriarchal notions of gender, as Wasserstrom and Antony maintain. Certainly, the complaint does not challenge the underlying logic of sex-segregated toilets and treats existing arrangements as inevitable, even if Banzhaf does consider alternatives to current arrangements elsewhere (1990, n.p.) Nearly two decades after Molotch's article, it appears that, given existing gender ideologies and notions of privacy, providing *more* toilets is still considered the best remedy for inequities in provision; yet it is clearly not always the best from a rational, gendered, not to mention environmental perspective (as summarized by Greed 2003, 111–29). Why is it so difficult for us collectively and imaginatively to explore other options?

Toilets, Dirt, and Social Order: Anthropological and Sociological Approaches

Anthropologists and sociologists, most notably Mary Douglas (*Purity and Danger*, 1966), have highlighted the ways in which notions of dirt and its management reflect and inform social arrangements. In works indebted to Douglas's insights, toilets become windows onto the processes by which cultures define, separate, and manage dirt, and thus they contribute to the maintenance or violation of ideal order. As Ben Campkin and Rosie Cox remark, an especially helpful aspect of Douglas's work is that it views definitions of dirt as central to the social classificatory systems of *all* cultures, whether scientifically advanced or "primitive," even though these are manifested very differently (Campkin and Cox 2007, 4). Douglas further argues that ideas about dirt are so naturalized that their regulatory social role is revealed only through cross-cultural comparison (Van der Geest 2002, 197–206) or at moments when they are threatened by transgression (pollution). For instance, the historians Patricia Cooper and Ruth Oldenziel (1999) attribute the visibility of bathroom discourse during World War II to the unsettling of normal gender and racial patterns. They conclude that in this situation of ambiguity, when women of both colors suddenly entered the male workplace, bathrooms were crucial to keeping social categories (black and white, women and men) from mixing with and contaminating each another. Cooper and Oldenziel's emphasis on social ordering allows them to maintain a critical perspective on what toilets represent: the inclusion symbolized by toilet provision comes at a price, as it quickly imposes familiar patterns of racist and sexist spatial segregation on users (1999, 20).

Pierre Bourdieu's concept of "habitus" (1979/2007) has also been used to relate dirt to cultural definition and social order. Notably, sociologist David Inglis (2001) identifies the management of dirt, especially of human waste, as constituting a distinctly Western, bourgeois fecal habitus, crucial to what Bourdieu calls "distinction"—the efforts of modern society to define its various members symbolically. Although the literature on female toilet usage inspired his interest in "defecatory matters," Inglis mainly addresses the issue of class in his own work. Yet he throws down the gauntlet to feminist scholars, asking, among his more provocative questions, "Why is toilet paper pastel?" (2001, 2). Inglis's seemingly idle musing is consistent with an approach held by many feminists and queer theorists, who now regard the process of social formation as embedded in seemingly mundane routines and consumption decisions. He has also inspired research from a "social constructionist" position by sociologists Martin Weinberg and Colin Williams, who consider how the fecal habitus is "mediated by sociocultural factors" (2005, 324). In interviews with 172 Indiana University students, the authors analyze their differing responses to "bodily betrayal" and fecal sights, sounds, and smells along the axes of gender and sexual identity and the threat these pose to self-presentation. In this, their work relates to sociologist Beverley Skeggs's identification of female toilets as potentially crucial sites for the enactment of femininity and the legitimatization of cultural capital necessary for symbolic power (2001). However, based on her research into the English gay bar scene, Skeggs notes that, in reality, the performances often do not function in such an affirmative way but instead highlight tensions between various social actors.

Lastly, the talk of self-presentation invokes the work of sociologist Erving Goffman, most famously *The Presentation of Self in Everyday Life* (1959), which considers our daily interactions as social performances and, following dramaturgical principles, divides spaces into front- and backstage regions; on the frontstage, we perform, whereas in the back regions, surrounded by props, we remove our social mask and prepare ourselves for the next act. Considering Goffman's definition, it might initially seem as if the bathroom is a classic backstage area. But, as Spencer Cahill points out, the backstage is actually the toilet stalls (Cahill et al. 1985, 33–38). The open area of the bathroom in front of the sinks and urinals is often an area of performance, governed by what Goffman calls "interpersonal rituals," some of which acknowledge other users while others leave them alone. Perhaps the most relevant of these interpersonal rituals is what Goffman calls "civil inattention," where one acknowledges the other but then withdraws one's attention before the other feels like "a target of special curiosity or design" (Goffman 1963, 84; Cahill et. al 1985, 38–42). Goffman's discussion bears an obvious relationship to the later work of queer theorists. In the context of their studies, however, the performance that takes place in bathrooms is always charged with sexual meanings—and one withdraws one's attention to avoid being called a queer.

Toilets, Subjectivity, and Symbolic Order: Psychoanalytical Approaches

Other writers have come to toilets via a psychoanalytical route, drawing from George Bataille's (1985) notions of abjection, excess, and waste or Julia Kristeva's (1982; 1997) more openly gendered notion of the abject. Perhaps the most madly energetic engagement with the subject (and closest to Bataille in spirit) is Dominique Laporte's *History of Shit* (1993). As Rodolphe El-Khoury (1993) notes, in this work Laporte was creating an account of the civilizing process as a devaluation of the senses. In addition to Laporte's debt to Freud's *Civilisation and Its Discontents* (1930/1961), this project can be related to that of sociologist Norbert Elias, who, in the groundbreaking *The Civilizing Process* (1939/2000), traced the rise of civility to the increasing control over bodily excreta. Yet Laporte's analysis privileges smell above other senses, as he sees the containment of olfactory offenses as central to bourgeois subjectivity and to the emergent capitalist economy.[6] He also believes it is the desire for containment that drives domestic design toward greater segregation—the internal partitioning of toilets into stalls is a good example—that extends ever outward to the city at large. But, while tracing these larger (infra)structural changes, Laporte does not lose sight of the role of waste in self-definition: "To touch, even lightly, on the relationship of a subject to his shit, is to modify not only that subject's relationship to the totality of his body, but also his very relationship to the world and to those representations that he constructs of his situation in society" (1993, 29).

In discussing how shit mediates between individual bodies and the world, Laporte makes little explicit distinction between different bodies. For a more specific account of how such relations define us as gendered beings, we might consider toilet training for girls and boys, which, as Simone de Beauvoir argued in *The Second Sex* (1949/1997), indoctrinates women into a subordinate (crouching) position. Or we might turn to the psychoanalyst Jacques Lacan. Famously, Lacan illustrated his account of how we enter the symbolic register and become subject to its arbitrary logic with reference to a public toilet, accompanied by a drawing of two identical doors marked "Ladies" and "Gentlemen." Lacan (1997) states that it is these signs, backed up by the "laws of urinary segregation," that fix sexual difference, at least in public. Literary theorist Elizabeth Abel also draws on the work of Lacan in analyzing how racially segregated bathrooms and drinking fountains inscribe differences between "Colored" and "White" (1999, 435–39).[7] Lacan—and Kristeva too—underscores that any disruption of the symbolic and spatial order creates anxiety and disgust. Through a complex and brilliant analysis, for instance, architectural theorist Lorens Holm notes that the shock one feels when confronted with scatological, racist, sexist toilet graffiti is caused by the fact that it is "matter out of place" (Douglas 1966, 36). Yet Holm makes clear that this is not "matter out of place" in the sense that Douglas defined it; rather, the displacement to which he refers is internal, destabilizing the representational boundary between inside and outside and thus reminding us of "the horror that simmers beneath any symbolic system"—the Real that the Symbolic has repressed (Holm 2007, 430).

Toilets and Spatial Order:
Architectural Approaches

When Marcel Duchamp was asked the question "What is the difference between architecture and sculpture?" his response was reputedly "Plumbing." Writers on architecture have subsequently found plumbing to be a useful means of probing the boundaries of modernism. Noting that modernism strove to create the appearance of light-filled, transparent, and functional spaces, for instance, the editors of the special "Toilet" issue of *Postcolonial Studies* point out that this, paradoxically, necessitated that other elements of building, its "underbelly," be hidden away. "At the very moment when the precursors to the internationalist school were pushing the use of glass and promoting the value of transparency in building form," they observe, "the private bathroom moves into the shadows as the one space/place where transparency does not reign" (Dutton, Seth, and Gandhi 2002a, 138). They ask: "Is the toilet the 'limit' of modernity, that which is occluded, repressed, displaced by the onward march of modernity? Or is it rather an essential part of the story of the modern by very virtue of its occlusion?" (2002a, 138). For these scholars, the toilet opens up a different story of the modern: a somatic one that is not dominated by vision. As such, it is related to the work of the historians Alain Corbin (1986) and David S. Barnes (2005), whose discussions of smells, stinks, waste, and sewers reintroduce an experiencing body to discourse—a body that senses, perceives, breathes, eats, smells, hears, sleeps, digests, and defecates.

Significantly in terms of this volume's aims, unlike the abstracted, ideal (male) body around which modern architecture is built, the body that emerges in these accounts is one differentiated by sex, race, ethnicity, and class. So, too, are the laborious rituals of cleaning upon which the maintenance of modernist purity depends. As the art historian Briony Fer reminds us, "Woman as a servant, or as a mother, is charged (and I mean Charged in both sense of responsibility and impugned guilt) with the management of dirt. Dirt and cleanliness are the women's prerogative" (quoted in Lahiji and Friedman 1997, 55; see also Lupton and Miller 1992, 11–15). (And surely, the image of woman as a high priestess of domestic cleansing answers David Inglis's question about the delicately colored hues of toilet paper?) Toilet studies allow architectural scholars to resurrect what modernism must suppress in order to construct itself: the irrational, the pathological, the psychic, the foreign, the erotic, the decorative, and, most crucial here, the feminine (Morgan 2002, 171–95).

These acts of resurrection and reconnection are driven by the desire to restore wholeness to a discipline, be it history or architecture, that is seen to be lacking in some way. One thinks, for instance, of Jun'ichiro Tanizaki's eulogy to the "spiritual repose" offered by traditional Japanese toilets in contrast to the sanitized glare of Western ones (1933/1977, 3–6). In such essays, the toilet emerges as a kind of crucial hinge between opposed states: the sacred and the profane, purity and abjection, private and public, moral and immoral (Frascari 1997, 165). While toilets are seen as the container of the unclean, at the same time they enable the ablutions that are so necessary to modern Western life. These ablutions are moments of what Helen Molesworth, following Deleuze and Guattari, calls "hooking up," where our bodies interact with machines (Molesworth 1997, 83).

It is worth pausing for a moment to consider Molesworth's development of "hooking up" in greater depth. Many have spoken of toilets as machines: in fact, toilets, in their gleaming, white, standardized perfection, have become iconic fetish objects not only for architects such as Le Corbusier and Adolf Loos but for historians of modernism. It is not for nothing that Margaret Morgan called the white porcelain of the toilet bowl "that grand signifier of twentieth-century modernism" (1997, 171). One of the best-known books on the subject, Lawrence Wright's Clean and Decent (1960), compiles sections of toilets, removed, as with Marcel Duchamp's Fountain, from the context of their use. Floating in the white space of the page, they appear as pieces of equipment defined by bowls and pipes, valves and flushes. Relieved of what Siegfried Giedion saw as the "grotesqueness" and daintiness of their "feminine" ornamentation, their functional, manly simplicity was perfectly in tune with modernist aesthetics (Giedion 1948, 691). The concept of hooking up, however, re-embodies these objects, reminding us of the gendered body who initiates use and of the machine/body relationships that are part of everyday life. Indeed, Molesworth argues that Fountain was so unsettling precisely because it made the urinal useless, effectively suspending machine-body interaction, everywhere highlighting "dirty bodies and full bladders" (Molesworth 1997, 83). The urge to restore wholeness is doubtless why exhibited toilets are such a provocation. One thinks of retired seed-merchant Pierre Pinoncelli's 1993 notorious attack on Fountain: prior to striking it with a hammer, he urinated into it in a pungent act of neo-Dadaist protest (Durantaye 2007).

Toilets and Sexual Identity: Queer Theory

The body is also the focus of queer theorists for whom public toilets resonate not only because they have historically been sites for homosexual encounters but because of their metonymic relationship to the "closet" of gay identity. Michel Foucault's notion of "disciplining" (1975/1991) is relevant here: as part of the drive to create "docile bodies," every aspect of the body, including sexual desire, is overseen and regulated. In Foucault's account, the partitioning of space into individualized cells (we might say, stalls) is key to enabling close and constant supervision. Significantly, Foucault uses the toilets at France's École Militaire as an example of "hierarchical observation," noting that they were installed with half-doors so that "the supervisor on duty could see the head and legs of the pupils, and also side walls sufficiently high 'that those inside cannot see one another'" (1991, 171–72). The stall arrangement makes students visible while simultaneously ensuring that they cannot see each other's genitalia, setting into motion a complex and coercive play of exposure and secrecy, repression and desire, the implications of which queer theorists explore.

Drawing on Judith Butler's notion of the performativity of gender (1990) and on Eve Kosofsky Sedgwick's definition of homosociality (1985), a number of scholars discuss the gender performances that take place within bathrooms and that identify one as homosexual or heterosexual (e.g., Edelman 1994, 1996; Halberstam 1998; Munt 1998; Houlbrook 2000; Barcan 2005). Literary theorist Lee Edelman notes that the men's room is unique in that it can strongly affirm heterosexual identity. However, a straight man can be sheltered only "so long as he performatively shelters the structural flaw that opens his body, by way of its multiple openings (ocular, oral, anal, genital), to the various psychic vicissitudes able to generate illicit desires" (1996, 152). Edelman particularly pays attention to the unwritten but tacitly understood behavioral codes that govern toilet use, termed "urinal etiquette" by the historian Matt Houlbrook (2000, 55). While the genitals are exposed at the urinal, other men should never look at them. Edelman writes, "The law of the men's room decrees that men's dicks be available for public contemplation at the urinal precisely to allow a correlative mandate: that such contemplation must never take place" (1996, 153). Equally, lesbians in gay bars speak of averting their gaze when they find themselves queuing with visibly feminine women (Skeggs, 2001, 301).

In these works, the bathroom emerges as a frontstage space where sexual identity, queer and straight, is performed and may be legitimated (e.g., Nilsson 1998). However, this performance is fraught with anxiety and, as the case of Senator Craig (and a long line of men attempting to engage in gay sex) reminds us, subject to rejection, police surveillance, or entrapment (Humphries 1970; Maynard, 1994; Chauncey 1996). Yet, considering the prosecution of men for cottaging in early-twentieth-century London, Houl-brook observes how the violations of "proper" urinal etiquette that trig-gered police action were often contested in courts of law. One man who found himself under suspicion on the grounds that he had been enter-ing one urinal five times in forty minutes later defended himself on the medical grounds that he had a "weak bladder" (2000, 52–70). The same ambiguous codes that could entrap men could be used to exonerate them. In this reading, homosexual conduct, like homosexual identity itself, is subject to testing and contestation, which, as queer theorists argue, often drives the violence against gay men. Edelman writes, "Where better to discern the full force of aggression implicit in the question—'Are you looking at *me?*'—that condenses our pervasive male cultural anxiety about the capacities of gay men to transform, or to queer? . . ." (1996, 154).

Toilets and Representation: Literature, Arts, and Film

It is important to note that academic criticism has discovered the toilet relatively late in the game. The toilet has long been a setting for literary, artistic, and film representations of gendered subjectivity and subjecthood, of abjection and mastery, of secrets and lies. It is not by coincidence that one of the most seminal feminist novels, Marilyn French's *The Women's Room* (1977), opens with its protagonist, Mira, hiding in the female toi-lets. Her traditionalism, alienation, and deepening personal crisis are im-mediately signaled by her response to graffiti scratching out the word "ladies" and replacing it with "women's." Mira, French tells us, called it a ladies' room "out of thirty-eight years of habit, and until she saw the cross-out on the door, had never thought about it. . . . But here she was at the age of thirty-eight huddled for safety in a toilet booth in the basement of Sever Hall, gazing at, no, studying that word and others of the same genre" (1997, 1). In French's novel, the crossing-out of "ladies" is meant as a meta-phor for the changes Mira will experience after her divorce. Yet its some-what naïve substitution of one term for another warns readers that a change of circumstances alone may not be enough to permit Mira to escape from the patriarchal system (as indeed proves to be the case).

Public toilets have also been a fertile site and provocation for visual and performance art, as chapters in this collection by Alex Schweder, Kathy Battista, and Robin Lydenberg demonstrate. Toilet doors themselves, with their gender-prescriptive signs, are designed to communicate. Graphic de-signer Lynne Ciochetto connects the now-ubiquitous signs for women and men to "the internationalism of commerce and culture that occurred in the post war period," driven by mass tourism in the United States and the rise of global events such as the Olympics (2003, 193–200). In areas that are less touched by mass tourism and multinational business, flourishing local vernacular traditions for depicting men and women remain on toilet doors (see examples in Ciochetto 2003, 203). Whatever their style, these signs reflect gender and cultural norms; that international pictograms are inherently Western, for instance, is revealed by their reliance on (dated) Western dress codes—the woman wears a skirt, the man, trousers—even in cultures or situations where this does not correspond to the clothing people wear (Munt 1998, 201–2). The 2005 exhibit "Toilet Doors of Melbourne" at the Museum Victoria drove home the point that we typically overlook such biases: "We don't often stop and think about the signs on toilet doors—we only really take notice of what the signs actually say when we're confused about which door is for us" (Horvath 2005).

Toilets have also made their mark in popular culture, especially on television: one need only think of *Ally McBeal*'s iconic unisex office bathroom. Whenever the camera zooms in on a stall, we know that we were about to witness confessions, eavesdropping, romantic encounters, or violence. Similarly, toilet spaces are often important settings in motion pictures, as Frances Pheasant-Kelly discusses in her contribution to this volume. Such fictional and mundane representations remind us that, however much we treat toilets as private spaces, they are actually saturated by publicity, as images of private moments, behaviors, embarrassments, and passions are circulated endlessly through various media.

There are also many exemplary documentary films that engage with public toilets and their gendered use, often with the specific aim of stimulating debates over social difference, equal rights, and public space. Given the significance of the bathroom in Peter Greenaway's *The Cook, the Thief, His Wife and Her Lover*, it is appropriate the British auteur directed one of the best films of this type. In *26 Bathrooms* (1985, 26 min.), Greenaway arranges the bathroom in encyclopedic alphabetical order, each bathroom corresponding to a letter: "A is for A Bathroom; B is for Bath," and so forth. Some categories are factual, some humorous, some ironic, such as "Q is for a Quiet Smoke"—a shot of a man on a toilet smoking and reading. Greenaway's "subjects" range from opulent, expensively designed, full-size bathrooms to a bleak, cupboard-like cubicle (referred to as "the Samuel Becket [*sic*] Memorial Bathroom"). Similarly, the users range from sybarites advocating bodily pleasures (in which they readily and nakedly indulge on screen), to fully-clothed soliloquists recalling painful youth experiences, to individuals recounting stories of bathroom renovations. These accounts are intercut with an interview with an expert ("X is for an Expert on Bathrooms") who provides snippets of history of private and public bathrooms, starting from the Victorian era. Bathroom use emerges in the film as a social experience—a place where intimate conversations between couples or cuddling between a mother and a baby takes place.

More recently, a number of documentaries have explored issues arising from bathroom use by transgender people. Perhaps the most influential among them is *Toilet Training* (2003, 30 min., dir. Tara Mateik), produced by the Sylvia Rivera Law Project, an organization that provides legal services to low-income transgender and gender-variant people. Appropriately, the video and accompanying handbook address the persistent harassment and violence that gender-variant people face in gender-segregated bathrooms. Through the real-life stories, the video raises problems with public bathroom access for a range of people: an African American trans woman who is arrested for using a women's room in the public park; a tomboy who dropped out of school because she was prohibited from using the men's room by staff, and from the women's room by female students; and a disabled man who notes, ironically, that gender segregation is lifted only in the context of disability. These stories are interspersed with interviews with lawyers, social workers, and activists that help explore current law and policy and highlight recent and future policy changes. The filmmakers pay close attention not only to gender and space but also to the ways these intersect with age, race, and class.[8]

A different aspect of gender performance is raised in a short video, *Tearoom Trade* (1994, 12 min. dir. Christopher Johnson). The video features an interview with two young gay men and their playful enactment of a "tearoom" (i.e., public toilet) encounter. These sequences are punctuated by homoerotic imagery from several films (in particular, Jean Genet's *Un chant d'amour*) and scenes from commercial gay pornography. By contrast, *Ferry Tales* (2003, 40 min., dir. Katja Esson) emphasizes the public toilet's homosociality. *Ferry Tales* is filmed in a women's bathroom on the Staten Island Ferry, a place that one of the characters calls "a great equalizer." The ferry's bathroom brings together commuters across races, classes, and ages. For thirty minutes every day, the women on a ferry form an unusual community. Always in a rush, these women use the time on a ferry to gather in front of the mirrors in the bathroom "to put our faces on," as one of the characters states; the diverse group of women—young, old, black, white, working-class, executive—are portrayed huddled together before the mirrors in one big lipstick-holding, hair-curling organism. Unlike the sexually charged, transgressive atmosphere of the men's room in *Tearoom Trade*, the ferry's "powder room" is a space of communion and sisterhood that feels to the women at times "like a family." And as in a family, not everything is smooth: conflicts exist alongside expressions of social and emotional support. What emerges is a conversation about identity: the women peer intensely in the mirrors at themselves and others not just to monitor the application of make-up but also to search for themselves.

The Iranian documentary *The Ladies Room/Zananeh* (2003, 55 min., dir. Mahnaz Afzali) also takes place inside a women's restroom, this time in a public park in Tehran. This bathroom also becomes a sort of a spontaneous social club; it brings together addicts, prostitutes, and homeless girls, as well as women who work nearby or pass through. Many are downtrodden, abused, or abandoned. And yet, the bleak space of the park restroom, with its yellowed tiles and basic plumbing, becomes a liberating zone for the women. As one of them exclaims on screen: "I go to the Laleh Park restroom. It's an ultimate pleasure!" In the ladies' room, these women feel comfortable enough to smoke and talk frankly with each other about marriage, sex, physical abuse and incest, relationships, and religion. They remove their veils—a radical gesture in itself, as women baring their hair on screen is a violation of Iranian cinematic and gender conventions. They create their own space, a place of female camaraderie in between private and public, sometimes a place of last resort. Despite its lack of clarity or commentary (a real disadvantage for cultural outsiders), the film stands as a rare attempt to draw out the invisible and the unrepresentable for cross-cultural audiences.

This also is true of the Indian documentary *Q2P* (2006, 54 min., dir. Paromita Vohra). *Q2P* (pronounced "queue to pee") tackles the culturally unmentionable subject of public toilets, in particular the shortage of women's facilities in India. The availability and conditions of public restrooms for women testify to the state of the city, its citizens, and their impressive yet disjointed efforts to move toward greater progress. The film takes us on a sweeping journey from the Westernized city center with its modern sleek bathrooms, though the poorer periphery where community toilets are scarce and scary, to the realities of the homeless, who bathe their newly born children in the street. Looking at the country through the lens of toilets allows the film to raise questions about gender, class, caste, and urban development in India. Even today, the city's sanitation workers come from the "untouchable" caste, and access to toilets correlates with both class and gender: according to the film, 700 million Indians still do not have toilets at home and rely on public latrines for their needs. Not surprisingly, such facilities are more commonly provided for men than for women. The film brings together different voices: it features interviews with a feminist architect, government officials responsible for public toilets, and staff of the Sulabh International Museum of Toilets. But we also hear voices of teachers at public schools in poor neighborhoods who suffer from health problems because of lack of toilet access; young girls who explain that they have a special "system" so they never have to use a toilet in public; women living in slums who develop strategies for using public toilets safely; even a contractor who builds illegal private toilets without proper drainage. The diverse cast of the film creates a rich and multidimensional picture of a problem and, like many of the other films discussed above, provides a humane and timely reminder of the role toilets have to play in creating a dignified and equitable society.

The Toilet Papers

Ladies and Gents aims to provide a cross-disciplinary and cross-cultural platform for the study of public toilets and gender. Despite coming from a wide variety of fields and covering many topics, the essays we received in response to our CFP fell under several distinct themes. These are reflected in this book's two-part structure: The first part, "Potty Politics: Toilets, Gender, and Identity," addresses issues of health, safety, and equality, as well as the role of toilets in defining notions of public and private and of cultural difference. The second part, "Toilet Art: Design and Cultural Representations," seeks to draw out more explicitly a discussion of public toilets as designed spaces and as spaces of representation.

The first part opens with a trio of essays that establish the importance of accessible, secure public toilets to the creation of inclusive cities, work, and learning spaces. We begin with planner Clara Greed's essay. Affirming the role of public toilets in making healthy cities, her essay traces a dispiriting picture of the reality of provision in the United Kingdom: over 40 percent of public toilets have been closed in the last decade, a situation that has a particularly negative impact on the mobility and health of women. Greed makes a powerful case for compulsory legislation, increased funding, and improved management to improve radically the status quo. Following on Greed's U.K.-based analysis, environmental designers Kathryn H. Anthony and Meghan Dufresne provide an overview of the situation in the United States, discussing moves to legislate equal access, especially "potty parity" laws and the backlash against them. They call for an end to what they call "potty privileging"—a systematic spatial discrimination against women. They conclude on a cautiously hopeful note, presenting new developments and technological inventions that speak to an increasing international will to address restroom issues. Then, educator Claudia Mitchell provides a deeply troubling account of the role unsupervised toilets play in enabling sexual violence against girls in sub-Saharan African schools. Analyzing children's drawings of toilets and interviews with teachers and pupils, she concludes that toilets carry the threat of violence and infection by AIDS and, as such, constitute a significant barrier to girls' education. Mitchell ends with a question as to how the situation can be remedied.

The following four essays assess the impact and meanings of campaigns and legal fights over female toilet provision, considering toilets as spaces of social definition or of cross-cultural encounter, and together provide a historical and cultural perspective on the contemporary situation. Historians Andrew Brown-May and Peg Fraser analyze the asymmetrical public toilet provision in Melbourne, Australia, from the 1850s on. Probing the fact that Melbourne's first municipal public toilet for men was erected some fifty years earlier than a toilet for women, they conclude that gender stereotypes and ideas about respectability were at play, shaping official definitions of the "public" citizen. In addition, they introduce the notion of "municipal interchange," the circulation of information and innovation between cities, to explain the simultaneous appearance and acceptance of female toilets in metropolitan centres from the United Kingdom to Australia at the turn of the century. In the next essay, legal scholar Jami Anderson dissects the 2004 decision *Everson v. Michigan Department of Correc-tions*, in which the court accepted the Michigan Department of Correc-tion's claim that "the very manhood" of male prison guards both threatens the safety of female inmates and violates the women's "special sense of privacy in their genitals" warranting the complete elimination of all male prison guards. Anderson argues that the *Everson* decision, while claiming to protect women prisoners from the harms of toileting exposure, actually reveals a long—though mostly implicit—custom of defining privacy as the "right to modesty" where women are concerned.

Continuing the theme of citizenship, belonging, and bodily privacy, Alison Moore considers toilets and toilet habits as markers of cultural dif-ference. Drawing on her own experience of traveling through North Africa and India, Moore examines touristic responses to excretion in public spaces and fears of gastrointestinal illness as represented by popular travel manuals such as *Lonely Planet*. Her analysis indicates that anxieties about public excretion and disease remain a crucial part of middle-class Western perceptions of the difference between postcolonizing and postcolonial cul-tures. The essay also questions what role middle-class anxieties about ex-cretion might play in relation to feelings of guilt about the colonial past and neocolonial present, especially for women tourists. Architectural the-orist Naomi Stead's essay also takes up issues of shame and obfuscation. Positioning herself as an amateur etymologist, Stead explores why it is that English speakers, especially women, have historically been so averse to calling a toilet a toilet. Stead argues that the persistent use of euphe-misms points to the ongoing links between taboo, gender, and language and suggests toilets will always be a necessary but unspeakable cultural presence.

In the second part, the first two essays specifically focus on aspects of toilet design, noting that they remain deeply, if invisibly, shaped by mascu-linist conventions. We begin with architect Deborah Gans's essay about designing refugee housing. As the main occupants of refugee camps are women of childbearing age, the camps pose special challenges to designers both in terms of architecture and in terms of human rights—challenges that are often not met by implicitly colonialist and male-centred Interna-tional Style camps. Consequently, Gans has designed and implemented an alternate camp design and layout that increases the woman's control over the patterning and maintenance of the household, permitting improved pri-vacy, hygiene, and child supervision. In a similar vein, Barbara Penner's essay questions the underlying logic of female public toilet design. Specifi-cally, in the face of unremitting complaints about women's public toilets—from long queuing times to cramped cubicles—why is it that their design has been so rarely reconsidered over the last century? Penner considers var-ious attempts from the 1890s to the present to introduce female urinals into public toilets and analyzes how each attempt questions the gendered conventions that govern toilet production and use.

The subsequent four essays focus specifically on toilets as a powerful subject of and site for visual art and site-specific installations. Theorist Robin Lydenberg provides an incisive overview of the legacy of Marcel Duchamp's *Fountain*. Using the work of Dorothy Cross and Ilya Kabakov, Lydenberg traces the Duchampian influence to three strands in contemporary art: one takes on his challenge to the isolation of "high art" institutions from everyday life; another aims at social change; and yet another focuses on the body, gender issues, and sexual orientation. Following on Lydenberg's third strand, art historian Kathy Battista considers feminist artists' reinterpretation of the toilet since the 1970s. Analyzing Judy Chicago's groundbreaking *Menstruation Bathroom* (1972) and Catherine Elwes' *Menstruation* performances (1977), Battista discusses how feminist artists have sought to undermine the artistic trope of women at their toilet in order to demystify female experience and the relationship of gender to biology. Her main interest, however, is the toilet-based photographic and sculptural work of British artist Sarah Lucas. Battista argues that in Lucas's pieces toilets challenge gender stereotypes and, through their complex array of connotations, resist any straightforward reading of a woman as a vulnerable or sexual creature.

Artist and architect Alex Schweder's essay mines the psychological potency of the spatial partitioning of public toilets. He presents four recent projects that, by dissolving clear boundaries, intensify anxieties sublimated in public bathrooms and destabilize normal codes of spatial occupation. Bushra Rehman follows with a more personal meditation on the cultural meaning of bathroom practices inspired by sister Sa'dia Rehman's installation *Lotah Stories* in the Queens Museum of Art's bathroom. Lotahs, small vessels that contain water for cleansing oneself after using the toilet, are commonplace throughout South Asia and in many Muslim countries. However, once South Asian and Muslim immigrants come to the United States, the pressure to assimilate forces many to make the transition from lotah to toilet paper, while others carry on using lotahs-in-disguise. Through interviews and anonymous communications, Sa'dia encouraged first-generation and second-generation South Asians to talk publicly about their lotahs. Bushra Rehman's conversation with her sister underscores the way dirt and cleanliness are shaped within culture.

The final three essays delve into the world of representation through film, theater, and popular culture. Taken together, they confirm the notion that, even though toilet practices are on one level private, on another they are only too public. Frances Pheasant-Kelly's essay examines representations of men in toilets in the films *Full Metal Jacket*, *Pulp Fiction*, and *There's Something about Mary*. Pheasant-Kelly argues that, cinematically, toilet spaces in Hollywood movies almost always denote a depleted masculinity and threaten an occasionally fatal loss of control and emotional composure. Yet she observes that this threat is often alleviated in films through the use of comedy, where the instabilities of masculinity are mitigated by laughter or by men dressing as women. Next, urban theorists Johan Andersson and Ben Campkin examine the meanings of "cottage" in mainstream and gay cultures. They show how the British media reinforce a link between male homosexuality and public conveniences: the emphasis on the toilet's relationship to waste in combination with the real dereliction of many "cottages" confirms gay men as society's dirty other. Andersson and Campkin draw out the ambivalence toward public toilets in gay culture itself, analyzing two contemporary plays where cottages are variously depicted as romantic, aggressively hygienic, or profoundly dirty. The cottages emerge as spaces of abjection—both oppressive and liberating, frightening and pleasurable, disgusting and fantastical, rather than being decisively one or the other. In his chapter, Nathan Abrams arrives at similar conclusions, but in a different context. Abrams examines the specific function of the toilet in Jewish popular culture, imagination, and memory. After establishing the importance of toilet practices to maintaining purity in the Torah and later Talmudic literature, Abrams moves on to examine how the toilet has functioned in Jewish American literature and film, in the representation and memory of the Holocaust, and in providing a space for Jewish fantasies and ordeals. Abrams concludes that the toilet suggests a range of oppositions: from ritual impurity to potential danger, from an ordeal to relief and fantasy.

The essays in this volume highlight the reality that toilet practices and spaces, like the toilet's representations, are unstable and inherently contradictory. They emerge as sites where various bodies compete for scarce resources and for recognition—and the stakes are high. It is not the intention of *Ladies and Gents* to try to smooth away these conflicts; and despite the fact that convincing cases are made throughout this book for more innovation in the financing, legislation, design, location, and maintenance of public toilets, its aim is not to prescribe specific remedies. Rather, the book emphasizes that, while there are no simple solutions, much may be gained by talking about toilets in all their material, social, symbolic, and discursive complexity. Such an approach may take readers down diverse paths. It may encourage research that takes into account the psychological, social, and physiological requirements of potential groups of toilet users or it may question the tenets of sex-segregated toilet design. It may enrich discussions surrounding urban theory, tourism, sociology, or anthropology with its demonstrations of how experiences, down to the most banal or natural, are inflected by one's gendered body. Wherever future directions may lead, the various contributions to *Ladies and Gents* testify to the importance of public toilets to our environment *and* to our scholarship, unspeakable no more.

Notes

1. A word about terminology: there are many different names for public toilets. A few of the most common include bathrooms, conveniences, facilities, lavatories, loos, resting places, restrooms, and washrooms. As much as possible, we have avoided standardizing our terminology and have retained whatever term would have been used in its original historical and geographical context.

2. It should be noted that fears of contagion along class lines are still in evidence in today's Britain. A recent article in *The Guardian* noted that the citizens of Romsey had to pay £5000 for a new toilet for exclusive use of the queen. She also has her own specially designed and never used "throne" in Government House in Hong Kong (Hoggart 2007, 25).

3. In his brilliant 1979 article "Sex Is Politics," Vidal also singles out Hilton Kramer—the founder of *The New Criterion*, which led the academic assault on our project—as one of those who have whipped up the country into a "state of terminal hysteria on the subject of sex in general and homosexuality in particular" (550–51).

4. In contrast to the West, where it is assumed that men urinate standing up, in Muslim cultures the practice is to sit down or squat. The justification for squatting is religious: when a man stands, urine might splash on one's body or clothes, thus rendering him ritually unclean. For the same reason, water ablution is used instead of toilet paper. Moreover, in Muslim etiquette, people relieve themselves in seclusion, or at least keep silent and avoid social contact in the bathroom.

5. Court decisions concerning female toilet provision in the United States have been made on various grounds, from anatomical differences (which take into account special female conditions such as menstruation and pregnancy) to the theory of "disparate impact," where it is accepted that inadequate toilet provision places a heavier burden on women and, hence, constitutes a form of sexual harassment (for a full account of relevant legal decisions and precedents, see Banzaf n.d. and Banzhaf 2002). In an e-mail communication with the editors dated January 16, 2008, Banzhaf informed us that his fight goes on: he most recently filed a potty parity complaint against the speaker of the U.S. House of Representatives, Nancy Pelosi, for failing to provide adequate toilet provision for the House's seventy female members.

6. It is also worth pointing out that Laporte sets out to foul language or, as El-Khoury writes, "to reverse the deodorization of language by means of a reeking syntax" (El-Khoury 1993, ix). Although his efforts follow a noble tradition in literature, beginning with Francois Rabelais and Jonathan Swift, Laporte's strategy is particularly noteworthy in an academic context as it highlights the extent to which scholarly discourse itself is usually sanitized and policed by protocols and conventions.

7. Interestingly, Abel argues that Lacan's discussion of sexual difference is already informed by race through his choice of the phrase "laws of urinary segregation"—a deliberate reference, she believes, to American Jim Crow laws.

8. While *Toilet Training* is the only documentary to focus exclusively on bathroom access for transgender people, several other documentaries discuss the issue of public bathrooms in the larger context of the performance of gender. Among them are *Outlaw* (1994, 26 min., dir. Alisa Lebow) and *You Don't Know Dick* (1997, 58 min., dir. Candace Schermerhorn and Bestor Cram). *Outlaw* is a cinematic profile of transgender activist, writer, and performer Leslie Feinberg, who presents the bathroom as a key test of gender performance. *You Don't Know Dick* is a collective portrait of several female-to-male transsexuals. In part of the latter film titled "Men's Room," the main characters talk about experiences of transgender men in the men's bathrooms, their strategies of access, and their behavior adjustments.

References

Abel, E. 1999. "Bathroom Doors and Drinking Fountains: Jim Crow's Racial Symbolic." *Critical Inquiry* 25 (3): 435–81.

Adams, M. 2005. "Piled Higher and Deeper." *Townhall*, June 2. Available at http://townhall.com/columnists/MikeSAdams/2005/06/02/piled_higher_and_deeper.

Alcoff, L., and L. Gray. 1993. "Survivor Discourse: Transgression or Recuperation?" *Signs* 18 (2): 260–90.

Allen, C. 2005. "Gender Theory Takes a Trip Down the Commode." Independent Women's Forum, June 3. Available at http://www.iwf.org/inkwell/show/16529.html.

Andrews, M. 1990. "Sanitary Conveniences and the Retreat of the Frontier: Vancouver, 1886–1926." *BC Studies* 87:3–22.

Anthony, K. 2001. *Designing for Diversity: Gender, Race, and Ethnicity in the Architectural Profession.* Urbana: University of Illinois Press.

Antony, L. 1998. "Back to Androgyny: What Bathrooms Can Teach Us about Equality." *Journal of Contemporary Legal Issues* 9:1–21.

August, O. 2004. "China Scrubs Up to Impress Global Elite of Sanitation." *The Times*, November 17. World News.

Banks, T. L. 1990. "Toilets as a Feminist Issue: A True Story." *Berkeley Women's Law Journal* 6 (2): 263–89.

Banzhaf, J. 1990. "Final Frontier for the Law?" *National Law Journal* (April 18). Available at http://banzhaf.net/pottyparity.html.

———. 2002. Copy of recent "Potty Parity" complaint against the University of Michigan. Available at http://banzhaf.net/docs/michigan.html.

———. N.d. "Is Potty Parity a Legal Right?" Available at http://banzhaf.net/docs/pparticle.html.

Barcan, R. 2005. "Dirty Spaces: Communication and Contamination in Men's Public Toilets." *Journal of International Women's Studies* 6 (2): 7–23.

Barnes, D. S. 2005. "Confronting Sensory Crisis in the Great Stinks of London and Paris." In *Filth: Dirt, Disgust and Modern Life* Ed. W. Cohen and R. Johnson. Minneapolis: University of Minnesota Press, 103–32.

Bataille, G. 1985. *Visions of Excess: Selected Writings, 1927–1939.* Trans. A. Stoekl, with C. R. Lovitt and D. M. Leslie Jr. Minneapolis: University of Minnesota Press.

Beam, A. 2005. "Academia Goes Down the Drain." *Boston Globe*, June 2.

Beauvoir, S. de. 1949/1997. *The Second Sex.* Ed. and trans. H. M. Parshley. London: Vintage.

Belkin, L. 1990. "*Houston Journal:* Seeking Some Relief, She Stepped Out of Line." *New York Times*, July 20.

Boris, E. 1998. "'You Wouldn't Want One of 'Em Dancing with Your Wife': Racialized Bodies on the Job in World War II." *American Quarterly* 50 (1): 77–108.

Bornstein, K. 1998. *My Gender Workbook.* London: Routledge.

Bourdieu, P. 1979/2007. *Distinction: A Social Critique of the Judgement of Taste.* Trans. R. Nice. Cambridge, Mass.: Harvard University Press.

Brunton, D. 2005. "Evil Necessaries and Abominable Erections: Public Conveniences and Private Interests in the Scottish City, 1830–1870." *Social History of Medicine* 18 (2): 187–202.

Butler, J. 1990. *Gender Trouble: Feminism and the Subversion of Identity.* New York: Routledge.

Cahill, S. E., W. Distler, C. Lachowetz, A. Meaney, R. Tarallo, and T. Willard. 1985. "Meanwhile Backstage: Public Bathrooms and the Interaction Order." *Urban Life* 14 (1): 33–58.

Campkin, B., and R. Cox, eds. 2007. *Dirt: New Geographies of Cleanliness and Contamination.* London: I. B. Tauris.

Carter, W. H. 2007. *Flushed: How the Plumber Saved Civilization.* New York: Simon and Schuster.

Case, A. M. 2001. "Changing Room? A Quick Tour of Men's and Women's Rooms in US Law over the Last Decade, from the US Constitution to Local Ordinances." *Public Culture* 13 (2): 333–36.

Cavanagh, S., and V. Ware. 1990. *At Women's Convenience; A Handbook on the Design of Women's Public Toilets.* London: Women's Design Service.

Chauncey, G. 1996. "'Privacy Could Only Be Had in Public': Gay Uses of the Streets." In *Stud: Architectures of Masculinity.* Ed. J. Sanders. New York: Princeton Architectural Press, 224–67.

Chess, S., A. Kafer, J. Quizar, and M. U. Richardson. 2004. "Calling All Restroom Revolutionaries!" In *That's Revolting: Queer Strategies for Resisting Assimilation*. Ed. M. Bernstein Sycamore. Brooklyn: Soft Skull Press, 189–207.

Ciochetto, L. 2003. "Toilet Signage as Effective Communication." *Visible Language* 37 (2): 208–22.

Cooper, A., R. Law, J. Malthus, and P. Wood. 2000. "Rooms of Their Own: Public Toilets and Gendered Citizens in a New Zealand City, 1860–1940." *Gender, Place and Culture* 7 (4): 417–33.

Cooper, P., and R. Oldenziel. 1999. "Cherished Classifications: Bathrooms and the Construction of Gender/Race on the Pennsylvania Railroad during World War II." *Feminist Studies* 25 (1): 7–41.

Corbin, A. 1986. *The Foul and the Fragrant: Odour and the Social Imagination*. Trans. M. L. Kochan. Cambridge, Mass.: Harvard University Press.

Cowen, D., U. Lehrer, and A. Winkler. 2005. "The Secret Lives of Toilets: A Public Discourse on 'Private' Space in the City." In *uTOpia*. Ed. J. McBride and A. Wilcox. Toronto: Coach House Books, 194–203.

Custer, R. 2005. "Parade of Pies and Potty Politics Highlight Campus Outrages." August 29. *Human Events Online*. Available at http://www.humanevents.com/article.php?id=8762.

Daley, C. 2000. "Flushed with Pride? Women's Quest for Public Toilets in New Zealand." *Women's Studies Journal* 16 (1): 95–113.

Davis, M. 1992. *City of Quartz: Excavating the Future in Los Angeles*. New York: Vintage.

De Hart, J. S. 1991. "Gender on the Right: Meanings behind the Existential Scream." *Gender and History* 3:246–67.

Douglas, M. 1966. *Purity and Danger: An Analysis of the Concepts of Pollution and Taboo*. London: Routledge.

Durantaye, L. de la. 2007. "Readymade Remade." *Cabinet Magazine* 7 (Fall). Available at http://www.cabinetmagazine.org/issues/27/durantaye.php.

Dutton, M., S. Seth, and L. Gandhi. 2002a. Editorial. "Plumbing the Depth: Toilets, Transparency and Modernity." *Postcolonial Studies* 5 (2): 137–42.

———, eds. 2002b. Special issue of *Postcolonial Studies* on toilets.

Edelman, L. 1994. "Tearooms and Sympathy; or, The Epistemology of the Water Closet." In *Homographesis: Essays in Gay Literary and Cultural Theory*. New York: Routledge, 148–70.

———. 1996. "Men's Room." In *Stud: Architectures of Masculinity*. Ed. J. Sanders. New York: Princeton Architectural Press, 152–61.

Edwards, J., and L. McKie. 1997. "Women's Public Toilets: A Serious Issue for the Body Politic." In *Embodied Practices: Feminist Perspectives on the Body*. Ed. K. Davis. London: Sage, 134–49.

Elias, N. 2000. *The Civilizing Process*. Vol. 1 of *The History of Manners*. Ed. E. Jephcott. Oxford: Blackwell.

El-Khoury, R. 1993. Introduction to *History of Shit*, by D. Laporte. Trans. N. Benabid and R. El-Khoury. Cambridge, Mass.: MIT Press.

Faludi, S. 1994. "The Naked Citadel." *New Yorker*, September 5, pp. 62–81.

Feinberg, L. 1996. *Transgender Warriors: Making History from Joan of Arc to Dennis Rodman*. Boston: Beacon Press.

Foucault, M. 1991. *Discipline and Punish: The Birth of the Prison*. Trans. A. Sheridan. London: Penguin Books.

Frascari, M. 1997. "The Pneumatic Bathroom." In *Plumbing: Sounding Modern Architecture*. Ed. N. Lahiji and D. S. Friedman. New York: Princeton Architectural Press, 163–82.

French, M. 1977. *The Women's Room*. New York: Ballantine Books.

Freud, S. 1930/1961. *Civilization and Its Discontents*. Trans. J. Strachey. New York: W. W. Norton.

Gedan, B. 2002. "Group Wants Transgender Bathrooms for UMass." *Boston Globe*, October 20.

Geisler, T. 2000. "On Public Toilets in Beijing." *Journal of Architectural Education* 53 (4): 216–19.

George, R. 2008. *The Big Necessity: Adventures in the World of Human Waste.* London: Portobello Books.

Giedion, S. 1948. *Mechanization Takes Command: A Contribution to Anonymous History.* New York: Oxford University Press.

Goffman, E. 1959. *The Presentation of Self in Everyday Life.* New York: Anchor Books.

———. 1963. *Behavior in Public Places.* New York: Free Press.

Gordon, B. 2003. "Embodiment, Community Building, and Aesthetic Saturation in 'Restroom World,' a Backstage Women's Space." *Journal of American Folklore* 116 (462): 444–64.

Greed, C. 1995. "Public Toilet Provisions for Women in Britain: An Investigation of Discrimination against Urination." *Women's Studies International Forum* 18 (5/6): 573–84.

———. 2003. *Public Toilets: Inclusive Urban Design.* Oxford: Architectural Press.

———. 2005. "Overcoming the Factors Inhibiting the Mainstreaming of Gender into Spatial Planning Policy in the United Kingdom." *Urban Studies* 42 (4): 1–31.

Gregory, M. E., and S. James. 2006. *Toilets of the World.* London: Merrell.

Guerrand, R.-H. 1997. *Les lieux, histoire des commodités.* Paris: La Découverte.

Halberstam, J. 1998. *Female Masculinity.* Durham: Duke University Press.

Hart-Davis, A. 1997. *Thunder, Flush and Thomas Crapper: An EncycLOOpedia.* London: Michael O'Mara.

Hoggart, S. 2007. "Simon Hoggart's Week: Cues, Royal Loos, and Money Down the Pan." *The Guardian*, October. 20.

Holm, L. 2007. "ES aitcH eYe Tee." *Journal of Architecture* 12 (4): 423–36.

Horan, J. 1996. *The Porcelain God: A Social History of the Toilet.* Secaucus, N.J.: Carol Publication Group.

Horvath. A. 2005. "Toilet Doors of Melbourne." Poster. Museum Victoria.

Houlbrook, M. 2000. "The Private World of Public Urinals: London 1918–1957." *London Journal* 25 (1): 52–70.

———. 2001. "For Whose Convenience? Gay Guides, Cognitive Maps and the Construction of Homosexual London: 1917–1967." In *Identities in Space: Contested Terrains in the Western City since 1850.* Ed. S. Gunn and R. J. Morris. London: Ashgate, 165–86.

———. 2005. *Queer London: Perils and Pleasures in the Sexual Metropolis, 1918–1957,* Chicago: University of Chicago Press.

Humphries, L. 1970, *Tearoom Trade: Impersonal Sex in Public Places.* Chicago: Aldine. Reprinted in Leap, W., ed. 1999. *Public Sex/Gay Space.* New York: Columbia University Press, 29–53.

Inglis, D. 2001. *A Sociological History of Excretory Experience: Defecatory Manners and Toiletry Technologies.* Lewiston, N.Y.: Edwin Mellen.

Ings, W. 2007. "A Convenient Exchange: Discourses between Physical, Legal and Linguistic Frameworks Impacting on the New Zealand Public Toilet." *Public Space: The Journal of Law and Social Justice,* 1 (1): 1–44.

Kimball, R. 2005. "Where Is Hercules When You Need Him?" *New Criterion*, May 30. Available at http://newcriterion.com.

Kira, A. 1966. *The Bathroom, Criteria for Design.* Ithaca, N.Y.: Cornell University Center for Housing and Environmental Studies.

———. 1976. *The Bathroom: New and Revised Edition.* New York: Viking Press.

Kithcin, R., and R. Law. 2001. "The Socio-Spatial Construction of (In)Accessible Public Toilets." *Urban Studies* 38 (2): 287–98.

Kristeva, J. 1982. *Powers of Horror: An Essay on Abjection.* Trans. Leon S. Roudiez. New York: Columbia University Press.

———. 1997. "Approaching Abjection." In *The Portable Kristeva.* Ed. K. Oliver. New York: Columbia University Press, 229–47.

Lacan, J. 1997. "The Agency of the Letter in the Unconscious, or Reason since Freud." In *Ecrits: A Selection.* Trans. Alan Sheridan. New York: W. W. Norton, 146–78.

Lahiji, N., and D. S. Friedman, eds. 1997. *Plumbing: Sounding Modern Architecture*. New York: Princeton Architectural Press.

Lambton, L. 1995. *Temples of Convenience and Chambers of Delight*. London: Pavilion Books.

Laporte, D. 1993. *History of Shit*. Trans. N. Benabid and R. el-Khoury. Cambridge, Mass.: MIT Press.

Lupton, E., and J. A. Miller. 1996. *The Bathroom, the Kitchen, and the Aesthetics of Waste: A Process of Elimination*. New York: Kiosk.

Maynard, S. 1994. "Through a Hole in the Lavatory Wall: Homosexual Subcultures, Police Surveillance, and the Dialectics of Discovery, Toronto, 1890–1930." *Journal of the History of Sexuality* 5 (21): 207–42.

Miller, S. 2002. "Down the Drain." *Independent Gay Forum*, October 22. Available at http://www.indegayforum.org/blog/show/30090.html.

Molesworth, H. 1997. "Bathrooms and Kitchens: Cleaning House with Duchamp." In *Plumbing: Sounding Modern Architecture*. Ed. N. Lahiji and D. S. Friedman. New York: Princeton Architectural Press, 75–92.

Molotch, H. 1988. "The Rest Room and Equal Opportunity." *Sociological Forum* 3 (1): 128–33.

Morgan, M. 1997. "Too Much Leverage Is Dangerous." In *Plumbing: Sounding Modern Architecture*. Ed. N. Lahiji and D. S. Friedman. New York: Princeton Architectural Press, 62–74.

———. 2002. "The Plumbing of Modern Life." *Postcolonial Studies* 5 (2): 171–96.

Morrison, K. 2008. "Spending a Penny at Rothesay; or, How One Lavatory Became a Gentleman's Loo." *Victorian Literature and Culture* 36 (1): 79–94.

Munt, S. 1998. "Orifices in Space: Making the Real Possible." In *Butch/Femme: Inside Lesbian Gender*. London: Cassell, 200–210.

Muntadas, A. 2001. *Ladies and Gentlemen*. Barcelona: Actar.

Newman, A. 2007. "Society's Politics, as Seen through a Porcelain Lens." *New York Times*, November 4.

Nilsson, A. 1998. "Creating Their Own Private and Public: The Male Homosexual Life Space in a Nordic City during High Modernity." *Journal of Homosexuality* 35 (3/4): 81–116.

Ohly, J. H. 1946. "History of Plant Seizures during World War II." Office of the Chief of Military History, Department of the Army, vol. 3, app. Z-1-a. Duplicated.

Otta, E. 1993. "Graffiti in the 1990s: A Study of Inscriptions on Restroom Walls." *Journal of Social Psychology* 133 (4): 589–90.

Penner, B. 2001. "A World of Unmentionable Suffering: Women's Public Conveniences in Victorian London." *Journal of Design History* 14 (1): 35–52.

Pierce, J. 2002. Posting on the *Daily Collegian* electronic discussion board in response to the article "Restroom Revolution Gathers at Stonewall," by Morris Singer, published on October 3, 2002, in the *Daily Collegian*. Available at http://media.www.dailycollegian.com.

"The Politics of Pee." 2002. *Minuteman*, November 26.

Quindlen, A. 1992. "Public and Private; a Rest(room) of One's Own." *New York Times*, November 11.

Rappaport, E. 2000. *Shopping for Pleasure: Women in the Making of London's West End*. Princeton: Princeton University Press, 79–85.

Reyburn, W. 1969. *Flushed with Pride: The Story of Thomas Crapper*. London: Macdonald.

Reynolds, R. 1946. *Cleanliness and Godliness*. New York: Doubleday.

Schuster, C. 2005. *Public Toilet Design: From Hotels, Bars, Restaurants, Civic Buildings and Businesses Worldwide*. New York: Firefly Books.

Sedgwick, E. Kosofsky. 1985. *Between Men: English Literature and Male Homosocial Desire*. New York: Columbia University Press.

Sheldon, L. P. 2002. "A Gender Identity Disorder Goes Mainstream." *Traditional Value Coalition*. October 25. Available at http://www.traditionalvalues.org/pdf_files/TVC-SpecialRptTransgenders1234.pdf.

Skeggs, B. 2001. "The Toilet Paper: Femininity, Class and Mis-recognition." *Women's Studies International Forum* 24 (3–4): 295–307.

Sulabh Sanitation Movement. 2007. Home page. Available at http://www.sulabhtoiletmuseum.org.

Tanizaki, J. 1933/1977. *In Praise of Shadows*. Chicago: Leete's Island Books.

Taranto, J. 2005. "How to Earn Your Pee h.D." *Wall Street Journal*, section Opinion Journal, May 31. Available at http://www.opinionjournal.com/best/?id=110006758.

TFFKAMM. 2005. "Toilet Papers: The Gendered Construction of Public Toilets." *Free Republic*, May 31. Available at http://www.freerepublic.com/focus/f-news/ 1413958/posts.

Vade, D. 2001. "Gender Neutral Bathroom Survey." Transgender Law Center, San Francisco, California. Duplicated.

Van der Geest, S. 2002. "The Night-Soil Collector: Bucket Latrines in Ghana." *Postcolonial Studies* 5 (2): 197–206.

Vidal, G. 1979/1993. "Sex Is Politics." In *United States: Essays, 1952–1992*. London: Abacus, 538–53.

Wasserstrom, R. A. 1977. "Racism, Sexism, and Preferential Treatment: An Approach to the Topics." *UCLA Law Review* 24:581–615.

Weinberg, S. M., and C. J. Williams. 2005. "Fecal Matters: Habitus, Embodiments, and Deviance." *Social Problems* 52 (3): 315–36.

Wenz-Gahler, I. 2005. *Flush! Modern Toilet Design*. Boston: Birkhauser.

Woolf, V. 1929/1994. *A Room of One's Own*. London: Flamingo.

Wright, L. 1960. *Clean and Decent: The Fascinating History of the Bathroom and the Water-Closet and of Sundry Habits, Fashions and Accessories of the Toilet, Principally in Great Britain, France, and America*. London: Routledge and Paul.

Filmography

Ferry Tales. 2003. Directed by Katja Esson. Available from Women Make Movies, http://www.wmm.com.

Inside Rooms: 26 Bathrooms, London and Oxfordshire. 1985. Directed by Peter Greenaway.

The Ladies Room/Zananeh. 2003. Directed by Mahnaz Afzali. Available from Women Make Movies, http://www.wmm.com.

Outlaw. 1994. Directed by Alisa Lebow. Available from Women Make Movies, http://www.wmm.com.

Q2P. 2006. Directed by Paromita Vohra. Available from Partners for Urban Knowledge Action and Research, http://www.pukar.org.in/pukar/genderandspace.

Tearoom Trade. 1994. Directed by Christopher Johnson.

Toilet Training. 2003. Directed by Tara Mateik. Available from the Sylvia Rivera Law Project, http://www.srlp.org.

You Don't Know Dick.1997. Directed by Candace Schermerhorn and Bestor Cram. Available from Berkeley Media, http://www.berkeleymedia.com.

Potty Politics

Toilets, Gender, and Identity

1

The Role of the Public Toilet in Civic Life

CLARA GREED

Most people imagine public toilets to be dirty, full of germs and the remains of other people's unsavoury habits (Greed 2003; Bichard, Hanson, and Greed 2007). Drawing on ongoing research, this chapter argues that people are justified in their assumptions about the unhealthy state of British toilets. Public toilets here are defined as both the traditional "on-street" public toilets (run by the local authority) and "off-street" toilets (run by private-sector providers) to which the general public has right of access (e.g., in shopping malls and railway stations) (BTA 2001).

The first section of this chapter outlines the issue of inadequate public toilet provision, highlighting the problems encountered by women. The second section discusses the role of public toilets as sites of germ transmission. The third section discusses the less obvious but equally worrying role of poor toilet design in contributing towards physiological problems for users. Section four discusses the health implications of tasks undertaken in toilets other than urination or excretion, and section five argues that many of the problems identified, which disproportionately affect women, derive from the male professional perspective, which informs toilet provision and design. The concluding section contends that toilet provision and cleaning need to be taken much more seriously as key elements in maintaining health and well-being. This can be achieved only by changes in toilet organisation and management.

The Problem: Unequal and Inadequate Provision

Research has demonstrated that public toilet provision constitutes the missing link that would enable the creation of sustainable, accessible, healthy, and inclusive cities (Bichard, Hanson, and Greed 2004; Hanson, Bichard, and Greed 2007). If the government wants to encourage people to leave their cars at home and travel by public transport, cycle, or walk, then the provision of public toilets is essential, especially at transit centres. Public transport passengers, pedestrians, and cyclists—unlike car drivers—cannot speed to the nearest service station to use the toilet when they find the local facilities have been closed.

In London alone, every day over 5 million people travel by bus, 3 million by tube, and 11 million by car. These travellers generate millions of "away from home" trips to the toilet per day. It should not be assumed that only a minority will need public toilets because private toilet options are available. Admittedly, some out-of-town shopping malls contain good facilities, but public toilets have been closed in many town centres. Men are more likely to use toilet facilities in licensed premises such as bars, clubs, and pubs. When women complain about a lack of public facilities, it is often suggested that they go to a pub. This is not necessarily an option for women. Women with small children may effectively be barred from using such facilities because of licensing law. Many more women would be hesitant to enter an unfamiliar pub by themselves because of safety concerns and the discomfort of being the only woman in a male space (Greed 2003; Penner 1996). Some religious group members may be wary of using toilets in buildings where alcohol or non-*halal* food is served.

Women are particularly in need of public toilets, as they are the ones most frequently out and about in the daytime, travel on public transport more than men, and often are accompanied by children or elderly or disabled relatives (Cavanagh and Ware 1991; Booth et al. 1996). And yet, there is less public toilet provision for women than for men in many British cities, in terms of both the number of toilets available and the ratio of male to female facilities (Greed 2003)—a situation replicated in many countries. Surveys have shown that one in four women in the European Union between thirty-five and seventy years of age suffers some degree of urinary stress incontinence, which restricts their freedom to travel. Moreover, urinary tract infections, problems of distended bladders, and a range of other urinary and gynaecological problems among women have increased in relation to further toilet closures (Edwards 1998a).

Although considerable attention has been given to accessible toilet (also called sometimes "disabled toilet") provision under disability legislation, not everyone's toilet needs have been met (Disability Discrimination Act 1995; Bright, Williams, and Langton-Lockton 2004). The so-called bladder leash impedes access and mobility in the city for many people (Bichard, Hanson, and Greed 2004). Standard (or abled) toilets may prove inaccessible for people with strollers or with luggage, the pregnant, and the elderly. Their access is restricted by narrow entrances, small stalls, and stairs (Greed 1996; Greed 2004). Automatic public toilets and toilets with a turnstile-controlled payment system also present difficulties for some users.

Government policies to promote the evening economy, the twenty-four-hour city, tourism, and public transport use have all increased the need for toilet provision, but, paradoxically, public toilets are being closed "to save money." The proliferation of city-centre pubs and bars has resulted in increased alcohol consumption, typified by a binge-drinking, male, youth culture (Tallon and Bromley 2002). This scenario is far from the European "city of culture" that was meant to attract a diverse and sophisticated evening population, as originally envisaged by policy makers (CCI 2002; Roberts 2003).

Adequate infrastructural back-up has not been forthcoming in terms of public toilets, public transport, street cleaning, policing, and public safety measures. Growth in licensed premises, combined with public toilet closure, has resulted in increased street urination by males. Even if bars and pubs provide toilets, men still urinate outside on their way home, after the closing time. There is also an element of bravado that dares young men to urinate openly in the streets. Ethnographically, it is significant that whilst women's space to urinate is heavily controlled and restricted to a small number of narrow stalls, men can claim the whole expanse of the street to do so without censure, for "only men are entitled to overflow on the public highway" (Chevalier 1936, 97). Only a minority of young women will chose to urinate in public; most women tend to defer urination until they can find a public toilet.

According to the Royal Society of Chemistry, the absence of sufficient public toilets, along with crumbling sewerage systems and neglect of drainage issues, is resulting in the spread of strains of *Cryptosporidium parvum* associated with diarrhoea (Hashmey, 1997) and the return of water-borne diseases, such as cholera, typhoid, and dysentery, that were prevalent in the nineteenth century (RSC 2002; Hawker et al. 2005). As a result of public health concerns, some local authorities have provided open-air male street urinals to counter the use of popular "wet spot" locations in city centres.

Toilets and Germ Transmission

While the problems caused by lack of adequate and equal provision demand an urgent resolution, the condition of existing public toilets is also of grave concern. Poor hygiene results in a proliferation of toilet-related diseases. However, hospital toilets, rather than street toilets, have been the primary focus of media concern because of their perceived role in the transmission of MRSA.

The term *MRSA* refers to a range of bacteria that have become resistant to antibiotics, use of which in the past might have mitigated the effects of inadequate cleaning and poor personal hygiene (Larson 1988). A major National Health Service hospital-focused campaign to encourage people to wash their hands after using the toilet has been introduced along with improved cleaning regimes (Rothburn and Dunnigan 2004). The contracting out of cleaning and maintenance services, along with privatisation of many health, welfare, and local authority functions, may have saved money, but it has also led to reduced in-house control over cleaning standards.

While MRSA in hospital toilets has grabbed the headlines, CA-MRSA, a different strain, may prove more lethal. It is found in shared and community facilities such as toilets and showers in prisons, orphanages, schools, correctional institutions, sports facilities, and hostels, as well as in public toilets and hospitals (O'Brien et al. 1999; Rothburn and Dunnigan 2004). CA-MRSA can be picked up by toilet users from unwashed surfaces, bacteria thriving in stagnant water, faecal remains, menstrual blood waste, and urine (Deslypere 2004). However, CA-MRSA seems to be in a blind spot for both media and government. Reasons for this include political unwillingness to admit the scale of the problem, inability of local authorities to assign more money and resources to toilet cleaning, and fear of legal action. Public toilet campaigners are wary of mentioning the problem, as it may be used as an excuse to close down the remaining toilets.

Public toilets are one of the main locations where complete strangers mix and use the same sanitary facilities, with all the related risks of bodily fluid exchange and contamination. Careless users may transmit germs to the outside world on unwashed hands that subsequently handle food, money, paperwork, and clothing and that touch other people. Deslypere (2004) has demonstrated that the chances of germ transmission are very high, as every door handle, tap, lever, lock, soap, toilet roll holder, and turnstile turns into a potential germ carrier. Yet most toilets have very limited washing facilities, and hot water is seldom available. Even modern, well-equipped toilets may present hazards. Electric hand driers (often imagined to be safer than towels) may be blowing germs back into the atmosphere (unless the filters are regularly changed or the drier is externally vented). Their use can contribute to the spread of Legionnaires' disease, which is transmitted through contaminated air and water systems (Rothburn and Dunnigan 2004, 65–66). Even flushing the toilet results in minidroplets of contaminated air passing into the respiratory system (Deslypere 2004). There is no need to become paranoid: humans carry around millions of bacteria, many of which are benign and essential to digestion. Nevertheless, vulnerable groups, such as the young and the weak, can be susceptible to infections.

Nowadays, concerns about new diseases such as SARS figure strongly in the public mind. With the expansion of international air travel, fear of catching even more exotic diseases, such as Ebola, are expressed by air passengers using airport toilets. The prevalence of E. coli both in Britain and internationally has led to a renewed concern with food hygiene. It can be transmitted through food, by infected water, and from person to person by touch (Larson 1988). But at source, all E. coli are dependent on poor human hygiene, especially in the toilet.

Because hygiene is so important in preventing disease transmission, one would expect toilets to be seen as front-line services in both the public and clinical health systems (Ayliffe 2000). One would imagine toilets would be subject to the highest levels of management, maintenance, cleaning, and pathogen control. Far from it: hospital toilets (and hospitals themselves) are surprisingly badly maintained. Little attention is given to such simple measures as separating patient and visitor toilets to prevent the spread of contagion (Morris 2005). Other public-realm toilets, such as school facilities, have also been the subject of criticism. Many children are wary of going to the toilet because of disgusting conditions. The levels of provision and male/female ratios of toilet provision in schools have remained inadequate as well (BSI 2006). Teachers may exacerbate the situation by closing toilets to reduce incidences of bullying, smoking, and drug taking, thus preventing children from legitimately using the facilities (Vernon et al. 2003).

The Debilitating Effect of Toilet Design

An equally important, but less visible, aspect of ill health is the design of toilet facilities. Women are particularly adversely affected because they need to sit down to use the toilet (at least in the United Kingdom, where Western toilets are dominant), but many have difficulty doing so because of the stall size and design. Inward-opening doors are the largest component restricting available stall space. Often, the edge of the door touches the outer rim of the toilet bowl. Presumably, many stalls are still designed by men, for men. Men do not need to get into the stall, close the door, do a three-point turn, and sit down before urinating; they sit down only to defecate. Sitting down for women may also be impeded by the positioning of a jumbo-sized toilet-roll holder and a sanitary product disposal bin beside the seat.

The "bin problem" is frequently raised by female respondents, often with extreme embarrassment. In England and Wales, disposal bins are provided within stalls under the requirements of Environmental Protection Act (1990) for "the safe disposal of clinical waste." Often the only place to put the bin in the stall is right beside the toilet bowl in an already very narrow compartment. So the bins rub against women's legs and outer thighs when they sit down on the toilet. Bins are infrequently emptied and often overflow with sanitary waste. Ironically, the purpose of the bins was to prevent contact with contaminated products and bodily secretions, all of which provide ideal cultures for bacteria and virus incubation (Monaghan 2002.) The bin may be so high and large that it prevents a woman from sitting down on the toilet seat, causing her to "hover" over the pan, tensing muscles and restricting urine flow (Blandy 2004).

Studies have long shown that around 80 percent of women hover over the seat to urinate when in public toilets, whereas they prefer to sit when using their toilet at home (Moore et al. 1991). Even if they can reach the seat unimpeded, many women are fearful of a contaminated toilet seat. Women are wary of sitting down on a wet seat, sprayed by the last users. While a lack of cleaning and poor toilet management deter some women from using the facilities, deeper cultural taboos prevent other women from sitting comfortably. Thus poor cleaning practices and restrictive stall design conspire to discourage women from sitting down, which causes major medical problems. Hovering contributes to residual urine retention, as the bladder cannot empty properly, leading to the development of continence problems (Parazzini et al. 2003; Moore et al. 1991).

Whereas women are often accused of being too fastidious in their toilet practices, a variety of pathogens indeed inhabit the toilet seat, causing gastrointestinal infections and urinary tract problems. Some women solve the problem by covering the seat with toilet paper, which is then flushed away—a practice that contributes to blocked toilets. Automatic toilet-seat-cover dispensers are available in some semi-private public toilets (such as in hotels or in doctors' offices), but in on-street public toilets, such dispensers are often vandalised or ill maintained. Instead of trying to solve the toilet seat problem, many recommend squatting rather than sitting, as is common in much of the world. Squatting is seen as a healthier and more hygienic position, which also ensures that the bladder and the bowels are fully emptied. In the Far East and across the Muslim world people are wary of using Western-style toilets, which are considered dirty because a seat there is shared by strangers.

The Importance of Changing

Public toilets not only provide for the excretory needs; they also serve as private spaces within the public realm where a range of other personal activities can take place. Changing and disposal facilities are necessary for many users, including menstruating women and people with urinary and anal/faecal incontinence. Indeed, "changing" is a major but underestimated function of the toilet.

At any given time, around a quarter of the female population of childbearing age will be menstruating—that is, around 5 million in the United Kingdom alone. And yet, public toilets often inadequately provide for the needs of menstruating women, including the need to dispose of sanitary products. The bin location and maintenance are often inadequate, as discussed above. If there are no toilets available, women who use tampons are facing a higher risk of infections (Armstrong and Scott 1992; Rothburn and Dunnigan 2004, 79).

Changing and disposal facilities are also necessary for people with incontinence: in women's as well as in men's toilets, in abled as well as in accessible toilets. Some elderly men are unlikely to venture out if there are no disposal facilities in the men's toilets. Men who need to discharge urine from a urostomy bag may decide to empty their bag in full view at the urinals if there are no usable stalls. Those changing colostomy bags (for faecal waste) need absolutely hygienic conditions, good lighting, shelves, and hooks for equipment, as well as hot and cold water supply. Discharging through a stoma (an opening made in the abdomen) requires particularly clean conditions, due to infection risks. Ideally, public toilets should be as clean as in a well-run hospital.

Even though there is now toilet provision for people with disabilities, especially wheelchair users, there is still little awareness of the wider epidemiological role of public toilets. Toilets may contribute to or prevent pathogen transmission; their design may increase or decrease the development of muscular disability and damage to internal organs.

Architects often give the impression that if they provide for the disabled, any requirement to pay attention to the needs of anyone else is absolved. Those experiencing urinary dysfunction, who desperately need toilet facilities, are likely to be treated with suspicion if they appear to be healthy and not eligible to use an accessible toilet reserved for people in a wheelchair. A divisive and judgmental mentality prevails. An inclusive approach is recommended, which would accommodate the needs of those in wheelchairs but also all people with disabilities (over 10 percent of the population), as well as the incontinent (at least 6 million more people) (Greed 2003, 155). But toilets should equally be available for meeting the needs of the other 80 percent of the population who, as ordinary human beings, need to go to the toilet several times a day. Otherwise "the micturating majority" will experience a deterioration in health and an increased propensity towards disability and disease themselves.

Women with babies, small children, and strollers are a large group whose needs are not met. They are not disabled but find regular toilets inaccessible and ill equipped (Cavanagh and Ware 1991). A minority of public toilets offer baby-changing facilities, often of poor standard (BTA 2001). But changing diapers requires cleanliness for both the baby and the mother, as well as bins and adequate washing facilities to ensure that subsequent users are not confronted with unsanitary conditions. Some women breastfeed in the toilet, the only refuge available from disapproving public glares. Risk of infection is high, and campaigners ask, "Would you eat your dinner in a public toilet?" In an ideal world, alternative facilities would be provided, such as those in some shopping malls, where toileting, baby changing, and breastfeeding are given separate spaces. But social attitudes need to change to allow maternal activities "in the open."

Toilets have become the location for all sorts of other activities (both benign and hostile) that are disapproved of in public or for which there is no space outside. A wide range of people frequent toilets for a variety of reasons, ranging from bona fide urinators, disabled users, and baby-changers to drug users and those engaging in antisocial behaviour or sexual activity (such as cottaging or cruising). The general public is also concerned about growth of tuberculosis infection and its association with homeless (who may use public toilets frequently). Fears about encountering other people's bodily fluids, mess, and "sharps" (used drug syringes) haunt many people. Some local authorities have introduced special blue ultraviolet lighting in the toilet so that intravenous drug users will have difficulty seeing their veins. But many people need good light in the toilet, especially those with medical conditions, and drug users have responded by using fluorescent marker pens to highlight their veins. Interestingly, the blue lighting has led to an increase in sexual activity in some toilets, apparently creating a night-club atmosphere, a touch of "risky glamour" (Greed 2003, 88). Addressing these challenges in an ad hoc, fragmented manner results in solving one problem and creating another.

Professional Subcultural and Organisational Constraints

There is a need for a holistic, inclusive, strategic, city-wide, policy-level approach to solving the problems of toilet provision and management. In terms of hygiene control, public toilets are not accorded the level of attention and importance given to other front-line health facilities such as hospitals, health centres, and local clinics. Instead, public toilets are generally the responsibility of relatively low-status, technical, operational departments in local government, often falling under the control of "parks and gardens," "municipal services," "refuse disposal," or "street cleansing." There is little strategic policy dimension and no proactive policy making. A reactive, "firefighting" approach prevails, wherein the authorities respond to problems of vandalism and disrepair by simply closing down the toilets and thus removing the problem zone. But no alternative is provided, for as one toilet manager commented, "The only good public toilet is a closed public toilet."

Many of these problems arise from the subcultural values of the decision makers themselves (Greed 2000). Those responsible for public toilet provision generally hail from an engineering rather than a medical or social policy background. A narrow quantitative approach informs their decision making, with little space for a reflective, sociological, "big picture" approach. A hundred years ago, medical experts, social reformers, intellectuals, engineers, and architects worked together, inspired by a sense of civic pride and social responsibility to equip Victorian and Edwardian cities with public toilets, along with libraries, hospitals, and public parks. In our times, such amenities are likely to be viewed by local government auditors as money-wasting and low-status matters, for "they know the cost of everything and the value of nothing" (Greed 2003). The professions have grown apart, and each now speaks its own language (with its own jargon and territory). There is little opportunity for communication, let alone collective thinking.

The sanitary engineering fraternity within the municipal public works subculture appears obsessed with "practical" issues such as the best size of piping; the amounts of water used in flushing; the minutiae of material specifications, dimensions, tolerances, and so forth. A lack of concern about user needs, ergonomics, and social considerations is evident. No one thinks about the actual users. When toilet users are considered, they are imagined to be male, because most of those who are responsible for toilet design, provision, and management are male (Greed 2002). In contrast, user needs and social issues are high on the priority list for health care and social policy professionals concerned about toilet provision and design. Unsurprisingly, they often tend to be women.

Women's issues have been marginalised within the male-dominated professional subcultures of sanitary engineering, medicine, architecture, city planning, and product design. But what is "good for men" is not necessarily "good for women." There are major biological, sexual, and gender differences in terms of toilet usage and design needs, for both abled and disabled users. Taking the male as norm resulted in extremely unsatisfactory provision for women. Within the world of municipal engineering, the women's toilet is an embarrassing topic and a source of extra cost. Women's needs are not seen as being as valid as those of men. The disabled may be seen as a more legitimate group, but they are seldom disaggregated into male and female, constituting some sort of third sex in the minds of some toilet providers. Yet disabled women and men have quite different physiological characteristics in terms of upper body strength, urination position, and average arm reach (Adler 2000).

The male/female divide is evident at all levels of toilet design and management. In seeking to tackle germs, cleaning is a critical issue. But responsibilities for cleaning services are often separated from technical departments whose main role is building and equipment maintenance. Hygiene matters appear to be of little concern to sanitary engineers (Greed 2004). Cleaning is a low-status, poorly paid area of employment, mainly undertaken by a female and ethnic minority workforce. But cleaning and caring are two of the largest industries in Britain, far larger than manufacturing (Gilroy 1999). Cleaners need to be recognised, trained, and respected as the front-line troops in infection control. But such is the gender divide between those who design and manage toilets, on one hand, and those who clean them, on the other, that the voice of cleaning experts is seldom heard within male professional and managerial toilet circles. Mary Schramm, a leading figure in cleaning science, commented that "architects never think about the problems trying to clean the buildings they design" (personal communication). But so much time, money, and effort could be saved if the experience of women cleaners, carers, and nurses was taken on board by male designers.

Concluding Comments: What Needs to Be Done

One would imagine that with so much emphasis put upon the importance of creating sustainable cities, public toilets would figure strongly in urban policy development. But there is no requirement that public toilet policy be included in town plans, urban policy documents, or urban regeneration policy (Greed 2003). There is not even a mandatory requirement for local authorities to provide public toilets (under the 1936 Public Health Act, still in force). Public toilet provision needs to be made a compulsory and adequately funded component of urban structure and services (Greed 2004). Public toilets are often seen as a waste of money, but surveys by the Association of Town Centre Managers have demonstrated "the business case," showing that better public toilet provision increases local business, shopping turnover, and tourist numbers (Lockwood 2001). Cleaner toilet provision would also undoubtedly reduce the amount of money spent by the National Health Service on urological and incontinence services (Edwards 1998b) and reduce the transmission of a wide range of viruses, bacteria, and other pathogens.

Society is taking a huge risk with respect to the nation's health and the chances of future epidemics in not paying attention to public toilet provision. Money needs to be put into ensuring that toilets be properly managed, frequently cleaned, well maintained, adequately equipped, and efficiently supervised. The initial capital expenditure of toilet construction and equipment may account for only 20 percent of the total toilet expenditure over five years. Toilet attendants should be put in every main toilet block; the cost of wages will be recouped by reductions in toilet damage and running costs (Greed and Daniels 2002). Attendants should be well trained, remunerated fairly, and valued as a key component in the local authority's toilet strategy. Arguably, cleaning should be made a key design consideration in all aspects of architectural training and professional practice and should figure very highly in the development of the local authority's total toilet strategy.

Instead of piddling around with ad hoc decisions at the technical, operational level, which usually results in toilet closure, public toilet provision needs to become a priority for the highest-status policy departments that deal with city planning, transportation, and urban policy making. Of course, not all toilets are run by local authorities. The provision of public toilets is currently fragmented, held by a variety of public and private bodies, on and off street, including retail facilities managers, bus and railway station managers, car parks, and others. Toilet providers are ill informed or even unaware of the level of toilet provision made by each other. The current shambles needs to be resolved by organisational change and liaison. A toilet strategy backed by an initial survey of what actually exists, what toilet facilities people require, and where people need toilets should be an integral part of city planning and policy making. This is already the case in some Far Eastern countries, for example, Japan, with equal provision for women being a high priority (Miyanishi 1996; Asano 2002).

To ensure that toilet provision is adequate, local government needs restructuring (Greed 2005). Departments, agencies, and professionals who are concerned with citizens' health and well-being need to make a major input in toilet decision-making. These might include representatives concerned with child care, elderly and disabled care, education, public health, and other group needs. This restructuring would ensure that a user perspective, along with a more social and medical outlook, would be mainstreamed into toilet policy making. Such a move would precipitate a culture change among toilet providers and counteract the current ethos of the sanitary engineering fraternity. Promoting a culture of cleanliness and care would result in better, more accessible provision for everyone. Availability of free and unrestricted use of the toilet remains one of the most basic requirements for good health and public safety.

References

Adler, D. 2000. *New Metric Handbook: Planning and Design Data.* Oxford: Butterworth.

Armstrong, L., and A. Scott. 1992. *Whitewash: Exposing the Health and Environmental Dangers of Women's Sanitary Products and Disposable Diapers.* Toronto: HarperCollins.

Asano, Y. 2002. *Number of Sanitary Fixtures: Mathematical Models for Toilet Queuing Theory.* Nagano: Faculty of Architecture and Building Engineering, Shinshu University.

Ayliffe, G. 2000. *Control of Hospital Infection: A Practical Handbook.* London: Chapman Taylor.

Bichard, J., J. Hanson, and C. Greed. 2004. *Access to the Built Environment—Barriers, Chains and Missing Links: Initial Review.* London: University College London.

———. 2007. Please Wash Your Hands. *Senses and Society* 2 (3): 385–90.

Blandy, J. 2004. *Lecture Notes on Urology.* Oxford: Blackwell Science.

Booth, C., J. Darke, and S. Yeandle. 1996. *Changing Places: Women's Lives in the City.* London: Paul Chapman.

Bright, K., P. Williams, and S. Langton-Lockton. 2004. *Disability: Making Buildings Accessible—Special Report.* London: Workplace Law Group.

BSI. 2006. BS6465 *Part 1: Code of Practice for the Design of Sanitary Facilities and Scales of Provision of Sanitary and Associated Appliances.* London: British Standards Institute.

BTA. 2001. *Better Public Toilets: A Providers' Guide to the Provision and Management of "Away from Home" Toilets.* Winchester: British Toilet Association.

Cavanagh, S., and V. Ware. 1991. *At Women's Convenience: A Handbook on the Design of Women's Public Toilets.* London: Women's Design Service.

CCI. 2002. *Licensing Reform: A Cross-Cultural Comparison of Rights, Responsibilities and Regulation*. London: Central Cities Institute, University of Westminster.

Chevalier, G. 1936. *Clochemerle*. London: Mandarin.

DCLG. 2007. *Improving Public Access to Better Quality Toilets: A Strategic Guide*. London: Department of Communities and Local Government. Available at http://www.communities.gov.uk.

Deslypere, J. 2004. "Effects of Public Toilets on Public Health." *Conference Proceedings of the World Toilet Association Summit*. November, Beijing, 179–84.

Disability Discrimination Act. 1995. Available at http://www.opsi.gov.uk.

Edwards, J. 1998a. "Local Authority Performance Indicators: Dousing the Fire of Campaigning Consumers." *Local Government Studies* 24 (4): 26–45.

———. 1998b. "Policy Making as Organised Irresponsibility: The Case of Public Conveniences." *Policy and Politics* 26 (3): 307–20.

Gilroy, R. 1999. "Planning to Grow Old." In *Social Town Planning*. Ed. C. Greed. London: Routledge, 60–73.

Greed, C. 1996. "Planning for Women and Other Disenabled Groups." *Environment and Planning A,* 28 (March): 573–88.

———. 2000. "Women in the Construction Professions: Achieving Critical Mass." *Gender, Work and Organisation* 7 (3): 181–96.

———. 2003. *Public Toilets: Inclusive Urban Design*. Oxford: Architectural Press, Elsevier Publications.

———. 2004. "Public Toilet Provision: The Need for Compulsory Provision." *Municipal Engineer: Proceedings of the Institution of Civil Engineers* 157:77–85.

———. 2005. "Overcoming the Factors Inhibiting the Mainstreaming of Gender into Spatial Planning Policy in the United Kingdom." *Urban Studies* 42, no. 4 (April): 1–31.

Greed, C., and I. Daniels. 2002. *User and Provider Perspectives on Public Toilet Provision*. Bristol: University of the West of England, Faculty of the Built Environment.

Hanson, J., J. Bichard, and C. Greed. 2007. *The Accessible Public Toilet Resource Manual*. London: University College London.

Hashmey, R. 1997. "Cryptosporidiosis in Houston, Texas: A Report of 95 Cases." *Medicine* 76 (2): 118–39.

Hawker, J., N. Begg, I. Blair, R. Reintjes, and J. Weinberg. 2005. *Communicable Disease Control Handbook*. Oxford: Blackwell.

Hung, H., D. Chan, L. Law, E. Chan, and E. Wong. 2006. "Industrial Experience and Research into the Causes of SARS Virus Transmission in a High-Rise Residential Housing Estate in Hong Kong." *Building Services Engineering Research and Technology* 27 (2): 91–102.

Larson, E. 1988. "A Causal Link between Hand Washing and Risk of Infection? Examination of the Evidence." *Infection Control and Hospital Epidemiology* 9:28–36.

Lockwood, J. 2001. *The Lockwood Survey: Capturing, Catering and Caring for Consumers*. Huddersfield: Urban Management Initiatives.

Miyanishi, Y. 1996. *Comfortable Public Toilets: Design and Maintenance Manual*. Toyama, Japan: City Planning Department.

Monaghan, S. 2002. *The State of Communicable Disease Law*. London: Nuffield Trust.

Moore, K., D. Richmond, J. Sutherst, A. H. Imrie, and J. L. Hutton. 1991. "Crouching over the Toilet Seat: Prevalence among British Gynaecological Outpatients and Its Effect upon Micturition." *British Journal of Obstetrics and Gynaecology* 98 (June): 569–72.

Morris, H. 2005. "Design Neglected in Health Care Funding: Would MRSA Be Such a Prominent Health Issue if Enough Thought Had Gone into the Design of Hospital Toilets?" *Planning*. Editorial (March 18): 11.

O'Brien, F., J. Pearman, M. Gracey, T. Riley, and W. Grubb. 1999. "Community Strain of Methicillin-Resistant *Staphylococcus aureus* Involved in Hospital Outbreaks." *Journal of Clinical Microbiology* 37, no. 9 (September): 2858–62.

Parazzini, F., F. Chiaffarino, M. Lavezzari, and V. Giambanco. 2003. "Risk Factors for Stress, Urge and Mixed Urinary Incontinence in Italy." *International Journal of Obstetrics and Gynaecology* 110 (January): 927–33.

Penner, B. 1996. *The Ladies Room: A Historical and Cultural Analysis of Women's Lavatories in London*. M.Sc. diss., Bartlett School of Architecture, University College London.

Roberts, M. 2003. "Civilising City Centres?" *Town and Country Planning* 7, no. 3 (March/April): 78–79.

Rothburn, M., and M. Dunnigan, eds. 2004. *The Infection Control, Prevention and Control of Infection Policy*. Liverpool: National Health Service Trust Hospitals, Mersey Manual.

RSC. 2002. *150th Anniversary of Public Toilets: Why Things Are Becoming Less Convenient*. London: Royal Society of Chemistry.

Tallon, A., and R. Bromley. 2002. "Living in the 24 Hour City." *Town and Country Planning* (November): 282–85.

Vernon, S., B. Lundblad, and A. Hellstrom. 2003. "Children's Experiences of School Toilets Present a Risk to Their Physical and Psychological Health." *Child: Care, Health and Development* 29 (1): 47–53.

2

Potty Privileging
in Perspective

Gender and Family Issues in Toilet Design

KATHRYN H. ANTHONY AND MEGHAN DUFRESNE

Although we are all forced to use them whenever we are away from home, public restrooms raise a host of problems: for women as well as men, for adults as well as children. Restrooms are among the few remaining sex-segregated spaces in the American landscape, and they remain among the more tangible relics of gender discrimination. How many times have you been trapped in long lines at the women's restroom? Why must women be forced to wait uncomfortably to relieve themselves, while men are not? Gender-segregated restrooms no longer work for a significant part of the population. Yet family-friendly or companion-care restrooms that allow males and females to accompany each other are still all too rare.

Why is this the case? And why have these problems persisted for so long? Architects, contractors, engineers, and building-code officials rarely contacted women to learn about their special restroom needs. And until recently, women were rarely employed in these male-dominated professions. Nor were women in a position to effect change. Even today, these professions remain clearly male-dominated. For example, as of 2001, women comprised just under 14 percent of all tenured architecture professors in the United States and only 13 percent of the American Institute of Architects (Anthony 2001). Yet, as more women gradually enter these professions, they increase the potential for change. And as we argue below, it is often a female legislator—or a male legislator who waited for his wife to use the restroom—who took the lead to address these pressing issues.

In recent years, feminist theorists have reexamined, reconceptualized, and recontextualized three philosophical categories: gender, power, and speech. Public restrooms can be viewed in light of all three categories. The

Portions of this article appeared in Kathryn H. Anthony and Meghan Dufresne, "Potty Parity in Perspective: Gender and Family Issues in Planning and Designing Public Restrooms," *Journal of Planning Literature* 21, no. 3 (2007): 267–94. Reprinted with permission from Sage Publications.

issues raised here challenge the binary gender classifications that have traditionally restricted public restrooms to either males or females. They question the power structure reflected in the planning and design of public restrooms that, in many respects, privileges men over women. And they call for a new language to identify yet another "problem with no name." In this respect, the power of labeling is key to legitimizing this problem. Just as sexual harassment, street harassment, and sexual terrorism existed long before the terms were invented, we propose that a new label, "potty privileging," signifies the ways in which public restrooms have long discriminated against certain segments of our society, especially women. And we argue for an end to potty privileging.

We begin this chapter by describing how public restrooms historically have been settings for privileging one group and discriminating against another. We turn our focus to gender discrimination issues and how restrooms have tended to discriminate especially against women. At the same time, we discuss how restrooms have also been troublesome for many men, posing serious problems that can no longer be ignored. We examine how public restrooms have presented special health and safety problems for women, men, and children—family issues that span many types of users. We then address events leading to the passage of recent "potty parity" legislation, examining the impacts of and backlash against these new laws. Sources of information include an eight-year extensive literature review including legal research and media coverage of these issues. We searched several library databases, including LexisNexis Academic Universe, Wilson, Article1st, and NetFirst, along with myriad Internet sources. This research is an outgrowth of our prior work in designing for diversity (Anthony 2001, 2008; Anthony and Dufresne 2004a, 2004b, 2005, 2007) and the first author's participation in the American Restroom Association (www.americanrestroom.org).

Relatively little has been written about gender and family issues in restroom design. Alexander Kira (1977) was among the first academics to examine both public and private restrooms in his landmark book *The Bathroom*. He covered the subject from multiple perspectives, including social, psychological, historical, and cultural. Marc Linder, a labor lawyer and political economist, and Ingrid Nygaard, a physician specializing in urogynecology, coauthored *Void Where Prohibited: Rest Breaks and the Right to Urinate on Company Time* (Linder and Nygaard 1998). While Linder and Nygaard do not focus on restrooms per se, they stress the physiological consequences that workers without legal protection face when not allowed rest breaks to urinate. Clara Greed's (2003) *Inclusive Urban Design: Public Toilets* was the first book to address toilets as an integral part of urban design. Greed argues that toilets should be seen as a core component of strategic urban policy and local area design. She provides compelling evidence that toilets are valuable features in their own right as manifestations of civic pride and good urban design that add to the quality and viability of a city. Rose George's *The Big Necessity: The Unmentionable World of Human Waste and Why It Matters* (2008) makes a strong case for improved sanitation worldwide.

Public Restrooms as Settings for Discrimination by Class, Race, Physical Ability, and Sexual Orientation

Placed in a broader framework, throughout American history public restrooms have reflected various forms of discrimination. Not only have they embodied gender discrimination, favoring the needs of men over those of women, but they have also mirrored social discrimination among classes, races, and persons of different physical ability and sexual orientation. Public restrooms provided by airports are a far cry from those found in Greyhound stations. Throughout much of the American South, until the passage of Title II of the Civil Rights Act in 1964, African Americans were forced to use separate restroom facilities from those of whites, due to the infamous Jim Crow laws. Such laws called for racially segregated hotels, motels, restaurants, movie theaters, stadiums, and concert halls, as well as transportation cars. It was not until the passage of the Americans with Disabilities Act (ADA) in 1990 that public accommodations in the private sector—including public restrooms—were required to eliminate physical, communication, and procedural barriers to access (Wodatch 1990, 3). The transgender population still can be at a loss in deciding which public restrooms to use. For gay men and lesbians, public restrooms have long provided a venue for derogatory graffiti as well as hate crimes.

While public restrooms have reflected discrimination according to gender, class, race, physical ability, and sexual orientation, only race and physical ability have been addressed through federal legislation in the United States. No such federal legislation provides equal access to public restrooms for women. Restrooms still remain common sites of gender discrimination.

Public Restrooms as Settings for Gender Discrimination

Gender discrimination in public restrooms can be seen in several spheres. In the workplace, legal scholar Sarah Moore (2002) argues, restroom inequality is a form of subtle sexism or sex-discriminatory behavior in office life. It often goes unnoticed and is considered normal, natural, or acceptable, but its effect is to maintain the lower status of women. Moore identifies four types of restroom inequity in the workplace and describes the results of courtroom battles for each of these:

- *Unequal restrooms,* where women's restrooms are fewer in number, smaller in size, or more distant than men's
- *Inadequate women's restrooms,* where women and men have equal facilities but lack of soap or running water makes restrooms unhealthy for women
- *Missing women's restrooms,* where women must share facilities with men
- *No restrooms at all,* where women must either "hold it" or seek whatever privacy nature might provide

Unequal restrooms often can be found where women as a group are new to the work environment. The U.S. Capitol Building in Washington, D.C., is one such example. On the House side is a "Members Only" bathroom behind the chamber; it still is a men's room. Off Statuary Hall is the "Lindy Boggs" room, named after the U.S. representative from Louisiana who, in the 1960s, corralled a suite with a restroom and sitting area for women members. Prior to that time, congresswomen lacked these basic necessities (Ritchie 2008). By contrast, congressmen walked a few feet away from the House floor, where their restroom had six stalls, four urinals, gilt mirrors, a shoeshine, a ceiling fan, a drinking fountain, and television. The ladies' restroom on the first floor of the House side was remodeled in 2000, just in time for the Million Mom March, resulting in seven stalls where there had been four (Moore 2002).

After the 1992 election, in order to accommodate the growing number of women senators, Senate Majority Leader George Mitchell announced that he was having a women's room installed just outside the Senate chamber in the U.S. Capitol Building. At that time, only a men's restroom was located there, with the telling sign "Senators Only," an implicit assumption that all senators were men. The two women senators who did not qualify for admission had to trek downstairs and stand in line with the tourists (Collins 1993). And it was not until 1994 that the U.S. Supreme Court, built in 1935, was renovated to include gender-equal facilities (Kazaks 1994). No doubt such oversights explain why potty parity has often been a pressing issue for women legislators, from the U.S. Capitol to fifty state capitals across the country.

The lack of potty parity can also be readily seen at places of assembly such as sports and entertainment arenas, musical amphitheaters, theaters, stadiums, airports, bus terminals, convention halls, amusement facilities, fairgrounds, zoos, institutions of higher education, and specialty events at public parks. Several journalists have argued for gender equity in publicly accessible restrooms. Their articles have appeared in the *New York Times, Redbook, Wall Street Journal,* and *Working Woman,* among others, as well as on ABC and BBC television. One of the more vivid accounts appeared in the *New York Times Magazine* (Tierney 1996):

I've seen a few frightening dramas on Broadway, but nothing on-stage is ever as scary as the scene outside the ladies' room at inter-mission: that long line of women with clenched jaws and crossed arms, muttering ominously to one another as they glare across the lobby at the cavalier figures sauntering in and out of the men's room. The ladies' line looks like an audition for the extras in *Les Miserables*—these are the vengeful faces that nobles saw on their way to the guillotine—except that the danger is all too real. When I hear the low rumble of obscenities and phrases like "Nazi male architects" I know not to linger.

The work of researcher Sandra K. Rawls sparked greater awareness about the long queuing times that women endured. Her research painstak-ingly documented the obvious: women take about twice as much time as men to use restroom facilities. While men took a mere 83.6 seconds, women took almost three minutes (Rawls 1988). Her findings have often been cited in media articles. Long lines in women's restrooms have com-mercial implications. Rather than face a long wait at the restroom, many women feel compelled to curtail or avoid liquid intake during sporting events. As a result, while men can purchase as many hot dogs, sodas, and beers as they wish, women are less likely to spend money on concessions, if they do so at all.

Some women have given up waiting in lines altogether. When, out of desperation, they choose to enter the men's restrooms, they can pay a hefty price. The most famous case is that of Denise Wells, a legal secretary. In 1990, Wells was arrested upon entering the men's room after waiting in a long line at a concert at Houston's Summit, a seventeen-thousand-seat au-ditorium. The charge was violating a city ordinance. She had to plead her case in a court of law. A police officer testified that twenty women were waiting to enter the ladies' room, and that the line spilled out into a hall-way, while the men's room line did not even extend past the restroom door. The jury, two men and four women, deliberated for only twenty-three minutes and found Wells not guilty (Woo 1994). Her case attracted widespread attention and letters of support from women all over the world (Weisman 1992).

Convention centers pose similar dilemmas for potty parity. In this regard, an innovative solution was designed into the Colorado Convention Center at Denver, built in 1990, where architect Curt Fentress separated men's and women's restrooms with a movable wall. When groups whose membership is primarily women—such as the Intravenous Nurses Soci-ety—hold their conventions, walls can be moved so that the women's rooms are three times larger than the men's. Conversely, when a group such as the American Association of Petroleum Geologists meets there, the ratio can be reversed (Woo 1994).

Even the famed Getty Center in Los Angeles, designed by world-famous architect Richard Meier at a cost of $1 billion, was plagued by restroom problems in its early days. When it opened in December 1997, no restrooms were included in the North or South Pavilions, causing long lines to form at a small set of women's restrooms in the West Pavilion. In this regard, *Chicago Tribune* architecture critic Blair Kamin (2004) acknowledged, "any space that doesn't attend to the basics is setting itself up for disaster." More restrooms have since been added (Creamer 2003; "Posh Museum Has Pictures, Lacks Potties" 1998).

John Banzhaf III, a professor at the George Washington Law School, is considered the "Father of Potty Parity" after authoring "Final Frontier for the Law?" where he presents major cases, studies, and products related to potty parity across the United States. He discusses potty parity as the new frontier of feminism (Banzhaf 1990). Banzhaf argues that limited restroom facilities impose a special burden on females because a significant number of women at public places will be either menstruating or pregnant. In either case, waiting can lead to medical and health complications (Banzhaf 2002).

Public Restrooms and Health

Public restrooms pose a myriad of health and safety issues for women and men, adults and children. Yet for many reasons—pregnancy, attending to feminine hygiene needs, breast-feeding babies, and accompanying small children—women may frequent public restrooms more often than men. And as a result, public restroom deficiencies may affect women and children more adversely than they affect most men. Women conceal feminine hygiene products such as tampons and sanitary napkins in purses, bags, and other gear—along with wallets, cash, identification cards, and personal grooming items—that inevitably accompany them to the restroom. All too often, women drop such paraphernalia on a filthy bathroom floor. Men carry no such gear, and their loose clothing allows them to place wallets in their pockets. One might argue that if men carried purses, toilet stalls would have been designed much more sensitively years ago.

Even worse, often babies and small children end up on the floor of bathroom stalls. When handicapped-accessible facilities are available, users have space to accommodate both themselves and small children. Yet when these stalls are occupied, or in parts of the world where they are not required, parents have no choice but to squeeze children with them into a standard stall and onto a dirty bathroom floor. Given what environmental microbiologist Charles Gerba's pioneering (2005) research has discovered—that the highest levels of microorganisms in public restrooms are found on floors in front of toilets—this situation is especially alarming.

Even while urinating, women generally have contact with the toilet seat. Although toilet seat covers are standard features in California's public restrooms, they are rarely found elsewhere. New and newly remodeled restrooms featuring automatic-flush toilets and touch-free faucets are a step toward improving this disparity.

Health dangers are especially problematic in educational settings. Because children face daily deplorable conditions in their school restrooms, many avoid them altogether and wait to use their bathrooms at home. The Opinion Research Corporation conducted a study on behalf of Kimberly Clark examining this issue. Their survey used a national probability sample of 269 adults who were parents and guardians of public school children from the seventh to twelfth grades. Results showed that almost 20 percent of middle and high school students avoid using school restrooms ("Parents Sound Off on School Restroom Conditions" 2002). More than one-third of restrooms at middle and high schools in the United States lack basic sanitary supplies such as toilet paper, soap, and paper towels (Barlow 2004; "Teens Blast School Restroom Conditions" 2004).

Even if the restroom is sparkling clean, when a woman has to hold her urine while waiting in long lines, she becomes a potential candidate for cystitis and other urinary tract infections that, if left untreated, can pose serious health problems such as renal damage. For pregnant women who must urinate often, waiting in long restroom lines can lead to urinary tract infections associated with low-birth-weight babies at risk for additional health problems (Banzhaf 2002b, Naeye 1979). Medical research reveals that constipation, abdominal pain, diverticuli, and hemorrhoids can result if individuals delay defecation (National Institutes of Health 1995).

Many individuals suffer from invisible disabilities, intermittent or chronic medical conditions that require unusually frequent restroom use. These include overactive bladder, urinary tract infections, and chronic digestive illnesses such as irritable bowel syndrome, ulcerative colitis, diverticular disease, and Crohn's disease that affect both genders (Benirschke 1996). The availability of public restrooms—or lack thereof—severely hampers their daily activities, causing many to stay home. Cold weather and side effects of certain medications can also cause individuals to need restrooms more often. Small children often face emergencies where they suddenly need to relieve themselves (Schmidt and Brubaker 2004).

A disorder called paruresis, making it impossible for someone to urinate in public if others are within seeing or hearing distance, affects over 20 million Americans, about 7 percent of the population. This condition is also known as shy bladder syndrome, bashful bladder syndrome (BBS), bashful kidneys, or pee-phobia. Nine of ten sufferers who seek treatment are men, although women, too, can have extreme cases. According to Steven Soifer, coauthor of *Shy Bladder Syndrome*, about 2 million people suffer so seriously from BBS that it interferes significantly with their work, social relationships, and other important activities. It can ruin lives and careers and even end marriages. Some boys become targets for bullying—not perceived as being "manly" enough to stand up, show their equipment, and use a urinal—merely by entering a toilet cubicle. The result can lead to lifelong problems stemming from feelings of powerlessness. People with paruresis are unlikely to be able to perform a urine test for jobs that require it as part of the employment application process, and hence are knocked out of the running. Improved restroom design—an end to urinal "troughs," greater space between urinals, the construction of floor-to-ceiling partitions between urinals, and doors on all toilet stalls—can have a strong impact on the symptoms of paruresis sufferers (Soifer et al. 2001; Wolf 2000). Recent plumbing codes have addressed this problem by requiring more sizable partitions between urinals in new construction and major building additions.

Public Restrooms and Safety

In the worst instances, the lack of alternatives to the standard men's room and women's room poses a serious risk to our personal safety. What happens when a single mother takes her young son to a restroom, or when a single father accompanies his young daughter? Sometimes allowing unaccompanied children to use a public restroom can place them in harm's way—and even lead to their death.

Take the tragic case of nine-year-old Matthew Cecchi, in Oceanside, California, a 1998 story that made national headlines (Reuters 1998). Matthew's aunt waited for him outside a public restroom at a paid camping area at the beach. While Matthew was using the men's room, a man entered, exited minutes later, and walked away. When Matthew failed to come out, his aunt realized something was wrong. Her nephew had been brutally murdered. The man who entered and exited the restroom, a twenty-year-old drifter, slashed young Matthew's throat from ear to ear. Although a rare occurrence, this could happen to any child when his or her caregiver of the opposite sex is forced to wait outside a public restroom. Such horrific criminal behavior has served as justification for closing public restrooms altogether. Yet avoiding the problem is not solving it. Instead, we argue that cases like Cecchi's underscore the need to develop new prototypes and transform restrooms into safe, family-friendly spaces.

In fact, public restrooms provide convenient hiding spots for criminals, and all are potentially vulnerable. One can argue that men's use of urinals renders them more likely than women to be victims of public restroom crimes. While women are locked away and temporarily protected in toilet stalls, men, while using the urinal, are much more vulnerable. Public men's rooms often are venues for drug deals, drug taking, and other criminal activities.

Furthermore, some individuals are vulnerable to danger in restrooms due to their fragile mental or physical conditions. As the baby boomer population reaches retirement age, the numbers of those with Alzheimer's disease, Parkinson's disease, cancer, and other mental and physical disabilities are increasing rapidly. Today, over 5 million persons suffer from Alzheimer's; in the past decade the numbers have skyrocketed to epidemic proportions. Those afflicted by such infirmities are often unable to use a restroom alone—yet now they are forced to do so. An anxious family member of the opposite sex must wait outside. The present alternative to this dilemma is for them to remain homebound, causing both patient and caregiver to become increasingly isolated from the everyday world.

Must we all face experiences like these to wake up to the reality that family-friendly restrooms are a right, not a privilege, that we all deserve?

Potty Parity Legislation as a Response

Potty parity legislation first made national headlines in 1974, when California Secretary of State March Fong Eu smashed a toilet bowl on the steps of the State Capitol in Sacramento as part of her successful campaign to ban pay toilets in her state. In 1975, New York State outlawed pay toilets in response to charges that they discriminated against women because all women were required to pay for toileting, while men could still use urinals for free. Pay toilets have since been outlawed across the United States. Yet in many parts of the world, pay toilets for women are still commonplace.

Potty parity laws requiring greater access to women's restrooms have been passed in several states. Currently, about twenty-one states and several municipalities have statutes addressing potty parity (Anthony and Dufresne, 2004a). While these laws have made great strides for women by increasing the number of available toilet stalls, they have not yet improved the quality of restrooms for women or for men. As a result, many public health and safety issues remain unresolved. Furthermore, almost all potty parity laws apply only to new construction or major renovations of large public buildings, where at least half the building is being remodeled. Despite the fact that these laws represent substantial progress, most of the older building stock remains unaffected. So in most cases, when nature calls, women still must grin and bear it.

Who has initiated such legislation? It is often either the rare female state legislator or the enlightened male state legislator who has been inconvenienced by waiting for his female companion. In 1987, California led the way when State Senator Art Torres (D.–Los Angeles) introduced such legislation after his wife and daughter endured a painstakingly long wait for the ladies' room while attending a Tchaikovsky concert at the Hollywood Bowl. The bill became law that same year (Woo 1994). In Chicago, Building Commissioner Mary Richardson-Lowry introduced potty parity, spearheading its integration into that city's Municipal Building Code. Chicago's potty parity ordinance passed in 2001 and was applauded by women in Chicago and around the country (Spielman and Hermann 2004). In 2005, New York City legislators passed the Restroom Equity Bill (Anderson 2005). It amended the city's building code by requiring all new bars, sports arenas, movie theaters, and similar venues to have a two-to-one ratio of women's to men's stalls.

The nature of potty parity laws differs in various states and cities. Most states require new ratios of two women's toilet stalls to one men's stall, while others require a three-to-two or simply a one-to-one ratio. A range of definitions exists about which places are and are not required to achieve potty parity. A key question has been raised in the legal literature about exactly what equality in restrooms means: is it equal square footage, equal toilets, or equal waiting time? In our opinion, Wisconsin's law is a model, as it defines potty parity terms of *equal speed of access* for women and men (Moore 2002).

But is potty parity legislation the only means by which gender discrimination in public restrooms can be remedied? In fact, a more powerful means exists in the revision of building codes that could set the standards for all buildings in all states. The 2003 International Building Code (IBC) called for more water closets in stadiums for both men and women than had been previously required. It also called for family restrooms in certain building types. Yet the 2003 IBC's "Minimum Number of Required Plumbing Facilities" still called for only equal numbers of water closets for men and women in nightclubs, bars, taverns, and dance halls (one fixture for forty occupants), as well as in restaurants, banquet halls, and food courts (one fixture for seventy-five occupants). (*International Building Code* 2003). Subsequent versions of the IBC show some additional improvements (*International Building Code* 2006).

Although such changes in building codes are steps in the right direction, they have not gone far enough. Regarding the number of toilets required, updated building codes, like potty parity legislation, apply only to new construction, major renovations, and additions—not to existing buildings. Once again, the vast majority of the older building stock remains fundamentally unchanged. Further changes to building codes—for example, if and when feasible, requiring upgrades of toilet facilities in existing buildings, as is required for ADA compliance—could lead to even more sweeping improvements in restroom design nationwide.

Impacts of Potty Parity and Its Backlash

What have been the impacts of potty parity legislation? While women rejoiced, men protested—especially in sports settings.

As a result of the Tennessee Equitable Restrooms Act that increased the proportion of female to male restrooms, at Nashville's new Adelphia Coliseum, built in 1999 for the Tennessee Titans football team, a snake-like line of forty men formed at the top level, forcing some to wait fifteen to twenty minutes to use the restroom. Security officers had to station themselves at the exits to some men's rooms in order to stop those who tried to avoid the line by entering the wrong way. One police officer was quoted as saying, "We're just trying to keep fights down" (Paine 1999).

Soon after it was built, an exemption from the state's new mandate of two women's toilets for every man's toilet (2:1 ratio) was filed for Adelphia Coliseum. Even the state architect acknowledged that the state's potty parity law needed more flexibility. Yet State Senator Andy Womack argued against the exemption bill, saying that lawmakers were "micro-managing. . . . The intent of the original bill is to give parity. Now we're carving out exceptions to parity" (de la Cruz 2000; Jowers 2000; "State's Potty Parity Too High" 2000). Ironically, in a matter of months, men could undermine a law that attempted to relieve decades of discomfort from women.

Soldier Field, the renovated stadium for the Chicago Bears that reopened in 2003, also prompted heated controversy. When new construction improved wait times for women's restrooms, men were forced to wait fifteen minutes or more at some restrooms, especially in the end-zone sections (Spielman and Hermann 2004). In response to complaints, five women's restrooms were converted to men's rooms. Measurements taken during summer 2004 after the change revealed that while the wait for men was reduced, the wait time for women increased. The city was to assess the situation at the end of 2004 to ensure that average wait times were balanced between male and female fans (Hermann 2004).

Los Angeles Times reporter Carla Hall lamented that "the laws governing women's bathrooms seem to change only when men are inconvenienced." We assume she refers to the fact that it was often sensitive males, frustrated by waiting for their female companions, who made the case for potty parity legislation. She noted that although the situation has improved slightly for women across the United States over the past decade, potty parity laws apply only to certain types of buildings, such as sports venues, concert halls, and theaters, whereas restaurants and clubs are generally omitted (Hall 2001).

Ironically, while women have waited in long ladies' room lines for years, the passage of potty parity laws created an uproar among some men who may never have had to wait in line before. Cutting in line, entering in the exits, and even fistfights resulted. More important, some men rushed to undo the new potty parity laws before the ink had even dried. The potty parity backlash leads us to question: will gender equity in restrooms ever be possible, or will it remain just a "pipe dream"?

Conclusion

In the future, improved technology may play a role in alleviating potty privileging. Some progress is already underway, such as the development of a female urinal, the She-Pee or TravelMate (Penner 2005; "Travelmate Urinary Products Overview" 2003). Yet gender equity in public restrooms is still a long way away.

In retrospect, public restrooms raise a host of complexities and contradictions. While attendants provide safety for women and children, they pose problems for men and women with paruresis. Reducing long lines for women can result in increased lines for men. The need to conduct private behavior in a public place can promote a sense of psychological discomfort and territorial invasion. Our feelings about the body, sex, elimination, privacy, and cleanliness are all called into question in public restrooms. In contrast to sacred spaces, such as houses of worship, that promote a sense of community, spirituality, and inspiration, restrooms are "secret spaces" into which we silently disappear, remaining faceless among strangers.

Whether we want to or not, we must visit them several times a day. Women and men, girls and boys, of every ethnic background, every social role, all use them. Virtually every building type must have them. In fact, they are among the most prevalent spaces in our built environment—and places that affect us all.

As we have shown, because of design decisions uninformed by women users, clients, code officials, and designers, millions of women, men, and children around the world suffer from poorly designed and maintained restrooms. As increasing numbers of women infiltrate the design and building construction professions, and as more women legislators enter the political system, a significant number of women's restrooms have gradually begun to improve. However, compared to the sweeping changes prompted by the Americans with Disabilities Act that mandated improvements benefiting persons with disabilities, the changes benefiting women have been achieved at a snail's pace. And most public restrooms still remain woefully inadequate for women's special needs—menstruation, pregnancy, breastfeeding and pumping—and men's basic needs for privacy.

Gender and family issues in restrooms must no longer be cloaked under the guise of modesty. They can no longer continue to be swept under the rug. Architects, building construction officials, and legislators around the world must call for an end to potty privileging—and the beginning of a new era of sensitive restroom design for women, men, and children.

References

Anderson, Lisa. 2005. "Anatomy and Culture Conspire against Women in Public Toilets. Now NYC Has Joined the Trend for Potty Parity." *Chicago Tribune*, July 1, sec. 1, pp. 1, 24.

Anthony, Kathryn H. 2001, 2008. *Designing for Diversity: Gender, Race and Ethnicity in the Architectural Profession.* Urbana: University of Illinois Press.

Anthony, Kathryn H., and Meghan Dufresne. 2004a. "Putting Potties in Perspective: Gender and Family Issues in Restroom Design." *Licensed Architect* 8 (1): 12–14.

———. 2004b. "Putting Potty Parity in Perspective: Gender and Family Issues in Public Restrooms." In *Design with Spirit: Proceedings of the 35th Annual Conference of the Environmental Design Research Association.* Ed. Dwight Miller and James A. Wise. Oklahoma City: Environmental Design Research Association, 210.

———. 2005. "Gender and Family Issues in Restrooms." In *World Toilet Expo and Forum 2005 Conference Proceedings.* Organized by the World Toilet Organization, Shanghai City Appearance and Environment Sanitation Administrative Bureau, 74–82.

———. 2007. "Potty Parity in Perspective: Gender and Family Issues in Planning and Designing Public Restrooms." *Journal of Planning Literature* 21 (3): 267–94.

Banzhaf, John. 1990. "Final Frontier for the Law?" *National Law Journal*, April 18. Available at http://banzhaf.net/docs/potty_parity.html. Accessed November 12, 2004.

———. 2002. "Is Potty Parity a Legal Right?" Article sent via e-mail from John Banzhaf on July 31, 2002. Available at http://banzhaf.net/docs/pparticle.html. Accessed November 12, 2004.

Barlow, Linda. 2004. "Teens Blast School Restroom Conditions. More Than One-Third of Student Restrooms in U.S. Lack Basic Sanitary Supplies." PR Newswire, August 16, Lifestyle Section.

Benirschke, Rolf, with Mike Yorkey. 1996. *Alive and Kicking.* San Diego: Firefly Press.

Collins, Gail. 1993. "Potty Politics: The Gender Gap." *Working Woman* 18 (March): 93.

Creamer, Anita. 2003. "Getty Center Matures Beyond Chic." *Sacramento Bee.com*, May 18. Available at http://www.sacbee.com/content/travel/southern_california/features/story/11142837p-7639972c.html. Accessed December 6, 2004.

de la Cruz, Bonna M. 2000. "Bill May Relieve Men's Restroom Lines at Adelphia." *Tennessean.com*, April 5. Available at http://www.tennessean.com/sii/00/04/05/potty05.shtml. Accessed January 30, 2004.

George, Rose. 2008. *The Big Necessity: The Unmentionable World of Human Waste and Why It Matters.* New York: Metropolitan Books, Henry Holt.

Gerba, Charles. 2005. "Microorganisms in Public Washrooms." In *World Toilet Expo and Forum 2005 Conference Proceedings.* Organized by the World Toilet Organization, Shanghai City Appearance and Environment Sanitation Administrative Bureau, 125–31.

Greed, Clara. 2003. *Inclusive Urban Design: Public Toilets.* Oxford: Architectural Press.

Hall, Carla. 2001. "Is 'Potty Parity' Just a Pipe Dream? Although Things Are Improving, Women Still Wait in Line to Use Facilities." *Los Angeles Times*, January 14, pp. E1, E3.

Hermann, Andrew. 2004. "Soldier Field Evens the Score with More Men's Restrooms." *Chicago Sun-Times*, August 29, News, p. 3.

International Building Code. 2003. Country Club Hills, Ill.: International Code Council, chap. 29, "Plumbing Systems," pp. 547–50.

———. 2006. Country Club Hills, Ill.: International Code Council, chap. 29, "Plumbing Systems," p. 521.

Jowers, Walter. 2000. "The Potty Penalty: Nowhere to Go at the Delph." *Weekly Wire.com*, January 24. Available at http://weeklywire.com/ww/01–24–00/nash_ol-helter_shelter.html. Accessed January 30, 2004.

Kamin, Blair. 2004. "Creature Comforts." *Chicago Tribune.com*, July 18. Available at http://www.chicagotribune.com/features/chi-0407180367ju118,1,5057471.story. Accessed December 6, 2004.

Kazaks, Julia. 1994. "Architectural Archeology: Women in the United States Courthouse for the District of Columbia." *Georgetown Law Journal* 83 (2): 559–74.

Kira, Alexander. 1977. *The Bathroom.* New and expanded ed. New York: Bantam Books.

Linder, Marc, and Ingrid Nygaard. 1998. *Void Where Prohibited: Rest Breaks and the Right to Urinate on Company Time.* Ithaca, N.Y.: Cornell University Press.

Moore, Sarah A. 2002. "Facility Hostility? Sex Discrimination and Women's Restrooms in the Workplace." *Georgia Law Review* 36:599–634.

Naeye, R. L. 1979. "Causes of the Excess Rates of Perinatal Mortality and the Prematurity in Pregnancies Complicated by Maternity Urinary Tract Infections." *New England Journal of Medicine* 300 (15): 819–23.

National Institutes of Health. 1995. *Publication No. 95–2754* (July).

Paine, Anne. 1999. "Coliseum Potty Ratio Makes Guys Squirm." *Tennessean.com*, December 20. Available at http://www.tennessean.com/sii/99/12/20/potty20.shtml. Accessed December 11, 2004.

"Parents Sound Off on School Restroom Conditions: Experts Warn of Risks Associated with Unclean, Unsafe, Unstocked Restrooms." 2002. Available at http://www.ncdjjdp.org/cpsv/Acrobatfiles/Restroom_Survey02.PDF. Accessed October 19, 2005.

Penner, Barbara. 2005. "Leftovers/A Revolutionary Aim?" *Cabinet* 19. Available at: http://www.cabinetmagazine.org/issues/19/penner.php.

"Posh Museum Has Pictures, Lacks Potties." 1998. *Des Moines Register*, March 17, p. 10A.

Rawls, Sandra K. 1988. "Restroom Usage in Selected Public Buildings and Facilities: A Comparison of Females and Males." Ph.D. diss., Department of Housing, Virginia Polytechnic Institute and State University.

Reuters. 1998. "Police Ask for Help in Child Murder Case." *CNN.com*, November 16. Available at http://www.cnn.com/us/9811/16/boy.killed. Accessed November 12, 2004.

Ritchie, Donald. 2008. Historical Office, Office of the Secretary, U.S. Senate, e-mail correspondence, December 2, 4, 5, 8, 17.

Schmidt, Jasmine, and Robert Brubaker. 2004. "The Code and Practice of Toilets in the United States of America." Paper presented at the World Toilet Summit, Beijing, China, November.

Soifer, Steven, George D. Zgourides, Joseph Himle, and Nancy Pickering. 2001. *Shy Bladder Syndrome: Your Step-by-Step Guide to Overcoming Paruresis.* Oakland: New Harbinger Publications.

Spielman, Fran, and Andrew Hermann. 2004. "Bears Ask for Potty Break." *Chicago Sun-Times*, April 23, News Special Edition, p. 10.

"State's Potty Parity Too High." 2000. *The Oak Ridger Online*, January 6. Available at http://www.oakridger.com/stories/010600/stt_0106000019.html. Accessed January 30, 2004.

"Teens Blast School Restroom Conditions." 2004. *Medical News Service.com*, August 17. Available at http://www.medicalnewsservice.com/ARCHIVE/MNS2487.cfm. Accessed December 15, 2004.

Tierney, John. 1996. "Bathroom Liberationists." *New York Times Magazine*, September 8, pp. 32, 34.

"Travelmate Urinary Products Overview." 2003. Available at http://www.travelmateinfo.com/page002.html. Accessed December 5, 2004.

Weisman, Leslie Kanes. 1992. *Discrimination by Design: A Feminist Critique of the Man-Made Environment.* Urbana: University of Illinois Press.

Wodatch, J. 1990. "The ADA: What It Says." *Worklife* 3:3.

Wolf, Buck. 2000. "Avoiding the Men's Room: When It Comes to Restrooms, Men Are the More Squeamish Sex." *The Wolf Files*, abcnews.com, December 17. Available at http://abcnews.go.com/Entertainment/WolfFiles. Accessed November 12, 2004.

Woo, Junda. 1994. "'Potty Parity' Lets Women Wash Hands of Long Lines." *Wall Street Journal*, February 24, pp. A-1, A-19.

3

Geographies of Danger

School Toilets in Sub-Saharan Africa

CLAUDIA MITCHELL

Pinky Pinky is an urban legend in South Africa, a kind of featureless bogeyman, a pink tokoloshe, half-human, half-creature, who lives between the girls and boys' toilets at school. The feared entity is a creature with one claw and one paw, and preys on little girls who it threatens to rape if they wear the colour pink. The visual artist, Penny Siopis says she was reminded of this icon of childhood fear when her son returned from school with the news that a classmate of his had presented an essay on the figment of childhood fear in a class discussion on urban mythology. So Siopis went on a personal exploration of the feared entity, producing a series of paintings. . . . Pinky Pinky seems to have emerged in 1994. A pink, hybrid creature, it is half-man half-woman, half-human half-animal, and half-dog half-cat [Figure 3.1]. Described sometimes as a white tokoloshe, albino, bogeyman, stranger, it is an imagined character that finds shape in various tellings of the myth. Pinky Pinky, for example, terrorizes prepubescent children, lying in wait for them at school toilets. . . . "Girls can see it but boys can't," Siopis told a small band of art enthusiasts on a walkabout tour at the Goodman Gallery.[1]

Penny Siopis's *Pinky Pinky* work presents a fascinating investigation into a whole range of issues around personal and public narratives in relation to fear and trauma in South Africa, particularly as experienced by schoolgirls. As the artist observes, *Pinky Pinky* "embodies the fears and anxieties that girls face as their bodies develop and their social standing changes. He can also be seen as a figure that has grown out of the neurosis that can develop in a society that experiences such change and tension as is found in Southern Africa. It is also a society in which rape and the abuse of women and children is extremely high" (artist's statement, 2002, cited in

Figure 3.1 Penny Siopis, *Pinky Pinky: Little Girl*, 2002, oil and found objects on canvas. (Courtesy of the artist.)

Nuttall 2005). Pinky Pinky, as Sarah Nuttall writes in her analysis of Siopis's installation, "is a creature that lives between toilets, those places that deal in that which must be hidden from public view—a foundational space, as George Bataille tells us, because we can have no society without its taboos; a space therefore, of potential transgression" (2005, 137). Nuttall goes on to note in an essay that explores the links between Siopis's *Pinky Pinky* series and her *Shame* paintings, which investigate more explicitly girlhood in South Africa:

> In placing the threatened, sexed body of the girl child at the center of these works, Siopis signals to scenes of the social in South Africa: to the gendered violence evident in high rates of rape and abuse, and also to the ways in which the child, especially the girls, is always the radical locus of the uncertain in society—the figure, that is, against whom the anxieties of societies are played out, given often perverse expression, and who often figures social transition itself. (Nuttall 2005, 141)

It is not just a coincidence that Pinky Pinky lurks in toilets, or that an artist like Penny Siopis has made such rich use of Pinky Pinky in her interrogations of girlhood. In this chapter I use Pinky Pinky as a way to frame fieldwork in Southern Africa on gender violence in and around schools, focusing in particular on the place of toilets in this work.[2] As both private (and emblematic of a private bodily function, particularly for girls) and public (in the sense of an official component of the school grounds and far from being private in terms of location, lack of doors, and so on) school toilets constitute a site for interrogating and deepening our understanding of the complexities of the lives of girls and women in sub-Saharan Africa. Emphasizing the visual—in this case, the photographs and drawings of twelve- and thirteen-year-old girls and boys in schools in Swaziland, South Africa, and Rwanda—I explore the powerful images of toilets that young people produced in relation to "safe" and "unsafe" spaces in and around their schools.

The chapter is divided into three sections. In the first section I look at some of the literature on toilets as a way to frame the fieldwork. In the second section I focus on the actual data on schoolchildren and toilets, data that come out of the use of photography and drawings as visual approaches to studying "safe" and "unsafe" spaces in schools. I contrast some of the girls' images with the images produced by the boys in response to the same prompts on safe and unsafe spaces. In the final section of the chapter, I consider the implications of this work within the idea of "remapping," returning to the mythical Pinky Pinky as symbolic of a new critical space for social change.

Toilets: A Critical Space

This chapter draws on three main areas of research, which, when taken together, provide a critical space for studying girls and toilets, particularly in sub-Saharan Africa: the literature on gender violence and school safety, the literature on school geographies, and the related literature on embodiment and pedagogy. From the first area, this study takes the position that schools are often sites of violence that is frequently gender-specific. This is a global phenomenon, but it is particularly prevalent in sub-Saharan Africa. This is an important point to emphasize because most parents and policy makers are accustomed to thinking that sending all children to school is a good thing (Leach and Mitchell 2006). Yet in many situations, as documented by, for instance, the "Scared at School" Human Rights Watch study in South Africa (2001), schools do not provide environments that are "girl-friendly," and girls must fear gender violence on a daily basis not only from boys and gangs but also from teachers. As one girl interviewed for the Human Rights Watch study observes: "All the touching at school—in class, in the corridors, all day everyday—bothers me. Boys touch your bum, your breasts" (cited in OCHA/IRIN 2005, 73).

Such comments lead us to the second point, drawn from literature on the geographies of the built environments of schools, which calls for a more attentive critical mapping of the environment. In the context of toilets, for example, we must consider where they are positioned, how they are maintained, and how they are regulated. Who can use them, and under whose supervision?

The third area, and one informed by both the work on gender violence in schools and that on school geographies, is the study of embodiment and pedagogy—what Lesko describes as the "body and curriculum" (1988). The "schooled" body (particularly the female schooled body), how it is regulated, and even how it is clothed has itself become a critical area of study (Mitchell and Weber 1999; Weber and Mitchell 2004). At the same time that the body has come to occupy a central position, at least theoretically, there remains a sense that real bodies are supposed to go unnoticed (hooks 1997; McWilliam and Jones 1997), a social taboo that prohibits paying much scholarly attention to the experience of embodiment we all have.

Doing Fieldwork on Gender Violence in Schools: Visual Representations of Safe and Unsafe Spaces

While the literature mentioned above provides a clear framework for a critical study of toilet spaces in schools, the most important evidence is that provided by the students themselves. In studies where they have been asked to document safe and unsafe spaces, girls in particular have used imagery of toilets to suggest their sense of fear and anxiety.

Swaziland

Seventh-grade students in a school just outside Mbabane in Swaziland participated in a photo-voice project where they were given disposable cameras and asked to photograph where they felt safe and not so safe. The one-day project, part of a larger study on participatory methodologies with youth for addressing issues of sexual abuse, was carried out in three short stages. In stage 1, the thirty or so young people gathered in group and were given a short explanation of the point of the project, which was to find out where they felt safe and not so safe in school—particularly in the context of sexual abuse. They were also given a short demonstration on the use of disposable cameras and were grouped with three or four others of the same sex. In stage 2, which lasted for approximately forty minutes, they were free to go anywhere on the school premises to take photographs. Stage 3 was the "looking at photographs" stage. The students gathered in small groups on the playground, and each was given an envelope of photos to look at and from which to choose several that the student wanted to write about, on the back of the photographs. During this process school ended, and teachers as well as other children at the school joined in for this phase of looking at the photos. Over and above the obvious enthusiasm the students had for the project, they were very serious about their "work" and clearly engaged, something that is evident in an accompanying video that was made of this kind of action-oriented fieldwork with young people.[3]

While more pictures depicted unsafe spaces than safe spaces, I comment on the safe spaces first, if only to point out that the fact that one of the safe spaces was the principal's office may have made it possible for students to feel free to comment on the unsafe spaces. The Home Economics room also figured in several "safe" photographs, and in a photograph that depicts one of the girls sitting in a desk in front of the chalkboard, the words "Safe Place" are written on the chalkboard behind her. Beyond the classrooms, the boys took photos of scenes that were environmentally unsafe (unclean water, garbage dumps) or hazardous in other ways. While both boys and girls identified some "unsafe spaces" in common, such as the bushes around the school, it was interesting to note that the boys were more likely to talk about snakes in the deep grass while the girls talked about the fact that you could be raped in the bushes. Indeed, elsewhere I provide a close reading on one photograph that depicts two girls enacting a rape scene (Mitchell and Larkin 2004; Mitchell 2005).

But it was the photographs of toilets that were particularly revealing. Included in the collection of close to three hundred photographs were quite a number of toilets. In some instances students wrote about how unsanitary toilets were, and indeed, the photographic evidence confirmed this. In other cases there were picture of toilets without doors, and the girls in particular commented on the fact that there was no sense of privacy. Others felt that they were too isolated. In still other cases, pupils mentioned that they were not safe for girls. "You can be raped in the toilets," wrote one of the girls (Figure 3.2).

The "making public" process itself was an interesting one. While we did not have an opportunity to mount an exhibition in the school, something that we regard as vital in this kind of work, we nonetheless were able to organize the viewing process in such a way that interested teachers were able to listen in and look at the informal displays.[4] Like our research team, they were totally intrigued by the students' images of toilets. On one hand, there may have been a slight sense of disapproval ("Why have they taken pictures of toilets, of all things?"). On the other hand, several commented that they had not thought about the significance of the toilets.

Showing these images of toilets in other settings—at a regional UNICEF workshop on girls' education, at an international workshop on Gender and Human Security, and at a conference on gender equity in South Africa—I have found that the image of the toilet has provoked a great deal of discussion among participants, and in the instance of UNICEF, whose focus on the physical environment of schools has been an important one, has led to

Figure 3.2 "You can be raped in the toilets." (Courtesy of the author.)

some new alliances between the Child Protection Unit and those working on Water and Sanitation.[5]

Rwanda

In another study in the region, Rwandan children were asked to draw places in and around school where they feel safe and unsafe.[6] In one primary school just outside of Butare, the students produced very detailed drawings of all parts of the school and surroundings—the classrooms, the toilets, the bushes, the road, the administrative block, and so on—and at the bottom of their drawings they provided a legend noting each area of danger. The toilets feature in many of these, as we see in the following captions from the drawings of three girls in an upper primary school:

> I fear behind the toilet because I can easily be raped from there or else they kill me.
> Inside the toilettes I fear there because a boy can rape me from there.
> Behind the school I fear there because every one can easily harm you from there.
> I fear in the corridor because some one can rape you from there when it is dark.

On the administration I fear there because the headmistress
   punishes us seriously.

On the toilets are bushes so we fear there because like a girl can
   easily be raped from there. On the road we fear there because
   car can knock you to death.

Behind the classes we fear there because of the bush and some one
   can rape you.
We fear the barracks because they can beat us from there and we
   meet bombs.
On the toilet I fear there and boys or men can easily catch me and
   rape me.
On the road I fear there because the car can knock me down.

Beyond the relevance of their drawings to this chapter, what is also worth
noting is that any one child can experience fear in relation to several forms of
violence or several places at the same time (Kanyangara 2006).

Sex, Power, and Toilets
It has been useful to look again at some of the features of sex and power in the
photographs of toilets. As noted above, the girls photographed the toilets and
drew pictures of the toilet blocks in order to point out dangers to their own
safety and security. Some of the boys also photographed toilets, although
their commentary tended to focus more on the unsanitary state of the toilets.
   However, several groups of boys took pictures of themselves peeing,
something that positioned them—and the toilets—in ways that caused our
research team to consider the social context of taking pictures. Drawing
from the work of Annette Kuhn (1995) and others who suggest the importance of including in any critical reading of a photograph questions such as
"Who took the picture?" "What is the relationship between the photographer and the photographed?" and "Who is going to see the picture?" my
research colleagues and I (all female) have been intrigued with what a critical reading on these peeing portraits might say in a study of hegemonic
masculinity or young masculinities. How, for example, do the boys discuss
the shot ahead of time? Who first suggests the idea of taking photographs
in the toilet area, and who decides which people are going to be "photo
subjects" and which is going to be the photographer? Do they know who is
going to see the picture (the group of female researchers)?
   Although the work on male-on-male bullying in schools in the region
suggests that the toilet area can be a site of violence, gender harassment is
a topic that does not easily come up in situations such as these, where boys
are working in groups and where the activity of picture taking has not necessarily been constructed within a framework for looking at gender criti-

cally. At the same time, though, these portraits raise questions about public and private spaces and about sex and secrecy. For the girls, the toilets are clearly both public and private. They are private in the sense that there is often no protection. No one knows what happens to you when you go to the toilet. Toilets in schools are perfect spaces for predators, bullies, and harassers. They are public in the sense that they do not serve as havens of safety. The girls who minded that there were no doors on the toilets in Swaziland cited privacy in relation to this. Others, however, spoke about the fact that the toilets were too far away from the rest of the school, and for that reason they were too private.

In several recent studies of gender violence in schools in sub-Saharan Africa that have taken a "through the eyes of children" participatory focus, there are numerous references to dangers on the playground, in the bushes close by, and in other areas that are unprotected. Deevia Bhana's detailed ethnographic work of performed sexualities on the primary school playground in several township schools in South Africa highlights the situation for both boys and girls. In "Show Me the Panties: Girls Play Games in the School Yard," she explores the specific ways in which girls' games serve as a type of resistance and agency in response to the actions of boys (Bhana 2005). In another article, she talks about the ways in which boys, even in the primary grades, have begun to take on masculine identities that are linked to sexual harassment and sexual violence (Bhana 2006). Similarly, the work of Rob Pattmann and Fatuma Chege (2004) in Southern Africa suggests a need for a more critical look at the space of school as a site both for protection and change

It is worth pointing out that the (woman) teacher's body is also a site of struggle in the schools I have been describing. While the more public issues tend to be pregnancy and HIV and AIDS, sexual harassment remains a critical issue, particularly in relation to promotions—as I found out when I asked women teachers in Zambia why they didn't put their names forward for promotion (Mitchell 1996). The bodily functions of women, including using the toilet, as the Afro-American activist bell hooks has pointed out, have long been a contested area in male-dominated institutions. Speaking of her early days as a teacher, hooks observes:

> Individuals enter the classroom to teach as though only the mind is present and not the body. To call attention to the body is to betray the legacy of repression and denial that has been handed down to us by our professional elders, who have been usually white and male. But our non-white elders were just as eager to deny the body. . . . When I first became a teacher and needed to use the restroom in the middle of class, I had no clue as to what my elders did in such situations. No one talked about the body in relation to teaching. What did one do with the body in the classroom? (1994, 191)

Deepening an understanding of the barriers for women in rural schools is a girl-focused project in and of itself. In many rural areas of sub-Saharan Africa the absence of women teachers may account for why parents do not send their daughters to school. Gladys Teni Atinga (2004), in her study of beginning teachers' perceptions of sexual violence, found there were many institutional practices and "geographies" that accounted for the fear that many female beginning teachers felt. Promotions, having one's grades altered by the typist-clerks, and difficulty in getting references were all aspects of the institution that could work against young women if they refused to have sex with particular male lecturers, male typists, and other administrators. Among these female teachers' concerns was the fact that the dormitories where they slept were at a great distance from the block of toilets designated for women. As one beginning teacher (female) stated, "We have been trying to get the administration to build another block of toilets closer to the dormitory. It's not safe." The compound where the college was housed was also poorly lit and poorly patrolled (and indeed, there was some concern that the men hired to patrol the grounds were themselves dangerous), so that women teachers often devised their own makeshift systems for going to the toilet during the night.

Remapping School Toilets in Sub-Saharan Africa

What the fieldwork and other studies noted above point to is a need for reconfiguring school spaces to take account of gender and human security—starting with the toilets. Heather Brookes, an anthropologist working with the Human Science Research Council, in her study of rural schools in South Africa has begun to document some of the practices that contribute to a safe school environment. One that is central to the discussion here is the finding that in schools where teachers monitor the toilet block, the number of reports of gender violence decreases (Brookes 2004). Clearly the issue of resources is a critical one, as we see in the case of open pit latrines and the cost of constructing toilet blocks where the toilet stalls have doors. A gender-sensitive design is also an issue, as one of the "gender focal persons" working within the provincial and national gender "machinery" of South African education observed at a meeting on the state of girls' education. As she noted, the design of most of the new portable toilets is not gender-sensitive in the sense that it is difficult for girls and women to position themselves in a very cramped space. Practically, then, the issues are about material resources but also about awareness and advocacy in relation to girls' security.

Below I list a number of questions that could be used as the basis for an audit of school toilets. Like the "walk safe" types of audits that many universities in North America have implemented, the toilet audit could form the basis for a more conscious and critical look at school spaces.

Toilet Audit

Where are toilets positioned? What are the consequences of having toilets as part of the main structure of the school, or at least close by? What happens (as in the case of most parts of sub-Saharan Africa) when they exist as separate toilet blocks at some distance from the teaching and administrative blocks or, worse, as open pit latrines set off at a great distance from the rest of the school, particularly in rural settings?

What is the condition of the toilets? What is the consequence of toilets without doors or with broken doors, or as pits set off in the bushes or tall grass?

What regulations and policies exist around toilets? Are there separate toilets for boys and girls? When can students use them? Who, if anyone, patrols them? To what extent are the toilets (and, indeed, the whole school area) separated by a gate or fences? What special attention is paid to menstruation of pubescent girls?

Conclusion

Beyond the obvious practical suggestions noted above, I argue that this work points to a need for feminist scholars to engage in new ways of looking at the meaning of toilets in studies of childhood and adolescent sexuality. While basic protection is one aspect of this, another is to see how childhood and youth studies might incorporate visual and other participatory approaches to researching the body, sexuality, and space. At recent annual conferences sponsored by the International Visual Sociology Association, several papers have taken up questions about the types of pedagogical and play spaces of schools. To date, however, little of this work has taken on what might be described as a feminist geography of school, one that places at the center "a girl's eye," or for that matter a girl's body. (Recent studies of youth and queer studies by Rasmussen [2004], along with the work of Leavitt, Lingafelter, and Morello [1998] and of Walton [1995], do suggest useful links between space, body, sexuality, and childhood or youth studies, and a multicountry study of children as visual researchers addressing violence in the community, conducted in Thailand, India, Columbia, and Nicaragua [Egg et al. 2004], points to the significance of "the child's eye.") There remains, as well, relatively little work within youth geographies more generally that focuses on toilets, although as we see in the work on bedroom culture (McRobbie and Garber 1991; Skelton and Valentine 1998; Brown et al. 1994), the study of girls' physical spaces is a generative area of research and advocacy. Michele Polak, in her work on "the menstruation narrative" of girls and young women (2006), observes that she was surprised in her initial research at how many women were anxious to talk about their menstrual cycle, and she concludes that it is critical to create new spaces for girls to speak and potentially to "rewrite" the narratives, which, as Catherine Driscoll notes, articulate "revelation, explication, reassurance, and disgust" (2002, 92).

Toilets in sub-Saharan African schools must be reconfigured as safe spaces for girls. Pinky Pinky can remain as a myth, but the real crimes against girls and young women need to disappear. Although toilets are, in some ways, simply emblematic of unsafe places (and if girls aren't raped in the toilets, they can still be raped in the bushes, in the ditches on the way to and from school, and even in the home of a teacher), they are an obvious place to start in terms of school practices and school policies. The participatory approaches noted in this chapter, along with the outlining of some concrete steps that educators and policy makers can take, suggest ways of challenging the regimes of sex and gender within school spaces.

Notes

1. Adapted from curatorial notes on *Pinky Pinky and Other Xeni*, by Penny Siopis, The Goodman Gallery, Johannesburg, 2002.

2. The data collection, part of a project on addressing sexual violence in schools organized by the Eastern and Southern African office of UNICEF, took place in 2003.

3. The Swaziland children photographing the safe and unsafe spaces of their school is documented in *Speak Out!*—a video documentary available through the UNICEF Eastern and Southern Africa Regional Office, Box 44145, Nairobi, Kenya.

4. Within the social science and development community there is a burgeoning interest in using arts and participatory elements for research designs that have a built-in "research as social change" orientation (Schratz and Walker 1995), with the work on children and other marginalized groups as first-time photographers as particularly useful approach. See, for example, the work of Wendy Ewald and James Hubbard, as well as the highly acclaimed Kids With Cameras documentary *Born into Brothels* (2005) and the follow-up book compiled by Zanta Briski (2005). For further work on the idea of "making public" using visual data (screenings, local exhibitions, and so on), see the International Visual Methodologies (for Social Change) Project Web site at http://www.ivmproject.mcgill.ca.

5. Here I acknowledge the Gender and Human Security Conference organized by Noala Skinner at the United Nations in New York, April 11–12, 2004.

6. The data collection, part of a project on testing out participatory methodologies for working with children and young people to address violence in and around schools, and organized by UNICEF in Kigali, took place in 2005.

References

Bhana, D. 2005. "'Show Me the Panties': Girls Play Games in the School Grounds." In *Seven Going on Seventeen: Tween Studies in the Culture of Girlhood*. Ed. C. Mitchell and J. Reid-Walsh. New York: Peter Lang, 163–72.

———. 2006. "Starting Early with Little Boys: Dealing with Violence." In *Combating Gender Violence in and around Schools*. Ed. F. Leach and C. Mitchell. London: Trentham Books, 171–79.

Briski, Z. 2004. *Born into Brothels: Photographs by the Children of Calcutta*. New York: Umbrage Edition Books.

Brookes, H. 2003 *Violence against girls in South African Schools*. Pretoria: Human Sciences Research Council.

Brown, J. D., D. R. Dykers, J. R. Steele, and A. B. White. 1994. "Teenage Room Culture: Where Media and Identities Intersect." *Communication Research* 21 (6): 813–27.

Burke, C., and I. Grosvenor. 2003. *The School I'd Like*. London: RoutledgeFalmer.

Driscoll, C. 2002. *Girls: Feminine Adolescence in Popular Culture and Cultural Theory*. New York: Columbia University Press.

Egg, P., B. Schratz-Hadwich, G. Trubwasser, and R. Walker. 2004. *Seeing beyond Violence: Children as Researchers*. Innsbruck: Hermann Gmeiner Academy.

Ewald, W. 1992. *Magic Eyes: Scenes from an Andean Girlhood*. Seattle: Bay Press.

———. 1996. *I Dreamed I Had a Girl in My Pocket*. New York: W. W. Norton.

———. 2001. *I Wanna Take Me a Picture: Teaching Photography and Writing to Children*. Boston: Beacon Press.

Holland, P. 2005. *Picturing Childhood: The Myth of the Child in Popular Imagery*. London: I. B. Taurus.

hooks, b. 1993. "Eros, Eroticism and the Pedagogical Process." *Journal of Cultural Studies* 7 (1): 58–63.

Hubbard, J. 1994. *Shooting Back from the Reservation*. New York: New Press.

Human Rights Watch. 2001. *Scared at School: Sexual Violence against Girls in South African Schools*. New York: Human Rights Watch.

Kanyangara, P. 2006. *Violence contre les enfants dans le système scolaire au Rwanda; à travers les yeux des enfants et des jeunes*. Kigali, Rwanda: UNICEF 2006.

Kincaid, J. 2002. *Child-Loving: The Erotic Child and Victorian Culture*. New York: Routledge.

Kuhn, A. 1995. *Family Secrets: Acts of Memory and Imagination*. London: Verso.

Leach, F., and C. Mitchell, eds. 2006. *Combating Gender Violence in and around Schools*. London: Trentham.

Leavitt, J., T. Lingafelter, and C. Morello. 1998. "Through Their Eyes: Young Girls Look at Their Los Angeles Neighbourhood." In *New Frontiers of Space, Bodies and Gender*. Ed. R. Ainley. New York: Routledge, 76–87.

Lesko, N. 1988. "The Curriculum of the Body: Lessons from a Catholic High School." In *Becoming Feminine: The Politics of Popular Culture*. Ed. L. G. Roman and L. K. Christian-Smith, with E. Ellsworth. New York: Falmer Press, 123–41.

McRobbie, A., and J. Garber. 1991. "Girls and Subcultures." In *Feminism and Youth Culture: From Jackie to Just Seventeen*. Ed. A. McRobbie. Cambridge, Mass.: Unwin Hyman, 1–15.

McWilliam, E., and A. Jones. 1996. "Eros and Pedagogical Bodies: The State of (Non)Affairs." In *Pedagogy, Technology and the Body*. Ed. E. McWilliam and P. Taylor. New York: Peter Lang.

Mitchell, C. 1996. *"Oh No, We Want to Go Further than That": Towards Strategizing on Increasing Female Participation in the Management of Education in Zambia*. GRZ/UNICEF PAGE (Programme for the Advancement of Girls' Education) Project, Lusaka, Zambia.

———. 2004. "Was It Something I Wore?" In *Not Just Any Dress: Narratives of Memory, Body and Identity*. Ed. S. Weber and C. Mitchell. New York: Peter Lang.

———. 2005. "Mapping a Southern African Girlhood in the Age of AIDS." In *Gender Equity in Education in South African Education, 1994–2004: Conference Proceedings*. Ed. L. Chisholm and J. September. Cape Town: HSRC Press, 92–112.

Mitchell, C., and J. Larkin. 2004. "Disrupting the Silences: Visual Methodologies in Addressing Gender-based Violence." Paper presented at Pleasures and Dangers Conference, Cardiff, June 29–July 1.

Nuttall, S. 2005. "The Shock of Beauty: Penny Siopis' *Pinky Pinky* and *Shame* Series." In *Penny Siopis*. Ed. K. Smith. Johannesburg: Goodman Gallery, 134–49.

OCHA/IRIN. 2005. *Broken Bodies, Broken Dreams: Violence against Women Exposed*. New York: United Nations Office for the Coordination of Humanitarian Aid.

Pattmann, R., and F. Chege. 2003. *Finding Our Voices: Gendered and Sexual Identities and HIV and AIDS in Education*. Nairobi: UNICEF.

Polak, M. 2006. "From the Curse to the Rag: Online GURLS Rewrite the Menstruation Narrative." In *Girlhood: Redefining the Limits*. Ed. Y. Jiwani, C. Steenbergen, and C. Mitchell. Montreal: Black Rose.

Rasmussen, M. 2004. "Safety and Subversion: The Production of Sexualities and Genders in School Spaces." In *Youth and Sexualities: Pleasure Subversion and Insubordination in and out of Schools*. Ed. M. L. Rasmussen, E. Rofes, and S. Talburt. London: Palgrave Macmillan, 131–52.

Skelton, T., and G. Valentine, eds. 1998. *Cool Places: Geographies of Youth Culture*. London and New York: Routledge.

Teni-Atinga, G. 2004. *Beginning Teachers' Perceptions and Experiences of Sexual Harassment in Ghanaian Teacher Training Institutions*. Unpublished Ph.D. diss., McGill University.

Walsh, S., and C. Mitchell. 2006. "'I'm Too Young to Die': Danger, Desire and Masculinity in the Neighbourhood." *Gender and Development* 14 (1): 57–68.

Walton, K. 1995. "Creating Positive Images: Working with Primary School Girls." In *What Can a Woman Do with a Camera?* Ed. J. Spence and J. Solomon. London: Scarlett Press, 153–58.

Weber, S., and C. Mitchell, eds. 2004. *Not Just Any Dress: Narratives of Memory, Body and Identity*. New York: Peter Lang.

4

Gender, Respectability, and Public Convenience in Melbourne, Australia, 1859–1902

ANDREW BROWN-MAY AND PEG FRASER

In late 2005, visitors to the City Gallery at the Melbourne Town Hall were amused and informed by a quirky exhibition titled "Flush! A Quest for Melbourne's Best Public Toilets in Art, Architecture and History." A selection of documents and photographs from the city's archives formed the core of the exhibition, including petitions for and against the provision of public toilets in the city, original architectural plans from the City Engineer's Office, and samples of historic toilet paper. The historic artefacts and archives were complemented by mixed-media artworks from creators who had been invited to respond to the themes of the collection, such as public space, local identity, and the gendered city. Mary Ellen Jordan's *Mrs. Bateman's Handbag* constructed an everyday accessory in woven paper out of a replica letter from a toilet attendant in 1917, while Nicola McClelland's delicate mixed-media collage responded to a handwritten petition of complaint asking for female public conveniences in 1901.

Architectural designs for a new city toilet filled out the display as part of the Caroma Golden Toilet III Awards. The competition brief called for a single cubicle, a basin and a mirror, to be sited on the median strip on Russell Street immediately north of Bourke Street, a site of some historical significance as the vicinity of Melbourne's first underground public toilet, opened in 1902, which was also the first public toilet for women. While entrants were asked to engage with the actual issues and opportunities of designing a public toilet for a busy Melbourne location, they were also invited to bring a sense of fun to what was a hypothetical brief. Placegetters had variously offered an architectural interpretation of the obligatory potty humour (Rory Hyde's *The Golden Turd*); responded to the site context as the location of a number of video-game parlours, with pop-culture graphics or arcade-influenced forms (George Huon and Peter Knight's *The*

Turdis); or played on the ritual or technology of toilets (Mick Moloney's *Public Loobery*).[1]

The tripartite display was mounted at a time when Melbourne's oldest extant underground public toilet (at the intersection of Collins and Queen Streets, 1905) reached its centenary. Hence, the double irony of the exhibition is both that women continue to experience discrimination through the lack of toilet facilities in the city and that the historic 1902 toilet had been decommissioned and sealed off in 1994, though according to city authorities its below-ground elements remain intact under a concrete cap. Four of Melbourne's first underground toilets were placed on the Victorian Heritage Register in 2007.

The Crystal Palace Exhibition of 1851 heralded the burgeoning of public toilet provision in England, a measure that at the time was considered a startling novelty (Kira 1976; Kilroy 1984; Pike 1967, 25–26, 34–51; Rudofsky 1969, 301–3). Scholarship on the introduction of women's public toilets has in more recent years usefully observed the ways in which concerns of gender underpinned the shaping of public space in relation to female facilities (Penner 2001; Cooper, Law, and Malthus 2000). Melbourne's first public toilet—a men's urinal—was erected in 1859, twenty-two years after the city's foundation. The first conveniences for women were opened in 1902. This chapter, in accounting for this discrepancy, asserts the social sequestration of public space as a male-dominated site that made some streets off-limits to women while encouraging in others a fear of harassment or breaches of decorum.[2] It traces historically the "colonisation of women by men" in cities (Fell 1991, 77), supports the assertion that "women have not enjoyed, historically . . . a 'freedom of the streets' comparable to that of men" (Lofland 1984, 13), and suggests that public toilet provision also helped shape a sense of masculinity as a controlled body hidden from public view.

We first establish in brief the particular demographic structure of colonial Melbourne and the notion of female delicacy that characterised Victorian society, before charting the introduction of toilet facilities to the city in the 1850s. A discussion of the relationship between the toilet and definitions of public nuisance then prefaces a more detailed analysis of the circumstances surrounding the introduction of women's facilities in the early twentieth century. In conclusion, we note the need for historians to take account not only of local social and political circumstances but of globalised networks of municipal exchange in explaining such aspects of urban change.

Women and Public Space

By the early twentieth century, the attention of first-wave feminist lobbyists was turned, if not directly towards questioning fundamental sex-role stereotypes, to issues of equality in relation, for example, to public facilities.

Women's claim on public space began to gain momentum. From the 1830s to the 1850s women, children, and the elderly had been a rare enough sight on the streets of the colonial city. Males outnumbered females by almost two to one in 1854 (Vamplew 1987, 27–28). "As to ladies," wrote the barrister and abolitionist George Stephen in 1855, "I have not yet seen one at large. If there are any, I conclude that they are secreted in the bush. They certainly are never visible in Melbourne or its environs." Many city establishments such as Spiers and Ponds Café de Paris did not admit women. The reporter William Kelly remarked in *Life in Victoria* that in the 1850s respectable women were not seen in public, and their territory was limited to a more restricted range of social settings outside the home than that of men. From 1837, when Robert Hoddle first laid out Melbourne's grid, the streets were ostensibly public zones but were broken up into a maze of gendered territories (Thorne 1980, 240; Davidoff and Hall 1983, 327–45): the male zones being outside the hotel, the barber's shop, or the cab stand, where the notoriously bad conduct of men "hooting, yelling, and pouting" at women was well known (O'Brien 1862); the female zones being outside women's public conveniences or underclothing establishments, often deliberately intruded upon by threatening male presence. "We have been very much annoyed by a lot of low class bookmakers standing about in front of our shop, as ours is a ladys [sic] shop you will understand how unpleasant it is & several ladies have complained about it" (Paterson 1897).

Even after the sex ratio levelled out by the end of the century, gender stereotypes continued to be employed to manipulate the public landscape of the streets, and women's value as the focus of male competitive exchange (Irigaray 1977/1993, 31–32) was recognised in the daily dealings of male ratepayers and their male municipal representatives. In other words, notions of female "delicacy," for example, were invoked by men in the mitigation of various perceived public urban ills (Figure 4.1). The nuisance of the noise of auctioneer's bellmen, recorded the *Port Phillip Patriot* (April 8, 1841), necessitated the female purchaser "stretching her voice to a roar:— who loves to hear a lady roar?" In the 1850s, according to the *Australasian Builder* (June 19, 1856), while "men can manage with their long boots to wade through the slush . . . how ladies contrive to perambulate is to us a perfect marvel." The noise of boys selling papers and race-cards in 1901 may have been "a great annoyance" to most people, but to ladies in particular it was deemed to be "distressing beyond measure" (Isaac 1901). The erection of a public urinal could even be charged with offending the respectability of private domestic space: "ladies & children sit in the upstairs room and cannot look out of the windows without noticing for what purpose it is used and therefore sufficient to convey ideas of indelicacy to young children" (Windsor 1878). The absence of footbridges over certain street corners, the use of back lanes as urinals, the poor condition of footpath and roadway, leaking verandahs—a host of municipal improvements were

Figure 4.1 Detail from "Street Sketches in Melbourne,"
Illustrated Australian News, August 20, 1887.

demanded on the basis of female respectability, the paradox being that the complaints in effect both reflected and recreated women's restricted access to public space.

Public Toilet Provision in Early Melbourne

On November 1, 1849, a ship's surgeon wrote to the *Sydney Morning Herald* on the question of Sydney's sanitary requirements. Duty required him to refer to the lack of urinals and water closets in that town, an oversight that was held to promote "the worst class of diseases." Growing awareness of the European vogue, coupled with the opening of the Yan Yean water supply in 1858, provided the impetus for Melbourne's first public toilets. Until 1859, public toilets in Melbourne were available only in hotels (hardly public), the alternative for the city visitor caught short being to seek out the most secluded corner of a street or park. In 1856 the Local Board of Health recognised the absence of public urinals and privies, noting that with the impending connection of the city water supply the matter would soon be under consideration.

In 1859 the Melbourne City Council (MCC) erected a urinal on the pavement in Bourke Street near Elizabeth Street. No doubt a paper presented to the Victorian Institute of Architects by their president, J. G. Knight, published in the *Argus* on June 2, 1857, and forwarded to the MCC "as the guardians of the health and morality of the citizens," had some bearing on this decision. The paper referred to facilities in Paris and suggested the formation of three trial establishments, two for men and one for women. All classes of residents, claimed Knight, deserved provision for "that which, though we affect to be too delicate to name, we can neither control nor supersede, and which in the absence of suitable arrangements, must either be checked at the risk of our health or indulged in at the peril of our morality." Knight advised against adoption of the French system (deemed too public for colonial sensibilities), opting instead for less-prominent establishments, to be euphemistically named Public Ablution Rooms.

The first public urinals were placed directly over the street channel, and it was not until after the establishment of the Melbourne and Metropolitan Board of Works (MMBW) in 1891 that connection with sewers commenced (Dingle and Rasmussen 1991). On September 12, 1860, the *Argus* reported on the siting of a *commodité*, "a neat little pagoda-kind of building" on a bluestone base, in the centre of the roadway at the intersection of Bourke and Swanston Streets. Its lower portion was constructed of iron panels, with upper glass panels carrying "sundry business announcements, readable only from the outside." On its roof were a clock and a vane, the whole structure being illuminated at night. By 1911 there were nineteen sets of closets with 151 stalls, seventy-one public urinals with 210 stalls, and five underground conveniences (three of these for men only). While a number of urinals were open free of charge, closet accommodation cost a penny via a slot machine, with extras (wash or brush) available for a further penny. There was little general complaint of the cost, although some correspondents to the MCC regarded the charge on public toilets as most unfair.

At least from the early 1850s, complaints were made of the "indecent nuisances" being committed in public streets and lanes of the city due to the want of public toilets. The euphemistic sign "Commit No Nuisance," which was prominent on the walls of many city rights-of-way, was little disincentive to those urgently needing to pee. The growing complaint of nuisances committed in the public places of the city was due in part to increasing population and lack of facilities, but perhaps also to a changing threshold of public decency. Practices admitted in a raw frontier town eventually came to be seen as out of step with the rise of an advanced urban community. It was not until the 1870s that complaint of public urination began to reach a crescendo, relating concerns both for public health as well as public morality.

Complaints of nuisances invariably focused on rights-of-way and lanes, often in the vicinity of theatres, markets, or restaurants or on vacant blocks of land or poorly lit building sites. As the central city was slowly furnished with public toilet accommodation, the outer stretches of the municipality became the focus of complaint. In 1891 "the stains on the fence about the neighbourhood" were a measure of male public behaviour on Carlton streets, while in South Yarra in 1919 "a man wishing to obey a call of nature usually does so, up against one of the fences."

In 1890, Russell Place was used as a place of convenience during intervals by those attending the Bijou Theatre and Gaiety Concert Hall; a nuisance that, according to the police, could not be alleviated until proper provision was made for public conveniences. Those men making use of the lane contended that it was hardly an offence to answer a call of nature if proper facilities were unavailable, and Senior Constable Blade reported that even "some of the leading men of the city sometimes are to be seen."

The stench of urine from the back lanes was one of the ubiquitous nineteenth-century city smells. It distracted the patrons in the dining room of the Melbourne Coffee Palace and of a Saturday and Sunday night was an unbearable nuisance to boarders off Latrobe Place. It was a persistent summer intolerance rising off the back walls at the workroom of Dibble and Wheaten, tailors of Bourke Street. Even the lessees of the Theatre Royal considered that the stench and danger of infection were jeopardising their theatre's success. Cab ranks were often singled out for complaint, and residents near a Carlton rank in 1892 could not "come out of their houses without seeing some man standing against the wheel of his cab or against an iron fence in the neighbourhood. . . . This state of things is very objectionable to females passing up and down the street." By 1900, new underground conveniences were about to be installed, and many urinals were already connected to the new sewerage system. Complaints of nuisances about the theatres slowly decreased.

A more sinister association was made between those committing nuisances in back lanes and a dark human underworld in which night, pitch-black rights-of-way and blind alleys, drunken sailors, prostitutes and larrikins (mischievous youths), lurking burglars and footpads, and stinking piles of unidentifiable or unmentionable matter were all bound up in a fearful urban pathology. In the battleground of the streets, safe social territory could be marked by the comforting beacons signifying and promoting urbanity: the street lamp, the cast-iron urinal, the street sign, the street tree, the fire plug.

The modern and forward-looking city was expected to provide its citizens with the latest in technological and social improvements, and public toilet provision was a hallmark of any civilised urban society:

> On Monday last at 9am I was taken very short, and being in the vicinity of Princes Bridge, I made for the place on the river side below the bridge, but imagine my disappointment, it was locked. . . . Now, when a person is in agony, as I was, has [sic] to go two or three hundred yards further before being relieved, is to say the least wrong, to say nothing of the danger of having to hold yourself in check so long.

Mr. Blakston's unabashed recounting of his inconvenience in 1909 was a sign of the times. The proper provisioning of public toilets was no longer simply a panacea for general urban dissolution, assuaging middle-class fear of pathological crime, dirt, and disease; it was an essential comfort for the individual in the city. In the 1880s a traveller versed in both cities had compared the inadequacies of Melbourne with the convenient and ubiquitous provisioning of Glasgow with public urinals. While public toilets may have been an accepted part of the urban landscape in Melbourne, their lack of numbers was yet cause for concern. Meanwhile, their use, though popularly sanctioned, was still provoking surreptitious behaviour in 1909: "The common spectacle of men lined up on the kerb of Collins Street waiting their turn to enter the wretched lattice urinal near the Town Hall . . . is a disgraceful sight as embarrassing for women as for men."

As early as 1860, when, owing to complaints of indecency, the first city urinal at the central corner of Bourke and Elizabeth streets was removed to a less prominent location, a strategic game had commenced in which the MCC parried the complaints of citizens adjacent to the new structures by removing them to other, hopefully less sensitive and less controversial pitches.

The presence of public toilets lessened the use made of lanes and trees for public urination, and despite the clamour against them, the MCC was determined to follow through a programme of proper sanitary accommodation in the city. Toilets had also been provided on roads leading in and out of the central city, especially for carters plying between the city and Brunswick. Though the residents of Parkville asked for a urinal's removal "from the view of windows and balconies of our private residences," as it was "like sacrilege to disfigure the most beautiful of the Roads leading out of the City," the City Surveyor regarded such objections as being "of sentimental and temporary nature." Reinforcing the negative image of the public toilet, detractors objected not only to their visual pollution but to their use as a haunt for stragglers and objectionable characters, their smell, the appearance of illegal posters and racist literature, and their general effect on public decency.

Negative social and psychological attitudes towards bodily functions were still evident in euphemistic language and spatial mechanisms, and the solution to the suggestion of indelicacy through defecation, urination, or sexuality in general was the underground public toilet. Public toilets were also provided more and more frequently in railway stations, libraries, hotels, and department stores, though limited by verbal and spatial circumscription. Psychologically, public facilities continued into the twentieth century to be associated with marginality and social deviance, with attention focusing on vandalism, graffiti, illegal advertising, drug taking, and homosexual liaison (Kira 1976, 93–107; Rudofsky 1969, 300–305).

City conveniences not only provided basic toilet requirements but sometimes furnished the public with a range of additional extras, such as brushes or towels, for the cost of a penny. The pilfering of towels was not uncommon, while in 1903 articles stolen from the ladies' lavatory at 407 Flinders Street included towels, soap, brushes, combs, table covers, window curtains, and toilet glass. Toilet attendants alone late at night were in a vulnerable position and occasionally were the victims not only of verbal harassment but of violent assault. As well as attending to the practical running of their establishments, they were required to fend off the predations of youths who, particularly on Friday nights, showered oyster shells on the heads of unsuspecting customers on the steps of underground facilities. Nighttime at the Viaduct W.C. in Flinders Street drew a certain "class of men and boys" who "are constantly writing filth and dirt and respectable citizens [sic] names if seen go in." If unmentionable bodily functions could be carried on behind cast-iron panels, those entering or leaving were often accused of breaching the spatial and moral partitioning of the act by adjusting their clothes in public view. "No matter when a urinal is erected," noted the Assistant Surveyor, "there is always a certain amount of captious criticism," and he recommended the placement of a notice, "'please adjust your dress before leaving' on the wall."

"The Wants of the Female Half of the Human Race"

The obvious solution to the distaste occasioned by the visibility of public toilets on city streets was to build them underground. As early as 1865, George Jennings predicted that city toilets would be constructed beneath the pavement (Davis and Dye 1898, 172). By 1895 the Town Clerk and City Surveyor were in possession of details of underground toilets in Aberdeen, London, Leeds, and Bournemouth. One correspondent blasted the above-ground urinals as "relics of a barbarous age"; the Town Clerk responded somewhat huffily that Melbourne had no need for—and could not afford—such "luxurious" conveniences as underground toilets. Perhaps more to the point was the fact that the necessary plumbing was not yet available for them.

The MMBW, established in 1891, was responsible for bringing sewerage services to the city, but progress was agonisingly slow due to financial difficulties and the shortage of skilled workers. With the initial emphasis on the provision of residential services, it was several years before the board could cater to the specialised demands of underground toilets. Designing and building the toilets was the responsibility of the city's Department of Public Works, under the supervision of the City Surveyor Adrien Charles Mountain, who had come from a similar appointment in Sydney in 1888—the year in which that city opened its first underground toilet for men.

Mountain appears to have relied heavily on Davis and Dye's *A Complete and Practical Treatise on Sanitation and Plumbing*, published in London in 1898, for the details of the first underground toilets in Melbourne. The book gave exhaustive instructions regarding the siting, plans, fixtures, and plumbing for the new conveniences. The first underground toilets were opened on June 23, 1902, in the traffic island at the intersection of Russell and Bourke

Figure 4.2 Interior, Russell Street underground toilets (male).
From City of Melbourne Annual Report, 1902.

Streets in the city, and they largely resembled the plans supplied in *A Complete and Practical Treatise* (Figure 4.2). Mountain's later correspondence would show that he also seemed to have imbibed Davis and Dye's opinions regarding the viability of public facilities for women.

With the opening of the Russell Street underground conveniences, Melbourne also acquired its first female public toilet. In addition to the problems of filth and nuisance, the aboveground urinals had involved another drawback: there was no provision for women. Women may have been a rare sight on the streets of the gold-rush town, but their numbers were increasing. Public urinals, however insanitary and unattractive they might be, were at least provided for men; women had to rely on the kindness of shopkeepers or on the few semi-private toilets available in tearooms or at the Eastern Market, or simply to hold on. A Ladies' Sanitary Association had been agitating in the early 1880s in London for provision of public toilet facilities for women, and in Melbourne in 1887 the Central Board of Health was suggesting the need for women's toilets in the city. In 1899 the Women's Political and Social Crusade (WPSC) presented the Melbourne City Council with a petition signed by doctors, from GPs in working-class neighbourhoods to distinguished Collins Street practitioners, supporting the establishment of women's toilets as "not only desirable but necessary" in the interests of public health.

By 1900 the City Council had resolved that female sanitary conveniences should be provided, perhaps spurred by the chastisement in a letter from Catherine Rickarby—a campaigner on issues such as women's employment and education—on behalf of "thousands of women and children who suffer in their visits to this 'City' through the neglect of the City Council. . . . The men are lavishly provided for everywhere privately and publicly. Women have the same natural wants as men and must necessarily suffer under the same circumstances, and as they pay equally with men to the City Council their wants should be equally attended to." But while the Health Committee might support such provision, progress on the part of the City Council was slow, and Catherine Rickarby wrote again at the end of 1900, "I think the Fathers and Husbands belonging to the Council might have a little more consideration for the wants of the female half of the human race than up to this they have exhibited."

Early 1901 found the city making preparations for the Federation of Australia and the visit of the Duke and Duchess of York to Melbourne to mark the occasion. Thousands were expected to throng the streets, and the Committee of Public Works received various correspondences requesting the provision of female public toilets. The Celebrations Committee of the Department responded by increasing the toilet provision for men and promising to consider temporary conveniences for women. The latter do not appear to have been built.

The MCC had, by this time, instructed the City Surveyor to draw up plans for an underground toilet incorporating facilities for both men and women. Mountain countered with a suggestion for building aboveground toilets for women in a nearby location and keeping the Russell Street site strictly for men, but eventually he compromised with a small kiosk structure over the ladies' entrance. Perhaps he had anticipated difficulties with the model selected for the site. The plan was lifted straight from the pages of *A Complete and Practical Treatise*. Davis and Dye were so pessimistic of the success of women's underground toilets that the building was engineered specifically to allow for this eventuation. The fault, they held, lay with the illogical nature of women:

It is now acknowledged that accommodation of the kind is an absolute necessity for the natural consequences of eating and drinking, and why there should be any false delicacy in recognising and providing for this cannot be explained. This strange form of modesty still prevails, however, with the weaker sex, as public conveniences for women are, as yet, more often failures, financially and practically, than a success; and in building such places with sections for each sex, it is commonly found that the whole can be easily converted for the use of men only, if the women's section is not appreciated and used. (1898, 172)

Davis and Dye's plans for underground toilets did not incorporate a ladies' private waiting room, despite their comment on its desirability "to avoid that publicity which is such a barrier to the use of these places by the opposite sex" (Davis and Dye 1898, 182).

The Melbourne plans went ahead with both male and female conveniences. Despite the prolonged lobbying from individuals and the WPSC, the first public toilet for women was hardly a roaring success. Barely four months after its opening, the City Surveyor was back reporting to Council that the September income from the ladies' side covered less than 25 percent of the month's running expenses: "it would appear that there are so many 'conveniences' for ladies all over the city (in tea-rooms, restaurants, shops, etc) that they do not really require such accommodation as has been provided." He proposed closing the ladies' facility and extending the men's convenience into that space, thereby saving the Council two pounds, ten shillings per week.

What Davis and Dye failed to acknowledge, and Mountain perhaps suspected, was that the design itself had failure built into the specifications. Although the City Surveyor claimed adequate provision for women existed—a debatable point, and one that women themselves disputed—the Town Clerk was made aware that the new facilities fell short of acceptable standards. The indefatigable Catherine Rickarby wrote to Council once again, outlining the faults of the new toilet: "It is only in extreme cases women will patronise the one in Russell St, the Stand at the back, where men are always coming and going . . . is subversive to all notions of female delicacy." Entering the toilet directly off a busy street, without the mitigating fiction of a "waiting room" and in close proximity to men using the male toilets, was too much for some women to face: "Myself and many others would often take advantage of the conveniences . . . but for the fact of it being so open & under the gaze of every tram & vehicle that passes."

Davis and Dye's unsympathetic dismissal of "a peculiar excess of modesty, or what is imagined to be modesty, among women" (1898, 194) was in fact the crux of the problem that many women had with the new conveniences. Rather than the product of an overrefined sensibility, the reluctance to be seen—especially by men—entering a public toilet was an inevitable reaction to the dilemma in which women now found themselves. On one hand was the opportunity to move through the city with a new freedom; on the other was the necessity to maintain the appearance of respectable female behaviour, which included the denial of the existence of bodily processes and needs. Toilets were especially fraught through being associated, rightly or wrongly, with immoral behaviour.

In October 1905, the WPSC, claiming an instrumental role in forcing the provision of women's "Sanatories," requested that the female lavatory attendants be allowed to finish work earlier in the evenings, as it was not safe for them after dark. In requesting that they be allowed to leave as soon as the theatres had closed, "as no respectable women will be out after that hour," the organisation was itself complicit in a gendering of space that upheld traditional patriarchal stereotypes of the sex-role ideology. The conflict between the behaviour expected of a respectable woman and the actions of a citizen inhabiting and fully participating in a modern urban environment can be described as "double conformity," the pressure to obey two simultaneous yet contradictory codes of behaviour. In the history of women's education, where the concept has informed debate on educational reforms in the nineteenth century, double conformity takes the nature of "the strict adherence . . . to two sets of rigid standards: those of ladylike behaviour at all times *and* those of the dominant male cultural and educational system" (Delamont 1978, 146). In this case the conflict was between the demands of ladylike behaviour and the chance to join men, as workers, consumers, and revellers, in their occupation of public space.

The clearest expression of the tensions thrown up by double conformity is in the words of the women themselves. Even individuals such as Catherine Rickarby, who never wavered in her lobbying of City Council for public toilet provision for women, expressed (perhaps unwittingly) the contradictions. Her earlier letter positions women as citizens with rights to which their taxpayer status entitles them; later, she invokes the passive female, defined by her relationship to men, who must appeal to the better natures of "Fathers and Husbands" to extend consideration.

A corollary to the idea of double conformity suggests that the greater the challenge that the new behaviour offers to accepted norms, the stricter must be the adherence to the forms and appearances of the old code. Correspondence from other women suggests that they chose the conservative option, "unable to shake off the fear of being characterised as unladylike, or worse still, unfeminine" (Delamont 1978, 160), and preferred to continue to suffer physically rather than cross the line of perceived respectability. Their solution, as evidenced by suggestions to the Town Clerk for the erection of screens, or for police to keep the area clear of idling men, was not to challenge established notions but to put into place mechanisms that allowed them to tread both paths of conformity without disaster.

Despite the recommendations of the City Surveyor, the Russell Street toilets kept their configuration for both men and women. Even if representatives of the Melbourne establishment objected to the building of public toilets in public places, others approved of the underground structures. In 1903, "Cleanliness" wrote to the *Argus* calling for more underground conveniences: "The one in Russell-street has been a great success financially, and I feel certain others would more than pay their way." In 1905 the Women's Political Association of Victoria resolved that "on aesthetic grounds as well as on grounds of sanitation and convenience all street and park lavatories be built underground." A second underground toilet was built in 1905, again following the principles laid out by Davis and Dye, but this included provision only for men.

It was not until 1907, with the opening of underground conveniences in Elizabeth Street, that a second public toilet for women became available. Financial reports from this time indicate that viability was no longer an issue: from July 1907 to June 1908, the two toilets that included accommodation for women each generated nearly five times the income of the men-only underground toilet in Queen Street (helped, no doubt, by the fact that the urinals in the men's toilets were free of charge). There was now little doubt that women really did require "such accommodation as has been provided."

The contrast in the reception received by each of the new women's toilets indicates a shift in women's use of the facilities. It is tempting but premature to attribute this to a radical shift in attitudes. The campaign to provide public conveniences for women, and the subsequent concern about their suitability, was largely driven by middle-class women who were as influenced by their class standing as by their gender, so many of their observations are concerned with activity outside the toilets, at the periphery where male and female territory intersected. It is unclear whether these women actually used the public facilities or opted for the conveniences provided by the better stores and tearooms. Perhaps working-class women did not share the same preoccupations with ladylike behaviour and had very different views of the suitability of public toilets.

Our exploration of public conveniences started with the separation of men's and women's roles in the streets of turn-of-the-century Melbourne. The next step is to dismantle the monolithic vision of "woman" and discover the nature and variety of the individuals who entered the ladies' loo.

Conclusion

There is little doubt that over the half century from the 1850s to the early 1900s, not only did the incidence of urination in streets and indecent exposure decline but an altered threshold of public decency eventually cordoned off the public toilet as the only appropriate place for such bodily functions. As Norbert Elias has noted, "shame" as social function increasingly determined the impoliteness of public urination. While the withdrawing of bodily functions from public (and the consequent "moulding of instinctual urges") was made possible by technological progress, Elias remarks that changes in sensibilities are also attributable to sociogenetic and psychogenetic factors (1939/1978, 131, 139–40). Whereas the sight of public toilets themselves was once as offensive as the back-street nuisances they sought to allay, they eventually found a place on city streets as essential and practical sites of containment. The ideological and actual separation of men's and women's roles in the streets of nineteenth- and early-twentieth-century Melbourne was reflected not only in the extent of toilet provision but in the spatial and temporal (e.g., in terms of opening hours) boundaries of those facilities themselves. Finally, that public toilets for women first proliferated, for example, in London, Melbourne, and Dunedin, in the decade around 1900 is due both to particular endogenous controversies and constructions of social order (cf. Hamlin 1994) and to a broader currency of ideas and knowledge as motors of social change (the copy of Davis and Dye we consulted in the Architecture Library at the University of Melbourne is the MCC's original copy, which Mountain clearly consulted).

Flows of information from metropolis to colony might be predominantly unidirectional, but understanding modulations of the imposition of social and moral order might usefully occur in a more broadly comparative framework, utilising more detailed local-level research (Silverman and Gulliver 2005). Cities and towns appear across colony and empire as social laboratories, adaptive proving grounds of technology and social innovation. So problematic, for example, were the tactics of location and relocation on urinals in 1860s Melbourne, in response to citizens' complaints, that the Councillors of Adelaide (in South Australia) were influenced against erecting urinals newly imported from England, news having reached them of the MCC's difficulties.

Geographers Felix Driver and David Gilbert, exploring the influence of imperialism on London, have cogently observed that while the hybridity of architectural, ceremonial, and other symbolic landscapes has come under the scrutiny of scholars of the imperial domain, historians have yet to turn adequate attention to the lived spaces of the networked city. The history of public toilet provision is part of a bigger consideration of the currency of ideas, mentalities, and commodities that produced hybridised or homogenised physical and social spaces. Here indeed, in contemplating cities as transnational actors, we might seek interconnections and affinities in the bringing of social and moral order to cities, to challenge simplistic understandings of the metropolis/periphery binary.

Notes

1. Sponsored by the City of Melbourne and curated by architect Kirsty Fletcher from the Rexroth Mannasmann Collective, artist Nicky Adams, and historian Dr. Andrew Brown-May, the exhibition ran from September 2005 to January 2006.

2. This chapter develops arguments first presented in chapter 4 of Brown-May 1998, "At Your Convenience: Street Facilities," which is a broader examination of the provision of street trees, seating, toilets, drinking fountains, water troughs, and street lights. Unless otherwise indicated, material on public toilets is drawn from the Melbourne Town Clerk's Correspondence files in the Victoria Public Record Office, VPRS 3181/653–686 (Nuisances) and 3181/970–971 (Urinals).

References

Brown-May, Andrew. 1998. *Melbourne Street Life*. Melbourne: Australian Scholarly Publishing.

Cooper, Annabel, Robin Law, and Jane Malthus. 2000. "Rooms of Their Own: Public Toilets and Gendered Citizens in a New Zealand City, 1860–1940." *Gender, Place and Culture* 7 (4): 417–33.

Davidoff, Leonore, and Catherine Hall. 1983. "The Architecture of Public and Private Life:

English Middle-Class Society in a Provincial Town 1780 to 1850." In *The Pursuit of Urban History*. Ed. D. Fraser and A. Sutcliffe. London: Edward Arnold, 327–45.

Davis, George B., and Frederick Dye. 1898. *A Complete and Practical Treatise on Plumbing and Sanitation etc.* London: E. and F. N. Spon.

Delamont, Sara. 1978. "The Contradictions in Ladies' Education." In *The Nineteenth Century Woman: Her Cultural and Physical World*, ed. Sara Delamont and Lorna Duffin. London: Croom Helm, 134–63.

Dingle, A. E., and Carolyn Rasmussen. 1991. *Vital Connections: Melbourne and Its Board of Works 1891–1991*. Melbourne: Penguin Books.

Driver, Felix, and David Gilbert, eds. 1999. *Imperial Cities: Landscape, Display and Identity*. Manchester: Manchester University Press.

Elias, Norbert. 1939/1978. *The Civilizing Process: The Development of Manners: Changes in the Code of Conduct and Feeling in Early Modern Times*. Trans. Edmund Jephcott. New York: Urizen Books.

Fell, Alison. 1991. "Penthesilia, Perhaps." In *Whose Cities?* Ed. Mark Fisher and Ursula Owen. London: Penguin Books, 73–84.

Hamlin, Christopher. 1994. "Environmental Sensibility in Edinburgh, 1839–40: The 'Fetid Irrigation' Controversy." *Journal of Urban History* 20, no. 3 (May): 311–39.

Irigaray, Luce. 1977/1993. *This Sex Which Is Not One*. Trans. Catherine Porter. Ithaca, N.Y.: Cornell University Press.

Isaac, Thomas. 1901. Letter to MCC. Victoria Public Record Office Series 3181 Unit 870, File 1534, April 6.

Kelly, William. 1859. *Life in Victoria or Victoria in 1853, and Victoria in 1858: Showing the March of Improvement Made by the Colony within Those Periods, in Town and Country, Cities and Diggings*. 2 vols. London: Chapman and Hall.

Kilroy, Roger. 1984. *The Complete Loo: A Lavatorial Miscellany*. London: Gollancz.

Kira, Alexander. 1976. *The Bathroom*. Harmondsworth: Penguin Books, chap. 16.

Lofland, Lyn. 1984. "Women and Urban Public Space." *Women and Environments* 6 (2): 12–14.

O'Brien, Louisa. 1862. Letter to MCC. Victoria Public Record Office Series 3181 Unit 332, October 10.

Paterson, E. 1897. Letter to MCC, Victoria Public Record Office Series 3181 Unit 865 File 943, March 23.

Penner, Barbara. 2001. "A World of Unmentionable Suffering: Women's Public Conveniences in Victorian London." *Journal of Design History* 14 (1): 35–51.

Pike, E. Roysten. 1967. *Human Documents of the Victorian Golden Age (1850–1875)*. London: Allen and Unwin.

Rudofsky, Bernard. 1969. *Streets for People: A Primer for Americans*. Garden City, N.Y.: Doubleday.

Silverman, Marilyn, and P. H. Gulliver. 2005. "Historical Anthropology through Local-Level Research." In *Critical Junctions: Anthropology and History beyond the Cultural Turn*. Ed. Don Kalb and Herman Tak. New York: Berghahn Books, 152–67.

Stephen, George. 1855. Letter, July 3. University Library, Cambridge, England.

Thorne, Robert. 1980. "Places of Refreshment in the Nineteenth-Century City." In *Buildings and Society: Essays on the Social Development of the Built Environment*. Ed. Anthony D. King. London: Routledge and Kegan Paul, 228–53.

Vamplew, Wray, ed. 1987. *Australians: Historical Statistics*. Broadway: Fairfax, Syme and Weldon Associates.

Windsor, A. 1878. Letter to MCC. Victoria Public Record Office Series 3181 Unit 662, File 663, June 1.

5

Bodily Privacy, Toilets, and Sex Discrimination

The Problem of "Manhood" in a Women's Prison

JAMI ANDERSON

Unfounded assumptions about sex and gender roles, the untamable potency of maleness and gynophobic notions about women's bodies inform and influence a broad range of policy-making institutions in this society. In December 2004, the U.S. Court of Appeals for the Sixth Circuit continued this ignoble cultural pastime when it decided *Everson v. Michigan Department of Corrections*.[1] In this decision, the Court accepted the Michigan Department of Correction's (MDOC's) claim that "the very manhood" of male prison guards both threatens the safety of female inmates and violates the women's "special sense of privacy in their genitals." MDOC argued that concern for the women prisoners' safety and rights to privacy warranted designating the prison guard positions in the housing units at women's prisons as "female only." The Everson Court accepted this argument and declared that the sex-specific employment policies were not impermissibly discriminatory. While protecting women prisoners from sexual abuse and privacy violations is of paramount importance for any correctional institution, I argue that the Sixth District Court's decision relies on unacceptable and offensive stereotypes about sex, gender, and sexuality, and it undermines Title VII's power to end discriminatory employment practices.

The *Everson* decision is ostensibly a Title VII case. But the significance of this case is the insight it affords us into the perpetuation of defining women's right to privacy in terms of their need for modesty.[2] Rather than evaluate employment policies for prison guards to ensure they are designed to protect women prisoners from sexual abuse, which is what the case purports to do, the court shifts its focus to the matter of protecting women prisoners from the shame of being seen by male guards while using a toilet.

Obviously, anxieties about privacy violations while using a toilet are profoundly strong in Western culture. Put simply, toilets are everywhere—at work, business, school, government buildings, stores, hospitals, and military facilities—and we carry our toileting anxieties with us wherever we go. So it is not surprising that we find the same anxieties surfacing in women's prisons. But not only is toilet anxiety an unsound basis for a Title VII decision, but cultural fears of genital exposure prevent us from realizing social equality. It is women who are paying a higher price. While claiming to protect women prisoners, this decision reinforces misogynistic and sexist assumptions about women. And these assumptions advance men's interests—*all* men—and oppress women—*all* women. If we are ever to realize a fairer, more equal society, we need radically to rethink our toilet anxieties. Toileting is a vital human activity; unjust toileting policies (such as "whites only" toilet policies) affect us in a deeply personal way. And prisons, because they institutionalize profound disparities of power, are sites in which we should be particularly certain to cast aside toilet anxieties and instead evaluate policies according to the highest standards of equality and fairness, not in terms of our fear of exposed genitals.

A "Special Sense of Privacy"

Before beginning my analysis of the *Everson* decision, I provide some background information about the events that brought this case to the courtroom. *Everson v. Michigan Department of Corrections* principally concerns a Title VII dispute. Title VII of the Civil Rights Act of 1964 is the primary federal protection against harassment and unequal employment opportunities in the private sector. Employers may not discriminate against any employee "with respect to his compensation, terms, conditions, or privileges of employment," nor can employers "limit, segregate, or classify" employees on the basis of their sex. Title VII was amended in 1972 so that it would apply to federal and state government.

Although Title VII was created in part to ensure equal employment opportunities for men and women, the courts have long accepted the claim that men and women are, when it comes to certain employment situations, importantly different. Indeed, our court system accepts that the differences between men and women are so significant and unerasable that employers can refuse to hire either men or women, choose to promote or advance men or women only, and segregate men and women into separate employment sectors (creating what some feminists refer to as "gender ghettoes" in the workplace). If an employer can successfully argue that a person's sex is a bona fide occupational qualification (BFOQ), then treating women and men employees differently is not a violation of Title VII. To establish a BFOQ defense, an employer must show three things:

1. The employer has a "basis in fact" for its belief that gender discrimination is "reasonably necessary"—not merely reasonable or convenient—to the normal operation of its business.[3]
2. The "job qualification must relate to the essence, or to the central mission of the employer's business."[4]
3. No reasonable alternatives exist to discrimination on the basis of sex.[5]

It is important to note that the BFOQ defense does not aim to show that sex discrimination is not taking place; rather, it argues that discriminatory treatment is justified.

In its recent decision, the *Everson* court reviewed the Michigan Department of Corrections employment policy stipulating that all COs (correctional officers) and RUOs (residential unit officers) in the housing units in the women's prisons would be female only. This sweeping sex-specific employment policy was created to eliminate the long-standing problem of sexual abuse and mistreatment of female inmates. During the 1990s, several human rights organizations reported that the sexual abuse of female prisoners by male guards was "rampant." Nothing was done to address prison conditions until a lawsuit by the U.S. Department of Justice and, barely a year later, a lawsuit by the female prisoners were initiated. Both lawsuits were decided against MDOC.

Highlights of the history of sexual abuse in MDOC's women's prisons during the 1990s include the following:

- In 1993, the Michigan Women's Commission advised the MDOC that "sexual abuse and harassment are not isolated incidents and that fear of reporting such incidents is a serious problem" (*Mich. Comp. Laws Ann.* § 10.71).
- In 1996, the Human Rights Watch concluded that "rape, sexual assault or abuse, criminal sexual contact, and other misconduct by corrections staff are continuing" and that male corrections staff routinely violate inmate privacy rights by "improperly viewing inmates as they use the shower or toilet" (*Everson v. MDOC* [2004]).
- In 1999, the UN Commission on Human Rights claimed that corrections officers retaliate against women who report sexual abuse.
- In May 1999, the Civil Rights Division of the U.S. Department of Justice settled a lawsuit against the MDOC after investigating allegations of sexual abuse of women prisoners in Michigan prisons. The lawsuit, reported "a pattern of sexual abuse, including sexual assaults by guards, 'frequent' sexual activity between guards and inmates, sexually aggressive acts by guards (such as pressing their bodies against inmates, exposing their genitals to

inmates, and fondling inmates during 'pat-down' searches), and ubiquitous sexually suggestive comments by guards . . . [as well as] improper visual surveillance of inmates, including the 'routine' practices of watching inmates undress, use the shower, and use the toilet." In the "*USA* agreement" emerging from the suit, the MDOC pledged to minimize one-on-one contact between male staff and female prisoners and to institute a "knock and announce" policy, which would require male officers to "announce their presence prior to entering areas where inmates normally would be in a state of undress" (*Everson v. MDOC* [2004]).

- In July 2000 a lawsuit initiated by female inmates (the "*Nunn* lawsuit," which charged the MDOC with tolerating "rampant sexual misconduct, sexual harassment, violation of privacy rights, and retaliation by correction officers" [*Everson v. MDOC*]) was settled, with an award of just under $4 million going to the inmates. In addition to the monetary relief, the MDOC pledged, among other things, to restrict pat-down searches of female inmates by male staff, to require male staff to announce their presence in female housing areas, and to "maintain areas where inmates may dress, shower, and use the toilet without being observed by male staff" (*Everson v. MDOC* [2004]).

Shortly after the two highly public and expensive lawsuits were settled, the newly appointed director of the MDOC decided that the best way to respond to the rampant sexual abuse of their prisoners was to eliminate all male guards from women's prisons.

The *Everson* court accepted MDOC's claim that "the female gender" is a bona fide occupational qualification for the prison guard positions in the women's prisons. In other words, the court determined that the nature of the job *requires* that it be done by a female, and though the MDOC is discriminating against males, it is not violating Title VII. In explaining this decision, the court focused on two lines of reasoning: (1) that courts must acknowledge the "unusual responsibilities" with which prison administrators are burdened and not "tie their hands" by limiting the means by which they fulfill those responsibilities and (2) that the safety and privacy concerns of female inmates make sex-specific employment policies reasonable. Let us first consider the first line of reasoning, that the "unusual responsibilities" with which prison administrators are burdened justify sex-specific employment policies. Relying on well-established precedent, the court cited the U.S. Supreme Court when claiming that prison officials "must grapple with the 'perplexing sociological problems of how best to achieve the goals of the penal function in the criminal justice system: to punish justly, to deter future crime, and to return imprisoned persons to society with an improved chance of being useful, law-abiding citizens.'"[6] In addition to achieving this complex cluster of penalogical goals, prison officials must provide a secure and safe environment that protects the legal rights of its inmates as well as its employees.

It is well accepted by both prison officials and the courts that realizing these goals necessitates the complete observation of inmates at all times. It is believed that this panoptic regime enables the guards to prevent inmates from harming the guards, other inmates, or themselves. Thus, while prison inmates suffer a loss of privacy that would violate the constitutional rights of nonincarcerated individuals, this loss is regarded as acceptable given the intolerable dangers that can arise behind closed doors and privacy screens. Bill Martin, director of the MDOC, testified that

> any time you put barriers in a facility from observation, *direct observation*, it puts I think inmates and staff at certain risk. For instance, if a window curtain is up on a cell door and an officer, male or female, it doesn't matter, can't see in, there's no way we can intervene in a suicide attempt because we don't know that's going on. We just don't know what's behind it, and it seems contrary then to other recommendations that you put windows in other doors [so] that you can always see in.[7]

George Camp, a "corrections consultant," testified that doors and screens are

> barriers [that] give inmates an opportunity . . . to do things that they ought not be doing, for the staff not to be aware, not to interact with them, and I think that runs counter to being alert, observant, and in the know, and you have to have that. . . . Once you abandon any part of the turf at *any time* or *any place*, you have sent a signal that this belongs to the inmates and it cannot, and once you do that, it leads to a creeping and eroding of the legitimate rights, *the legitimate obligation of a prison staff to be everywhere*, to be informed, to be alert.[8]

So guards have not only the right but the duty to observe inmates at all times, including when they dress, shower, and use the toilet. But the question before the *Everson* court is this: Does requiring *male* guards to observe unclothed *female* inmates violate the female inmates' right to privacy to an intolerable degree? And this brings us to the Sixth District Court's second line of reasoning: that the safety and privacy interests of female inmates support the claim that all guards in women's housing units must be female.

Consider the court's discussion of the inmates' right to safety first. Declaring that "no amount of sexual abuse is acceptable," the *Everson* court agreed with the MDOC that it must adopt employment policies that ensure, as much as reasonably possible, the elimination of the sexual abuse of female inmates.[9] The MDOC argued that the only way adequately to protect female inmates was to hire only female prison guards. To hope to screen out the abusive male guards from the nonabusive ones was deemed unreasonable, since "some male officers possess a trait . . . a *proclivity for sexually abusive conduct*—that cannot be ascertained by means other than knowledge of the officer's gender."[10] Thus, to use the language of the BFOQ defense, the MDOC has claimed that it is a "basis in fact" that those with a proclivity for the sexual abuse of females are males, and that barring all males from employment as prison guards is a "reasonably necessary" means of ensuring that individuals with this "proclivity" are not unwittingly employed. So while the *Everson* court did not assert that *all* male guards will necessarily sexually abuse female inmates, it did assert that the very fact that a guard is a man gives sufficient reason to conclude that he may have "the proclivity" to be sexually abusive. Moreover, the MDOC argued, and the court agreed, that all other employment policies intended to protect male guards' right to equal employment opportunities (such as requiring that they be paired with a female guard) would necessarily compromise the inmates' safety. The court agreed with the MDOC that the complete elimination of all male guards from women's housing units was a reasonably necessary means of protecting female inmates from those guards with the "proclivity" for sexual abuse.

Notably absent from this discussion of sexual abuse proclivities is a defense of the assumption that female inmates will be safe (or, at least, substantially safer) in the hands of female guards. It seems the court believed either that no woman has a proclivity to abuse women sexually or that if some women do have such a proclivity, they are so rare that a female-only hiring policy does not put the female inmates in an unacceptably unsafe situation. Alternatively, the court may have been assuming that the sexual abuse of female prisoners by female guards is a less serious problem (that is, that it creates a less serious violation of an inmate's interest in safety) than the sexual abuse of female prisoners by male guards. I suspect that the notion of the sexual abuse of women prisoners by women guards was simply outside the court's conceptual framework. I return to these questionable assumptions later.

Of greater interest for the *Everson* court than the safety of the female inmates was the question of the right to privacy. Does a female prisoner's right to privacy necessitate the elimination of male guards? The court argued that it does. While acknowledging that all prisoners "lose many of their freedoms at the prison gate,"[11] the court claimed that a prisoner "maintains some reasonable expectations of privacy," particularly when it concerns forced exposure to strangers. Justice Rogers, writing for the *Everson* court, stated that most people have a special sense of privacy in their genitals, and involuntary exposure of them in the presence of people of the other sex may be especially demeaning and humiliating. . . . *We cannot conceive of a more basic subject of privacy than the naked body.* The desire to shield one's unclothed figure from view of strangers, and particularly strangers of the opposite sex, is impelled by elementary self-respect and personal dignity.[12]

The court noted that this "special sense of privacy" goes beyond shielding one's bare genitals while showering, dressing, or toileting, for it includes sleeping, waking up, brushing one's teeth, and requesting sanitary napkins.

The housing unit serves as inmates' "home," the place where they "let their hair down" and perform the most intimate functions like "showering, using the toilet, dressing, even sleeping." In the housing units, inmates spend a great deal of time in close contact with the officers, who supervise "the most intimate aspects of an inmate's life in prison, what time they go to sleep, where they sleep, when they get up, brush their teeth, use the restroom, shower, dress." [Moreover,] inmates must request sanitary napkins and other personal items from the officers.[13]

With this, the *Everson* court established that brushing one's teeth is an act of intimacy on a par with defecating. And with this alarmingly expanded notion of genital privacy, the court certainly ensured that there is no way to keep women inmates safe from male guards—for as long as a male guard can see the female inmate engaging in any act of intimacy (which he certainly *must* be able to do, to fulfill the requirements of his job), he is violating her "special sense of privacy."

Interestingly, this "special sense of privacy in our genitals" causes not only humiliation for the exposed person humiliation but discomfort for the "modest" observer as well. George Sullivan, a "corrections professional," testified that "as a simple matter of their own self-consciousness and modesty, most male staff are very reluctant to search women's garments, personal care/sanitary items, observe them nude in showers or while using toilets."[14] George Camp testified that male guards are "tentative" around female prisoners. Michael Mahoney, a corrections expert for the Department of Justice, testified that when male guards are "reluctant . . . to view females in a state of undress, in the use of toilet facilities, in dressing, and other kinds of situations, they may reluctantly, not pursue vigorously their supervision requirements because of the natural reluctance to not do that."[15] The unease male guards allegedly experience is so intense that the court claimed it reasonable to assume that they are incapable of competently performing their duties.

This line of reasoning is interesting for several reasons. First, safety and privacy interests, which began as two distinct matters, have merged and are now connected. Requiring the male guards to view the female inmates' acts of intimacy so discomforts the guards that they are incapable of fulfilling their job requirements, which therefore places them, the other guards, and all the prisoners at risk. Second, notice that the court has transformed a case inspired by the "rampant sexual abuse" of female prisoners—abuse that included horrific accounts of rape, sexual violence, degradation, and intimidation—into a discussion centered on the male guards' discomfort and modesty. The women prisoners are no longer victims of the male guards' sexual abuse; instead, it is the male guards who are incapacitated by their crippling embarrassment from having to see women prisoners use a toilet.[16]

But perhaps the most striking feature of this analysis of genital shame is the court's claim that male guards violate a female inmate's "special sense of privacy" through no fault of their own; it is their "very manhood" that is the source of the problem. I am not entirely clear what this "manhood" is (the presence of a certain set of genitals, the absence of another kind, specific levels of hormones, types of sexual desires and experiences, a sense of self-identification), since the court provides no indication. I do know that the court concludes it is because of the "manhood factor" that *no* male guard—no matter how conscientious, professional, and committed to justice—is able adequately to respect female inmates' privacy and maintain prison security.

Toilets and Sanitary Napkins

The court's reasoning in *Everson v. MDOC* is alarming: it rests on unjustifiable assumptions about sex and sexuality, in particular the notion of the untamable potency of maleness and necessary modesty of femaleness, and it prioritizes the validation of these assumptions over an interest in ending discriminatory employment practices.

Let's take a closer look at the claim that women have a special sense of privacy in their genitals. We saw that this special sense of privacy includes far more than the exposure of one's genitals to members of the "opposite sex" but extends to include brushing one's teeth, sleeping, and requesting a sanitary napkin. But how are we to make sense of the court's claim that a female prisoner's privacy is violated if she has to ask a male guard for a sanitary napkin (and the implied claim that her privacy is *not* violated if she makes the same request to a female guard)?

The most logical reason to request a sanitary napkin is so that one can attend to one's menstrual activities. Menstruation is a quintessentially female activity. Despite the fact that we all know that, in theory at least, most (if not all) the women prisoners will menstruate at some time while in prison, the particulars of these experiences are hidden from others. However, the moment one requests a sanitary napkin, this experience becomes public. Not literally—no one will see her menstruate. But that request makes public that she will menstruate or is menstruating right at the time of the request. And it must be something about that fact that is the source of embarrassment.

Iris Marion Young discusses societal attitudes about menstruation and the resulting imperative that women hide all evidence of their menstrual experiences:

> On the one hand, for a culture of meritocratic achievement, menstruation is nothing other than a healthy biological process. . . . On the other, from our earliest awareness of menstruation until the day we stop, we are mindful of the imperative to conceal our menstrual processes. . . . Keep the signs of your menstruation hidden—leave no bloodstains on the floor, towels, sheets, or chairs. Make sure that your bloody flow does not visibly leak through your clothes, and do not let the outline of a sanitary pad show. Menstruation is dirty, disgusting, defiling, and thus must be hidden.[17]

Young identifies the anxious bind menstruating women are in: they are normal and decent members of society as long as they are hiding the fact that they are menstruating. If they give any sign that they are at that moment bleeding—if they leak, let a tampon fall from their purse or pocket, allow a pad to bulge through their clothing, or talk about it in any way except in urgent whispers ("Do you have a tampon I can use? I got my period early!")—then they are disgusting and indecent. And while nonincarcerated women can hope to keep their menstruation out of the public eye, women prisoners cannot possibly keep their menstruation hidden from others. As long as they are under complete surveillance, as concerns for prison safety allegedly require, every aspect of their life, including their menstrual experiences, is on full view.

No wonder the *Everson* court cites having to ask a male guard for a sanitary pad as being a source of intense humiliation for a female prisoner—a humiliation so intense that requiring her to announce her menstrual needs is a violation of her constitutional rights. Of course, the exposure of one's genitals is not required when requesting a sanitary napkin, but the request makes clear that she *has* genitals, and that they are the kind of genitals that generate a bodily need that the male guard, as a male, does not have. So even though her genitals are politely hidden, her request publicizes those genitals as effectively as a strip search. The court is careful to insist that there is nothing about the male guard in particular that violates her privacy—nothing he believes, says, or does. Rather, it is his body—his "very manhood"—that causes the humiliation. Given the nature of her body and its dirty business, there is simply no way for him not to cause her humiliation. With this line of reasoning, the court clearly accepts the attitudes about menstruation that Young identifies. (Just what are we to make of that woman who unashamedly asks male guard for a sanitary pad or tells all and sundry about her menstrual cycle? She's a vulgar hussy—no wonder she's in prison!)

But what if we believed that all humans are essentially the same insofar as we all have bodies that need maintenance, that these maintenance activities are not shameful, and that to be observed engaging in such activities is not humiliating—no more humiliating than to be seen eating, for example? And what if we believed that a woman's body, though in some minor ways different from a man's, is not *essentially* different? And what if we believed that menstruation is a normal, healthy bodily activity? If we did hold these beliefs, then the notion of an adult woman feeling embarrassment when asking a man for a sanitary napkin is unremarkable—no more embarrassing than asking for a Kleenex.

In addition to disturbing attitudes about menstruation, the court's discussion of bodily privacy implicitly accepts the notion that men are less vulnerable to injury than women. Part of the very notion of "maleness" is the idea that men can easily (naturally?) tolerate experiences that would harm (or, perhaps worse, "toughen") women. Despite the court's claim to the contrary, this special sense of privacy concerning women's genitals does not seem to be universal, for when we look to the language of this case (and of the cases it cites as precedent), we see that U.S. courts treat a male prisoner's right to bodily privacy very differently—and far more cavalierly— than a female's. The *Everson* court states that the basis for this "right against the forced exposure of one's body to strangers of the opposite sex" is to be found in the Fourth and Eighth Amendments to the U.S. Constitution, as well as in the due process clause of the Fourteenth Amendment.[18] But the discussions of bodily privacy in these cited cases are not entirely consistent. The cases that concluded inmates have a right to be free of forced exposure to members of the opposite sex all concerned male guards subjecting female inmates to body searches, urinalysis tests, and strip and "pat-down" searches. The cases concerning male inmates being viewed by female guards were decided rather differently; in these, the courts argued that while male prisoners indeed have a *prima facie* right to bodily privacy, that right does not outweigh the needs of prison administration. For example, *Cornwell v. Dahlberg*—a case repeatedly used by the Sixth District Court as precedent for their decision in *Everson*—concerns a male prisoner's claim that being subjected to a body search in view of female guards was cruel and unusual and, therefore, was unconstitutional.[19] *Cornwell* concluded that the question is not whether or not a prison can permissibly subject a male prisoner to a body search in front of female prison guards—

the court declared that there is no doubt that it can—but instead whether or not the manner in which they conducted the body search violated the prisoner's constitutional rights. So, according to the *Cornwell* court, the discussion should focus on whether or not needless violence was used during a body search or a more comfortable location for the body search could have been found. In the *Cornwell* case, the body search was conducted outside on the cold, muddy ground. But since the body search took place right after a prison uprising, the court concluded that in such instances the needs of the prison can legitimize body searches of prisoners on cold, muddy grounds in full view of female prison guards. *Cornwell* concluded that blanket policies forbidding the exposure of prisoners' genitals before prison guards of the opposite sex would restrict the needs of the prison administration unduly.

The *Everson* decision that the female prisoners' rights to privacy entail ensuring that no male guards ever see their exposed genitals is a radical departure from precedents concerning male prisoners and a dramatic development of the (few) decisions concerning female prisoners. So why do our courts claim that prison administrators are free to subject male prisoners to treatment that, when inflicted on female prisoners, violates "simple human decency"? Perhaps it is that "manhood" factor of which the court speaks, which apparently inures men to privacy violations; for it certainly seems that a female's "womanhood" is nothing but a source of vulnerability. As evidence for the existence of "womanhood" and its nature, the *Everson* court cites a U.S. Supreme Court decision concerning the employment of female guards in Alabama maximum-security prisons. There the U.S. Supreme Court stated that

> the essence of a correctional counselor's job is to maintain prison security. A woman's relative ability to maintain order in a male, maximum-security, unclassified penitentiary of the type Alabama now runs *could be directly reduced by her womanhood*. There is a basis in fact for expecting that sex offenders who have criminally assaulted women in the past would be moved to do so again if access to women were established within the prison. There would also be a real risk that other inmates, deprived of a normal heterosexual environment, would assault women guards because they were women.[20]

The *Everson* court argues that, just as the "very womanhood" of a female guard will undermine prison security in men's prisons, so, too, does the "very manhood" of a male guard undermine his capacity to provide security in women's prisons. Notice, though, that a female guard's "womanhood" places her at risk of being victimized by male prisoners—her womanhood instigates her sexual victimization. But the male guard's "manhood" places the female prisoners at risk—his manhood victimizes them.

These twin assumptions—that women are by nature sexually seductive victims and that men are by nature sexual predators—perpetuate the most invidious and intolerable myths about men and women. And yet our courts are consistently relying on these myths when making decisions about the employment policies of prisons and about the treatment of its prisoners.

Privacy, but Not Safety

At first glance, *Everson* seems to be a victory for both women prison guards and women prisoners. Not only are women prison guards guaranteed access to certain employment opportunities at women's prisons in Michigan but, perhaps more important, women prisoners are guaranteed protection from the sexually abusive antics of male prison guards. Yet this victory is a pyrrhic one. As to the first concern, this case actually ensures that women prison guards will have dramatically reduced employment opportunities. Only about 4 percent of Michigan prisoners are women, and despite an increase in the general prison population in Michigan, the percentage of women prisoners is shrinking.[21] Thus, while women have been guaranteed access to a small number of jobs in women's prisons, that number is minuscule compared to the jobs that are being closed to them at men's prisons.[22]

As to eliminating sexual abuse, the *Everson* court claims that MDOC's sex-specific employment policy will eliminate sexual abuse perpetuated by male guards against female inmates. But there is no reason to believe that the policy will eliminate the sexual abuse of female inmates, for of course sexual abuse is not limited to incidents of men abusing women. Explaining its support of the elimination of male guards, the court mentions that 60 percent of the sexual misconduct charges lodged against COs between 1994 and 2000 were against male officers. This implies, of course, that 40 percent of the charges were against female officers. So a sex-specific employment policy will not eliminate, or even drastically reduce, the number of sexual assault cases that we can expect to occur in future years, when all the guards in the housing units are female. Why, then, does the court conclude that this sex-specific guard policy is the only way to ensure prisoner safety?[23] Perhaps the court is less concerned with the number of assaults committed by guards than with the kind of assaults committed. That is, perhaps they regard female-inflicted sexual assault as a less serious threat to female prisoner safety. Although such a belief would be hard to defend, it is in keeping with the idea developed earlier, that "manhood" is imbued with a kind of potency that makes manhood-motivated sexual assault a terrible harm. If one believes that "womanhood" is weak and prone to injury, it would make sense (in a very strange sort of way) to think that female-inflicted sexual assault is, while a bad thing, not nearly as damaging as male-inflicted sexual assault.[24]

Perhaps the court assumes that any same-sex sexual assault is less horrific than "cross-sex" sexual assault because same-sex sexual assault does not involve opposite-sex genital exposure and therefore avoids causing genital shame. But the sexual assault of male prisoners (by male prisoners and male guards) is considered a serious problem in our society, and all evidence suggests that incidents are on the rise. And I doubt anyone would take seriously the suggestion that male prisoners would be safer if all men's prisons followed MDOC's lead and adopted same-sex employment policies, so that male prisoners were victimized only by men.[25]

To understand the reasoning behind the MDOC employment policy, one must attend to the fact that sex-specific hiring applies only to female guards in the housing units, where, as the court stated, the women prisoners "let their hair down." The court cannot possibly think that housing units are the only sites for sexual assaults against women prisoners. Therefore, since male guards will continue to be employed in other locations within the women's prisons, they will still have ample opportunity to sexually assault the female prisoners. Despite the assurances of MDOC and the *Everson* court, we have no reason at all to think that this employment policy will reduce the number of sexual assaults committed by male guards.[26] So again we are back to the idea that there must be something very precious about those private moments during which one brushes one's teeth and hair, showers, sleeps, and uses a toilet. To be sure, most people would prefer to maintain a sense of modesty and not to be forced to expose their genitals to others. But I do not think anyone's objection to being sexually victimized stems from or is even essentially connected to their sense of modesty. Nor do I think anyone would prioritize privacy while using the toilet over security from sexual assault while in the dining hall or laundry. And, despite claiming to design an employment policy that will protect women's prisoners constitutionally guaranteed rights to safety *and* privacy, the *Everson* court has prioritized the right to privacy—and a patently gender-specific one at that—at the expense of the right to safety. Rather than focus on the serious injustices the women prisoners are suffering in these prisons, the court chooses to focus on the discomfort felt when asking for sanitary pads. In doing so, the court grossly trivializes sexual assault, undermines Title VII, and squanders the opportunity to require that the MDOC confront and resolve the myriad of problems within its prisons. The women prisoners may be spared the shame of being forced to urinate in view of male guards, but they are not safe, and the far-too-long-standing tradition of protecting female modesty at the cost of other interests continues.

Notes

1. *Everson v. Michigan Department of Corrections*, 391 F.3d 737 (2004).

2. For fuller discussions of the development of women's right to privacy being defined essentially in terms of protecting female modesty, see Anita L. Allen and Erin Mack, "How Privacy Got Its Gender," *Northern Illinois University Law Review* 10 (1990): 441–78; and Carol Danielson, "The Gender of Privacy and the Embodied Self: Examining the Origins of the Right to Privacy in U.S. Law," *Feminist Studies* 25, no. 2 (Summer 1990): 311–39.

3. *Dothard v. Rawlinson*, 433 U.S. 321 (1977); see also *Diaz v. Pan Am. World Airways, Inc.*, 442 F.2d 385 (1971).

4. *Workers of Am. v. Johnson Controls, Inc.*, 499 U.S. 187 (1991).

5. *Reed v. County of Casey*, 184 F.3d 597 (1999).

6. *Rhodes v. Chapman*, 452 U.S. 337 (1981).

7. *Everson v. MDOC* (2004); emphasis added.

8. *Everson v. MDOC* (2004); emphasis added.

9. *Everson v. MDOC* (2004).

10. *Everson v. MDOC* (2004); emphasis added.

11. *Everson v. MDOC* (2004), citing *Covino v. Patrissi*, 967 F.2d 73 (1992).

12. *Everson v. MDOC* (2004), citing both *Lee v. Downs*, 641 F.2d 1117 (1981), and *York v. Story*, 324 F.2d 450 (1963); emphasis added.

13. *Everson v. MDOC* (2004), citing testimony of Michael Mahoney, director of John Howard Association, a private, not-for-profit prison reform group and expert for the Department of Justice.

14. *Everson v. MDOC* (2004).

15. *Everson v. MDOC* (2004).

16. For an interesting discussion of the problems created for employers when female modesty and bathroom privacy are prioritized over employment equality, see Ruth Oldenziel, "Cherished Classifications: Bathroom and the Construction of Gender/Race on the Pennsylvania Railroad during World War II," *Feminist Studies* 25, no. 1 (Spring 1999): 7–41.

17. Iris Marion Young, *On Female Body Experience* (Oxford: Oxford University Press, 2005), 106–7.

18. *Everson v. MDOC* (2004).

19. *Cornwell v. Dahlberg*, 963 F. 2d 912 (1992).

20. *Dothard v. Rawlinson*, 433 U.S. 321 (1977); emphasis added.

21. My impression from this court case is that Michigan's prison population trends are typical and that this discussion can be extended to other state prison populations.

22. MDOC is not prohibiting men from holding all CO and RUO positions in women's prisons; rather, its female-only policy applies to guard positions in the housing units only. But the scope of *Everson* extends beyond women's prisons. The *Everson* court cites previous cases that considered the legitimacy of sex-specific employment policies in other contexts, including psychiatric hospitals, dormitories, and mental health care facilities. Yet none of the cases cited by the *Everson* court determined it legitimate to eliminate completely the employment of any member of one sex from all positions. Rather, each of the previous cases argued that reserving a small percentage of certain positions for members of one sex does not violate Title VII. (For example, an employer can specify that the third-shift janitor in a female dormitory be female but cannot employ only female janitors.) The *Everson* court has swept aside all of these previous efforts to balance equal employment interests with sex-segregation interests and instead has provided the groundwork for prioritizing sex discrimination over equality. And, given the history of employment discrimination women have faced in this society, I suspect that women will pay a high price for the preservation of their right to privacy.

23. The court does not reveal the relative percentage of male and female correctional officers, which makes a fully informed decision concerning the relative dangers of male and female guards impossible.

24. It is tempting to believe that the wrong of sexual acts between guards and prisoners stems not from the alleged "special sense of privacy in their genitals" but from the disparate

power relations between the guards and prisoners. Notice that if a female prisoner's genitals are exposed to a male guard, she is seen to have suffered a harm; yet, when a male guard exposes *his* genitals to a female prisoner, she *again* is seen to be a victim. Thus it would seem that it is not genital exposure per se that shames a person but the role one occupies (and whether or not one is choosing to expose one's genitals) that determines whether or not one is shamed. Yet consider this: three female prison guards who worked in the Baraga prison units in Michigan were charged with "having illegal sexual activity" with male inmates. Yet the perceived victims in this case are the women guards, not the male prisoners. This is because although the women guards chose to have sexual relations with the male prisoners, they are seen to have been duped by the male prisoners. County prosecutor Joseph O'Leary claims that the male prisoners "used that relationship to get into their worlds and lure them into [theirs]." Because the women were not raped (and not even being considered is the possibility that the men were raped by the women), O'Leary added that "there's no victim in the traditional sense." So why are criminal charges being brought against the three women guards, if no one believes the male prisoners were harmed and it is believed that the women were exploited? MDOC director Patricia Caruso explained the need for prosecution: "This type of activity is not acceptable," and the punishment of the guards sends a "loud and clear message" to other guards (John Flesher, "Female Prison Workers Accused of Sex with Male Inmates," Associated Press State and Local Wire, March 2, 2006). No doubt a message is being sent, but that message is not that any prisoner is vulnerable to the abuses of guards but that *women*—as prisoners *or* guards—are vulnerable to the abusive harms of "manhood." The real wrong the women guards committed, it seems, was in falling victim to the seductive manhood of the male prisoners.

25. The court's discussion of opposite-sex genital observation assumes that sex categories are binary and that all guards and prisoners are either male (with fully effective "manhood" powers) or female (with a fully existent "womanhood" in place). It seems that intersexual, transsexual, and transgendered guards and prisoners are simply not a conceptual possibility. Yet intersexuals, transsexuals, and transgendered guards and prisoners do exist, and their existence necessarily calls into question the court's simplistic assumptions about gender and sex.

26. Since the sex-specific employment policy has been in place, reports of sexual assault committed against female prisoners by male guards have increased. Deborah LaBelle, an attorney representing four hundred women prisoners in Michigan, stated, "The number of sexual assaults is on the rise. I think that it's a consistent system of denial. If you continue to deny that it's happening, you create the culture that's happening now." Patricia Caruso, the current MDOC director, responded, "Anyone can make a complaint, it doesn't make it true." See Amy F. Bailey, "Corrections Department Director Says Changes Are Keeping Abuse Down," Associated Press State and Local Wire, May 24, 2005.

6

Colonial Visions of "Third World" Toilets

A Nineteenth-Century Discourse That Haunts Contemporary Tourism

ALISON MOORE

In 1998, I spent three months in Tunisia studying Arabic and taking a much-needed holiday from my Ph.D. studies. An Australian woman of mixed heritage (including Cherokee Indian), my multilingualism, physical smallness, black hair and eyes, and yellow-toned skin allow me to blend in, or at least to defy categorisation, in a range of cultures. As a woman travelling alone in that region, I attracted an inordinate amount of attention but was also, perhaps due to my liminal status as an anomaly, privy to some insightful confessions and revelations from Tunisians and Algerians I met there.

I first began to think about the intersection between gender, colonialism and attitudes towards excretion as a result of this trip and other ones to India, Thailand, and various parts of Europe, where I saw multiple examples of the construction of codified attitudes towards toilet practices embedded in the politics of cultural difference. The most overwhelmingly common examples of this consisted of travellers who identified as "Western" experiencing disgust and discomfort at having to use squat toilets and having to go without toilet paper, and the (sometimes legitimate) fears of female travellers that public toilet use might expose them to sexual danger or unwanted sexual attention, which they associated with the "third world" nature of the cultures they were visiting. I also heard complaints from locals about the toilet practices of foreign travellers—namely, bemused or horrified attitudes towards the use of toilet paper, since it does not clean as effectively as the water used for postexcretory cleansing in a range of non-industrial and semi-industrial societies; or mockery of the common occidental inability to squat comfortably, due to the habit of daily chair sitting. These locals associated toilet paper with the polluting and wastefulness of the West and foreign toilet practices generally with the hypocrisy of Western attitudes of superiority towards their cultures.

In contemporary global tourism, those who have inherited the privileges and affluence provided by past colonial exploitation at times stand face to face with the inheritors of the very cultures who were dispossessed of an autonomous socioeconomic development by that colonial past. Ongoing inequalities between debtor and indebted nations moreover make the politics of (neo)colonial difference more than merely a vestige of some forgotten power exchange.

This chapter focuses on the anxieties of the Western gaze on excretory practices in less-affluent postcolonial cultures, arguing that these anxieties stem from a continuous and pervasive notion of the inherent relationship between progress, or the civilising process, and excretory control.[1] While contemporary tourists may often indeed demonstrate deeper respect for and knowledge about the cultures they encounter than any nineteenth-century colonist or exoticist ethnographer, their fears about filth, disease, and sexual danger associated with another culture's toilet practices are nonetheless still informed by assumptions of excretion as a signifier of social progress. But I also draw attention to the more complex way in which this heritage is played out across an axis of gender and cultural difference. In responding to this gaze and its incumbent assumptions, postcolonial subjects at times target gender as the point at which to challenge neocolonial power as expressed through the touristic demand for "Western" toilet facilities and toilet paper. Female tourists to these regions may also often internalise tensions around these issues in a gender-specific way. Stereotypes in some postcolonial cultures about sexually available Western women make all bodily practices seem more vulnerable for women travelling there, but in some cases their own conditioning around feminine propriety and dignity make adaptation to new toilet practices problematic.

Anecdote 1: Singapore airport. This is a scenario I have observed on numerous occasions, and anyone wishing to do the same need only visit the ladies toilets in the transfer terminal there. Squat toilets are the popular choice in Singaporean society, but tourists from wealthy industrial countries who use Singapore airport as a transfer point to travel between Europe and the United States or Australia are commonly unaccustomed to them. As a flight disembarks, a crowd of bowel- and bladder-full tourists cram into the first available toilets before looking for their transfer. In most female toilets there are three or four "Western" sit-down toilets and one or two squat toilets. The queue often runs out the door, since there are no more women's toilets than men's and the social need for cubicles makes the waiting far longer.[2] But no matter how great the urgency, the majority of female tourists prefer to wait rather than use the vacant squat toilets. Singaporean cleaners shake their heads with wry smiles at the fifteen-person queue for the sit-down toilets while the squat ones remain empty. For me the choice is clear, and one cleaner smiles warmly and nods encouragement at me as I opt for the squat.

Anecdote 2: Barcelona, January 1994. Before boarding an early-morning Sunday train to Paris, I decide to go to the toilet. A man around forty years old is sitting smoking a cigarette nearby and watches me intently as I pass. While on the toilet, I notice there is an evenly carved hole in the door and I hear slow footsteps heading towards my cubicle. A man's eye appears before the hole. In my paranoia I am well prepared and poke a finger sharply through the hole before the eye can focus. I hear the same footsteps retreat away, this time faster. It is the first time it occurs to me that using public toilets might expose women (myself) to sexual violation.

Anecdote 3: Tozeur, Tunisia, September 1998. Accustomed to the lack of toilet paper, and in any case content with the water-washing technique more common there, I take an empty bottle with me to fill at the tap before entering a posh hotel to use the toilet. The security guards ask me, "Hey what's the bottle for?" And I answer vaguely that it is to collect some water. They ask why. They know what it would be for if I were Tunisian, but perhaps they are baffled to see a foreigner resort to this in a fancy tourist hotel where toilet paper is supplied in anticipation of "Western" sensibilities. Perhaps, too, they are indignant that I imagine I might not find any there. Perhaps they are teasing me in a way that is funny only because I am woman and they know it would be improper for me to answer them honestly. From their curious combination of deeper knowing, surface uncertainty, feigned indignation, and humour, I suspect it is a combination of all these things.

Discussions of toilet practices and excretory taboos have formed a hidden but nonetheless consistent part of colonial and postcolonial discourses since the very beginning of modern European imperial expansion. How the other excretes and deals with excretory waste, or how one's own practices signify civilisation and progress—these ideas were embedded in European visions of conquered peoples from the sixteenth century. While constituting only minor and occasional observations in the early modern period, such claims were massively intensified throughout the nineteenth century in discourses about urban reform and in ethnographic theory. They were, moreover, imbued with a set of gendered assumptions about the colonising and civilising processes as a masculine agenda. Colonial inequalities underwent a pronounced domestication in the European metropolis in this period. The growth of ethnographic writing, the expansion of settler societies in colonised lands, and the importation of exotic consumer commodities all made for a European middle class that was unprecedentedly aware of its colonised other.[3] This heritage, too, lies beneath current-day visions of toilet practices as signifiers of "first" and "third" worlds, beneath the way in which excretion is problematically engendered by contemporary writers of travel guides, of journalistic exposés, and of Weblog exchanges in the late twentieth and early twenty-first century.[4]

Female travellers today invoke the spectre of these discourses most clearly due to their own marginal and ambivalent subject position within those older visions of civilisation and progress. Construed by many nineteenth-century thinkers as a "retarding force" in the masculine work of civilisation, women were situated both as targets for exotic consumer desire and as "cloacal" (and therefore primitive) in their imagined connection to the body and to matter. At the same, nineteenth-century visions of women as genteel and delicate made it a matter of great impropriety for them to use public toilets or for their excretory needs to be imagined, considered, or discussed. Moreover, the notion of women as less athletic, active, and dynamic than men made them subjects for the concerns of doctors writing about constipation. In psychoanalytic thought, it is the mother who stands at the forefront of both toilet training and sexual identity. Throughout the nineteenth century, then, women both constituted excretory conditioning and were denied it as a public convenience. Excretion itself, by contrast, was bound into notions of the primitive body that must be disciplined in the civilizing and colonising processes.

Excretion, Progress, and Civilisation

There is no doubt that from the second half of the nineteenth century well into the twentieth, toilet technologies were seen by many as signifiers of a stage of progress imagined along a universal social-evolutionary timeline. In an article arguing in favour of sewage recycling for agriculture, one late-nineteenth-century Parisian engineer could not resist the temptation to align what was in his view an archaic toilet technology (individual septic systems) with *la barbarie*, quipping, "Look what is tolerated . . . in a city that pertains to be at the head of progress in all things."[5] The notion that toilet practices reflect a culture's level of development was likewise expounded by early-twentieth-century sociologist Norbert Elias. Arguing that European table manners, habits of cleanliness, and excretory taboos were inherent to the creation of complex social structures and hierarchies in early modern Europe, Elias portrayed modern Western toilet functions as universally embedded in "the civilising process."[6]

Indeed, it was the metaphor of colonialism that Sigmund Freud used to describe the relationship of the civilised man to his own body.[7] Equating "the process of civilization" with "the libidinal development of the individual,"[8] Freud claimed that it was only through a collective sublimation of sexual and anal desire that civilisation could be achieved—that the accumulated energy of this sublimation was the fuel for the immense creative work of civilisation. "In this respect," Freud remarked, "civilization behaves towards sexuality as a people or stratum of its population does which has subjugated another one to its exploitation."[9] According to the Freudian schema, then, sexuality is itself collectively colonised through the develop-

ment of civilised society. But on the level of individual bourgeois accultura-
tion, excretion figures just as heavily. The development from childhood to
adulthood echoed that of the social evolution from primitivity to modernity. The (implicitly male) European child constructs his excreta as a "gift"
to the mother and must learn to "give up" his feces to the potty and subli-
mate the pleasure of defecating into an interest in money. Hence money
and excrement were, for Freud, "interchangeable" in the unconscious: to
be a wealthy was to be *filzig* (filthy) and to spend wildly was to be a *Dukat-
enscheisser* (shitter of ducats).[10] Excrement thus helped to construct the hi-
erarchy of matter by which civilised man learned to distinguish that which
was most valuable from that which was valueless. But at both extremes of
the spectrum, the two concepts merged within unconscious processes, with
the mother standing at the pivot. In the Freudian schema, then, while
women operate as the enabling mechanism for masculine Oedipal development of the individual, in the social evolution from primitive to civilised
they are living embodiments of the sexual instinct that must be repressed
for cultures to develop. They threaten the work of civilisation with their
"retarding and restraining impulses," since they represent "the interests of
the family and of sexual life" versus those of work and progress: "The
work of civilization has become increasingly the business of men, it con-
fronts them with ever more difficult tasks and compels them to carry out
instinctual sublimations of which women are little capable."[11] The individual (masculine subject) is "at loggerheads with the whole world."[12] Repression of desire is thus a uniquely masculine problem, one in which
women are a constant hindrance.

As Anne McClintock demonstrated in her landmark cultural history of
gendered colonial racism, *Imperial Leather*, feminine bodies and sexualities formed the symbolic framework for a specifically spatial mapping of
colonial wealth in the European imagination. The Portuguese explorer Jose
de Silvestre provided a literal example of this in a 1590 diagram of King
Solomon's Mines (redrawn in Henry Rider Haggard's novel of 1885) that
showed the location of the hidden bounty of colonial conquest as a woman's breasts and genitals, with the treasure itself lying just beyond the anal
entrance.[13] But similar symbolism lay even in visions of the European metropolis. Paris of the mid-nineteenth century contained great resources of
capitalist wealth, with its toiling masses and consuming middle classes,
while its essentially medieval sanitary system heaved under the strain of the
unprecedented population growth of the early 1900s. Urban planners
spoke of the Parisian absorption of outlaying townships as a kind of colonisation, while hygienists wrote about the revolutionary French working
classes as a primitive mass, the source of disease that must be tamed, contained, and sanitized.[14] As a number of historians have demonstrated, the
mid-century technologization of the Paris sewerage system, along with
concerns about urbanization and disease, formed a distinct discourse that

related cleanliness, odorlessness, and the masculine conquest of the filth of city life to the path of civilising progress.[15] In the 1830s, the French town planner Parent-Duchâtelet explicitly related prostitutes to excrement, noting that an abundance of both was inevitable in an urban district, and hence "the authorities should take the same approach to each": regulation, sanitization, and concealment.[16] Victor Hugo's 1862 novel *Les Misérables*, bound criminality to the sewers of Paris and nicknamed the early-nineteenth-century urban engineer Bruneseau the Christopher Columbus of the "cloaca."[17] Donald Reid notes the mentality that emerged under the regime of Napoléon III, during which time the Préfet de la Seine, Baron Georges Haussmann, led a major reconstruction of Paris, both above and below ground. The word *cloaque* (cloaca = the singular excretory, urinary, and generative orifice of birds), with its biological connotation, was increasingly replaced by the term *égout* (sewer), connoting a technological construction; as Reid puts it, "less a natural organ than a natural form subordinated to man's use."[18]

The late-nineteenth-century historian Aldred Franklin devoted an entire volume to the history of hygiene in his seven-volume study of *La Vie privée d'autrefois* (Private life in olden times), showing how the growth of glory of the French state and the moral rectitude of the French people coincided with the banning of public excretion and urination, with the deodorisation of Paris, and with the creation of an efficient sewage system. In Franklin's vision, the dirty, unrestrained habits of the medieval past are clearly bound up with an imagined lack of civilisation, understood in both socioeconomic and moral terms.[19] Franklin claimed that the first toilets in France were constructed in churches under the reign of Louis XVI and were referred to as *des lieux à l'angloise*, or "English-style places."[20] More commonly, though, when French writers discussed the virtues of Parisian excretory technology, it was in a tone of national pride. The writer Alfred Mayer, in his entry in the 1867 *Guide-Paris*, described the technologized sewers of Paris at that time as a clear sign that French civilisation had at last surpassed the grandeur of Ancient Rome.[21] The opening of the Paris sewers for public visits under the Second Empire was in part an issue of national rivalry, following the British Crystal Palace exhibition of 1851. Like all trade fairs and exhibitions in Europe of the late nineteenth century, the Crystal Palace exhibition had displayed exotic products from the colonies as tokens of national glory but also, more uniquely, was home to a spectacular electric lighting display. It also housed Europe's first flushing public lavatories.[22] Female public toilets in this period, however were rare, and unlike men's, they were more often paying facilities.[23] Sanitary engineers complained that women rarely used the facilities built for them, hence the reason few were built to begin with.[24] The discrepancy served to encourage the limitation of women to the private sphere, with forays into the public only as long as the intervals between bladder and bowel movements.

Taboos around female excretion, combined with the scarcity and expense of toilets, made it impractical for women to rely on public facilities.

In ethnographic writing, too, there was a symbolic association drawn between sublimated excretion, masculinity, and civilisation. From the very beginning of European colonial expansion, notions of inappropriate excretory practices figured amongst the signifiers of primitivism used to reassure colonisers of the moral legitimacy of disenfranchising conquered peoples. Seventeenth-century German Jesuit Jacob Baegert, for example, described the American Indians of Lower California as "a race of naked savages who ate their own excrement."[25] But the association of primitivity with excretory ingestion was primarily a late-nineteenth-century fixation. Anthropologist Peter Beveridge was so shocked by an excremental ritual he claims to have observed amongst a Victorian Riverina Aboriginal culture in southern Australia that the passage (concerning the use of young women's excreta to bring a dying person back to life) in his 1889 work appears in Latin.[26] The amateur American ethnologist John G. Bourke devoted an entire volume to the study of excremental practices amongst various "primitive" cultures, ranging from Tibet, the Philippines, and Mexico to the ancient Assyrians and medieval Europeans. Bourke tells us that the Romans worshipped a Goddess named Cloacina, guardian of the cloacas, sewers, and privies. Moreover she may have been confused with the goddess Venus, since statues of Venus were often said to be found at the cloacae of Ancient Rome. This slippage between deities of excrement and deities of sexual love appears in several of the cultures Bourke surveys: the Aztec mother of all gods, Suchiquecal, is said to eat *cuitlatl* (shit), though there is also an Aztec goddess of ordure, Tlaçolteol, mentioned by several sources, who presided over lovers and carnal pleasures, was the goddess of "vices and dirtiness," of *"basura ó pecado"* (ordure and sin), and "eater of filthy things." The Assyrians, Bourke says, offered excrement and flatus as oblations to Venus, while witches of the medieval Europe kissed the anus of Satan in worship.[27] The implication in Bourke's compendium is that excretory rituals follow from a lack of "civilisation." Europeans, while once prone to such behaviour, had progressed to another stage of social development, and those who still practiced excretory rituals were embodiments of what Europeans once were in the timeline of progress. Notably, the only examples Bourke cites of such behaviour involve mad people and a woman, who consumed her husband's excrements. A pregnant farmer's wife from the town of Hassfort on the Main "ate the excrements of her husband, warm and smoking."[28]

As Mary Douglas notes, early anthropologists tended to characterise "primitive" attitudes towards bodily functions as "autoplastic"—revelling in the body and its products—unlike the "alloplastic," "civilised" man, who abjects fecal matter as filth.[29] Excretion functioned as a signifier of progress in the modernist schema precisely because it represented the ultimate valueless matter. As James Frazer argued in the seminal anthropological work of 1890, *The Golden Bough*, "savage societies" were primarily characterised by a failed or inverted system of value: "the conception[s] of holiness and pollution" were "not yet differentiated." Dirty things such as excrement and menstruation could be esteemed as ultimately valuable, while chiefs, hunters, and other powerful figures could be marked as taboo.[30] Fraser's coupling of excrement with menstrual blood is revealing of the symbolic associations of this time. While discussion of real women's toilet needs within metropolitan public space functioned as "unspeakable" in the late nineteenth century, women by nature were nonetheless inherently imagined to be closer to excretion than men.

Late-nineteenth-century Europe also saw the emergence of an unprecedented fixation with intestinal health. Hygiene manuals and medical writings emphasised intestinal stasis as the source of all ill health, advising readers in the use of purgative medicines, enemas, diet, exercise, and lifestyle control and often depicting constipation as the quintessential disease of the civilised European, due to the emergence of sedentary lifestyles of the burgeoning middle classes.[31] Stimulant sweets, coffee and tea, and new consumer commodities derived from colonial exploitation of South American, African, and Indian produce were increasingly used by Europeans and were often recommended by medical guides and even by government officials as valuable props for stamina in the working day—or, more particularly, as cures for constipation and urinary stagnation.[32]

Women were seen as more likely than men to suffer from constipation, due the growing bourgeois gender demarcation that relegated women to the domestic sphere, where minimal physical activity would stimulate the body's excretory processes.[33] That male and female excretion was not the same was something that had already been claimed by medical writers at the end of the eighteenth century: in a 1785 text about toilet technologies, M. Hallé of the Faculté de Médecine de Paris stated, as a well-known fact, that men's excreta were large and firm, while women's were small and soft.[34] No doubt because of the gender-divided public and private spheres, and perhaps also because of assumptions about women excreting less than men, public toilets for women in nineteenth-century Europe were nonexistent before 1859 and few and far between after that date.[35] As historians such as Christopher Forth, Michael Hau, and Ina Zweininger-Bargielowska have shown, French, German, and British concerns about hygiene of the body were often profoundly gendered.[36] Constipation, for instance, was seen as linked to weight gain, and contrary to late-twentieth-century discourses that tended to view fatness in women as the object of far greater cultural obsession than in men, in the late nineteenth century masculine corpulence occupied the thoughts of many hygienists and medical writers, who viewed it as a deviation from normative masculinity and as a sign of the degeneration of the national physique.[37] While some writers viewed women as more likely to develop constipation due to inactivity, many saw men's obesity (and hence, implicitly, men's constipation) as a more serious problem. Referring to masculine constipation as "the white man's burden," early-twentieth-century British hygienist Frederick Arthur Hornibrook looked to images of healthy, fit "native" men as models of abdominal health.[38]

Colonial Diarrhea

Perhaps of greatest interest as background to a study of contemporary tourism in the postcolonial world is the body of texts that related colonial enterprise in the nineteenth century to prevailing concerns about the health and hygiene of European subjects. Although hygienic fears about intestinal health and notions of sublimated excretion as "civilised" were clearly a part of European self-reflection in metropolitan societies, they were uniquely pronounced and aggravated when faced with cultural difference in colonial settlements across the seas. While the bourgeois French, British, and German city was imagined to be naturally constipated by the sedentary lifestyle of European modernity, the colonial world was seen almost systematically as a coherent geographic zone that inflicted diarrhea on the European males who lived there. Dr. Georges Treille was professor of navy hygiene and exotic diseases and Inspecteur Général of the French Colonial Health Services during the 1890s. His 1899 book *Principles of Colonial Hygiene* stated well the relationship between metropolitan and colonial hygiene concerns: if *Hygiène* (with a capital H) was essential to European civilisation generally, then it was doubly so in the colonies.[39] Using interchangeably the terms *the colonies* and *the hot countries* or *the tropical countries*, Treille argued that a concerted effort was required to ensure both the good health of European settlers and their successful governance in lands so "inhospitable to the European race."[40] While stating from the beginning that it is not the climate that determines disease in the tropics or colonies, but rather "crimes committed against hygiene,"[41] Treille devoted the majority of his book to an explanation of how heat, humidity, and the abundance of microbes in Africa resulted in a higher number of serious epidemics and greater general ill health resulting from diarrhea or other fevers and infections. "Tropical climatology" was thus, "in biological sense, more hostile to the European."[42]

It becomes clear what Treille imagined to be the central "hostility" at stake when he stated: "All the experience of my career has led me to consider gastro-intestinal dyspepsia to be universal amongst Europeans in the hot countries." It was the source of all other illness even in Europe, he claimed, and in the colonies was practically inescapable.[43] Ironically, Treille acknowledged that it was often European settlement that resulted in epidemiological crises in Africa—the diseases that afflicted French colonies in Africa in the late nineteenth century (cholera, typhoid, etc.) were indeed European importations.[44] The hasty construction of administrative centres governed by strategic military imperatives rather than consideration of water-drainage geography was frequently the source of poor sanitation in expanding towns, such as in Kayes and Bafoulalé in the Sudan and Saint-Louis and Grand-Bassam on the Ivory Coast; indeed, the French were forced to abandon the latter settlement in 1899 due to an epidemic of cholera.[45] Unsurprisingly, Treille's study has nothing to say about the effect of these diseases on the colonised peoples of these lands. Somehow, it is their land that is hostile to Europeans, and not Europeans to them. "Contrary to popular opinion," claimed Edouard Henry in 1893, places with hot climates did not systematically cause illness;[46] good health was possible for Europeans in the colonies, but only if they exercised moderation in their lifestyle habits, in particular with regard to food.[47]

Another 1901 text on health in the colonies by Paul d'Enjoy is devoted almost entirely to a description of gastrointestinal illnesses, such as the exotically nicknamed Asian diarrhea he calls La Cochinchinite (Cochinitis).[48] A 1933 work by the doctor Adolphe Bonain echoed late-nineteenth-century claims: colonial troops must be fed better than those stationed in Europe, in order to ensure their intestinal health.[49] The exotic substances so treasured by Europeans as stimulants (coffee, tea, sugar) were to be avoided in the colonies due to their tendency to aggravate nervous conditions, even if the drive to consume them—sociability—was one of the "most legitimate aspirations of civilised man."[50]

Contemporary Tourism and Postcolonial Toilets

Comparing these accounts to a present-day French medical travel guide, one sees vestiges of the nineteenth-century mingling of excretion, gender, and colonialism. The 2003 travel guide by Dr. Evelyne Moulin reiterates the nineteenth-century adage that diarrhea in the tropics is the source of all ills for visiting Europeans. The argument here, though, is more modern: the presence of diarrhea suggests exposure to a harmful micro-organism, which could mean that one has also been exposed to more serious bacteria, viruses, and so forth; or, if one has not already been exposed, having diarrhea weakens the immune system and could leave the traveller more susceptible to serious infections in the future.[51] While I am not suggesting there is anything inherently racist about informing travellers of the likelihood of intestinal disturbance from exposure to unfamiliar bacteria, it is nonetheless revealing to examine the language used by contemporary travel writers when they talk about the health issues of their assumed "Western" public. Moulin's advice on how to avoid traveller's diarrhea is fairly standard: do not drink the water, and avoid raw foods and shellfish. Yet she repeatedly uses the term *La Turista* to describe the phenomenon of traveller's diarrhea, a term employed widely by travellers to South America but which resonates a curious exoticism, implying diarrhea itself to be both inherently foreign and feminine.[52] (The word is feminised because *diarhée* is a feminine noun in French, as its equivalent is likewise in other Romance languages, but *la turista* means also "the female tourist.") A recent general travel guide to Mexico City by John Noble repeats the use of this word while offering an alternative nickname for the diarrhea experienced by travellers to Mexico: "Montezuma's revenge," a fascinating construct that implies diarrhea to be the punishment of Westerners by the spirit of the Aztec king who mistook Hernán Cortés for a god in the original colonial conquest of Tenochtitlán in 1519.[53] Implicitly in these accounts, then, traveller's diarrhea hovers symbolically somewhere between the feminine and the colonial, marking and linking both.

Warnings about diarrhea and about toilet usage appear in a large number of travel guides to poor countries[54] but rarely appear in travel guides to more affluent ones or to countries with no colonial past. Travel guides generally attempt to prepare the traveller for unfamiliar or unexpected differences in daily habits, yet toilet practices differ even from one European culture to another (for instance, the prevalence of bidets in France and Italy, or of flat toilet bowls that do not allow excreta to slip directly in the water that one finds commonly throughout central Europe). Somehow, though, the differences between cultures that squat and wash and those that sit and wipe are seen as more traumatic than any other kind. This difference is overwhelmingly the focus of travel-guide accounts of foreign toilet experiences. Mexican public toilets rarely stock toilet paper, John Noble tells us; "it's worth carrying a little of your own."[55] Travellers to South India and to Bangladesh are reassured by several recent travel guides that there is no need to adapt to local customs of left-hand water washing, since "toilet paper is widely available."[56] In Central America, by contrast, one should "never assume that because there is a toilet there is paper."[57] In Java "it is seldom supplied in public places, though you can easily buy your own."[58] In Turkey, we are told, "Carry your own";[59] in Taiwan, "Toilet paper is seldom available in public toilets so keep a stash of your own with you at all times. If you do forget to take some there are vending machines that dispense paper—keep some change handy."[60] Curiously, none of the travel guides I have consulted actually suggests to travellers that they simply follow local custom and forget about toilet paper in favour of left-hand water washing, although one guide acknowledges that this is an option if one forgets one's stash of toilet paper.[61]

Traveller's Weblogs are consistent with published accounts on this issue and, because anonymous, are often more explicit, though problematic, sources.[62] Under the heading of "Squatting Questions," one Lonely Planet Southeast Asia Thorn Tree blogger asked of experienced travellers to this region: "Do they sell toilet paper everywhere, even in the countryside? Or do I have to stock up in the large cities?" and "Have any of you lost your balance while squatting and gotten a little messy? I have read that diarrhea is very common in SEA. Does it ever spray on your shoes or legs? I have never squatted before. I am not looking forward to it. I am thinking about practicing now, so I don't lose my balance when I am there. Does one lean forward while squatting, so that your butt is pointed out more? Or do you get your butt as close to the ground as possible in a relaxed squat? Are there bars or handles you can grab to balance yourself? I know the questions are a bit odd. I am just curious." An enthusiastic range of replies included complaints about squat toilets and bad smells, as well as advice about carrying one's own toilet paper and using facilities in hotels and restaurants.[63]

While some guides do discuss the reason for water washing in many cultures, others patently fail to advise travellers that using toilet paper in plumbing systems not designed for such slow-degrading matter is highly irresponsible, as it can result in plumbing blockages that render the toilets of an establishment unusable.[64] One guide, assuming there to be a natural evolution from water washing to toilet-paper usage, describes toilet systems not equipped for paper as "antiquated": "designed in the pre-toilet paper era."[65] Here there is an assumption that toilet technology follows a simple linear development from squatting and washing to sitting and wiping—an assumption perhaps fuelled by a new dynamic in which postcolonial societies do appear to be moving in this direction in order to attract more income to the tourist industry.

Different continents' toilet structures, physical adjustments to them, and their smells receive wide discussion and comparison in travel media. On the Lonely Plant Africa Thorn Tree Web site, one traveller recounts, "I've gotten used to squat toilets even though I swore I never would (though I still hate, um, going #2 in them)."[66] Another blogger counters that "dirty filthy squat toilets are something I never get used to. I came to love the clean squats that I experienced in south-east Asia, but the dirty scary foul smelling public squats of Africa are forever ingrained in my mind."[67] Many accounts assume the reader to have the stereotypically stiff hips attributed to chair-sitting Westerners. Robert Storey tells us, "It takes some practice to become proficient at balancing yourself over a squat toilet."[68] A Thorn Tree blogger explains, "Squatting is a completely natural pose. In Asia and Africa adults use the pose as well, but westerners 'forget' how to squat like that when they grow up so when you first have to do it after twenty years you'll find your calf muscles are no longer used to it. It is just a matter of training and stretching."[69] One account acknowledges that "the experts who are employed to study such things (scatologists?) claim that the squatting position is better for the bowels," though the travel writer notes that the absence of seat toilets in Taiwan does mean that there is "no seat for you to sit on while you read the morning paper."[70] Turkey's toilets consist of two kinds, we are told: the "familiar" raised-bowl commode and the squat-type *alaturka*.[71] In West Africa, too, there are "two main types of toilet: Western sit-down style, with a toilet-bowl and seat; and African squat style, with a hole in the ground."[72]

The assumption that a squat toilet is an inferior technology appears widespread amongst both guide books and Web accounts. Seatlike toilets are clearly associated for many travellers with "Westernisation," modernisation, and progress. "A sign of change in Delhi is the swish new public toilets," one guide book announces happily; however, "in older parts of Delhi little has changed and there is a pervasive smell of dried urine."[73] In Java, we are told gloomily, "Another thing which you may have to get adjusted to is the Indonesian toilet. It is basically just a hole in the ground . . . over which you squat and aim." But on the bright side, "In tourist areas and big cities, Asian toilets are fading away as more places install Western-style toilets."[74] The imagined evolution from squat to sit again here looms like an inevitable force of progress. It is curious, moreover, that toilets are seen as being divided into two types, when in fact there are multiple variations of design of seat and squat toilets, some of which combine both possibilities (one guide book refers to these as "weird hybrids").[75] Even more curious is the notion that a seatlike toilet is "Western" while a squat toilet is "Asian," "alaturk" (in the Turkish style), or "African." Squat toilets are indeed common in many parts of the world—they were the norm in France throughout the early twentieth century and exist there still in many old buildings—and seat toilets are the norm in many cultures not commonly deemed "Western," for instance, in South America and Japan. Toilets, however, are largely imagined to fall neatly along a dichotomous axis of East/West, with the former seen as more primitive, holding out like some stubborn force of nature against the technological tide of modernity, progress, and civilisation.

Money is an issue that appears in a number of travel accounts about toilets. A Southwest China guide tells us, "Be careful in public toilets. Quite a few foreigners have laid aside their valuables, squatted down to business, and then straightened up again to discover that someone had absconded with the lot."[76] Another guide tells us, "While you are balancing yourself over one of these devices [squat toilets], take care that your wallet, keys and other valuables don't fall out of your pockets into the abyss."[77] In Turkey, "most public toilets require payment of a small fee (around US$0.25),"[78] and in Central America, "occasionally, a public toilet will have an attendant offering toilet paper for a small tip."[79] One blogger recounted with horror how in the Philippines the writer was questioned by a "comfort room" attendant about whether he or she intended to urinate or defecate and was told it would be five pesos for the first and ten for the latter (for the use of additional toilet paper).[80] Another blogger claimed that in Turkey, "u [sic] can see a note like this on the doors of toilet . . . : 'kucuk' . . . 'TL, buyuk' . . . 'TL; kucuk literally means 'little' but refers to 'pee' and buyuk literally means 'big' but refers to 'poo' and of course having 'buyuk' is more expensive than having 'kucuk' . . . TL = turkish lira." A reply by another blogger reads: "And you're [sic] point is . . . you're complaining of US$0.20 you have to pay to take a shit?"[81]

These tourists are horrified to find a price placed on their differentiated bodily functions, because social conditioning within their own cultures glosses over the specifics of defecation and urination, subsuming both under a polite and disembodied notion of "going to the toilet" or "going to the bathroom." In middle-class circles in the United States, someone who announces the precise bodily practice they will undertake can expect to receive the quip "That is too much information." And so the delineation of defecation and urination in postcolonial cultures is regarded as a violation of propriety. Charging money for individual bodily acts, moreover, is seen as beyond the pale of decency. In a Freudian analysis, this could be read as simply too close to the bone: excretion, which is sublimated to understand money, cannot thereafter be costed itself.

Concerns about how public toilet use affects women also feature in many travel accounts and guides. Under the heading of "Things You Could Never Get Used to in Africa," Thorn Tree bloggers recount how they "found it very difficult to get used to the unisex toilets in the bars in Ethiopia. Not cool and hip unisex but, you often had to walk past the urinal lined up with drunk and randy men to get to the squat toilets."[82] In Turkey, "some women report that when trying to use toilets in cheap restaurants, they've been told the facilities are unsuitable."[83] In Pakistan, "for women the lack of public toilets is no laughing matter, and requires daily planning." The authors advise male travellers to follow local custom and defecate in public using a *salwar kameez* to cover themselves, but for women they suggest using toilets in top-end hotels or returning to one's own hotel room each time one needs to go.[84] Curiously, there is little speculation about how local women deal with the absence of toilets (either public or private). Indeed, the scant availability of toilets in India, Bangladesh, and Pakistan is the subject of a great deal of gender speculation not only by travellers but by a range of social commentators. One *New Statesman* journalist claims, "The majority of Indian women have to wait until after it gets dark before they can answer the call of nature."[85] None of these writers seems to consider that the use of long skirts or tunics by the majority of Indian women provides a measure of privacy for public bodily functions in the same way that the use of long tunics does for men. In cultures where female exclusion from public life is traditional, public toilet facilities for women will invariably be poor, but this deeper problem of gender-differentiated zones is an uncomfortable one for many to acknowledge because of the tendency to imagine this as parallel to the exclusion of women from public life in European's own past. Gender inequality is often imagined along a simplistic binary evolutionary timeline—the liberated "our days" and the repressive "olden days"—that ignores the reality that female public excretion became a European problem only in the nineteenth century. Precisely for fear of drawing the conclusion that postcolonial women have no public toilet practices because they are not "yet" liberated like the West, the problem of female public excretion is left vague.

One British *Handbook for Women Travellers* discusses this issue in some detail, complaining, "Very few guide books mention loos at all, let alone tell you where they can be found," and stating that "it is a particularly female problem." This, the writers claim, is because men can "relieve themselves with relative decency." [86] Presumably here they mean urination, as their claim would not appear to stand up in the case of defecation. Quotations from women travellers in this collection reveal a wide range of variations amongst the cultures within which women travel. One traveller to Morocco complained of toilets that are "unisex and deplorable." One traveller to Afghanistan (in the 1980s) complained that bus stops were never long enough to go in search of a bush or other covering, so both local and tourist women stayed seated for the full six-hour journey. By contrast, we are told that Peruvians "are used to seeing women squatting."[87] Over the years I have heard numerous travellers describe their disgust, even horror at the sight of Indian men squatting to excrete in front of others during train stops. Based on a similar observation, French scatology writer Jacques Frexinos characterises India as land of free inhibitions in relation to excretory taboos, but he ignores the restraints more commonly placed upon women.[88] Julia Kristeva, too, was intrigued by this question in her seminal text on the symbolism of abjection, *Powers of Horror*. Her claim is that while the lower-body generally is mapped as both a site of taboo and desire in Indian-subcontinent cultures, public urination or defecation passes in these cultures via a dualistically hovering field in which impurity and law may interact but are not unified.[89]

So while European thinkers find in India a useful point of contrast to their own symbolic systems surrounding public excretion, few seem prepared to consider the problem from a gendered perspective, and those who do consider gender (because their book is about women travellers) only generalise about it as a "feminine problem" but give no analysis of how systems of public excretion and gendered propriety function and differ across postcolonial tourist destinations. Defecation hovers in this text as an unvoiced negation: "Unless you're just having a pee" begins the sentence about outdoor squatting. The something else one must be doing if not "just having a pee" appears unspeakable.[90]

On the whole, discussions of bad smells, inadequate sewage systems, and poor plumbing feature consistently in a range of visions of the "third world." A lack of "civilisation" is still imagined to be manifest in laissez-faire attitudes towards bodily functions or in a lack of abjection of excretory matter. As one blogger complains, "If you have been to some of the countries in West Africa, you will see many people use the beaches for toilets. Ugh!" [91] Another remarks, "Public urination . . . that always bothers me. I guess when you have to you have to go. Cosmo you know what I mean after travelling to Guinea-Bissau right?" [92] Further, the genre of news article about population growth in India and China that is so popular amongst neoliberal journalists almost systematically invokes the issue of poor sewage systems and lack of public toilets. Adam Hochsfield writes of

Bangladesh that "sewage leaks into freshwater lines and some two million people are without access to private or public toilets."[93] Edward Luce, in an article about how India and China will dominate the world economy by 2050, remarks that "less than a third of Indian homes have an indoor toilet. Public toilets barely exist."[94] A Web site called India: An Insider's View states, "Quite a few foreigner have a dread of Indian toilets," and provides a several-hundred-word survival guide on how to use squat toilets most hygienically, how to clean oneself afterward, and how to buy tissue paper in India.[95] Clearly, India does have massive sanitation concerns that are the topic of much discussion amongst Indian public health campaigners.[96] These discussions typically focus on the problem of disease, while non-Indian diatribes emphasise the filth and horror of poor sanitation.

A concern about building toilets is not itself a sign of some deeper continuity with nineteenth-century visions of sublimated excretion as progress, but when the language of description is one imbued with dread and otherness, there is reason to believe an older symbolism to be active still.

Conclusion

Toilet anxieties and intestinal health issues remain ongoing concerns for Western-identifying tourists today because it is primarily via these corporeal zones that such tourists imagine the lands they visit to be inhospitable. While the concerns travel advisors raise about diarrhea and toilet safety may be legitimate, complaints about excretory discomfort and expressions of disgust function as a kind of dumping ground for a range of resentments and traumas relating to cultural difference, or to an awareness of the colonial past. Although complaining about unfamiliar customs is not necessarily a signifier of colonially inspired cultural difference, the language of progress that travel writers use in their descriptions of toilet technologies in poor countries suggests the older discourse outlined in the first half of this chapter is still at play in contemporary attitudes.

According to psychoanalytical mappings of the body, the anus acts as the zone through which the Superego is constructed, that part of the self that ensures conformity, respect for authority, and comprehension of money. Spanking of a child on the buttocks reinforces this association of anality with authority, but the association exists already with the requirement to "give up" one's excreta or to give up the pleasure of retention and "spend." The emotional drive behind the Superego is always guilt. It is guilt that determines that we censor ourselves, control ourselves without the need for external authority. If travellers to postcolonial cultures experience anxiety about excreting or disturbance of their excretory functions, perhaps it is the shadow of the colonial past that haunts the contemporary body.

Lonely Planet guides are the richest source for such anxieties precisely because they are geared towards lower-income travellers who aim to travel cheaply and with a greater level of awareness of the cultures they visit. High-income travellers with unlimited disposable income are less likely to be forced to confront toilet differences, as they are able to rely on posh hotels and avoid material discomfort.

The characterisation of "non-Western" toilet models as belonging to some antiquated stage of development that has not "yet" been affected by the tide of globalised change suggests that a patronising gaze still constructs postcolonial cultures as being to "the West" what a child is to an adult. One blogger defending squatting nonetheless reiterates this logic: "Children all over the world can do it without a problem."[97] Some travellers indeed take seriously the challenges of cultural adaptation; not coincidentally, bloggers who propose that travellers simply adopt local toilet customs also tend to be those who invoke social responsibility about, for instance, not using toilet paper in countries where plumbing systems are not commonly designed for such behaviour. What travel blogs and guides cannot tell us, of course, is what the attitude is towards these issues amongst people who plan never to travel in poor countries, precisely due to an aversion to the filth they expect to encounter there. *Lonely Planet*, it is worth remembering, is probably not an example of the worst ethnocentrism that exists around this issue.

The reliance of many poor countries on tourist dollars is already forcing many cultures to provide so-called Western-style toilet facilities more widely, hence validating the vision of an evolution to sit-down toilets with toilet paper as a natural form of progress, in spite of the dubious nature of these practices both for intestinal health and for environmental sustainability. In Pakistan, "mid-range tourist hotels are now joining the top-end ones in going over to clean, tiled bathrooms and sit-down toilets, apparently under pressure from western group tour operators."[98] If female tourists cannot merely squat beneath their *salwar kameez*, as male tourists are encouraged to do, then they are implicitly invoked as the pressuring force on the colonial world to adapt it toilet customs to the needs of the affluent visiting West. If the naughty children of the underdeveloped world will not willingly give up their excremental autoplasticism to the parental will of the West, then the power of money will make them do so. Tourist dollars that create pressure on the postcolonial world to conform toilet practices to "Western" sensibilities also reinforce myths about the shift to sit-down toilets with paper as inevitable progress, coupled with "advanced" technology.

That women are especially implicated in this dynamic due to their own cultural inhibitions about toilet practices is consistent with older discursive associations between gender and excretory sublimation. While the feminised, cloacal primitivity of the postcolonial world is seen as requiring subjection to the masculine work of progress, women, too, function as objects within the Oedipal drama, this time played out as a neocolonial demand for tourist industries in struggling third world economies. Female tourists create a pressure on tourist industries of the postcolonial world to adopt

"Western" facilities. At times, women's role in this schema relates to their own toilet conditioning; at times, to how they disrupt gendered divisions of public and private life in cultures where there is a strict demarcation. As in the nineteenth century, envisioning toilet technologies as a binary of East versus West, old versus new, continues to use gender as the pivot.

Notes

1. This is not to deny the reality of the epidemiological dangers that can result from inadequate sewage treatment systems in underdeveloped economies, nor the reality of intestinal illness experienced by Western travellers exposed to unfamiliar bacteria in Africa and Asia. However, all the sources I discuss here share a discursive thread that predates modern medical definitions of bacteriology.

2. See Barbara Penner, "Female Urinals: Taking a Stand," in *Room 5: Arcade*, no. 2, ed. Nina Pearlman (London: London Consortium), 25–37.

3. See Timothy Morton, *The Poetics of Spice: Romantic Consumerism and the Exotic* (Cambridge: Cambridge University Press, 2000); also Alison Moore, "Kakao and Kaka: Chocolate and the Excretory Imagination of Nineteenth-Century Europe," in *Cultures of the Abdomen: Diet, Digestion and Fat in the Modern World*, ed. Christopher E. Forth and Ana Carden-Coyne (New York: Palgrave Macmillan, 2005), 51–69.

4. The Lonely Planet Thorn Tree Web site houses an English-language Weblog for travellers, grouped under regional headings, and provides a forum for the exchange of information and personal experiences about travel from those who have undertaken tourism or who intend to do so. All the pages cited here are available at http://thorntree.lonelyplanet.com.

5. My translation: Anonymous, "Construire des fosses à notre époque c'est de la barbarie, c'est du gaspillage de la fortune publique," *Bulletin de l'Industrie de Paris* 1 (August 1863): 5.

6. Norbert Elias, *The Civilizing Process*, trans. Edmund Jephcott (Oxford: Blackwell, 1978).

7. Indeed, Ranjana Khanna has recently argued that psychoanalysis itself needs to be understood as a form of knowledge arising out of colonial relations, as a "theorization of nationhood and selfhood as they were developed in response to colonial expansion." Ranjana Khanna, *Dark Continents: Psychoanalysis and Colonialism* (Durham: Duke University Press, 2003), 28.

8. Sigmund Freud, "Civilization and Its Discontents," in *The Freud Reader*, ed. Peter Gay (London: Vintage, 1989), 742.

9. Ibid., 746.

10. Sigmund Freud, "On the Transformation of the Instincts with Especial Reference to Anal Erotism," in *Freud: Collected Papers*, vol. 2, ed. John D. Sutherland, trans. Joan Rivière et al., (London: International Psycho-Analytical Library, 1950), 168; Sigmund Freud, "The Dissolution of the Oedipus Complex" in *The Freud Reader*, 661–64; Sigmund Freud, "Character and Anal Erotism," in *The Freud Reader*, 294–97.

11. Freud, "Civilisation and Its Discontents," 745–46.

12. Ibid., 729.

13. Anne McClintock, *Imperial Leather: Race, Gender and Sexuality in the Colonial Conquest* (New York: Routledge, 1995), 1–3.

14. Catherine J. Kudlick, *Cholera in Post-Revolutionary Paris: A Cultural History* (Berkeley: University of California Press, 1996), 213–16. Also, David Harvey, *Paris, Capital of Modernity* (New York: Routledge, 2003), 1–20.

15. Alain Corbin, *Le Miasme et la jonquille: l'odorat et l'imaginaire social, xviiie–xixe siècles* (Paris: Editions Aubier Montaigne, 1982), 167–88; François Delaporte, *Le Savoir de la maladie: Essai sur le cholera de 1832 à Paris* (Paris: Presses Universitaires de France, 1990), chap. 5; Dominique Laporte, *L'Histoire de la merde* (Paris: C. Bourgois, 1993); Donald Reid, *Paris Sewers and Sewermen: Realities and Representations* (Cambridge, Mass.: Harvard University Press, 1991).

16. Alexendre Jean-Baptiste Parent-Duchâtelet, *De la prostitution dans la ville de Paris, considérée sous le rapport de l'hygiène publique, de la morale et de l'administration: Ouvrage appuyé de documents statistiques puisés dans les archives de la Préfecture de police, avec cartes et tableaux*, vol. 1 (Paris: J. B. Baillière, 1837). I am indebted in this observation to the superb social history by Reid, *Paris Sewers and Sewermen*, 23–24.

17. Victor Hugo, *Les Misérables*, in *Oeuvres Complètes*, ed. Jean Massin, vol. 11 (Paris: Club Français du Livre, 1969), 879.

18. Reid, *Paris Sewers and Sewermen*, 36.

19. Alfred Franklin, *La Vie privée d'autrefois*, vol. 8: *L'Hygiène; Arts et métiers, modes, moeurs, usages des Parisiens du douzième au dix-huitième siècle d'après des documents originaux ou inédits* (Paris: Librairie Plon, 1890).

20. Ibid., 176.

21. Alfred Mayer, "The Canalisation souterraine de Paris," in *Guide-Paris, par les principaux écrivains et artistes de la France*, ed. Corinne Verdet (Paris: Découverte/Maspero, 1983), 184.

22. Reid, *Paris Sewers and Sewermen*, 39–44. Jacques Frexinos, *Les Ventres serrés: Histoire naturelle et sociale de la constipation et des constipés* (Paris: Editions Louis Pariente, 1992).

23. Jacques Frexinos, *Voyage sans transit: géographie mondiale de la constipation* (Paris: Editions Médigone pour les Laboratoires Beaufour, 1997), 33.

24. George B. Davis and Frederick Dye, *A Complete and Practical Treatise upon Plumbing and Sanitation, Embracing Drainage and Plumbing Practice etc., with Chapters Specifically Devoted to Sanitary Defects, and a Complete Schedule of Prices of Plumbers' Work* (London: E. and F. N. Spon, 1898), 172.

25. Cited in John G. Bourke, *Compilation of Notes and Memoranda Bearing upon the Use of Human Ordure and Human Urine in Rites of a Religious or Semi-Religious Character among Various Nations* (Washington, D.C.: U.S. War Department, 1888), 13.

26. Peter Beveridge, *The Aborgines of Victoria and Riverina as Seen by Peter Beveridge* (Melbourne: M. L. Hutchinson, 1889), 53.

27. John G. Bourke, *The Scatologic Rites of All Nations: A Disseration upon the Employment of Excrementitious Remedial Agents in Religion, Therapeutiques, Divination, Witchcraft, Love-Philters, etc., in All Parts of the Globe*, ed. Louis Kaplan (New York: Morrow, 1994), 3, 32–72.

28. Bourke, *Compilation of Notes*, 31.

29. Mary Douglas, *Purity and Danger: An Analysis of Concepts of Pollution and Taboo* (London: Routledge and Kegan Paul, 1966), 116–17.

30. James Frazer, *The Golden Bough: A Study in Magic and Religion*, vol. 1 (New York: Macmillan, 1947), 223.

31. For a detailed discussion of this phenomenon, see James C. Whorton, *Inner Hygiene: Constipation and the Pursuit of Health in Modern Society* (New York: Oxford University Press, 2000).

32. Pierre Fauvel, "Action du chocolat et du café sur l'excrétion urique," *Extrait des comptes rendues des séances de la Société de Biologie*, Séance du 16 Mai 1908, vol. 64, 854. See also C. Choqart, *Aux consommateursde chocolat et de thé: Histoire d ces deux aliments, leurs propriétés hygiéniques, leur fabrication et leur commerce; recettes les meilleures pour les préparer* (Paris: Chocolaterie Impériale, 1868), 39.

33. Le Docteur Amable Cade, "Cure remarquable d'une constipation de 40 jours en 10 minutes par l'electro-thérapie indutive," *Lyon Médical*, deuxième année, vol. 4 (1870): 242–44. See also James Chalmers, "Remarkable Constipation: Inability to Empty the Bowels during Three Years," *London Medical Gazette* 1, n.s. (1842–43): 20–21.

34. M. Hallé, *Recherches sur la nature et les effets du méphitisme des fosses d'aisance* (Paris: L'Imprimerie de Ph.-D/Pierres, 1785), 115.

35. Frexinos, *Voyage sans transit*, 33–34.

36. Ibid.

37. Forth and Carden-Coyne, eds., *Cultures of the Abdomen*; Michael Hau, *The Cult of Health and Beauty in Germany, 1890–1930* (Chicago: University of Chicago Press, 2003);

Ina Zweiniger-Bargielowska, "The Culture of the Abdomen: Obesity and Reducing in Britain, circa 1900–1939," *Journal of British Studies* 44, no. 2 (April 2005): 239–74.

38. Frederick Arthur Hornibrook, *Culture of the Abdomen: The Cure of Obesity and Constipation* (London, 1924), 6.

39. Georges Treille, *Principes d'hygiène coloniale* (Paris: Georges Carré et C. Naud, 1899), i–ii.

40. Ibid., i.

41. Ibid.

42. Ibid., 24.

43. Ibid., 43–45.

44. Ibid., 3.

45. Ibid., 126–27.

46. Edouard Henry, *Hygiène coloniale* (Imprimerie centrale A. La Morinière, 1893), 5.

47. Ibid., 36.

48. Paul d'Enjoy, *La Santé aux colonies: Manuel d'hygiène et de prophylaxie climatologiques; médecine coloniale* (Paris: Société d'Editions Scientifiques, 1901), 163.

49. Docteur Adolphe Bonain, *L'Européen sous les tropiques: Causeries d'hygiène pratique* (Paris: Henri Charles-Lavauzelle, éditeur militaire, 1933), 209.

50. Ibid., 244.

51. Dr. Evelyne Moulin, *La Préparation santé de son voyage* (Ardenais: Les Asclepiades, 2003), 7.

52. Ibid., 7, 80–81.

53. John Noble, *Mexico City*, 2nd ed. (Hawthorn, Australia: Lonely Planet, 2000), 65–66.

54. In addition to Noble, *Mexico City*, 63–66, see Robert Storey, *Taiwan*, 5th ed. (Footscray, Australia: Lonely Planet, 2001), 66, 107; Peter Turner, *Java*, 1st ed. (Footscray, Australia: Lonely Planet, 1999), 104; Bradley Mayhew and Thomas Huhti, *South-West China* (Footscray, Australia: Lonely Planet, 1998), 123; Mary Fitzpatrick, *Read This First: West Africa* (Hawthorn, Australia: Lonely Planet, 2000), 83; Christine Niven, *South India*, 1st ed. (Footscray, Australia: Lonely Planet, 1998), 82, 131; Tom Brosnahan, *Turkey*, 5th ed. (Hawthorn, Australia: Lonely Planet, 2003), 63; Richard Plunkett, Alex Newton, Betsy Wagenhauser, and Jon Murray, *Bangladesh*, 4th ed. (Footscray, Australia: Lonely Planet, 2000), 57; Verity Campbell and Christine Niven, *Sri Lanka* (Hawthorn, Australia: Lonely Planet, 2001), 61; John King and Bradley Mayhew, *Pakistan*, 3rd ed. (Footscray, Australia: Lonely Planet, 1998), 86–87; David Zingarelli and Daniel Schechter, *Central America on a Shoestring*, 4th ed. (Footscray, Australia: Lonely Planet, 2001), 59; Patrick Horton, *Delhi*, 3rd ed. (Footscray, Australia: Lonely Planet, 2002), 54–55; Tom Brosnahan and Nancy Keller, *Guatamala, Belize and Yucatan: La Ruta Maya*, 3rd ed. (Hawthorn, Australia: Lonely Planet, 1997), 54.

55. Noble, *Mexico City*, 63.

56. The phrase appears in Niven, *South India*, 82, and in Plunkett et al., *Bangladesh*, 57.

57. Zingarelli and Schechter, *Central America*, 59.

58. Turner, *Java*, 104.

59. Brosnahan, *Turkey*, 63.

60. Storey, *Taiwan*, 66.

61. Brosnahan, *Turkey*, 63.

62. Weblogs rarely reveal any information about the participants (such as gender or cultural background), nor guarantee that the experiences recounted are genuine. However, I include some mention here of exchanges about toilet practices on the Africa and Southeast Asia sections of Lonely Planet Web site because I have found these to be consistent with discussions I heard myself when travelling in North Africa and southern Asia, as well as with the range of print travel guides examined in this chapter.

63. Lonely Planet Thorn Tree, January 25, 2006–February 16, 2006. Asia–South East Asia Islands and Peninsula, accessed February 16, 2006.

64. See Turner, *Java*, 104, for a good explanation of this issue.

65. Storey, *Taiwan*, 66.

66. Lonely Planet Thorn Tree, Africa, October 23, 2005–February 16, 2006, accessed February 16, 2006.

67. Lonely Planet Thorn Tree, Africa, October 23, 2005–February 16, 2006, accessed February 16, 2006.

68. Storey, *Taiwan*, 66.

69. Lonely Planet Thorn Tree, January 25, 2006–February 16, 2006. Asia–South East Asia Islands and Peninsula, accessed February 16, 2006.

70. Storey, *Taiwan*, 66.

71. Brosnahan, *Turkey*, 63.

72. Fitzpatrick, *West Africa*, 83.

73. Horton, *Delhi*, 54.

74. Turner, *Java*, 104.

75. Plunkett, *Bangladesh*, 57.

76. Mayhew and Huhti, *South-West China*, 123.

77. Storey, *Taiwan*, 66.

78. Brosnahan, *Turkey*, 63.

79. Zingarelli and Schechter, *Central America*, 59.

80. Lonely Planet Thorn Tree, January 25, 2006–February 16, 2006. Asia–South East Asia Islands and Peninsula, accessed February 16, 2006.

81. Lonely Planet Thorn Tree, January 25, 2006–February 16, 2006. Asia–South East Asia Islands and Peninsula, accessed February 16, 2006.

82. Lonely Planet Thorn Tree, Africa, October 23, 2005–February 16, 2006, accessed February 16, 2006.

83. Brosnahan, *Turkey*, 57.

84. King and Mayhew, *Pakistan*, 86.

85. Edward Luce, "One Land, Two Planets: The Economy Will Overtake That of the US by Roughly 2050: Along with China, India Will Dominate the Twenty-first Century. But It Is Still a Terrible Place to Be Poor," *New Statesman* 135, no. 4777 (January 30, 2006): 23–33.

86. Maggie Moss and Gemma Moss, *Handbook for Women Travellers* (London: Piatkus, 1987), 112

87. Ibid., 114–15.

88. Frexinos, *Voyage sans transit*, 11.

89. Julia Kristeva, *Pouvours de l'horreur: Essai sur l'abjection* (Paris: Editions du Seuil, 1983), 89.

90. Moss and Moss, *Handbook for Women Travellers*, 117.

91. Lonely Planet Thorn Tree, Africa, October 23, 2005–February 16, 2006, accessed February 16, 2006.

92. Lonely Planet Thorn Tree, Africa, October 23, 2005–February 16, 2006, accessed February 16, 2006.

93. Adam Hoschfield, "Underworld: Capturing India's Impossible City," *Harper's* 310, no. 1857 (February 2005): 90–94.

94. Luce, "One Land, Two Planets," 28.

95. Available at http://www.indax.com/toilets/html, accessed February 24, 2006.

96. See, for instance, this interview with public health campaigner Bindeswar Pathak, "India Needs Another Freedom Struggle!" *India Together*, October 22, 2006, available at http://www.indiatogether.org/2003/dec/hlt-pathak.htm, accessed October 22, 2006.

97. Lonely Planet Thorn Tree, January 25, 2006–February 16, 2006. Asia–South East Asia Islands and Peninsula, accessed February 16, 2006.

98. King and Mayhew, *Pakistan*, 87.

7

Avoidance

On Some Euphemisms for the "Smallest Room"

NAOMI STEAD

Since the invention of the flush toilet—one of the wonders of nineteenth-century technology—literally hundreds of euphemisms have been coined to evade mentioning its existence.
— Judith S. Neaman and Carole G. Silver, *A Dictionary of Euphemisms*

Vulgarity is a cultural construct, and the evidence suggests that it was the new courtly tradition of the Middle Ages which, by creating gentility, also created vulgarity.
— Jennifer Coates, *Women, Men and Language*

This chapter is about linguistic diversion, about verbal circumlocution and ellipticism, about terms used to obfuscate and disguise. It is about the many fascinating words, their variations and curiosities, that have been generated in the long attempt to avoid calling a toilet a toilet. But even there we are held back, by "toilet"—seemingly the plainest and most straightforward word, it is, in fact, itself a euphemism. There is literally no direct word of English origin for this humble object. Observing the ways and means that English speakers have avoided the unmentionable, then, is a fascinating linguistic wild goose chase, one that reveals much about society and culture; as Judith Neaman and Carole Silver note, "Attitudes towards secretions and excretions represent a cultural history of the world."[1]

A true scholarly study of the subject would cross etymology, sociolinguistics, and psychology and take in the related areas of social taboo, the theory of politeness, and the study of gender and language. But while this chapter touches on these fields, it is more the perspective of an amateur etymologist, a word-fancier if you like, drawn to the richly inventive, sometimes salty, and often amusing lexicon of euphemisms for the "smallest room."

Euphemisms serve to avoid direct reference to, and therefore a potentially embarrassing or shameful confrontation with, certain culturally determined taboo objects and activities. Such taboos vary but can include "sex; death; excretion; bodily functions; religious matters; and politics."[2]

The toilet is placed squarely in the category of taboo object through its close association with bodily fluids and the process of excreting them. In *Roget's Thesaurus* we find *latrine* falling under the general heading of "uncleanness," in the company of beastliness, grottiness, filthiness, squalor, pollution, defilement, corruption, taint, putrescence, contamination, infection, and badness.[3] These are some of the strongest and most potent words in the English language, and they give a sense of just how deeply this taboo state is encultured and reviled. It appears there is a relationship of inverse proportion between the vehemence of these words and the dissimulating mildness of the euphemisms for toilet. Peter Farb, writing about the history of linguistic prohibition, notes, "The habit of creating euphemisms dates back at least to the Norman conquest of England in 1066. At that time the community began to make a distinction between a genteel and an obscene vocabulary, between the Latinate words of the upper class and the lusty Anglo-Saxon of the lower. This is why a duchess *perspired* and *expectorated* and *menstruated*—while a kitchen maid *sweated* and *spat* and *bled*."[4] Farb's subjects here—the duchess and the kitchen maid—are surely chosen advisedly, and they serve to point out the class and gender implications of taboo activities and the euphemisms that surround them. Elsewhere, he writes that amongst nineteenth-century upper-class American society, "women were insulated against the raw sights and sounds of life. A man might curse and tell 'dirty' stories, but a proper lady was expected to swoon if she heard the taboo word *leg* instead of the more appropriate *limb*."[5] The supposed delicacy and prudery of women, their apparent physical inability (not to mention unwillingness) to cope with raw, crude, or "dirty" things, meant that linguistic prohibitions were even stronger in their presence.

Jennifer Coates, in a recent work on gender and language, has argued that "the courtly tradition of the Middle Ages, which put women on a pedestal, strengthened linguistic taboos in general, and also condemned the use of vulgar language by women, and its use by men in front of women."[6] Coates discusses the historical belief that women are more disposed to the use of euphemism than men, citing Otto Jespersen's 1922 claim, "There can be no doubt that women exercise a great and universal influence on linguistic development through their instinctive shrinking from coarse and gross expressions and their preference for refined and (in certain spheres) veiled and indirect expressions."[7] Coates also discusses Robin Lakoff's later survey of received ideas about women's use of language, that "women don't use off-color or indelicate expressions; women are the experts at euphemism."[8] Coates concludes that while the perception or expectation that women's language should be "more polite, more refined—in a word, more ladylike" is longstanding, the interrelationship of taboo, gender, and language is more complex than such stereotypes admit.[9] As a counterpoint to this, it is perhaps amusing to recall the actions of the American humorist Dorothy Parker. "Distressed that she was meeting no men at her office, she hung a simple sign over her door. It said 'Gentlemen.' Miss Parker's office was soon inundated by a veritable stream of male visitors."[10] The humour of this misappropriation, the disingenuous use of a euphemism as though it were a simple and transparent direction, serves to reveal the absurdity of it but also underlines the continuing sexual associations, and the more general taboo, of toilets.

Amongst the hundreds of euphemisms for toilet are some discernable themes. First are words of non–Anglo Saxon derivation, which furnish us with some of the most widely used terms, including *lavatory, latrine, loo,* and *toilet* itself.[11] *Lavatory* and *latrine* are simple enough—they derive from the Latin *lavare,* "to wash."[12] The origin of *loo,* however, is contested. While there are several plausible origins for it (all of them French), Michael Quinion argues that "there are few firm facts . . . and its origin is one of the more celebrated puzzles in word history."[13] Possibilities include a corruption of the French *lieu* (the place) or *lieux d'aisances* (literally, "places of ease").[14] Another theory is that it is a shortening of "Gardy loo!"—the warning cry of Edinburgh housewives when emptying bedpans out the window, itself a version of "*Gardez l'eau!*" or "Watch out for the water!" Alternatively, it may have derived from the "the eighteenth-century French word *bourdalou(e)* used to describe a urinal or chamber pot intended mainly for the use of ladies while travelling," which was itself an eponym, named after "the famous French preacher Louis Bordalou (1632–1704), whose sermons at Versailles were so popular that his congregations assembled hours in advance."[15] Finally, there is speculation that the word may derive from Waterloo. But whatever the truth of it, the relatively polite and homely *loo* is now the most popular such term in Britain and Australia.

The origin of *toilet,* also from the French, is clearer. The *Oxford English Dictionary* contains a lengthy entry on the word, demonstrating the complexity of its interrelated senses.[16] The root is *toilette,* itself the diminutive of the French *toile,* or cloth, and this leads to the original meaning of toilet: a cloth for wrapping clothes. Other senses are of a cloth covering for the shoulders during hair dressing; a cloth covering for a dressing table; the items on that table, namely, "the articles required or used in dressing; the furniture of the toilet-table, toilet service"; and the table itself.[17] The word also expands outwards to encompass "the action or process of dressing, or, more recently, of washing and grooming" and the now obsolete practice of receiving visitors during this process.[18] Toilet has historically also been used to mean clothes themselves and the way they are worn: "a manner or style of dressing; dress, costume, 'get-up,' also a dress or costume, a gown."[19] It is only then that the *OED* comes to the contemporary, conventional meaning of toilet, as a "dressing-room; . . . a dressing room furnished with bathing facilities. Hence, a bath-room, a lavatory; (contextually), a lavatory bowl or pedestal; a room or cubicle containing a lavatory."[20]

What is interesting about this procession of meanings are the spatial implications—beginning with the accoutrements and processes of dressing, moving outwards to the dressing room, then sideways to the dressing room with lavatory facilities, and then inwards again to the lavatory object itself. This procession offers a hint of the way in which euphemism tends to operate metonymically—that is, it refers to the container to mean the contained. Unlike metaphor, which expands and deepens the sense of a word, metonym diffuses, sidesteps, and turns the sense passive.[21] This can be seen in numerous examples, including *bathroom* (ubiquitous in the United States but causing confusion in Britain, where it still means a room with a bath), *washroom, lounge, cloak room, powder room, chamber* (also *chamber of commerce*, underlining the Freudian connection between excretion and money), *outhouse*, and *head*, the last of which derives from the position of the toilet on many ships, on or near the bulkhead.[22] Rawson discusses variations on these from other languages: the German *Abort* ("away place"); the Russian *ubornaya* (reportedly meaning "adornment place"), the Dutch *bestekamer* (best room), and the Maori *whare-iti* ("small house").[23] There is also the Hebrew-based Yiddish euphemism *bey-sakise*, "house of the throne."[24] Other variations refer to the smallness and secrecy of the space and its sometime location deep within a house, namely, *the smallest room, privy, closet* (also *water closet* and *earth closet*), *sanctuary, private office*, and the ironic *sanctum sanctorum* and *holy of holies*.

A range of terms refer to the toilet as a place of relief from a pressing need, for instance, *convenience, comfort station* (which took on another, more sexual and sinister meaning in the "comfort stations" provided to Japanese soldiers during World War II), *seat of ease, commode*, and *the necessary*. Neaman and Silver note the relationship between the last two, since "the word 'necessary' originally meant commodious or convenient. The growing technology of toilets transformed a necessity into a convenience and, by 1851, commode meant both a chamber pot and the often elegant article of furniture that enclosed it."[25] It is also interesting to note the idea of "the necessary" as a levelling device, pertaining to an activity necessary to all people, of all classes, throughout history. This is evidently also the impulse behind expressions such as the Yiddish and Russian "to go where even the king/tsar goes on foot."[26]

There are a number of terms that refer to the artefact or equipment of the toilet whilst carefully avoiding mention of its function, namely, *throne, close stool, stool, can* (which also has the American slang meaning of "buttocks"), and *jerry* (derived from *Jeroboam*, "a large bottle and also a chamber pot").[27] All these terms evidently date from before the advent of the flush toilet, when the device was often some variation of a seat or stool mounted above a receptacle.[28] The blank and instrumental *facilities, amenities*, and *the utensil* perhaps also fall into this category, which is related to the variety of convoluted "official" terms for public toilets, namely, *public convenience, municipal relief station*, and *guest relations facility*.[29] In a different register, the term for toilets in a restaurant can be a source of amusement; as Neaman and Silver note, "American national squeamishness" on the subject of public toilets can be seen in "the coy 'Gulls' and 'Buoys' favoured by some seafood restaurants."[30] This is a play on the gender-segregated *ladies/gentlemen* (also verbally "the gents"), *women/men*, and the infantile spoken form *little boys'/little girls' room*, which appears to be unused outside the United States.

On top of these relatively respectable euphemisms, there is a whole world of slang and "toilet humour" in common circulation. Many a schoolchild's joke would have been incomplete without a *crapper, thunderbox, bog, shithouse, splashhouse, dunny,* or *growler*.[31] Likewise, a special category of terminology in use in university student circles throughout the United States, Great Britain, and Australia relates to the act of vomiting—for instance, "driving the porcelain bus" and "bowing to the porcelain god." In this context, it is important to note that the use of slang and deliberate vulgarity can be a means of demonstrating and reinforcing membership of a particular subculture or group; for including selected individuals whilst excluding others. There is also an appeal, for some people, in breaking linguistic taboos. While Farb notes that "people living in Western cultures have long looked upon their verbal taboos as hallmarks of their advanced 'civilization,'"[32] Wardhaugh argues that "there are always those who are prepared to break the taboos in an attempt to show their own freedom from such social constraints or to expose the taboos as irrational and unjustified."[33]

It is not for nothing that taboos are described as "unmentionables." They are far more potent in speech than in writing, since the potential for direct embarrassment or loss of face is much greater. The counterpart to the noun forms of euphemism, then, is the multitude of ways to avoid saying where you are about to go. Many of these take the form of "going to . . ." sentences, such as "going to see a man about a dog/horse," "to cash a cheque," "to Cannes" (a famous watering spot, and evidently also a play on "can"),[34] "to water the lawn/petunias" (to explain an outdoor journey), "to pay a visit to the old soldier's home," "to visit Mrs. Jones" (derived from "visit the john"),[35] "to go and mail a letter," "to spend a penny" (from the price of using a public toilet),[36] "to shake the dew off my lily" (this expression specifically for men, obviously), and the popular "to answer the call of nature," "to freshen up," and, for women specifically, "to powder my nose." American schoolchildren are taught to make the request, as polite as it is vague, "may I please be excused/please leave the room."

As is obvious from the list above, explanations of where one is going and why are often gendered and sometimes also sexualised. Part of the appeal of the expression "shaking the dew off my lily," for example, presumably lies in the flirtatious suggestiveness of the double entendre—a wink-and-nod acknowledgement of the true nature of the lily being referred to. Neaman and Silver also note that in the late nineteenth century the expression "see a man about a dog" meant to visit a woman for sex, although this meaning is now obsolete. A *convenience* has also been used to refer to a prostitute, and there is a coincidence between "the john"—one of the most common euphemisms in the United States—and the anonymous male name given to a prostitute's customer. In fact, the john is an evolution of the earlier (and more vulgar) *jack*, *jakes*, *Jacques*, and *Ajax*; "in the sixteenth century, 'jakes' meant not only the privy but also filth or excrement."[37] But the sexual possibilities and connotations of (especially public) toilets clearly remain and are still a source of anxiety and taboo amongst mainstream contemporary society. The term *cottage*, for a public toilet in Britain, has given rise to the term *cottaging*, referring to the use of a public toilet for anonymous sexual encounters amongst gay men. Such locations are also known as *beats*, and although this term refers not only to toilets but to any location where men might "cruise" for casual sex, public toilets provide the ideal level of privacy and seclusion, and also the ostensibly "innocent" or pragmatic cover, for illicit sexual activities. In this sense, a public toilet beat is doubly a "closet," a private space where secret identities are revealed and enacted, a "queer space" in which activities outside of heteronormative constraints can take place.

In the etymology of the terms I have discussed here, euphemism piles upon euphemism: once a word's cover is blown, it needs to be disguised again, wrapped in other clothing in order to be made respectable again. "New euphemisms are constantly being invented because after a while even the substituted words become too infected for use in polite society."[38] In light of this, there is a case for seeing the toilet as the supreme euphemism, synonymous with the word itself. Hugh Rawson reports the usage "Ivan Lendl has gone to the euphemism" (from a tennis commentator explaining an unexpected break in the 1985 French Open final).[39] This is perhaps the ultimate and most apt expression of the impossibility of referring to this, an instrument that fulfils the most fundamental of functions, without evasion.

Notes

1. Judith S. Neaman and Carole G. Silver, *A Dictionary of Euphemisms* (London: Hamish Hamilton, 1983), 45.

2. Ronald Wardhaugh, *An Introduction to Sociolinguistics*, 4th ed. (Oxford: Blackwell Publishers, 2002), 237.

3. George Davidson, ed., *Penguin Reference Roget's Thesaurus of English Words and Phrases*, 150th anniversary ed., (London: Penguin Books, 2002).

4. Peter Farb, *Word Play: What Happens When People Talk* (London: Jonathan Cape, 1974), p. 80.

5. He continues on, noting that "pianos were even draped with cloth pantalets to conceal from feminine eyes those obscene supports which are now unblushingly called *piano legs*" (Farb, *Word Play*, 50–51).

6. Jennifer Coates, *Women, Men and Language: A Sociolinguistic Account of Gender Differences in Language*, 3rd ed. (Harlow, England: Pearson Longman, 2004), 14.

7. Otto Jespersen, *Language: Its Nature, Development and Origin* (London: George Allen and Unwin, 1922), 246; quoted in Coates, *Women, Men and Language*, 15.

8. Robin Lakoff, *Language and Women's Place* (New York: Harper and Row, 1975), 55; quoted in Coates, *Women, Men and Language*, 15.

9. Coates, *Women, Men and Language*, 13.

10. Neaman and Silver, *Dictionary of Euphemisms*, 46.

11. It is interesting to note that this borrowing of terms is not only in the one direction. The most common term throughout mainland Europe is reportedly W.C., from the English

water closet. Interestingly, there is a relatively direct term in both English and French for a fixture for urination: both *urinal* and *pissoir* are unusually explicit in this context. One could conjecture about whether this is because urine is a less-alarming bodily excretion or because these facilities are used solely by men.

12. Writing about the Latin and French origin of many euphemisms, Farb retells Robert Graves's amusing story "of the soldier who had been shot in the ass. When a lady visitor to the wards asked where he had been wounded, he replied: 'I'm sorry, ma'am, I can't say. I never studied Latin'" (Farb, *Word Play*, 79).

13. Michael Quinion, *Port Out, Starboard Home: And Other Language Myths* (London: Penguin Books, 2004), 179.

14. Ibid., 180.

15. Neaman and Silver, *Dictionary of Euphemisms*, 69.

16. *The Oxford English Dictionary*, vol. 18, 2nd ed., prepared by J. A. Simpson and E.S.C. Weiner (Oxford: Clarendon Press, 1989), 193–94.

17. Ibid., p. 193.

18. Ibid., p. 194.

19. Ibid.

20. There is another, specifically surgical meaning, that of cleaning a wound after an operation, and a whole range of related terms "of or pertaining to the toilet," such as *toilet-can, toilet-soap, toilet block, bowl, lid, seat, stall,* and so on. The verb *toilet* means "to perform one's toilet, to wash and attire oneself," or "to assist or supervise in using a toilet" (ibid.).

21. Peter Stockwell writes, "Idioms . . . often rely for their meaning on metaphorical interpretations. . . . Conversely, euphemism can be seen not so much as a lexical replacement by a dissimilar word as a replacement by a closely associated word (a metonymy rather than a metaphor). 'The rest room' is not a metaphor; rather it conveys slightly different, more pleasant associations than the other possibilities ('bog,' 'crapper,' 'thunderbox,' 'shithouse,' and many others)." Peter Stockwell, *Sociolinguistics* (London: Routledge, 2002), 30.

22. "Head(s), the," in R. W. Holder, *A Dictionary of Euphemisms: How Not to Say What You Mean* (Oxford: Oxford University Press, 2003), 185.

23. "Toilet," in Hugh Rawson, *Rawson's Dictionary of Euphemisms and Other Doubletalk*, 1995, available at xreferplus, http://www.xreferplus.com/entry/991162, accessed January 19, 2006.

24. My thanks to the anonymous reviewer of this chapter for this reference.

25. Neaman and Silver, *Dictionary of Euphemisms*, 65.

26. To go where even the king/tsar goes on foot: "*geyn vu der meylekh geyt tsu fus/idti kuda sam tsar' khodit peshkom.*" I thank the anonymous reviewer of this chapter for this reference.

27. "Toilet," in Rawson, *Rawson's Dictionary of Euphemisms.*

28. See Lawrence Wright, *Clean and Decent: The Fascinating History of the Bathroom and the Water Closet* (London: Routledge and Kegan Paul, 1960).

29. "Toilet," in Rawson, *Rawson's Dictionary of Euphemisms.*

30. Neaman and Silver, *Dictionary of Euphemisms*, 46.

31. The Australian slang *dunny* is derived from *dunnekin*, meaning "privy," "originally an unsewered outdoor privy, now used loosely of any lavatory." Joan Hughes, ed., *Australian Words and Their Origins* (Melbourne: Oxford University Press, 1989), 185.

32. Farb, *Word Play*, 78.

33. Wardhaugh, *Introduction to Sociolinguistics*, 237.

34. "Powder my nose, I have to," in Rawson, *Rawson's Dictionary of Euphemisms*, accessed January 19, 2006.

35. Neaman and Silver, *Dictionary of Euphemisms*, 66.

36. Wright attributes this to George Jennings, who was responsible for installing public lavatories in the Crystal Palace. See Wright, *Clean and Decent*, 201.

37. Neaman and Silver, *Dictionary of Euphemisms*, 68.

38. Farb, *Word Play*, 80.

39. "Euphemism, the," in Rawson, *Rawson's Dictionary of Euphemisms*, accessed January 20, 2006.

Toilet Art

Design and Cultural
Representations

8

Were Our Customs Really Beautiful?

Designing Refugee Camp Toilets

DEBORAH GANS

War is gendered. Traditionally, classically, it is the theater of manhood, with backstage realms of womanhood—the bedroom of Lysistrata, the burial ground of Antigone. As part of our current overturning of gendered norms, we are intent to desegregate the male battlefield; but there remain other gendered precincts of war yet unexamined, in particular, the refugee camp.

The primary population of refugee camps is women of childbearing age, for the obvious reason that the parallel population of men is often in the midst of active conflict. Typically, these women must support and care for children and elders by themselves and maintain the household, including the gathering of fuel and water for cooking meals. If they are lucky and the camp has some sort of internal economy beyond the dole, they need to figure out how to finance and work their business while caring for the family simultaneously. Their nontraditional role of economic provider can be in conflict with their desire or others' expectations that they sustain domestic tradition. And these social tensions can have physical repercussions, such as vulnerability to rape while requesting physical assistance in tasks, while foraging for fuel, or while traveling to the latrine. The physical distance of the bathroom from the home is representative of the many displacements of domestic custom within the culture of the camp.

The United Nations and related agencies are increasingly sensitive to the travails of female refugees. A body of international law deriving from the Declaration of Human Rights of 1948 has grown to protect them from abuse and to guarantee equality of gender, to call out the family and mothers as subjects of special interest, and to require the schooling of young children. In 1991 the UN High Commission on Refugees issued "Guidelines on the Protection of Refugee Women" in recognition of the widespread need but also in affirmation of the declaration's fundamental freedoms of individual thought, assembly, property, and movement.[1] In 2001 the United Nations changed the guidelines' title to read "Protection/ Gender Equality of Refugee Women," emphasizing the extent to which female vulnerability emerges from broad-based cultural patterns rather than the violence of war per se. The current position of the United Nations is the "mainstreaming" (their word) of gender in all aspects of refugee planning.[2]

The texts of refugee planning, such as the widely respected "Sphere Guidelines" and the planning manual of the nongovernmental organization (NGO) Doctors without Borders, incorporate UN attitudes toward gender and cultural difference in their directives on hygienic practice and in other, overlapping areas of shelter design. They mandate that user need should guide the facility design, and that those users include specifically women, the elderly, and the infirm. They suggest that the users even be consulted in the design process. They require that adequate toilets be sufficiently close to dwellings to allow rapid, safe, and acceptable access at all times of the day and night. Based on the lessons learned from field observation, these texts state that toilets shared by families are preferable to those shared by strangers and that these socially networked facilities are generally better kept, cleaner, and therefore more regularly used when the families have been consulted about their siting and design and have the responsibility and means to keep them clean. They ask that camp planners accommodate cultural differences in cleansing by water or ash, paper or hand. They call out the differences in practices related to menstruation, such as the use of cloths, which need to be washed in private conditions, versus paper, which needs to be disposed of.

Environmental concerns can conflict with cultural sensitivities and trump them—for good reason, given the deadly consequence of a contaminated water supply or vector-borne diseases such as malaria. So while the guidelines call for toilets proximate to living quarters or not more than thirty meters distant, the actual regulated distances, determined by soil conditions such as limestone or bedrock, can require a distance of one hundred meters, and a similar one hundred meters between water point and latrine. A high water table can require the use of a septic field or of toilets elevated over two-hundred-liter drums so that latrines must be ganged, centralized and organized by gender rather than family. In the end, because so many camps are situated in inauspicious terrain on short notice, the undomesticated rationality we associate with military tents arranged in a relentless grid, with trench latrines at distant albeit regular intervals, fulfills the initial refugee camp demands for rapid deployment and delivery of goods, surveillance, fire protection, and quarantine of disease.

Because of the similarity in operation of refugee and military camps, it is more than ironic coincidence that a popular alternative to the tent campground site is a disused military barracks. Take, for example, the compound in Nagyatad, Hungary, for Bosnian refugees. After lying idle for eighteen months, the former army camp opened as a transitional refugee settlement in 1991 without any dramatic physical change. Besides the mess hall and infirmary there stood four-story barrack buildings of large, undivided rooms, built to accommodate fifty soldiers each, with gang bathrooms obviously built for men. The only way families achieved privacy in each barrack was to hang sheets between spaces. Throughout the camps there had been no locks, and none were installed. Nonetheless, during its three-year occupation the camp became known as "the refugee village," with an infirmary; elementary, middle, and high schools; a post office; a Muslim prayer room, with fifty rugs donated by the Indonesian embassy; a library; club and TV rooms; and a craft room funded by the Peruvian embassy. In the same three years, thirty babies were born (a low number because of the dominance of women in the camp population) and seventy people died. Children attended school; men and women deprived of their usual agrarian occupations visited and crocheted, played cards, and drank coffee; neighbors squabbled. Muslims and ethnic Hungarians bickered over the use of the facilities—the Muslims squatting above the lavatories, the Hungarians sitting on the seat, each convinced of the unsanitary consequence of the other's practice.[3]

The disaster relief housing we designed in response to a competition organized by Architecture for Humanity, seeking better shelter for Kosovar refugees, was an argument first against the long-term camp per se. Our larger goal was to enable refugees to return home before the restoration of large-scale infrastructural systems such as water, sewage, and electricity, and thereby to halt the devolution of the social as well as physical city fabric that occurs in the absence of citizens. The strategy was to provide the families with a shelter that included a small-scale, individualized infrastructure of water power and waste they could take with them when they left the camp and install on the sites of their future—or former—homes. In other words, we argued that toilets and water, rather than a better tent, were the central issues of staking out home, wherever it might be located. The shelter consists of two small, demountable and transportable rooms that look like hollow columns, one housing a shower, cistern, and stove and the other a privy. The rooms are literally columns in that they are strong enough to support the framing for a roof or even second story. Placed at a distance from one another, the privy column and cistern column frame the living space and support the roof and walls. Initially, the columns might stand within a refugee camp and be sheathed by tarps. They could later be transported to the ruined shell of a house, where they would supply the domestic infrastructure and support conventional beams and sheathing. The core of the toilet and shower or cistern is like the seed of the house—or, indeed, of the reconstructed city—standing within the old husk

Figure 8.1 Prototype of paired columns with privy installed at Slought Foundation, Philadelphia, 2003. (Courtesy of the architect.)

and providing goods immediately needed as it is gradually absorbed by the growth of the house around it (Figure 8.1).

The specific appearance and mechanisms of the core depend on the local climate, soil conditions, and natural resources and on the customs that the refugees bring with them. As in the UN and NGO guidelines, there is a tension between the need for ecological and self-sustaining systems and the desire to respect cultural mores. For example, while solar cookers and boilers reduce the search for fuel and the consequent deforestation, opportunities for rape, and waste of time that attend it, in some regions of Africa they are rejected by the refugees because they require pots be open to the air without lids, which potentially allows bad spirits to enter the food and water. While wood as a building material might be locally available and culturally appropriate, the deforestation it entails might make the use of prefabricated, imported cores of plastic the better choice. Thus far we have built cores of bamboo and of engineered folded paper, which have the advantage of being very light, very strong, and sustainably produced. The roof and base of the core are lightweight concrete palettes with center openings that accommodate a toilet vent/wind turbine and cistern pipe at the top and a composting toilet pit or drain in the floor. Based on the San-Plat™ design, the slab has an elevated footrest cast into it to help define user position at night if there is no seat. We have explored a range of technologies for the other internal workings of the cores: ceramic jiko pots, which hold heat like a thermos; solar cookers; photovoltaic tarps in which filaments are embedded in the fabric and attached to a battery. The goal is a core that is as universal in its potential for deployment as a tent but adaptable through its material to environmental factors, and through its workings to cultural ones.

While the primary goal is to facilitate the right of return where possible, a secondary goal of the core dwelling would be increased domestication of the refugee camp itself through the closer integration of hygiene, ablution, and its surrounding rituals into the house. By eliminating exposure to the larger camp population in matters of hygiene, the family toilet mitigates the spread of disease. The columnar system allows for the interior to adapt to specific mores; for example, the privy can face the interior of the house or the exterior, away from Mecca or toward the kitchen. The columns can group to form clustered dwellings as well, with expanded and shared cooking, which has energy and environmental benefits, or shared toilets and showers, which would allow for group bathing. The clustered cores can shape the shared space among houses, defining courtyards for safe play of children, public thresholds for cottage industry or the display of goods, and collective places for leisure and assembly. It would be possible to construct a larger gathering space with ganged privies along one edge and grouped cooking facilities along the other for cultures in which those activities must be separated.

While the domestication of the camp is in itself feminizing, the structure has attributes specifically geared to women. The ability to shape and cluster the houses increases the woman's control over the patterning and maintenance of the household. The placement of communal spaces within the domestic block allows for shared chores and child supervision. The core itself can be erected with something like a car jack independent of help and the obligations that might entail (the conceit being that every woman can change a tire).

Refugee planning tends, reasonably, to prioritize human rights issues surrounding *non refoulement*, the non-extradition of refugees back to their abandoned states, and mortal threats such as deadly cholera outbreaks and internecine violence. Given these overwhelming concerns, and the unassailable price point of the tarp and latrine, who would question the tried-and-true procedures for setting up basic camps military fashion? There are some venture capitalists interested in producing our latest folding design; but their attraction to the unit and their vision of it as a commodity is based on its material lightness rather than on its integrated infrastructure—specifically its toilet, which they have not figured into their marketing or financial equation. It takes a larger cost-benefit analysis that includes arenas of sanitation, health, economic productivity, social well-being, and the safety of women for the alternative shelter with its toilet to make economic sense. Then the overlay of a domestically scaled infrastructure of water, fuel, and waste on the camp's abstract grid of services appears not as redundant but as an affordable way toward a reintegrated existence, where a refugee can move among work and water, hygiene and planting, cooking and community as in everyday life, and may begin to answer the query asked by a Bosnian woman: "Were our customs really beautiful or am I just imagining things?"[4]

Notes

1. *The Declaration of Human Rights*, United Nations, 1948.

2. Women's Commission for Refugee Women and Children, *United Nations High Commission of Refugees Policy of Refugee Women and Guidelines on Their Protection; An Assessment of Ten Years of Implementation* (New York: United Nations, 2002).

3. Joel Halpern and David Kideckel, eds., *Neighbors at War: Anthropological Perspectives on Yugoslav Ethnicity, Culture and History* (Collegeville, Pa.: Penn State University Press, 2000), 346.

4. Julie Mertus, ed., *The Suitcase: Refugee Voices from Bosnia and Croatia* (Berkeley: University of California Press, 1999), 71.

9

(Re)Designing
the "Unmentionable"

Female Toilets in the Twentieth Century

BARBARA PENNER

In 2004, a radical improvement was introduced at one of the United Kingdom's largest music festivals, Glastonbury: She-Pee, a pink, fenced-off enclosure containing urinals for the exclusive use of women. Once past the guarded entrance, female users were supplied with a P-mate, effectively a disposable prosthetic penis made of cardboard that enabled them to stand up to pee. The British media reported widely and positively on She-Pee. And once they figured out how to use P-mate—place the funnel where your underwear should be, straighten out your knees, point and shoot—the army of female concertgoers gave it thumbs-up too. One woman enthused to the BBC: "The She-Pees were cleaner, with no queues really and you didn't have to touch anything, so it was more hygienic."[1] While a few hailed She-Pee and P-mate as a form of empowerment for women, most simply expressed relief at being able to bypass Glastonbury's grimy and oversubscribed portaloos.

P-mate was distributed free at Glastonbury but normally retails for £2.50 (US$4.50) for a pack of five. As any woman who does rock climbing or other adventure sports knows, P-mate is just one of many cheap and uncelebrated devices available today that allow women to urinate in any situation. (Other popular models include the Whiz and Feminal.) And even these are hardly as revolutionary as they might initially seem. Along with chamber pots and Bourdaloues, female urinals made of glass or pottery have been around for centuries, long before water closets were ever invented.[2] (See Figure 9.1.) Yet Glastonbury 2004 should be recognized as a milestone of sorts, as it is one of the few attempts in recent times to tackle the age-old problem of the queue for the ladies' room on a mass scale.

The scarcity of serious or inventive attempts to redesign female public

Figure 9.1 Glass, bottle-shaped women's urinal, 1701–30.
(Courtesy of the Science and Society Picture Library.)

toilets is not surprising. Female lavatories, while a highly visible feature in everyday life, remain more or less invisible in discourses around design. Thanks to queer theory and feminist interventions in planning, there is now some scholarly interest in how public toilets are used and experienced, but there is almost no discussion of how they are currently produced or how they might be produced in future.[3] This myopia is reproduced in legislation such as the American "potty parity" bills or the more recent Women's Restroom Equity Bill in New York.[4] While it is undeniably important that women have adequate provision in public buildings, potty parity simply ensures that more female lavatories are built, without exploring new and potentially more spatially compact design and ecologically friendly solutions. The ladies' room—complete with water closet, stall, lock, and door—is still ubiquitous, having not been seriously reconsidered for well over a hundred years.

My aim in this chapter is to make visible three attempts to redesign the female toilet from 1890s to present. Each project, in a different way, demonstrates that the true problem with rethinking the female toilet is that it is not simply a functional response to a physical need but a cultural product shaped by discourses about gender, the body, privacy, and hygiene. As such, the planning of ladies' rooms owes less to female physiology or the realities of use than to deep-rooted historically and culturally specific conventions, from prohibitions on bodily display to the binary gender division. Motivating my excavation of these projects is a question: can challenging the assumptions that underlie the design of female lavatories open up the possibility of subverting them?

Urinettes

A short-lived experiment took place in London circa 1898, when so-called urinettes were installed on a trial basis in an unnamed women's public lavatory. Smaller than conventional water closets, with curtains instead of doors, they automatically flushed like a man's urinal. What was perhaps more progressive than their design, however, was that only a halfpenny was to be charged for their use.

To understand why this proposal was so radical, it is important to set it into the context of late-Victorian London. Women then seeking public lavatory accommodation had to contend with two major obstacles: first, they had to locate facilities; and second, they had to be able to pay for using them. While men were able to use urinals at no cost and paid a penny only for a water closet, women were charged one penny every time—which, as George Bernard Shaw correctly observed, was an "absolutely prohibitive charge for a poor woman."[5] According to Shaw, "no man ever thought of [this difficulty] until it was pointed out to him." Shaw blamed this widespread ignorance on "the barrier of the unmentionable," which prevented the open and free discussion of female needs.[6] For the most part, women's bodily functions—pregnancy, menstruation, defecation, urination—were uncharted territory, a "tangled snaky darkness" that evoked the spectre of sexuality and the uncontrollable female body in the popular mind.[7]

Urinettes, however, attempted to provide an engineering solution to the penny charge problem. Like urinals, urinettes were cheaper and more space-efficient than traditional water closets. Furthermore, despite the fact that women's dress in the 1890s was still restrictive, their underclothing would have been open at the crotch, without buttons or fastenings. This openness meant that female urinals might well have been more convenient and easier for women to use than they would be today.

But even though they continued to be installed at least into the 1920s, urinettes never appeared to gain widespread acceptance. A female patient of Havelock Ellis, Florrie, referred to the presence of a urinette in Portsmouth only to note that it was spectacularly unpopular.[8] Though there is no historical evidence for why such experiments failed, they were most likely the victims of a larger problem facing women's conveniences. Looking at the 1898 ground plan for the convenience with urinettes, for instance, one is struck by a strangely familiar sight: while the women's side is equipped with four water closets, three urinettes, and one lavatory, the men's side has seven water closets, fifteen urinals, and two lavatories. (See Figure 9.2.) This asymmetry was no accident but was standard in conveniences at this time.[9]

As the engineers George Davis and Frederick Dye explained in 1898, the problem was that women often did not make use of their side, with the consequence that conveniences for "the weaker sex" were "more often fail-

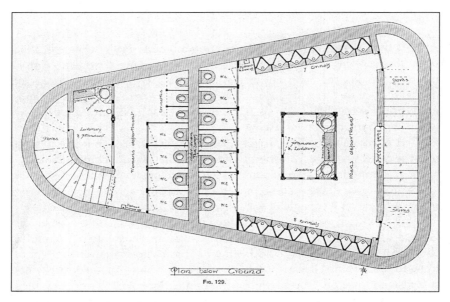

Figure 9.2 Plan of 1898 London public lavatory with female urinettes. From George B. Davis and Frederick Dye, *A Complete and Practical Treatise upon Plumbing and Sanitation*, 1898. (Collection of the author.)

ures, financially and practically, than a success."[10] Consequently, fewer were provided for them. The reason why ladies' conveniences were notorious financial duds, however, was not simply because poorer women could not afford to use them. The reality was that, far from being universally put to use by women, public lavatories were often shunned by them, whether out of fear, distaste, or, as Davis and Dye put it, a "peculiar excess of modesty" that forced their closure.[11]

With this revelation, the picture becomes considerably more complex. Women's public toilets were clearly shaped by contemporary notions of decency and femininity. But the closure of female facilities also reminds us that Victorian women were as invested in these discourses as Victorian men, to the extent that it often overrode their own physical needs when in public.

The Bathroom

Writing sixty years later, the architect Alexander Kira recognized the degree to which toilets continued to be caught up in societal taboos. However, he believed that these taboos could be sympathetically accommodated in design and set about to do just that. Between 1958 and 1965, Kira directed a major study at Cornell University whose purpose was to rethink bathroom design completely, according to the principles of human engineering or ergonomics. Published in 1966, the book detailing the study's results, *The Bathroom*, is the only serious study of the toilet published in the twentieth century that attempts to consider all aspects of human lavatory requirements, physical and psychological, in an objective, scientific way.[12]

Perhaps the best example of this attempt at neutrality was how Kira, keen to break away from the prejudices surrounding his subject, invented a scientific terminology to describe bathroom activities: toilets became "hygiene facilities," bathing became "body cleansing," and urinating or defecating became the rather sinister "elimination." By reducing what takes place in the toilet to a mechanical function, Kira attempted to contain its psychosexual dimension, treating the body as machine. Similarly, Kira blanked out the faces of the female models in his photographic studies of cleansing activities in what appears to have been a preemptive (and not totally successful) gesture to head off public outrage. It is worth noting, however, that by the time of the book's revised edition in 1976, the models not only appeared naked but also were photographed urinating.

The Bathroom's most significant section, part 2, records laboratory investigations into the functional and physiological activities of the bathroom. The purpose of these explorations was to establish a basic set of criteria for bathroom design and to suggest how these might ultimately be applied to new equipment. As Kira wanted to design for the optimal number of users, he made abundant use of diagrams and statistical charts. These set out anthropometric data, drawn from military studies of body dimensions, on the height, width, and range of movement of potential users. Despite designing for a universal user, Kira was sensitive to the anatomical and cultural differences between men and women and studied them performing their various personal hygiene activities separately in order to provide eventually for both.

On the subject of female urination, however, Kira's conclusions were bleak. He observed that many experiments had taken place over the years to provide a stand-up public urinal for women but that all had failed due to the unwieldiness of female clothing and to women's "psychological resistances to being publicly uncovered."[13] Kira also noted that women face a third, equally pernicious problem: that of aim. He stated that, while men learn the "ability to control the trajectory of the urine stream" early on, women have no such control and soil themselves when they attempt to urinate standing up. Subsequently, although men "can urinate equally conveniently . . . from either a sitting/squatting, or standing position," Kira recommended that women pee exclusively from a seated position.[14]

In the revised edition of his book, he amended this view where public facilities were concerned. Acknowledging that, due to fears of contagion, women generally hover over public toilets to urinate rather than sit on them as at home, Kira proposed a women's toilet/urinal that replaced the conventional seat with angled thigh-high pads. This supported them in an optimal hovering position with a minimum of bodily contact.[15] Kira's radical yet commonsense design proposition was never taken up by any major American manufacturer, even though at least one contributor to his study, American Standard, had already tried to respond to the "hovering" problem in female facilities. From 1950, it promoted its own model of a female urinal, Sanistand, by assuring women that they did not need "to sit or touch [it] in any way." But the design was quietly pulled from production in 1973 and is now only occasionally sighted in restrooms around America, a curiosity from another era.

FEMME™ pissoire

Normally attentive both to gender differences and to the social impact of toilet behaviour, Kira's discussions of female urination dwelt largely on the practicalities (or the *im*practicalities) of the act, leaving to one side the question of what the control of urine might mean psychologically to men and women—a less surprising oversight when we recall that *The Bathroom* opens with Freud's famous maxim "anatomy is destiny."[16] Kira, above all a pragmatist, observed existing habits of use and reproduced them in his design. But others have been much more interested in the social consequences of urinary control, from Karen Horney to Simone de Beauvoir, who devoted several pages to the subject in *The Second Sex*. Beauvoir believed that the Western convention that women squat to urinate "constitutes for the little girl the most striking sexual differentiation." She explained, "To urinate, she is required to crouch, uncover herself, and therefore hide: a shameful and inconvenient procedure."[17] The erect position in our society, she noted, is reserved for men. This question of control, among others, intrigued the architect J. Yolande Daniels in New York when she began working on FEMME™ pissoire in 1991–92. To what extent is controlling the flow of urine a personal freedom for men? What might mastering this act mean for women?

To give a brief description: FEMME™ pissoire consists of a basic ensemble (stainless steel bowl and spout, supply and return hose, mirror, instructional floor mat) that was installed at a series of different locations, from hotel rooms to art galleries, between 1996 and 1998. (See Figure 9.3.) With each shift in site, there is a corresponding shift in theoretical emphasis.[18] While it is engaged with a changing bundle of questions, a key interest of the project is how the relationship between designed objects, social convention, female anatomy, and subjectivity is mediated. By playfully challenging every custom currently governing toilet design and protocol, Daniels puts them to the test: is anatomy and social convention destiny?

Before answering this question, we must first consider in greater detail the specific ways in which FEMME™ pissoire transgresses custom. Rejecting the "backing on and squatting" stance of most models of female urinal,

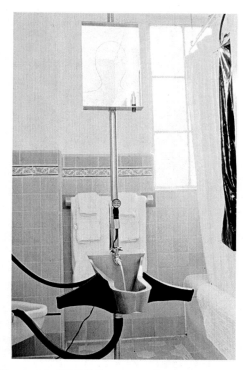

Figure 9.3 FEMME™ pissoire, Chateau Marmont.
(Courtesy of J. Yolande Daniels.)

FEMME™ pissoire opts for a "standing and facing" position that enables women stand directly over the toilet bowl. Standing up encourages women to learn to direct the stream of urine themselves, as boys are trained to do from a young age. As Beauvoir observes, this aspect of boys' toilet training contrasts strongly with that of girls: whereas boys are taught to control their urine stream through handling their own penis, the girls are taught that their sexual organs are taboo.[19] With FEMME™ pissoire, women would get used to touching themselves in order to direct the urinary stream until, over time, this gesture would potentially become everyday and unremarkable, "an automatic reflex."[20]

Although Kira believed women would never use urinals in public unless these were afforded the same visual privacy as water-closets, FEMME™ pissoire is stall-less and curtainless. Daniels tackles the problem of privacy by removing the need for women to disrobe so completely. She designed the P-system pant with two zippers: one that opens like a conventional zipper, another that opens at the crotch.[21] (See Figure 9.4.) The redesigned trousers become an integral aspect of the redesigned toilet, addressing not only the "pants-around-the-ankles" complaint that repeatedly surfaces with female

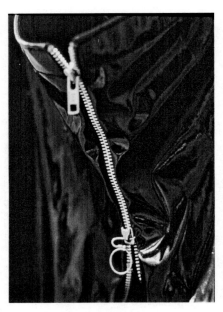

Figure 9.4 FEMME P-system pant.
(Courtesy of J. Yolande Daniels.)

urinals but also the way in which female genitalia is generally left unarticulated in design, a "lack," in comparison to the male. In the same way the front zipper on trousers articulates male anatomy, the FEMME P-system pant now articulates and makes visible the female.

Last, FEMME™ pissoire's project of rendering women visible is pushed further by the mirror. Typically used for the application of make-up, the mirror is, in Daniels's words, where we "verify the surface application of the feminine—the proper."[22] Not merely a reflective surface, it is a point of mediation between the personal and collective self, where women may "put on" their public face. By contrast, the mirror of FEMME™ pissoire, placed directly at eye level, ensures that female users confront images of themselves as they urinate standing up, actively challenging fixed ideas about what is "proper" feminine behaviour and fostering an awareness of the acquired character of the conventions that govern toilet protocol. Watching themselves standing erect in the act of urination, female users may see in the mirror the possibility of reconfiguring these relationships and of reshaping their selves.

"Hey! Stand and Deliver"[23]

While the FEMME™ pissoire project exists primarily as a propositional object, the goal is for it to be mass-produced and commonplace. Nor is it the only model that aims to go mainstream. A new generation of women's urinals have been developed since the 1990s including the Lady P by Gustavberg Sphinx and the Lady Loo by Goh Ban Huat Berhad. Despite their elegant designs and the high level of publicity they have received, most of these are currently purchased for their novelty appeal and installed singly in nightclubs or theatres.[24] For all of their appeal, this crop of urinals for women is too expensive and fixed to supplant the water closet in any kind of systematic way.[25]

This chapter is not necessarily an attempt to convince readers of the benefits of the female urinal, although this analysis shows that it does offer advantages in certain scenarios (e.g., temporary events such as festivals, where large numbers of women congregate) and is appealing for reasons of hygiene as well. Rather, this brief survey intends to demonstrate how the prevalent design of female toilets responds not to the experiences or needs of women as much as to an ideologically dominant idea of femininity as modest, discreet, and hidden. Yet the dominant ideal of femininity is not unassailable. As interventions into the status quo, female urinals push against collective expectations and stretch them to include new objects and conventions of behaviour such as women standing to urinate. While not a grand gesture that will single-handedly bring the binary gender system crashing down, urinals for women point to the fact that small subversions can be built into design: small shifts in existing boundaries that can be embraced—or contested—in their turn. For Daniels, the true emancipatory potential of FEMME™ pissoire and the women's urinal lies in the possibility that, through use, it might one day become banal, perhaps even unnecessary. As she observes, "In using the object, the object itself becomes obsolete."[26]

Notes

1. "Girls Beat Glasto Toilet Nightmare," BBC News, Wednesday, June 30, 2004, available at http://news.bbc.co.uk/1/hi/entertainment/music/3849381.stm, accessed June 14, 2005.

2. There is little written about how and in what context these vessels were used. Some seemed intended for women to use in public: for instance, the sauceboat-shaped Bourdaloue reputedly took its name from a Jesuit priest, Père Bourdalou, whose sermons were so brilliant but long-winded that women needed to relieve themselves while he spoke. By contrast, other vessels are shaped in such a way as to suggest that they were used privately while women were reclining or confined to their beds. In addition to being made of porcelain, like chamber pots, these female urinals were often made of clear glass, which suggests they also might have been used for diagnostic purposes (e.g., for uroscopic inspection). One scholar who begins to consider these vessels is Johan J. Mattelaer, "Some Historical Aspects of Urinals and Urine Receptacles," *World Journal of Urology* 17 (1999): 145–50. For more on chamber pots, see Lucinda Lambton, *Temples of Convenience and Chambers of Delight* (London: Pavilion, 1998).

3. See, for instance, Lee Edelman, "Men's Room," in *Stud: Architectures of Masculinity*, ed. Joel Sanders (New York: Princeton Architectural Press, 1996), 152–61; Sally R. Munt, "Orifices in Space: Making the Real Possible," in *butch/femme: Inside Lesbian Gender*, ed. Sally R. Munt (London: Cassell, 1998), 200–209.

4. Publicly acknowledging that its 1984 potty parity legislation had not done enough, in 2005 New York City Council unanimously pushed through a much tougher Women's

Restroom Equity Bill, which requires that most new public buildings install two women's bathrooms for every one men's in place of the one-to-one ratio that existed previously.

5. George Bernard Shaw, "The Unmentionable Case for Women's Suffrage," in *Practical Politics*, ed. Lloyd J. Hubenka (Lincoln: University of Nebraska Press, 1976), 104.

6. Ibid., 103.

7. Jennifer Bloomer, "The Matter of the Cutting Edge," in *Desiring Practices*, ed. Duncan McCorquodale, Katerina Redi, and Sarah Wigglesworth (London: Black Dog, 1996), 15.

8. Florrie notes that the women ran away from the urinette "in horror." Quoted in Simone de Beauvoir, *The Second Sex*, ed. and trans. H. M. Parshley, (1949; London: Vintage, 1997), 303.

9. This asymmetry continues to present. A study by the American Department of the Environment in 1992 determined that the average ratio of male to female toilets in theatres and cinemas is fifty-three to forty-seven. The ideal would be about thirty-eight to sixty-four. Grace Bradberry, "Why Are We Waiting?" *The Times*, September 6, 1999, sec. 3, p. 37.

10. George B. Davis and Frederick Dye, *A Complete and Practical Treatise upon Plumbing and Sanitation Embracing Drainage and Plumbing Practice etc.* (London: E. and F. N. Spon, 1898), 171–72.

11. Ibid., 182.

12. Alexander Kira, *The Bathroom* (1966; New York: Bantam Books, 1967).

13. Ibid., 140.

14. Ibid., 140–41.

15. Alexander Kira, *The Bathroom*, rev. ed. (New York: Viking Press, 1976), 232–37.

16. Kira *Bathroom* (1966), 1.

17. Beauvoir, *Second Sex*, 301–4. Beauvoir argues that the freedom boys exhibit when urinating and their seeming omnipotence contribute to the penis envy of girls. She stresses, however, that it will have this effect only on girls who have not been "normally reared." Freud also cited cases of young girls urinating standing up as evidence of their "envy for the penis." Sigmund Freud, "The Taboo of Virginity," in *The Pelican Freud Library*, vol. 7, ed. Angela Richards, trans. James Strachey (Middlesex: Penguin, 1977), 278.

18. As part of Daniels's interest in provoking a public discourse, FEMME™ pissoire was installed in two hotels: the Gramercy Hotel, New York, and the Chateau Marmont, Los Angeles. The urinal, hooked up to the existing sink and toilet, was fully functional in both sites but was used more frequently in the Chateau Marmont, where there was a door. It was used by both sexes. The project was also installed in two galleries: the Whitney Independent Studios and the Thomas Healy Gallery. In the former it functioned as a fountain, and in the latter it was installed as a pure object. J. Yolande Daniels, e-mail to author, March 5, 2001.

19. Beauvoir, *Second Sex*, 302.

20. Daniels, e-mail to author, March 5, 2001.

21. Daniels, e-mail to author, March 13, 2001.

22. Yolande Daniels, "OUR Standard FEMME pissoire," *Young Architects: Scale* (New York: Princeton Architectural Press, 2000), 20.

23. The heading for this section comes from the opening lines of "Piss Manifesto" in the U.K. underground girlzine *Girlfrenzy*, which originally provided Daniels with the inspiration for her project. It carries on: "GIRLS—YOU'VE BEEN BRAIN-WASHED. . . . Get yourself on your feet and stand proud and PISS WITH PRIDE." See Mandie Beuzeval, "Piss Manifesto," *Girlfrenzy*, no. 3, (n.d.): 32; and Daniels, e-mail to author, March 5, 2001.

24. For instance, see Ingrid Wenz-Gahler, *Flush! Modern Toilet Design* (Basel: Birkhäuser, 2005), 110.

25. A critique of existing designs has been produced by Orde Levinson. His paper "The Female Urinal: Facts and Fables" is available at http://www.femaleurinal.com/factsandfables.html, accessed June 9, 2005.

26. Daniels, e-mail to author, March 5, 2001.

10

Marcel Duchamp's Legacy

Aesthetics, Gender, and National Identity in the Toilet

ROBIN LYDENBERG

> I will have (later) only a public toilet or
> underground W.C. in my name.
> —Marcel Duchamp, January 25, 1967[1]

In 1917, Marcel Duchamp submitted an entry, under the pseudonym Richard Mutt, to the first exhibition of the American Society of Independent Artists. The sculpture, which he titled *Fountain*, consisted of a mass-produced ceramic urinal mounted on a pedestal upside down and on its back, signed and dated by the "artist" R. Mutt. Although the bylaws of the society stipulated that anyone paying the membership fee of six dollars was entitled to a showing of his or her artwork, Duchamp's entry was rejected by the committee on the grounds that "the fountain may be a very useful object in its place, but its place is not an art exhibition, and it is, by no definition, a work of art" (Anon. 1917, 6).

The brief scandal that ensued at the time and the flood of mixed outrage and reverence that has persisted for almost a century in response to this work seem concentrated precisely on issues of "definition." *Fountain* belongs to a series of works Duchamp called "readymades"—ordinary objects removed from their original context and function, titled, signed, and designated as "art." Many critics have struggled to define this enigmatic genre, about which the artist himself remarked, "The curious thing about the readymade is that I've never been able to arrive at a definition or explanation that fully satisfies me" (qtd. in Tomkins 1996, 159). What Duchamp undoubtedly did find satisfying about the readymades was their disruption of the very systems of definition they defied.

Beginning with Duchamp's infamous urinal, toilets in art have been used over the decades to disrupt the systems of classification by which we attempt to define and stabilize the uncertain psychological and cultural terrain of modernity. The appearance of the urinal in the context of aesthetics undoes the binary opposition not only of art and everyday life but also of public and private, male and female, heterosexual and homosexual, insider and outsider, mind and body, sacred and profane. This chapter explores the critical reception of what came to be known as the "Richard Mutt Case"[2] and the impact of Duchamp's legacy in a continuing avant-garde tradition of toilet art by contemporary artists Dorothy Cross and Ilya Kabakov.

The intense anxiety provoked by Duchamp's destabilizing intervention in 1917 manifested itself first in the outrage expressed by some members of the exhibition committee: "'We cannot exhibit it,' [the artist George] Bellows said hotly, taking out a handkerchief and wiping his forehead. . . . 'It is indecent! . . . gross, offensive!'" (Wood 1985, 29). As recently as January 2006, a replica of the original urinal (Duchamp produced eight) was subjected to more direct critique—by a hammer-wielding performance artist. Clearly, *Fountain* still has the subversive power to provoke; and in the work of some contemporary artists, one often detects an ambivalent desire simultaneously to deflate and emulate Duchamp's genius.[3]

When five hundred art professionals were recently asked to name the single most influential work of modern art, Duchamp's *Fountain* edged out Pablo Picasso's *Les Demoiselles d'Avignon* and *Guernica* and Andy Warhol's *Marilyn Diptych* to win first place (Higgins 2004). This is an honor rich in irony. Duchamp's creation of this readymade was intended to undermine the pretensions of high culture, the aura of the originality of the artist, and the uniqueness of the work of art. Yet if the "influence" of a work of art can be measured by the sheer volume of critical debate generated and by the number of artists who have appropriated, imitated, denounced, or celebrated it, Duchamp's *Fountain* has clearly earned its honorific.

The earliest defense of this work was made (although not without irony) on aesthetic grounds. During the debates over the urinal's suitability for exhibition in 1917, Walter Arensberg remarked, "A lovely form has been revealed, freed from its functional purpose, therefore a man clearly has made an aesthetic contribution" (Wood 1985, 30). In the first essay to address the transformed urinal, Louise Norton defended it against those "atavistic minds" offended by what she coyly referred to as a "certain natural function," asserting that "to any 'innocent' eye how pleasant is its chaste simplicity of line and color!" (Norton 1917, 5–6).

Alfred Stieglitz's photographic portrait of *Fountain* emphasized through careful lighting and placement what he referred to as the urinal's "fine lines" and aesthetic quality (qtd. in Camfield 1991, 141). Another colleague of Duchamp interpreted his transformed urinal in retrospect, and without apparent irony, as a gesture meant to reveal that "beauty is around you wherever you choose to discover it" (Roche 1959, 87).

Duchamp, however, specified that his selection of the objects that became his readymades, including the urinal, was never "dictated by aesthetic delectation" but rather by "a reaction of visual indifference" (Duchamp 1973,

141). Writing to a friend from his early days in the Dada movement, Duchamp complained, "When I discovered the readymades I thought to discourage aesthetics. In Neo-Dada they have taken my readymades and found aesthetic beauty in them. I threw the bottle-rack and the urinal into their faces as a challenge and now they admire them for their aesthetic beauty" (qtd. in Richter 1965, 207–8).[4] Appreciations of *Fountain* on aesthetic grounds, whether ironic or sincere, obscure the sharp political thrust of Duchamp's readymades, which challenge institutions and markets that reduce art to the level of a commodity while retaining their pretensions to what John Berger (1972, 23) calls the "bogus religiosity" attached to works of high art.[5]

The transgressive nature of Duchamp's sculpture is captured more clearly in those commentaries that embellish their formalist appreciations with a hyperbolic spiritual discourse, adopted in mockery of the "bogus religiosity" that cloaks much aesthetic discourse. The title of Louise Norton's essay "Buddha of the Bathroom" sets the tone early on. Contemporary celebrations of *Fountain* often echo this provocative use of religious metaphors to describe a piece of bathroom plumbing. The sculptor Robert Smithson, for example, wittily declares Duchamp "a spiritualist of Woolworth . . . a kind of priest . . . turning a urinal into a baptismal font" (1973, 47).[6]

Duchamp's *Fountain* and much of its artistic and critical legacy clearly reflect the artist's desire to unsettle basic epistemological categories that separate the aesthetic from the everyday, the sacred from the profane. Given the original function of Duchamp's selected object for this readymade, it is not surprising that one of its most intriguing effects is its challenge to the binary opposition of the sexes. In his definitive study of *Fountain*, William Camfield describes the convergence of genders in the sculpture: "A masculine association cannot be divorced from the object because the original identity and function of the urinal remain evident, yet the overriding image is one of some generic female form—a smooth, rounded organic shape with flowing curves. . . . [Duchamp] transfigured . . . a fixture serving the dirty biological needs of men to a form suggestive of a serene seated buddha or a chaste veiled madonna" (Camfield 1989, 33–35).

Such gender confusion is not just an expression of Duchamp's personal predilections and humor; it is also characteristic of the particular historical moment at which *Fountain* was created. In the first decades of the twentieth century in the West, Victorian culture's segregation of male (public) and female (domestic) spheres began to give way under the pressure of shifting gender roles. This evolution was exemplified by the androgynous figure of the New Woman—a mythical icon of (allegedly) liberated and empowered modern women who were penetrating the public worlds of work and politics. A cartoon published in Germany in 1925, captioned "Lotte at the Crossroads," depicts such a cosmopolitan woman, dressed in a masculine tailored suit incongruously adorned with a flower, hair slicked back, and cigarette in hand, hesitating before two lavatory doors clearly marked *Damen* and *Herren*. This New Woman is confronted by the discontinuity between the absolute categories of sexual difference regulated by public toilet signage, on one hand, and her own more complex gender identity, on the other.[7]

In contrast to those who were made anxious and resentful by this destabilizing of sexual difference (the New Woman provoked a flood of misogynistic literary and artistic attacks), Duchamp was happy to add to the confusion. His most elaborate contribution to the undermining of gender identity was his adoption of a female alter ego. Rrose Sélavy (whose name puns on the phrases "Eros, c'est la vie" [Eros, that's life] or "arroser la vie" [to water life]) was incarnated by Duchamp posing in female drag in several photographs and by a female mannequin displayed in masculine drag (in a man's jacket, shirt, tie, and hat but nude below the waist) at a 1938 exhibition of Surrealist art. Duchamp's casual practice of alternating genders dissolves Lotte's anxious dilemma into an opportunity for performance and play.

Rrose Sélavy did produce several visual and textual works specifically under her own name, and she shared Duchamp's taste for somewhat pornographic puns and aphorisms. For example, in the obscure notes accompanying his major work *The Bride Stripped Bare by Her Bachelors, Even*, he offers the following enigmatic declaration: "—one only has: for *female* the public urinal and one *lives* by it" (Duchamp 1973, 23).[8]

To read this aphorism as degrading to women seems incompatible with what we know about Duchamp's work and life. One might hear in it instead an effort to mask behind a rather adolescent witticism the sad confession of an impossible desire that finds only solitary satisfaction. Duchamp depicts such lonely autoeroticism in his representation of the bachelor figures in *The Bride Stripped Bare*. Fated never to possess the bride, each bachelor is condemned, as the artist euphemistically puts it, "to grind his chocolate himself," while repeating the bachelor's litany: "Slow life, Vicious circle, Onanism, Horizontal, round trip for the buffer, Junk of Life" (Duchamp 1973, 56).

The convergence of male and female forms in Duchamp's urinal has been analyzed by art historians in the context of this doomed heterosexual drama.[9] Recent "queer" readings of *Fountain*, however, have shifted attention from the anxiety aroused by its destabilization of gender categories to the threatened collapse of the heterosexual/homosexual divide.[10]

In his meticulously researched and carefully argued essay "Object Choice: Marcel Duchamp's *Fountain* and the Art of Queer Art History," Paul Franklin sets *Fountain* in the context of the gay male subculture flourishing in public toilets in Paris and New York in the early decades of the twentieth century. He argues that one strategic intention of Duchamp's political and aesthetic manifestation was to associate avant-garde artistic practice with repressed queer sexualities, especially with those illicit activities (of exhibitionism and voyeurism) associated with public toilets.[11]

In his account of the history of pissoirs, Franklin describes how as early as the 1860s these public facilities had become popular venues for homosexual cruising and targets for police surveillance and arrests. Franklin argues that the pissoirs were scandalous meeting grounds not only because of the sexual mingling that occurred there but because they offered a space of *cultural* mingling in which "the most entrenched cultural divisions of sexuality, race, ethnicity, class and geography" were transgressed (Franklin 2000, 29).

The public toilet, even before Duchamp's transformation of it, was perceived from its inception in the nineteenth century as a threat to systems of definition, segregation, and social control. This general epistemological destabilization produced a collective anxiety that found concrete expression in moral and sanitary objections to these perceived havens for homosexual activity. As his adoption of a female alter ego indicates, Duchamp did not share the homophobia of many of his contemporaries. Like Freud, he readily acknowledged the homosexual component in his collaborative work with other men, describing such relations as a form of "artistic pederasty." He remarked with characteristic indifference about his relationship with André Breton, "One could even see in it a homosexual element, if we were indeed homosexuals. We were not, but it is all the same" (qtd. in Franklin 2000, 44).

In the second half of the twentieth century, the association of public toilets with homosexual activity has more explicitly political repercussions. In "Tearooms and Sympathy, or, The Epistemology of the Water Closet," Lee Edelman describes postwar American culture of the late 1950s and early 1960s as dominated by the desire to fortify American national identity and ideology against the perceived threat of global communism. Focusing his analysis on the role of the intensely charged site of the public urinal in a contemporary political scandal, Edelman reveals how anxieties about contamination by communism became entangled in the collective imaginary with anxieties about exposure to homosexuality. Like communism, homosexuality threatened the ideological construction of American middle-class respectability and norms: "Thus the postwar machinery of American nationalism operated by enshrining and mass-producing the archaic, bourgeois fantasy of a self-regulating familial sanctuary" (1992, 269).

Such defensive "heterosexual mythologizing," as Edelman puts it, was undermined by the existence of the public men's room as a site of sexual transgression. He argues that although the gender signs on public toilets seem to assure the certainty of sexual difference and segregation, there is no signage to protect heterosexual from homosexual patrons. As a result of the exposure of this unregulated "difference within," the masculine preserve of the men's room becomes a site of "epistemological crisis," where the "fracturing of the linguistic and epistemic order" (1992, 277) destabilizes all defining categories, personal as well as national.[12]

The innate vulnerability of definitional signs to such fracturing has been explored in more theoretical terms by Jacques Lacan in "The Agency of the Letter in the Unconscious, or Reason since Freud." Lacan offers as a concrete illustration of his argument an image of the signage on public lavatories. His essay begins with a familiar equation from structural linguistics: the word *tree* (the "signifier") is set over the image of a tree (the "signified"), and the two combine to produce the composite and communicable "sign." To emphasize the arbitrariness of such an equation, Lacan substitutes another example: images of two identical doors are labeled with the different signifiers, "LADIES" and "GENTLEMEN" (1977, 151; Figure 10.1). He suggests provocatively that what we perceive as the natural given of sexual difference is actually an arbitrary cultural and linguistic construction fortified by "the laws of urinary segregation" (1977, 151).

To show this fundamental *méconnaissance* at work, Lacan puts these lavatory signs into an anecdote about a brother and sister sitting opposite each other on a train. As the train pulls into the station, the similarity between enamel station signs and enamel toilet signs leads the brother to announce, "Look . . . we're at Ladies," to which the sister responds, from her different perspective, "Idiot! . . . Can't you see we're at Gentlemen?" (Lacan 1977, 152).

Lacan is pessimistic about the repercussions of our captivation by such arbitrary constructions of difference: "For these children, Ladies and Gen-

Figure 10.1 Lacanian diagram laws of urinary segregation.

tlemen will be henceforth two countries toward which each of their souls will strive on divergent wings, and between which a truce will be the more impossible since they are actually the same country" (1977, 152). Lacan's analogy here between national difference (and, indeed, all forms of "factionalism") and sexual difference suggests that both are cultural and linguistic illusions. Our defensive attachment to these stabilizing structures of binary opposition—whether political or sexual—makes any unmediated and undistorted relationship with the "other" impossible.

In the general drift of late-twentieth-century thought, explorations of the relations between the sexes, between nations, and between self and "other" have increased in political and psychoanalytic complexity. The legacy of Duchamp's *Fountain* in contemporary manifestations of toilet art, particularly in works by Dorothy Cross and Ilya Kabakov, reflects these developments.[13] The installations by these two artists stand apart from much contemporary toilet art by combining political seriousness with the conceptual wit and playfulness of Duchamp's original gesture.

Dorothy Cross's *Attendant* is a site-specific installation that explores the unconscious sources of a specific history of political conflict. The artist created this work in 1992 as part of the *Edge Biennial*, a group exhibition held simultaneously in London and Madrid. Cross sought out in each of these world capitals a hidden or abandoned territory where the dominant culture's repressed but constitutive fantasies lay buried. The two spaces she selected—a nun's residence in Madrid and an abandoned underground pissoir in London—represent in concrete architectural form the segregation of the realms of church and state, private and public, spiritual and corporeal, female and male. By leading her audience literally down into these segregated spaces, however, Cross reveals a breach deep within each one, where everything excluded as abject and "other" has made its secret habitation. Moving from private convent to public urinal, the artist takes us from a primal territory of the maternal, where male and female are still inchoate, to an explicitly male preserve where rigid definitions of masculinity and power will be unsettled by the return of repressed desires and fears.

Attendant was situated in an abandoned public facility whose distinctly Victorian tile work calls up that era's repressive attitudes toward the body and bodily functions, attitudes reinforced spatially by its underground placement. Visitors to the site descend the stairs to a landing where two painted signs direct them to proceed to the left or to the right. Instead of the usual lavatory choice of "Ladies" or "Gentlemen," the visitor must choose to descend as "English" or "Irish" (Figures 10.2 and 10.3). Both stairways, however, lead to the same lower area, where the original fixtures have been replaced by two bronze urinals cast by the artist: one in the shape of England, the other in the shape of Ireland. Mounted on the tiled wall, each map/bowl tapers below into an anatomically correct penis-shaped drain pipe (Figure 10.4).

Figure 10.2 Dorothy Cross, *Attendant,* at *Edge Biennial,* London and Madrid, 1992. (Courtesy of the artist.)

Figure 10.3 Dorothy Cross, *Attendant,* at *Edge Biennial,* London and Madrid, 1992. (Courtesy of the artist.)

The history of British efforts to segregate the Irish, even within Ireland, is mockingly reversed in this staging of an intimate confluence of the two peoples below the surface of Britain's own national capital. The title of the installation refers to the not-so-distant past when one of the few jobs available to Irish immigrants in London was that of "attendant" in a public toilet. The meeting of the two nations in Cross's underground facility is designed to suggest curiosity and desire rather than exclusion or hostility. The penises incline toward each other in what appears to be a natural and spontaneous response that is perhaps possible only in the relative seclusion of this underground space.

Cross's meticulously, even tenderly, crafted bronze urinals have a very different impact from the conceptual chill of Duchamp's piece of commercial plumbing. Unlike *Fountain,* which was liberated from its conventional use, Cross's urinals are incorporated into a social site, made anthropomorphic and functional. The implied invitation to viewers to make use of one or the other bowl reenacts on a bodily level the linguistic choice already made on the landing above: to identify with and follow the directional signs for either "English" or "Irish" users of the facility. In Cross's installation, such definitional categories and identifications are exposed as illusory; the two nationally segregated stairways lead to the same space below, and both nationally distinct urinal maps are positioned to drain into the

Figure 10.4 Dorothy Cross, *Attendant,* at *Edge Biennial,* London and Madrid, 1992. (Courtesy of the artist.)

same hole in the floor. As one critic puts it, "inevitably, as with all such neat divisions, these signs lead you astray" (Isaak 1995, 26).

Cross is more optimistic than Lacan about the possibility of a productive encounter of self and other that might take place beyond this domain of misleading signs. Although the index fingers in the signs on the landing point in opposite directions, they are replaced below by the penises inclining tentatively toward one another. The sly hint at homoeroticism in this underground meeting place is only one aspect of Cross's broader exploration of masculine identity, nationalism, and power.

Cross's casting of the urinals in the shape of maps calls up the conflicted history of centuries of British invasion, remapping, and renaming of Irish territories. In Cross's installation, the playing field is leveled because England and Ireland are both represented only in outline, without names or borders. No longer a system of knowledge, an exercise in the power of dividing and naming, the map becomes instead an empty receptacle, its three-dimensionality as a urinal opening it up to the instability of multiple and temporary meanings. In *Attendant,* mapping becomes participatory, an open pathway to chance encounters above- as well as belowground.

In the same year as the *Edge Biennial,* the town of Kassell, Germany, hosted the prestigious international exhibition of contemporary art *Docu-*

menta. As several critics noted at the time, quite a few of the works on display dealt with bodily functions.[14] Although by the 1990s scatology, like pornography, had exhausted its ability to shock the art world, one of those works did provoke something of a scandal—Ilya Kabakov's *The Toilet*. The objections that were raised about the Soviet artist's installation, however, were quite different from those that greeted Duchamp's *Fountain*.

For each *Documenta* exhibition, some of the most influential and innovative artists from around the world are invited to produce a new work for the occasion. Kabakov understood his inclusion in this august company as an invitation to create a work that was explicitly "Russian-Soviet." As the "representative of the Soviet motherland," he explained, he felt he "should take the position which corresponded to its position in the world. . . . That place, of course, was in the rear. . . . [In] the front [of the main exhibition space of the neo-classical Fridericianum] was America, Europe was in the middle, and Russia was in the back" (qtd. in Wallach 1996, 222).

In that unobtrusive and uncontested space, Kabakov recreated a public toilet exactly like those he remembered seeing throughout Russia during the 1960s and 1970s, "sad structures with walls of white lime turned dirty and shabby, covered with obscene graffiti that one can't look at without being overcome with nausea and despair" (Kabakov 1995, 162). Visitors patiently lined up by gender, as directed by the familiar signage on the two entrances (Figure 10.5). Upon entering, they found that the space, still containing open stalls with only crude holes for squatting, had been transformed by the artist into a typical, modest two-room Soviet apartment—the living room and kitchen on the "Men's" side, the bedroom on the "Women's" side (Figures 10.6 and 10.7). As Svetlana Boym describes the impact

Figure 10.5 Ilya Kabakov, *The Toilet*, at *Documenta IX*, Kassell, Germany, 1992. (Courtesy of the artist.)

Figure 10.6 Ilya Kabakov, *The Toilet*, at *Documenta IX,*
Kassell, Germany, 1992. (Courtesy of the artist.)

Figure 10.7 Ilya Kabakov, *The Toilet*, at *Documenta IX,*
Kassell, Germany, 1992. (Courtesy of the artist.)

of the installation, "Here, side by side with the black hole, everyday life continues uninterrupted" (1998, 505).

Articles in the Russian press perceived Kabakov's toilets as "symbols of national shame," and many of the artist's countrymen were scandalized that such a degrading image of their culture had been exposed to an audience of "outsiders." "Russian national mythology," Boym explains, "had no place for ironic nostalgia" (1998, 511). Although they misunderstood the artist's intentions, these media accounts were perhaps more accurate in their anticipation of how some members of *Documenta*'s international audience would interpret Kabakov's art.

The Toilet belongs to a series of works the artist describes as "total installations" of Soviet life (one project is titled simply *This Is Where We Live*).[15] Despite the artist's repeated efforts at clarification, these projects have often been interpreted literally instead of metaphorically. Seen as *literal* recreations—of public toilets, communal kitchens, workers' barracks— these constructed "scenes" appear to some as confirmation rather than contestation of the West's dehumanizing stereotypes of Russian life. The artist himself reports with a characteristically witty ingenuousness:

A woman came to me: "Mr. Artist, please tell me . . . is it really true all people in the Soviet Union live in the toilet?" I said: "Yes." "But what percent," people asked. I said "Two years ago it was seventy-five percent; today practically everyone." . . . And a man came to me and said: "I understand why Russians live in toilets, because they're so lazy they have no time to go to a toilet." This is tragic, but also funny, because I understand well what kind of concept people have of Russians. (qtd. in Wallach 1996, 88)

Determined to "demystify Western perceptions of the Soviet Union, communism and 'the evil empire'" (Schlegel 1999, 99), Kabakov invites viewers into a total environment where despite indications of the grimmest poverty, there is always evidence of the persistence of human dignity: attentiveness to detail, efforts to preserve the most worn objects and to adorn the most hopeless space with scraps of beauty. To notice such gestures of tender domestication is to recognize the lived humanity behind the stereotypes, to discover our common desire to make a home.

Yet what is the effect of staging this human drama inside a public toilet? As its history reveals, the public toilet has been, from its inception, a paradoxical space where public and private converge. In the context of Soviet life, this confusion is emblematic of the particular nature of lived intimacy in a culture in which the private or personal was often subjected to the constraints of communal living (shared kitchens and bathrooms) and to the official goals of a utopian collectivity (Boym 1998, 499–503). Kabakov's work reflects this peculiarly Soviet "dystopian" intimacy in which the ordinariness of everyday life is displayed and cherished without being idealized, in which the experience of home, for the Soviet citizen as for the exile, is always somewhat alienating and uncanny.

One impetus behind *The Toilet* was Kabakov's desire to show how even in the rubble of the failed utopian promise of the Soviet system or in the displacement of exile, a certain vitality survives; the "indestructible, ordinary, almost vegetative human existence overcomes destruction" (Biro 1996, 59). The piece also has a personal source in Kabakov's childhood memory. The artist describes his mother's circumstances when he was accepted into a Moscow boarding school for art students. Because he was a young boy, his mother wanted to be nearby, so she took a job as a housekeeper at the school. Unable to afford an apartment, she lived clandestinely for a brief period in a pantry that had originally been a small public toilet. The humiliation of his mother's eventual ejection even from this pathetic little corner is made endurable for Kabakov only by his insistence on the dignity with which she survived her homelessness (Wallach 1996, 221).

In *The Toilet*, Kabakov pays tribute to his mother's endurance, and following her example, he demonstrates in Kassel as elsewhere his ability to make a home of art wherever he finds himself. The habitations he creates are never idealized fantasies but environments in which the concrete specificity of each object, each chipped plate or frayed jacket, even each stain on the wall has been meticulously created by the artist with the care and tenderness that lies at the heart of home—even in a public toilet.

Paradoxically, the public or communal toilet, where taking care of one's private business is sometimes a matter of public knowledge, can also provide a temporary refuge. The shared toilets Kabakov remembers from his childhood evoke for him the possibility, even in communal living, of treasured moments of solitary pleasure. For an installation titled *Toilet in the Corner* (1991), Kabakov constructed a shabby bathroom door in the corner of a gallery. Through the opaque windows in the door a dim light could barely be seen, but viewers could hear clearly a voice coming from within, singing Neapolitan songs with abandon. Behind the peeling door of this communal toilet some anonymous individual lets himself dream. Kabakov associates this installation with his childhood memory of the pleasure of hiding in a dresser. From within that "dark shelter," removed from the "torment" of constantly being with others, he could observe the ordinary life of the family, unseen (qtd. in Stooss 2003, vol. 1, 339).

Kabakov reminds us, then, that the public restroom, communal toilet, or clothes dresser can be transformed into an island of refuge even within the clamor of collective living. Yet he is also thinking beyond those temporary and cramped retreats, to imagine more utopian possibilities. For example, his plan for an installation titled *Toilet by the River* consists of a double public latrine open at the front, giving each user a beautiful view of the river and landscape beyond. The artist describes the paradoxical convergence here of "two 'meditative' states: sitting in the toilet and dreaming in quiet, wonderful nature . . . [in] isolation from the social world surrounding and frustrating each of us; a marvelous feeling of solitude, tranquility and peace" (qtd. in Stooss 2003, vol. 2, 332).[16] In his conversation with the artist, Joseph Bakshtein points out the many obstacles to a successful realization of this project, the insurmountable incompatibility of a functioning outhouse and a "poetic" communing with nature. Kabakov responds that perhaps the most important aspect of the project is that very impossibility. Truly utopian, it can exist, perhaps, "only in the imagination." After all, he concludes, "The dream, the desire, is more important than anything" (qtd. in Stooss 2003, vol. 2, 133, 135).

This brief analysis of the tradition of toilet art in the twentieth century has taken us from Duchamp's witty displacement of the urinal from a plumbing supply store to an art gallery, to the exploration by artists such as Cross and Kabakov of the displacement of people in our increasingly urbanized global culture. Duchamp "threw the urinal in our faces," but Cross and Kabakov open up the strangely intimate space of the public toilet to unexpected human encounters—with our own repressed desires and dreams, with that alien "other," and even with the beauty of nature. The transformative power of art gives asylum to the humble urinal, allowing it to dream its way not only to Duchamp's new intellectual regions but to unexpected new identities and functions that exceed all definition.

Notes

1. Qtd. in J. Gough-Cooper and J. Caumont, "Ephemerides on and about Marcel Duchamp and Rrose Sélavy, 1887–1968," in P. Hulten, *Marcel Duchamp: Work and Life.*

2. I am deeply indebted to the scholarship of Camfield and Franklin, in particular, for their insightful analyses of Duchamp's work, and also for their meticulous gathering of information and bibliographical resources on *Fountain.*

3. During the final days of a Dada exhibition at the Pompidou Center in Paris, a seventy-seven-year-old performance artist, Pierre Pinoncelli, attacked *Fountain* with a hammer, repeating his 1993 demonstration in Nîmes, where he urinated in the sculpture before attacking it. A similar provocation was executed by the "guerilla artists" Yuan Cai and Jian Jun Xi, who paid homage to Duchamp by urinating in *Fountain* while it was on display at the Tate Modern in 2000. See "Dada Artist Accused of Vandalizing Duchamp Piece," *USA Today,* January 6, 2006.

4. Octavio Paz asserts the irrelevance of aesthetics to the readymades and emphasizes their critical edge: "It would be senseless to argue about their beauty or ugliness, firstly because they are beyond beauty and ugliness, and secondly because they are not creations but signs, questioning or negating the act of creation. . . . It is criticism in action" (1978, 22).

5. Two contemporary artists following Duchamp's lead in using the trope of the toilet to challenge art institutions are Gavin Turk (who labeled a series of toilet basins with the names of major art institutions) and Michael Craig-Martin (who painted a portrait of *Fountain* in hot red in the lobby of MOMA). Others have introduced toilets into art galleries in a less critical manner, simply asking viewers to give the same respect and attentiveness to the things of everyday life that they reserve for the contemplation of art (Takashi Homma and Tatsurou Bashi).

6. Taking this witty form of veneration to an extreme, the artist Mike Bidlo spent two years producing 3,254 drawings of *Fountain*, varying the image in scale and position, applying palimpsest and collage techniques. Following Bidlo's remark that "these drawings were like daily meditations," one reviewer describes the drawings as "surrogate fonts and shrines [that] almost glow with unearthly light, like rows of votive candles" (Rosenblum 1999, 102).

7. This cartoon is reproduced in *cut with a kitchen knife: the weimar photomontages of hannah höch*, by Maude Lavin (1993, xviii).

8. Duchamp's equation of the female genitals and the urinal, both receptacles for male fluids, is certainly not original; it belongs to the familiar lexicon of misogynistic jokes. In 1967 the feminist artist and writer Kate Millet used the insulting analogy critically to expose the debasement of women in a male-dominated culture. Her installation titled "City of Saigon" included a row of urinals behind bars, each one positioned between a pair of female legs in high heels. Millet's specific political target here was the mistreatment of women prostitutes in the sex markets flourishing in Saigon under the patronage of American soldiers (O'Dell 1997, 49). The joke was repeated uncritically as recently as 2004, in Virgin Atlantic's design for the urinals in its clubhouse restroom at JFK Airport. "Kisses," as the urinals were named, were ceramic fonts in the shape of huge, open, red-lipped female mouths. Public outrage soon sent the company's designers back to the drawing board (Saul 2004, 8).

9. See Krauss 1977 and Jones 1994.

10. See Franklin 2000 and Hopkins 1998.

11. As Franklin suggests (2000, 27), it is not difficult to see the connection between these activities and the kind of display and viewing that take place in art galleries and museums. Visitors to the Philadelphia Museum of Art, for example, can view Duchamp's *Etant donnés* only through the peepholes in a wooden door. The scene revealed is a strange diorama featuring a naked female figure, legs spread and genitals exposed.

12. Several contemporary artists have used the trope of the toilet to raise issues about violence against gays. See especially the work of Hugh Steers.

13. Some of the contemporary artists working in this vein, focusing on issues of homelessness, poverty, urban devastation, and global exploitation, are Richard Posner, Damian Ortega, Marjetica Potrc, and Achim Mohne.

14. In his interview with Ilya Kabakov about *Documenta IX*, Boris Groys remarks, "It should be said that very many artists in that *Documenta* without concurring with each other produced works that in one way or another related to an anal system. There was the installation with the bathroom with the ancient depictions in it, the fake bathroom in the garden, the system of children's bathrooms, there was the not-so-bad work by the French artist with bathroom signs, a ceramic depiction of shit, etc." (qtd. in Wallach 1996, 222).

15. See Yvette Biro 1996 on Kabakov's total installations *This Is Where We Live* and *The Communal Kitchen*.

16. In a related utopian plan, Kabakov imagines placing a single outhouse on the precipice of a mountain, where it is "transformed into a type of 'Chinese pavilion' intended for meditation." Even more dramatically than the toilet on the river, this mountain facility offers "a withdrawal from people, total isolation, seclusion, a 'heavenly' high point from which to view the world" (Kabakov and Kabakov 2004, 239).

References

Anon. 1917. "His Art Too Crude for Independents." *New York Herald*, April 11, p. 6.

Berger, John. 1972. *Ways of Seeing*. London: Penguin Books.

Biro, Yvette. 1996. "Digging around the Ruins of Utopia." *Performing Arts Journal* 18, no. 3 (September): 58–65.

Boym, Svetlana. 1998. "On Diasporic Intimacy: Ilya Kabakov's Installations and Immigrant Homes." *Critical Inquiry* 24 (Winter): 498–524.

Camfield, William. 1989. *Marcel Duchamp: Fountain*. Houston: Menil Collection and Fine Art Press.

―――. 1991. "Marcel Duchamp's *Fountain:* Aesthetic Object, Icon or Anti-Art." In *The Definitively Unfinished Marcel Duchamp.* Ed. Thierry de Duve. Cambridge, Mass.: MIT Press, 133–78.

Duchamp, Marcel. 1973. *The Writings of Marcel Duchamp.* New York: Da Capo Press.

Edelman, Lee. 1992. "Tea and Sympathy, or The Epistemology of the Water Closet." In *Nationalisms and Sexualities.* Ed. Andrew Parker, Mary Russo, Doris Sommer, and Patricia Yaeger. New York: Routledge, 263–84.

Franklin, Paul B. 2000. "Object Choice: Marcel Duchamp's *Fountain* and the Art of Queer Art Theory." *Oxford Art Journal* 23 (1): 23–50.

Higgins, Charlotte. 2004. "Work of Art That Inspired a Movement . . . a Urinal." *The Guardian,* December 2, 2004. Available at http://guardian.co.uk/ok/2004/ dec/02/arts. artsnews1.

Hopkins, David. 1998. "Men before the Mirror: Duchamp, Man Ray and Masculinity." *Art History* 21, no. 3 (September): 303–23.

Isaak, Jo Anna. 1995. *Laughter Ten Years After.* Geneva, N.Y.: Hobart and William Smith Colleges Press.

Jones, Amelia. 1994. *Postmodernism and the En-gendering of Marcel Duchamp.* Cambridge: Cambridge University Press.

Kabakov, Ilya. 1995. *Installations 1983–1995.* Paris: Centre Georges Pompidou.

Kabakov, Ilya, and Emilia Kabakov. 2004. *The Utopian City and Other Projects.* Stuttgart: Kerber Verlag.

Krauss, Rosalind. 1977. *Passages in Modern Sculpture.* London: Thames and Hudson.

Lacan, Jacques. 1977. "The Agency of the Letter in the Unconscious, or Reason since Freud." In *Ecrits: A Selection.* Trans. Alan Sheridan. New York: W. W. Norton, 146–78.

Lavin, Maude. 1993. *Cut with a kitchen knife: The weimar photomontages of hannah höch.* New Haven: Yale University Press.

Norton, Louise. 1917. "Buddha of the Bathroom." *The Blind Man,* no. 2 (May): 5–6.

O'Dell, Kathy. 1997. "Fluxus Feminus." *TDR* 41, no. 1 (Spring): 43–60.

Paz, Octavio. 1978. *Marcel Duchamp, Appearance Stripped Bare.* Trans. Rachel Phillips and Donald Gardner. New York: Seaver Books.

Richter, Hans. 1965. *Dada Art and Anti-Art.* New York: McGraw-Hill.

Roche, Henri-Pierre. 1959. "Souvenirs of Marcel Duchamp." In *Marcel Duchamp.* Ed. Robert Lebel. New York: Grove Press, 87.

Rosenblum, Robert. 1999. "Bidlo's Shrines." *Art in America* 87, no. 2 (February): 102.

Saul, Michael. 2004. "Potty Mouth!" *New York Daily News,* March 20, p. 8.

Schlegel, Amy Ingrid. 1999. "The Kabakov Phenomenon." *Art Journal* 58, no. 4 (Winter): 98–101.

Smithson, Robert. 1973. "Robert Smithson on Duchamp, an Interview." *Artforum* 12, no. 2 (October): 43.

Stooss, Toni. 2003. *Ilya Kabakov Installations, 1983–2000: Catalogue Raisonne I and II.* Dusseldorf: Richter Verlag.

Tomkins, Calvin. 1996. *Duchamp: A Biography.* New York: Henry Holt.

Wallach, Amei. 1996. *Ilya Kabakov: The Man Who Never Threw Anything Away.* New York: Harry Abrams.

Wood, Beatrice. 1985. *I Shock Myself: The Autobiography of Beatrice Wood.* Ojai, Calif.: Dillingham Press.

Toilet Training

Sarah Lucas's Toilets and the
Transmogrification of the Body

KATHY BATTISTA

The woman at her toilet has been an abiding trope in the history of art. From Titian to Picasso and Renoir, artists—almost always male—have depicted idealized images of women in their most private spaces. Their nude or scantily clad subjects are typically seen bathing, applying makeup, or adorning themselves, producing a sensuous, intimate look at femininity. Take, for example, Renoir's *Bather Arranging Her Hair* (ca. 1885). The nude woman is seen from behind, arranging her hair with raised arms: her undergarment is pulled down, revealing her breasts, swollen stomach, and buttocks for the (presumably male) viewer's gaze. Similarly, Degas' sumptuous treatment of female nudes presents a romanticized notion of ballerinas and models who were, in fact, living in penury and quite often working as prostitutes.[1]

Women artists historically have avoided the theme of the nude at her toilet. When painting scenes of female domesticity, they have instead concentrated on the nurturing aspects of the female sex. A typical depiction is Elisabeth Vigée Le Brun's *Self-Portrait with Her Daughter Julie* (1789) and Mary Cassatt's *Young Mother Sewing* or *Little Girl Leaning on Her Mother's Knee* (1902).[2] In these scenes, femininity is expressed not through the sexualized body but through the mother-and-child relationship. The female body is seen as a sign of fertility and unconditional love rather than an eroticized subject for voyeuristic contemplation.

In the 1970s feminist artists undermined the classic female nude in practices that were increasingly concerned with demystifying women's experiences and exploring debates around gender and biology. For example, Judy Chicago's *Menstruation Bathroom* (1972) from the Feminist Art Program's *Womanhouse* exhibition is an installation in a domestic toilet that is filled (and literally overflowing) with detritus related to menstruation: bloody tampons and sanitary towels, douches, an enema bag, and feminine

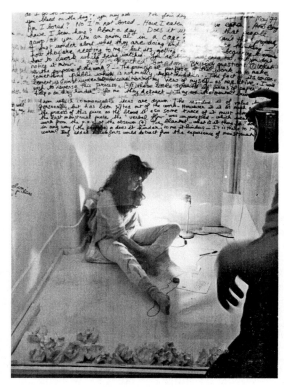

Figure 11.1 Catherine Elwes, *Menstruation II*, 1977.
(Courtesy of the artist.)

hygiene products refer to society's inability to cope with this taboo subject. Here Chicago presents the female bodily functions as untidy, uncontained, and abject. Interestingly, viewers were not allowed into the installation but saw it only through a thin veil of gauze.[3] This created a similar voyeuristic feel as that created while viewing a Degas or Renoir nude, although it might be argued that most of the audience for this exhibition would have been women sympathetic to the feminist cause.

Similarly, Catherine Elwes' *Menstruation* performances literally turned the viewing space into a toilet. While a student at the Slade School of Art in London during the late 1970s, and a burgeoning feminist practitioner, Elwes created two performances on the topic of menstruation. *Menstruation I* and *Menstruation II* (1977; Figure 11.1) took place in spaces at the Slade. In each of these performances, the artist sealed herself into cubicle-like spaces where she bled for the duration of one period.[4] Elwes' performances, like Chicago's installation, used abjection and female experience as catalysts for radical, confrontational work that expressed the political ethos of their generation, both in the United Kingdom and the United States.

The feminist interpretation of the woman at her toilet is witnessed more recently in the work of British artist Sarah Lucas.[5] In the first section of this chapter, I discuss her early photographic series and in particular works such as *Human Toilet Revisited* (1998), where she uses the toilet as a substitute for and an extension of the female form. (She has also used food as a substitute for human physiognomy.) In the second section, I examine how Lucas has employed toilets throughout much of her sculptural work. From a real ceramic toilet plumbed into her dealer Sadie Coles's gallery to polyurethane casts of toilets, Lucas uses the form as a stand-in for the human figure and as a symbol of lavatory humor. Lucas's work is discussed in relation to Robert Gober's and Hadrian Pigott's work on similar themes. This chapter attempts to understand Lucas's complex practice and her use of such imagery. Why does she portray herself as a toilet or on toilets, and how is this related to her female sexuality? And why is she fixated on the toilet as a sculptural form? How does this relate to other artists, notably male, who have engaged toilets in their practice? How does this relate to their sexuality?

Anthropomorphism: Toilets as Extensions of and Substitutions for Human Physiognomy

Sarah Lucas rose to prominence in the British group of artists who gained international critical attention and became known as the "YBAs" in the 1990s. Her colleagues include Damien Hirst, Tracey Emin,[6] Gavin Turk, and Gary Hume. Lucas's practice ranges across media, including photography, sculpture, and installation. Her work is characterized by a confrontational approach and often contains puns based on crass notions of sexuality. This can be illustrated through the use of ephemeral materials that suggest bodily parts, as in *Two Fried Eggs and a Kebab* (1992), where the eggs are a substitute for breasts and the kebab, genitals. This reference to food, and thus the digestive system, foreshadows work later in the decade where she turned to the depiction of herself as toilet, and thus the receptacle for digestive waste.

Take, for example, *Human Toilet I* and *Human Toilet II* (1996), from the series *Self Portraits 1990–1998*. In the first of these Lucas is seen in the photograph straddling the toilet bowl, with its lid raised, and holding the cistern in front of her face. She transmogrifies into a cartoon-like character, half woman, half toilet. The bag of rubbish seen behind her in the studio setting completes the composition with a wry joke. The overall theme of waste says much about how Lucas positions herself and the status of a woman artist. Perhaps it also refers to a more general comment on female identity and women's position in the contemporary art world.[7]

In *Human Toilet II* the artist portrays herself naked on the bowl of the toilet, cradling the black cistern in her arms. The cistern covers her torso, thus eradicating a view of the indicators of her sex, for example, breasts and genitals. It creates an androgynous effect, as only an oblique view of her face, legs, and arms is visible.[8] Her body is literally incorporated into the apparatus. The figure occupies the centre of the composition and is lit with a soft light, which seems to emanate from a window nearby. These works lack her trademark confrontational stare, witnessed in earlier photographs such as *Got a Salmon on #3* (1999) and *Eating a Banana* (1990). They are not, however, idealized views. In each case, the toilet is located in a semi-industrial space, perhaps the artist's studio, with dilapidated brick walls. The look is one of griminess and disarray rather than any idealized notion of a female toilet.

If Lucas portrays herself as a toilet in a soiled environment, is she saying that the female artist is literally "shit" or a "receptacle for excremental waste"? Matthew Collings has written that Lucas's *Human Toilet II* "really expresses what it's like to be knocked out by patriarchy."[9] This reading of the work, while alluding to earlier feminist art practice as well as theory, relies on a biographical reading of Lucas's piece. Has she, in fact, been knocked by patriarchy? I disagree: Lucas has enjoyed great success. She is one of the most respected and sought-after female artists of her generation, with shows at major public institutions,[10] a solid market for her work,[11] and the respect of her peers.[12] Lucas's work is more complex, and perhaps ambivalent, than a straightforward social commentary. That Lucas is both artist and model is an important factor in this discussion. Like other artists of her generation, including Jemima Stehli, Tracey Emin, Hayley Newman, and Elke Krystufek, Lucas turns the camera on herself, resulting in a narcissistic role as the subject and object of the gaze.[13] If there is an indictment of women as objects, seen elsewhere in her work and in popular culture, she is both victim and perpetrator. While assuming the "feminine" role of the object and the "masculine" role of the artist, she combines both the problem and the critique of voyeurism in her work.

In *Human Toilet Revisited* (1998; Figure 11.2), Lucas revisits this subject. Here she is seen sitting on the toilet, legs scrunched underneath her, smoking a cigarette.[14] As in *Human Toilet II*, her face is averted from the camera and gazes down toward the floor. Lucas is clad only in a gray T-shirt, which may suggest that she has just got out of bed or in fact that a sexual act has just taken place. If so, does the cigarette suggest a lonely postcoital moment? Here the toilet is a private resting place where one can ponder uninterrupted. In this photograph, the window is visible as well as the various cleaning products—Sturgene, Ariel—beside the toilet. The inclusion of these cleansers suggests the role of hygiene in today's cleanliness-obsessed culture. That domestic cleaning[15] is traditionally the role associated with the female sex further complicates this work.[16] Roland Barthes writes that the cleaning products we surround ourselves with carry signs:

Figure 11.2 Sarah Lucas, *Human Toilet Revisited*, 1998.
(Copyright by the artist and courtesy of Sadie Coles HQ, London.)

Powders . . . are selective, they push, they drive dirt through the texture of the object, their function is keeping public order not making war. This distinction has ethnographic correlatives: the chemical fluid is an extension of the washerwoman's movements when she beats the clothes, while powders replace those of the housewife pressing and rolling the washing against a sloping board.[17]

Barthes' discussion of detergents and cleaning agents is inextricably linked to the female sex, traditionally responsible for such household duties within the division of labor in the family. Compare this to Lucas's idea around toilets as sites for the washing away of dirt: "The toilets are a kind of rock bottom. . . . Hidden, dirty, removers of everything we don't want around. . . . We're all too familiar with them as receptacles and also as shapely objects."[18] If the toilet is an agent of removal for the hidden and dirty in society, and the toilet is an extension of the female in Lucas's work, then it is indeed the woman who is concerned with the muck and dirt. Lucas's self-portraits as toilets convey the idea of the women as the receptacle, the remover of the shit that society does not want. However, the self-portraits with toilets at the same time challenge gender stereotypes and resist any straightforward reading. The woman here is a far cry from earlier, idealized notions of women in toilets by male artists. Instead, these photographs raise a complex array of connotations. Lucas is at once masculine and feminine, vulnerable and confrontational. The toilets are seen as extensions of the female body as well as places of refuge.

Toilets as Sculptural Form: Lucas, Gober, and Pigott

Lucas's fascination with toilets carries across to her sculptural work. Indeed, the toilet and urinal have taken the central form of many of her installations as well. Take, for example, *Old In and Out* (1998), a urine-colored cast of a toilet base. In contrast to the toilets in her photographs, which were used for their grubby appearance, this sculpture is sanitized and aesthetically appealing. It is made of polyurethane and has the translucent quality of some of Rachel Whiteread's sculpture, for example, *100 Spaces* (1995).[19] The "old in and out" is cockney slang for a burglary and is a double entendre meaning sexual intercourse. The form of the sculpture, while suggestive of a female form in the void of the toilet, is also indicative of male sexual organs, with its protruding pipe at the side of the base. Thus the sculpture becomes a hermaphrodite, suggesting a confusion of the sexes.

The saggy version of this sculpture, *Old In and Out Saggy* (1998; Figure 11.3), pushes the confusion even further. Ambivalent sexuality is then wilted as the detumescent sculpture suggests something the opposite of its erect counterpart. Whereas *Old In and Out* is forceful and intact, the

Figure 11.3 Sarah Lucas, *Old In and Out Saggy*, 1998.
(Copyright by the artist and courtesy of Sadie Coles HQ, London.)

Old In and Out Saggy is weak, spent, and lacking vitality. Interestingly, the Victoria and Albert Museum chose this work as part of their Close Encounters program, where works of art were rotated through a series of domestic venues. Each family could place the work wherever they chose, and most chose to place it in the living room, creating an unusual context. One of the hosts of this work, Mari, commented:

> You definitely want to touch it—because it's translucent I suppose. On the other hand it's a toilet so you don't want to touch it. It's quite Salvador Dali—melting clocks and melting objects. At the same time it's quite British. The British are into toilet humour. *Carry on at Your Convenience*—Sid James cracking double-entendres in a factory making lavs.[20]

The tenuous divide between attraction and repulsion is indeed witnessed here. Mari's tendency to want to touch it is hampered by the idea of it being a toilet, with all the scatological implications that apply.[21]

Lucas's reference to Marcel Duchamp's *Fountain* (1917), an upturned urinal signed R. Mutt, is obvious. Duchamp's urinal has mythical status in the history of twentieth-century art. Just what is it about the urinal that sustains our captivation with this object? Indeed, artists from Bruce Nauman (*Self Portrait as Fountain*, 1965) to Alex Schweder[22] have paid homage to Duchamp's work.[23] Sherrie Levine, perhaps the ultimate post-modern artist in that her entire oeuvre is appropriated from earlier artworks by male artists, recreated Duchamp's urinal in *Fountain: After Marcel Duchamp A.P.* (1991). Levine's sculpture is a bronze cast of a contemporary urinal rather than an actual readymade, thus creating an individual and unique work. Her casting of it in a precious material says much about the legacy and mythology of the earlier male artist. Indeed, this may also be a nod to Piero Manzoni's *Merda d'artista* (1961), which is a tin—it is an editioned work—of the artist's shit. While Manzoni sought to create a personal and intimate work for collectors, he valued his shit per gram at the price of gold, a reference to the tradition of artist as alchemist that is associated with Yves Klein, Joseph Beuys, and Duchamp.[24]

Lucas has used urinals in her work: for example, the recent sculpture *Toilet and Urinal* (2003; Figure 11.4) where Lucas pairs a urinal and a toilet bowl, both covered with bar towels. Lucas's work suggests a pairing of the sexes yet blurs the distinction between them. The bar towels again represent the basest idea of masculinity in British society—lager lads, pubs, and yob culture—as seen through the eyes of the artist. They also hint at the ultimate site of all that drinking—the toilet or urinal and eventually the sewer. One might also reflect on the associations the sculpture

Figure 11.4 Sarah Lucas, *Toilet and Urinal*, 2003.
(Copyright by the artist and courtesy of Sadie Coles HQ, London.)

has with class connotations, with the pub as the center of working-class British social life.

A. C. Grayling writes eloquently on Lucas's use of crass symbols for women:

> Her point, or at least a major part of it, seems to be that much of the sexual aspect of life consists of attitudes and anxieties formed in exactly such caricatures, and that even women more than half buy into them. In fact, her sculptures make one ask whether women invite, expect or even enjoy the reductive view of themselves—and at the same time whether they are covertly laughing at boys as wankers, and at the boys' fear of the female that makes them mouth and enact such denigrations of it.[25]

Grayling's hypothesis that women may actually invite the reductive view of their sex makes perfect sense in terms of the culture in which Lucas lives. So-called ladette culture has been witnessed in Britain during the last decade. Certainly, Lucas seems to delight in the use of such crass symbols of female sexuality and to enjoy the toilet humor involved.

Toilet and Urinal fetishizes abjection through the bar towels. Using either apparatus would result in relieving oneself onto the fuzzy, thick bar towels. The idea of towels soaked in piss is reminiscent of the beer-soaked towels found on the bar in any local pub. In the sculpture Lucas suggests that alcohol quickly turns to piss. Lucas seems to take the Beuysian notion of transformation of materials on board; however, her transformation is less alchemical and more grounded in social observation. Here she invokes both a body subject to the whims of the digestive system and one that is part of the economy of the city.

The toilet may also be considered the initial site for transformation of the scatological into a less-contaminating material. Dominique Laporte writes of the transformation of feces into fertilizer in the tenth-century Byzantine empire:

> Human scybala can only be used for fertilizer after a lengthy process of transformation. First, waste must be allowed to lie fallow, to precipitate and decant so that its qualities will mutate from the negative pole of their origin to the positive outcome, a noble and matchless pole. . . . What is burned and dried up fertilizes and nourishes, rank odors turn into perfume and rot into gold.[26]

One can imagine that although the process of transformation may have changed today, there is little development in ten centuries of civilization. Humans still shit, and that still poses a problem to cities: where and how do we dispose of it?

Toilet and Urinal becomes a fetishized pair of objects for a culture as obsessed with binge drinking as it is with hygiene and sexual stereotypes. The sculpture also characterizes both female and male, respectively. The pairing of the forms suggests man and woman, husband and wife. This work puts Lucas's previous forays into toilets in perspective. If the toilet is the female equivalent of the urinal, Lucas replaces Duchamp's accessory with its female counterpart, thus subverting the Duchampian paradigm so prevalent in contemporary art. Here Lucas's biography becomes important: the artist pays homage to Duchamp and yet simultaneously redresses the lack of the female artist in the history of twentieth-century avant-garde practice.

Lucas's work is reminiscent of other artists who have investigated and exploited the possibilities of urinals while undermining their status as icons of male sexuality. Robert Gober's[27] practice during the 1980s was concerned with domestic objects, ranging from sink units to drains.[28] These were often abstracted and attached to or embedded into unusual surfaces, such as tables or walls. *Untitled* (1985) is a hybrid of a sink and a urinal. Its white ceramic body suggests something of the Duchampian *Fountain*, yet it transcends this in its physical form, which is much less straightforward, with an attenuated and bastardized shape. Gober's sculpture appears to have been fabricated in the same manner as standard toilet apparatuses. However, the artist painstakingly makes each of these by hand.

Gober's references, like Lucas's, are based on political issues. Where Lucas positions herself in a debate around depictions of gender, sexuality, and the abject in contemporary British culture, Gober's stance is that of a

Figure 11.5 Hadrian Pigott, *Dysfunction*, 1994.
(Courtesy of the artist.)

homosexual male in American society. His work was synchronous with the onset of the AIDS epidemic, and its preoccupation with notions of hygiene, sterility, and contamination may be seen as representative of the fear and panic around the virus at that time.[29] *Drains* (1990) are pewter drains that suggest an orifice. Knowing Gober's biography and the context of his work, one can safely assume it is an anal orifice. If one accepts the drain as an anus, then the cross of the object becomes symbolic of the struggle against homophobia and hysteria around the epidemic. Seen in today's light, with the development of combination drug therapy and education around the topic, Gober's works are a testament to a particular moment in American culture, much as Lucas's work is indicative of a certain generation of British culture. Britain in the 1990s witnessed the return of lads' magazines such as *Loaded* and *FHM*, as well as "ladette" culture. Far enough detached from the feminist backlash of the 1980s, the next decade saw a resurgence in men reveling in bad behavior and the abolition of political correctness. It was once again about tits and ass, and this is what Lucas's work examines.

Both Lucas and Gober can be considered alongside the work of Hadrian Pigott.[30] His sculptural work in the 1990s consisted of an in-depth examination of sinks and other domestic appliances. While these objects are initially functional, Pigott renders them dysfunctional by altering their physical form. Like Gober, he painstakingly made this body of work by hand. Works such as his *Dysfunction* series (1994; Figure 11.5) are large-scale pieces, sculpted from soap and most often exhibited on the ground, without a plinth.[31] His *Re Surface* (1997) is a small, podlike sculpture that suggests an inverted sink or bathroom apparatus. While its material appearance is suggestive of a sink, its form is completely dysfunctional. Instead of containing a void, *Re Surface* is a bulbous form, which means that water or any liquid would just pour off of its surface. This white ceramic[32] shell is punctuated only by a hole, presumably the drain, with a plug attached by a chain. Like Gober's *Drains*, Pigott's drain evokes a bodily orifice. The sculpture can be exhibited either way, plugged or unplugged; in each case it suggests something different—containment or excess. It can be considered as male or female, or perhaps an amalgamation of both, in its physical qualities. While it features an orifice, which can be read as male or female, it also contains the means for plugging that orifice. Here Pigott turns a household object into something layered with meaning and allusions. Like Gober's work and Lucas's *Old In and Out Saggy*, Pigott's sculpture exudes a haptic quality. One wants to touch it, to run one's hands across its surface, which seems cool, smooth, and soothing.

Pigott was in fact inspired by Richard Hamilton's[33] *Homage à Chrysler Corps* (1957), which is an image of a car melded with the shape of a female. In this painting, emblematic of postwar consumption and desire for consumer goods, Hamilton equates bodily desire with the lust for household goods so prevalent in postwar England. Pigott was intrigued by Hamilton's interest in society's predilection for household goods[34] and began to make his sculptural series based around these ideas. The coloration of his sculptural works, such as the *Dysfunction* series and *Re Surface*, is a direct response to Hamilton's muted, fleshy tones in his *Chrysler* painting. Also, Pigott translates Hamilton's Cadillac ears, seen as breasts in the painting, to the bulbous forms found in works such as *Flesh Cadillac* (from the *Dysfunction* series).

Pigott's *Dream: Of Wanting, Wetness, and Waste* (1995; Figure 11.6) can be considered an extension of this phenomenon. In this six-minute video a protagonist (the artist himself) is embodied only by his hands. This figure becomes abnormally and obsessively engaged with a sink. After washing his hands he begins to wash the sink, caressing it with his soapy wet hands. His fingers penetrate the safety holes where the water would

Figure 11.6 Hadrian Pigott, still from *Dream: Of Wanting, Wetness, and Waste*, 1995. (Courtesy of the artist.)

normally drain, suggesting a sexual encounter with the object. As Lucas does with her human toilet, Pigott here crosses a boundary between human and household object, where the relationship has gone awry. The sink becomes fetishized in its anthropomorphism, and the protagonist crosses a boundary with the object. This is further emphasized as the protagonist begins to lick the surface of the sink, transgressing any normal relationship between the human and the apparatus. Throughout the video, the sound of trickling water is amplified at each point of transgression, creating a soundtrack akin to a dramatic plot.

Pigott's video encapsulates several of the themes found in the work of Lucas and Gober. First, the sink is anthropomorphic in that it is suggestive of a human form. This relates directly to Lucas's self-portraits with toilets and her sculptures, as well as Gober's urinals, which take on human characteristics. The unhealthy relationship between human and toilet is typified in Pigott's *Dream*. As in Lucas's photographs, the distinction between the human and the apparatus becomes blurred, with the body becoming part or joined with the fixture. Pigott has remarked on the blurred boundary between the body and the toilet fixtures in his work:

> I had already been seeing "body" in all these pieces, whether soap sculptures like Dysfunction where the body emerged, albeit in abstract form, as the chrome fittings and functions were stripped away and the locations of such notional functions shifted position across the forms, or, as in Dream, with the possibility of reading or misreading body into an inanimate object, particularly where that object has been designed to accommodate the human form in an intimate way.[35]

This double reference to the body—as formal inspiration as well as the inanimate becoming animate—relates to the work of Lucas and Gober. The latter's sinks become animate objects, while Lucas intermingles her body with that of the toilet.

Conclusion

The curious proliferation of toilets and related infrastructure is an abiding element of contemporary art. Lucas uses the toilet as an extension or a substitute for the body as well as a reference for the scatological by-products of society. Her predecessor Gober and her YBA colleague Pigott also entertain the toilet as an anthropomorphic entity. Perhaps it is fitting that toilets stand in for the human form, as they have been in existence almost as long as human beings. Plumbing is one of the first signs of civilization and, indeed, responsible for eradicating the spread of disease caused by waste. However, toilets become more than just infrastructure for Lucas and her male colleagues. They represent various forms of the human anatomy, as well as of sexuality. Gober's drains and dysmorphic sinks represent a fear of sexual contamination. Pigott's sculptures seem to suggest the anthropomorphic possibilities of domestic objects, in particular those that the body contacts in close proximity. Indeed, the transgression of a human and a fetishized object is predominant in his work. Lucas's toilets, while at times suggesting a sexual act, are indicative of the female body and its orifices and the metaphorical topics that they suggest. Her work above may be read as a subversive and humorous reworking of the Duchampian imperative: by morphing the female body into a readymade and depicting toilets in her sculptural work, she examines the scatological as a pervasive theme in the history of art.

Notes

1. See Anna Greutzner Robins and Richard Thomas, *Degas, Sickert and Toulouse-Lautrec: London and Paris 1870–1910* (London: Tate Publishing, 2005), 92; see also Richard Kendall and Griselda Pollock, eds., *Dealing with Degas: Representations of Women and the Politics of Vision* (London: Rivers Oram Press/Pandora List, 1992).

2. See Griselda Pollock, *Differencing the Canon: Feminist Desire and the Writing of Art's Histories* (London: Routledge, 1999), 204–10.=

3. See Amelia Jones, *Sexual Politics: Judy Chicago's* The Dinner Party *in Feminist Art History* (Los Angeles: UCLA at the Armand Hammer Museum of Art and Cultural Center in association with University of California Press, 1996), 191.

4. See Catherine Elwes, *Video Loupe* (London: KT Press, 2000), 56–57.

5. Lucas here plays with the notion that toilet refers both to the act of dressing oneself up as well as the object itself.

6. Emin and Lucas met at City Racing, the artist-run gallery in London. They worked side by side for a time in the 1990s. For a short while they ran a shop in a dilapidated Victorian house in Bethnal Green, in the East End of London. They sold ephemeral bits of art in the shop, à la Oldenberg's Store. See Kathy Battista, "Domestic Crisis: Women Artists and Derelict Houses in London 1974–1998," in *Surface Tension, Problematics of Site*, ed. Ken Ehrlich and Brandon LaBelle (Los Angeles: Errant Bodies, 2003). See also Matt Hale, Paul Noble, and Pete Owen, eds., *City Racing: The Life and Times of an Artist-Run Gallery 1988–1998* (London: Black Dog, 2002).

7. Recently Channel 4 broadcast a program called *What Price for Art*, which was presented by Lucas's colleague Tracey Emin. In this program she tried to understand the reasons that the work of women artists is still valued at less than that of their male colleagues. *What Price for Art*, Channel 4, March 15, 2006.

8. Her face is directed not toward the camera but outside of the window.

9. Matthew Collings, *Sarah Lucas* (London: Tate Publishing, 2002), 70.

10. Lucas has recently had solo shows at the Kunsthalle Zurich (2005) and Tate Liverpool (2005).

11. Available at http://www.artnet.com, http://www.artfacts.net, or http://www.the-artists.org. Lucas has consistently broken record prices for her work.

12. Lucas has historically been shown with her male peers, unlike many of her feminist predecessors who were marginalized from the gallery system. In fact, Damien Hirst selected her work in his watershed show *Freeze* in the London Docklands in 1988. *Minky Manky*, curated by Carl Freedman in 1995, also featured Lucas's work. Lucas was featured in the landmark show *Sensation* at the Royal Academy of Art in 1997. One of the most recent examples is *In-a-Gadda-da-Vida*, Tate Britain, March 3–May 31, 2004, where she showed alongside Damien Hirst and Angus Fairhurst.

13. See Laura Mulvey, "Visual Pleasure and Narrative Cinema," in *Visual and Other Pleasures* (Bloomington: Indiana University Press, 1989).

14. Cigarettes are an abiding theme in Lucas's work. They take different roles, ranging from accessories in self-portraits to material itself for a series of sculptural works. One might argue that they are phallic registers in her images. In one series, thousands of cigarettes are pieced together like matchstick houses to make toilet bowls, garden gnomes, bra and breasts, even a car. Her exhibition *The Fag Show* at Sadie Coles HQ in London (March 16–April 18, 2000) consisted of works made entirely out of cigarettes. Lucas has said, "I first started smoking when I was nine. And I first started trying to make something out of cigarettes because I like to use relevant kind of materials. I've got these cigarettes around so why not use them. There is this obsessive activity of me sticking all these cigarettes on the sculptures, and obsessive activity could be viewed as a form of masturbation. It is a form of sex, it does come from the same sort of drive, And there's so much satisfaction in it. When you make something completely covered in cigarettes and see it as solid it looks incredibly busy and it's a bit like sperm or genes under the microscope." Sarah Lucas, interview with James Putnam, January 2000.

15. Lucas has made sculptures of vacuum cleaners with breasts.

16. The reference to domestic labor calls to mind Mary Kelly's *Post-Partum Document* (1973–76), which measured the mother's labor through the son's feces. See Mary Kelly, *Post-Partum Document* (London: Routledge and Kegan Paul, 1981); Mary Kelly, *Imaging Desire* (Cambridge, Mass.: MIT Press, 1996); and Sabine Breitwiser, ed., *Rereading Post-Partum Document Mary Kelly* (Vienna: Generali Foundation, 1999).

17. Roland Barthes, *Mythologies* (1957; reprint, London: Vintage, 2000), 36.

18. Beatrix Ruf, "Conversation with Sarah Lucas," in *Sarah Lucas: Exhibitions and Catalogue Raisonné 1989–2005*, ed. Yilmaz Dziewior and Beatrix Ruf (Liverpool: Tate Publishing, 2005), 30.

19. This installation consists of one hundred casts of the space underneath chairs, done in different-colored resin. This also can be compared to Bruce Nauman's *A Cast of Space under My Chair* (1965–68).

20. Http://www.vam.ac.uk/collections/contemporary/past_exhns/close_encounters/old_in_out/mari.

21. Mari also touches upon an issue that has been seen as an important factor in readings of Lucas's work. Her reference to Dali is appropriate, as Lucas's sculptures have often been referred to in the legacy of Surrealism.

22. For more information, see http://www.alexschweder.com.

23. It is important to acknowledge that the Duchampian imperative may be exaggerated in some cases. Conceptual artist Dan Graham has said, "Everybody talks about Duchamp. We all hated Duchamp. We thought he was an asshole." Here Graham refers to himself as well as the group of Minimalist artists with which he is often associated. Daniel Graham, conversation with the author, January 21, 2006.

24. For more on Manzoni's *Artist's Shit*, see Germano Celant, *Piero Manzoni* (Paris: Musée d'art moderne de la ville de Paris, 1991); and Freddy Battino, *Piero Manzoni: catalogue raisonné* (Milan: Vanni Schweiler, 1991).

25. A. C. Grayling, "An Uncooked Perspective on the Nature of Sex," *Tate Etc*, no. 5 (Autumn 2005): 94.

26. Dominique Laporte, *History of Shit* (1978; reprint, Cambridge, Mass.: MIT Press, 2000), 34–35. This again can be related to the themes of Levine and Manzoni—turning shit to bronze or gold in the literal sense.

27. Gober is an American artist, born in 1954 in Wallingford, Connecticut.

28. For more information on Gober, see Robert Gober and Brenda Richardson, *Robert Gober: A Lexicon* (New York: Steidl/Matthew Marks Gallery, 2006); Robert Gober, *Robert Gober* (Chicago: Art Institute; Washington. D.C.: Hirshhorn Museum, 2001); Paul Schimmel, Hal Foster, and Robert Gober, *Robert Gober* (Zurich: Scalo, 1998).

29. There is a large body of literature on this topic. One of the most informative and accessible is Randy Shilts, *And the Band Played On: Politics, People, and the AIDS Epidemic* (New York: St. Martins Press, 1987).

30. Pigott is a British artist, born in 1961 in Aldershot. He has been included in several important group shows of 1990s art, including *Sensation* (1997) and a solo show at the

Saatchi Gallery. Most recently, his work *Rifiuti* was shown at the Wordsworth Trust in Cumbria in 2005 and continued his interest in mechanisms of waste.

31. An interesting side note to this is that Pigott suffered from severe toxic shock syndrome as a result of modeling sculpture out of soap, which, absorbed through the skin in large doses, can be toxic. Because he shaped the soap sculptures by his own hand, too much of the harsh chemicals seeped into his skin and thence his system. As a result, he could not use any soap products. From Hadrian Pigott, discussion with the author, January 23, 2006.

32. Pigott had this sculpture (which is in fact an edition of ten) constructed at Carradon Bathrooms in Kent, a factory that manufactures toilets. He worked on site with the factory manager to construct the mould and fire the sculptures. The factory workers thought Pigott was making lamp bases. Hadrian Pigott, e-mail to the author, January 29, 2006.

33. For more information on Hamilton, see Richard Morphet, *Richard Hamilton* (London: Tate Publishing, 1991); Etienne Lullin, ed., *Richard Hamilton Prints and Multiples Catalogue Raisonné* (New Haven: Yale University Press, 2004).

34. Hamilton was inspired by James Joyce and illustrated scenes from Ulysses. Joyce was famously obsessed with the scatological. See Richard Hamilton and Steven Coppel, *Imaging James Joyce's Ulysses: Richard Hamilton's Illustrations to James Joyce's Ulysses 1948–1998* (London: Gardner Books, 2003). Joyce's delight in scatology is witnessed throughout *Ulysses*. For example, in episode 4, Leopold Bloom sits on the toilet and reads the newspaper. Joyce writes: "Midway, his last resistance yielding, he allowed his bowels to ease themselves quietly as he read, reading still patiently slight constipation of yesterday quite gone. Hope it's not too big bring on piles again. No, just right. So. Ah! Costive" (see James Joyce, *Ulysses* [1922; reprint, London: Bodley Head, 1986], 56).

35. Hadrian Pigott, e-mail to the author, January 22, 2006.

12

Stalls between Walls

Segregated Sexed Spaces

ALEX SCHWEDER

Architects design buildings to order the world, embody morality, and reflect societal fantasies. Once built, designed spaces are occupied and inform the way that occupants of those environments think of themselves; the spaces we subjectively create then create us as occupying subjects. For this reason, buildings can be used as mirrors with which we can examine the way we want to see both ourselves and others. Both our desires for an ideal world and our anxieties about the experienced world can be read through the way we parse space, separate it into different functions, and then arrange these spaces in relation to one another. Public bathrooms are arguably the most divided and divisive rooms within buildings, making them ideal sites to investigate how architectural boundaries segregate rooms according to gender. Divided into stalls, public bathrooms keep their occupants from crossing sexual boundaries.

Buildings give materiality to the behavior that we consider orderly and, ultimately, enforce this order. Policing (manifested in public bathrooms as architectural partitions) necessitates a criminal, which in the case of bathrooms is formlessness. My pursuit of this idea is not to prove guilt or innocence but to understand how formlessness participates in our construction as subjects. Through the writings of thinkers such as Georges Bataille, Rosalind Krauss, Dennis Hollier, and Mark Cousins, I have come to understand formlessness as a process where boundaries dissolve, a process in which the distinction between subjects and objects, as well as that between subjects, loses clarity. In public bathrooms the policing of formlessness creates distance from and borders between us and dirt (subject and object) as well as us and other users of the bathroom (subject and subject). I explore these ideas separately and then, in conclusion, as parts of the same anxiety.

Bathrooms are the sites we have designated for our bodies to return to dirt (the landscape). Hair, urine, feces, blood, saliva, semen, and vomit are all ruptures in the fantasy that our bodies are seamless extensions of our subjective will. These liquid moments of explicit entropy show us that we are fleshy bodies contingent on a world that we cannot completely control. Within the toilet stalls, we see our bodies leaking and the boundary between our bodies' insides and their outsides becoming unclear. We see our inner bodies transgressing the boundaries of our skin. And we are reminded that our bodies are continually moving from a state of individuality toward undifferentiated form. Bataille equates this particular process of formlessness with both ecstasy and death. Bodily leakings are daily reminders that a hermetic and unchanging (thereby undying) body is a fiction. In an effort to turn away from this, users expect the space of public bathrooms to draw clear boundaries between our puddlings and us. Where others might see our bodies returning to soil, we place partitions. Where we must see our liquid traces, they are quickly removed from view. Toward this end bathroom surfaces are designed to remove, completely and quickly, such evidence from our sight.

While pursuing such a reading, it is important to distinguish between physical and psychological cleanliness. As Mary Douglas describes in *Purity and Danger* (2002, 36), the concept of dirt has to do with matter being out of place. When our insides become our outsides through our waste products, they become perceived as filthy. But not until the Victorian era was human waste associated with disease. This is not to say that waste and disease are unrelated but rather to point out that the "sickness" inspired in us is at least partially psychological. For example, bathrooms that are white allow users to see the dirt that might cause disease. The same color allows us to see a pubic hair in the sink, which is a reminder of our body's entropy and sex. In order for it potentially to harm us physically, we would have to come in contact with it, yet simply seeing it makes us feel "sick."

Another type of formlessness that bathrooms are designed to prevent is sexual or subject-to-subject formlessness. When two bodies mingle, fluids exchange and the boundaries between them become unclear. During orgasm it is difficult to tell where one body ends and the other begins. Bataille (1986, 170) used the term *petite mort*, "little death," to make a connection between sex and death. As he discusses, when human bodies unite, a loss of boundaries occurs similar to when cadavers turn to dirt and mingle.

Sexual formlessness is not only the literal mixing of bodies; it is also the mixing of gender roles. Contemporary bathrooms are designed to be stages on which reductive gender roles are played out and reinforced. By going into separate rooms, we are choosing which role we will play in the performance of gender. A cross-dresser reveals the element of choice and performance when he or she makes the decision to enter either the ladies' or the gents'. The objections raised when people choose the "wrong" door/identity reveal the widespread desire for a stable correlation between the gender and sex.

Sexual difference exists, as Elizabeth Grosz observes in *Volatile Bodies*. By understanding our bodies as dissimilar yet treating them as equal, the resulting exploration of unlike but nonetheless positive experiences can constitute a contemporary model of feminism. Public bathrooms, as conventionally constructed today, are based on a Freudian model, where women's bodies are men's bodies that lack a penis. Conventional women's rooms are basically men's rooms without urinals. The absence of female urinals in public spaces emphasizes women's lack of a penis and all the potency that Freud associated with penises. Grosz's model of contemporary feminism suggests urinals in both bathrooms, which would allow both men and women to reflect on what it means to have bodies and, specifically, genitals that leak. Here the use of urinals would prompt users to reflect on lateral rather than hierarchical differences between the sexes. *How* bodies leak would be the focus of thought, instead of *if* bodies leak.

When male or female bathrooms are entered, we encounter separate stalls. In relation to the policing of sexual identity, these divisions keep bodies both discrete and discreet from others of the same sex and in line with sanctioned heterosexual behavior. The only moment in either men's or women's rooms where congregation is encouraged is when we make ourselves "clean" at the sinks. This cleansing is psychological as well as physical, to the extent that we are performing acts of cleansing for our neighbors, announcing ourselves as free of bodily and sexual formlessness.

As Julia Kristeva discusses in *The Powers of Horror* (1982, 69), things that confound our constructs of order, our sense of the way the world should be—things that are ambiguous—are moved outside that invented system of order. Abjection, as she defines it, is the process of removing what does not make sense—what contradicts the agreed-upon order, what has become repulsive—to where it cannot be seen. Contemporary bathrooms are those places where the evidence of formlessness, in both messy materiality and slippery sexuality, is kept out of sight. Kristeva also points out that things kept in the margins are there not only because they confound categorization but also because they are potent. For these reasons, the periphery contains fertile ground for an exploration of our identities.

Projects

At the intersection of art and architecture, my practice has been informed at times by a desire to tap the psychological potency of bathrooms. The stakes of engaging these public partitioned places, either in theory or practice, are to change the relationships for occupants with both their own bodies and those bodies around them. The projects of mine that follow are

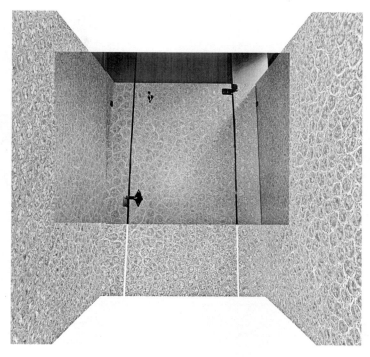

Figure 12.1 *Liquid Ghosts*, Museum of Sex, New York, 2002.
(Photo: Alex Schweder.)

not intended to illustrate the theory I have outlined, nor vice versa. Rather, my aim is to provide experiential and textual perspectives on the related issues of formlessness, sexual difference, and abjection.

Liquid Ghosts (plastic laminate, 60" × 30" × 60", 2002) and *Lovelorn Walls* (edition of three, vitreous china and silicone sealant, 84" × 36" × 57", 2004) both alter bathroom partitions as a way of being explicit about the permeability of occupied space and occupying subjects. *Liquid Ghosts*, a permanent installation at New York's Museum of Sex, situates an occupant within an immersive image of the cell structure of a human colon, incorporated into the plastic laminate of partitions between toilet stalls. The installation is not explicit about what the imagery depicts. Instead, it allows the reading of the imagery to remain ambiguous, something bodily versus something architectural, something repulsive (the cells of a human colon) versus something covetable (a floral pattern). Here boundaries are confused when the inside of a human body is used to decorate the outside, the occupied space.

Working conversely, from the outside in, is *Lovelorn Walls*, a permanent installation at the Tacoma Convention and Trade Center made during an Arts/Industry residency at the Kohler plumbing fixture factory in Wis-

Figure 12.2 (*above*) *Lovelorn Walls*, overview, Tacoma Convention and Trade Center, 2004. (Photo: Alex Schweder.)

Figure 12.3 *Lovelorn Walls*, detail, Tacoma Convention and Trade Center, 2004. (Photo: Alex Schweder.)

consin. This work replaces the plastic partitions with the vitreous china used to make toilets, tiles, and tableware, to offer occupants of these stalls (one in the men's room and one in the women's) a way of thinking about ingesting the space around them. Some of the normal grid of tile blocks becomes bodily by sprouting spigots that imply the possibility of sucking something out of them. These blocks also allude to edibility through the application of small portions of the caulk with a serrated cake decorator.

Peescapes (vitreous china, 60" × 48" × 28", 2001) and *Bi-Bardon* (vitreous china, 32" × 34" × 14", 2001) were both made during an earlier residency at Kohler's Arts/Industry program. These fully functional works complicate normative boundaries of gender, bodies, and buildings. Each urinal removes boundaries usually drawn between bodies. *Peescapes* is a series of male and female diptych urinals that place men and women in the same spaces as they urinate. *Bi-Bardon* removes the boundary of having two discrete urinals between occupants of already homosexual space.

Peescapes slows down the process of bodies becoming buildings in order to achieve an aesthetic rather than an economic experience. Urine is choreographed by biologically referenced interventions in the urinals that give the fluid shape as it returns to the landscape. *Bi-Bardon* grafts the imagery of an anomalous body onto a white and symmetrical plumbing fixture, crossing the line between building and biology.

Figure 12.4 (*above*) *Peescapes*, overview, 2001. (Photo: Alex Schweder.)

Figure 12.5 *Peescapes*, female quahog detail, 2001. (Photo: Alex Schweder.)

Figure 12.6 *Bi-Bardon,* overview, 2001.
(Photo: Alex Schweder.)

Figure 12.7 (***below left***) *Spit Skin,* detail,
2006. (Photo: Richard Barnes.)

Figure 12.8 *Spit Skin,* overview, 2006.
(Photo: Alex Schweder.)

Spit Skin (2006) explores the permeability of occupied space and occupying bodies by making a moisture-sensitive skin with saliva and biodegradable loose-fill packing (peanuts) in a leaking bathroom. As wetness acts on this skin through either the body or the building, a new topography of this exchange emerges. Locations of liquids deform the once perfect skin through holes and bulges. This bathroom mirrors the inevitable changes in its occupants' bodies.

References

Bataille, Georges. 1986. *Erotism: Death and Sensuality.* San Francisco: City Lights Books.
Douglas, Mary. 2002. *Purity and Danger: An Analysis of Concepts of Pollution and Taboo.* London: Routledge Classics.
Grosz, Elizabeth. 1994. *Volatile Bodies: Toward a Corporeal Feminism.* (Theories of Representation and Difference.) Bloomington: Indiana University Press.
Kristeva, Julia. 1982. *The Powers of Horror: An Essay on Abjection.* New York: Columbia University Press.

13

"Our Little Secrets"

A Pakistani Artist Explores the Shame and Pride of Her Community's Bathroom Practices

BUSHRA REHMAN

We were in the kitchen, my mother and I, when she turned to me and said, "Did you know Amreekans keep medicine in the bathroom?"

I waited, not quite sure where she was going with this. She looked at me as if I was slow and then continued, "They keep it in the bathroom, and then they eat it." There was triumph in her voice when she added, "And they say we're dirty."

I was surprised, not by the information, or that my mother had just found this out after living in the United States for thirty years. I was surprised that she, a proud woman who spent most of her time with people in our Pakistani community, had internalized the stereotype that we immigrants, Pakistanis, were considered dirty.

It was this conversation with my mother that I remembered when my sister Sa'dia, a visual artist, and I were discussing ideas for an art installation in the bathroom of the Queens Museum of Art in New York. Sa'dia was writing a proposal for an upcoming show and had just discovered that one of the only places left for an emerging artist like herself to exhibit was the bathroom.

In her last exhibition, *More Milk, Lighter Skin, Better Wife*, at the Gallery ArtsIndia in Manhattan, Sa'dia had created an installation using teacups. Each cup was handmade and branded with comments like "You'll look beautiful in gold" or "First comes marriage, then comes love." They were the kind of remarks made by aunties to young women over tea.

Sa'dia realized, however, that teacups were not going to work in the bathroom. I suggested that instead of teacups, she use lotahs. Sa'dia laughed, thinking I was making another one of my bad jokes, but when I spoke to her again, she had developed the idea into the installation *Lotah*

Previously published in *ColorLines* 8, no. 2 (Summer 2005), available at www.colorlines .com. Reprinted with the permission of *ColorLines* magazine, www.colorlines.com.

Stories. Both of us had no clue at the time that we were about to discover an underground world.

Hiding from Roommates, Even Lovers

A Hindustani word, *lotahs* are water containers used to clean yourself after using the toilet. They look like teapots without covers and are made of metal or plastic. With one hand, you pour the water and with the other, you wash yourself clean. Lotahs are commonplace throughout South Asia, and in many Muslim countries they are used for cleansing yourself before prayer. However, once South Asian and Muslim immigrants come to the United States, the pressure to assimilate forces many of us to make the transition from lotah to toilet paper. But there are some South Asians who refuse to cross over. Instead, they find themselves living double lives, using lotahs-in-disguise.

As Sa'dia began creating her art installation *Lotah Stories*, it quickly evolved into a community art project. For months, people who had been solicited via e-mail and word of mouth met in her apartment to decorate individual lotahs and record their stories. One hundred lotahs were collaged with labels from water bottles and soda bottles—common lotahs-in-disguise.

I had the opportunity to participate in this community project by creating lotahs and accompanying Sa'dia on her interviews with people who used lotahs. We soon discovered a secret society, one of closeted lotah users. We met people in streets and in cafes, even in their homes. These were strangers who were willing to lay themselves bare, not for money or fame (almost all

Figure 13.1 Sa'dia Rehman, *Lotah Stories*, Queens Museum of Art, New York, 2005. (Courtesy of the artist. Photo: Tahir Butt.)

the submissions were anonymous) but for the sake of being able finally to talk about their lotahs. We received e-mails from teachers, teenagers, high-powered lawyers, statisticians, artists, and first-generation and second-generation South Asians. Most of them were nervous and excited during the interviews and e-mails, but talking about lotahs seemed to free them somehow. Even though Sa'dia and I were strangers to them, the interviewees opened their homes to us and shared their secret lotah practices.

Listening to their stories, I was amazed by the depth of people's shame and the lengths that they had gone to in order to hide their lotahs from coworkers, roommates, even live-in partners. And I wondered again, where did we get this shame? How did it sink so deep into our skin? Why did lotahs feel so dirty, when using water was more clean? But I knew that as immigrants, we've always been made to feel ashamed. The dominant culture knows that if you can make people feel shame, you can make them do anything.

During the project, one of the participants, let's call him T., finally confessed to his white roommate that he had secretly been using a lotah. The roommate answered, "Dude, why didn't you just tell me?" T. was relieved, but he told us that he had to spend the rest of the evening listening to jokes made at his expense and constant reminders to wash his hands.

Turning Secrets into Art

Lotah Stories is part of *Fatal Love: South Asian American Art Now*, an exhibit at the Queens Museum of Art in New York that ran until June 6, 2005. The exhibit features both well-established Shazia Sikander and emerging artists such as Rina Banerjee and Chitra Ganesh.

Most museum visitors don't expect to find art in the bathroom, but at the Queens Museum, whether they are waiting in line, using the toilet, or washing their hands, visitors can experience *Lotah Stories*. When visitors enter the bathroom, they will find lotahs suspended from the ceiling and in the window niches by the sinks. The lotahs are covered with collaged paper cut up from water-bottle labels. Some labels are torn, some carefully cut out and glued. The lotahs are placed near the sinks so that viewers can't avoid looking at them while they are washing their hands. While visitors are waiting in line for a stall to open or are using the toilet, they listen to an audio loop of stories recorded from people who use lotahs. Some of these stories are full of shame and others full of humor. Most have an element of both.

I sat down with Sa'dia in her Brooklyn apartment during one of the lotah community parties leading up to the installation's opening. The apartment was covered with cat hair and water-bottle labels. There were people—Indian, Pakistani, Bengali—spread out on the carpet, cutting and gluing labels, laughing and joking.

How did you decide to use the bathroom for your installation space?
Well, to submit an art proposal for the exhibit, I had to take a tour. I went with one of the curators to the second floor gallery. She showed me the space and said, "We want this artist here and this artist there [naming well-known artists]." She said, "If you have something that fits the corner we'll look at it and see if the dimensions will fit." It seemed like every place was already covered.

When she saw I looked discouraged, she said, "That's just an idea. We don't know if they're going to be in the show." She showed me spaces like the elevator and the ramp. And then, laughing, she said, "You could even do something in the bathroom."

I said, "Can you show me the bathrooms?"

We went in there, and I liked the light in the morning time. There were windows, a niche, between the sinks. I saw my father doing wudu in the bathroom [cleansing before prayer] and how it is always embarrassing to do wudu in a public space. So it was with this memory of shame and love that *Lotah Stories* was born.

When did you decide to do the interviews? At first, I was going to have lotahs in all the stalls, but I didn't want people using them as a trashcan to throw garbage in. And the title from the beginning was *Lotah Stories*. While I was discussing the installation with my friends, they would be very excited and they would start telling me their funny lotah stories. I wanted to have the stories in their voices.

What did you think of the interviewees? They seemed so relieved to finally talk about it. When we were actually recording, they were open, but once you clicked the button off they became very concerned that we would reveal their names and tell people their secret.

What was the lotah-making process? I first began collecting the labels. I asked all my friends to collect labels. Not to go out of their way but whatever they drank. Sometimes I would sneak downstairs into the trash bins, and I would take the labels off of the water bottles and soda bottles. But I'd wash them.

Why use water-bottle labels? I was using water-bottle labels because these were common things that a lot of Pakistani use when they hide the fact that they use a lotah in a public restroom. You can't just whip out your lotah, but you can use something that carries water but that wouldn't bring too much attention to itself.

So, of course, a water bottle. People use other things instead of water bottles and soda bottles. They use plastic cups and Styrofoam cups or small water jugs. One woman was using a measuring cup. I chose to use water-bottle labels because it's something that's familiar. I know that some people will get it. They've used water bottles as a disguised lotah. They've been in that situation.

Why do you think there is so much secrecy around lotah use? It's different from the ideas of "cleanliness" in American culture. Americans think that their way is right and everything else is wrong.

How do you feel the project turned out? It helped a lot of people come out to people they used to hide their lotahs from. One friend finally told her boyfriend that she lives with, that the watering can in the bathroom wasn't for the plants.

So what's the future of Lotah Stories? In the beginning, I wasn't expecting that great of a response, but I feel all these people that e-mailed us and who we had the opportunity to interview, they inspired me to show it in other places, not only New York. I want it to be a much bigger installation, more overwhelming to represent how much it's hidden. I'd like to show it in bathrooms across America.

Excerpts from Interviews

Tips on Using Lotahs

1. If you live in a college dorm, use a plastic cup. Preferably khaki, black or some other nondescript color to avoid attracting unnecessary attention. It can sit discreetly in your shower caddy until its services are needed.
2. Act completely nonchalant when you walk in the bathroom and get your cup from your caddy. Go to the sink, stare at your reflection, pretend to fix your hair, anything, while filling it up.
3. Now slowly walk over to your stall; placement is very important. Make sure you hold it in a way that would be least visible to any person in the bathroom with you.
4. Ignore the impulse to explain what you are doing, even to friends. Unless someone has been using a lotah all their lives, the benefits completely escape them and you seem to them to be a freak.
5. At work, due to the extra pressure to assimilate, the need for discretion is paramount. Take your time at the sink until whoever else [is] in the bathroom with you is no longer within sight.
6. If you are sharing an apartment with a non-desi roommate, keep a plant in the bathroom. That would comfortably explain why you keep a small watering can in your cabinet.

—Anonymous

Cappuccino Boyfriend

It's funny now but it's kind of gross. What happened was there was this phase where I would wake up every morning and for some reason I would find my lotah on the kitchen counter. And I just didn't understand it. Then one day, my boyfriend, my German boyfriend, had just moved in. And he said, "Why do you always take the measuring cup to the bathroom?" It turns out that he had been using it to measure the milk for his cappuccino machine and had been drinking it.

Well, as you can imagine, after I told him he went off cappuccino for a year. But he got used to it. He agreed with me. I think I almost converted him.

—Anonymous

College Dorms

I grew up in a Muslim household, and I used a lotah all my life. When I went away to college it was the first time I realized how much I had gotten used to using one. Living with roommates who didn't use a lotah, I felt very ashamed that I did, but, of course, wanting to be as Americanized as I could possibly be, I didn't use it for a while.

But I began to really miss feeling that clean. So there were times I would take an old McDonald's cup in the bathroom, or I'd pretend I was still drinking water from my own cup and just happened to walk into the bathroom with it. There were even times I used cups that my roommates used in the bathroom where they would keep their toothbrushes . . . or their toothpaste. I always hoped that no one would find out. Especially since the insides of their cups were so dirty, and after I was done they would be clean.

—Anonymous

14

In the Men's Room

Death and Derision in Cinematic Toilets

FRANCES PHEASANT-KELLY

Toilets are troublesome spaces, particularly for men and especially for Hollywood. A survey of recent mainstream American film shows that toilets tend to be sites of extreme violence and bloody death. Alternatively, they are spaces of crude comedic rupture. While the on-screen toilet might be an appropriate location for secret or illicit acts to occur, its appearance has some undesirable ramifications. It has a sordid realism that depletes Hollywood of its glamour. Furthermore, the possibility of the penis on display and the homoerotic connotations of the anus threaten heteronormative masculinity. Ultimately, any propensity to linger in a space aligned with seepage and fluidity suggests a body out of control. Such proximity to the abject is potentially feminising and reflects a masculinity under threat. I therefore argue that the ways in which toilet spaces are represented in mainstream American film reflect certain sociocultural anxieties. I suggest that, despite structural and signifying differences between "the men's" and "the ladies'," the toilet is inherently feminising and is therefore represented in film as threatening to men.

The appearance of the toilet in film is a fairly recent phenomenon. Mostly invisible in the history of American cinema,[1] they have become increasingly apparent in films since the 1960s. While toilets appear to exert a special fascination for some directors, such as Quentin Tarantino and Alfred Hitchcock, the toilet scene is not director- or even genre-specific. Toilet scenes are found across a diverse range of genres, including science fiction, action, romantic comedy, and horror. This incidence across genres suggests that the toilet has a more fundamental meaning. Closer examination reveals that men's toilets, and indeed men's penises, are often pivotal to the plot. They are, however, also depicted as places of horror, abjection, and bloody death. This threat materialises mostly in relation to men, specifically marking toilets as places of vulnerability for them.

I argue that toilets in film are potentially hazardous spaces for men for several reasons. The threat of seepage and proximity to bodily fluids is consistent with feminisation, while toilets are unequivocally related to bodily orifices. Acknowledging these breaks in the boundaries of the body is potentially problematic to heterosexual men, since a body perforated is a vulnerable one and uneasily close to homosexuality. Further, toilets are linked to loss of control and abjection and are seen as places of "letting go." The anxieties that toilets may present for men are represented explicitly in mainstream film[2] through extreme violence and death. However, the narrative may also alleviate such anxieties for the viewer by the use of comedy, where the instabilities of masculinity are mitigated by laughter. While literary and cultural scholar Loren Glass (2001) suggests that this current hysterical preoccupation with the penis has been prompted by President Bill Clinton's revelations about Monica Lewinsky, I argue that, instead, this trend reflects a masculinity that is under threat more generally.

This chapter examines the representation of men in the most vulnerable of private spaces, the cinematic toilet. I also consider the narrative function of the toilet scene and the implications for masculinity relating to the space of the toilet. Film directors in Hollywood reinforce the gendered construction of toilets (on-screen) by reinterpreting connotations associated with "loitering." These aspects of men's toilets, especially the potential for homoerotic contact, therefore steer film narratives in specific ways. Referring to *Pulp Fiction*, *Full Metal Jacket*, and *There's Something about Mary*, I show that men's toilets in film are consistent with abjection, emasculation, or homoeroticism and, as scholar of gender Ruth Barcan (2005, 8) suggests, are "dirty spaces." I therefore argue that the gendered division of the public toilet is mediated and amplified through mainstream Hollywood film.

Full Metal Jacket

Directed by Stanley Kubrick, *Full Metal Jacket* contains an interesting example of a toilet scene that is narratively significant and that conflates issues of masculinity and abjection. The film charts the transformation of young American males into fighting machines through the processes of a boot camp, supervised by Sergeant Hartman (Lee Ermey). The practices of institutionalisation work here to repress individuality and are ultimately infantilising and emasculating. This is suggested in the opening scenes, where the new recruits have their heads shaved, and subsequently through Hartman's barrage of abuse, which largely focuses on a denigration of their masculinity. Comments such as "I will unscrew your head and shit down your neck" and "I will definitely fuck you up" both humiliate and feminise the cadets. Masculinity is measured by the ability to kill and is articulated through the cadets' use of their rifles. The cadets, who are ordered to give girls' names to their rifles, perform their rifle drill whilst lying on their beds. The equation between sex and violence is further suggested by their marching chant: "This is my rifle, this is my gun, this is for firing, and this [as they hold their crotches] is for fun." This has particular resonance for cadet Private Pyle (Vincent D'Onofrio) and for the gendering of the toilet scene. Pyle is represented as being overtly emasculated, partly through his soft and rounded physique. Cinematography, especially the use of the close-up, repeatedly emphasizes his fatness, which cultural studies scholar Antony Easthope (1992) suggests is feminising. By contrast, masculinity, he asserts, is bound to musculature: "For the masculine ego the body can be used to draw a defensive line between inside and outside. So long as there is very little fat, tensed muscle and tight sinew can give a hard clear outline to the body. Flesh and bone can pass itself off as a kind of armour" (1992, 52–53).

Pyle's emasculation is further highlighted by a conversation with Hartman, who renames him Lawrence of Arabia (which refers to homosexuality), the conversation going thus:

Hartman: What's your name, fat body?
Private: Sir, Leonard Lawrence, sir!
Hartman: Lawrence? Lawrence what? Of Arabia?
Private: Sir, no sir!
Hartman: That name sounds like royalty. Are you royalty?
Private: Sir, no sir!
Hartman: Do you suck dicks?
Private: Sir, no sir!
Hartman: Bullshit. I'll bet you could suck a golf ball through a garden hose. I don't like the name Lawrence. Only faggots and sailors are called Lawrence. From now on you're Gomer Pyle.

The name Gomer Pyle here makes reference to a television show featuring the character Gomer Pyle, played by an allegedly homosexual actor. Pyle's masculinity is again called into question by his physical inability to complete the assault course. Consequently, he is made to suck his thumb as punishment by Hartman, which further infantilises him.

The incessant psychological trauma that Pyle experiences leads him to kill Hartman and then himself in the communal toilet. The relevant scene opens with Private Joker checking the dormitory at night. He opens the bathroom door and shines his torch on Private Pyle, who is sitting on a toilet. The toilet is pristine and unusual in design—it is one of a regimented row of communal toilets, lidless and completely devoid of privacy. The stalls and urinals that usually characterise the male toilet are absent. Barcan suggests that men's toilets are where "heteronormative masculinity is defined, tested and policed" (2005, 7) and are designed to disavow the homoerotic connotations of the anus. In this scene, however, bodily orifices cannot be concealed. Kubrick's deliberate insertion of the toilet scene[3] suggests that its narrative function and design are specifically significant. It seems that issues of sex, violence, and masculinity, implicit in the film, are condensed into the toilet scene. The open and lidless design means not only that anuses are on display but also that the process of defecation is a public one. Easthope (1992) asserts that men need to keep tight control of bodily orifices, not only because of the possibility of homosexual penetration but also because the abject inner body detracts from masculinity and needs to be concealed.

Several studies establish a relationship between the female body and the abject. For Julia Kristeva (1982), the abject inner body is always threatening to emerge through the processes of childbirth, menstruation, excretion, and death. While considering that "the corpse . . . is the utmost of abjection" (1982, 4), she emphasises the feminine body and a disgust derived from female bodily fluids, notably those arising during childbirth and menstruation. It is clear that she considers the female body closer to abjection than the male, stating that "polluting objects fall, schematically into two types: excremental and menstrual. Neither tears or sperm, for instance, although they belong to the borders of the body, have any polluting value" (1982, 71). Elizabeth Grosz (1994) also aligns women with fluidity and seepage of bodily fluids. However, whilst Grosz recognises that "seminal fluid is understood primarily as what it makes, what it achieves, a causal agent and thus a thing, a solid: its fluidity, its potential seepage, the element in it that is uncontrollable, its spread, its formlessness, is perpetually displaced in discourse onto its properties, its capacity to fertilise, to father, to produce an object" (1994, 199), she does take issue with this and argues that semen is polluting.

The contaminating effects of semen are suggested by Hartman's words to Pyle, who is unable to climb over an obstacle: "I'm going to wring your balls off so you can't contaminate the rest of the world." Whilst this might suggest that disease and abjection are related to seminal fluid, in light of Hartman's tirade against Pyle, it may imply that Pyle is contaminating in the same way as a woman. It is, however, feasible to argue that men's toilets carry the threat of feminisation both because of this fluidity, particularly since the penis is used for both urine and seminal fluid, and because of the potential for homoerotic penetration. Thus the communal toilet depicted in *Full Metal Jacket* is particularly feminising, since its open design renders men vulnerable to penetration. Further, it denies the ability to maintain borders between disgust and cleanliness and thereby prevents the sociocultural processes of adulthood. For both reasons, the toilet scene brings men closer to abjection.

Both the cinematography and mise-en-scène of the toilet scene in *Full Metal Jacket* reinforce these potentially emasculating effects. Pyle is sitting on the toilet with a rifle magazine between his legs. His body is particularly feminised by its softness, lacking the hard contours defined by Easthope (1992) and infantilised by his white underwear. The rifle, an obvious phallic symbol, stands for the fully fledged masculine adulthood that he desires in order to escape the "shit" in which he exists. He begins to load the magazine, Joker asking him, "Are those live rounds?" Pyle responds to Joker's question with "seven six two millimetres, full metal jacket,"[4] indicating that his rifle is fully loaded and primed. Joker attempts to reason with him, saying, "If Hartman comes in here, we'll both be in a world of shit." This is ironic considering their location, although the orderliness depicted here opposes any suggestion of abjection. It does, however, anticipate the imminent chaos. Pyle, looking increasingly deranged, suggested by his rolling eyes, gaping mouth, and half-lit face, replies, "I *am* in a world of shit," defining his metaphoric and literal status.

Hartman enters the bathroom dressed in his hat and his underwear. Both mise-en-scène and framing make him appear both ridiculous and smaller in the frame than Pyle, who, since he has a loaded weapon, is temporarily masculinised. Pyle makes a final grasp for masculinity by shooting Hartman and emits a sigh as he does so, suggesting sexual satisfaction. The order of the toilet is disrupted as blood ejaculates from the drill instructor's chest in slow motion. Violence between men is here equated with sex but is potentially a male rape or homosexual act. (This is a theme reiterated throughout the rest of the film, where extreme violence against women is equated to rape.) In a final loss of control, Pyle slumps back on the toilet seat, places the rifle in his mouth, and shoots himself through the head, the whiteness of the tiles splattered with his blood. While the act is in itself shocking, the aesthetic, bloody spectacle distracts the viewer from any homoerotic connotations. As the space of the ordered toilets becomes abject, there is a shift from masculinity to femininity.

Literary scholar Susan White also sees the toilet scene as a display of male homoerotic desire, commenting that "Pyle cannot leave behind the confusing miasma of his own infantilism, the blood and violence and desire for male love (the toilet on which he kills himself, like his name, might be seen as a sign of his fixation on the anal) that form the infrastructure of the Corps but that must be externalised onto women and the enemy" (1988; in Anderegg 1991, 209). Indeed, White acknowledges that the potential for homoerotic encounters exists "at every juncture, [where] the line between male bonding and the baldly homoerotic is a fine one" (1988; in Anderegg 1991, 208).

Pyle's feminisation in relation to the toilet scene is significant in that it dissects the narrative. The second half of the film, which directly follows the toilet scene, moves to Vietnam and ends with the death of a female sniper. Pyle, represented as feminised and dangerous, is thereby aligned with the woman sniper who kills the other soldiers towards the end of the film. Therefore, while the scene is narratively significant in its dissection and repetition of story lines, it functions to render Pyle's masculinity precarious and ultimately unattainable. The physical architecture of the toilet space makes the cadets susceptible to penetration whilst simultaneously demanding a high degree of control in order to maintain masculinity. Pyle is particularly feminised through his rounded physique, which is exaggerated through cinematography and mise-en-scène. His feminisation and inability to attain a stable adult masculinity are suggested ultimately by the representation of homo-sex as violence and his own suicide. The killing of Hartman, I suggest, is a homosexual rape, whilst the splattering of Pyle's brains against the white tiles carries the implication of menstrual blood. The film, through the toilet scene, suggests that the abject cannot be repressed through the forces of discipline, and institutions, where order should prevail, are most susceptible to its eruption.

Pulp Fiction

The representation of masculinity takes a different but related form in *Pulp Fiction*. While the film is renowned for its extreme violence closely linked with humour, there is a similar preoccupation with anality, excrement, and emasculation. These anal scenarios are invariably related to a number of toilet scenes, which are a frequent feature of Tarantino films. In *Pulp Fiction*, Vincent Vega (John Travolta) visits the toilet at key narrative junctures that film scholar Sharon Willis defines as "both world-making and earth-shattering" (1995, 41). However, while narratively implicated, the toilet scenes also anticipate or witness moments of disgust and extreme abjection. They include the diner robbery scene, Mia (Uma Thurman) Wallace's overdose, the clean-up scene after the shooting of Marvin, and Vincent's killing.

While these narrative events are significant, they are crucially linked to Vega's extended disappearances to the toilet. Robyn Longhurst's (2001) study of men and toilets indicates that an inclination to linger is denoted as feminising (in that women spend more time in toilets than men do) or alludes to masturbation and bodies out of control. The notion of the toilet space as feminising is relevant since one of *Pulp Fiction's* main themes is that of homosexuality. While Vincent Vega is never overtly identified as homosexual, these bathroom scenes mark moments of vulnerability for him. It is here that his masculinity is called into question, often suggested through seepage and abjection. References to bodily function are explicitly stated in that Vincent Vega is going to the toilet "to jerk off," "take a piss," or "take a shit." There are also direct allusions to menstruation. Lingering in the toilet leads ultimately to Vega's death. While several authors acknowledge the pervasiveness of anality within the film (e.g., Dinshaw 1999; Willis 1995), there is little focus on the significance of the space of the toilet scenes in relation to gender. However, Carolyn Dinshaw asserts that this film is centrally related to homosexuality and what she terms "anal surveillance" (1999, 188), arguing that part of the film's premise is "to reassure the audience that anuses are used for shitting" (1999, 188).

Toilet space in *Pulp Fiction* functions slightly differently from its role in *Full Metal Jacket*; even though, as Willis notes, "the bathroom anchors a dense nexus that connects blood and violence to anal eroticism" (1995, 41). I suggest that the implications of lingering and constriction of space render men vulnerable and feminised—literally "caught with their pants down" (Willis 1995, 41).

The first key toilet scene in *Pulp Fiction* occurs when Vincent escorts Mia Wallace out to dinner. He takes her home and goes to the bathroom. This toilet scene finds Vincent talking himself out of sleeping with Mia Wallace; looking in the mirror, he says to himself, "Say goodnight, go home, jerk off and that's all you're gonna do." Vega's lingering in the on-screen toilet has further connotations. The toilet functions as a potential place to masturbate and is therefore a site where the male body struggles to control itself. Vega's narcissistic looks in the mirror, whilst making reference to *Saturday Night Fever*,[5] further denote this space as feminising. However, the link with abjection is forged here since the toilet scene cuts to a close-up of the overdosed Mia Wallace covered in blood and vomit. As Vincent lifts her head, vomit dribbles out of her mouth. The feminine body is here closely aligned with disgust, and its proximity to the toilet scene establishes a link between abjection, femininity, and the toilet. Moreover, it anticipates Vincent's death, which later occurs whilst he is again lingering in the toilet.

In the following scene, Butch (Bruce Willis), after killing a boxer in a fight, returns to his apartment to retrieve his father's gold watch. This scene is important for its completion of Butch's Oedipal trajectory in his reclaiming of the watch.[6] Entering the apartment, he notes a gun on the kitchen worktop. He picks up the weapon when he hears the toilet flush. He turns to the bathroom door and, as Vincent Vega opens it, he shoots him. The camera cuts to a dead and bloody Vincent framed tightly within the space of the toilet, which is splashed with blood.

The restricted space in this toilet has implications for representations of masculinity. Until recently, Hollywood has generally suppressed any hint of homoeroticism on-screen. However, there is a danger that male viewers looking at men on screen not only identify with their hero but also gaze admiringly. Looks between male characters may also be ambivalent. Film scholar Steve Neale (1983) argues, therefore, that the male figure is subject not only to a narcissistic gaze but also to a contemplative one. He suggests that these voyeuristic, potentially feminising looks are usually displaced from the male body to the hero's movement through vast landscapes or cityscapes or, alternatively, by graphic violence and bloodshed. Neale's essay is relevant here in that he considers how far on-screen space allows differentiation between an active male body, one that may legitimately be identified with, and the passive male body to be contemplated. In contrast, restricted space, such as that found in the toilet, allows for little such virilising activity. The space frames its hero tightly, focussing the fixed gaze of the spectator on the male protagonist in a potential state of undress. This is, according to Laura Mulvey (1975), essentially objectifying and voyeuristic (a private space made public) and therefore feminising. There is nothing for the arrested gaze of the spectator to be diverted to in this restricted space, except graphic violence or comedic rupture. Neale's (1983) and Mulvey's (1975) theories support my argument that men in (cinematic) toilets may be feminised, particularly since these men are subject to extreme violence or humiliation.

It is evident that the space of the toilet in Vega's death functions in a similar way. Whilst there are the implications of lingering, he is also in a restricted space and framed within the toilet. Further, Vincent is feminised by the dance sequence, his refusal to sleep with Mia, and his narcissistic looking in the mirror. Bloody violence, while distracting from his immobilisation, signifies a proximity to seepage, menstruation, and abjection, assuring his feminisation.

Although bloodshed is a familiar feature of the gangster genre, it has a particularly sustained focus in *Pulp Fiction*. The inner abject body is ultimately highlighted by Vincent's accidental shooting of Marvin. The resulting spray of blood, brains, and skull fragments leads to the next bathroom scene, where Jules (Samuel Jackson) and Vincent attempt to wash away the blood. Again, the proximity of the two men in the restricted space of the bathroom might generate some anxiety. This is further exacerbated by the blood, which they cannot deal with. There is a direct reference here to menstruation as Jules reprimands Vincent about his cleaning habits, referring to the towel he has used as a "maxi-pad." This calls to mind Grosz's (1994) work on seepage and the female body, as well as Kristeva's (1982) disgust in relation to menstruation. It again directly feminises Vega and reiterates the pattern of femininity, abjection, and violence found in the on-screen toilet scene.

While Willis focuses her argument on the equation of blood with shit and the humour associated with what she terms "smearing" (2000, 281), she also considers that such detritus and waste represent the film's recycling of fragments of popular culture. However, I suggest that the excessive bloodletting is related to the abject feminine body and the anality that pervades the film (but is generic to a range of films). Indeed, the film has attracted discussion around its arguably most controversial scene, the rape of Marsellus Wallace. As a result of the anal rape, Marsellus shoots the perpetrator in the crotch, thereby both castrating him and feminising him, causing him to bleed like a woman.

The focus on bodily function is iterated in the return to the opening diner scene at the end of the film, which finds Vincent and Jules engaged in conversation that relates to another key aspect of abjection: that of food abomination. Jules comments that he does not eat pork because "pigs are filthy animals, I don't eat filthy animals, they sleep and root in their own shit." Vincent then announces that he "is gonna take a shit," affirming his own proximity to filth and also leaving the diner at another key narrative juncture. While the toilet space is not visualised here, it functions to consolidate Vincent's links to the abject. Furthermore, in his absence the lengthy diner scene takes place, with its mise-en-scène of guns and action. This scene, consistent with masculinity, contrasts with Vincent's lingering in the vulnerable space of the toilet.

The toilet scenes in *Pulp Fiction* variously illustrate how this space functions as a place of emasculation. They are linked to excessive bloodshed, seepage, and abjection. Further, in the constricted space of the toilet, the masculinising activities that male characters typically engage in are impossible. The male body is therefore tightly framed and positioned as feminised spectacle. Longhurst's (2001) study also suggests a feminisation of Vega through his tendency to linger in the toilet and his preoccupation with anality. This is consistent with a film that has homosexuality as a central theme.

There's Something about Mary

In this romantic comedy, emasculating comedic humiliation, rather than violence, is used as a device to distract the viewer from the potential homoerotic implications of men together in the toilet. This takes the form of a bloody, literal castration for its protagonist. While blood loss is implied, it is not visualised, although the film's key comedic shot is an extreme close-up of Ted's damaged genitalia.

The film begins in flashback, as Ted (Ben Stiller) recounts the events resulting from his high school crush on Mary (Cameron Diaz) to his analyst. Ted is physically short and fairly unattractive, which is emphasised through several close-up shots. The focus on his dental braces highlights both his juvenility and his physical unattractiveness. Mary invites him to the school prom, and when they meet, he visits the bathroom. This is visually constructed as a feminine space, with pink and blue wallpaper and lace curtains. The sound of Ted urinating, which appears to be amplified, therefore seems especially incongruous and disgusting. As he stands at the toilet, Mary's mother looks down at him from a bedroom window and mistakenly thinks that he is masturbating. When Ted realises this, he quickly zips up his trousers, also zipping in his genitals, providing the main comedic scene. The camera then cuts to an extreme close-up of Ted's genitals zipped into his trousers. As a number of people crowd into the bathroom to view his predicament, this private space becomes completely public, especially since a policeman leans in through the window, saying, "Neighbours said they heard a lady scream." The onlookers recoil in a mixture of hysterical amusement and horror as they peer at his genitals.

Ted is confined to a corner of the bathroom (and the frame) and is the object of the male characters' and the viewer's gaze. The scene infantilises and feminises Ted and fixes him at an Oedipal level. There are visual and verbal references to him being castrated and to him "shitting himself." As the policeman attempts to unzip Ted's trousers, the scene cuts to that of an ambulance crew shouting, "We got a bleeder"—bleeding, as in *Pulp Fiction* and *Full Metal Jacket*, being synonymous with feminisation. As Ted is pushed into the ambulance, there are shouts of "He was masturbating!" Again, this is relevant to a body that is out of control and, therefore, feminised.

As Ted finishes recounting this story to his analyst, he comments that after suddenly thinking about Mary, he pulled off the road and stopped at a rest area. His analyst replies, "You know, rest areas are homosexual hangouts," retrenching the feminising implications of this scene.

This scene is key to the narrative, as it is the point at which Ted loses contact with Mary. A second toilet scene is also significant, as it is the point at which they are reacquainted. In this toilet scene, men's bodily fluids are literalised as disgusting and contaminating. Ted has been advised by his friend to "clean [his] pipes" before going out with Mary, saying that "it's like going out with a loaded gun . . . dangerous." (This equation between sex and violence occurs in *Full Metal Jacket*.) His friend then adds that after "cleaning the pipes," "you're thinking like a girl," suggesting that the act of masturbation is feminising. The comic moment comes in a second toilet scene, after Ted does, indeed, "clean his pipes." The doorbell rings, and he hurriedly cleans the bathroom but is unable to locate the seminal fluid. As Mary asks him if he has hair gel on his ear and applies it to her own hair, it becomes hilariously apparent where the ejaculate is now located. This humour is combined with repulsion for the audience and discomfort for Ted, who stares continually at Mary's stiff, upswept hair. Thus the second bathroom scene actually does find Ted masturbating and defines the uncontrollable, previously castrated male body as a source of humour and disgust.

The space of the toilet in both scenes is suggested as abject. Ted's castration and loss of control situate him closer to the feminine body. Cinematography and mise-en-scène reinforce this emasculation by both framing him tightly in the bathroom space and emphasising his infantilism. The scrutiny of male genitalia by other men, which could generate anxieties about homosexuality, is also objectifying. However, this toilet scene uses humour rather than violence as a strategy for distraction.

Conclusion

The space of the cinematic toilet has implications for heteronormative masculinity. While there are directors who employ toilet scenes frequently, the scenes are not restricted to those directors or to specific genres. It is evident that toilet scenes in mainstream film are inserted for specific purposes and are not generally incidental to the narrative: they provide private, secretive spaces within which transgressive acts that are crucial to the plot may occur. It seems, however, that the space of the on-screen toilet carries the inevitability of threat to masculinity. In these films, this threat manifests in anxieties about homosexuality, abjection, and emasculation. The hard, muscular, impenetrable body that is active and moves easily and without resistance through the frame defines contemporary masculinity. By contrast, an isolated, restricted body that discloses its abject interior is susceptible, as is the body that cannot control its emissions. It renders men vulnerable in a space that is aligned with seepage, penetration, and bodily fluids.

The loss of control that the on-screen toilet suggests may materialise as insanity, drug overdose, or very often a dark and inevitably bloody death. Alternatively, it provides a humiliating or emasculating comedic experience in which the male is literally (as in *There's Something about Mary*) or symbolically castrated. What is interesting is that this is often aligned with excrement or the spectacle of graphic death, suggestive of menstrual blood. Furthermore, the toilet tends toward Oedipal scenarios, with males unable to achieve a stable, coherent adult masculinity, as seen in *Full Metal Jacket*, *Pulp Fiction*, and *There's Something about Mary*.

While this chapter suggests that the space of the on-screen toilet is feminising, it is interesting to note that the space functions differently for female characters. Much less evident in American mainstream film, the appearance of women in toilets has very different connotations. Again often a narrative space of secrecy or illicit activity, the women's toilet is simultaneously most commonly signalled as a communal, friendly place, with a focus on appearance and cosmetics. It lacks the dangerous frisson of "the men's" and, more significantly, is likely to be a clean space. While women are killed in bathrooms in mainstream cinema,[7] their death tends to be contiguous with cleanliness rather than dirt. The bath's or shower's identification as a place of vulnerability is rendered through relaxation and nudity rather than homoerotic possibility. These are clean spaces, as opposed to the "dirty spaces" of the men's toilet. It is rare to see men bathing in film. Acts of cleansing and purity therefore seem to be associated with women, and consequently, narratives that demand a private space for violence towards women tend to occur in bathrooms rather than toilets.

The dominance of male directors in mainstream American film may be relevant to the depiction of vulnerable masculinities. By comparison, toilet scenes in British film tend to be less threatening. Ranging from the surreal

(*Trainspotting*, 1996) to the mundane (*Secrets and Lies*, 1996), U.K. toilet spaces function differently and, although narratively pertinent, are much less inclined to violence and death.

In much of American film, therefore, it is evident that the toilet scene is consistent in its tendency for disorder. The implications are that masculinity can be considered in a different way, and that the toilet space in film is articulated as a threatening space for heterosexual men. While this fairly recent phenomenon in film might be influenced, as Glass (2001) suggests, by the Clinton controversy, it more likely reflects anxieties about masculinity under threat, from both the legalisation of homosexuality and the heightened status of women. Thus it appears that directors of mainstream Hollywood film, who generally tend to be male, extend and reinforce notions of a gendered division in the space of the toilet. While a useful space to insert illicit activities, the toilet scene also features mostly violent or humiliating acts towards men. These function to detract from homoerotic implications, to facilitate a narrative that suggests feminisation of the male character, or to concretise links between abjection, violence, and feminisation. Thus, while men's toilets "aim to keep excretion, defecation and sexuality apart" (Barcan 2005, 11), the threat of emasculation is pervasive and fails to keep everything in its right and proper place, materialising in mainstream American film as death or derision for the male protagonist. This examination of three mainstream films from different genres confirms that the space of the on-screen toilet is inherently unstable and, as Barcan further claims, is "a physical-psychical space, . . . too culturally laden, too uncontrollable, too ambiguous, to keep categories watertight" (2005, 11).

Notes

1. Alfred Hitchcock was the first director to show a toilet flushing on screen in *Psycho*.
2. "Mainstream" is used here to indicate Hollywood film.
3. In the original novel, *The Short Timers*, the place of Hartman's death was a barracks.
4. This is the scene that gives the film its title and, in the context of this chapter, gives further illumination as to its meaning.
5. In *Saturday Night Fever*, Travolta played the character of a narcissistic dancer, preoccupied with his appearance.
6. The watch has been passed from father to son over several generations. Captain Koons (Christopher Walken), an ex-Vietnam officer, visits the young Butch to pass on to him his father's gold watch. He recounts to the young Butch how Butch's father, and then Koons himself, had hidden "this uncomfortable hunk of metal up [the] ass." This implication of anal exchange enforces the anality that pervades the film.
7. Films include *The Virgin Suicides*, *Girl Interrupted*, *Fatal Attraction*, and *Psycho*.

References

Barcan, R. 2005. "Dirty Spaces: Communication and Contamination in Men's Public Toilets." *Journal of International Women's Studies* 6 (2): 7–23.

Dinshaw, C. 1999. *Getting Medieval: Sexualities and Communities, Pre- and Postmodern*. Durham, N.C.: Duke University Press.

Easthope, A. 1992. *What a Man's Gotta Do*. London: Routledge.

Glass, L. 2001. "After the Phallus." *American Imago* 58 (2): 545–66.

Grosz, E. 1994. *Volatile Bodies: Towards a Corporeal Feminism*. Bloomington: Indiana University Press.

Inglis, D. 2002. "Dirt and Denigration: The Faecal Imagery and Rhetorics of Abuse." *Postcolonial Studies* 5 (2): 207–21.

Jeffords, S. 1989. *The Remasculinisation of America: Gender and the Vietnam War*. Bloomington: Indiana University Press.

Kristeva. J. 1982. *Powers of Horror: An Essay on Abjection*. New York: Columbia University Press.

Longhurst, R. 2001. *Bodies: Exploring Fluid Boundaries*. London: Routledge.

Mulvey, L. 1975. "Visual Pleasure and Narrative Cinema." *Screen* 16 (3): 6–18.

Neale, S. 1993. "Masculinity as Spectacle." In *Screening the Male*. Ed. S. Cohan and I. Hark. London: Routledge, 9–20.

Polan, D. 2000. *Pulp Fiction*. London: BFI.

Robinson, S. 2000. *Marked Men: White Masculinity in Crisis*. New York: Columbia University Press.

White, S. 1988. "Male Bonding, Hollywood Orientalism, and the Repression of the Feminine in Kubrick's Full Metal Jacket." In *Inventing Vietnam*. Ed. Michael Anderegg. Philadelphia: Temple University Press, 204–30.

Williams, P. 2003. "'What a Bummer for the Gooks': Representations of White American Masculinity and the Vietnamese in the Vietnam War Film Genre 1977–87." *EJAC* 22 (3): 215–34.

Williams, S., and G. Bendelow. 1998. *The Lived Body: Sociological Themes, Embodied Issues*. London: Routledge.

Willis, S. 1995. "The Fathers Watch the Boys' Room." *Camera Obscura* 32:41–73.

———. 2000. "Style, Posture, and Idiom: Quentin Tarantino's Figures of Masculinity." In *Reinventing Film Studies*. Ed. Christine Gledhill and Linda Williams. London: Arnold, 279–95.

Filmography

Full Metal Jacket. 1987 (U.S.A.). Directed by S. Kubrick.

Psycho. 1960 (U.S.A.). Directed by A. Hitchcock.

Pulp Fiction. 1994 (U.S.A.). Directed by Q. Tarantino.

Secrets and Lies. 1996 (U.K.). Directed by M. Leigh.

There's Something about Mary. 1998 (U.S.A.). Directed by Bobby and Peter Farrelly.

Trainspotting. 1996 (U.K.). Directed by D. Boyle.

15

"White Tiles. Trickling Water. A Man!"

Literary Representations of Cottaging in London

JOHAN ANDERSSON AND BEN CAMPKIN

At least since 1726, when the *London Journal* ran a front-page editorial listing "markets" and "bog-houses" where men met "to commit Sodomy" (quoted in Norton 1992, 66), the British media have reinforced a link between male homosexuality and public conveniences. Despite a general liberalization of attitudes towards gay sex and relationships in recent years, certain parts of the media remain obsessively preoccupied with this association. An extreme example can be found in the homophobic polemics of British tabloid columnist Richard Littlejohn, who has written more than thirty pieces on the topic in the last decade.[1] Aside from the tabloids and popular references to "cottaging," such as the video accompanying George Michael's song *Outside* (1998),[2] more serious representations have emerged in works of gay fiction, reinforcing the association of gay male identity and "gentlemen's" rooms, while also eroticising public toilet sex. These literary images of cottaging—so called because of the cottage-like domestic appearance of some British public conveniences (Figure 15.1)—are deserving of our attention, not least because they point to some of the underlying historical, social, and psychological factors that have influenced certain men to seek sexual encounters in these spaces.

In what follows, we first consider a selection of indicative accounts of cottaging across a number of different academic disciplines and cultural representations. From this foundation we then explore two recent plays about cottaging set in the East End of London: Chay Yew's *Porcelain* (1992) and Philip Ridley's *Vincent River* (2000). We conclude by reflecting on these representations in reference to theoretical debates about dirt and abjection.

Accounting for the use of public toilets for cottaging is logistically and ethically problematic from the perspective of formal urban research because of the hidden nature and illegality of such activities, and because of

Figure 15.1 Public Toilet, Pond Square, Highgate, London. (Courtesy of Matt Hucke.)

the need to protect participants' anonymity. The first academic studies of cottaging were published by North American ethnographers, who carried out observational research in selected "tearooms" (the American term for a cottage) (Humphreys 1970; Delph 1978). However, preceding these accounts, cottaging already featured in official urban records and discourse. Matt Houlbrook has shown that a guidebook to London's public toilets published in 1937 was in fact offering "an ironic—if heavily veiled—indictment of contemporary sexual mores" (Houlbrook 2005, 51; Pry 1937). Yet, as David Bell has argued, the first true "ethnographers of public sex (apart from the participants themselves)—and the producers of the first maps of these erogenous zones—were the police, with plain-clothes officers on entrapment operations painstakingly recording 'offences' in public toilets or at after-dark parks" (Bell 2001, 88–89). Frank Mort also elaborates this thesis in reference to 1950s London, showing how the Metropolitan Police effectively constructed a map of homosexual spaces in the metropolis, charting informal meeting places including parks and cottages. He contends, "Utilising the 19th-century genre of social investigation [this] map of the city was at once inquisitorial, classificatory and interpretative" (Mort 1998, 890). Cultural and legal histories of queer London in the late-nineteenth and twentieth centuries that have mapped the city's homosexual geography using criminal records have repeatedly focused on the public toilets in Piccadilly Circus Underground Station as one of the key sites for illicit encounters (Cook 2003; David 1997; Houlbrook 2005).

Although subsequent sociological research on public sex has been more radical and participatory in its approach (see, e.g., Califia 1994 and van Lieshout 1997), many of the more insightful representations of cottaging are found in gay fiction and autobiographical work by gay writers. The British filmmaker and queer activist Derek Jarman, for example, manages to capture both the attraction to and history of public sex in his diaries and essay anthologies, published in the early 1990s. According to Jarman, legal oppression is the root of cottaging because society "fought the opening of the bars . . . and anything that might suggest we led normal lives" (Jarman 1993, 60). Before male homosexuality was partly decriminalised in 1967, bars and commercial meeting places were frequently raided by the police. Cottages and cruising areas were the only meeting places that did not require a detailed knowledge of the hidden commercial scene or access to personal networks for information. As Jarman suggests, the stigma attached to these places contributed to the exclusion of homosexual men from identification with "normal lives." This is supported by Houlbrook's detailed historical analysis of the legal response to cottaging in London:

> In 1917, 81 percent of homosexual incidents resulting in proceedings at Bow Street Police Court were detected in locations positively identifiable as public conveniences. Arrested primarily in urinals, the homosexual was constructed in the image of that place. Harold Sturge, Old Street magistrate, made explicit the connection between the dirt and defecation of the lavatory and the homosexual. Homosexual acts were, he argued, "morally wrong, physically dirty and progressively degrading" (Houlbrook 2000, 62).

This account emphasises how, historically, the legal establishment mobilised an image of homosexual men as dirty and contaminating through reference to the soiled space of the cottage.

The literary response to such stigmatisation has often been the aestheticisation of the very aspects of gay life that violate conventional notions of romance and intimacy. Homosexual French writer Jean Genet pioneered a form of subversive aesthetics that reversed conventional moral values and, in the North American novelist Edmund White's words, "transformed degradation into saintliness" (White 2005, 333). In Britain, playwright Joe Orton was influenced by Genet, although he claimed Genet's style to be unconsciously comical since a "combination of elegance and crudity is always ridiculous" (Orton 1996, 70). Orton's descriptions of cottaging in 1960s London are stylistically sparse in contrast with Genet's elaborate prose, but he transposes the unapologetic tone into his own work.[3] As White has pointed out, Orton "never seems particularly anguished by his homosexuality" (White 2004, 88), and cottaging is presented matter-of-factly as a form of underworld activity, more often than not located literally underground, in

Figure 15.2 Still from Fernando Arias, *Public Inconvenience, 2004.*
(Courtesy of the artist.)

subterranean public lavatories (Orton 1996). Between a tube and bus journey to and from London's Holloway Road, he describes experiencing a
"scene of a frenzied homosexual saturnalia" in "the little pissoir under the
bridge," listing, with minimal emotion, the details of who did what to whom
while "no more than two feet away the citizens of Holloway moved about
their ordinary business" (Orton 1996, 105). The juxtaposition between the
"ordinary business" of the people of Holloway on street level and the "frenzied homosexual saturnalia" underground is poignantly choreographed in
Stephen Frears's biopic of Orton, *Prick Up Your Ears* (1987). While the playwright has sex in the blacked-out toilet, acoustically animated by the sounds
of dripping cisterns, the feet of passersby are visible as shadows walking
across the glazed bricks that form a light well from the pavement.

Other literary representations portray the cottage as a space of guilt
and disgust. In White's novel *The Beautiful Room Is Empty* (1988), the
narrator is compulsively addicted to the sex he finds on tap in the toilets of
his university campus. Although White eroticises cottaging, the sexual
pleasure experienced by his character is quickly overshadowed by feelings
of intense shame: "After I ejaculated I felt full of self-hatred every time, and
every time I swore I'd never return to the toilets" (White 1988, 59). In this
example the toilet is both a space where homosexual relations can be forged
in relative security—a place of (limited) freedom for sexual experimentation—and, simultaneously, a kind of prison, the oppressive setting of sexual
compulsion and stigmatisation.

Yew's play *Porcelain* (1992) and Ridley's *Vincent River* (2000) also
present the cottage as a paradoxical space. On the one hand, they display a
subversive tendency to eroticise even the "dirtiest" aspects of cottaging; on
the other, they focus attention on the themes of disgust and self-disgust. As
abject spaces, these fictional cottages hover between different meanings:
they are at once hygienic and filthy, oppressive and liberating, banal and
functional, while also constituting spaces of erotic fantasy. They are the

setting for feelings of nausea, contamination, discomfort, and panic—characteristics outlined by William Ian Miller in his theory of disgust, an emotion he links to dirt as an instrument of social control (Miller 1997). At the same time they hold associations of pleasure, safety, and the fulfilment of sexual desire.

Yew and Ridley are consistently vague about the formal architecture of the toilet spaces, concentrating instead on their phenomenological qualities. These particular cottages could be drawn from any of the myriad forms taken by London public conveniences, from the boom Victorian period of toilet construction—in which ornate new conveniences crowned London's new sewage system at surface level—to later, more modest and functional modernist examples.

In Yew's play, *Porcelain*, Cambridge University–bound, nineteen-year-old gay Asian John Lee becomes obsessed by an older white builder, William Hope, whom he meets in a cottage in Bethnal Green. The plot develops through John Lee's psychotherapeutic analysis after his confession to the murder of Hope, an act that takes place at the beginning of the play in the cottage itself. Through an exchange amongst five anonymous voices, Yew explores Lee's motives for participating in cottaging and the ultimately abusive relationship he enters into with Hope, who drunkenly beats and rapes him. At the outset of the play, the psychologist secretly admits his feelings about the case: "I think the whole case is—sick. Public sex is an offence. Murder is an offence. Well, let me put it in simple words—a queer chink who indulges in public sex kills a white man. Where would your fucking sympathies lie? Quite open and shut isn't it" (Yew 1992, in Clum 1996, 359). The play draws out many of the central issues in ongoing debates about cottaging. The psychotherapist's homophobic statement, which presents the "indulgence" of public sex as morally "open and shut," is countered later on by the voices of "straight" men who admit to cottaging as an easy route to sexual relief (Yew 1992, in Clum 1996, 368).

During the course of the play, we are given retrospective insights into the feelings of social alienation and the experience of racism on the commercial gay scene that drive Lee to seek sex, and love, through cottaging. On the scene, he is used to meeting older men who are "looking for a house boy. Trying to relive the old colonial days" (Yew 1992, in Clum 1996, 373). In contrast, the cottage offers Lee an environment where he feels socially equal, and equally desirable, to other men. A dialogue amongst four anonymous voices conveys various different motivations for cottaging, comparing the cottage to an anonymous and exclusive gentleman's club, to a convenience supermarket for sex, and to parks, back alleys, offices, and planes—places where "people like to fuck" because of the element of danger and risk of discovery.

John Lee's therapy focuses on an image of the fairytale *Beauty and the Beast*, which Lee is reminded of through a book he has been reading on the history of Chinese art: "The fascinating thing about porcelain is the process. Coarse stone powders and clay fused by intense temperatures to create something so delicate, fragile, and beautiful: Two extremes, two opposites thrown together only to produce beauty. Like the fairy tale *Beauty and the Beast*" (Yew 1992, in Clum 1996, 364). This image forms the intersection between several themes. The porcelain of the play's title works on different metaphorical levels. It refers at once to the material properties and aesthetics of the toilet—the tiles and the bowl of the lavatory itself, a receptacle for urine and faeces—and the skin of the ironically named William Hope, whom Lee romanticises as his lover. As Lee's therapy unfolds, it becomes apparent that Hope is both desirable "beauty" and flawed "beast"; the cottage is the site of both desire and of repulsion; and Lee has contradictory feelings about himself as at times attractive and at others irreversibly contaminated:

> I just want to be held by these men. For a moment, they do. Hold me. And almost all the time, I treasure that moment. The moment they smile. Then I go back and take a long hot shower. Washing every memory, every touch, and every smell. Only it never quite leaves me. No matter how hard or how long I wash. The dirt, filth penetrates deep into your skin. And for a time I'd try to stay away from the toilet until that familiar loneliness—the need to be held. It's strange. This feeling. This marriage of dirt and desire. (Yew 1992, in Clum 1996, 374)

Ridley's play *Vincent River*, also set in the East End of London, features similar themes to *Porcelain* around dirt and desire, homophobia and violent death. The play is structured as a dialogue between the mother (Anita) and the lover (Davey) of Vincent, the victim of a fatal queer-bashing assault in a cottage in Shoreditch. As in *Porcelain*, cottages are paradoxically represented as spaces of both hygiene and filth, safety and violence. In one oneiric recollection of a sexual encounter in a public toilet, Davey describes a cottage in the following stark terms, evoking the sounds, smells, and hygienically bright strip-lighting: "Bleach! Brilliant white light. White tiles. Trickling water. A man! He's leaning against the porcelain. . . . He smells of aftershave. Makes me giddy. He's holding my hand. Leading me into a cubicle. Closes the door. Smell of bleach gets stronger. Water trickles louder. Everything's so clean and peaceful. He's undoing his belt" (Ridley 2000, 65).

The emphasis on the colour of white—a "quasi-universal signifier of purity" (Shonfield 2001, 42)—and the sound of trickling water give this cottaging episode an almost innocent setting (something that is also underlined by the men holding hands). However, for most parts of the play this imagery of purity is replaced with a darker emphasis on dirt and disgust in relation to cottaging and homosexuality. Heterosexual society's disgust at homosexuality in general, and cottaging in particular, are personified by Anita, who finds it difficult to accept that her son, Vincent, is gay. She finds out about Vincent's sexuality only when a local newspaper describes the murder site as "a haunt for gay men seeking sex" (Ridley 2000, 14), and she discovers a cardboard box full of gay pornographic magazines underneath his bed. When she tries to get rid of these magazines, no place seems dirty enough for their disposal: first she walks to the "dust bins," then to the "rubbish bins," and then to the Regent's Canal, before finally taking a bus to the end of the route, where she dumps the magazines in "a pile of rubbish" tucked "between two cardboard boxes" in a "side street" (Ridley 2000, 18–19). The identification of homosexuality with waste in this episode is reflected not only in the rubbish itself but in the urban landscape as a whole: the only locations deemed appropriate dumping grounds for Vincent's "filthy" magazines are a dark canal and a littered side street. In his doctoral thesis, Jon Binnie has commented on this association of homosexuality with what he calls "the ruins of the urban landscape": "Queers are associated with the discarded, the derelict—the ruins of the urban landscape. In homophobic discourse, gay men have been commonly represented as the 'waste of modernity'—as the Other. Non-productive sexualities have been seen as wasteful—surplus to the system of reproduction. So homosexuality is literally seen as a negation of life force and creativity" (Binnie 1997, 153).

The historically hidden location of commercial gay nightlife in semi-derelict, rundown neighbourhoods may have contributed to this association of queers with "the ruins of the urban landscape," but as Aaron Betsky has pointed out, informal cruising grounds also tend to occur "where the supposed rationale of the urban structure falls apart because it is not functional" (Betsky 1997, 147; see also Andersson 2009). The murder site in *Vincent River*, a cottage in a disused railway station, corresponds to this image of the "abandoned" city and is described as "Just ruins really. . . . Big hole in the roof. The walls are enamelled tiles. Cracked sink. Should've been a row. Most ripped out. Brickwork showing. At the far end . . . Cubicles. Five. Doors missing. Wooden frames. Graffiti" (Ridley 2000, 25–26). Although this is a threatening environment, the erotic appeal of the cottage is linked to its derelict state and vandalised appearance. Davey cannot have sex with Vincent in the safety of his home because it is less exciting than in the urban ruin of the cottage: "Vince and me. We didn't do anything that night. I couldn't get it up. . . . I told him it wasn't his fault. It was the place. Bedroom and stuff. It was too safe" (Ridley 2000, 79). As opposed to the domestic setting of the bedroom, this particular cottage represents a disordered, filthy, and dangerous space that is nevertheless erotically exciting (or, indeed, erotically exciting precisely because it is disorderly, dirty, and dangerous).

The cottage as evoked by Yew and Ridley is a space that prompts us to rethink the rigidity of the "dirt is matter out of place" theory that social anthropologist Mary Douglas developed in the 1960s, which has remained dominant in discussions of polluted space and hygiene aesthetics (Douglas 1966/2000; Campkin and Cox 2007; Campkin 2009).[4] As William Cohen writes, we now need to recognise that "contradictory ideas—about filth as both polluting and valuable—can be held at once" (Cohen 2005, xiii). The sense in which the cottage is dirty in Douglas's terms is insofar as it represents a confusion of established categories; it conveys an architectural imagery of hygiene, and yet it comes to be associated with dirt and waste: material, bodily, sexual, and social. Instead of considering cottage spaces as simply dirty, they can be categorised more usefully as "abject" (Kristeva 1982), a nuanced notion more equipped to account for their spatial and social ambivalences.

Geographer Steve Pile understands abjection as an exclusionary force, "a perpetual condition of surveillance, maintenance, and policing of impossible 'cleanliness'" (1996, 90). Recent responses to cottaging in the United Kingdom—including the obsessive surveillance and closure of public toilets[5] and the criminalisation of toilet sex[6]—as cultural manifestations of this process. As the literary examples above have suggested, even for those who engage in cottaging the status of these spaces is equivocal. This is, as David Woodhead has observed, reflected in their spatial contradictions: "the contained space is also a containing space which leaves those men using the cottage in a vulnerable situation" (1995, 239). It is this paradoxical spatial and social character that both Yew and Ridley's dramatizations of cottaging strongly reinforce.

Notes

1. This figure was obtained through a search using the LexisNexis database. For more information on Littlejohn's views and a biography, see his Wikipedia entry, available at http://en.wikipedia.org/wiki/Richard_Littlejohn, accessed September 2, 2006.

2. The song and video made clear reference to Michael's arrest by an undercover police officer for "engaging in a lewd act" in a public restroom in a park in Beverly Hills, California. *Outside* reached number 2 in the U.K. singles chart.

3. An equivalent in contemporary visual art can be found in London-based Colombian artist Fernando Arias's work *Public Inconvenience* (2004; Figure 15.2), the most sexually graphic work in the U.K. Architecture Foundation's controversial 2006 *Glory Hole* exhibition. Apparently shot with a hidden camera in a now-closed cottage, south of London's Tower Bridge, the film provides a voyeuristic glimpse of men cruising, their faces blurred to prevent identification (see Campkin and Andersson 2006).

4. For detailed discussion of the interpretation of Douglas's theory in relation to architecture, space, and cities, see Campkin and Cox 2007 and Campkin 2009.

5. Katherine Shonfield notes the irony of "the flowering of illicit sexual activity within the [obsessively clean and orderly] lavatory itself" and the "unspoken and unspeakable rationale" behind the mass closure of public toilets in late-twentieth-century London: the fact that these spaces allowed "the possibility of open scrutiny and enjoyment of others' genitals" (Shonfield, in Hill 2001, 39).

6. Sexual Offences Act (2003), section 71.

References

Andersson, J. 2009. "East End Localism and Urban Decay: Shoreditch's Re-emerging Gay Scene." *London Journal* 34 (1).

Bell, D. 2001. "Fragments for a Queer City." In *Pleasure Zones: Bodies, Cities, Spaces*. Ed. D. Bell, J. Binnie, R. Holliday, R. Longhurst, and R. Peace. Syracuse, N.Y.: Syracuse University Press, 84–102.

Betsky, A. 1997. *Queer Space: Architecture and Same-Sex Desire*. New York: William Morrow.

Binnie, J. 1997. "A Geography of Urban Desires: Sexual Culture in the City." Unpublished Ph.D. diss., University of London.

Califia, P. 1994. *Public Sex: The Culture of Radical Sex*. Pittsburgh: Cleis Press.

Campkin, B. 2009. "Dirt, Blight and Regeneration: Urban Change in London." Unpublished Ph.D. diss., University College, London.

Campkin, B., and J. Andersson. 2006. "Glory Hole Outs the Relationship between Architecture and Gay Sex." *Building Design* 1731 (July 21). Available at http://www.bdonline. co.uk/story.asp?sectioncode=429&storycode=3070986.

Campkin, B., and R. Cox, eds. 2007. *Dirt: New Geographies of Cleanliness and Contamination*. London: I. B. Tauris.

Cohen, W. A. 2005. "Introduction: Locating Filth." In *Filth: Dirt, Disgust and Modern Life*. Ed. W. A. Cohen and R. Johnson. Minneapolis: University of Minnesota Press, vii–xxxi.

Cook, M. 2003. *London and the Culture of Homosexuality, 1885–1914*. Cambridge: Cambridge University Press.

David, H. 1997. *On Queer Street: A Social History of British Homosexuality 1895–1995*. London: Harper Collins Publishers.

Delph, E. W. 1978. *The Silent Community: Public Homosexual Encounters*. Beverly Hills, Calif.: Sage Publications.

Douglas, M. 1966/2000. *Purity and Danger: An Analysis of the Concepts of Pollution and Taboo*. London: Routledge.

Frears, S., dir. 1987. *Prick Up Your Ears*. Screenplay by A. Bennett. Classic Collection DVD, Carlton International Media.

Houlbrook, M. 2000. "The Private World of Public Urinals." *London Journal* 25 (1): 52–70.

———. 2005. *Queer London: Perils and Pleasures in the Sexual Metropolis, 1918–1957*. Chicago: University of Chicago Press.

Humphreys, R.A.L. 1970. *Tearoom Trade: A Study of Homosexual Encounters in Public Places*. London: Gerald Duckworth.

Jarman, D. 1993. *At Your Own Risk: A Saint's Testament*. London: Vintage.

Kristeva, J. 1982. *Powers of Horror: An Essay on Abjection*. Trans. L. Roudiez. New York: Columbia University Press.

Lieshout, M. van. 1997. "Leather Nights in the Woods: Locating Male Homosexuality and Sadomasochism in a Dutch Highway Rest Area." In *Queers in Space: Communities, Public Places, Sites of Resistance*. Ed. G. B. Ingram, A.-M. Bouthillette, and Y. Retter. Seattle: Bay Press, 339–56.

Michael, G. 1998. *Outside*. Epic Records.

Miller, W. I. 1997. *The Anatomy of Disgust*. Cambridge, Mass.: Harvard University Press.

Mort, F. 1998. "Cityscapes: Consumption, Masculinities and the Mapping of London since 1950." *Urban Studies* 35 (5–6): 889–907.

Norton, R. 1992. *Mother Clap's Molly House: The Gay Subculture in England 1700–1830*. London: GMP Publishers.

Orton, J. 1996. *The Orton Diaries*. Ed. J. Lahr. New York: Da Capo Press.

Pile, S. 1996. *The Body and the City: Psychoanalysis, Space and Subjectivity*. London: Routledge.

Pry, P. 1937. *For Your Convenience: A Learned Dialogue Instructive to All Londoners and London Visitors, Overheard in the Thélème Club and Taken Down Verbatim by Paul Pry.* London: G. Routledge and Sons.

Ridley, P. 2000. *Vincent River.* London: Faber and Faber.

Sexual Offences Act. 2003. The Crown Prosecution Service Publications. Available at http://www.opsi.gov.uk/Acts/acts2003/ukpga_20030042_en_1. Accessed April 18, 2008.

Shonfield, K. 2001. "Two Architectural Projects about Purity." In *Architecture—The Subject Is Matter.* Ed. J. Hill. London: Routledge, 29–44.

White, E. 1988. *The Beautiful Room Is Empty.* London: Picador.

———. 2004. *Arts and Letters.* San Francisco: Cleis Press.

———. 2005. *My Lives.* London: Bloomsbury Publishing.

Woodhead, D. 1995. "Surveillant Gays": HIV, Space and the Constitution of Identities. In *Mapping Desire: Geographies of Sexualities.* Ed. D. Bell and G. Valentine. London: Routledge, 231–44.

Yew, C. 1992. *Porcelain.* Reprinted in *Staging Gay Lives: An Anthology of Contemporary Gay Theatre.* Ed. J. M. Clum. Boulder, Colo: Westview Press, 1996.

16

The Jew on the Loo

The Toilet in Jewish Popular Culture, Memory, and Imagination

NATHAN ABRAMS

In the BBC television sitcom *Blackadder Goes Forth* (1989), the German character of the Red Baron declares, "How lucky you English are to find the toilet so amusing. For us, it is a mundane and functional item. For you it is the basis of an entire culture." Swap "English" for "Jewish" here and the quote would ring just as true, for the toilet plays an important part in Jewish culture. Indeed, the act of elimination has its own dedicated *brachah* (blessing):

> Blessed are You, o Lord, our God, King of the Universe, Who formed man with intelligence, and created within him many openings and many hollow spaces; it is revealed and known before the Seat of Your Honor, that if one of these would be opened or if one of these would be sealed it would be impossible to survive and to stand before You (even for one hour). Blessed are You, o Lord, Who heals all flesh and does wonders.

The function of the blessing is no doubt to imprint on the mind the oft-appearing words "*Da lifnei Mi atah omed*" (Remember before Whom you stand). While both this blessing and the reminder might be gender nonspecific, the words *man* and *stand* may be read in a masculine fashion, referring to the act of urination as it is commonly performed by men. Taking this cue, then, this chapter explores a series of vignettes to highlight and illustrate the use of the toilet in Jewish popular culture, memory, and imagination, broadly defined, and argues that the space of the toilet, both public and private, is gendered differently for women and men and is a boundary marker between Jews and non-Jews.

Ritual Purity

Much emphasis was placed in the Bible on personal cleanliness as an essential requirement for both physical fitness and holiness, specifically, ritual purity. Consequently, latrines were situated beyond the confines of the military encampment in order to keep it clean, and each soldier was equipped with a spade (spike or trowel) so he could dig a hole to bury his excrement. As it is written in the Torah:

> Thou shalt have a place also without the camp, whither thou shalt go forth abroad. And thou shalt have a paddle among thy weapons; and it shall be, when thou sittest down abroad, thou shalt dig therewith, and shalt turn back and cover that which cometh from thee.
>
> For HaShem thy G-d walketh in the midst of thy camp, to deliver thee, and to give up thine enemies before thee; therefore shall thy camp be holy; that He see no unseemly thing in thee, and turn away from thee. (Deuteronomy 23:13–15)

A literal reading of the language here seemingly refers only to the act of defecation, since it uses the word *sitting* and not *standing*, but later Talmudic literature (*Berakhoth* 25a) insists that this includes the act of urination. Since it is used in the context of establishing a military camp, it is referring to public, homosocial, and male space. The later rabbis also required that one's hands be washed after urination and defecation and spent much time discussing whether a male Jew could pray in or near a toilet and under what conditions. The concern here was that the toilet and its contents would defile such a holy act as prayer, and much thought and ink were deployed in establishing a clear distinction between sacred and profane (that is, toilet) space. In a similar vein, both the Torah (Leviticus 15:19–31) and the Talmud (*Tractate Nashim*) are indirectly concerned with female toileting practices, in particular *niddah* (impurity), whereby any menstruating woman may not have any contact with her husband. This period is marked by psychological and physical separation (Daniels 2008, 79–80). Although *niddah* is not, strictly speaking, toilet practice, it is related. Nevertheless, the public toilet, as it then was, appears to be an exclusively male space.

Anxiety, Danger, and Dehumanization

The toilet has represented a gendered threat in many situations where the male Jew has been compelled to hide his religion and ethnicity, in order to pass as gentile or white, and as a way to move up the socioeconomic ladder. The toilet hence becomes a site for the potential unmasking of his invisibility by displaying the primary signifier of Jewish masculinity: the circumcised penis. This is typically a feature in films dealing with the subject of anti-Semitism and especially the Holocaust. In films such as *School Ties* (Robert Mandel, 1992), *The Believer* (Henry Bean, 2001), and *Europa, Europa* (Agnieska Holland, 1991), some of which were based on true stories, a male Jew attempts to pass himself off as gentile. In these cases, the public toilet or bathroom represents a clear and present danger for the real identity of the Jew, who can be unmasked. In the toilet, the naked male Jew is at his most physically and emotionally vulnerable.

Significant with respect to the Shoah is the use of the toilet as a means of humiliation and degradation. When the Jews were herded into cattle cars and transported eastward to the death camps, the trains did not contain any toilets, nor were there any toilet stops—for the Jews, at least. Consequently, the acts of defecation and urination are remembered as very public and humiliating spectacles, designed by the Nazis, according to Primo Levi (as elaborated in his *If This Is a Man*, first published in Great Britain in 1979), incrementally and collectively to dehumanize the Jews before killing them. The disgusting physical state in which the Jews arrived would have facilitated the Nazis' murder machine, for it significantly distanced the Jews from their humanity and therefore helped the individuals responsible for administering the death camps to believe they were not, in fact, killing fellow human beings but rather destroying "pieces"—the Nazis' preferred term for Jewish prisoners (Levi 2000, 22).

The humiliation continued for the camp prisoners. Given the sheer numbers of Jews, there the toilet was most likely coded as "Jewish space." Life in the camps rotated around food, sleep, and "elimination" of waste. Because "elimination" was only at particular time, and collective, the importance of performance on these occasions was literally vital, as an inmate might not have another chance to go during the day. The pervasive lack of privacy in daily functions such as toilet use was paramount during the Shoah. Primo Levi recalled how it was forbidden to go there alone even during working hours. The Nazis assigned the weakest and clumsiest of the Kommando with the duty of *Scheissbegleiter*, "toilet companion" (Levi 2000, 74). Like Levi's, Holocaust memoirs recall toilet facilities of an identical nature: wooden boards on which inmates sat in rows, perhaps eighty to ninety people at a time. Survivor David R. Katz recalled, "The sanitary facilities were located in a wooden barrack in the center of the camp, and consisted of the latrine, with trenches along one wall, over which were some long wooden planks with a round hole about every two feet or so, with a small partition between them" (Katz 2008). Levi described how, in Auschwitz, there was one latrine for each group of six to eight "Blocks," or wooden huts, into each of which he estimated were crammed 200 to 250 inmates. By this count, anywhere between 1,200 and 2,000 men were attempting to use the one toilet. These pressures on the latrines were exacerbated as some were designated off-limits to Jews and were *"nur fr Kapos"* or *"nur fr Reichsdeutsche"* (Levi 2000, 37–40).

At nights the inmates used a bucket in the hut. Levi recalled how "every two or three hours we have to get up to discharge ourselves of the great dose of water which during the day we are forced to absorb in the form of soup to satisfy our hunger" (Levi 2000, 67). As a consequence, the toilet once again functioned as a gendered public space, not so much by sight as by sound. Since a rule operated that the last user of the bucket was required to empty it in the latrines, another humiliating and disgusting practice, "old members of the camp have refined their senses to such a degree that, while still in their bunks, they are miraculously able to distinguish if the level is at a dangerous point, purely on the basis of the sound that the sides of the bucket make" (Levi 2000, 67). Women fared little better than men, and many female survivors recalled a loss of menstruation (Chodoff 1997, 150; Friedman 2001, 9). Those women who did menstruate were not provided with proper hygiene articles, and one can only imagine the lengths they had to go to deal with their menstruating bodies and public toilet needs. Such public toilet conditions were designed to strip the inmates of any vestige of human dignity.

Refuge and Resistance

At the same time, however, the latrines and washrooms became a site for resistance against the Nazis' dehumanization policy. Levi recalls how at least one inmate used the latrines as a means to maintain his dignity and humanity by continuing the act, if only an illusory one, of washing himself. In this way, he was preserving "the skeleton, the scaffolding, the form of civilization" (Levi 2000, 47). Furthermore, a key part of the memory of the Holocaust is how the public toilet provided refuge. Chaya Ostrower (2000) observed how former camp inmates recalled that the latrines had a name, RTA, which stood for Radio Tuches ("buttocks" in Yiddish) Agency, because there camp inmates exchanged information, news, barter, gossip, and even jokes. Thus the public toilet was remembered not only as a public space in which the Jewish inmates were somewhat obscured from their oppressors but also as a location for humanizing interaction. In addition, since the latrines were located on a border of the section between men and women, a trip to the latrines was as a potential occasion for communication with inmates on the other side. During the day, the latrine permitted a brief respite from the daily grind of back-breaking labor; Levi recalled it as "an oasis of peace" (Levi 2000, 74).

The latrines have also been remembered as functioning as places of refuge and safety in a further respect, as children hid, literally, in the shit to escape being rounded up and selected for the gas chambers. This was illustrated most graphically in *Schindler's List* (1993), Steven Spielberg's film adaptation of Thomas Keneally's book *Schindler's Ark* (1982). A final example here is the memoir of Ana Novac (née Zimra Harsanyi), who recorded her impressions during six harrowing months in Auschwitz and Plaszow concentration camps, from June to November 1944, on sheets of toilet paper, which she hid in her shoes.

Humor, Cancer, Constipation, and Masturbation

On a less serious note than the accounts from the Shoah, everyday Jewish culture revolves around going to the toilet. Apart from essential biological requirements, it has become a staple of Jewish humor in which the toilet and toileting practices play a central role. One Yiddish joke, for example, goes thus:

> In a men's room in Warsaw in 1910: two men are standing at adjoining urinals when one of them feels a stream of urine running down his right pant leg. He asks: "Well, how are things in Klodova?" The second man responds: "How did you know I am from Klodova?" First: "Who doesn't know the work of Reb Moishe the Lefthander, the Klodover Mohel?"

In the United States, it is a trope of contemporary American Jewish literature that at least one, and usually always a male, member of the family must suffer from a chronic toilet-related ailment, such as constipation or irritable bowel syndrome. In such literature, this is attributed to a diet rich in salt and fat, which he is forced to eat in copious quantities by his overbearing mother and then, later, his wife. Consequently, the toilet has provided much grist for the mill in Jewish literature. In 1949 the Jewish American New York poet Isaac Rosenfeld wrote an extremely contentious piece, "Adam and Eve on Delancey Street," a Freudian rendition of the laws of Kashrut. The most controversial part of the piece focused on a joke that occurs in the toilet, which Rosenfeld used to illustrate his argument that food taboos were actually sex taboos:

> *Milchigs*, having to do with milk, is feminine; *fleshigs*, meat, is masculine. Their junction in one meal, or within one vessel, is forbidden, for their union is the sexual act. (The Jewish joke about the man with cancer of the penis bears this out. He is advised by the doctor to soak his penis in hot water. His wife, finding him so engaged, cries out, "Cancer shmancer. *Dos iz a milchig tepple!*— who cares about cancer? You're using a *milchig* pot.") (Rosenfeld 1949, 387)

Rosenfeld concluded that the dietary laws were thus injunctions against forbidden sexual practices; the careful circumscription of food mirrored

Jewish sexual repression. The location of the joke in the toilet, with its subject of cancer, further suggests the nexus of male body parts, sexuality, defilement, and disease. Rosenfeld had introduced here a kind of speculative, half-humorous inquiry into matters in which the author Philip Roth would specialize and satirize, to great consternation, more than a decade later.

In 1969, Roth published his classic and controversial novel *Portnoy's Complaint*. The father of the eponymous narrator of the title, Mr. Portnoy, suffers from constipation, and one of the narrator's "earliest impressions" is of "my father reading the evening paper with a suppository up his ass" (Roth 1971, 3). Meanwhile, his son, Alexander, competes with his father for toilet time by masturbating there. In a section titled "Whacking Off," the reader is treated to a long and detailed treatise about Alex's masturbatory exploits on the toilet, which take place at home, in the movie theater, and even at school: "In the middle of class I would raise a hand to be excused, rush down the corridor to the lavatory, and with ten or fifteen savage strokes, beat off standing up into a urinal" (Roth 1971, 18). Not only is public toilet space used here, but Alex does not even seek to mask his actions by utilizing a cubicle; indeed, he stands and "whacks off" with seemingly no concern that he might be discovered. Ironically, then, when at home, Alex seeks to hide the amount of time he spends on the toilet devoted to his self-abusing obsession by telling his parents he has diarrhea, which only causes his mother further concern and his father jealousy. The space of the toilet is gendered here because Portnoy (like Roth and, arguably, American Jewish literature in general) ignores the topic of women's toilet practices and use of toilets as both a space of refuge and relief of sexual urges.

The Ordeal of Civility

Following on from literature, Jewish-related film in America has made much use of the toilet; however, the toilet in film often functions as a gendered space of anxiety for the Jew. The toilet serves to code the clash between Jewishness and gentility, or what John Murray Cuddihy (1978) called "the ordeal of civility." By this reasoning, the toilet becomes a distancing device for establishing the cultural divide between Jews and gentiles. For example, in any number of films, male Jewish characters are confronted with toilet-related situations as a source of social danger and humor in which they have to overcome an obstacle or test in order to obtain the object of their respective affections, typically a non-Jewish and blonde female: *There's Something about Mary* (Bobby and Peter Farrelly, 1998), *Meet the Parents* (Jay Roach, 2000), *Meet the Fockers* (Jay Roach, 2004), *Along Came Polly* (John Hamburg, 2004), and *The Fantastic Four* (Tim Story, 2005), to name just a few. Thus the toilet represents a test to demonstrate that the male Jew is worthy of being accepted into gentility, as genteel and gentile. (Incidentally, the masturbation scene in *There's Something about Mary*, referred to in Chapter 14, almost replicates exactly a similar sequence in the novel *Portnoy's Complaint*. Playing on or with the Portnoy episode, the film has thus utilized the space of the toilet as a source of Jewish-related humor.)

Jewish Space and Fantasy

A significant number of male Jewish characters on television are placed in the bathroom, to the extent that some claim anyone on the toilet on screen is instantly recognized as Jewish by a media-savvy audience able to detect and decode the signs. For example, the character of George Costanza (Jason Alexander) in the seminal sitcom *Seinfeld*, while not explicitly a Jewish character but clearly playing a Jewish archetype modeled on the show's creator Larry David, is constantly in the bathroom, usually at Jerry's apartment. He is often shown taking in something to read, too, thus elongating his stay and reinforcing the connection.

Larry David's own show, *Curb Your Enthusiasm*, makes much play of the toilet. In one incident, Larry is caught short and in his desperation uses the "disabled toilet," as the others are occupied. Meanwhile, however, a wheelchair user enters the bathroom and is unable to use the designated toilet. When Larry leaves, the wheelchair user admonishes him and tells him never to use "our" toilets again. Later in the film, Larry enters the same toilet and discovers that all but the disabled toilet are occupied. He remembers the admonition and refrains from using the disabled toilet, only to witness that the aforementioned wheelchair user is using one of the nondisabled lavatories. A smile crosses Larry's face as he tells the wheelchair user that he should never use one of "our" toilets. As is typical for *Curb Your Enthusiasm*, the episode uses the public toilet as a means for Larry to fulfill his revenge fantasies against those who have slighted him in the past.

In the Christmas 1997 episode of *South Park*, the male Jewish character Kyle Broflovski sings a frustrated song about being a lonely Jew on Christmas, since he is marginalized from the mainstream celebration of the festival. In its place, he privately invents a nonreligious substitute for Santa Claus, Mr. Hankey, the Christmas Poo, who, as his name suggests, is a talking turd that emerges from the family toilet when Kyle is alone there. As a consequence, the toilet becomes not only a marginalized Jewish space but also a site for fantasy and wish fulfillment unavailable to Kyle in the wider society of which he is a part. Such occasions also occur on film: for example, in *La Haine* (Mathieu Kassovitz, 1995), when Vinz (Vincent Cassels), a disaffected *banlieue*-dwelling working-class Jew, is depicted in the bathroom as he practices acting out the part of Scorsese's Travis Bickle from *Taxi Driver* (1976)—a part he later tries to perform beyond the confines of the toilet, but in which he fails and is upstaged by his rival. As a result of the multiplicity of these television and film toilet-related scenes, the toilet becomes semiotically coded as gendered and Jewish space, reinforcing the sense of Jewish male Otherness and marginalization. Yet it is also a site in which the Jewish male can achieve what he is denied elsewhere in the host society.

A final example concerns another gender dimension to the toilet. Comedian Sarah Silverman, in her show, performances, and movie *Jesus Is Magic* (2005), makes much of her bowels and toilet humor. The opening credits of her television show, for example, depict her sitting on the toilet, facing a camera and singing, "I always have to watch myself when I go pee," thus transforming the bathroom from private to a gendered public space. Meanwhile, her song continues: "If I find a stick I'll put it your momma's butt and pull it out and stick the doody in her eye." In this way, Silverman issues a direct challenge to the notion of toilets as the sole domain of men in American Jewish popular culture and attempts to rescue the toilet as a gendered space for American Jewish women and their revenge fantasies too.

References

Chodoff, Paul. 1997. "The Holocaust and Its Effects on Survivors: An Overview." *Political Psychology* 18, no. 1 (March): 147–57.

Cuddihy, John Murray. 1978. *The Ordeal of Civility: Freud, Marx, Lévi-Strauss, and the Jewish Struggle with Modernity*. Boston: Beacon Press.

Daniels, Jyoti Sarah. 2008. "Scripting the Jewish Body: The Sexualised Female Jewish Body in Amos Gitai's *Kadosh*." In *Jews and Sex*. Ed. Nathan Abrams. Nottingham: Five Leaves, 73–83.

Friedman, Jonathan. 2001. "Togetherness and Isolation: Holocaust Survivor Memories of Intimacy and Sexuality in the Ghettos." *Oral History Review* 28, no. 1 (Winter–Spring): 1–16.

Katz, David R. 2008. "Autobiography." Available at http://www.holocaust-trc.org/dkatz_autobio.htm. Accessed January 2008.

Keneally, Thomas. 1982. *Schindler's Ark*. London: Hodder and Stoughton.

Levi, Primo. 2000. *If This Is a Man*. London: Abacus.

Novac, Ana. 1997. *The Beautiful Days of My Youth: My Six Months in Auschwitz and Plaszow*. New York: Henry Holt.

Ostrower, Chaya. 2000. "Humor as a Defense Mechanism in the Holocaust." Ph.D. diss., Tel-Aviv University.

Rosenfeld, Isaac. 1949. "Adam and Eve on Delancey Street." *Commentary* 8, no. 4 (October): 385–87.

Roth, Philip. 1971. *Portnoy's Complaint*. London: Corgi.

Filmography

Along Came Polly. 2004. Directed by John Hamburg.
The Believer. 2001. Directed by Henry Bean.
Blackadder Goes Forth. 1989. BBC television series.
Curb Your Enthusiasm. 2000–. HBO television series.

Europa, Europa. 1991. Directed by Agnieska Holland.
The Fantastic Four. 2005. Directed by Tim Story.
Gentleman's Agreement. 1947. Directed by Elia Kazan.
La Haine. 1995. Directed by Mathieu Kassovitz.
Meet the Fockers. 2004. Directed by Jay Roach.
Meet the Parents. 2000. Directed by Jay Roach.
Sarah Silverman: Jesus Is Magic. 2005. Directed by Liam Lynch.
The Sarah Silverman Program. 2007. Comedy Central television series.
Schindler's List. 1993. Directed by Steven Spielberg.
School Ties. 1992. Directed by Robert Mandel.
Seinfeld. 1990–98. NBC television series.
South Park. 1997–2007. Comedy Central television series.
Taxi Driver. 1976. Directed by Martin Scorsese.
There's Something about Mary. 1998. Directed by Bobby and Peter Farrelly.

Afterword

Some years ago I made a short film called *Inside Rooms—26 Bathrooms* which, with ironic alphabetical ordering, attempted to demonstrate what went on in the smallest room in the English house. It was to be about washing, bathing and batheing, showering, soaking, drying, cleaning, masturbating, playing with rubber ducks, reading damp books, cutting toenails, brushing teeth, gargling, singing to enjoy the echo, expectoration, some copulation, though not so much (too many hard surfaces), considerable looking in mirrors, picking spots, trying to see a good view of your own backside, some vomiting (voluntary and involuntary), and of course urinating and defecating. Urinating and defecating, peeing and shitting, micturating and general elimination. Bodily fluids, as you might expect, were strong on the agenda. Which maybe is as it should be—why not? Bodily fluids make the body go round.

Much in the investigation was expected, but as much again was not. Which is about true with all investigation into apparently familiar territories. The old wives tales and the urban myths and the apocrypha were legion. But unprovable—so if I was set on telling you the truth—could I use them? Women pee on average five times a day compared to men who own up to seven—nothing particularly physiological—just down to the construction and the convenience of bathroom conveniences which were obviously not very convenient. Most women never sit down on the seat of a WC. The urine smells of a city are exclusively male. Several dead tramps in 1978 in the railway tunnels of East London had burnt genitals—an ammonia-heavy urine stream was a fast track between electrified rail and penis. Wearing white knickers makes you pee less. Never completely empty your bladder, because the deflated bladder walls might stick together through something called "dermal adhesion."

In the event the funding of this *26 Bathrooms* film restricted travel to largely Greater London. The bourgeois, surprisingly, were less uptight than the proletariat to let us watch them in their bathrooms, hence a criticism that 1980's middle-class London and the Home Counties mores were on show and not therefore indicative of life in general, but life in particular—could any survey be anything other than life in particular? We did visit the public washrooms, but we were indeed fascinated by L is for Lost Soap, N is for Newt and J was for Jacuzzi. So foggy, no-ventilation bathrooms in Hampstead, greenhouse shitting facilities in Chelsea, and a stylish customized Jacuzzi in North London were investigated. A young woman and a young man were to show us how a Jacuzzi worked; she came by public transport, he came by bike. They had never met before. They stripped naked, avoiding one another's eyes as they got into the foaming, spuming, artificially turbulent water of a Golders Green bathroom. Tentatively they relaxed with us, and then they relaxed with one another. We left them gossiping when we went for the afternoon tea-break. Nine months and one week later I was invited to the christening party of their first-born. They had called him Jonah. J is for Jonah who was spewed into the foaming, spuming, naturally turbulent brine of the Red Sea.

The English were late with Jacuzzis; indeed they were late with bathrooms, like the Dutch were late with staircases. Dutch staircases and English bathrooms were tacked onto houses at the very last moment, just before the builders departed. The English were not very clean anyway—never had been. And that story that the first English domestic baths were used for keeping coal was true in my grandmother's case, but that had more to do with—true to form—the bathroom being built in the backyard—my great grandfather much preferred to wash off the coal-dust in a tin bath before the warm fire in the parlor. S was for the Samuel Beckett Memorial Bathroom, a very cold, unheated, drafty, inclement space where you could not flush the shit (and cigarette-ends) away till the ice melted in the toilet bowl.

Nowadays toilets and bathrooms are very different spaces. For a start, in the English home with no central heating above the first floor, every bedroom and bathroom used to be freezing spaces in winter. You rushed in, did what you had to do as quickly as possible and then rushed out. We researched toilets that were libraries of pornography, toilets that were entirely unscreened and your visitors could watch you wiping your backside, toilets that were communal dining-rooms, which reminds me of that Borges short story of the tribe that ate in excessive privacy and defecated in public. I remember the shitting fields outside the barbed wire perimeter fence at Singapore Airport—in the eighties—countless neat holes in the ground as far as the eye could see—for shitting into as the planes came in from New

York and Sydney and Tokyo. The hole users in the early morning as the sun came up, were oblivious that these metal birds contained fascinated voyeurs used to white porcelain, heated loo seats, hot and cold water, flushing bidets and a domestic supply per house of twenty miles of pink toilet paper per year.

The queen and Mrs. Thatcher were provided with special toilet seats in the mid-eighties, wherever they traveled, never used before, never used after. My documentary might have appealed to these two ladies. But the documentary had an admittedly bizarre poetry about it. I went looking for that sort of bizarre poetry in this book and found it hard to find. Subjects in my eighties film were often wry and ironic about their lavatorial habits—curiously affectionate and understanding about the demands of their bodies as though their bodies were children in need of particular understanding, special care and vetted creature comforts. And so they should be. We are into harder stuff in this book—the politics of the urinal is ever-present. Julio Romano apparently preserved all his turds labeled and dated. There was that sixties Italian artist who canned and labeled his turds and sold them to a nervous public. Some were recently auctioned at decent saleroom prices, though no one took a tin-opener to discover how the contents had behaved. The labeled cans could have been empty and it could all have been a con-trick—the artist knew he probably would not be rumbled.

That sweet infamous book by Alexander Kira is mentioned and acknowledged. I am glad—the ergonomics of shitting and peeing complete with diagrams and photographs—a naked subject stands, squats or crouches in a Muybridge squared-up room so we can measure the arc of the urine flow, the splash back of the urine. Many a naked man has, I am sure, whilst peeing from a standing position into a domestic toilet bowl, felt the fine spray on his bare legs—and young boys take it to be manly and masculine to pee standing up when in the interests of hygiene they should be limiting the universal spray by sitting down.

Gone, thank God, is the communal Roman sponge on a stick dipped in vinegar to cleanse the buttocks, gone the left hand reserved for the anus and the right hand for the mouth—I was told that was really the reason for the left-handed being condemned—no relying on the Latin etymology of the word sinister. I remember doing student teaching-practice at Wandsworth Prison, and the prisoner replying, when asked what was the worst thing about prison-life? "The rough unsympathetic toilet paper. Could I please smuggle in something softer when I came back next week?" Comforts and conveniences have reached new standards. New standards of proprietary have eroded some of the fear and guilt. This book usefully helps us a little more—though there is still some considerable way to travel. You could well make this book your present guide. But male understanding of female practices is still under-developed. Have we progressed that much further beyond Swift's irony?

> *Strephon, who heard the fuming rill*
> *As from a mossy cliff distil,*
> *Cried out, Ye Gods, what sound is this?*
> *Can Chloe, my heavenly Chloe, piss?*

Peter Greenaway
January 2009

Contributors

NATHAN ABRAMS is a senior lecturer in film studies and the director of graduate studies at Bangor University. He has written widely on Jewish history, politics, popular culture, and film, including the following books: *Caledonian Jews: A Study of Seven Small Communities in Scotland* (McFarland, 2009); *Norman Podhoretz and Commentary: The Rise and Fall of the Neo-Cons* (Continuum, 2009); *Jews and Sex* (Five Leaves, 2008); *Commentary Magazine 1945–1959: "A Journal of Significant Thought and Opinion"* (Vallentine Mitchell, 2006); *Studying Film* (Arnold, 2001), coauthored with Ian Bell and Jan Udris; and *Containing America: Production and Consumption in Fifties America* (Birmingham University Press, 2000), coedited with Julie Hughes. He is currently working on a project that examines Jews, Jewishness, and Judaism in contemporary cinema.

JAMI ANDERSON is an associate professor in the Philosophy Department at the University of Michigan at Flint. Her primary research interests are critical race theory, gender theory, and philosophy of law. She has published a philosophy textbook, *Race, Gender, and Sexuality: Philosophical Issues of Identity and Justice* (Prentice Hall, 2003). She is currently completing a monograph, *Bodies and Embodiment: A Hegelian Analysis of Race, Gender, and Sex*.

JOHAN ANDERSSON is a visiting scholar at the Graduate Center, City University of New York. He is working on a collaborative research project called "Sexuality and Global Faith Networks" at the University of Leeds. He completed his doctoral work at University College London in 2008.

KATHRYN H. ANTHONY is a professor at the School of Architecture, University of Illinois at Urbana–Champaign, where she also serves on the faculty of the Department of Landscape Architecture and the Gender and Women's Studies Program. Anthony is the author of three books—*Running for Our Lives: An Odyssey with Cancer* (Campus Publishing Services, University of Illinois at Urbana–Champaign, 2004), *Designing for Diversity: Gender, Race, and Ethnicity in the Architectural Profession* (University of Illinois Press, 2001, 2008 [paperback]), and *Design Juries on Trial: The Renaissance of the Design Studio* (Van Nostrand Reinhold, 1991)—and over one hundred other publications. She received the 2005 Achievement Award from the Environmental Design Research Association, the 2003 Collaborative Achievement Award from the American Institute of Architects, and the 1992 Creative Achievement Award from the Association of Collegiate Schools of Architecture. She serves on the board of directors of the American Restroom Association and has presented her restroom research at the 2005 World Toilet Forum in Shanghai and the 2006 World Toilet Forum in Bangkok.

KATHY BATTISTA is a writer, lecturer, and curator. She is currently the director of Contemporary Art at Sotheby's Institute of Art, New York. Her doctoral research centered on the work of feminist artists in 1970s London. She is a coauthor of *Art New York* (Ellipsis, 2000) and *Recent Architecture in the Netherlands* (Ellipsis, 1998). Her articles have appeared in *Arcade: Artists and Placemaking* (Black Dog, 2006), *Surface Tension: Supplement 1* (Errant Bodies, 2006) and *Surface Tension: Problematics of Site* (Errant Bodies, 2003), as well as in the journals *RES, Art World, Third Text, Frieze,* and *Art Monthly.* She is on the editorial board of *Art and Architectural Journal* and is the New York correspondent for *PhotoIcon.* She has taught at Birkbeck College, Kings College, the London Consortium, the Ruskin School of Art, and Tate Modern.

ANDREW BROWN-MAY is an associate professor in the School of Historical Studies at the University of Melbourne, Australia. He is a principal editor of *Encyclopedia of Melbourne* (Cambridge University Press, 2005). His articles on urban social history have appeared in such journals as *Urban History* (United Kingdom), *Storia Urbana* (Italy), and *Historic Environment* (Australia).

BEN CAMPKIN is a lecturer in architectural history and theory at the Bartlett School of Architecture, University College London, and a codirector of the University College London Urban Laboratory. With Paul Dobraszczyk, he coedited a special issue of the *Journal of Architecture* (2007) on architecture and dirt, and with Rosie Cox he coedited *Dirt: New Geographies of Cleanliness and Contamination* (I. B. Tauris, 2007), a collection of essays exploring conceptions of dirt and cleanliness in relation to domestic, urban, and rural space. He is currently completing research examining discourses of dirt, blight, and regeneration within processes of urban change in modern and late-modern London.

MEGHAN DUFRESNE is a writer, architectural designer, and graphic designer currently working at PDA Associates in Natick, Massachusetts. She received her master's degree from the School of Architecture at the University of Illinois at Urbana–Champaign and has taught as an adjunct professor at Suffolk University in Boston. Together with Kathryn H. Anthony, she has been conducting research and lecturing on restroom design for several years. Currently she is researching sustainable design strategies.

PEG FRASER is a postgraduate student in the Public History and Heritage program in the School of Historical Studies at the University of Melbourne. She has recently completed a history of colonial Australian needlework samplers in the context of gender, migration, and female education.

DEBORAH GANS is the principal of Gans Studio and a professor in the Architecture School at Pratt Institute. She is an editor of *Bridging the Gap: Rethinking the Relation of Architecture and Engineering* (Van Nostrand Reinhold, 1991), which was honored by the American Institute of Architects International Book Awards, and the anthology *The Organic Approach* (Academy Press, 2003). She is also the author of *The Le Corbusier Guide* (Princeton Architectural Press, 2000), now in its third edition. A prototype of her studio's disaster relief housing was exhibited in the United States Pavilion of the Venice Biennial 2008.

OLGA GERSHENSON is an assistant professor of Judaic and Near Eastern studies at the University of Massachusetts Amherst. She is the author of *Gesher: Russian Theatre in Israel—a Study of Cultural Colonization* (Peter Lang, 2005) and an editor of *Volumes: New Insights into the Gendered Construction of Space/s*, a special issue of *Journal of International Women's Studies* (2005), coedited with Valerie Begley. Gershenson's interdisciplinary research has been published in numerous edited collections and scholarly journals, including *Journal of Israeli History, Journal of Film and Video, Journal of Modern Jewish Studies, Jewish Cultural Studies, Intercultural and International Communication Annual*, and *Journal of International Communication*.

CLARA GREED is a professor of inclusive urban planning at the School of Architecture and Planning at the University of the West of England at Bristol. She is a town planner and chartered surveyor interested in the social aspects of planning and urban design, including public toilets. She holds an MBE for her contributions to urban design. She is the author of several influential books, including *Social Town Planning* (Routledge, 1999); *Approaching Urban Design* (Longman, 2001), coauthored with Marion Roberts; and *Public Toilets: Inclusive Urban Design* (Architectural Press, 2003; China Machine Press, 2005 [in Chinese]). She is a member of the British Toilet Association and the British Standards Institute committee responsible for revising the national standards for sanitary installations and a founding member of the World Toilet Organization.

ROBIN LYDENBERG is a professor of English at Boston College. Her research interests include the interdisciplinary study of the avant-garde, psychoanalysis, visual culture, and literary theory. She is the author of GONE: Site-Specific Works by Dorothy Cross (McMullen Museum of Art, Boston College, 2005) and *Word Cultures: Radical Theory and Practice in William S. Burroughs' Fiction* (University of Illinois Press, 1987). She is a coeditor of *Feminist Approaches to Theory and Methodology: An Interdisciplinary Reader* (Oxford University Press, 1999) and *William S. Burroughs at the Front: Critical Reception, 1959–8* (Southern Illinois University Press, 1991).

CLAUDIA MITCHELL is a James McGill professor in the Faculty of Education, McGill University, Canada, and an honorary professor at the University of KwaZulu-Natal, South Africa. She has published extensively in girlhood studies, development studies, and teacher education. She is a cofounder and coeditor of *Girlhood Studies: An Interdisciplinary Journal* (Berghahn Press), with the 2008 inaugural issue. Most recently, she edited two collections: *Combating Gender Violence in and around Schools* (Trentham, 2006), coedited with Fiona Leach, and the two-volume *Girl Culture Encyclopedia* (Greenwood, 2007), coedited with Jacqueline Reid-Walsh.

ALISON MOORE is a postdoctoral research fellow at the University of Queensland, Australia, in the Centre for the History of European Discourses. She is the author of *Sexual Myths of Modernity: Sadism, Masochism and Historical Teleology* (Lexington Books, 2009). Her articles on sexual and gender issues in historical memory in France and Germany and on attitudes toward sexuality and toward excretion have appeared in *Journal of the History of Sexuality, Gender and History, Sexualities, Australian Feminist Studies*, and *Lesbian and Gay Psychology Review* and in numerous edited collections. With Peter Cryle, she wrote a book on the concept of feminine sexual frigidity in French medical and literary texts and is now completing a book manuscript on the history of fecal symbolism in European cultures.

BARBARA PENNER is a lecturer at the Bartlett School of Architecture, University College London. Her interdisciplinary research explores the intersections between public space, architecture, and private lives, focusing on everyday spaces from public toilets to honeymoon resort hotels. Her work has been published in numerous edited collections and scholarly journals, including *Journal of International Women's Studies* (2005), *Negotiating Domesticity* (Routledge, 2005), *Architecture and Tourism: Perception, Performance and Place* (Berg, 2004), and *Winterthur Portfolio* (Spring 2004). With Jane Rendell and Iain Borden, she coedited *Gender Space Architecture* (Routledge, 2000). Her new book is *Newlyweds on Tour: Honeymooning in Nineteenth-Century America* (University Press of New England, 2009.)

FRANCES PHEASANT-KELLY is a senior lecturer and M.A. coordinator in the Department of Film Studies at the University of Wolverhampton, United Kingdom, where she lectures on aspects of representation, authorship, gender, and science fiction. She recently completed her doctoral work on abjection, space, and institution in American film from the University of East Anglia. Further areas of research include masculinity and abjection, representational practices in science fiction and the medical drama, and abjection as an aesthetic approach.

BUSHRA REHMAN is a Brooklyn-based writer and coeditor of *Colonize This! Young Women of Color on Today's Feminism*. Her memoir about being a Pakistani little rascal and her on-the-road adventure novel are available at www.bushrarehman .com.

ALEX SCHWEDER is the 2005–6 Rome Prize fellow in architecture. Since being awarded the fellowship, Schweder has been experimenting with time- and performance-based architecture, including *Flatland* at New York's Sculpture Center 2007; *Homing MacGuffin*, during New York's Homebase III project 2008; and *A Sac of Rooms All Day Long*, to be shown at the San Francisco Museum of Modern Art in 2009. He is a three-time artist-in-residence at the Kohler Company and will be in residence at the Chinati Foundation in the fall of 2009. Schweder has been a guest professor at the Southern California Institute of Architecture. Images of his work can be found at www.alexschweder.com.

NAOMI STEAD is a senior lecturer in architectural theory, philosophy, and cultural studies at the University of Technology at Sydney. Her research interests include architecture and literature, etymology, the history and theory of museums, architectural criticism, questions of representation in and of architecture, and intersections between architecture and the visual and performing arts. Most recently, her essays have been published in anthologies including *Critical Architecture* (Routledge, 2007) and *Architecture and Authorship: Studies in Disciplinary Remediation* (Black Dog, 2007).

Index

British Standards Institute (BSI), 39
British Toilet Association (BTA), 35, 41
Brookes, Heather, 70
Brunton, Deborah, 5
building codes, 57
built environment: architectural boundaries
and gender segregation, 25, 182–88; in
colonial Melbourne, 77–78, 79–80, 81,
82, 87; design of toilet facilities in refugee
camps, 24, 136–40; and female access
and spatial organization, 11–12; the
paradoxical space of "cottages," 211–12,
213, 215; toilets and spatial order, 16–17;
of toilets in Sub-Saharan schools, 64–65,
70–71; women's toilet provision in
nineteenth-century Europe, 110, 112. See
also architectural designs; design
Butler, Judith, 18

Cahill, Spencer, 14
Call For Papers (CFP), 1–4, 22–26
Camfield, William, 153
Camp, George, 94, 96
Campkin, Ben, 13
cancer, 223
Capitol Building, Washington, 51
Cassatt, Mary, Young Mother (painting),
167
castration, in film, 202, 203–4
Cecchi, Matthew, 55
Central Cities Institute (CCI), 37
changing facilities, in public toilets, 40–41
charges. See pay toilets
Chege, Fatuma, 69
Chicago, Judy, Menstruation Bathroom
(installation), 25, 167–68
Chicago, potty parity in, 56, 58
children: in concentration camps, 221; and
gendered violence, 62, 63–64; and
health and safety in public restrooms,
53–54, 55; and lack of public toilet
facilities, 36, 41
China, 10, 117
Chodoff, Paul, 221
cinema. See American film, toilets in;
British film, toilets in; films
Ciochetto, Lynne, 19
circumcision, 219
cities, public toilet provision in, 5, 22, 23,
35–37. See also Chicago, potty parity in;
London; Melbourne; New York and
potty parity legislation; Paris
"civil inattention," 14
civility, 223–24

civilization, Western concepts of, and
excretion, 108–13
The Civilizing Process (Elias book), 15, 87,
108
Civil Rights Act (1964): Title II, 50; Title
VII, 90, 91–92, 102
civil rights movement, 7
class. See social class
Clean and Decent (Wright book), 5, 17
cleanliness: differences in cultural practice,
136, 189–94; hygiene and women's
domestic roles, 16–17, 170–71; in Jewish
religious practices, 219–20; physical and
psychological, 183, 184; and postexcretory cleansing practices, 105–8, 115–16,
190–94; standards of, and disease in
U.K. public toilets, 37–39, 43, 44; and
women's toilets in film, 205. See also
health; hygiene
cloaques (cloacae), 110, 111
closet accommodation charges, 79. See
also stalls
closure, of U.K. public toilets, 37, 38, 42
clothes. See dress
Coates, Jennifer, 127
Cohen, William, 215
college campuses: and transgender
students, 7–8, 50; and transgender toilet
provision, 7; and women's toilets, vii
Collings, Matthew, 170
Collins, Gail, 51
colonialism, gender, and attitudes toward
excretion, 24, 105–22
Colorado Convention Center, Denver,
52
comedy. See humor
communal toilets, 163–64, 198
A Complete and Practical Treatise (Davis
and Dye), 82, 84–85, 86, 143–44, 144f
concentration camps, 220–22
constipation, 112–13, 223
contamination. See dirt; marginality;
uncleanliness; waste
control: loss of (see abjection); of public
toilet provision in the United Kingdom,
42–43, 44–45; urinal, 145–48
conveniences. See men's toilets; pissoir;
public toilets; school toilets; toilet(s);
urinals; women's toilets
convention centers and problems of potty
parity, 52–53
conventions. See cultural conventions;
taboos; toilet practices

metropolis, 109–10. *See also* cities; *names of cities*
Mexico, 115
Michael, George, *Outside* (song), 208
Michigan Department of Correction (MDOC): discriminatory employment practices in, 24, 90, 93, 101; equal employment opportunities in, 91–92; and sexual abuse allegations, 92–93
military academies: "hierarchical observation" in, 18, 197; women's access to, 9
military barracks: latrines in, 219, 220–22; as refugee camps, 137
Miller, William Ian, 212
Les Misérables (Hugo novel), 110
Mitchell, Senator George, 51
modernism/modernity, 16, 151–54
modesty: and design of female urinals, 144, 149; of male prison guards, 97–98; toilets and sanitary napkins, 97–100; and women prisoners' right to privacy, 24, 90–91, 102; and women travelers' toilet practices, 106, 108. *See also* female "delicacy"; marginality; taboos; uncleanliness
Molesworth, Helen, 17
Molotch, Harvey, 12
Moore, Sarah A., 50, 51, 57
morality, public, 8, 17. *See also* female "delicacy"; marginality; taboos; uncleanliness
Morello, C., 71
Morgan, Margaret, 17
Morocco, 119
mother figure and psychoanalytic concepts of excretion and toileting, 108, 109
Moulin, Evelyne, 114
Mountain, Adrien Charles, 82–83, 84
Mulvey, Laura, 202
"municipal interchange," 23, 42–44, 77–79
murder, 212, 214. *See also* death; Holocaust
Museum of Sex, New York, 185
Muslims, toilet practices, 10, 40, 137
Mutt, Richard (Duchamp pseudonym), 151

National Health Service (United Kingdom), 37–39
national identity: American, 6, 155; Irish, 157–58

National Institutes of Health, 54
Nazis/Nazism, 219, 220
Neale, Steve, 201, 202
Neaman, Judith, 126, 129–30
neo-colonialism, 24, 106, 121
New Woman, 153–54
New York and potty parity legislation, 49, 57, 142
New York Times Magazine, 51
niddah (impurity), 219
Noble, John, 115
Norton, Louise, 152, 153
Novac, Ana, 221–22
nudity, in art, 167
number of public toilets: in colonial Melbourne, 80–81; in India, 22; in Los Angeles, 9. *See also* accessible provision; equality/inequality; gender: ratios
"*Nunn*" lawsuit, 93
Nuttall, Sarah, 62–63
Nygaard, Ingrid (and Marc Linder) *Void Where Prohibited,* 49

O'Brien, Louisa, 77
observation: toilet stalls designed for, 18, 197; of women prisoners, and loss of privacy, 94–97
Oldenziel, Ruth, 9, 13
Old In and Out Saggy (Lucas installation), 172f, 177
Orton, Joe, 211
Ostrower, Chaya, 221
"other," 157, 159, 214, 225
Outside (Michael song), 208
Oxford English Dictionary, 128

Paine, Anne, 58
Pakistan: stereotypes of Pakistanis, 189; toilet practices, 118, 121
Parent-Duchâtelet, Alexandre Jean-Baptiste, 110
parents, and child's use of public restrooms, 55
Paris, 109–10
Parker, Dorothy, 127–28
paruresis (bashful bladder syndrome), 54–55
patriarchal repression, 12, 13, 170
Pattmann, Rob, 69
pay toilets: charges for female toilets, 6, 143, 144; income from, 85, 87; legislation to ban, 56; various charges, 79, 81, 117

Sulabh Sanitation Movement, 10
Sullivan, George, 96
Superego, 120
Supreme Court, 51
Surrealist art, 154
Swaziland, 65–67
Sydney Morning Herald (Australian newspaper), 78
Sylvia Rivera Law Project, 21
symbols/symbolism: of feminine sexuality, 109; of Lacan's "laws of urinary segregation," 15, 156–57; and psycho-analytical body mappings, 109, 110, 120; rifles as phallic symbols, 197, 199; washing as symbolic action, 213, 221; of women, 174–75

taboos: and design of female urinals, 143, 144, 146; dietary and sexual, 222; and euphemisms for "toilet," 127–28, 130, 145; of menstruation, 167–68; and postcolonial toilet practices, 107–8, 111, 112–13, 119. *See also* euphemisms
Tacoma Convention and Trade Center, 185
Taiwan, 115, 116
Talmud, 219
Tanizaki, Jun'ichiro, 17
Tarantino, Quentin, *Pulp Fiction* (film), 25, 200–203
Taxi Driver (Scorsese film), 225
tearooms, 83, 87, 209
"Tearooms and Sympathy" (Edelman essay), 18, 19, 155–56
Tearoom Trade (Johnson documentary), 21
technology: and excretion, progress, and civilization, 108; and improvements in "potty parity," 58–59. *See also* plumbing; sanitation and sanitary engineering; sewerage systems
Tehran, 21–22
television shows: Jewish characters in, 26, 224–25; toilets in, 20. *See also* American film, toilets in; British film, toilets in; films
Tennessee Equitable Restrooms Act, 57
There's Something about Mary (Farrelly brothers film), 25, 203–4, 223, 224
third world toilet practices, 24, 105–22
Thorne, Robert, 77
Tierney, John, 51
Title II (Civil Rights Act, 1964), 50
Title VII (Civil Rights Act, 1964), 90, 91–92, 102

The Toilet (Kabakov installation), 160f, 160–64, 161f
Toilet and Urinal (Lucas installation), 172, 174f, 174–75
toilet: anxiety, 91, 195–96, 220–21; art, 19–20, 25–26, 151–64, 167–79, 184–88 (*see also* aesthetics; American film, toilets in; British film, toilets in; Cross, Dorothy; Duchamp, Marcel; exhibitions; films; installations; Kabakov, Ilya; Lucas, Sarah; Schweder, Alex; television shows); attendants, 44, 59, 75, 82, 85, 117, 158; training, 15
toilet(s): euphemisms for, 126–31; as feminizing and hazardous spaces, 195, 196, 198–204, 205; in film, 20–22, 25–26, 195–206, 223–25 (*see also* American film, toilets in; British film, toilets in); in Jewish popular culture, 218–24; traditional Japanese, 17; UN guidelines on toilet facilities, 135–36. *See also* pissoir; public toilets; school toilets; urinals
The Toilet by the River (Kabakov installation), 163–64
The Toilet in the Corner (Kabakov installation), 163
toilet paper: and cleanliness of toilet seats, 40; and postexcretory cleansing, 105–6, 115–16; as writing paper, 221–22
toilet practices: as emasculating, 200–201, 203; female, and gendered space, 21–22, 37, 223; gender, colonialism, and attitudes toward excretion, 24, 105–22; and Jewish ritual, 219; in *Lotah Stories*, 191–94
Toilet Training (Mateik documentary), 21
Torah, 219
Torres, Art, 56
tourism/tourists: and global culture, 19; and postcolonial toilet practices, 105–8, 114–20
trains, toilet facilities of, 107–8
transgender people, use of public toilets by, 7–8, 20–21, 50
travel: and global culture, 19; guides, 24, 107–8, 110, 114–20, 121; and postcolonial toilet practices, 105–8, 114–20
Traveller's Weblogs, 107–8, 115–22, 119
TravelMate, 59
Treille, Georges, *Principles of Colonial Hygiene* (book), 113
Tunisia, 105, 107
La Turista (travelers' diarrhea), 114